Facticity and the Fate of Reason After Kant

Facticity and the Fate of Reason After Kant

G. ANTHONY BRUNO

OXFORD
UNIVERSITY PRESS

OXFORD
UNIVERSITY PRESS

Great Clarendon Street, Oxford, OX2 6DP,
United Kingdom

Oxford University Press is a department of the University of Oxford.
It furthers the University's objective of excellence in research, scholarship,
and education by publishing worldwide. Oxford is a registered trade mark of
Oxford University Press in the UK and in certain other countries

Published in the United States of America by Oxford University Press
198 Madison Avenue, New York, NY 10016, United States of America

British Library Cataloguing in Publication Data
Data available

Library of Congress Control Number: 2024941137

ISBN 9780198875673

DOI: 10.1093/9780191987533.001.0001

Printed and bound by
CPI Group (UK) Ltd, Croydon, CR0 4YY

MIX
Paper | Supporting
responsible forestry
FSC® C013604

The manufacturer's authorised representative in the EU for product safety is Oxford University Press España S.A. of El Parque Empresarial San Fernando de Henares, Avenida de Castilla, 2 – 28830 Madrid
(www.oup.es/en or product.safety@oup.com). OUP España S.A. also acts as importer into Spain of products made by the manufacturer.

For Sarah, my love

Contents

Acknowledgments

This book emerged from a series of essays, courses, discussions, and obsessions whose interconnection revealed an unexpected unity, which, for me, makes its completion all the more pleasing. As with all of my work, its composition has been a consciously social affair and so calls for many thanks.

The mark that Paul Franks continues to leave on my thinking is indelible largely because my awareness of it is typically belated. Part of the gift of my conversations with Paul and engagement with his work consists in finding myself on paths of thought struck, once again, by his foresight about where I might be heading.

Material in this book has been developed through longstanding and expanding conversations with many experts and patient friends in the field.

For helpful discussions, I thank Jojo Amoah, Michael Blezy, Karin de Boer, Daniel Breazeale, Martijn Buijs, Aiden Cahill, Joseph Carew, Rebecca Comay, Steven Crowell, Matthew Delhey, Tarek Dika, Naomi Fisher, Manfred Frank, Paul Franks, Sebastian Gardner, George di Giovanni, Sol Goldberg, Sacha Golob, Gabriel Gottlieb, Edward Guetti, Simon Gurofsky, John Hacker-Wright, Karl Hahn, Thimo Heisenberg, Boris Hennig, Till Hoeppner, Stephen Houlgate, Tobias Keiling, Jeffery Kinlaw, James Kreines, Thomas Land, Jessica Leech, Eliza Little, Sebastian Luft, Wayne Martin, Colin Marshall, Colin McLear, Colin McQuillan, Gregory S. Moss, Dalia Nassar, Karen Ng, Jens Pier, Jesper Lundsfryd Rasmussen, Karl Schafer, Johannes-Georg Schülein, Simon Schüz, Paula Schwebel, Matthew Shockey, Sean M. Smith, Nicholas F. Stang, Robert Stern, David Suarez, Kevin Temple, Clinton Tolley, Tyler Tritten, Owen Ware, Andrew Werner, Daniel Whistler, and George Williams.

For helpful feedback, I thank: attendees at meetings of the 2011 North American Kant Society Southern Study Group, the 2015 North American Schelling Society, the 2017 Canadian Philosophical Association, the 2017 Pacific American Philosophical Association, the 2019 North American Neo-Kantian Society, and the 2020 Eastern American Philosophical Association; workshop participants at the New York German Idealism Workshop, Utrecht University, the University of Florence, McGill University, the University of California San Diego, the University of Guelph, the University of Toronto, and Royal Holloway University of London; conference participants at the University of Toronto and the University of Leuven; and panelists at book manuscript workshops at the University of Toronto and the University of Warwick.

My work on various stages of completing this book benefited from the hospitality of several academic hosts and the support of several funding bodies: Markus

Gabriel, who hosted my Alexander von Humboldt Postdoctoral Research Fellowship at the University of Bonn; Philip Buckley and George di Giovanni, who hosted my SSHRC Postdoctoral Research Fellowship at McGill University; Ulrich Schlösser, who hosted my Alexander von Humboldt Alumni Fellowship at the University of Tübingen; James Conant, who hosted my Forschungskolleg Analytic German Idealism Experienced Research Fellowship at the University of Leipzig; and Tobias Rosefeldt, who hosted my Alexander von Humboldt Alumni Fellowship at the Humboldt University of Berlin.

Developing the arguments in this book has been aided immensely by my time teaching at Royal Holloway University of London, for which I thank my colleagues and, most especially, my students.

I am grateful to Peter Momtchiloff, April Peake, and Jamie Mortimer for helping to see this project through to completion.

Expanded versions of material from previous publications appear with the kind permission of the publishers. Chapter 1 includes material from "Genealogy and Jurisprudence in Fichte's Genetic Deduction of the Categories" in *History of Philosophy Quarterly* 35 (1) (2018), "Determinacy, Indeterminacy, and Contingency in German Idealism" in *The Significance of Indeterminacy: Perspectives from Asian and Continental Philosophy* (Routledge, 2018), and "Post-Kantian Idealism and Self-Transformation" in *Transformation and the History of Philosophy* (Routledge, 2024). Chapter 2 includes material from "Facticity and Genesis: Tracking Fichte's Method in the Berlin *Wissenschaftslehre*" in *Fichte-Studien* 49 (2021). Chapter 3 includes material from "*Hiatus Irrationalis*: Lask's Fateful Misreading of Fichte" in *European Journal of Philosophy* (2021), "'All is Act, Movement, and Life': Fichte's Idealism as Immortalism" in *Life, Organisms, and Cognition: Understanding Nature Between Classical German Philosophy and Current Debates* (Springer, 2023), and "Quietism, Dialetheism, and the Three Moments of Hegel's Logic" in *Metaphysics as a Science in Classical German Philosophy* (Routledge, 2023). Chapter 4 includes material from "The Facticity of Time: Conceiving Schelling's Idealism of Ages" in *Schelling's Philosophy: Freedom, Nature, and Systematicity* (Oxford University Press, 2020). Chapter 5 also includes material from "*Hiatus Irrationalis*: Lask's Fateful Misreading of Fichte."

The quotations for this book's epigraph appear with the kind permission of Peter Lang Group, SUNY Press, and Verlag Vittorio Klostermann.

I thank my brothers for the worlds that they have opened for me. Mike Countryman illuminates the connection between creativity and authenticity and is a model of diligence. Moreover, I have him to thank for daring me to take my first philosophy class. Alastair Cheng illuminates the connection between philosophy and therapy and is a model of care. David Suarez illuminates the connection between self-understanding and communication and is a model of generosity.

I could not have pursued a life that I truly value without the love, sacrifice, and encouragement of my parents, Aurelia and Joseph Bruno, and my sisters, Tina

Soda, Rosanna Modica, and Elisa Davey. Having begun living this life, I want nothing more than to honor their efforts.

This book is primarily about radical contingency. Two examples of contingency that fill my mind with admiration and reverence are philosophy and love. It is as an inner voice that philosophy continues, without any genuine guarantee, to turn me toward questions that disturb and fascinate me. And it is as an outer calling that Sarah Halonen continues, beyond anything that I might dare to explain or calculate, to draw me toward lessons and adventures that improve my soul and sweeten my existence. She is beyond words the most precious because she gives me a life that is worth living.

"Only reason is ... We are in its hand and remain there, and no one can tear us out of it. We are eternal because it is."

– Fichte BM | SW II: 302

"To [Fichte], the world is only a ball which the I has thrown forth, and which it again catches in the act of reflexion!"

– Schiller's letter to Goethe, October 26, 1794, in Schiller and Goethe 1994: 19

"According to Fichte, it is the I that throws the world. But according to *Being and Time*, the I does not first throw the world; it is rather Dasein, essentially presencing before all humanity, which is thrown."

– Heidegger MDI | GA 49: 161

"[Dasein] is thrown in such a way that it is the 'there' as being-in-the-world. The expression 'thrownness' is meant to suggest the *facticity of its being delivered over*."

– Heidegger SZ | GA 2: 135

Introduction

0.1 Modesty and Contingency

In 1781/1787's *Critique of Pure Reason*, Immanuel Kant draws our philosophical attention away from the objects of special metaphysics, namely, the soul, the world, and God, and toward the necessary conditions of human experience. This Copernican turn coincides with a logical turn that has profound metaphysical consequences. Kant exposes the futility of relying exclusively on general logic, that is, the science of the "absolutely necessary rules of thinking, without which no use of the understanding takes place," as a means to resolving longstanding metaphysical disputes. General logic "abstracts . . . from all content of cognition, i.e., from any relation of it to the object, and considers only the logical form in the relation of cognitions to one another, i.e., the form of thinking in general."[1] The abstractness of general logic in this respect entails its indifference to distinctions among various classes of objects, for example, appearances and things in themselves. It also entails general logic's tolerance for internally consistent yet mutually inconsistent metaphysical doctrines, for example, libertarianism and determinism, which is why it is powerless to bring to an end what, in the A-edition Preface, Kant calls the "battlefield" of controversy in metaphysics.[2]

In order to satisfy reason's rightful metaphysical aspirations, Kant introduces a new logic, namely, transcendental logic, that is, the science of "the laws of the understanding and reason, but solely insofar as they are related to objects *a priori*."[3] Transcendental logic has the advantage of abstracting only from the empirical content of cognition, which enables it to deduce not merely the "form of thinking in general," but rather "the form of a possible experience."[4] This shift in logical focus guides the science of thinking toward a metaphysically appropriate class of objects, namely, objects insofar as they can appear to us, and thereby toward defensible metaphysical doctrines, namely, such doctrines as can articulate the nature of our autonomous standpoint on manifest objectivity. Transcendental idealism is the result of this turn.

Kant's logical turn reorients metaphysics from mere thinking toward possible experience. Ending metaphysical anarchy in this manner subjectivizes

1 Kant KrV A52/B76, A55/B79.
2 Kant KrV Aviii.
3 Kant KrV A57/B81-2. Cf. Kant's 1800 *Jäsche Logic* (Kant JL | AA 9: 9, 15).
4 Kant KrV A246/B303.

Facticity and the Fate of Reason After Kant. G. Anthony Bruno, Oxford University Press.
 DOI: 10.1093/9780191987533.003.0001

metaphysics insofar as it restricts universal and necessary claims about actuality to what can appear to us. However, it is not simply that Kant's logical turn limits the scope of metaphysics. It is also that this turn regards the grounds of metaphysics as brute, which this study will treat as synonymous with their being ultimately groundless or radically contingent. The first *Critique* provides no first principle from which to deduce the *a priori* conditions of experience, which include space and time, that is, the forms of sensibility by which objects of experience are given to us, the categories, that is, the pure concepts of the understanding by which we think of given objects, the forms of judgment, that is, the functions by which the understanding combines representations and propositions, and the ideas of reason, that is, the concepts with which reason unifies cognitions as a whole. According to Kant, our situation calls for modesty. Despite our rational desire for ultimate grounds, we must accept these *a priori* conditions as groundless grounds, that is, as "peculiar" facts about human subjectivity, which facts "attach" to "the subjective constitution of our mind."[5] Their necessity for possible experience is brute rather than absolute, since they are not deducible from a first principle. However unavoidable for us, the conditions of experience are radically, which is to say, at root, contingent.

The modesty and contingency that jointly characterize the metaphysical consequence of Kant's logical turn raise a question that both immediately and continually divides post-Kantian philosophy and that therefore has both historical and contemporary significance. In light of Kant's logical turn, it becomes crucial to decide whether the *a priori* conditions of experience are not merely necessary for us, but instead are absolutely necessary. Indeed, it becomes crucial to decide this question more generally for what I will call any putative 'conditions of intelligibility,' where such conditions include the categories, thought-determinations, and existential structures that *a priori* render experience, thought, and existence possible in their significance, truth, and meaning. Moreover, it becomes crucial to decide, for a systematic account of the conditions of intelligibility, that is, for what I will call a 'science of intelligibility,' whether bruteness is either impermissible or unavoidable. The post-Kantian question accordingly arises: can a science of intelligibility tolerate any conditions of intelligibility as brute facts? We find that two major philosophical traditions flow from this question.

On the one hand, those who deem bruteness impermissible aim to eliminate it from the science of intelligibility. Thus, nineteenth-century German idealists like Johann Gottlieb Fichte and Georg Wilhelm Friedrich Hegel claim that the conditions of intelligibility are absolutely necessary because, when properly deduced either from or as an absolute ground, that is, a first principle, no putatively contrary set of conditions is consistently thinkable. Logically deducing conditions of intelligibility from an absolute ground that is intuitively posited at the beginning

[5] See Kant KrV Avii, A23/B37-8, A35/B51, B145-6.

of science, as Fichte would have it, or deducing the conditions of intelligibility as the conceptual articulation of the absolute ground in which science culminates, as Hegel would have it, removes the appearance that such conditions are radically contingent and thereby promises to systematize philosophy.

On the other hand, those who deem bruteness unavoidable regard it as making the science of intelligibility possible in the first place. Thus, twentieth-century phenomenologists like Martin Heidegger claim that *a priori* conditions of intelligibility are facts that, while philosophically interpretable, are nevertheless undeducible and thus ultimately brute. Whereas empirical facts are not radically contingent insofar as they necessarily conform to the conditions of intelligibility, brute facts that function as conditions of intelligibility are radically contingent insofar as they are inescapable for any meaningful pursuit, including the pursuit of a science of intelligibility, yet are not logically deducible from or as a first principle and in this respect lack absolute necessity. Brute facts of this kind occupy what I will call the 'unique modal space' of conditions of intelligibility whose necessity is not logical yet whose contingency is not empirical. Denying such facts by purporting either to reduce them to the properties of objects or to deduce them from the content of logic is indeed thinkable. However, for Heidegger, this denial exhibits a kind of inauthenticity, that is, a dogmatic slumber of sorts.

Classical phenomenologists employ the term 'facticity' to signify such conditions of intelligibility as spatiality, temporality, sociality, embodiment, and mortality. Facticity is the character of the bruteness, which is to say, the ultimate groundlessness or radical contingency, of a condition of intelligibility. Unlike an empirical fact, which might be the case at some point, a brute fact of this sort is always already the case yet logically undeducible. The concept of facticity is typically associated with the work of Heidegger, Jean-Paul Sartre, Simone de Beauvoir, and Maurice Merleau-Ponty. However, since the source of this concept is generally although not entirely neglected, scholars remain largely unaware of the concept's century-long pre-phenomenological career and, in particular, of its Fichtean origin.[6]

This book provides the first history of the concept of facticity and demonstrates that the coining, transmission, and repurposing of this concept by major thinkers after Kant leaves a deep and lasting divide concerning the post-Kantian question of the relation between brute facts and the science of intelligibility. This divide is expressed as a fundamental methodological opposition between Fichte and Hegel's German idealist project of expunging apparent bruteness by deductive means, on pain of disowning reason's freedom and inviting its annihilation, and Heidegger's phenomenological project of interpreting genuine bruteness by hermeneutical means, on pain of evading our finitude and ignoring our thrownness.

[6] On Fichte's neologism, see Carvalho 2010, Denker 2000, Kisiel 2000, and Kisiel 2008. The *Historical Dictionary of Philosophy* traces 'facticity' only as far back as Heidegger's 1927 *Being and Time* (Fahrenbach 1972: 386–7).

My primary historical claim will be that we cannot fully understand the path from Kant to German idealism to phenomenology without understanding the momentous trajectory of the concept of facticity. My primary philosophical claim will be that we find in phenomenology's revival of the Kantian senses of modesty and contingency a defensible and, indeed, superior response to the post-Kantian question.

0.2 Dialectic or Hermeneutics?

Fichte's neologism originally names a problem that necessitates the first post-Kantian logical turn. Coined in 1799 amid the atheism dispute that forces him from the University of Jena to Berlin, 'facticity' is his term for what he regards as intolerable bruteness in philosophy and, in particular, in Kant's science of intelligibility. By referring to conditions of intelligibility whose necessity is ultimately groundless, the term signals the very sort of haphazard or rhapsodic determination with which Kant charges Aristotle's search for the categories. According to Fichte, what, for Kant, is the apparent facticity of space, time, the forms of judgment, the categories, and the ideas of reason can and must be eliminated by deducing their absolute necessity from an irrefutable first principle, namely, the absolute freedom of reason or, equivalently, the I. A true science of intelligibility, according to what he considers to be the spirit as opposed to the letter of transcendental idealism, demands the removal of the appearance that any condition of intelligibility could exceed reason's power of self-determination. Indeed, the primacy of practical reason consists in satisfying precisely this demand. This is the philosophical project that unifies Fichte's Jena and Berlin periods, which latter is recently receiving the attention of Anglophone scholarship.[7]

As we will see, Fichte's method of deducing the conditions of intelligibility typically takes the form of a dialectical movement of thought in which a contradiction in a putative condition is revealed and subsequently resolved by a successor condition that synthesizes the former's opposing inner elements. His deductive method accordingly signals the first post-Kantian logical turn, for it determines conditions by appeal not to brute facts about human subjectivity, but rather to a series of resolvable contradictions that arise from the I itself. Despite retaining 'transcendental logic' as a name for the science of determining the conditions of intelligibility, Fichte effectively invents dialectical logic as a means to eliminating the factical results of the science that Kant pursues under that same name and thereby as a means to realizing the spirit of transcendental idealism as a true science. In order to understand the trajectory of post-Kantian philosophy, it is crucial to register both the context and the impact of Fichte's logical turn.

[7] See Breazeale and Rockmore (ed.) 2008, Bruno 2021a, Crowe and Gottlieb (ed.) 2024, Martin 2003, Nuzzo 2010, Schlösser 2010, and Zöller 2016b.

First, regarding the context of Fichte's logical turn, several early post-Kantians are sympathetic to many of the conclusions of the first *Critique* yet reject its premises for their bruteness. Jakob Sigismund Beck, Fichte, Hegel, Salomon Maimon, Karl Leonhard Reinhold, and Friedrich Wilhelm Joseph Schelling each in their own way demand the removal of radical contingency from the conditions of intelligibility. A rhapsodic determination of such conditions leaves open the possibility that their ultimate ground not only eludes Kant, but also rules out the freedom and purposiveness of human reason, namely, a first principle to which Kant has no cognizably unconditioned alternative, in particular, Baruch Spinoza's conception of God or nature. This open possibility entails a threat that motivates the German idealist project and that, if taken seriously, shows this project to be less of a philosophical aberration than it might appear to Kantians and to others.

The threat in question is not only that Kant lacks a first principle from which to derive absolutely necessary as opposed to brute or factical conditions of intelligibility. It is also that Spinoza provides a principle that supports precisely this derivation yet reduces all things to causally necessitated modes of God or nature, thereby entailing the incoherence of human freedom and purposiveness.[8] In the 1785 first edition of *Concerning the Doctrine of Spinoza in Letters to Mr. Moses Mendelssohn*, Friedrich Heinrich Jacobi says that the "spirit of Spinozism" is "nothing other than the ancient [principle] *a nihilo nihil fit* [nothing comes from nothing]," a negative formulation of the principle of sufficient reason according to which nothing finite exists without an external condition, which itself has an external condition, and so on *ad infinitum*, from which it follows that nothing finite exists with an intrinsic capacity or property, for example, the capacity for freedom or the property of purposiveness. According to Jacobi, this reduces objects to fleeting and futile "*non-entia* [non-entities]."[9] This, he warns, is tantamount to the annihilation of true individuals, a consequence for which he coins the term "*nihilism*" in 1799's open letter to Fichte,[10] the same year that Fichte coins 'facticity.' Jacobi registers the threat of nihilism well before naming it, namely, in the *Doctrine of Spinoza*:

[8] See Spinoza's posthumous 1677 *The Ethics*: "human beings believe they are free because they are conscious of their own volitions and their own appetite and never think, even in their dreams, about the causes which dispose them to want and to will because they are ignorant of them ... [T]hat nature has no purpose laid down for it and that all final causes are nothing but human fancies—requires little argument ... [for] it would be the final things for the sake of which the prior ones were made that would be the most excellent of all. Then, this doctrine takes away the perfection of God. For if God acts for the sake of a purpose, he is necessarily seeking something that he lacks" (Spinoza 2002: E1 Appendix).

[9] Jacobi LS 131 | 1994: 220. Cf. Jacobi: "What distinguishes Spinoza's philosophy from all the other, what constitutes its soul, is that it maintains and applies with the strictest rigor the well-known principle, *gigni de nihilo nihil, in nihilum nil potest reverti* [from nothing, nothing is generated; into nothing, nothing returns]. If Spinoza has denied a beginning to any action whatever, and has considered the system of final causes the greatest delirium of the human understanding, he has done so only as a consequence of that principle" (Jacobi LS 59–60 | 1994: 205). See Spinoza: "For every thing a cause or reason must be assigned either for its existence or its non-existence" (Spinoza 2002: E1 P11 Second Proof).

[10] Jacobi BF 39 | 1994: 519. Jacobi first charges Fichte with nihilism, depicting the *Wissenschaftslehre* as an "*inverted* Spinozism" that reduces objects to rationally necessitated acts of the I or "pure and

> If there are only efficient, but no final, causes, then the only function that the faculty of thought has in the whole of nature is that of observer; its proper business is to accompany the mechanism of efficient causes . . . The inventor of the clock did not ultimately invent it; he only witnessed its coming to be out of blindly self-developing forces . . . We only *believe* that we have acted out of anger, love, magnanimity, or out of rational decision. Mere illusion![11]

Indeed, Jacobi reports falling "into a kind of swoon" when imagining the impossibility of his own autonomy.[12] Facing the threat of nihilism upon reading his text, the German idealists demand a principle that both can ground intelligibility conditions of the appropriate necessity and is exclusively accessible from the standpoint of our rational autonomy.[13] Only such a principle can eliminate factical conditions of intelligibility while avoiding what I will call the 'nihilistic consequence of Spinozism.'

Second, regarding the impact of Fichte's logical turn, Hegel lauds Fichte's campaign against facticity yet critiques its execution, in particular, the bruteness of presupposing the I as a first principle. Hegel subsequently develops dialectical logic into a presuppositionless science of the conditions of intelligibility, that is, a truly absolute science. Both philosophers endorse a logic that is neither general, in that its conditions make experience as well as thought possible, nor transcendental, in that its conditions are not brute facts about human subjectivity, but is rather dialectical, in that its deductions of conditions make productive use of contradictions that emerge from thought thinking itself. They thereby overcome both general logic's tolerance for anarchy in metaphysics and transcendental logic's tolerance for subjectivity in metaphysics. However, whereas Fichte's logic seeks to eliminate undeduced presuppositions as far as possible, that is, up to yet not including the presupposition of the I as an underivable or first principle, Hegel's logic seeks to eliminate them at all costs so as to deduce nothing less than presuppositionless intelligibility, that is, so as to demonstrate rationality without remainder.

Interrogating Hegel's completion of Fichte's logical turn, Schelling gradually mounts an internal critique of the German idealist project that, in the 1790s, he

empty consciousness" (Jacobi BF 4 | 1994: 502). However, we will see in Chapter 1 that, in the Jena texts that provoke Jacobi's charge, Fichte clearly aims to refute Spinozism's nihilistic consequence.

[11] Jacobi LS 18–9 | 1994: 189. Cf. Friedrich Adolf Trendelenburg's 1840 *Logical Investigations*: "because [Spinoza] gives no place to purpose, the value of individual life disappears for him, swirling around like dust upon substance only to sink into this great grave of necessity" (Trendelenburg 1862: 24, translated by Beiser 2013: 51).

[12] Jacobi LS 328–30 | 1994: 362. Cf. John Stuart Mill's 1873 *Autobiography*: "during later episodes of dejection the doctrine of philosophical necessity weighed on my existence like an incubus. I felt as if I was scientifically proved to be the helpless slave of antecedent circumstances; as if my character and that of all others had been formed for us by agencies beyond our control, and was wholly out of our own power" (Mill 2018: 97).

[13] On nihilism's role in the formation of German idealism, see Franks 2005.

helps to initiate. In texts that span three decades and culminate in his highly anticipated 1841–42 Berlin lectures, Schelling charges Hegel with presupposing not only the free endorsement and the guiding purpose of a science of intelligibility, but also existence itself, without which the conditions of intelligibility would be empty forms. That anything at all exists such as to be intelligible is a brute fact that contributes to intelligibility yet defies the deductions of dialectical logic. Existence is, in this respect, the undeducible remainder of science, which accordingly refutes the latter's claim to presuppositionlessness. For Schelling, *contra* Hegel, existence is that to which we are factically open in experience. As we will see, Schelling proves to be a pivotal yet neglected figure in the history of the concept of facticity, specifically, through his presentation of the science of experience that he calls 'positive philosophy.' Indeed, he marks the beginning of what I will call 'the transition from the primacy of the practical to the primacy of the factical,' at whose culmination reason's absolute freedom is unmasked and revealed to be its absolute thrownness. Moreover, Schelling's defense of the concept of facticity prefigures its eventual yet circuitous revival by phenomenology.

Heidegger inherits the concept of facticity from Emil Lask, a neo-Kantian philosopher whose 1902 doctoral thesis on Fichte's Berlin period exerts a deep and acknowledged impact on Heidegger's early work. On Lask's reading, Fichte regards facticity as the essential character of individuals, whose material particularity resists deduction from the I. As we will see, Lask misreads Fichte as discovering in individuality a deductively insuperable presupposition. In other words, he misreads Fichte as endorsing facticity's enshrinement rather than its elimination, at least beyond the presupposition of the I. Lask's is a productive misreading, however, for it directs Heidegger toward the factical character not of individual existents, but rather of our existence, that is, our Dasein or being-there. For Heidegger, Dasein's conditions of intelligibility, while philosophically interpretable, are factical in that they are undeducible. And they are undeducible because they make meaningful pursuits, including the pursuit of a science of intelligibility, possible in the first place. Thus, whatever its advantages over general logic and transcendental logic, dialectical logic unavoidably exhibits such brute facts as Dasein's being-in-the-world, being-with-others, being-ahead-of-itself, being-toward-death, and being-time.

In addition to inheriting the concept of facticity from Lask, Heidegger inherits the result of Wilhelm Dilthey's effort to develop hermeneutics from the art of interpreting canonical texts to the method on whose basis the human sciences interpret our lived experience. In lecture courses that culminate in 1927's *Being and Time*, Heidegger argues that Dilthey confines hermeneutics to its derivative, ontic role as the method of a human science such as psychology, which interprets lived experience third-personally as a distinct object. By contrast, Heidegger pursues hermeneutics in its originary, ontological role as the method of the science of intelligibility, which interprets lived experience first-personally as the situation into which Dasein's meaningful pursuits, including phenomenology itself, are always already thrown. In this respect, hermeneutics has the post-Kantian methodological advantage of wittingly exhibiting the factical conditions of intelligibility that it interprets, namely, in a hermeneutic circle. Heidegger thus extends Dilthey's efforts toward a hermeneutics of facticity, the genitive in which is simultaneously subjective and objective in that its interpretation of the factical conditions of our situation belongs to that very situation. The understanding that such a first-personal hermeneutics affords is accordingly a genuine kind of self-understanding.

A hermeneutical interpretation of the conditions of intelligibility is both enriching and transformative. On the one hand, hermeneutics intensifies the richness of the intelligibility that an initial condition affords, namely, through repeated interpretation. This repetition reveals that Dasein's factical worldliness contains its sociality, concernfulness, mortality, and temporality. As Heidegger says in *Being and Time*, "[p]hilosophy will never seek to deny its 'presuppositions,' but neither may it merely admit them. It conceives them and develops with more and more penetration both the presuppositions themselves and that for which they are presuppositions."[14] Rather than "merely admit" a factical condition, philosophy hermeneutically "penetrat[es]" its ultimate significance for Dasein's situation. On the other hand, hermeneutics transforms the prevailing conception of the conditions of intelligibility from logically necessary characteristics of being to radically contingent characteristics of our being-there. As Heidegger puts it in his 1920–21 winter lectures in Freiburg, *Introduction to the Phenomenology of Religion*, "through the explication of factical Dasein, the entire traditional system of categories will be blown up—so radically new will the *categories of factical Dasein be*."[15] By "blow[ing] up" the "traditional" conception of categories, hermeneutics allows us to conceive them as existential structures of Dasein and thus to convert an inauthentically unquestioned inheritance into an authentically critical appropriation.

Heidegger shows that the conditions of intelligibility are not dialectically deducible, but rather are hermeneutically interpretable, which signals hermeneutics as the methodological successor to dialectical logic. This methodological succession reflects the post-Kantian shift from German idealism's architectonic interest in logical systematicity toward phenomenology's existentialist interest in radical contingency. In line with my primary historical claim, we will see that we can best track the post-Kantian methodological shift only by tracking the coincident shift in facticity's role from being the obstacle to a science of intelligibility to being the groundless ground of that science, that is, from being the fundamental threat to philosophical rigor to being the fundamental topic of philosophical interpretation. In line with my

[14] Heidegger SZ | GA 2: 310.
[15] Heidegger EPR | GA 60: 54.

primary philosophical claim, we will see that the post-Kantian methodological shift marks a justified, if qualified, return to Kantian modesty and contingency.

0.3 Resoluteness and Finitude

Heidegger emerges in this study as the most exemplary thinker of facticity after Kant, at least by the 1930s. Earlier post-Kantians misguidedly seek to eliminate facticity, whether nearly entirely, as in Fichte, or entirely, as in Hegel. As we will see, they commit this error in the name of what I will call the 'enlightenment ideal of rational cognition,' which Kant initially defines and the German idealists subsequently radicalize. For Kant, rational cognition demands that reason be the sole source of the form of cognition and so demands thinking's independence from anything that is presupposed as being externally given concerning this form. In order to eliminate facticity, Fichte and Hegel absolutize Kant's conception of rational cognition by demanding thinking's independence from presuppositions as far as possible and at all costs, respectively. However, this demand neglects its own thrownness, that is, it neglects the factical conditions on which it depends, which conditions cannot be dialectically deduced, but rather must be hermeneutically interpreted. According to Heidegger, our situation calls for resoluteness. Despite our rational desire for presuppositionlessness, we must face up to what, in his 1929 inaugural lecture in Freiburg, "What is Metaphysics?," he calls the "strangeness" of intelligibility, namely, its radical contingency or groundlessness.[16] This is just to say that we must face up to the finitude of our thinking, which, since it cannot cognize an absolute ground for intelligibility, must accept that the conditions of intelligibility are ultimately groundless. We lack resolve when we flee from groundless grounds and, pursuing a radicalized enlightenment ideal of rational cognition, demand thinking's infinitude. We thereby exhibit the inauthenticity of evading our own finitude.

The resoluteness and finitude that characterize Heidegger's hermeneutical turn revive, respectively, the modesty and contingency that, for Kant, constitute a science of intelligibility with a human face. However, this is not an unqualified return. Although Kant anticipates an affirmative answer to the post-Kantian question of whether a science of intelligibility can tolerate brute facts, Heidegger motivates a richer account of such facts, one that draws on a wider array of capacities and experiences while critiquing the broadly idealist methods of deduction that precede him. Moreover, whereas Kant claims that metaphysics is the lone science whose "perfect unity" makes its "unconditioned completeness not only feasible but also necessary,"[17] Heidegger implies that hermeneutical interpretation is essentially

[16] Heidegger WM | W: 18.
[17] Kant KrV Axx.

incomplete. It is not only that *Being and Time* is an unfinished text that assigns Dasein's "primordial structure" to temporality, only to end with the question of how temporality itself is "to be interpreted." It is also that the text's final section announces that analyzing Dasein's structure is "only *one way*" to interpret temporality, that is, "[n]ot 'the' sole way," and, moreover, is only the "*right*" way on the assumption that "we have *followed* it."[18] Indeed, several days before his death and in lieu of an unfinished preface to his collected works, Heidegger writes the motto "ways—not works."[19] This motto suggests that the self-understanding that hermeneutics affords cannot be fixed into a doctrine, but rather is a path to be taken and maintained, one on which we are at every point vulnerable to going astray and so can at no point lay claim to perfectly authentic orientation.

The present study charitably motivates and rationally reconstructs central arguments by its main figures, while signaling and articulating their supersession by superior arguments. Thus, we will see that while Fichte rightly detects factical grounds in Kant's science of intelligibility, Hegel rightly detects vestigial facticity in Fichte's science and, in turn, Schelling rightly detects factical presuppositions in Hegel's science, which prefigures Heidegger's eventual rehabilitation of a philosophical account of factical conditions. The history of the concept of facticity accordingly emerges with Fichte, pivots with Schelling, and leads to Heidegger. However, far from a triumphant present's chronicle of past errors, this study reveals the extent to which the competing responses to the post-Kantian question rightly tend to restore modesty and contingency to the science of intelligibility and thereby to regain the spirit, if not the letter, of Kant's Copernican turn.

My broader scholarly aim is to engage readers of Kant, German idealism, neo-Kantianism, and phenomenology by illuminating deep historical and systematic connections among these traditions that become visible through the lens of facticity. This study does not deny the demonstrable importance of the concepts of reason, freedom, nihilism, and systematicity for understanding the philosophical path from Kant to Heidegger. Instead, it shows how these concepts are maximally organized by the concept of facticity. In other words, the problem that the concept of facticity raises is neither one to which other motivating problems of post-Kantian philosophy reduce nor simply one problem among many, but rather is the problem that most comprehensively coordinates its other motivating problems. Thus, for Fichte, nihilism threatens reason's freedom just insofar as it impedes reason's capacity to derive the conditions of intelligibility from itself and thereby remove the appearance of facticity from such conditions. And, for Heidegger, a science of intelligibility ultimately avoids nihilism just insofar as it authentically understands its own conditions as inescapably factical.

[18] Heidegger SZ | GA 2: 436–7, 437n.
[19] Von Herrmann 1972: 437–8.

Admittedly, Fichte and Heidegger use the term 'facticity' more often than Schelling, while Hegel apparently never uses it. However, we can regard the concept of facticity as co-extensive with the concept of finitude insofar as facticity is inevitable for any standpoint whose finitude consists primarily in the inability to cognize an absolute ground for the conditions of intelligibility. Thus, it is only because the Fichtean I and what Hegel calls 'thought' are infinite that they are said to be able to derive such conditions from themselves and thereby rule out their apparent facticity, whereas it is only because the Kantian I and what Heidegger calls 'Dasein' are finite that they are said to be unable to deduce such conditions from a first principle and thereby overcome their facticity.

Recent scholarship on Kant, German idealism, neo-Kantianism, and phenomenology makes possible the present study's contributions, including its ability to fill various interpretive lacuna. First, I examine Fichte's Jena period, which Daniel Breazeale, Wayne Martin, and Frederick Neuhouser lucidly articulate,[20] in order to provide context for the coining of 'facticity' in his Berlin period. Second, I offer a systematic reading of the development of German idealism beyond 1807, extending pioneering presentations of this tradition's founding arguments and methods by Frederick Beiser, Eckart Förster, and Paul Franks[21] so as to clarify its subsequent fissures. Third, like Karin Nisenbaum, I illuminate a problem that unifies nineteenth- and twentieth-century post-Kantian philosophy,[22] although I include Hegel within this unity. Fourth, like Karen Ng, I trace Hegel's logic to its early German idealist origins,[23] although I place more emphasis on his commitment to presuppositionlessness. Fifth, following Stephen Houlgate's resolute reading of Hegel's commitment to presuppositionlessness,[24] I show that Schelling's critique of Hegel is in fact cognizant of that commitment. Sixth, building on Steven Crowell's and Theodore Kisiel's work on Lask's reading of Fichte and impact on Heidegger,[25] I detail the complicated transmission of the concept of facticity from German idealism via neo-Kantianism to phenomenology. Seventh, I provide the German idealist pre-history of the momentous neo-Kantian and phenomenological debates, which Michael Friedman and Peter E. Gordon elucidate,[26] concerning the priority relation between rational spontaneity and existential thrownness. Eighth and finally, I explain the post-Kantian philosophical development that culminates in Heidegger's critique of Hegelian logic, which critique Robert Pippin recently defends.[27]

[20] See Breazeale 2013, Martin 1997, and Neuhouser 1990.
[21] See Beiser 1987, Beiser 2002, Förster 2012, and Franks 2005.
[22] See Nisenbaum 2018.
[23] See Ng 2020.
[24] See Houlgate 2006.
[25] See Crowell 1992, Kisiel 1995, and Kisiel 2000.
[26] See Friedman 2000 and Gordon 2010.
[27] See Pippin 2024.

Due to the scope of my primary historical and philosophical claims, the present study involves several necessary limitations. First, in order to trace the transition from German idealism's architectonic interest in logical systematicity toward phenomenology's existentialist interest in radical contingency, I focus on the pivotal role of Schelling and so leave out post-Kantian critiques of presuppositionlessness by Arthur Schopenhauer, Søren Kierkegaard, and Friedrich Nietzsche, which I register in footnotes. Second, in order to demonstrate Schelling's pivotal role in the history of the concept of facticity, I draw mainly on his later work and so omit earlier phases of his sprawling oeuvre, which I explore in previous publications. Third, in order to explain Heidegger's inheritance of Dilthey's hermeneutical method, I offer a brief account of modern hermeneutics that does not include later contributions by Hans-Georg Gadamer and Paul Ricoeur. Fourth, in order to articulate Heidegger's hermeneutics of facticity, I stop short of post-1930s theories of facticity by Sartre, de Beauvoir, and Merleau-Ponty, who, while they lack Heidegger's engagement with the pre-phenomenological sources, meanings, and provocations of the concept of facticity, indicate how the history of this concept continues into the hermeneutical, phenomenological, and existentialist traditions and, indeed, into our own time.

0.4 *Ich bin* or *Es gibt*

While Kant is evidently a philosopher of facticity *avant la lettre*, Heidegger is arguably the philosopher of facticity *par excellence*. In the historical interval that binds them, reason's peculiar fate is to transform from an infinite activity that deduces conditions of intelligibility from itself into a thrown activity whose conditions of intelligibility are radically contingent. In other words, and as this book's epigraph indicates, reason is transposed from the hand that unconditionally holds the world to the thrown activity of being-in-the-world. Moreover, reason's reorientation in this respect is itself factical, since it exhibits the undeducibly historical character that any meaningful pursuit must exhibit. In other words, it is in virtue of historicity that reason endures the post-Kantian methodological crises that yield the succession from transcendental logic to dialectical logic to hermeneutics.

Reason's fate after Kant might seem tragic to the extent that it sacrifices the logical rigor of deduction for the incompleteness and potential inauthenticity of hermeneutical interpretation. However, we can understand this fate as corrective in a Kantian sense.

In the B-edition Preface to the first *Critique*, Kant says that critique's "**negative**" utility is that it restricts speculative reason to "the boundaries of experience" and thereby "removes an obstacle that limits or even threatens to wipe out the practical use of reason." The "obstacle" is the assumption that objects of experience are things in themselves, from which it follows that the principle of causality is "valid of all things in general," that the "human soul" in particular is "subject to natural necessity, i.e., that it is not free," and that morality is therefore impossible. By rejecting this assumption, critique's "**positive**" utility is that it "convince[s]" us that reason has a "practical use," that is, a "moral use." The corrective power of critique is accordingly "to deny **knowledge** in order to make room for **faith**," where knowledge is the result of applying the principle of causality beyond the bounds of possible experience, yielding moral faithlessness.[28]

Similarly, for Heidegger, the assumption that thinking presupposes nothing, in accordance with the radicalized enlightenment ideal of rational cognition, is an obstacle to understanding our factical situation. By rejecting this assumption, hermeneutics enables us to pursue an authentic self-understanding. The corrective power of hermeneutics is accordingly to deny enlightenment in order to make room for authenticity, where enlightenment is the result of applying the demand for presuppositionlessness beyond the facticity of lived experience, yielding existential faithlessness. However, whereas Kant regards critique as exposing an evasion of freedom that he says is "dangerous to the schools" yet "can hardly be transmitted to the public,"[29] Heidegger regards hermeneutics as exposing an evasion of facticity that is observable not just in philosophy, but also in everyday life. Reason's fate after Kant thus affords a hermeneutical method for resisting a truly ubiquitous inauthenticity, against which, however, this very method, being a mode of Dasein's self-understanding, cannot guarantee its own immunity.

Reason's fate after Kant ultimately becomes our own. This is because, by virtue of philosophizing in light of the Copernican turn, we inherit the tension between the competing responses to the post-Kantian question of whether a science of intelligibility can tolerate brute facts. As post-Kantians, we must therefore ask anew whether bruteness is impermissible or unavoidable. We must ask anew whether we are incipiently at home in an intelligible world or face the uncanniness of being in that very world. We must ask anew whether we are held by the absolute autonomy of reason or thrown into the groundless givenness of being. *Ich bin* or *Es gibt*. There is, it seems, no third.

We should not be surprised to find ourselves faced with the post-Kantian question. The history of philosophy is not a chronicle of past positions that might provoke our curiosity, but is rather a living tradition that invites us to reflect on and reimagine how we think today. Indeed, the history of philosophy is not just a proper domain of inquiry, but is always also a persistent reminder of our critical responsibilities as philosophers, that is, as thinkers who are committed both to taking responsibility for our unseen intellectual inheritance and to assessing our unspoken assumptions about what counts as worthy philosophical study.

[28] Kant KrV Bxxiv–xxx.
[29] Kant KrV Bxxxiii.

Thus, we might dread nihilism and come to see why being the puppet of either nature or reason torments Jacobi and spurs Fichte to posit freedom as a first principle. We might lament that a culture without metaphysics is spiritually deadened and come to understand why, insofar as metaphysics is threatened by presuppositions, Hegel aims to eliminate them entirely. We might feel vertigo at the arbitrariness of the meaning of being who we are and come to appreciate why human existence drives Schelling to ask why there is meaning rather than meaninglessness. And we might experience anxiety at the absence of an absolute ground of beings and come to realize why the groundlessness of beings overwhelms Heidegger. To the extent that we philosophize in any of these ways, the history of philosophy reveals itself to be fraught with live problems, which is to say, problems that are livable and, often in our own lives, lived.

0.5 Overview

Fichte sets the terms of the post-Kantian question of whether a science of intelligibility can tolerate brute facts. This is because his philosophy bears what I will call the 'twin birth' of the coining of 'facticity,' which is his name for the alleged problem of groundless conditions of intelligibility, and the invention of dialectical logic, which is his method of deriving such conditions from the contradictions of reason or the I. In what follows, Part I registers this twin birth so that Parts II and III can trace the lineage that follows from each child. Moreover, each Part stages what I will call a 'crisis of method,' that is, a decisive point in the ongoing response to the post-Kantian question at which a method of determining the conditions of intelligibility is judged to be in need of change for the sake of the flourishing of philosophy as the science of intelligibility.

I will now provide a brief chapter overview.

Part I concerns the philosophical problems that Fichte inherits after Kant's turn from general logic to transcendental logic.

In Chapter 1, I will provide an analysis of the questions to which Kant's metaphysical and transcendental deductions are answers, namely and respectively, the question *quid facti*, concerning the origin of the categories, and the question *quid juris*, concerning our right to use the categories. Next, I will explain Fichte's critique of Kant's metaphysical deduction as a radically contingent and thus inadequate premise on which to rest the conclusions of Kant's transcendental deductions. I will then show that, in his Jena period, Fichte proposes a 'genetic' deduction of the categories, which proceeds by a dialectical movement of thought, in order to answer Kant's two questions simultaneously and thereby to secure scientific rigor for a transcendental idealist account of the categories as conditions of intelligibility. I will conclude by observing that Hegel develops Fichte's dialectical logic into a presuppositionless and thus truly absolute science of intelligibility, thereby distinguishing the extent to which they each strive to eliminate radical contingency. This will anticipate my full analysis of the nature and limitations of Hegel's presuppositionless logic in Part II.

In Chapter 2, I will detail the origin of Fichte's neologism in texts from his early Berlin period, showing that 'facticity' refers to the same intolerable radical contingency to which his logical innovation in Jena is the intended solution. Next, I will demonstrate the methodological continuity between the Jena and Berlin presentations of the *Wissenschaftslehre*, that is, the doctrine of science, which consistently divide this science into two parts, namely, the intellectual intuition or 'insight' into the I as first principle and the genetic deduction or 'genesis' of the conditions of intelligibility from the I. I will then detail Fichte's observation in the 1804 spring lectures in Berlin, which he delivers at his home, that his own doctrine of intellectual intuition contains an ideal form, namely, the thought of the I, and a real content, namely, the intuition of the I, that are factically and thus unacceptably presupposed, and I will reconstruct his genetic deduction of this form and content from the nature of the I itself. I will conclude by observing that although Heidegger shares the anti-nihilistic spirit of Fichte's idealism, they endorse diametrically opposed conceptions of facticity. This will anticipate my full analysis of the advantage and promise of Heidegger's hermeneutics of facticity in Part III.

Part II concerns the philosophical problems that Schelling diagnoses after Hegel's turn from transcendental logic to dialectical logic.

In Chapter 3, I will explain Kant's enlightenment ideal of rational cognition, according to which reason is the source of the form of cognition. Next, I will demonstrate Fichte's radicalization of this ideal in his pursuit of an absolute science of intelligibility. I will then show that, despite commending Fichte for inspiring this pursuit, Hegel argues in his own Jena period that Fichte falls short of total presuppositionlessness insofar as he tolerates the radical contingency of the opposition of the I and the not-I. This brute fact renders any genetic deduction of conditions of intelligibility on its basis rhapsodic and therefore unscientific. Diverging from a tendency among scholars, I will show that Hegel critiques Fichte's idealism not for being subjective as opposed to objective, but rather for being factical as opposed to scientific. I will conclude by articulating the logical method by which Hegel dialectically removes the last vestige of facticity in the *Wissenschaftslehre*, thereby completing the German idealist response to Kant's question *quid facti*.

In Chapter 4, I will introduce what I will call Kant's 'doctrine of epistemic reciprocity' and explain how it is meant to prove the objective reality of the categories through their application in sense experience and thus how this doctrine provides an answer to what I will call the 'question *quid indicii*.' Next, I will articulate Maimon's skepticism about any such answer, which he expresses in the empty formalism challenge against both Kant's categories and Reinhold's first principle. I will then show that Schelling appropriates Maimonian skepticism as a partial means to exhibiting the twofold factical presupposition of Hegel's science of intelligibility.

On the one hand, Hegel's science presupposes its own endorsement and purpose, which Schelling represents with the non-empirical concepts of the past and the future, respectively. On the other hand, Hegel's science presupposes the brute fact of existence as such, whose intelligibility requires, according to Schelling, not simply a negative science of thought-determinations that by themselves would be merely empty forms, but also a reciprocally dependent positive science of the experience of existence. I will conclude with an account of how Schelling's critique of Hegel provides the first post-Kantian defense of the philosophical plausibility of facticity.

Part III concerns the philosophical problems that Heidegger hermeneutically diagnoses in the post-Kantian logical turn.

In Chapter 5, I will consider Lask's claim that Fichte coins 'facticity' in order to name the limit of genetic deduction, namely, the material particularity of individuals that resists deductions from the I. Next, I will show that Lask mistakes the task of a genetic deduction and thereby mistakes the specific problem that Fichte's neologism names. The problem is not the haecceity of individuals, which I will call their 'material facticity,' but is rather the rhapsodic and thus unscientific determination of the conditions of intelligibility, which I will call their 'formal facticity.' This alone explains Fichte's explicit and repeated commitment to expunging facticity as far as possible from the *Wissenschaftslehre*. I will then show that, despite his misreading, Lask's conception of the facticity of individuals' existence prefigures Heidegger's conception of the facticity of Dasein's existence yet does not discourage the latter's phenomenological critique of what I will call Fichte's 'rationalist recoil from facticity.' I will conclude by introducing Dilthey's conception of the hermeneutical method and explain why, according to Heidegger, it demands a turn toward a hermeneutics of the facticity of Dasein.

In Chapter 6, I will show that Heidegger diverges from German idealism by dissolving rather than solving the rhapsody problem. I will argue that whereas the German idealists regard this problem as demanding a deductive solution, Heidegger denies that determining conditions of intelligibility can ultimately be deductive, since philosophical deduction, like any meaningful project, presupposes factical conditions that can only be hermeneutically interpreted. I will then demonstrate that Heidegger improves on various aspects of Schelling's, Lask's, and Dilthey's critical responses to German idealism. Next, I will show how Heidegger's hermeneutics of facticity reveals an unspoken truth in '*nihil ulterius*,' which is Kant's phrase in the first *Critique* for the groundlessness of the conditions of intelligibility. The truth is that there is no intelligible existence without what he calls 'the nothing,' a strange phrase that denotes the radical contingency that there are beings at all. Heidegger thereby effects a return to and intensification of Kant's tolerance for radical contingency, thereby casting reason's peculiar fate less in the theoretical terms of undeniable and unanswerable questions of metaphysics and more in the concrete terms of the lived experience into which we are always already thrown.

PART I
A CRISIS OF METHOD
Transcendental Logic

1

Nihil Ulterius

Fichte's Solution to Kant's Rhapsody Problem

1.1 Introduction

In the Preface to the first *Critique*, Kant warns that freedom and morality "give way to the mechanism of nature" if we defer to reason's speculative use, which, since it is restricted to the "natural necessity" of appearances, renders its "practical extension . . . impossible." It is in light of this that he resolves to "deny knowledge in order to make room for faith" of the sort that can withstand "all unbelief conflicting with morality."[1] In the Doctrine of Method, Kant concludes that, by preventing speculative "devastations" to freedom and morality, critique allows us to "return to metaphysics as to a beloved from whom we have been estranged" and to pursue the "essential ends of humanity," especially moral ends, to which mathematical, scientific, and empirical knowledge have "value" strictly as "means."[2] This foregrounds Kant's claim in the Dialectic of 1788's *Critique of Practical Reason* that "all interest is ultimately practical and even that of speculative reason is only conditional and is complete in practical use alone," from which he infers that we avoid "a conflict of reason with itself," not by a "contingent" juxtaposition of speculative and practical reason, but rather by a "necessary" union of speculative and practical reason in which "the latter has primacy."[3]

In §5 of the 1796–99 Jena lecture transcripts that compose the *Wissenschaftslehre Nova Methodo*, Fichte observes that Kant rightly "insists upon the primacy of practical reason," but asserts that he "has failed to show decisively that the practical is the source of the theoretical."[4] In the First Introduction, Fichte announces that these lectures "present philosophy *as a whole*, in the exposition of which theoretical and practical philosophy are united. This presentation follows a much more natural path, beginning with the practical sphere . . . in order to explain the [theoretical sphere] in terms of the former."[5] While Fichte agrees with Kant that practical

[1] Kant KrV Bxxvii–xxx.
[2] Kant KrV A849–50/B877–8.
[3] Kant KpV | AA 5: 121.
[4] Fichte NM | GA IV/2: 61. Cf. Fichte: "[Kant] speaks of an interest of speculative reason and of an interest of practical reason and opposes these two to each other. From the perspective of Kant's philosophy this is correct, but it is not correct in itself; for reason is always one and has only one interest. The interest of reason lies in confidence in one's own self-sufficiency and freedom, and reason's interest in unity and coherence is a consequence of this prior interest" (Fichte NM | GA IV/2: 17).
[5] Fichte NM | GA IV/2: 10.

Facticity and the Fate of Reason After Kant. G. Anthony Bruno, Oxford University Press.
 DOI: 10.1093/9780191987533.003.0002

reason has priority over theoretical reason, he interprets this priority in absolute terms. As he says in §5, "[i]f there is no acting, then there is no experience," for "it is only by means of such acting—and moreover, only insofar as it is a hindered or arrested activity—that we obtain any consciousness whatsoever of what is actual. Only thereby is *experience* possible."[6] It is our agency that originally opens up a world of objects, namely, as means, ends, and obstacles, from which it follows that reason is primarily practical. It is because practical reason has absolute primacy that Fichte demands that theoretical reason originate in or derive from it, lest their division threaten the unity of reason.

Throughout his Jena period, Fichte articulates the primacy of practical reason in terms of the absolute freedom of reason or the I, from which he aims to derive the necessary conditions of the possibility of intelligibility, namely, the forms of sensibility, the forms of judgment, the categories of the understanding, and the ideas of reason. Only such a starting point can secure the systematicity that is lacking in Kant's presentation of transcendental idealism, which is otherwise vulnerable to refutation by the theoretical possibility of Spinozism, with its denial of human freedom and purposiveness.

Fichte takes his derivational construal of the primacy of practical reason to capture the spirit, if not the letter, of Kant's philosophy. In 1797–98's *Attempt at a New Presentation of the Wissenschaftslehre*, whose Preface cites the motto of the B-edition first *Critique* that is taken from Francis Bacon's 1620 *The Great Instauration*,[7] Fichte says that his system is "nothing other than the *Kantian* [system]; this means that it contains the same view of things, but is in method quite independent of the *Kantian* presentation."[8] Fichte and Kant share an "idealistic" spirit that locates the "explanatory ground of experience" in the first-person standpoint.[9] Fichte contrasts this spirit with that of "the modern philosophers," whom he calls "*dogmatists*" because they assign the explanatory ground of experience to the third-person standpoint of things in themselves.[10] This, he says, "leaves an enormous gap between things and representations" made from the first-person standpoint.[11] Although Kant avoids this explanatory gap, his presentation

6 Fichte NM | GA IV/2: 60–1. Cf. Fichte's 1800 *Vocation of Man*: "We do not act because we know, but we know because we are meant to act; practical reason is the root of all reason . . . We cannot renounce [practical] laws without having the world and, with it, ourselves sink into absolute nothingness" (Fichte BM | SW II: 262).

7 Fichte VND | SW I: 419.

8 Fichte VND | SW I: 420. Cf. Kant: "Following Aristotle, we will call these concepts **categories**, for our aim is basically identical with his although very distinct from it in execution" (Kant KrV A79–80/B105).

9 Fichte VND | SW I: 428, 429n.

10 Fichte VND | SW I: 429n. On why Fichte's conception of idealism is not inconsistent with realism, see Martin 1997: 30–54. On why his conception of dogmatism is not identical with transcendental realism, see Beiser 2002: 262–72.

11 Fichte VND | SW I: 438. On this gap's relation to the hard problem of consciousness, see Bruno 2021c.

of transcendental idealism lacks a derivation of theoretical reason from practical reason, which calls for a new way of presenting "the same view," that is, a new "method" for expressing the idealist spirit. Fichte's *Wissenschaftslehre* is designed to supplement transcendental idealism by providing this derivation and, hence, by demonstrating the unity of reason.

How are we to understand Fichte's claim to articulate the same philosophical content as Kant but in a different form? How can Fichte espouse Kant's system yet maintain methodological independence? Indeed, what is the nature of the method by which the *Wissenschaftslehre* expresses the spirit of transcendental idealism?

In the first *Critique*, Kant develops two distinct sciences in order to account for our experience of nature. Whereas the transcendental aesthetic is the science of the rules of sensibility, namely, space and time, transcendental logic is the science of the rules of thinking of objects *a priori*, namely, the categories.[12] The conclusions of these sciences are that the forms of sensibility and the categories are necessary conditions of experience. Some of Kant's earliest readers, including Fichte,[13] Hegel,[14] Maimon,[15] Reinhold,[16] and Schelling,[17] call for a basic premise in the

[12] See Kant KrV A21/B35–6.

[13] See Fichte's letter to Friedrich Philipp Immanuel Niethammer, December 6, 1793: "Only by reaching Kant's results in one's own way will one have understood Kant, and then the world will really be astonished" (Fichte B | 1988: 368). Cf. his letter to Heinrich Stephani, mid-December 1793: "Kant's philosophy, as such, is correct—but only in its results and not in its grounds. This singular thinker looks more marvelous to me every day. I believe that he possesses a genius which reveals the truth to him without showing him why it is true" (Fichte B | 1988: 371).

[14] See Hegel's 1816 review of Jacobi's 1816 *Works, Volume 3*: "the narrative manner of Kant (whose own main concern was only to establish the basis of universality and necessity in cognition) gives just cause to assume that the materials of his story of thought, feeling, time and space, imagination, understanding, and finally reason are quite as contingent in respect to each other as their coincidence in a mere story would make them appear . . . [I]n Kant it is rather the *lack of necessity*, the *contingency* and *externality*, that characterize the determinations of the mind and their relation to each other" (Hegel JW | GW 15: 16–7).

[15] See Maimon's letter to Kant, December 2, 1793: "since the appearance of the *Critique*, there have been several attempts to bring particular disciplines into accord with its requirements, yet no one has attempted a reconstruction of logic. I am convinced that logic, as a science, is just as much in need of the *Critique*. *General* logic must of course be distinguished from *transcendental* logic, but the former must be revised in light of the latter . . . The rectification of logic will occur when people see the error of *abstracting* logical forms from their use, an error that early logicians, even Aristotle, committed. Something foreign to logical forms still remains attached to them thereby" (Kant B | AA 11: 470–1).

[16] In 1789/95's *Essay on a New Theory of the Human Capacity for Representation*, Reinhold describes his 1786–87 "Letters on the Kantian Philosophy" as an "attempt to present [Kant's] results independently of the Kantian premises" (Reinhold VNT 57 | 2011: 23). In 1790's *Contributions to Correcting Previous Misunderstandings of the Philosophers*, he charges that the first *Critique* provides "no first principle of all philosophy" and thus no principle from which to derive its "theory of sensibility, understanding, and reason." Reinhold's text consequently "leads to the same results" as the first *Critique* "through a completely different path" so as to secure a "confirmation of Kant's discoveries" and thereby establish the "elementary philosophy" (Reinhold BB | 1790: 262–3, 273).

[17] See Schelling's letter to Hegel, January 6, 1795: "Philosophy has not yet reached its end. Kant has given the results: the premises are still lacking. And who can understand results without the premises?" (Hegel B | 1984: 29). Cf. Schelling in 1795's "Of the I as Principle of Philosophy, or On the Unconditioned in Human Knowledge": "Kant's deductions tell us at first glance that they presuppose superior principles. Thus Kant names the only possible forms of sensible intuition, space and time, without having examined them according to a principle (as for instance the categories according to the principle of logical functions of judgment). The categories are set up according to the table of the

form of either a first principle or a dialectical logic that can serve as an absolute ground for some, if not all, of the conclusions of his logical and aesthetic sciences and thus can unify these conclusions into a single science. Without this premise, these conclusions might reflect no more than our subjective constitution or fail to compose a rigorous system. Kant's conclusions about the structural role that space, time, the forms of judgment, the categories, and the ideas play in experience might thereby lack absolute necessity.[18] In other words, whereas Kant regards "the critique of pure reason" as a "special science" that oversees the determination of conditions of intelligibility by aesthetic and logical sub-sciences,[19] critique for these early readers must become a doctrinal science that deduces such conditions from a first principle or a dialectical logic in order to guarantee their objectivity, rigor, and necessity. To this end, Fichte demands absolute necessity for Kant's conclusions and charges its absence with rhapsody or what in 1799 he calls 'facticity.' Fichte is the first to pursue a systematically rigorous post-Kantian logic, that is, a single, "absolute" science of the conditions of intelligibility.[20] Such a logic requires a new method for determining conditions, specifically, a new form of deduction.

Although Fichte alters his presentation of the *Wissenschaftslehre* throughout his career, he remains committed to a methodological division of labor between positing a first principle and deducing the conditions of intelligibility from that principle. In the *Nova Methodo*, he says that the *Wissenschaftslehre* consists of "precisely two parts," namely, positing the I as "the true object of consciousness" and "the foundation of everything else," on the one hand, and deducing "the conditions from which consciousness" is "to be constructed," on the other hand.[21] Earlier,

functions of judgment, but the latter are not set up according to any principle... This essay proposes to establish the principles [on which Kant's thoughts rest]" (Schelling IPP | SW I/1: 153–5; cf. 152, 210).

[18] See Beck's 1796 *The Only Possible Standpoint from which Critical Philosophy Must be Judged* (Beck 2000), Fichte VND | SW I: 441, and Maimon's 1794 *Attempt at a New Logic, or Theory of Thinking with Appended Letters of Philalethes to Aenesidemus* (Maimon VNL 407–32 | 2000: 186–96).

[19] Kant KrV A11/B24. Cf. Kant KrV A52/B76.

[20] Fichte NM | GA IV/2: 21n.

[21] Fichte NM | GA IV/2: 179. Cf. Fichte's claim in 1796's *Foundations of Natural Right* that our insight into the I is "the exclusive condition of all philosophizing," after which we must give a "deduction" of the necessary conditions of self-consciousness (Fichte GN | SW III: 2, 9). A similar methodological division characterizes 1794–95's *Foundations of the Entire Wissenschaftslehre*, which proceeds from an analysis of three basic principles to a derivation of theoretical and practical categories (Fichte GWL | SW I: 87). Fichte declares in 1798's *The System of Ethics* that the moral law must be "derived from the highest and absolute principle, that of I-hood," a "deduction" that thus proceeds from the "foundation of the entire *Wissenschaftslehre*" (Fichte SS | SW IV: 14–15). Indeed, the full titles of his texts on right and ethics, namely, *Foundations of Natural Right According to the Principles of the Wissenschaftslehre* and *The System of Ethics According to the Principles of the Wissenschaftslehre*, indicate that their deductions follow methodologically from philosophy's first principle. See also *Wissenschaftslehre*'s division in the 1804 spring lectures in Berlin into a doctrine of being, which yields insight into the absolute, and a doctrine of appearances, which deduces the structural disjunctions among phenomena (Fichte WL04 | GA II/8: 84–5). Cf. Fichte's twofold method with the analytic and synthetic methods by which Kant, in the Preface to 1785's *Groundwork of the Metaphysics of Morals*, abstracts the "supreme principle" of practical cognition and then combines the former with the latter (Kant GMM | AA 4: 392) and, in the Preface to the second *Critique*, forms the "*architectonic*" idea of a pure rational faculty as a whole and then derives the mutual relations of that faculty's parts (Kant KpV | AA 5: 10).

Fichte describes the latter task as "exhibit[ing] the conditions that make it possible for the I to posit itself and to oppose a not-I to itself... demonstrat[ing] these conditions by means of a deduction."[22] Positing the I is an act of affirming one's freedom as primary and irreducible, that is, it is positing oneself as self-positing.[23] Positing the I in this sense is meant to refute competing first principles, particularly the dogmatist's not-I as it is exemplified by Spinoza's conception of nature, whose nihilistic consequence is the denial of human freedom and purposiveness. By contrast, a deduction identifies the conditions that are necessary for exercising or realizing the I's freedom in experience. Such conditions are "categories" insofar as they are "the ways in which the I goes beyond simply thinking of itself and thinks of something else," that is, the ways in which the I "divides itself into a manifold—though in such a way that it nevertheless continues to remain a unity."[24] Deducing the categories from the freedom of the I secures precisely the derivation of theoretical reason from practical reason that Fichte finds lacking in Kant's philosophy and demands for the sake of the unity of reason.

The specific problem that Fichte's deduction is meant to solve is the ultimate groundlessness or radical contingency of Kant's metaphysical deduction of the categories in the first *Critique*, which aims to show that the categories "spring pure and unmixed from the understanding" by proving their "complete coincidence" with the logical forms of judgment.[25] Kant claims that this proof avoids the "haphazard search for pure concepts" that he attributes to Aristotle,[26] a charge that Fichte returns to Kant. Implicitly addressing Kant in the *New Presentation*, Fichte says: "To a critical idealist . . . who does not derive the presumed laws of the intellect from the very nature of the intellect, one may address the following question: How did you obtain any material acquaintance with these laws? I.e., how did you become aware that the laws of the intellect are precisely these laws of substantiality and causality?"[27] According to Fichte, if we deduce or, equivalently, derive[28] categories like 'substance' and 'causality' from the logical forms of judgment, that

[22] Fichte NM | GA IV/2: 8.

[23] On Fichte's conception of self-positing, see Henrich 1982 and Franks 2016a.

[24] Fichte NM | GA IV/2: 198. Cf. Fichte: "Idealism considers the intellect to be a kind of *doing* and absolutely nothing more... What has to be derived now are *determinate* representations of a material, spatial, etc., world... Accordingly, what idealism presupposes is the following: The intellect acts; but, as a consequence of its very nature, it can act only in a certain, specific manner. If one considers the intellect's necessary modes of acting in isolation from any [actual] acting, then it is quite appropriate to call these the 'laws of acting.' Hence there are necessary laws of the intellect" (Fichte VND | SW I: 441).

[25] Kant KrV A67/B92, B159.

[26] Kant KrV A81/B106–7. Cf. P | AA 4: 322–4. On Kant's claim to the completeness of Aristotle's logic, see Lu-Adler 2016.

[27] Fichte VND | SW I: 442. Cf. Schelling's 1841–42 Berlin lectures: "For ten to twenty years, the Kantian table of twelve categories has maintained a reputation in German philosophy scarcely less than that of the tables of the ten commandments, and everyone has believed that they must deal with everything according to this table; however, upon closer examination they may very well be subject to a significant reduction" (Schelling BV-B | SW II/3: 48).

[28] See Fichte RA | SW I: 23, Fichte NM | GA IV/2: 8, and Fichte SS | SW IV: 14.

is, through what he calls "a detour through logic," and if we presuppose these forms of judgment, as Kant does, instead of deriving them from a first principle, then we cannot prove that these and only these categories necessarily are the "immanent laws of the intellect," as opposed to properties of things in themselves.[29] Deducing both the forms of judgment and the categories from the activity of the I is meant to avoid this problem and thereby demonstrate the unity of reason. As Fichte says in 1794's *Concerning the Concept of the Wissenschaftslehre*: "every logical proposition and logic in its entirety must be deduced from the *Wissenschaftslehre*. We have to show that the forms that are established within logic really are the forms of a particular content within the *Wissenschaftslehre*. Logic, therefore, derives its validity from the *Wissenschaftslehre*, but the validity of the latter is not derived from the former."[30]

Inquiring into the nature of the *Wissenschaftslehre*'s methodological innovation accordingly draws our attention to Fichte's original idea of a deduction. In §7 of the First Introduction to the *New Presentation*, he explains that a deduction

> *shows that what is first postulated as the first principle and immediately established within consciousness is not possible unless something else occurs as well, and that this second thing is not possible apart from the occurrence of some third thing. It continues in this manner until all of the conditions of the first principle have been completely exhausted and its possibility has become completely comprehensible.*[31]

For Fichte, the absolute freedom of reason or, equivalently, the I is philosophy's "*first principle*."[32] Moreover, our immediate awareness or what he calls our

[29] Fichte VND | SW I: 442–3. Cf. Reinhold BB | 1790: 315.

[30] Fichte BWL | SW I: 68. In his capacity as co-editor of *Philosophical Journal of a Society of German Scholars*, Fichte appends a note to a passage in Johann Christian August Grohmann's anonymous 1798 "Fichte and Kant, or An Attempted Comparison between the Fichtean and the Kantian Philosophy" concerning the charge that the *Wissenschaftslehre* is guilty of "*empty circularity*," replying to the charge thusly: "Yes indeed, just think of it: the *Wissenschaftslehre* derives the laws of reason by thinking in accordance with the laws of reason! Is it then supposed to accomplish its derivations by thinking in a manner contrary to the laws of reason?—Granted, Kant himself is not guilty of this circularity; instead, he is guilty of the unpardonable circularity of deriving the laws of reason from logic. The Kantians themselves have not acquired any grey hairs from worrying about how such logic is itself supposed to have come into being. Anything that lies beyond the *Critique* is for them an unknown world" (Fichte ZFK | GA I/4: 487).

[31] Fichte VND | SW I: 446.

[32] See Fichte's 1795 summer lectures in Jena: "'Reason' is the name for the entire power and essence of the intellect or I-hood. 'I' and 'reason' are one and the same" (Fichte GA IV/1: 248, translated by Breazeale 2013: 412). Cf. Fichte: "it is the very nature of I-hood to determine itself unconditionally, to be what is absolutely first {in every moment of reflection} and never to be anything secondary {—for otherwise it would not be an I}. Consequently, this act of reflection is absolutely free . . . The 'pure I' of the published *Wissenschaftslehre* is to be understood as reason as such or in general, which is something quite different from personal I-hood" (Fichte NM | GA IV/2: 157, 220). Cf. also Fichte GWL | SW I: 253 and Fichte GN | SW III: 1, 22, 53, 58.

'intellectual intuition' of the I constitutes philosophy's sole proper starting point,[33] given the nihilistic consequence of idealism's only theoretically consistent systematic rival, namely, Spinozism.[34] However, grasping philosophy's first principle incurs the further task of determining the conditions under which the I can be realized, which task is served by a deduction. Such a deduction is "genetic" insofar as it is the method by which the I derives these conditions from itself.[35] The notion of genesis is meant to capture the sense in which determining the conditions of intelligibility is "*completely exhausted*" by the productive activity of the I reflecting on itself.

In order to comprehend Fichte's claim to articulate the same view as Kant in a different form and thus to comprehend the *Wissenschaftslehre*'s methodological independence from Kant's presentation of transcendental idealism, it is crucial to distinguish genetic deduction from the sorts of deduction that Kant offers. I propose to interpret genetic deduction as the simultaneous fulfillment of two tasks, namely, the genealogical task of deriving the categories from a first principle and the jurisprudential task of establishing our right to use them as necessary conditions of intelligibility. While the second task represents Fichte's agreement with the aim of Kant's transcendental deduction, which is to prove our right to use the categories, the first task reflects his dissatisfaction with the execution of Kant's metaphysical deduction, insofar as the latter derives the categories from an ultimately groundless or radically contingent origin, namely, the logical forms of judgment. For Fichte, we derive the categories from the I as first principle just if we establish our right to use them.

My reading draws on a Kantian distinction on which the secondary literature on Fichte is silent. In the first *Critique*, Kant distinguishes between the question *quid facti*, which concerns the origin of our possession of a concept, and the question *quid juris*, which concerns our right to use a concept. Kant's metaphysical and transcendental deductions of the categories are his respective responses to these questions. It is therefore imperative to interpret Fichte's methodological innovation in light of the questions *quid facti* and *quid juris*, for, as I will argue, the genealogical and jurisprudential tasks that these questions respectively raise jointly define the unified task that he assigns to a genetic deduction.[36]

[33] On Fichte's notion of intellectual intuition, see Ameriks 2000, Beiser 2002: 294–301, Breazeale 2013, Bruno 2022b, Gram 1981, Henrich 1982, Neuhouser 1990, Talbot 1900, and Zöller 1998: 33–8, and cf. Rödl 2013. For responses to Henrich 1982, see Zöller 2016a and Frank 2019.

[34] See Fichte's 1807 Königsberg lectures: "Before Kant, all philosophizing was a blind groping, and the most consistent of these blind gropers was Spinoza" (Fichte GA II/10: 113, translated by Breazeale 2018: 136).

[35] Fichte VND | SW I: 495.

[36] Martin hints that Fichte "does not think of philosophical enquiry as being concerned primarily with the *quid juris*" (Martin 1997: 151 n12). Rockmore refers to Kant's distinction in passing, but cites an inaccurate formulation of it (Rockmore 2001: 64). On why Schelling's claim in 1795–96's "Philosophical Letters on Dogmatism and Criticism" that philosophy's "last great question" is "to be or not to be" (Schelling PB | SW I/1: 339) expresses a radical form of the question *quid juris*, see Bruno (forthcoming).

In this chapter, I will offer an analysis of Kant's two questions (Section 1.2) and explain Fichte's critique of Kant's metaphysical answer to the question *quid facti* (Section 1.3). I will then examine Fichte's genetic answer to this question, underscoring the genealogical character of his answer while keeping in view its jurisprudential character (Section 1.4). Next, I will articulate the dialectical movement of thought in a genetic deduction and detail this movement's guidance by the principle of determinability (Section 1.5). I will conclude by observing how Fichte's dialectical thinking impacts Hegel's pursuit of a presuppositionless science of intelligibility, while distinguishing the extent to which they each strive to eliminate radical contingency (Section 1.6). This will anticipate my analysis of Hegel's dialectical logic in Part II.

1.2 The Questions *Quid Facti* and *Quid Juris*

Kant only briefly discusses the questions *quid juris* and *quid facti* in the first *Critique*.[37] In §13 of the Transcendental Analytic, he states that the question *quid juris* concerns our lawful "claim" or "entitlement" to use a concept, which a transcendental deduction is designed to prove. By contrast, an empirical deduction demonstrates not the "lawfulness" with which we use a concept, but rather "the fact from which the possession has arisen." It is with such an origin of acquisition that the question *quid facti* is in general concerned.[38] This brief definition of the question *quid facti* might give the impression that only an empirical deduction qualifies as an answer to it, which would imply that we only come to possess concepts empirically. However, when we broaden our interpretive frame, we see that the question *quid facti* admits of another sort of answer, namely, what Kant calls a 'metaphysical deduction,' according to which we acquire certain non-empirical or pure concepts through the understanding alone.[39]

An early-1780s reflection repeats the distinction made in §13, directing the question *quid facti* to the "way one has first come into the possession of a concept" and the question *quid juris* to the "right [by which] one possesses and uses it." Kant then adds that the "universality and necessity in the use of the pure concepts of the understanding betrays their origin," namely, that it "must not be empirical."[40]

[37] A version of this discussion appears in Bruno 2018c.

[38] Kant KrV A84–5/B116–7.

[39] See Kant: "An empirical concept arises from the senses through comparison of objects of experience and attains through the understanding merely the form of universality. The reality of these concepts rests on actual experience, from which, as to their content, they are drawn. But whether there are *pure concepts of the understanding* (*conceptus puri*), which, as such, arise merely from the understanding, independently of all experience, must be investigated by metaphysics . . . The origin of concepts in regard to their *matter*, according to which a concept is either *empirical* or *arbitrary* or *intellectual*, is considered in metaphysics" (Kant JL | AA 9: 92, 94).

[40] Kant NF | AA 18: 267 (R5636).

A transcendental deduction demonstrates that the pure concepts or categories have warranted use because they are universal and necessary features of human experience, that is, conditions of its possibility, whereas non-empirical concepts that cannot make experience possible and so have no warranted use, for example, 'fate' and 'fortune,' are "usurpatory."[41] But then the origin of the categories cannot be empirical, since they make experience itself possible. This points to a non-empirical origin and therefore to a non-empirical answer to the question *quid facti*. It points, in other words, to a metaphysical deduction of the categories.[42]

This raises the question of how a metaphysical deduction and a transcendental deduction are related. How can such diverse tasks as tracing the origin of the categories and proving our right to use the categories, tasks that are intended to answer such distinct questions as the questions *quid facti* and the question *quid juris*, both count as deductions?

Ian Proops clarifies this issue in light of Dieter Henrich's seminal work on the first *Critique*. Henrich shows that the context for Kant's conception of a transcendental deduction is the eighteenth-century legal practice of justifying a claim to a contested possession.[43] Proops observes that this narrowly jurisprudential sense of deduction is distinguishable from a broader sense that descends from the Latin '*deducere*,' which means 'to draw out' or 'to derive from a source.' He argues that this broader, derivational sense of deduction captures Kant's idea of a metaphysical deduction.[44] As Kant says in the first *Critique*, it is through a metaphysical deduction that the categories are meant to be "systematically generated from a common principle, namely, the faculty for judging (which is the same as the faculty for thinking)."[45] Moreover, in 1783's *Prolegomena to Any Future Metaphysics That Will Be Able to Come Forward as Science*, he describes the categories' generation equivalently as their "derivation or deduction."[46] The equivalence of these terms in this particular context distinguishes the metaphysical deduction's genealogical function from the jurisprudential function of a transcendental deduction. Given these two senses of deduction, we can see how metaphysical and transcendental deductions track the problems that are voiced, respectively, by the question *quid*

41 Kant KrV A84/B117. On Kant's account of usurpatory concepts, see Thielke 2006.

42 Such a deduction is as concerned with the origin as with the precise kind and number of the categories, since it aims both to "systematically generat[e]" them from the "faculty for judging" and to secure their "completeness" (Kant KrV A80–1/B106–7). Knowing which concepts are categories is thus inseparable from knowing their metaphysical origin. A "physiological derivation" cannot identify their origin, for it merely traces "the first endeavours of our power of cognition to ascend from individual perceptions to general concepts" (Kant KrV A86/B118-9), which Proops says is "an account of which sense impressions first provoke the exercise of a particular concept" and thus "does not address the deeper question of *how* this concept comes to be present in the mind in the first place" (Proops 2003: 217–8).

43 Henrich 1989.

44 Proops 2003: 216.

45 Kant KrV A80–1/B106.

46 Kant P | AA 4: 324. Cf. Kant JL | AA 9: 114.

facti and the question *quid juris*. A metaphysical deduction derives the fact of our possession of the categories from a non-empirical origin, while a transcendental deduction establishes the right by which we "posses[s] and us[e]" them.

Proops helpfully draws attention to the genealogical character of the derivation that is provided by a metaphysical deduction. In the A-edition Preface to the first *Critique*, Kant personifies metaphysics as the queen of the sciences, to whom he says we attribute a false "genealogy" if we trace her birth to the "rabble of common experience."[47] Shortly after introducing the distinction between the questions *quid juris* and *quid facti*, he says that an "entirely different birth certificate than that of an ancestry from experiences must be produced" for the categories.[48] These passages show that the question *quid facti* demands a non-empirical lineage for the categories. Moreover, in the *Prolegomena*, Kant credits David Hume with recognizing that, if restricted to relations of ideas, reason only "pretends to have generated [the category of causality] in her womb" and so falsely takes it "for her own child."[49] This passage indicates that the categories' provenance cannot be ascertained through mere conceptual analysis, which Hume recognizes is powerless to rule out the negation of the concept of causality, but instead requires a non-empirical or metaphysical certification.

I turn now to the metaphysical deduction itself, by which term Kant refers to §§9–12 of the Analytic, prior to what in the B-edition he calls the first step or "beginning" of the transcendental deduction in §21.[50] We find that the metaphysical deduction proceeds in an explicitly genealogical manner in that it traces the categories to their "birthplace" and "ancestral registry" in the understanding.[51] This deduction "establishe[s]" the categories' "origin" through their "complete coincidence" with the logical forms of judgment.[52] These forms are the ways in which the understanding combines concepts and propositions in judging, for example, the categorical form of judgment is a way of combining subject-concepts and predicate-concepts, the hypothetical form of judgment is a way of combining assumed propositions and inferred propositions, and so on. Kant observes that the forms of judgment have two uses. On the one hand, these forms provide the unity of "different representations in a judgment," whether these representations are concepts or propositions. They do so in abstraction from any sensory content, that is, without reference to an object of intuition. On the other hand, these forms provide the unity of "different representations in an intuition," namely, when sensory content is given in intuition to the understanding. Whereas the first use of the forms of judgment is merely logical insofar as it abstracts from all content, the second is

[47] Kant KrV Aix.
[48] Kant KrV A86/B119.
[49] Kant P | AA 4: 257.
[50] Kant KrV B144.
[51] Kant KrV A66/B90, A81/B107.
[52] Kant KrV B159.

real insofar as it determines a sensory manifold. These uses are nevertheless isomorphic because, Kant says, they are actions of the "same understanding."[53] It is the introduction of intuition that occasions the shift in that same understanding's activity from the logical to the real use of the forms of judgment. In this shift, intuition transforms the forms of judgment into categories that can determine a sensory manifold so as to yield empirical cognition, for example, the categorical form of judgment generates the category of substance, the hypothetical form of judgment generates the category of causality, and so on. By tracing the categories' origin to the logical forms of judgment, the metaphysical deduction provides an answer to the question *quid facti* concerning how we have "first come into the possession" of the categories.

Crucially, Kant qualifies the explanatory depth of the metaphysical deduction:

> for the peculiarity of our understanding, that it is able to bring about the unity of apperception *a priori* only by means of the categories and only through precisely this kind and number of them, a further ground may be offered just as little as one can be offered for why we have precisely these and no other functions for judgment or for why space and time are the sole forms of our possible intuition.[54]

This is a striking admission, one that will draw Fichte's criticism and inspire him to revolutionize both the idea of a deduction and the idea of logic. In this passage, Kant indicates that if a condition of possible experience has no "further ground" that we can cognize, then, as far as our cognition is concerned, it is groundless, which is to say that it is radically contingent or brute. In particular, he claims that while the metaphysical deduction answers the question *quid facti* by deriving the categories from their ground in the forms of judgment, this ground is itself ultimately groundless, for we are "just as little" able to "offe[r]" a further ground for "why we have precisely these and no other" forms of judgment as we are for why we have our specific forms of sensibility, namely, space and time.[55] The claim that the

[53] Kant KrV A79/B105.

[54] Kant KrV B145–6.

[55] On the radical contingency of our forms of sensibility, see Kant KrV A27/B43, B72, B150, A230–1/B283, Kant P | AA 4: 350–1, and Kant's posthumous 1804 "What Real Progress Has Metaphysics Made in Germany since the Time of Leibniz and Wolff?" (Kant W | AA 20: 267). Kant distinguishes between reasons for why space and time are forms of sensibility and reasons for why they are our forms of sensibility. In the Aesthetic's metaphysical exposition, he argues that experience must involve an *a priori* form of intuition. Experience gives us objects, which requires intuition. But since the form of intuition is not the content of experience, but is rather presupposed by experience, this form must be *a priori* (Kant KrV A20–2/B34–6). Kant then argues that space and time count as (1) *a priori* forms, since (a) outer and inner experience presuppose them, respectively, and (b) we can imagine the absence of extended and persisting objects, but not of space and time, and (2) intuitions, since (a) any spatial region or temporal duration presupposes a unitary space or time, and (b) such unitary wholes are given as unbounded and containing all regions and durations (Kant KrV A23–5/B38–41, A30–2/B46–8). However, there is no reason for why space and time are our forms of sensibility. No further ground is offered for this by a metaphysical exposition, just as no further ground is offered for why the forms of judgment are ours by a metaphysical deduction. On the relation between the radical contingency of the

conditions of possible experience are radically contingent is not the claim that entirely different conditions could suddenly make our experience possible, but is rather the claim that these conditions are not derivable from any ultimate ground, that is, any absolute first principle, that we can cognize, even if there is such a ground beyond our cognition.[56] This is why, in the passage, Kant says that the categories exhibit a "peculiarity of our understanding" and why, in the Appendix to the Analytic of Principles, he says that "the origin of our sensibility" is a "mystery" that is "too deeply hidden for us."[57] In their role as conditions of possible experience, space, time, the categories, and the forms of judgment exhibit what I will call 'anthropic necessity' insofar as they are unavoidable from the human standpoint yet lack a cognizably ultimate ground.

Kant's commitment to the radical contingency of the conditions of possible experience is further evident in several contemporaneous texts. In a letter to Marcus Herz, May 26, 1789, he says that "we are absolutely unable to explain further how it is that a sensible intuition (such as space and time), the form of our sensibility, or such functions of the understanding as those out of which logic develops are possible."[58] In the second *Critique* in Book I, Chapter I, "On the Principles of Pure Practical Reason," Kant says that "all human insight is at an end as soon as we have arrived at basic powers or basic faculties, for there is nothing through which their possibility can be conceived, and yet it may not be invented and assumed at one's discretion."[59] And in the Concluding Remark to 1785's *Groundwork of the Metaphysics of Morals*, he says that "[reason] restlessly seeks the unconditionally necessary and sees itself constrained to assume it without any means of making it comprehensible to itself, fortunate enough if it can discover only the concept that is compatible with this presupposition."[60]

forms of sensibility and the necessity of the categories, see Gomes, Moore, and Stephenson 2022. On Heidegger's agreement with Kant on the apriority of space and time, see Bruno 2015a.

[56] The absence of a cognizable first principle is consistent with Kant's claim in the A-edition Preface that metaphysics is "the **inventory** of all we possess through **pure reason**," from which nothing is "hidden" insofar as reason derives this inventory "entirely out of itself." In this derivation, reason's spade may well turn, namely, when it discovers brute facts among the conditions of experience, without thereby sacrificing the "unconditioned completeness" of metaphysics (Kant KrV Axx). Cf. Kant's claim in the A-edition Introduction that what "cannot remain hidden from us" regarding the understanding's "*a priori* cognition" of "the nature of things" is this cognition's "supply," not its origin (Kant KrV A12–3).

[57] Kant KrV A278/B334. Gurofsky claims that Kant can avoid the bruteness of the forms of sensibility by arguing that the concept of a non-spatio-temporal form of sensibility is meaningless in that such a form cannot be given to our sensibility (Gurofsky 2020: 9). This claim presumes the identity of thinkability and meaningfulness. However, since general logic and the ideas of reason allow us to think what cannot be given to our sensibility, the presumed identity would entail the meaninglessness of what we think on the basis both of general logic, for example, the content of dogmatic metaphysics and the content of certain works of fiction, and of ideas of reason, for example, the ideal of pure reason. Moreover, the presumed identity would prevent Kant from claiming that dogmatism plays the important role of reason's "childhood," which serves reason's teleological development toward the "mature and adult power of judgment" (Kant KrV A761/B789).

[58] Kant B | AA 11: 51.

[59] Kant KpV | AA 5: 46–7; cf. 91.

[60] Kant GMM | AA 4: 463.

To be sure, Kant assigns the metaphysical deduction with deriving the categories "from a common principle," namely, the "faculty for judging."[61] However, he provides no such derivation. Some scholars argue that Kant has the resources to derive the categories from the forms of judgment and to derive the forms of judgment from a first principle.[62] Nevertheless, we might wonder whether, for example, apperception can satisfy the role of such a principle, given its formal emptiness absent sensibly given matter.[63] More to the point, the above passage still leaves us with, first, the groundlessness of the forms of sensibility and, second, their explicit comparison in precisely this respect with both the forms of judgment and the categories.[64] Thus, while Kant regards the metaphysical deduction as a genuinely satisfactory answer to the question *quid facti*, it is subject to what he regards as the cognitive limit of "all human insight," which "is at an end" when it comes to conceiving the "possibility," that is, the ultimate grounds, of our "faculties" and hence of the conditions of possible experience that these faculties provide. This cognitive limit accordingly confronts us with the radical contingency or bruteness of such conditions.

Kant evokes the cognitive limit to which the metaphysical deduction is subject at the end of Book II, Chapter I of the Transcendental Dialectic, "The Paralogisms of Pure Reason." He there calls rational psychology "an imagined science" that arises from hypostatizing the idea of "our thinking being," that is, from fallaciously treating the referent of the idea of the soul as a cognizable object, whereas it is an idea to which no sensible intuition can be adequate. He then adds that critique liberates us from our "imagined happiness" with this imagined science by

> limit[ing] all our speculative claims merely to the field of possible experience, not by stale mockery at attempts that have so often failed, or by pious sighing over the limits of our reason, but by means of a complete determination of reason's boundaries according to secure principles, which with the greatest reliability

[61] Kant KrV A80–1/B106–7. Cf. Kant's invocation of "an **idea of the whole** of the *a priori* cognition of the understanding" by virtue of which the categories find "**connection in a system**" (Kant KrV A64–5/B89; cf. Kant KrV A67/B92).

[62] See Brandt 1995, Hoeppner 2022, Longuenesse 1998, Longuenesse 2006, Reich 1986, Stang (forthcoming), Wolff 1995, and Wolff 2017. Contrast Krüger 1968 and Thöle 2001.

[63] See Franks 2005: 62.

[64] In the Analytic, Kant adopts the biological metaphor of pure reason's "epigenesis," whereby reason generates the categories, proving that they are not externally necessary, as if implanted on God's whim, deposited through natural change, or inculcated by local custom, but rather are internally necessary, stemming from reason itself (Kant KrV B166–8). Cf. Kant P | 4: 319n and Kant's letter to Herz, February 21, 1772 (B | AA 10: 131). While epigenesis partly anticipates Fichte's idea of a genetic deduction, it still lacks the rigor that this idea demands, for it raises the question of why reason generates precisely the kind and number of categories that Kant describes. As Kant himself says in his 1785 review of Johann Gottfried von Herder's 1784–91 *Ideas for the Philosophy of the History of Humanity*, epigenesis develops only the "limitations, not further explicable, of a self-forming faculty, which latter we can just as little explain or make comprehensible" (Kant RI | AA 8: 62–3). Without a first principle from which to derive the categories, the necessity of their kind and number remains external to reason. On epigenesis, see Genova 1974 and Helbig and Nassar 2016.

> fastens its *nihil ulterius* [nothing further] on those pillars of Hercules that nature has erected, so that the voyage of our reason may proceed only as far as the continuous coastline of experience reaches, a coastline that we cannot leave without venturing out into a shoreless ocean, which, among always deceptive prospects, forces us in the end to abandon as hopeless all our troublesome and tedious efforts.[65]

The "principles" that "determin[e]" reason's "boundaries" establish the "field of possible experience" and in this sense function as the latter's conditions. Kant implies the ultimate groundlessness of the conditions of possible experience when he says that their determination "fastens" reason's "*nihil ulterius* [nothing further]" on the "pillars of Hercules." This is a metaphor for reason's inability to cognize a further, ultimate ground, namely, a first principle, from which to derive these conditions.[66] However, rather than "moc[k]" reason's cognitive limit, critique discloses it in order to prevent reason from falling into the deception of an imagined science. And rather than "sig[h]" over reason's cognitive limit, critique works within it in order to facilitate the aesthetic and logical sciences that provide the sensible and intellectual rules for reason's proper field of intelligibility, namely, possible experience. The metaphysical deduction thus contributes to the critical project of pursuing an appropriate science of the conditions of intelligibility. For Kant, this project reveals that there is nothing further to the conditions of intelligibility than their anthropic necessity, that is, that there is no cognizably ultimate ground for

[65] Kant KrV A395–6.

[66] In Greek mythology, the headlands that flank the Strait of Gibraltar are the pillars of Hercules, which mark the extent of his westward travels and represent the limit of human navigation. This limit yields the implicit ancient motto '*non plus ultra* [not further beyond],' which the Holy Roman Emperor Charles V negates in 1516 into the explicit modern motto '*plus ultra* [further beyond]' in order to reflect the territorial expansion of the kingdom of Spain (see Rosenthal 1971). Bacon adopts the modern motto in order to reflect the intellectual expansion of modern science, stating in 1608's unpublished "Refutation of Philosophies": "*Nos nostrum 'plus ultra' antiquorum 'non ultra' haud vane opposuimus* [It was not in vain that we opposed our 'further beyond' to the 'not beyond' of the ancients]" (Bacon 1829: 475). The frontispiece of his *Great Instauration* depicts a ship passing between the pillars of Hercules and expresses the modern motto thusly: "*Multi pertransibunt et augebitur scientia* [Many shall pass through and knowledge shall increase]." We might think that Kant endorses the modern motto when he quotes Bacon's *Great Instauration* in the epigraph to the B-edition first *Critique*. However, Kant instead endorses the ancient motto, given the passage that the epigraph quotes: "each may well hope from our instauration that it claims nothing infinite, and nothing beyond what is mortal; for in truth it prescribes only the end of infinite errors, and this is a legitimate end" (Kant KrV Bii). His preference for the ancient motto is also clear from the passage in the Paralogisms above that describes critique as restricting reason's "voyage" to the "continuous coastline of experience," that is, to a land-bound sea, and protecting it from the "deceptive prospects" of a "shoreless ocean." Cf. Kant: "the land of pure understanding... is an island, and enclosed in unalterable boundaries by nature itself. It is the land of truth (a charming name), surrounded by a broad and stormy ocean, the true seat of illusion, where many a fog bank and rapidly melting iceberg pretend to be new lands and, ceaselessly deceiving with empty hopes the voyager looking around for new discoveries, entwine him in adventures from which he can never escape and yet also never bring to an end" (Kant KrV A235–6/B294–5). Cf. Mensch 2013: 146–9.

them beyond their brute unavoidability for the human standpoint.[67] In this respect, and as we will see in Part III, he prefigures phenomenology's existentialist interest in radical contingency.

Kant's metaphysical deduction locates an origin for the categories and thereby provides an answer to the question *quid facti*. Nevertheless, this answer may not be satisfying given that the origin that it traces is as groundless as the forms of sensibility. Insofar as a groundless ground exceeds our cognitive limit, it escapes reason's theoretical power of self-explanation. As we saw in the Introduction, this leaves open the possibility that the cognizably ultimate ground of the conditions of intelligibility is in fact Spinozistic nature, whose nihilistic consequence is to rule out the autonomy of reason. Fichte will seek to remove groundlessness from the conditions of intelligibility by proposing a new, non-imagined science that can deduce these conditions from reason's practical power of self-determination. In this respect, as we will see, he champions German idealism's architectonic interest in logical systematicity.

Reinhold already expresses this architectonic interest in 1791's *The Foundation of Philosophical Knowledge* when he states that the findings of Kant's first *Critique* cannot be "universally binding" unless they are "secured" on a first principle. Universal validity eludes Kant's philosophy until it is "raised to the status of the science of the faculty of cognition," a science whose "*materials*" the first *Critique* provides, "but never the idea, let alone the actual *foundation*." Only for a philosophy that rests on a first principle "can it be established" that space, time, the categories, and the ideas are necessary conditions of experience.[68] Since Kant demands "*systematic form*" for philosophy, but does not secure "its foundation" in a "highest" principle, his conclusions are the "result" of a higher philosophy that is yet to be established.[69]

One reason that Reinhold adduces for the subordinate status of Kant's philosophy is that it relies on general logic for the "clue" to discovering the categories, despite the fact that general logic "has hitherto lacked a recognized first principle" and

> can offer no certainty, therefore, as to whether [its principles] are complete in number, or how they rank . . . In this situation of the logic, it is not difficult to understand that there was little, if anything at all, that Kant could safely take over from the *general* logic into his *transcendental* logic. He could draw little that was

[67] See Kant: "philosophy is the science of the relation of all cognition to the essential ends of human reason (*teleologia rationis humanae*), and the philosopher is not an artist of reason but the legislator of human reason. It would be very boastful to call oneself a philosopher in this sense and to pretend to have equaled the archetype, which lies only in the idea" (Kant KrV A839/B867). For a defense of Kantian modesty, see Ameriks 2000.

[68] Reinhold FPW 70-3 | 2000: 67–8.

[69] Reinhold FPW 115–7 | 2000: 87.

> profitable from the previous texts concerning the characteristics of the concepts that he needed as his *starting points*, i.e., those of *intuition, sensation, concept, judgment*, etc. (These are the concepts whose incomplete expositions he put at the base of his complete ones.)[70]

In the absence of a first principle from which he can derive the "number" and "rank" of the laws of general logic, Kant must inherit them from observed tradition. But philosophy cannot be said to "safely take over" any such uncritical inheritance, which is why it requires a first principle. To this end, Reinhold posits as "the *first* principle of all of philosophy" what he calls the "principle of consciousness." This principle states that "*in consciousness representation is distinguished through the subject from both object and subject and is referred to both*" and its "source" in consciousness, he says, is "an *actual fact*."[71]

Fichte's debt to Reinhold's pursuit of philosophy's "*systematic form*" is genuine yet critical.[72] In a letter fragment, March/April 1795, he tells Reinhold: "[Kant] showed that one must begin with an investigation of the subject; you showed that the investigation must proceed from a single first principle."[73] In another letter to Reinhold, April 28, 1795, he complains that Kant leaves the faculties of knowledge, feeling, and desire "merely coordinated" and should have "subordinated" them "to a higher principle." While Fichte acknowledges Reinhold's attempt to secure the "*foundation of all philosophy*" on the principle of consciousness, he takes this principle merely to ground reason's "theoretical faculty," for it is posited as a mere "*fact*" of consciousness, rather than an act of consciousness. Only an act can express the primacy of reason's practical faculty, that is, the irreducible freedom of the I. Hence Fichte tells Reinhold:

> I am in complete agreement with you that these faculties [namely, knowledge, feeling, and desire] must be subordinated to a higher principle, but I do not agree that the theoretical faculty can serve as the highest principle in question ... What I subordinate them to is the principle of subjectivity as such. You cut this path off completely with your elementary philosophy.[74]

[70] Reinhold FPW 119–21 | 2000: 88. On Reinhold's critique of Kant, see Ameriks 2000: 81–162, Beiser 1987: 226–5, and Henrich 2003: 113–39.

[71] Reinhold FPW | 2000: 70.

[72] On Fichte's debt to and critique of Reinhold, see Breazeale 1982 and Franks 2005: 219–37.

[73] Fichte B | 1988: 384.

[74] Fichte B | 1988: 389. Cf. Fichte's letter to Reinhold, March 1, 1794: "I am unable to grant that your principle of consciousness possesses those distinctive features which, as we both entirely agree, characterize any first principle" (Fichte B | 1988: 376). As Franks shows, one such feature is that a first principle must be heterogeneous with yet immanent in that which it conditions (Franks 2005: 225–8). Another is that it must be practical, as Fichte indicates in his 1794 review of Gottlob Ernst Schulze's 1792 *Aenesidemus, or Concerning the Foundations of the Elementary Philosophy Propounded in Jena by Professor Reinhold, Including a Defense of Skepticism Against the Pretensions of the Critique of Pure Reason*: "the principle of consciousness is a theorem which is based upon another first principle, from which, however, the principle of consciousness can be strictly derived, *a priori* and independently of all

As we will see in Section 1.6, Fichte's doctrine of intellectual intuition is meant to demonstrate our immediate apprehension of the I as first principle, where this is no mere fact, but is rather a free act.[75] His argument will be that this doctrine alone can establish the primacy of practical reason and thereby ground the true science of intelligibility.[76]

I will now turn to Fichte's critique of Kant's metaphysical deduction, which, while qualifiedly inspired by Reinhold, is where he develops his unique conception of the spirit as opposed to the letter of transcendental idealism, a spirit that he identifies with the *Wissenschaftslehre*.

1.3 Fichte's Critique of Kant's Metaphysical Deduction

We saw that Fichte expresses dissatisfaction with Kant's metaphysical deduction in the *New Presentation* when he claims that, by making a "detour through logic," namely, general logic, it raises the question of how we know that the categories that it deduces are the precise "laws of the intellect." The only satisfactory answer to this question, he claims, is one that unconditionally derives these laws "from the very nature of the intellect." Fichte echoes this criticism in the *Nova Methodo*:

> Kantian philosophy . . . is a proven philosophy, and everyone who understands it must admit that it is true. But it is not our vocation to be satisfied with this. We are destined for complete and systematic cognizance. It is not sufficient that our doubts be resolved and that we be consigned to tranquility; we also want science. Human beings have a need for science, and the *Wissenschaftslehre* offers to satisfy this need. The conclusions of the *Wissenschaftslehre* are therefore the same as those of Kant's philosophy, but the way in which these results are established is quite different. Kant does not derive the laws of human thinking in a rigorously scientific manner. But this is precisely what the *Wissenschaftslehre* is supposed to do.[77]

experience. The initial incorrect presupposition, and the one which caused the principle of consciousness to be proposed as the first principle of all philosophy, was precisely the presupposition that one must begin with a fact. We certainly do require a first principle that is material and not merely formal. But such a principle does not have to express a *fact*; it can also express an *act*" (Fichte RA | SW I: 8).

[75] See Fichte's claim that Reinhold "does not go far enough, for even representing is not the essence of the being [of the I], but only a particular determination of the same," since the I's essence is the identity of "[a]ction and deed" (Fichte GWL | SW I: 96, 100). See also Fichte's letter to Stephani, mid-December 1793: "It is amusing when Reinhold tries to make everything that happens in the human soul into a representation. Anyone who does this can know nothing of freedom and the practical imperative. If he is consistent, he must become an empirical fatalist" (Fichte B | 1988: 371). On Fichte's charge of empirical fatalism against Reinhold, see Bruno 2022b.

[76] See Fichte's letter to Johann Friedrich Flatt, November or December 1793: "even after the labours of Kant and Reinhold, philosophy is not a science" (Fichte B | 1988: 366).

[77] Fichte NM | GA IV/2: 7.

This passage criticizes the metaphysical deduction, but it does not criticize the transcendental deduction. It posits as a first criterion of "systematic" philosophy the resolution of "doubts" and the attainment of "tranquility." It is not difficult to see how Kant's transcendental deduction meets this anti-skepticism criterion. First, the transcendental deduction resolves the skeptical doubts that are raised by Hume concerning our right to use the categories, to which Fichte alludes just prior to this passage.[78] Second, by resolving these doubts, the transcendental deduction avoids one of skepticism's weaknesses, which, as Kant says in the *Prolegomena*, is its inability to warrant "even the tranquility of a permitted ignorance."[79] The transcendental deduction's achievements in this regard are precisely what Fichte calls the shared "conclusions" of the *Wissenschaftslehre*.

However, Fichte adds that "it is not our vocation to be satisfied" with these achievements. The transcendental deduction's conclusions are "not sufficient" without a crucial premise on which they can be "established," namely, the fulfillment of our "need for science." By "science," Fichte means not empirical inquiry, but rather a "rigorou[s]" derivation of the categories from a non-empirical source. Fulfilling our scientific need would satisfy, in addition to systematic philosophy's anti-skepticism criterion, a second, scientific criterion. According to Fichte, this scientific criterion is not met by Kant's metaphysical deduction, since it traces the origin of the categories to the forms of judgment, an origin that, like the forms of sensibility, is radically contingent or ultimately groundless. This leaves open the possibility that a further ground explains the necessity of these forms, namely, Spinozistic nature, which rules out the very idea of rational autonomy and thus the very idea that reason is free to critique itself and to determine the forms of cognition. The conclusions of Kant's transcendental deduction, while "true," lack a premise that is essential for establishing their truth, namely, an origin that supports a rigorous derivation of the categories' precise kind and number. This origin must be "a single, fundamental law" of reason rather than a brute fact, for only such an origin can ensure that the categories "constitute a single system."[80]

Grasping Fichte's criticism of the metaphysical deduction's unscientific character helps to clarify a related criticism that he makes earlier in the *Nova Methodo*: "Kant proves his philosophy only by means of induction and not through deduction."[81] We know that Kant's deductive failure is not transcendental, since the transcendental deduction satisfies the anti-skepticism criterion of systematic philosophy and thereby yields conclusions that are shared by the *Wissenschaftslehre*. His

78 See Fichte NM | GA IV/2: 5. Cf. Fichte RA | SW I: 3.

79 Kant P | AA 4: 274.

80 Fichte VND | SW I: 441. Cf. Fichte in 1793–94's unpublished "Personal Meditations on Elementary Philosophy": "Can one demonstrate, as Reinhold wanted, the categories and the forms of sensibility, time and space—sensibility, understanding, reason, faculty of cognition, faculty of desire—the necessity of all these things—or more precisely, can the whole of philosophy be built on a single fact, or must one take several to help?" (Fichte EM | GA II/3: 26).

81 Fichte NM | GA IV/2: 6.

deductive failure must therefore rather be metaphysical. But in what sense is his metaphysical deduction inductive?

In the context of this criticism, Fichte construes Kant's metaphysical deduction as arguing that experience is explicable if we assume "the operation of this or that [category]." Fichte infers that such a deduction achieves merely "hypothetical validity."[82] A hidden premise supporting his inference concerns the antecedent. If there is any doubt about the precise kind and number of the categories, then there is doubt about just which categories we may assume to be in "operation." The metaphysical deduction takes to be operative those categories which coincide with the logical forms of judgment that Kant observes from traditional general logic, a logic that is said to have already followed "the secure course of a science"[83] and whose use by the understanding is announced at the beginning of the metaphysical deduction as the "Clue" to the discovery of the categories.[84] Kant takes these forms as given and, as we saw, admits that their source is radically contingent. It is on their basis that he infers that the categories will be operative in all judging. But this inductive inference apparently spoils the metaphysical deduction, for, by tolerating radical contingency, it cannot support a rigorous derivation of categories that are absolutely necessary and thus have categorical validity. At most, this deduction supports a derivation of categories of "hypothetical validity."

We see, then, that Fichte's criticism of Kant's metaphysical deduction posits two criteria of systematic philosophy that jointly provide a job description for his successor notion of genetic deduction. The first criterion is that philosophy must resolve skepticism and achieve tranquility. Kant proves his philosophy to the extent that he satisfies this criterion on the strength of his transcendental deduction of our right to use the categories. The second criterion is that philosophy must rigorously derive the categories from their non-empirical origin. Kant's metaphysical deduction fails to satisfy this criterion because it locates a radically contingent origin. Meeting the first, anti-skepticism criterion is insufficient for systematic philosophy without meeting the second, scientific criterion.[85] For Fichte, like some of Kant's earliest readers, this is to offer a conclusion without an essential premise.

[82] Fichte NM | GA IV/2: 6.

[83] Kant KrV Bviii. Contrast Hegel: "Kant thought further of logic, that is, the aggregate of definitions and propositions that ordinarily passes for logic, as fortunate because, as contrasted with other sciences, it was its lot to attain an early completion; since Aristotle, it has taken no backward step, but also none forward, the latter because to all appearances it seems to be finished and complete. If logic has not undergone change since Aristotle—and in fact, judging from the latest compendiums of logic, the usual changes mostly consist only of omissions—then surely the conclusion to be drawn is that it is all the more in need of a total reworking; for the two thousand years of spirit's continuous labor must have procured for it a higher consciousness about its thinking and the purity of its inner essence . . . For the dead bones of logic to be quickened by spirit and become substance and content, its *method* must be the one which alone can make it fit to be pure science" (Hegel WL | GW 21: 35–6).

[84] Kant KrV A67/B92.

[85] Cf. Fichte's criteria with Reinhold's discussions of systematicity and skepticism in *Contributions* as presented in Breazeale 1982: 792–7.

The deductive method of a truly systematic philosophy must satisfy both criteria at once, establishing our right to use the categories precisely by deriving them from a non-arbitrary origin. Hence, it must simultaneously answer the question *quid juris* and the question *quid facti*, which is to say that it must be jurisprudential as well as genealogical. We will see that Fichte's deductive innovation not only sets a methodological agenda for Hegel's logic, but also specifies a criterion, namely, the scientific criterion, whose violation characterizes the determination of false conditions of intelligibility for which Fichte will coin the term 'facticity' in Berlin. For now, I will show that the methodological innovation of Fichte's genetic deduction satisfies the unified constraint of a simultaneously jurisprudential and genealogical account of the categories.

1.4 Fichte's Definition of a Genetic Deduction

We saw that Kant's metaphysical and transcendental deductions of the categories answer the questions *quid facti* and *quid juris*, respectively, and that Fichte charges the metaphysical deduction with failing to satisfy systematic philosophy's scientific criterion of deriving the categories from a non-arbitrary origin. We will now see that Fichte devises a new, genetic deduction in order to satisfy this criterion. While his deduction aims to overcome the limits of Kant's metaphysical deduction, it also aims to support the conclusions of Kant's transcendental deduction.

In the *New Presentation*, as we saw, Fichte describes a deduction as a proof that the I as first principle is "*not possible unless something else occurs as well*," namely, a set of conditions that must be "*completely exhausted*" if the I is to be "*completely comprehensible*." In the First Introduction to the *Nova Methodo*, he provides a definition of a deduction that indicates that such a proof is at once jurisprudential and genealogical:

> Whatever is required in order for the I to be able to posit itself and to oppose a not-I to itself is necessary. The *Wissenschaftslehre* demonstrates these conditions by means of a deduction. A deductive proof proceeds as follows: We can assume that it is the very nature of the human mind to posit itself and to oppose a not-I to itself; but if we assume this, we must assume much else as well. This is called 'deducing,' i.e., deriving something from something else. Kant merely asserts that one always proceeds in accordance with the categories, whereas the *Wissenschaftslehre* asserts that one must proceed in accordance with the categories—just as surely as one posits oneself as an I. The conclusions are the same, but the *Wissenschaftslehre* connects them to something higher as well.[86]

[86] Fichte NM | GA IV/2: 8.

According to this definition, a deduction demonstrates the conditions that are necessary for the I to posit itself over against a not-I. By "not-I," Fichte means a world of which the I can have cognition. Cognizing such a world is possible only given certain conditions, which the *Wissenschaftslehre* must deduce. Such conditions are "categories" to which one is entitled "just as surely as one posits oneself as an I" insofar as the latter is unintelligible without the former. In this respect, Fichte's definition of a deduction conveys the narrower, jurisprudential sense that characterizes Kant's transcendental answer to the question *quid juris*.

But the passage also defines a deduction as "deriving something from something else." Fichte specifies that deriving here must lead to "something higher." Given that he does so through an explicit contrast to Kant, we can infer that the derivational destination to which he refers is not merely another "something," namely, another category, but is rather the source of the categories. This is further supported by his claim that a deductive proof is drawn from "the very nature of the human mind," for we saw that the nature of the mind is precisely the origin from which Fichte thinks Kant's metaphysical deduction should have drawn. Hence, the definition also expresses the broader, genealogical sense of deduction that characterizes, even if it is not adequately served by, Kant's metaphysical answer to the question *quid facti*. Fichte is explicit, shortly after, that a genetic deduction's genealogical function satisfies the scientific criterion of systematic philosophy: "In this manner, the need for science is satisfied, and we then obtain a cognition that is not merely discursive and pieced together from experience, but systematic, in the sense that it all can be derived from a single point to which everything else is connected."[87]

The First Introduction's definition of genetic deduction is not the only evidence that Fichte regards it as equally jurisprudential and genealogical. The dual character of a genetic deduction is borne out by texts throughout the Jena period. In 1794–95's *Foundations of the Entire Wissenschaftslehre*, Fichte claims to deduce the necessity of the categories, following Kant's answer to the question *quid juris*, while arguing that they must arise "originally and absolutely" from "*the absolute I*," redeeming Kant's answer to the question *quid facti*.[88] This text expresses the mutual dependence of deduction's jurisprudential and genealogical tasks when it states that the categories by which it is possible for the I to realize itself in experience and the I from which the categories must be derived are warranted only reciprocally, a mutual relation that Fichte says "constitutes a circle, though an unavoidable one (see §7 of *Concerning the Concept of the Wissenschaftslehre*)."[89] The circle in question is unavoidable insofar as the categories condition the I's realizability just if the I grounds the categories' absolute necessity. Thus, a "*completely exhausted*" deduction of the categories starts from the I and ends by rendering the I "*completely*

[87] Fichte NM | GA IV/2: 9.
[88] See Fichte GWL | SW I: 99–123, 232, 272.
[89] Fichte GWL | SW I: 92; cf. Fichte BWL | SW I: 72–5.

comprehensible," such that we return to where we begin yet understand it for the first time. Moreover, the *New Presentation* states that the "proper task" of transcendental idealism is to deduce the "system" of the conditions of intelligibility, while insisting that each such condition "becomes, in turn, something that is itself conditioned and whose condition has to be discovered," that is, superseded by a successor condition until their "sum total" is completely derived.[90]

For its part, the *Nova Methodo* portrays genetic deduction jurisprudentially as securing "conditions that make it possible for the I to posit itself and to oppose a not-I to itself," that is, "categories" that are "present within us necessarily,"[91] while also portraying deduction genealogically as tracing the successive "foundation" of each condition.[92] Echoing the *Foundations*, moreover, the *Nova Methodo* observes that the reciprocity of the two functions of a deduction yields an unavoidable and therefore virtuous circularity, which Fichte calls a "circle of reason."[93] Indeed, the simultaneously jurisprudential and genealogical character of Fichte's genetic proofs explains why he often uses the terms 'deduction' and 'derivation' interchangeably. Such proofs, as we have seen, must convey both the broad and the narrow sense of a deduction if they are to agree with the conclusions of Kant's transcendental deduction while providing their missing premises.

We will now see that Fichte's deductive proof is governed by a dialectical logic, that is, that it consists in the detection and supersession of self-contradictory categories. According to this new logic, a putative category provides a condition of the I's positing itself over against a not-I, until it turns out that that category contains an opposition and so cannot stably be thought in its role as a condition without thinking of a more adequate category that can synthesize its opposing elements, which latter condition is thereby derived as a condition of the former condition. This dialectical movement of thought proceeds until no further contradiction is detected and the complete set of the conditions of intelligibility is secured.

1.5 The Dialectical Character of a Genetic Deduction

Fichte's definition of a deduction in the *Nova Methodo* states that when we assume a category in a deductive proof, "we must assume much else as well." Such a proof does not present a fixed set of ready-made categories, but instead shows how assuming one category necessarily leads us, in the broader, genealogical sense of deduction, to assume another category. Contemporaneously with the *Nova Methodo*,

[90] Fichte VND | SW I: 445–6.
[91] Fichte NM | GA IV/2: 8–9.
[92] Fichte NM | GA IV/2: 35.
[93] Fichte NM | GA IV/2: 167.

the *New Presentation* states that a deduction "proceeds in an uninterrupted progression from what is conditioned to the condition of the same. Each condition becomes, in turn, something that is itself conditioned and whose condition has to be discovered."[94] Deriving categories in this manner yields "the sum total of all of the conditions of that with which [idealism] began," namely, the absolute freedom of reason or the I.[95] Two preliminary conclusions can be drawn from this. First, insofar as a genetic deduction begins with the I and not, for example, the forms of judgment, it satisfies the scientific criterion of systematic philosophy. Second, insofar as a genetic deduction does not assume a distinction between sensible and intellectual rules of experience, it does not assume Kant's corresponding distinction between aesthetic and logical sciences, which means that the categories that a genetic deduction derives from the I can be regarded as the rules of a single science. As we will see in Section 1.6, Hegel will adopt and radicalize this deductive method in the decades following Fichte's Jena period.

To clarify the dialectical character of a genetic deduction, we must consider the rule that guides a scientific account of the system of the conditions of intelligibility.[96] Fichte adopts several names for this rule. In the *Nova Methodo*, he says that a deduction follows the "law of reflective opposition."[97] Following this rule consists in determining a condition through its opposite. Another name for this rule is the "law of reflection," according to which "determining" something occurs "by means of opposition."[98] Fichte eventually refers to this rule as the "principle of determinability."[99] As a rule for deducing conditions of intelligibility, determination through opposition has the advantage of ensuring that no conditions are introduced rhapsodically, for example, by an inductive appeal to observed forms of judgment inherited from traditional logic. It proceeds instead by positing a putative condition, discovering that it contains an opposition, and generating a successor condition to resolve this opposition.[100]

[94] Fichte VND | SW I: 446.
[95] Fichte VND | SW I: 446.
[96] A version of this discussion appears in Bruno 2018b.
[97] Fichte NM | GA IV/2: 38.
[98] Fichte NM | GA IV/2: 44.
[99] Fichte NM | GA IV/2: 2, 51. On the Maimonian roots of this principle, see Breazeale 2013: 42–69 and Melamed 2021. On the Spinozistic background of Maimon's principle, see Melamed 2004.
[100] Fichte hints at the dialectical movement of thought that characterizes a genetic deduction in the *Foundations*: "That action in which, in comparing two items, one seeks the characteristic feature through which they are *posited as opposites* is called the *antithetic* way of proceeding. This is commonly called the *analytic* way of proceeding, though this term is less apt than 'antithetic,' in part because the term 'analytic' may give rise to the opinion that something can be developed out of a concept that one has not first placed there by means of *synthesis*, and in part because the designation 'antithetic' more clearly indicates that this way of proceeding is the opposite of the synthetic way of proceeding. The *synthetic* way of proceeding consists precisely in the fact that one is seeking to discover in things posited in opposition to each other that characteristic feature in which they are *the same*" (Fichte GWL | SW I: 112–3). Unlike "*synthetic*" thinking, which seeks the "characteristic feature" through which two items that are "posited in opposition" are simply "*the same*," "*antithetic*" thinking seeks the feature through which two items are "*posited as opposites*," that is, the higher concept through which the contradiction between two opposing items can be affirmed and thereafter resolved.

The passage immediately following Fichte's definition of deduction in the *Nova Methodo* offers a compressed expression of a dialectical movement of thought, one in which I posit myself as free, but discover that I cannot do so without positing a world in opposition to my freedom: "The essence of reason consists in my positing myself; but I cannot do this without positing a world in opposition to myself, and indeed, a quite specific world: a world in space, within which appearances follow one another sequentially in time."[101] This movement of thought begins with a putative category, namely, 'self-positing freedom,' that reveals an inner tension and a subsequent need for a category that can resolve that tension. Expanding Fichte's expression of this movement, we can say that I am free, but that my freedom cannot be thought unless my action is directed at something that limits my freedom and thus in relation to which I am unfree, since otherwise my action is indeterminate. This requires thinking of a world in which my action can be rendered determinate by its surroundings, goals, and obstacles. However, a world that renders my action determinate cannot be thought unless it is one in which my action can progress from aim to success and thus render the world determinate, since otherwise my action is indistinguishable from a mere event. This requires thinking of a world that is structured by spatially contiguous regions and temporally continuous phases through which my action can be said to progress.[102]

A more detailed dialectical movement of thought occurs in 1796's *Foundations of Natural Right*, a text in which Fichte gives a "genetic proof"[103] of the external world, other rational beings, and the material body,[104] among other conditions of intelligibility.[105] I will illustrate the principle of determinability's application at an

[101] Fichte NM | GA IV/2: 9.

[102] Neuhouser 2014 traces the dialectical movement of Fichte's deductive proofs back to the *Foundations*, whose theoretical and practical parts derive the categories of reality, negation, determination, and striving through a progressive series of inner oppositions. Cf. Forster 1989: 130–5.

[103] Fichte GN | SW III: 77.

[104] Whereas Kant argues that "[o]ne can never represent that there is no space" (Kant KrV A24/B38), Merleau-Ponty argues in 1945's *Phenomenology of Perception* that "there would be for me no such thing as space if I did not have a body" (Merleau-Ponty 2012: 104). According to Fichte, with space comes not only my body, but also the bodies of others: "[t]he person cannot ascribe a body to himself without positing it as standing under the influence of a person outside him" (Fichte GN | SW III: 61). Cf. Merleau-Ponty 2012: 365–7 and Husserl's 1912 *Ideas Pertaining to a Pure Phenomenology and to a Phenomenological Philosophy, Second Book: Studies in the Phenomenology of Constitution* (Husserl IRP2 | 1989: 166, 294). In *Being and Time*, Heidegger says that Dasein "is spatial by way of circumspectly discovering space so that it is related to beings thus spatially encountered," but then asserts that the "spatialization of Dasein in its 'corporeality'... contains a problematic of its own not to be discussed here" (Heidegger SZ | GA 2: 108). This prompts Sartre's reproach in 1943's *Being and Nothingness* that while the body has a "differentiated structure" and "consequently" a "particular sexual structure," Heidegger's existential analytic of Dasein "does not make the slightest allusion to sex" or, indeed, to embodiment (Sartre 1956: 382–3). In a conversation with Medard Boss, March 3, 1972, Heidegger replies to Sartre's reproach by saying that "the bodily is the most difficult [to understand]," a topic about which he "was unable to say more" in *Being and Time*, but which he now says "must always start with" our "basic constitution" as "standing-open-toward-the-world" with a "non-objectifiable, optically invisible capacity to receive-perceive the significance of what it encounters" (Heidegger ZoS | GA 89: 292–3).

[105] Such conditions include the problematic character of mutual recognition, which, for Fichte, is deducible from the concept of right (Fichte GN | SW III: 46–7). By contrast, for Kant, as he says in the Fourth Proposition of 1784's "Idea for a Universal History With a Cosmopolitan Aim," this problematic

early stage of this proof in which the concept of freedom is discovered to contain the opposing concept of a sensible world, the tension between which concepts generates the concept of other minds, which resolves this tension.

Like other texts in the Jena period, *Natural Right* posits I-hood as the "exclusive condition of all philosophizing." "I-hood" denotes a rational subject's existence as free or self-determining, that is, as "an acting upon itself."[106] Drawing on the idea of a genetic deduction, Fichte claims that certain "necessary actions . . . follow from the concept of the rational being" that condition its possibility.[107] We can ascertain the first such condition by applying the principle of determinability, for we find that the concept of freedom contains an opposition: "This activity is *constrained* and *bound*, if not with respect to its form (i.e., that the activity occurs), then with respect to its content (i.e., that the activity, once it occurs in a particular case, proceeds in a certain way)."[108] While freedom has the form of self-determining movement, it is an empty form without some "content" that can distinguish its movement. In other words, "that" freedom occurs is a condition of philosophizing, but the "way" that it occurs owes in part to the world. Hence, if free activity is to be "an *efficacy* directed at objects," then some "world-intuiting" must limit it.[109] The concept of freedom accordingly contains the concept of a sensible world that stands in opposition to it.

Fichte acknowledges that common sense naturally grants existence to the world without philosophy's aid, but he asserts that this bestowal must itself be explicable.[110] Philosophy allows us to "bracket" common sense in order to explain why we naturally assume that the content of the world must exceed our rational agency or I-hood, that is, to explain "why we can posit ourselves only as altering the form of things, but never the matter."[111] On Fichte's dialectical account, it is specifically

character is a feature of our "*unsociable sociability*," i.e., our "inclination," which "lies in human nature" as a brute fact, both "to *individualize* (isolate)" ourselves against "expect[ed] resistance" and "to become *socialized*" so as to "obtain . . . a rank among [our] fellows" (Kant IAG | AA 8: 20–1). See Radrizzani 2016 for a reconstruction of a Fichtean deduction of historicity.

[106] Fichte GN | SW III: 1–2.

[107] Fichte GN | SW III: 2. While Fichte's deduction supports Kant's response to Humean skepticism, it also responds to Maimonian skepticism. Kant's transcendental deduction shows that experience is impossible without the categories. While this proves our right to use the categories *contra* Hume, it leaves open whether we actually apply them, i.e., whether they have objective reality and are not empty forms, a challenge that Maimon raises in 1790's *Essay on Transcendental Philosophy*. Fichte responds to this challenge in the *Foundations* when he says that Maimonian skepticism is refuted by the origin "from which every category is derived: the I, as absolute subject," whose reality is "transferred to" the categories (Fichte SW I: 99; cf. 121n). Hence he calls the categories "necessary actions" rather than mere concepts. Cf. Fichte: "Logic furnishes us with the *rules* that govern the act of determining an object; therefore, I should think, logic presupposes, as a fact of consciousness, this act of determining as such" (Fichte VND | SW I: 498). On the actuality problem that Maimon raises, see Franks 2005: 243–9.

[108] Fichte GN | SW III: 18.

[109] Fichte GN | SW III: 19.

[110] Cf. Hegel's 1807 *Phenomenology of Spirit*: "the familiar, just because it is familiar, is not cognitively understood" (Hegel PG | W 3: 35). Cf. also Hegel: "what is well known in this manner [namely, by being always on our lips] is usually what is most unknown" (Hegel EL | GW 20: §24 Addition 2).

[111] Fichte GN | SW III: 24, 27, 29.

our inability to posit I-hood without an opposing not-I that explains why we must posit the independent matter of the sensible world.[112]

A contradiction arises from the opposition within the concept of freedom. On the one hand, a rational subject limits the world insofar as it can alter the world's form. On the other hand, it does not limit the world insofar as it cannot create the world's matter. A "prior moment" therefore must precede the subject's limitation of the world, one in which the world limits the subject. However, this moment is itself preceded by one in which the subject, in virtue of its I-hood, limits the world, "and so on *ad infinitum*," producing a regress in which subjective form alternatingly does and does not limit worldly content. Assuming that the application of subjective form and the provision of worldly matter exhausts the possibilities of limitation, Fichte says that this regress "can be cancelled only if it is assumed that *the subject's efficacy* is synthetically unified with the *object* in one and the same moment." Only a synthetic unity of subject and object here can prevent a regress of alternating limitation between them. In particular, a synthetic unity of the subject and that which opposes it requires an event that "leave[s] the subject in full possession of its freedom to be self-determining." Fichte locates this event in another's summons, since a summons regards "the subject's being-determined as *its being-determined to be self-determining* . . . calling upon it to resolve to exercise its efficacy."[113] Your summons limits me by opposing my agency. But it also limits itself by assuming and inviting the exercise of my agency in the form of my response to you as summoner.[114] Our mutual recognition thereby secures the requisite synthesis of the subject and that which opposes it, resolving the contradiction between subjective and worldly limitation.[115]

The dialectical resolution of the opposition within the concept of freedom reveals that the world that initially opposes freedom is not simply sensible, but rather is always also social. In a social world, a summons' final cause or "ultimate end" is that its addressee's freedom "*ought* to exist."[116] You purposefully make room for my agency in a way that a merely sensible world cannot. The "undivided event" of "*free reciprocal efficacy*" between subjects thus emerges as a successor condition of intelligible experience.[117]

[112] As Gottlieb 2015 shows, Fichte's deduction of the sensible world is ultimately motivated by ethical rather than epistemic skepticism.

[113] Fichte GN | SW III: 31–3.

[114] As Franks 2016b puts it, your summons imposes a "*normative* limitation" rather than a "factual limitation" on me (100). Cf. Rödl 2014.

[115] Fichte does not imply the concept of the summons in the *Foundations* when he says "No thou, no I; no I, no thou," for he uses this phrase simply to "express" the mutual "mediat[ion]" of the I and the not-I "in more ordinary language" (Fichte GWL | SW I: 188–9). On the connection between Fichte's concept of the summons and the Kabbalistic concept of ẓimẓum, i.e., the self-limiting contraction of God, see Franks 2016b.

[116] Fichte GN | SW III: 33, 36.

[117] Fichte GN | SW III: 34. Fichte suggests that mutual recognition functions not only in a categorial sense as an intermediate condition of intelligibility, but also in a foundational sense as the ultimate condition of constructing a science of the conditions of intelligibility. In the Second Lecture of

The concept of another subject summoning me to action stabilizes the concept of freedom. Fichte arrives at this intermediate deductive result by applying the principle of determinability: "*In this process of distinguishing through opposition, the subject acts in such a way that the concept of itself as a free being and the concept of the rational being outside it (as a free being like itself) are mutually determined and conditioned*."[118] Resolving the contradiction arising from the opposition within the concept of freedom yields the first in a series of derived conditions of intelligibility. This series progressively articulates a rigorous system rather than a rhapsodic aggregate because it arises exclusively from the I's reflection on the possibility of its realization in the world. In other words, the series of conditions composes a true science because it is genetically deduced from a first principle.[119]

By grasping the simultaneously jurisprudential and genealogical character of a genetic deduction, we now see how Fichte can claim to present the results of transcendental idealism in a methodologically unique fashion. Consequently, we are able to register the *Wissenschaftslehre*'s impact on the development of post-Kantian logic, to which I now turn.

1794's "Concerning the Difference Between the Spirit and the Letter Within Philosophy," he says that, by elevating us from "that which is *represented*," namely, the object of consciousness, to "that which *represents*," namely, the subject of consciousness, philosophy raises us from the "material world" to a "higher world," i.e., from mere materiality to apperceptive materiality. He then implies that our initial emergence into mere materiality and our subsequent elevation to apperceptive materiality are both conditioned by our relation to others when he says that the "same difficulty that kept us from entering the first world also prevents us from entering this second one." The difficulty that is involved in each birth is our dependence on another. For our first birth, "parents" summon us by creating our existence. For our second birth, a "teacher" summons us by inviting our self-conscious response (Fichte UGB | 1988: 202–3, 207). Cf. Fichte VND | SW I: 507–9. The difficulty of each birth is only overcome when another summons us, namely, by creating our existence or by inviting our response. Of course, in one's first birth one's dependence on another is not reciprocal, whereas in one's second birth it is reciprocal. Fichte can invite us to attain self-consciousness, but he cannot perform this "instance of free acting" for us. He cannot successfully serve as midwife for our second birth without our response. Hence he says that "if one wants to communicate [the *Wissenschaftslehre*] to someone else, one has to ask the other person to perform the action in question" (Fichte NM | GA IV/2: 28, 38). Speaking from the position of a "teacher" in the Second Lecture, Fichte expresses to his students the reciprocal dependence that philosophy requires: "We are fortunate if we possess philosophy ourselves, but we cannot give it away. All of our philosophical assertions are 'bodies' and nothing more. And we hand these bodies over to you in order to help you to develop philosophy out of and through your own self—not that you could not also do so without the help of these 'bodies'" (Fichte UGB | 1988: 207). Cf. Fichte GGZ | SW VII: 37. A teacher gives a student no more than the letter of philosophy, i.e., the audible "bodies" of its assertions or, "without the help of these," the visual bodies of its writings. A student can study and memorize the spoken or written letter of philosophy, but in order to "possess" philosophy themselves, they must exhibit its spirit by responding.

118 Fichte GN | SW III: 42. Cf. Fichte GN | SW III: 11.

119 For an account of why, for Fichte, second-person knowledge in reciprocal recognition derives from first-person knowledge of a first principle, see Bruno 2020b.

1.6 Toward a Presuppositionless Logic

In its genealogical function of making productive use of contradiction in order to generate the categories from reason or the I, Fichte's genetic deduction prefigures the speculative analysis of the categories that becomes the hallmark of Hegelian dialectic. For reasons that Hegel himself indicates, the *Wissenschaftslehre*'s impact runs deep.

In the *Encyclopedia Logic*, Part I of 1830's *Encyclopedia of the Philosophical Sciences*, Hegel claims that logic, by which he means the science that provides a rigorous determination of the categories, "should be preceded by *universal doubt*, i.e., by total *presuppositionlessness*."[120] We can hear in this scientific criterion an echo of Fichte's complaint that Kant's answer to the question *quid facti* presupposes forms of judgment that lack a further, ultimate ground and are therefore dubious. Hegel's criterion states that logic cannot presuppose anything whose doubt could be so entertained. In other words, it cannot tolerate radical contingency or bruteness. As he says earlier in the *Encyclopedia*:

> We are all well aware that Kant's philosophy took the easy way in its *finding* of the categories. 'I,' the unity of self-consciousness, is totally abstract and completely undetermined. So how are we to arrive at the *determinations* of the I, or at the categories? Fortunately, we can find the *various kinds of judgment* already specified empirically in the traditional logic. To judge, however, is to *think* a determinate object. So, the various modes of judgment that have already been enumerated give us the various *determinations of thinking*.—It remains the profound and enduring merit of Fichte's philosophy to have reminded us that the *thought-determinations* must be exhibited in their *necessity*, and that it is essential for them to be *deduced*.—Fichte's philosophy ought to have had at least this effect upon the method of presenting a treatise on logic: that the thought-determinations in general, or the usual logical material, the species of concepts, judgments, and syllogisms, are no longer just taken from observation and thus apprehended only empirically, but are deduced from thinking itself. If thinking has to be able to prove anything at all, if logic must require that *proofs* are given, and if it wants to teach us how to prove [something], then it must above all be capable of proving its very own peculiar content, and able to gain insight into the necessity of this content.[121]

[120] Hegel EL | GW 20: §78 Remark.

[121] Hegel EL | GW 20: §42 Remark. Cf. Hegel: "The empirically universal way of knowing about what is rational is that of prejudgment and presupposition" (Hegel EL | GW 20: §82 Addition). Cf. also Hegel's 1812–16 *Science of Logic*: "Kantian philosophy . . . pick[ed] a portion of [the concepts of ordinary logic], namely, the functions of judgment, for the determination of the categories, and simply accepted them as valid presuppositions . . . [C]ritique has therefore removed the forms of objective thinking only from the thing, but has left them in the subject as it originally found them. That is to say, it did not consider them in and for themselves, according to their proper content, but simply took them over from subjective logic in the manner of lemmas. There was no question, therefore, of an immanent

Hegel lauds Fichte for recognizing that the categories cannot be derived "empirically" or, to use the latter's term, inductively.[122] If thought-determinations are the categories that condition the possibility of intelligibility, then they "must be exhibited in their *necessity*." This constraint means that they cannot be "taken from observation" of "traditional logic," which is a contingent origin absent some further ground, but instead must be "deduced from thinking itself," construed as an absolute ground.[123] Hegel's praise for Fichte's recognition of this constraint is reflected in his claim in 1812–16's *Science of Logic* that logic "cannot presuppose any of these [customary] forms of reflection, these rules and laws of thinking, for they are part of its content and they first have to be established within it."[124] We can hear in this claim Fichte's demand that, rather than derive the categories from a "detour" through assumed logical forms of judgment, we must derive them from reason alone, namely, by thinking dialectically through the contradictions of initial categories toward successor categories. Only this provides a satisfactory answer to the question *quid facti* and, with it, a path toward a true science of intelligibility.[125]

One of the *Wissenschaftslehre*'s chief insights for post-Kantian logic, then, is genetic. In order to complete the genealogical task that is inherited unfulfilled from Kant, we must remove contingency from the generation of the categories by showing that they emerge from reason alone, thereby avoiding the nihilistic

deduction of such forms, or also of deducing them as logico-subjective forms, still less, of a dialectical treatment of them . . . In the customary treatment of logic, a variety of *classifications* and *species* of concepts are adduced. It immediately strikes one as inconsequential that the species are introduced in this way: '*There are*, as regards quality, quantity, etc., the following concepts'. The 'there are' conveys no other justification than that *we find* the named species and that they show up in *experience*. What we have in this manner is an *empirical* logic—an odd science indeed, an *irrational* cognition of the *rational* . . . In this context, the Kantian philosophy incurs a further inconsequence by *borrowing* the categories for the *transcendental logic*, as so-called root concepts, from the subjective logic where they were assumed empirically. Since the Kantian philosophy admits the latter fact, it is hard to see why transcendental logic resorts to borrowing from such a science rather than directly helping itself from experience . . . Kant made the profound observation that there are *synthetic* principles *a priori*, and he recognized as their root the unity of self-consciousness, hence the self-identity of the concept. However, he takes the specific connection, the relational concepts, and the synthetic principles, *from formal logic as given*; the deduction of these should have been the exposition of the transition of that simple unity of self-consciousness into these determinations and distinctions; but Kant spared himself the effort of demonstrating this truly synthetic progression, that of the self-producing concept" (Hegel WL | GW 12: 28, 31, 43–4, 205). And cf. Hegel's 1825–26 Berlin lectures on the history of philosophy: "Kant adopts [the categories or universal thought-determinations] empirically, just in the way they have been ordered in logic. He does not think about proceeding from unity to the kinds or determinations of unity—about developing the distinctions out of unity" (Hegel VGP3 | V 9: 153). On Hegel's critique of Kant's reliance on formal logic, see McNulty 2023.

122 On the connection between Kant's "empiricism" and his "insufficiently transcendental logic" according to Fichte's 1812 lectures, see Nuzzo 2010: 196. On the lectures' apparently implicit critique of Hegel's *Science of Logic*, see Lauth 1998.

123 On the Fichtean elements of Hegel's philosophy, see Pippin 2019.

124 Hegel WL | GW 21: 27. Cf. Hegel's claim that presuppositions must "be given up when we enter into the science" (Hegel EL | GW 20: §78).

125 This is not to deny that Hegel's radicalized genetic deduction simultaneously answers the question *quid juris*. On this, see Cooper-Simpson 2021, but contrast Pippin 2019: 122.

consequence of Spinozism that the categories are imposed on reason. Another way of expressing this insight is that we must eliminate the appearance that the categories' origin, in addition to their kind and number, is external to reason by showing that their origin does not transcend reason's power of self-determination, but rather is unthinkable independent of that power.[126] As Hegel concludes the Introduction to 1807's *Phenomenology of Spirit*: "In pressing forward to its true existence, consciousness will arrive at a point at which it gets rid of its semblance of being burdened with something alien."[127]

I will conclude this chapter by distinguishing the extent to which Fichte and Hegel each strive to eliminate radical contingency. This will set the stage for my analysis, in Part II, of Hegel's presuppositionless logic and his related critique of Fichte's abiding tolerance for presupposition.

First, for Hegel, a presupposition is "an arbitrary *assurance*,"[128] since it lacks a further ground. Insofar as it is ultimately groundless, a presupposition "takes its *start* from the *contingent*," that is, from bruteness.[129] Hegel's commitment to presuppositionlessness is accordingly a commitment to eliminating radical contingency. His commitment extends to logic's very essence, which, he says, "cannot say what it is in advance."[130] We cannot externally assume anything about logic, not even that it must derive the categories in a dialectical manner. Instead, logic must internally generate its own method. As Stephen Houlgate shows, dialectic "may well *turn out* . . . to be the proper method for philosophical thought . . . but this is only because thought is required to become dialectical by the concepts it is led to consider." Dialectic cannot be presupposed as logic's proper method, but only gradually "proves to be inherent in presuppositionless thought itself."[131] As Hegel says in the *Encyclopedia*, dialectic is "not brought to bear on [logic's] thought-determinations from outside; on the contrary, it must be considered as dwelling within them."[132] Logic may not presuppose dialectic for the same reason that a metaphysical deduction may not presuppose the forms of judgment, namely, presupposition imports intolerable arbitrariness into philosophy, for example, at the origin of the categories or in the method of their deduction. Hence, although Hegel

[126] On eliminating externality, see McDowell 2009, Rödl 2007, and Rödl 2018.

[127] Hegel PG | W 3: 81. See William James' 1882 "Rationality, Activity, and Faith": "idealism gives to the nature of things such kinship with our personal selves. Our own thoughts are what we are most at home with, what we are least afraid of. To say then that the universe essentially is thought, is to say that I myself, potentially at least, am all. There is no radically alien corner, but an all-pervading *intimacy*" (James 1882b: 70).

[128] Hegel EL | GW 20: §78.

[129] Hegel WL | GW 11: 388.

[130] Hegel WL | GW 21: 27.

[131] Houlgate 2006: 34–5. Cf. Maker 1994: 99–100. Cf. the non-presuppositional character of dialectic with the concept of life in Gentry 2020 and Houlgate 2022.

[132] Hegel EL | GW 20: §41 Addition 1. Cf. Hegel: "Philosophy lacks the advantage, which the other sciences enjoy, of being able to *presuppose* its *objects* as given immediately by representation. And, with regard to its beginning and advance, it cannot *presuppose* the *method* of cognition as one that is already accepted" (Hegel EL | GW 20: §1).

follows Fichte toward a dialectical method, his science can only discover that this method "dwell[s] within" it. By contrast, as we saw, Fichte's science assumes in advance that logic, guided by the principle of determinability, must give a dialectical account of the conditions of intelligibility.[133]

Second and more importantly, Fichte derives the categories from the I as first principle without eliminating the radical contingency of positing this principle.[134] In Chapter 3, I will reconstruct Hegel's early charge of uneliminated radical contingency or bruteness against Fichte, which reprises Kant's similar charge against Aristotle and Fichte's against Kant. For now, we can anticipate Hegel's charge by considering the brute fact that Fichte neither eliminates nor regards as eliminable, namely, the act of positing the I as first principle.

In the *New Presentation*, Fichte claims that philosophy's first "task" is to posit the "explanatory ground" or first principle of experience.[135] Such a principle is meant to serve as the derivational source of the conditions of intelligibility. One can either posit reason or the I as first principle and, like Fichte, endorse "*idealism*" or posit nature or the not-I as first principle and, like Spinoza, endorse "*dogmatism*."[136]

Between idealism and dogmatism, a metaphilosophical dispute ensues that, Fichte argues, cannot be resolved theoretically, that is, through conceptual analysis:

[133] However, see Fichte: "our division of the *Wissenschaftslehre* into theoretical and practical parts is purely problematic (which is why we mention this division only in passing and are unable to draw any sharp boundary, since we do not yet recognize any such boundary). We do not yet know whether we shall be able to complete the theoretical part nor whether we might yet stumble upon a contradiction that is purely and simply beyond resolution. Even less can we know whether we will be driven from the theoretical part into a distinctively practical one" (Fichte GWL | SW I: 127).

[134] A version of this discussion appears in Bruno 2024a.

[135] Fichte VND | SW I: 423.

[136] Fichte VND | SW I: 425–6. Prior to developing the *Wissenschaftslehre*, Fichte undergoes a conversion from dogmatism to idealism. See his 1807 Königsberg lectures: "as a young man I was much more deeply rooted in the same Spinozism to which young people today, on far weaker grounds than those that I then repudiated, wish me to return" (Fichte GA II/10: 114, translated by Breazeale 2018: 105). See his letter to Friedrich August Weisshuhn, August/September 1790: "I have been living in a new world ever since reading the *Critique of Practical Reason*. Propositions that I thought could never be overturned have been overturned for me. Things have been proven to me which I thought could never be proven—for example, the concept of absolute freedom, the concept of duty, etc.—and I feel all the happier for it" (Fichte B | 1988: 357). See the draft of his letter to Heinrich Nikolaus Achelis, November 1790: "The influence that [Kant's] philosophy, especially its moral part (though this is unintelligible apart from a study of the *Critique of Pure Reason*), exercises upon one's entire way of thinking is unbelievable—as is the revolution that it has occasioned in my own way of thinking in particular. I particularly owe it to you to confess that I now believe wholeheartedly in human freedom and realize full well that duty, virtue, and morality are all possible only if freedom is presupposed. I realized this truth very well before—perhaps I said as much to you—but I felt that the entire sequence of my inferences forced me to reject morality. It has, in addition, become quite obvious to me that very harmful consequences for society follow from the assumption that all human actions occur necessarily" (Fichte B | 1988: 360-1). And see 1795's "On Stimulating and Increasing the Pure Interest in Truth": "intellectual power is strengthened and increased through use. And we derive pleasure from such an increase in our power, because it is something we have earned. It provides us with the elevating consciousness that is expressed in the following words: 'I was a machine, and I could have remained one. Motivated by myself and by means of my own strength, I have made myself into an autonomous being[']" (Fichte BE | SW VIII: 352).

> Neither of these two systems can directly refute the opposing one; for the dispute between them is a dispute concerning the first principle, i.e., concerning a principle that cannot be derived from any higher principle. If the first principle of either system is conceded, then it is able to refute the first principle of the other. Each denies everything included within the opposite system. They do not have a single point in common on the basis of which they might be able to achieve mutual understanding and be united with one another. Even when they appear to be in agreement concerning the words of some proposition, they understand these same words to mean two different things.[137]

Fichte gives three reasons for why the dispute between idealism and dogmatism is theoretically insoluble. First, each competing first principle is an ultimate explanatory ground and so "cannot be derived from any higher principle." Neither principle can be proven, since each is a presupposition on which all proof rests.[138] Second, each principle grounds a rigorous and complete account of the conditions of intelligibility, that is, a system of intelligibility. Once "conceded," each principle rules out anything that is inconsistent with the system that it grounds. Thus, positing the I grounds an autonomous human experience that rules out the putative experience-transcendence of the not-I, whereas positing the not-I grounds a deterministic universe that rules out the putative self-determination of the I.[139] Third,

[137] Fichte VND | SW I: 429. Cf. Fichte VND | SW I: 499, 509–n. Cf. James' "The Dilemma of Determinism", a lecture to the Harvard Divinity School, March 18, 1884: "[Indeterminism] admits that possibilities may be in excess of actualities, and that things not yet revealed to our knowledge may really in themselves be ambiguous . . . To that view, actualities seem to float in a wider sea of possibilities from out of which they are chosen . . . Determinism, on the contrary, says [possibilities] exist *nowhere*, and that necessity on the one hand and impossibility on the other are the sole categories of the real . . . Now, can *science* be called in to tell us which of these two point-blank contradicters of each other is right? Science professes to draw no conclusions but such as are based on matters of fact, things that have actually happened; but how can any amount of assurance that something actually happened give us the least grain of information as to whether another thing might or might not have happened in its place? Only facts can be proved by other facts . . . What fills up the gaps in our minds is something not objective, not external. What divides us into possibility men and anti-possibility men is different faiths or postulates—postulates of rationality . . . [F]rom any strict theoretical point of view, the question is insoluble" (James 1884: 198–200, 205). Cf. Balog 2012 on the theoretical insolubility of the dispute between physicalism and anti-physicalism.

[138] Cf. Fichte: "Every philosophy presupposes something that it does not demonstrate on the basis of which it explains and demonstrates everything else" (Fichte NM | GA IV/2: 17). Cf. also Fichte BWL | SW I: 54.

[139] Cf. Fichte's claim that, with "a correct inference" from their first principle, a dogmatist can discredit an idealist's alleged "fact" of spontaneity as "an illusion and a deception" (Fichte VND | SW I: 430). Cf. also his claim that a dogmatist "rejects the self-sufficiency of the I" by explaining "everything that occurs within consciousness," including "our opinion that we are free," as "a product of a thing in itself" (Fichte VND | SW I: 431). And cf. Fichte: "the system of universal necessity . . . barren and heartless indeed, but inexhaustible in its explanations, will explain even this desire for freedom, and this aversion to the contrary doctrine [of necessity]. It explains everything which I can cite from my own consciousness against it" (Fichte BM | SW II: 194–5). These passages conflict with Neuhouser's claim that the "inadequacy of dogmatism consists in the fact that, by starting from the thing itself, it will never be able to arrive at an account of the consciousness of things and therefore will prove incapable of constructing a single, all-encompassing system" (Neuhouser 1990: 58). Since dogmatic explanations are "inexhaustible," they indeed include an explanation of consciousness, according to which the "fact" of

each principle renders the system of the opposing principle unrecognizable, such that words in one system repeated in the other system "mean two different things." Thus, an idealist cannot recognize the mechanistic event that a dogmatist signifies with the words 'humans act,' just as a dogmatist cannot recognize the free activity that an idealist signifies with those same words.[140]

Fichte infers from the theoretical insolubility of the dispute between idealism and dogmatism that this dispute must be resolved practically. An idealist can practically resolve the dispute by attaining consciousness of their freedom. Since this is consciousness not of a mere fact, but rather of an act, it is consciousness not of something that I receive, but rather of something that I produce. Such consciousness therefore cannot be imposed on me, but must instead be solicited from me. Hence Fichte says that an idealist can only be "summoned" to exhibit the freedom of which they can attain conscious.[141]

In the Jena lectures whose transcripts compose the *Nova Methodo*, Fichte summons his students to exhibit their freedom by inviting them to think for themselves. He does so by asking them to think about the wall in the lecture hall, to think about themselves thinking about the wall, and to become aware of the identity of "the thinker and the thought" in this second thought.[142] Whereas a difference between thinker and thought involves the passivity of one's being given something other than oneself about which to think, an identity of thinker and thought involves the activity of one's giving oneself a thought about which to think. In thinking about myself thinking about the wall, then, I determine the content of my thought. More generally, in thinking for myself, I determine myself. To attain an awareness of my self-determination is to attain an immediate consciousness, which Fichte also calls an "intellectual intuition,"[143] of my freedom. Crucially, in order to attain consciousness of my freedom, I must exhibit or realize the very freedom of which I attain

or "desire" for freedom is deemed illusory. We will see that dogmatism's inadequacy rather consists in its performative contradiction.

[140] Cf. Fichte: "I have stated that I have nothing whatsoever in common with certain other philosophers and that they do not now occupy and never will be able to occupy the standpoint from which I write. People appear to have treated this declaration more as an indignantly expressed hyperbole than as something I am completely serious about, for they have not ceased to reiterate their demand that I should prove my theory to them. I must therefore solemnly declare that I intend this claim to be taken in the most literal sense, that I am completely serious about it, and that it expresses my deepest conviction . . . [Dogmatists and idealists] find themselves in two completely different worlds" (Fichte VND | SW I: 509n).

[141] Fichte VND | SW I: 461. Cf. Fichte: "we cannot force anyone to accept [idealism], since the acceptance of this system is something that depends on freedom" (Fichte VND | SW I: 499). Cf. also Fichte: "In the course of ordinary consciousness, one encounters no concept of the I, no self-reverting activity. Nevertheless, one is able to think of one's I when a philosopher calls upon one to do so; and then one discovers this concept by means of free activity, and not as something given" (Fichte NM | GA IV/2: 17).

[142] Fichte NM | GA IV/2: 29.

[143] See Fichte NM | GA IV/2: 31–2.

this consciousness. In doing so, I instantiate the absolute freedom of reason or the I. I thereby practically resolve the dispute in favor of idealism.

Underscoring the non-theoretical character of this way of resolving the dispute, Fichte says that consciousness of one's freedom cannot be "demonstrated by means of concepts," but rather must be "discovered immediately within [one]self," namely, by "perform[ing]" a "free act" and "becom[ing] conscious of it."[144] Responding to Fichte's summons to think for oneself, then, one engages not in a mere thought experiment, but rather in what I will call an 'act experiment.'

However, Fichte recognizes that, in attaining consciousness of their freedom, idealists resolve the dispute "*for [themselves]*," but not "*for [dogmatists]*."[145] This is because attaining the consciousness in question depends on performing the very act whose possibility the dogmatist denies, that is, whose possibility is refuted by the nihilistic consequence of Spinozism. The dogmatist posits the not-I as first principle, from which everything is meant to follow with causal necessity, thereby ruling out human freedom. If the dispute is to be genuinely resolved, the dogmatist must somehow conceal an incipient capacity for freedom in virtue of which they refute their own position. Fichte offers two main arguments to this conclusion in the *New Presentation*, which I will now reconstruct.

What I will call the 'argument from normativity' runs as follows. First, positing a first principle is a normative activity. This is because it is a response to the first task of philosophy, a response that one regards as correct and for which one therefore regards oneself as responsible. Second, a normative activity presupposes freedom, namely, the freedom to successfully or unsuccessfully satisfy the norm that governs that activity. Hence Fichte says that positing a first principle occurs "by means of a free act of thinking."[146] Third, a dogmatist posits the not-I as first principle, the consequence of which is to rule out the very freedom that their positing presupposes. In other words, in positing their first principle, a dogmatist commits the performative contradiction of smuggling freedom into their purportedly deterministic system. Hence Fichte says that a dogmatist "is not well prepared to defend [themselves] against [an idealist's] attacks, for there is something within [their] own inner self which agrees with [their] assailant."[147]

[144] Fichte VND | SW I: 449, 463.

[145] Fichte VND | SW I: 510.

[146] Fichte VND | SW I: 425.

[147] Fichte VND | SW I: 434. Insofar as Fichte summons his students to exhibit a consistency between their inescapable freedom and their first principle, a consistency that he models by summoning rather than coercing them, he arguably pursues the goal of what Michel Foucault explains is the philosophical practice of *parrhesia* or free speech: "*Bios* is the focus of Socratic *parrhesia*. On Socrates' or the philosopher's side, the *bios-logos* relation is a Dorian harmony which grounds Socrates' parrhesiastic role and which, at the same time, constitutes the visible criterion for his function as the *basanos* or touchstone. On the interlocutor's side, the *bios-logos* relation is disclosed when the interlocutor gives an account of his life, and its harmony tested by contact with Socrates. Since he possesses in his relation to truth all the qualities that need to be disclosed in the interlocutor, Socrates can test the relation to truth of the interlocutor's existence. The aim of this Socratic parrhesiastic activity, then, is to lead the

Fourth, a dogmatist therefore betrays a capacity for freedom and so refutes themselves.[148]

What I will call the 'argument from validity' runs as follows. First, a dogmatist "presuppos[es] the thoroughgoing validity of the mechanism of cause and effect." According to "mechanism," everything is determined by external causal relations and, ultimately, by the not-I. Second, the act of presupposing the validity of mechanism is a counterexample to it. This is because the relation between thinking and the thought of something's validity is not a causal relation. Hence Fichte says that a dogmatist's act of presupposing the validity of mechanism "is an act that lies outside the realm of mechanical determinism." Third, a dogmatist's act of presupposing the validity of mechanism is independent of causal relations and is therefore an act of freedom. Hence Fichte says that "[o]nly a free consciousness" can grasp the act of presupposing the validity of mechanism. Fourth, once again, a dogmatist therefore betrays a capacity for freedom and, since "[w]hat they say stands in contradiction with what they do," they refute themselves.[149]

The dispute between idealism and dogmatism is genuinely resolved, then, because, as the argument from normativity and the argument from validity each show, a dogmatist refutes their principle simply by positing it. Their act of positing comes too late to vindicate their deterministic system, for it is unavoidably an act of

interlocutor to the choice of that kind of life (*bios*) that will be in Dorian-harmonic accord with *logos*, virtue, courage, and truth" (Foucault 2001: 101).

[148] Cf. Fichte's argument in the *Foundations* that a Spinozist who abstracts from the I in order to posit nature as an absolute substrate "*also* thinks, without noticing it, of the *absolute subject*, as intuiting this substrate," and so "one tacitly adds in thought precisely that from which one professed to have abstracted and thereby contradicts oneself" (Fichte GWL | SW I: 97). Cf. also Hans Jonas' claim that "materialist monism" effectively "denies itself the status of an argument" by treating its argument as "the epiphenomenon of physical occurrences determined by necessities of sequence entirely foreign to 'meaning' and 'truth'" such that "there is no way on the part of those engaged in the argument, marionettes as they are to those necessities, to evaluate the issue on its merits" (Jonas 2001: 129–30). Cf. too Pippin: "To assume [dogmatism] would still be to determine oneself to act as if determinism were true. But that would make it a norm for action and so to refute oneself" (Pippin 2000: 158). And cf. Wood 2012: 130–2.

[149] Fichte VND | SW I: 510. Cf. Fichte: "Life, as giving oneself up to the mechanism, [is] not [possible] without the freedom that gives itself up, even if the latter were not to come to (actual) consciousness" (Fichte RAF | GA II/5: 182, translated by Zöller 2000: 67). Cf. also Kant's 1783 review of Johann Heinrich Schulz's 1783 "Attempt at an Introduction to a Doctrine of Morals for All Human Beings Regardless of Different Religions": "[the fatalist] has assumed in the depths of his soul that understanding is able to determine his judgment in accordance with objective grounds that are always valid and is not subject to the mechanism of merely subjectively determining causes, which could subsequently change; hence he always admits freedom to think, without which there is no reason" (Kant RS | AA 8: 14). Cf. too Jacobi's claim that we err when we "make to the principle of mechanism the absurd request that it too, if it is to be granted objectivity, exhibit a mechanism" (Jacobi LS 429 | 1994: 377). And cf. Schelling's 1797 *Ideas for a Philosophy of Nature as Introduction to the Study of this Science*: "The dogmatist, who assumes everything to be originally *present* outside us (not as *coming to be* and *springing forth from* us) must surely commit himself at least *to this*: that what is *external* to us is also to be explained by *external* causes. He succeeds in doing this, as long as he remains within the nexus of cause and effect, despite the fact that he can never make it intelligible how this nexus of causes and effects has *itself* arisen. As soon as he raises himself above the individual phenomenon, his whole philosophy is at an end; the limits of mechanism are also the limits of his system" (Schelling IPN | 1988: 30).

freedom. This is why Fichte says in the *Nova Methodo* that a dogmatist contains the "antidote" and "cure" for their own position.[150] If a dogmatist unavoidably engages in an act experiment and thereby refutes themselves, then one can only inconsistently posit the not-I as first principle and can only consistently posit the I as first principle. As Fichte says: "I am only active. I cannot be driven from this position. This is the point where my philosophy becomes entirely independent of all arbitrary choice and becomes a product of iron necessity—to the extent, that is, that free reason can be subject to necessity; i.e., it becomes a product of *practical* necessity."[151] The standpoint of freedom is inescapable because its denial is self-refuting.

This claim provides important context for understanding Fichte's dictum that "[t]he kind of philosophy one chooses thus depends upon the kind of person one is."[152] We might take the dictum to suggest that one can genuinely choose either idealism, given an idealistic personality, or dogmatism, given a dogmatic, that is, a Spinozistic, personality. It therefore might be taken to suggest Fichte's endorsement of metaphilosophical dualism, that is, the view that there are two possible types of philosophy.[153] However, since he regards dogmatism as self-refuting, the dictum rather entails Fichte's endorsement of metaphilosophical monism, that is, the view that there is only one type of philosophy. Hence he concludes that "[t]he only type of philosophy that remains possible is idealism."[154] The corollary of this conclusion regarding "the kind of person one is" is therefore rather strict. One can either choose idealism or else fail to see that idealism is one's only choice. But then one can only be an idealistic kind of person, whether wittingly or unwittingly.[155]

[150] Fichte NM | GA IV/2: 16.

[151] Fichte VND | SW I: 466–7. Cf. Fichte's 1798 "On the Basis of Our Belief in a Divine Governance of the World": "I am unable to doubt this freedom and this determination thereof without, at the same time, renouncing myself... I can go no further so long, that is, as I do not wish to destroy my own inner self. Therefore, the sole reason why I cannot go any further is because I cannot *will* to go any further. Here lies that which sets a limit to the otherwise unbridled flight of argumentation, that which binds the mind because it binds the heart. Here is the point where thinking and willing are united, where they become one and bring me into harmony with myself. To be sure, I could, in principle at least, proceed further if, that is, I wanted to place myself in contradiction with myself; for argumentation possesses no immanent limit within itself" (Fichte GGW | SW V: 181–2). Cf. also Fichte: "I remain purely passive, a quiet stage upon which certain representations are succeeded by other ones; but I am not the active principle that might have produced these representations. Yet I make precisely this latter assumption, and I cannot abandon this assumption without abandoning myself" (Fichte VND | SW I: 465).

[152] Fichte VND | SW I: 434. On Fichte's dictum and opposing interpretations of it by Schelling and Jacobi, see Bruno 2024a.

[153] On early Schelling's commitment to a minimally pluralistic metaphilosophical dualism in the "Philosophical Letters," see Bruno 2014a, Bruno 2016, and Bruno 2020d. I rebut Kemp and Iacovetti's objection to my pluralist reading of Schelling (Kemp and Iacovetti 2020) in Bruno 2022a.

[154] Fichte VND | SW I: 438. Cf. Fichte's 1801 "Public Announcement of a New Presentation of the *Wissenschaftslehre*": "one is either a '*one-sole philosophy philosopher*' or else one is *no philosopher at all*" (Fichte A | GA I/7: 164). On the limitations not only of Fichte's metaphilosophical monism but also of early Schelling's metaphilosophical dualism, Jacobi's metaphilosophical pluralism, and Hegel's metaphilosophical holism, see Bruno (2024b).

[155] Fichte claims that someone "whose character is naturally slack or who has been enervated and twisted by spiritual servitude, scholarly self-indulgence, and vanity will never be able to raise himself to the level of idealism," and says that he "does not expect to make any converts among people who are *already firmly set in their ways*" (Fichte VND | SW I: 434–5). As he tells Reinhold in a letter, July 4, 1797,

Crucially, for Fichte, choosing idealism is a brute fact, that is, a radically contingent act. As he says in the *New Presentation*, one's "decision" between idealism and dogmatism is "determined by *inclination* and *interest*," where "[o]ne's supreme interest and the foundation of all one's other interests is one's *interest in oneself*" and where one's self-interest ultimately expresses one of two "immediate" beliefs, namely, the dogmatic "belief in the self-sufficiency of things," which we saw is performatively contradictory, and the idealistic "belief in [one's] own self-sufficiency."[156] Being unmediated, both beliefs are simply brute. Moreover, Fichte says in the *Nova Methodo* that although consciousness of freedom is "the ultimate reason" on which idealism rests, "no reason can be given" for attaining it. In attaining consciousness of oneself as free, "one posits oneself as self-positing." But "[n]o grounds can here be adduced for this action, for we have reached the limit of all reasons."[157] As he tells Reinhold in a letter, July 2, 1795: "One enters my philosophy by means of what is absolutely *incomprehensible*."[158]

Nevertheless, to modify Kant's phrase from the Concluding Remark in the *Groundwork*,[159] we can say that one's entrance into the *Wissenschaftslehre* is comprehensibly incomprehensible. That positing the I as first principle is incomprehensible is itself comprehensible because this act could not have any condition, since it would thereby not be the positing of a first, that is, unconditioned, principle, but would rather be the positing of a conditioned principle. Positing the I is a brute fact because neither "reasons" nor "grounds" can be given for this act. It

the *Wissenschaftslehre* "assumes that every true human being is *naturally* conscious of his freedom (i.e., of his I-hood and independence). Whoever lacks and cannot obtain such consciousness is beyond help" (Fichte B | 1988: 421). Like "[m]ost human beings," such people, as he says in the *Foundations*, "would rather consider themselves to be a piece of lava in the moon than an *I*" (Fichte GWL | SW I: 175n). And yet he suggests in the *Nova Methodo* that experience naturally drives us "back into ourselves, where we discover our own freedom" and that, where dogmatism remains "predominant in a particular person," they "cannot endure this way of thinking for very long" because it leads "to fatalism" (Fichte NM | GA IV/2: 16). Cf. Aron Gurwitsch: "The fact that nihilism was able to develop and that the consequences thereof have taken on a greater and greater historical reality, the fact that the experience seems to confirm conceptions which themselves are inspired by nihilism—all this proves only the corruptibility of man. But this corruptibility is not at all identical with thoroughgoing degradation. By virtue of his full and authentic nature man is far from being in the state of decay, since he is *animal rationale*, a free and rational being; he is, however, constantly exposed to the danger of decay" (Gurwitsch 1945: 197).

[156] Fichte VND | SW I: 433–4.

[157] Fichte NM | GA IV/2: 31, 47.

[158] Fichte B | 1988: 399.

[159] See Kant: "[reason] restlessly seeks the unconditionally necessary and sees itself constrained to assume it without any means of making it comprehensible to itself, fortunate enough if it can discover only the concept that is compatible with this presupposition. It is therefore no censure of our deduction of the supreme principle of morality, but a reproach that must be brought against human reason in general, that it cannot make comprehensible as regards its absolute necessity an unconditional practical law (such as the categorical imperative must be); for, that it is unwilling to do this through a condition—namely by means of some interest laid down as a basis—cannot be held against it, since then it would not be the moral law, that is, the supreme law of freedom. And thus we do not indeed comprehend the practical unconditional necessity of the moral imperative, but we nevertheless comprehend its *incomprehensibility*; and this is all that can fairly be required of a philosophy that strives in its principles to the very boundary of human reason" (Kant GMM | AA 4: 463).

instead consists in a commitment to oneself as capable of commitment, that is, a commitment to oneself as free. In other words, it consists in what I will call 'taking a practical stand.' We can comprehend the incomprehensibility of positing the I, then, in terms of the radical contingency of performing this act. Insofar as this act is in some sense arbitrary, it is virtuously arbitrary insofar as its alternative is the performative contradiction of positing the not-I as first principle. Moreover, such arbitrariness does not threaten the necessity of the deductions that rest on it, for their necessity would lack any significance without initially taking the practical stand of exhibiting the activity of reason or the I.

The act of positing the I is no more contingent than the pursuit of enlightenment, which is to say that taking a practical stand is contingent in the way that emerging from self-incurred minority is contingent. Just as, for Kant, pursuing enlightenment depends on the resolve to use one's understanding without external direction,[160] so too, for Fichte, entering the *Wissenschaftslehre* depends on the resolve to exhibit the activity of reason without external determination. I will develop this idea in Section 3.2 in order to frame Hegel's charge of uneliminated radical contingency against Fichte.

Although Fichte campaigns against facticity, the *Wissenschaftslehre* clearly admits of at least one brute or factical element. By contrast, Hegel more thoroughgoingly adopts Fichte's genetic insight that a fully satisfying answer to the question *quid facti* must eliminate bruteness from the conditions of intelligibility. Hegel aims to do so by developing logic as a presuppositionless science, making him a foil for post-Kantians like Schelling, Schopenhauer, Kierkegaard, and Nietzsche, who challenge the very idea of presuppositionlessness through philosophical investigations of freedom, the will, subjectivity, and perspective. Fichte's methodologically innovative notion of a genetic deduction thus establishes an early crossroads for post-Kantian philosophy, one at which reason's systematic ambitions face serious questions about its apparently brute limitations.

[160] See Kant A | AA 8: 33. On Kant's theory of enlightenment, see Proops (forthcoming).

2
Annihilating Facticity
Fichte's Berlin *Wissenschaftslehre*

2.1 Introduction

In *Being and Time*, Heidegger pursues an answer to the "forgotten" question of the "meaning of being," one that avoids those "achieve[ments]" of Plato and Aristotle that "ha[ve] been preserved in various distorted and 'camouflaged' forms down to Hegel's *Logic*."[1] Heidegger's answer to this question accounts for the conditions on which being can be intelligibly disclosed to we who are Dasein or being-there. These conditions of intelligibility include being-in-the-world, being-with-others, being-ahead-of-itself, being-toward-death, and being-time.[2] Sharing the predicate of 'facticity,' such conditions are not empirically contingent discoveries, for they make possible our empirical openness to the world. As Heidegger says, "*[f]acticity is not the factuality of the* factum brutum *of something objectively present, but is a characteristic of the being of Dasein taken on in existence, although initially thrust aside*. The 'that' of facticity is never to be found by looking."[3] Nor are such conditions of intelligibility logically necessary derivations, for their denial yields no logical contradiction. As Heidegger says, it is due to the "methodically unrestrained tendency to derive everything and anything from a simple 'primordial ground'" that "it has often been disregarded in ontology" that the "characteristics of being" are "existentially equiprimordial," which is to say, groundlessly given conditions of Dasein.[4] 'Facticity' thus denotes a set of radically contingent conditions of intelligibility, that is, conditions that are inescapable for us as Dasein, but at whose root there is no reason insofar as they are not deducible from any first principle or dialectical movement of thought.[5] The term accordingly signifies the unique modal space of conditions of intelligibility whose necessity is not logical yet whose

[1] Heidegger SZ | GA 2: 2.

[2] See Heidegger's 1925 spring lectures in Kassel, "Wilhelm Dilthey's Research and the Contemporary Struggle for a Historical Worldview": "The *being-there* of Dasein *is* nothing other than *being-time*. Time is not something that I encounter out there in the world, but is what I myself am" (Heidegger WD | 2002: 169). Cf. his 1928 summer lectures *The Metaphysical Foundations of Logic*: "The primal fact, in the metaphysical sense, is that there is anything like temporality at all" (Heidegger MA | GA 26: 270).

[3] Heidegger SZ | GA 2: 135. Cf. Heidegger: "'Factical' does not mean naturally real or causally determined, nor does it mean real in the sense of a thing" (Heidegger EPR | GA 60 1: 9).

[4] Heidegger SZ | GA 2: 131.

[5] See Heidegger in *Being and Time* on the facticity of historicity, sociality, language, truth, and normativity (Heidegger SZ | GA 2: 19–21, 117–8, 162–3, 229, 267–8) as well as a circa-1929 note on the facticity of temporality (translated by Kisiel 2010: 28).

Facticity and the Fate of Reason After Kant. G. Anthony Bruno, Oxford University Press.
 DOI: 10.1093/9780191987533.003.0003

contingency is not empirical. This is why Heidegger describes facticity in terms of "thrownness."[6] Although we can hermeneutically interpret facticity, as we will see in Chapter 6, we are ineluctably given over to it.

The concept of facticity is philosophically important, not only in its own right, but also in light of what we can learn about its German idealist heritage, for it is crucial that Heidegger's analysis of the modal space of radically contingent conditions is neither unprecedented nor unprompted. On the one hand, as we saw in Section 1.2, Kant thematizes just this space, which sets a precedent for Heidegger's existential phenomenology. On the other hand, Fichte and Hegel's project of removing bruteness from the science of intelligibility serves as a foil that prompts Heidegger's existential analysis of Dasein as thrown. It is therefore well worth considering the German idealist origin of the concept of facticity.

In the first *Critique*, Kant locates conditions of possible experience at the modal register of anthropic necessity, a register in which they are unavoidable for us yet radically contingent insofar as they derive from no principle of reason.[7] Thus, despite being necessary for human sensibility, there is no rational ground for why space and time are our forms of intuition. They belong to a "kind of representation that is peculiar to us," a kind of sensibility whose "origin" is a "mystery."[8] And despite our ability to derive the categories of the understanding from the logical forms of judgment, there is no rational ground for why just these forms, and hence just these categories, are ours. As we saw in Section 1.2, the precise kind and number of the categories is a "peculiarity of our understanding."[9] Moreover, whatever common root grounds sensibility and understanding, that is, "the two stems of human cognition," is "to us unknown."[10] Such claims to the bruteness of transcendental conditions position Kant as a philosopher of facticity *avant la lettre*.[11]

As noted in Section 1.1, some of Kant's earliest readers demand a first principle that can ground his conclusions about the conditions of intelligibility, lest such conditions derive from an origin that either is radically contingent or, even worse, is Spinozistic and so precludes the possibility of rational autonomy. Fichte posits as a criterion of systematic philosophy the elimination of radical contingency and charges its presence with rhapsody or what he eventually calls 'facticity,' a term that he coins in 1799 on the eve of his Berlin period. Texts from this period maintain his earlier view that conditions of intelligibility are not brute facts, but rather

[6] See Heidegger SZ | GA 2: 135.

[7] Cf. Stanley Cavell: "Wittgenstein's view of necessity is, as one would expect, internal to his view of what philosophy is. His philosophy provides, one might say, an anthropological, or even anthropomorphic, view of necessity; and that can be disappointing; as if it is not really *necessity* which he has given an anthropological view of" (Cavell 1999: 118–9).

[8] Kant KrV A35/B51, A278/B334.

[9] Kant KrV B145.

[10] Kant KrV A15/B29.

[11] On the compatibility of facticity and transcendental philosophy, see Bruno 2017b, Crowell 2002, and Lafont 2015.

must be genetically deduced from the absolute freedom of reason or the I. Fichte's neologism thus names the same problem of bruteness to whose solution he is committed in Jena. Apparently factical conditions of intelligibility are shown to follow necessarily from the I through a process that Fichte now calls 'genesis.' As he says in the 1804 spring lectures in Berlin,[12] "an *absolutely given fact*... bears in itself the mark of its insufficiency as a *highest* principle for the *Wissenschaftslehre*," the mark of a "facticity" that we must "master ... genetically."[13] He adds in 1805's *Erlangen Propaedeutics* that "all facticity can become genetic"[14] and calls for the "absolute annihilation of all facticity" in that year's *Principles of the Doctrine of God, Ethics, and Jurisprudence*.[15] Fichte's critical response to apparently radically contingent conditions of intelligibility is to show that they are in fact absolutely necessary conditions that the I generates from itself, independent of empirical givenness. Genesis in this sense prefigures Hegel's conception of logic as a science that is "capable of proving its very own peculiar content, and able to gain insight into the necessity of this content."[16]

Facticity is thus a conceptual watershed in post-Kantian philosophy. For Fichte, it denotes the final obstacle to systematic philosophy. For Heidegger, it denotes the intelligibility conditions on which meaningful pursuits, including philosophy itself, depend. Yet the history of this concept remains neglected. German idealism scholarship still strongly favors Kant and Hegel, while Anglophone Fichte literature so far relies mostly on his Jena texts. This has the unfortunate effect of obscuring Fichte's role in the development of post-Kantian logic, overlooking the origin of a core concept for phenomenology, and disregarding the tension between Fichte's pioneering critique of Kant and Heidegger's qualified return to the factical elements in Kant's critical philosophy. It is therefore crucial to explore the Berlin *Wissenschaftslehre* for the origin of such a historically and systematically decisive philosophical concept.

In this chapter, I will first trace the origin and development of Fichte's neologism (Section 2.2). I will then review the Jena period's methods of intellectual intuition and genetic deduction (Section 2.3). Intellectual intuition exhibits our awareness of the I's absolute freedom, establishing it as philosophy's first principle. Genetic deduction derives from the I the necessary conditions of its realization in experience, avoiding any rhapsodic appeal to radically contingent origins. Next, I will illustrate the Jena period's continuity with the Berlin period's methods of insight and genesis. Insight yields unconditional knowledge of the oneness of a first principle,

12 For these lectures, I cite the English translation of GA II/8 using the page ranges that are denoted by number pairs in square brackets, which correspond to facing pages that are drawn from the SW and *Copia* versions of the lectures.

13 Fichte WL04 | GA II/8: 180–1.

14 Fichte PE | GA II/9: 54.

15 Fichte PGSR | GA II/7: 354. It is thus mistaken to suggest, as Denker does, that Fichte "remain[s] silent in wonderment" at and "graciously accept[s] the gift of facticity" (Denker 2000: 119).

16 Hegel EL | GW 20: §42 Remark.

while genesis deduces the multiplicity of the conditions of experience by showing that they emerge from this principle's own "self-construction" (Section 2.4).[17] I will then observe an important methodological clarification in 1804, when Fichte detects radical contingency within his own doctrine of intellectual intuition, whose "ideal" form and "real" content he says remain "at their root *factical*."[18] I will reconstruct his argument for why a proper insight into the I must itself be genetic, that is, it must deduce the I's form and content from the I itself. Such a deduction removes this deeper instance of facticity and thereby proves reason's "absolute self-sufficiency,"[19] which remains the *Wissenschaftslehre*'s abiding principal concern (Section 2.5). I conclude by observing that while Heidegger shares the anti-nihilistic spirit of Fichte's idealism, they endorse opposing conceptions of facticity (Section 2.6). This will anticipate my analysis of Heidegger's hermeneutics of facticity in Part III.

2.2 A Fateful Neologism

The first philosophical use of 'facticity' occurs around the turn of the nineteenth century,[20] beginning in the same year that Jacobi coins 'nihilism.'[21]

In the posthumous 1845–46 *Recollections, Answers, Questions*, which is written in 1799, Fichte says that "what is actual," namely, that which in perception is "factically recognizable [*factisch erkennbar*]," differs from that which is, in a "logical" sense, "absolutely first," namely, freedom as the "principle of possibilities."[22] This claim can be read alongside two related claims from 1806's *The Way Towards the Blessed Life, or the Doctrine of Religion*. First, Fichte says there that the absolute's existence is "factical and accidental [*factisch und zufällig*]" if it is viewed with a "merely factical glance [*factischen Blicke*]," whereas, for "decisive truthful thinking," the absolute's existence "necessarily follows" from its "inner being."[23] Second, he says that while the "historical" is "factical [*factisch*]," that is, an "absolute fact [*absolutes Factum*], existing for itself alone and isolated from everything else, not explained or deduced from a higher reason," the "metaphysical" is deduced from reason and thus "cannot be grasped merely as fact [*lediglich als*

[17] Fichte WL04 | GA II/8: 196–7.
[18] Fichte WL04 | GA II/8: 180–1.
[19] Fichte WL04 | GA II/8: 44–5.
[20] See Carvalho 2010, Denker 2000, Kisiel 2000, and Kisiel 2008.
[21] A version of this discussion appears in Bruno 2021a.
[22] Fichte RAF | SW V: 360. *Recollections* is composed just before Fichte's departure for Berlin. Breazeale observes that although the appearances of 'factical' in this text are published in SW, i.e., the collected works that Fichte's son, Immanuel Hermann Fichte, edits, but not in GA, i.e., the critical edition of Fichte's collected works, the editors of GA attribute passages in SW that differ from GA to Fichte's son without ruling out the possibility that his son's edition includes texts that Fichte in fact writes yet no longer survive.
[23] Fichte ASL | SW V: 509.

Factum]."[24] These cases indicate that the factical is a mark of contingency, whether this pertains to the actuality of what is given to perception, the absolute's existence conceived as merely accidental, or the historical event viewed in isolation from its explanation.[25] Moreover, in these cases, such contingency contrasts, respectively, with the necessity of freedom as an "absolutely first" principle, the necessity of the absolute's existence according to "truthful thinking," and the necessity of "higher reason" for the deduction of metaphysical facts. We have seen that freedom, the absolute, and reason all coincide, for Fichte, in the I. We can therefore infer that the contingency of the factical is to be distinguished from the necessity of the I and of the deductions that arise from it.[26]

Similarly, 1801–02's *Presentation of the Wissenschaftslehre* associates facticity with contingency. Fichte claims that knowing the absolute requires not mere

[24] Fichte ASL | SW V: 567. Fichte's pairing of '*factisch*' and '*Factum*' in the *Blessed Life* opposes his use of '*Thathandlung*.' In the *Aenesidemus* review, he claims that "the first principle of all philosophy" need not express "a *fact [Thatsache]*," for it "can also express an *act [Thathandlung]*" (Fichte RA | SW I: 8). In the Second Introduction, he explains this claim by saying that philosophy cannot "begin" with "a fact [*Thatsache*]," since this would restrict us to "a world of being and finitude," i.e., a world of causally determined objects, with no "path leading from this world to an infinite and supersensible one." Instead, it must begin with "an act [*Thathandlung*] (i.e., with a pure activity that presupposes no object, but, instead, produces its own object, and therefore with an *acting [Handeln]* that immediately becomes a *deed [That]*)," since this act reveals "the precise point where these two worlds are connected with each other and from which they can both be surveyed in a single glance" (Fichte VND | SW I: 468). Cf. Fichte NM | GA IV/2: 28. An "*act*" that produces itself, i.e., an "*acting*" that "becomes a *deed*," accordingly contrasts with facticity insofar as it "presupposes no object" that brutely limits it. Fichte's opposition of '*factisch*' and '*Factum*' to '*Thathandlung*' diverges from Kant's use of "*Factum*" to describe consciousness of the moral law, which consciousness expresses the act of adopting the standpoint of freedom (Kant KpV | AA 5: 31) and so prefigures Fichte's use of '*Thathandlung*,' on which, see Franks 2005: 276–98.

[25] Cf. Fichte's 1804–05 Berlin lectures, published as 1806's *The Characteristics of the Present Age*: "universal time . . . presupposes a *world-plan*, which, in its primitive unity, may be clearly comprehended and from which may be correctly deduced all the great epochs of human life on earth, so that they may be distinctly understood both in their origin and in their connection with each other" (Fichte GGZ | SW VII: 5). Cf. also Fichte's 1810–11 Berlin lectures, published as the posthumous 1817 *The Facts of Consciousness*: "the natural man is merely a historical intelligence, who can very well take hold of facts, re-image them in his reproductive power of imagination, substitute and exchange one for the other, but has also in this the limit of his range of vision. Whenever the problem is no longer merely to exchange facts for facts, but to rise beyond all facticity in its absolute form to its absolute ground by pure thinking, the faculty of the natural man is at an end; he must die, and a new one must be born in his place" (Fichte TB | 2017: 95–6). And cf. Hegel's 1822–23 Berlin lectures on the philosophy of world history: "What is the purpose of all these singular events, which interest us all? There is more to them than their particular aims. This enormous cost must be for some ultimate purpose . . . [I]t is a truth that such a final end is what governs and alone consummates itself in the events that occur to peoples, and that therefore there is *reason in world history*. This affirmative answer to the question is presupposed here; the proof of its truth can be found in the treatment of world history itself because history is the image and deed of reason . . . [H]istory is empty; nothing is to be learned from it if we do not bring reason and spirit with us" (Hegel VPW1 | GW 18: 20–2).

[26] Cf. Reinhold's *Contributions*: "A first principle, indeed, an absolutely *first* principle is indispensable to any science which is not merely *historical*, that is to say, to any science which is supposed to consist in knowledge of what is universal and necessary . . . Thus all of the propositions which make up the content of a philosophical science must be determined by syllogisms, i.e., each proposition in the science must either be derived from premises, among which is included a necessary and universal higher proposition (a *first principle*), or must itself be such a first principle" (Reinhold BB | 1790: 115–9, translated by Breazeale 1982: 792).

intuition "in its immediate facticity [*unmittelbaren Facticität*]," but rather an intuition that is "completely one with thinking," that is, intellectual intuition.[27] He extends this claim later by saying that the *Wissenschaftslehre* itself is "absolutely factical [*schlechthin factisch*] from the side of intuition," for the latter apprehends mere "facticity [*Facticität*]" unless it forms a "necessary unity" with thinking.[28] He concludes by explaining that "the absolute insight into an absolute form of knowledge" consists in distinguishing "factical knowledge [*factischen Wissen*]," which is "contingent," from the "absolute knowledge" according to which all knowledge "is necessarily grounded on freedom."[29] With this third text in view, we can now see that facticity is specifically a mark of a contingency that impedes a science of intelligibility insofar as it presents a false condition of intelligibility, that is, a condition that lacks the necessity that is demanded by systematic philosophy.[30] Mere intuition without thinking is a spurious condition of intelligibility, while merely contingent knowledge cannot be its own condition. Moreover, we once again find that the relevant sense of necessity concerns the I, for it is the I whose "freedom" grounds knowledge, whose intuition must be intellectual and thus in an absolute "unity" with thinking, and whose deductions articulate the "absolute form of knowledge."

The early Berlin texts use 'facticity' to designate the problematic contingency of conditions of intelligibility whose determination lacks systematic rigor. Unlike a factical condition of intelligibility, a true condition of intelligibility has absolute priority, as Fichte says in *Recollections*, or is deducible from a condition that has such priority, as he says in the *Blessed Life*, or is that whose intuition is intellectual, as he says in the *Presentation*.

Facticity is not to be confused with facts. Facticity is radically contingent insofar as it characterizes a purported condition of intelligibility that lacks the necessity of either a first principle or a deduction from that principle. Facts, by contrast, are empirically contingent yet compatible with systematic necessity, since, simply by appearing, they conform to true conditions of intelligibility. Facticity thus consists not in the sensible givenness of empirical actuality, but rather in the brute givenness of unthought or underived conditions of intelligibility, that is, conditions whose origin is obscure or unknown and whose necessity consequently lies in doubt.[31] As Fichte says in the *Presentation*, the factical must be "renounced" and a "higher" point of reflection adopted, from which such conditions as space and time can be derived from a knowledge that is "always remaining in itself."[32] Thus,

[27] Fichte DWL | SW II: 47.
[28] Fichte DWL | SW II: 161–2.
[29] Fichte DWL | SW II: 54–5.
[30] See Fichte's 1800–01 "Commentaries on Schelling's *Transcendental Idealism* and *Presentation of My System of Philosophy*," in which he charges Schelling with leaving the distinction between the "in itself and not in itself" as an underived "facticity" (Fichte S | 2012: 128).
[31] As Carvalho observes, factical consciousness "masks the unsolved problem of its origin" and is groundless insofar as it rests on hidden or unknown premises (Carvalho 2010: 230, 232).
[32] Fichte DWL | SW II: 132–3.

although Fichte distinguishes facticity from facts, as Heidegger will over a century later, unlike Heidegger, he holds that facticity must be eliminated by the absolute freedom of reason or the I.

The early Berlin texts display Fichte's sustained commitment to avoiding what in the metaphysical deduction Kant describes as the problem of deriving the categories "rhapsodically from a haphazard search for pure concepts, of the completeness of which one could never be certain, since one would only infer it through induction, without reflecting that in this way one would never see why just these and not other concepts should inhabit the pure understanding."[33] As we saw in Section 1.3, Fichte returns the rhapsody charge to Kant throughout the Jena period. Fichte agrees with Kant about the categories' necessity for human experience. However, since Kant traces their origin to forms of judgment that are inherited from traditional logic and that he admits lack an absolutely rational ground in the same way as do the forms of sensibility, Fichte must derive them from "something higher,"[34] namely, the I as first principle. As Fichte tells Reinhold in a letter, March 1, 1794: "To derive [the categories] from the logical forms of judgment presupposes that logic provides the rules for philosophy, and this I cannot accept."[35] Fichte echoes this complaint during his 1812 summer lectures in Berlin, "On the Relation of Logic to Actual Philosophy," when he says that Kant "was not so disinclined as he ought to have been [toward general logic]" and "had not recognized that his own philosophy requires that general logic be destroyed to its very foundation."[36] Rather than take a detour through traditional logic that subordinates reason's absolute freedom by deferring to a groundless authority, Fichte remains committed to eliminating radical contingency from the conditions of intelligibility. The rhapsody problem is accordingly a precursor to the facticity problem, for it exposes seemingly brute facts about intelligible human experience and indicates that they in fact arise from reason's power of self-determination, that is, from I-hood.

To the extent that the rhapsody problem prefigures the facticity problem, we should expect that Fichte's solutions to them are methodologically related. I will present the methods of the Jena and Berlin periods in Sections 2.3 and 2.4,

[33] Kant KrV A81/B106–7.

[34] Fichte NM | GA IV/2: 8.

[35] Fichte B | 1988: 376. Gottlob Benjamin Jäsche's Preface to the *Jäsche Logic* says that the possibility of a "deduction" of general logical principles raises the "highly significant question" of "an *absolutely first principle* of all cognition and science" and cites Fichte's and Schelling's claims to this principle's discovery (Kant JL | AA 9: 7).

[36] Fichte SW IX: 111–2, translated by Martin 2003: 35–6. Cf. Fichte: "One could say from another side that [the *Wissenschaftslehre*] consists in a transcendentalization of logic itself and arises from it, for if a logician wanted to ask himself . . . 'but how do I arrive at my assertions?', he would have to get into the *Wissenschaftslehre*" (Fichte DWL | SW II: 159–60). Cf. Husserl's 1929 *Formal and Transcendental Logic*: "Kant's purely formal logic concerns the ideal formations produced by thinking. And, concerning them, Kant fails to ask properly transcendental questions of the possibility of cognition. How does it happen that he regards a formal logic, with its apriority, as self-sufficiently grounded? How is it comprehensible that he never thought of asking transcendental questions about the sphere of formal logic, taken as a sphere in and for itself?" (Husserl FT | 1969: 260).

respectively, in order to demonstrate their continuity in precisely this regard. We will see how Fichte's dual method of intellectual intuition and genetic deduction in Jena are meant to solve the rhapsody problem and how this sets a methodological precedent for his solution to the facticity problem in Berlin.

2.3 Fichte's Twofold Method in Jena

In the Second Introduction to the *New Presentation*, Fichte asks:

> What then is the overall gist of the *Wissenschaftslehre*, summarized in a few words? It is this: reason is absolutely self-sufficient; it exists only for itself. But nothing exists for reason except reason itself. It follows that everything reason is must have its foundation within reason itself and must be explicable solely on the basis of reason itself and not on the basis of anything outside of reason, for reason could not get outside of itself without renouncing itself. In short, the *Wissenschaftslehre* is transcendental idealism.[37]

It may seem unlikely to those familiar with the letter of Kant's idealism to learn that it affirms either reason's absolute self-sufficiency, given our dependence on sensibility, or reason's absolute existence, given our affection by the thing in itself. But Fichte distinguishes the letter of Kant's idealism from its "spirit," which consists in "divert[ing] the attention of philosophy away from external objects and to direct it within ourselves," this as a means to proving that "a systematic derivation of all consciousness or, what comes to the same, a system of philosophy, would have to set out from the pure I, exactly as is done in the *Wissenschaftslehre*."[38] Fichte's main textual evidence for transcendental idealism's spiritual identity with the *Wissenschaftslehre* consists of passages from §§16–7 of the transcendental deduction:

[37] Fichte VND | SW I: 474. Cf. Fichte's claim that the "supreme law of reason" is the "law of self-sufficiency" (Fichte VND | SW I: 456).

[38] Fichte VND | SW I: 477, 479. Contrast Kant's 1799 "Declaration Concerning Fichte's *Wissenschaftslehre*": "I regard Fichte's *Wissenschaftslehre* as a totally indefensible system . . . [T]he system of the *Critique* rests on a fully secured foundation, established forever . . . There is an Italian proverb: may God protect us especially from our friends, for we shall manage to watch out for our enemies ourselves" (Kant B | AA 12: 370–1). Evidently, Kant rejects Fichte's response, at the end of the eighteenth century, to the invitation that the first *Critique* issues in its final sentence: "If the reader has had pleasure and patience in traveling along in my company, then he can now judge, if it pleases him to contribute his part to making this footpath into a highway, whether or not that which many centuries could not accomplish might not be attained even before the end of the present one: namely, to bring human reason to full satisfaction in that which has always, but until now vainly, occupied its lust for knowledge" (Kant KrV A855/B883).

> **original apperception** . . . is that self-consciousness which, because it produces the representation **I think**, which must be able to accompany all others and which in all consciousness is one and the same, cannot be accompanied by any further representation . . . The supreme principle of all intuition in relation to the understanding is that all the manifold of intuition stand under conditions of the original synthetic unity of apperception.[39]

By themselves, these passages do not convey the precise affinity between Fichte's and Kant's idealism. Accordingly, Fichte must ask: "what, summarized in a few words, is the gist of the Kantian philosophy?" What, in other words, is the nature of original apperception, that is, the presupposition that "manifests itself on every page of Kant's writing" and is "the same presupposition the *Wissenschaftslehre* makes"?[40]

Fichte explains that original apperception is the "pure self-consciousness" that is "the same in all consciousness, and thus it is not determinable by anything contingent within consciousness. The I that appears within pure self-consciousness is determined by nothing but itself, and it is determined absolutely."[41] This explanation implies two criteria for systematic philosophy, which will reflect Fichte's methodological position that the *Wissenschaftslehre* consists of "precisely two parts."

The first criterion is that the I is "determined absolutely" and "determined by nothing but itself," which is just to say that the I is absolutely self-determining. Given the nihilistic threat of Spinozism against which Fichte develops his system, I will call this the 'anti-nihilism criterion.' It is the requirement that the I is absolutely free and hence that its function is not, as Jacobi fears, "to accompany the mechanism of efficient causes," which would render its freedom an "illusion." To satisfy this criterion is to enshrine the I's freedom as a first principle. It is to posit a self-grounding activity that can thereby ground a derivation of the conditions of intelligibility or, "what comes to the same," a philosophical system.

The second criterion is that the I "is not determinable by anything contingent within consciousness." Given Fichte's criticism of Kant's metaphysical deduction for deriving the categories from a radically contingent origin, I will call this the 'anti-rhapsody criterion.' It is the requirement that no brute conditions of intelligibility, for example, the forms of judgment or the forms of sensibility, can be imposed on the I. This criterion is the negative formulation of what we saw, in Section 1.3, is the scientific criterion that the categories must be derived from a non-arbitrary origin, namely, the I.

Fichte denies that Kant satisfies the anti-nihilism criterion, since, by holding that the 'I think' is "a thinking, not an intuiting," and by proscribing intellectual

[39] Kant KrV B132, 136, corrected citation from Fichte VND | SW I: 475–6.
[40] Fichte VND | SW I: 474.
[41] Fichte VND | SW I: 476.

intuition of the actuality of the I or, indeed, of any being,[42] Kant leaves idealism's first principle uncognized and so leaves unchallenged Spinozism's opposing and cognizable first principle, namely, nature or the not-I. As Fichte says in the Second Introduction: "The intellectual intuition of which the *Wissenschaftslehre* speaks is not directed toward any sort of being whatsoever; instead, it is directed at an acting—and this is something that Kant does not even mention (except, perhaps, under the name 'pure apperception')."[43] Intellectual intuition would prove the actuality of the I beyond its mere thought, for such an intuition consists in the immediate consciousness of the actuality of my free activity, that is, of my instantiation of I-hood, and would thereby refute Spinozism's first principle and its nihilistic consequence. Fichte's parenthetical remark implies that, although the letter of Kant's philosophy does not satisfy the anti-nihilism criterion, its spirit does insofar as pure apperception is the activity whereby the I absolutely determines its own unity.[44] As Kant says between the passages that Fichte quotes from the Analytic, the apperceptive I is "**original**" because it unifies my representations in "an act of **spontaneity**" and is therefore not a derivative product of experience.[45] In other words, apperception does not accompany the mechanism of nature as its mere effect, but rather accompanies the experience of nature as its necessary ground. However, by restricting apperception to a mere form that receives matter via sensibility, Kant does not affirm apperception's actuality and thereby fails to posit a cognizably supreme principle that can refute the actuality of its Spinozistic rival. This is why Fichte claims in §5 of the *Nova Methodo* that the *Wissenschaftslehre* provides a "superior explication of the Kantian proposition that our concepts refer only to objects of experience." Such objects presuppose the apperceptive I as their principle of unity. But the I only "catches sight" of objects because it originally discovers itself "*as acting*," namely, among, toward, and away from objects. That our concepts refer to objects is thus only explicable by the fact that concepts "originate through acting and exist only for the sake of acting; only acting is absolute."[46] In other words, the "Kantian proposition" must be explicated not theoretically, but rather practically, such that what accompanies all my representations is not merely

[42] Kant KrV B157; cf. B72, B307, A252/B308.

[43] Fichte VND | SW I: 472.

[44] But see Kant's "Declaration": "Since some reviewers maintain that the *Critique* is not to be taken literally in what it says about sensibility and that anyone who wants to understand the *Critique* must first master the requisite 'standpoint' (of Beck or of Fichte), because Kant's precise words, like Aristotle's, will kill the mind, I therefore declare again that the *Critique* is to be understood by considering exactly what it says and that it requires only the common standpoint that any cultivated mind will bring to such abstract investigations" (Kant B | AA 12: 370–1). Reiterating the Second Introduction, Fichte responds to Kant's "Declaration" in the "Announcement" by clarifying that his use of 'intellectual intuition' is meant to signify the apprehension not of an object, but rather of reason's own activity, i.e., the "*cognition of reason itself by means of reason itself*" (Fichte A | GA I/7: 159). For a defense of Fichte's response, see Bruno 2022b.

[45] Kant KrV B133.

[46] Fichte NM | GA IV/2: 61.

apperceptive thought, but rather apperceptive action, that is, not simply the "I **think**,"[47] but rather what I will call the 'I act.' This reflects Fichte's charge, with which we began in Section 1.1, that Kant fails to properly vindicate the primacy of practical reason.

Similarly, Fichte denies that Kant satisfies the anti-rhapsody criterion, since, as we saw in Section 1.2, Kant derives the categories from forms of judgment whose origin is ultimately as groundless as the forms of sensibility. Fichte's criticism implicitly distinguishes between the letter and spirit of Kant's philosophy:

> I know full well that Kant has by no means actually *constructed* a system . . . I also know that Kant has by no means *proven* that the categories he has postulated are conditions for the possibility of self-consciousness, but has merely asserted that this is so . . . Nevertheless, I am equally certain that Kant has entertained the *thought* of such a system, that all of the things he has actually presented are fragments and results of this system.[48]

Kant could have "*proven*" that the categories are conditions of self-conscious experience had he shown that they are the "results" of a grounded system, that is, had he derived them from a first principle. Fichte's last remark implies that, despite the unsystematic letter of Kant's philosophy, its spirit assumes the "*thought*" of a system, namely, the thought of consciousness grounded on the apperceptive I as a supreme principle. This thought, Fichte adds shortly after, is "the spirit and the innermost soul of Kant's entire philosophy, and it is also the spirit and soul of the *Wissenschaftslehre*."[49] But Kant imperfectly expresses this spirit by failing to derive the forms of sensibility and judgment, and hence also the categories,[50] from

[47] See Kant KrV B131.

[48] Fichte VND | SW I: 478. Cf. Fichte's letter to Niethammer, December 6, 1793: "There is only one original fact of the human mind, a fact which is the foundation of philosophy in general, as well as of its two branches, theoretical and practical philosophy. Kant was certainly acquainted with this fact, but nowhere did he state it" (Fichte B | 1988: 369).

[49] Fichte VND | SW I: 479. Förster shows that "[i]n order to avoid the common misunderstanding that Kant really meant to speak of 'given concepts' and of 'objects that affect us', Beck insisted that one begins with the productive activity of the understanding, what he calls the 'original representing'. For sensibility and understanding, according to Beck, have a common root in the original act of representing, an act from which space, time, and the categories originally emerge, not as concepts of objects, but rather as ways of representing, and as ways of achieving the original synthetic unity of consciousness through which I can apprehend an object in the first place." He notes that while Beck's account conflicts with the first *Critique*, it "looks more plausible (and more Kantian) from the point of view of self-positing that Kant developed in the [posthumous 1936–38] *Opus Postumum*" (Förster 2005: 163–4). For an argument that Kant removes the radical contingency of space and time in the *Opus Postumum*, see Shuster 2014.

[50] In a footnote, Fichte claims that the categories "can be defined only *by showing how each category is determinately related to the possibility of self-consciousness*, and anyone who is in possession of these definitions is necessarily in possession of the *Wissenschaftslehre*." Kant lacks this definition because he does not rigorously demonstrate the categories' relation to the I, namely, through a genetic deduction. Fichte cites as evidence Kant's claim that he "deliberately spare[s]" himself a definition of the categories and that whereas in "a system of pure reason one could rightly demand these [definitions]," in the first *Critique* "they would only distract us from the chief point of the investigation" (Fichte VND

the I and thus by failing to affirm the I's supremacy, that is, its absolute power of self-determination. Consequently, Fichte charges that, in the Kantian edifice, "the construction materials—though already well prepared—are jumbled together in a most haphazard manner."[51] He repeats this charge in Berlin in 1800's *New Version of the Wissenschaftslehre*: "'The I think that is able to accompany all of my representations.' . . . This is what Kant says in a rhapsody entitled: Deduction of the Categories, where he carries out everything except a deduction."[52] Admitting "anything contingent" into idealism in this way betrays its spirit. Hence Fichte must satisfy the anti-rhapsody criterion by providing the necessary premises for Kant's "fragments and results."[53]

The criticism of Kant, along with the clarification of idealism's spirit, yield a twofold job description that Fichte upholds throughout the Jena period. First, the *Wissenschaftslehre* must satisfy the anti-nihilism criterion by intellectually intuiting the I's absolute freedom.[54] Second, it must satisfy the anti-rhapsody criterion, that is, the scientific criterion, by genetically deducing the system of the conditions of intelligibility from the I. While we saw, in Section 1.3, that Kant's transcendental deduction satisfies the anti-skepticism criterion by proving our right to use the

| SW I: 479n, citation from Kant KrV A82–3/B108–9). Cf. Kant: "in philosophy the definition, as distinctness made precise, must conclude rather than begin the work" (KrV A730–1/B758–9). On Kant's didactic method of definition, see Pier (forthcoming).

[51] Fichte VND | SW I: 479n. Cf. Fichte RA | SW I: 25.

[52] Fichte NB | 2012: 104.

[53] We can partly trace Kant's and Fichte's diverging views about idealism's spirit to differing notions of completeness. In the Introduction to the first *Critique*, Kant says that while critique can "guarantee" the completeness of the principles of pure reason, it is "not yet" the "complete system" of transcendental philosophy, which "would also have to contain an exhaustive analysis of all of human cognition *a priori*." Thus, although he claims to give "a complete enumeration of all of the ancestral concepts that comprise the pure cognition in question," namely, of the categories (Kant KrV A13–4/B27–8, A81/B107), this enumeration is not an "exhaustive analysis" of *a priori* cognition, which would include the forms of sensibility and the forms of judgment whose ultimate ground Kant regards as obscure. This reveals an ambiguity in his claim that "what reason brings forth entirely out of itself cannot be hidden, but is brought to light by reason itself as soon as reason's common principle has been discovered" (Kant KrV Axx) and his claim in the *Prolegomena* that the first *Critique* "takes no foundation as given except reason itself" and "therefore tries to develop cognition out of its original seeds without relying on any fact whatever" (Kant P | 4: 274). Cf. Kant P | 4: 329–30. Such "discover[y]" and "develop[ment]" are not exhaustive by Kant's lights, which incompleteness is consistent with his claim that sensibility and understanding "arise from a common but to us unknown root" (Kant KrV A15/B29), his claim in the Introduction to 1790's *Critique of the Power of Judgment* that the faculties of the soul "cannot be further derived from a common ground" (Kant KU | AA 5: 177), and his trust in traditional logic to provide the forms of judgments. For Fichte, by contrast, completeness is impeded by trust in any authority beyond reason's ability to generate the system of the forms of cognition from itself, which is why the spirit of idealism demands reason's absolute freedom.

[54] 'Intellectual intuition' does not appear in the *Foundations*. Fichte uses the term in his review of Schulze's *Aenesidemus* a year prior and resumes its use in the *Nova Methodo* the following year. However, we find the concept behind the term at work in the *Foundations* when we compare the latter with Fichte's description of a first principle in the *Aenesidemus* review. For this comparison, see Bruno 2020d: 139 and Tilliette 1967, but contrast Philonenko 1966. On the role of ancient skepticism in Schulze's *Aenesidemus*, see Berry 2022 and Dunphy 2023. On Fichte's *Aenesidemus* review, see Breazeale 1981, Franks 2005: 219–37, and Messina 2011.

categories, this only secures conclusions for transcendental idealism, whereas its premises require satisfying both the anti-nihilism criterion and the anti-rhapsody criterion.

In order to satisfy the anti-nihilism criterion, it is insufficient for an idealist to complete what Fichte calls philosophy's first "task" of locating the "explanatory ground" or first principle of intelligible experience in the absolute freedom of reason, since this leaves open the logical possibility that this principle is in fact Spinozistic nature, that is, a cause of which experience, including reason itself, is a necessary effect. An idealist must therefore also fulfill what Fichte calls philosophy's "first demand" of turning away from objects and "look[ing] within [one]self," for only then can I cognize the absolute freedom of reason, namely, by intellectually intuiting myself as exhibiting this freedom through my rational autonomy.[55] Intellectual intuition thus secures not merely the thought of the logical possibility of I-hood, but rather the knowledge of the actuality of I-hood, an actuality that is accessible only from my first-person awareness of my freedom, that is, from my "immediate consciousness that I act."[56]

Moreover, in order to satisfy the anti-rhapsody criterion, it is insufficient for an idealist to prove our right to use the categories as necessary conditions of experience, as Kant's transcendental deduction does, if such a deduction relies on their metaphysical deduction from a radically contingent origin. We must also prove that the categories' source is not "contingent within consciousness," but rather arises "from the very nature of the intellect,"[57] namely, through a genetic deduction. As we saw in Section 1.5, the dialectical movement of thought in a genetic deduction demonstrates that the categories are necessary conditions of intelligibility just if they arise from the I's reflection on itself.

In the Jena period, the rhapsody problem concerns the metaphysical deduction of the categories and not the intellectual intuition of the I as first principle. We will now see that, in the Berlin period, Fichte traces this problem, under the name of 'facticity,' back to his own doctrine of intellectual intuition.

[55] Fichte VND | SW I: 422–3. Cf. Fichte: "a postulate is also a starting point, which is not further proven, and thus it is a first principle. A first principle is any cognition that cannot be further proven . . . The *Wissenschaftslehre* proceeds in this manner as well, and it employs the term 'act' to designate its postulate. This term *was* not understood; but it means no more—and is meant to mean no more—than this: one is supposed to act internally and observe what one is doing. This means that if one wants to communicate this philosophy to someone else, one has to ask the other person to perform the action in question. In this sense, one does have to postulate something" (Fichte NM | GA IV/2: 27–8). Cf. Schelling: "The first postulate of all philosophy, to act freely, seemed to [me] as necessary as the first postulate of geometry, to draw a straight line. Just as little as the master of geometry proves the straight line should the philosopher try to prove freedom" (Schelling IPP | SW I/1: 243).

[56] Fichte VND | SW I: 463.

[57] Fichte VND | SW I: 442.

2.4 Methodological Continuity in Berlin

In Section 2.2, we saw that Fichte coins 'facticity' in order to name an architectonically intolerable contingency, namely, the apparent radical contingency, bruteness, or ultimate groundlessness of the conditions of intelligibility. The problem of facticity is accordingly another guise of rhapsody, since it undermines the possibility of systematic philosophy by subordinating the absolute freedom of reason or the I to brute facts that allegedly exceed reason's power of self-determination. In *Recollections* and the *Blessed Life*, 'factical' denotes the sheer givenness of perceptual content, the dependence of the absolute on an external cause, and the insulation of historical events from explanation. In the *Presentation*, 'facticity' denotes a principle whose intuition is divorced from thought and thus not intellectual. In each case, a purported condition of intelligibility turns out to be false because its determination is brute, whether perceptually, causally, historically, or intuitively so. A true condition of intelligibility, by contrast, has absolute necessity insofar as it is an intellectually intuitable first principle or else is deducible from such a principle.

A far more extensive investigation of facticity than appears in these texts occurs in Fichte's 1804 spring lectures in Berlin. I will turn now to these lectures in order to demonstrate their methodological continuity with the Jena period's strategy of eliminating radical contingency and systematizing transcendental idealism.

Fichte begins the Sixth Lecture by asserting that the *Wissenschaftslehre* "has the task of *tracing* all multiplicity *back* to absolute oneness" and "*deduc[ing]* all multiplicity *from* oneness."[58] We can see how this assertion contains a restatement of the methodological division of labor that Fichte adopts in Jena by examining the concepts of oneness and multiplicity.

First, Fichte describes oneness in the First Lecture in terms of the "unconditionally true." He explains that "whoever would have [this truth] must produce it entirely out of [themselves]. The presenter can only provide the terms for insight; each individual must fulfill these terms in [themselves]."[59] Insight into oneness evokes the Jena doctrine of the intellectual intuition of the I, which, in response to philosophy's first task, is an immediate awareness of the explanatory ground or first principle of intelligibility and which, in response to philosophy's first demand, "everyone has to discover immediately within [themselves]."[60] As Fichte now puts it, in insight, "[w]hat we genuinely comprehend becomes part of ourselves, and if it is a genuinely new insight, it produces a personal transformation."[61] As we saw in Section 1.6, such a transformation consists in one's elevation of oneself to the

[58] Fichte WL04 | GA II/8: 84–5. Cf. Fichte: "[the philosopher] reciprocally conceives multiplicity through oneness and oneness through multiplicity" (Fichte GA II/8: 8–9).
[59] Fichte WL04 | GA II/8: 4–5.
[60] Fichte VND | SW I: 463.
[61] Fichte WL04 | GA II/8: 18–9.

standpoint of freedom, a transformation that the "presenter," namely, Fichte himself, can summon, but cannot enforce.

Second, Fichte describes multiplicity not in terms of the "mere empirical givenness" of objects, but rather in terms of those "distinctions" that can be "established in the *mind*." Such distinctions, he explains later in the Thirteenth Lecture, are "modes of consciousness [that] must be deduced from self-consciousness" in "proper genetic fashion."[62] Deducing *a priori* distinctions, construed as modes of consciousness, evokes the genetic deduction of the categories, which distinguish and relate substance and accident, cause and effect, mind and world, self and other, and so on, and which, in order to satisfy systematic philosophy's anti-rhapsodic, that is, scientific, criterion, must show that the categories are "immanent laws of the intellect"[63] and not dictated by tradition.[64] As Fichte expresses the point in Berlin, no such categorial distinctions can be "merely factical," but rather "must become genetic."[65]

In the Sixteenth Lecture, Fichte confirms the methodological continuity of his Jena and Berlin periods by reiterating a decade-old view with the claim that the *Wissenschaftslehre* has "two main parts." The first part is the "doctrine of reason and truth," which provides "a single insight" into a "fundamental principle." The second part is the "doctrine of appearance and illusion" or "*phenomenology*," which "deduce[s] from the first part, as necessary and true appearances, everything which up to now we have let go as merely empirical."[66] We can explicate this new characterization of the two parts of the *Wissenschaftslehre* by drawing on the opening assertion of the Sixth Lecture. Regarding the first part, insofar as a doctrine of reason and truth affords "insight" into the oneness of a "fundamental principle," it must secure knowledge of the I. We will see in Section 2.5, however, that this insight is more complicated than Fichte acknowledges in Jena. Regarding the second part, insofar as, on the basis of the doctrine of reason and truth, the doctrine of appearance and illusion deduces "as necessary" that which "up to now we have let go as merely empirical," it must genetically deduce from the I the multiplicity of the conditions of intelligibility, that is, the multiplicity of conditions that we might otherwise rhapsodically assign to empirical sources that are external to the I. These are conditions whose necessity pertains both to our right to use them, in

[62] Fichte WL04 | GA II/8: 84–5, 200–1.

[63] Cf. Fichte VND | SW I: 442.

[64] By refusing to credit the categories to tradition, genetic thinking transforms ordinary assumptions about their content. Cf. Fichte's claim in *Natural Right* that philosophy must "bracket" the commonsense notion of the world's existence so as to "deduce" it from the I (Fichte GN | SW III: 24) with his claim in the Twenty-Second Lecture that "*transcendental* knowing" must "genetically" ground the "tacitly assumed premises" of "ordinary knowing" (Fichte WL04 | GA II/8: 336–7).

[65] Fichte WL04 | GA II/8: 148–9. Cf. Fichte's description of the historical event in the *Blessed Life* with his claim in the First Lecture that "merely apprehending multiplicity, as such in its factical occurrence, is history" (Fichte GA II/8: 8–9).

[66] Fichte WL04 | GA II/8: 206–7, 228–9, 242–3. For a survey of pioneering uses of 'phenomenology' in Johann Heinrich Lambert, Kant, Reinhold, and Fichte, see Piché 2010.

the narrow, jurisprudential sense of a deduction, and to their origin, in the broader, genealogical sense of a deduction. That the conditions of intelligibility or modes of consciousness are "true appearances" yet non-empirical indicates that they rise and fall not in perception, but rather in thinking, as we would expect from the dialectical movement of thought that characterizes a genetic deduction. Indeed, since deduction concerns conditions that are "established in the *mind*," a doctrine of appearance and illusion must pertain not to perceptual illusion, but rather to thinking's illusion regarding the origin, kind, and number of the categories, which illusion dialectic detects and overcomes. We can accordingly conclude that the Berlin period's methods cohere with the Jena period's by, first, demonstrating our insight into the oneness of the I as a fundamental principle and, second, deducing the multiplicity of conditions that, as modes of consciousness, make the I's realization in experience possible.[67]

Now, whereas Fichte levels the rhapsody charge against Kant's metaphysical deduction of the categories in Jena, he claims in the Thirteenth Lecture that the threat of radical contingency, now under the name 'facticity,' lies even deeper: "the primary error of all previous systems has been that they began with something factical and posited the absolute in this."[68] Fichte no longer scrutinizes merely the categories' necessity, but now also scrutinizes the necessity of philosophy's "absolute" first principle. Nevertheless, he once again targets Kant. Fichte claims that, in Kant's 1790 *Critique of the Power of Judgment*, we find "the confession that the sensible and supersensible worlds must come together in a common but wholly unknown root." He objects that if this root is "inscrutable, then while it may indeed always contain the *connection* [of the two worlds], [he] at least can neither comprehend it as such, nor collaterally conceive the two [worlds] as originating from it."[69] By "factically discover[ing] the distinction between the sensible and supersensible worlds" and leaving their ultimate ground in the dark, Kant degrades philosophy's first principle "from genetic manifestness," where genesis is the method whereby the doctrine of appearance and illusion deduces "necessary and true appearances," to "merely factical manifestness, completely contravening the inner spirit of the *Wissenschaftslehre*."[70] Moreover, Kant leaves open the possibility that Spinozism provides an unrivaled and cognizable principle, namely, nature, which grounds absolutely necessary conditions that rule out human freedom and purposiveness. As we saw from the early Berlin texts in Section 2.2, facticity spoils the necessity of any purported condition of intelligibility, whether it is intelligibility's derivative conditions, that is, the categories, or its original condition, that is, the first

[67] On the continuity of Fichte's Jena and Berlin periods, see Gueroult 1930, Hyppolite 1971, Schmidt 2004, and Talbot 1901. On Fichte's methodological division within the Berlin period, see Piché 2010 and Zöller 2016b.

[68] Fichte WL04 | GA II/8: 202–3.

[69] Fichte WL04 | GA II/8: 32–3.

[70] Fichte WL04 | GA II/8: 60–1.

principle. A first principle is factical if it is brutely unfathomable, that is, inscrutably imposed on reason. It can therefore be no true condition of intelligibility.

Remarkably, Fichte denies having yet given a presentation of the I as first principle that definitively escapes the threat of facticity. He states that the task of demonstrating the "*oneness*" of the I is "*entirely new* and has not even arisen in the earlier presentations of the *Wissenschaftslehre*."[71] Fichte's statement implies that when, for example, in his 1794 review of Gottlob Ernst Schulze's anonymous 1792 *Aenesidemus, or Concerning the Foundations of the Elementary Philosophy Propounded in Jena by Professor Reinhold, Including a Defense of Skepticism Against the Pretensions of the Critique of Pure Reason*, he describes the I as a first principle that we must intellectually intuit as "express[ing]" not only "a *fact*" but also "an *act*,"[72] he simply assumes the oneness of fact and act in this principle without demonstrating it. This raises the unprecedented challenge that the I's oneness must itself be deduced, that is, that insight into the I must itself be made genetic. Fichte's methodological clarification in Berlin is accordingly to maintain his distinction between the insight into the I and the genesis of conditions of intelligibility, but also to provide insight with its own genetic deduction, lest facticity spoil the very root of the *Wissenschaftslehre*. As he says in the Fourteenth Lecture, we require "the genetic deduction of the I."[73] This explains why Fichte specifically demands that his system's first part, "as a doctrine of truth and reason, expunges all facticity from itself."[74] This also contextualizes his assertion that insight into the I is "the only truly difficult part" of his system, the second part being the "brief and easy affair" of "deducing all possible modifications of apparent reality" as derivative, categorial conditions of intelligibility.[75] It turns out that the 1804 spring lectures offer no deduction of the categories that are familiar from the Jena period. Nevertheless, the lectures do claim to detect and remove facticity from our insight into the I, without which no such deduction could begin. I turn now to reconstruct Fichte's argument for this claim.

2.5 Uprooting A Deeper Facticity

In the Seventeenth Lecture, Fichte asserts that "a genuine derivation must have a reliable principle. Otherwise . . . one deduces from the intrinsically contingent something else which is also contingent . . . As if a good, proper, and reliable standpoint could arise when one had two terms, neither of which could stand by itself,

[71] Fichte WL04 | GA II/8: 242–3.
[72] Fichte RA | SW I: 8, 10.
[73] Fichte WL04 | GA II/8: 216–7. Cf. Fichte: "let us make this insight itself genetic" (Fichte GA II/8: 248–9).
[74] Fichte WL04 | GA II/8: 206–7.
[75] Fichte WL04 | GA II/8: 132–3.

each relying reciprocally on the other."[76] Earlier in the lectures, he stresses the importance of seeing what the principle of the *Wissenschaftslehre*, that is, what the I, "authentically is" and then describes seeing what "we really *are* in our highest peak," namely, instances of I-hood, as a matter of "ascend[ing] from factical terms to genetic ones."[77] What are the "factical terms" that preclude seeing what the I "authentically is," which is to say, what we "really *are*"? And how do such factical terms prevent the I from serving as a "reliable," that is, non-contingent, principle for the "genuine derivation" of a systematic philosophy?

An answer lies in the Ninth Lecture, where Fichte detects a "disjunction" at the foundation of the *Wissenschaftslehre*, namely, within the cognition of its first principle. On the one hand, the I has epistemic priority as the "inner essence of knowing," since no knowledge is possible without the idea of the I. On the other hand, the I has ontological priority as "knowing's formal being," since no knowledge exists outside the actuality of the I. The I's twofold priority yields two aspects that are essential to the cognition of the I. First, we must think of the I's idea or "concept" as the essence of knowing. Second, we must intuit the I's actuality or "light" as the being of knowing. However, the disjunction between thinking the I's essence and intuiting the I's being imposes a "task," namely, that of "finding the oneness" of these two cognitive aspects: "The essence of knowing [is] not without its being, and vice versa, nor intellectual knowing without intuition and vice versa, which are to be understood so that the disjunction that lies within them must become one in the oneness of the insight."[78] The disjunction between thinking and intuiting is intolerable because neither aspect of cognizing the I is adequate for a genuine insight into it. On the one hand, merely thinking the I raises a question of actuality, for this thought could be empty, lacking light. On the other hand, merely intuiting the I raises a question of ideality, for this intuition could be non-rational, lacking concept. Hence, neither cognitive aspect is self-standingly intelligible. As Fichte says above, the "reliable standpoint" of a first principle is inaccessible if our cognition of it relies on "two terms, neither of which could stand by itself." Moreover, if the epistemic and ontological terms for the two aspects of cognizing the I are not self-standingly intelligible, then these terms themselves are factical insofar as they fail to grasp a true condition of intelligibility. Such factical terms must, as Fichte puts it, be raised "to genetic ones," that is, to terms that stand together and grasp the I as the ultimate condition of intelligibility. Failing this, we lack insight into the I's authentic nature as a first principle and, consequently, we lack insight into our own nature as instances of I-hood, that is, into who we "*are*."

[76] Fichte WL04 | GA II/8: 260–1. Cf. Fichte: "only principles can enter the circle of our science. Whatever is not in any possible respect a principle, but is instead only a principled result and phenomenal, falls to the empirical level" (Fichte GA II/8: 86–9).

[77] Fichte WL04 | GA II/8: 40–1, 76–7.

[78] Fichte WL04 | GA II/8: 138–9.

Fichte's detection of a disjunction within the cognition of the I modifies his conviction in Jena that, in philosophy, we must cognize the I as the "foundational principle of all human knowledge," which "express[es] that *act* which neither appears nor can appear among the empirical determinations of our consciousness, but instead lies at the basis of all consciousness and alone makes consciousness possible."[79] According to this earlier view, we simultaneously think the I as internal and essential to knowing, lest it be externally and accidentally imposed onto knowing, and intuit the I's being immediately, unmediated by an intervening and endless series of empirical states. But in Berlin, Fichte identifies the thought and intuition of the I with what, in the Fifteenth Lecture, he calls, respectively, "*idealistic*" and "*realistic*" maxims that "are at bottom *factical*."[80] The Twelfth Lecture describes the idealistic maxim as assuming a "standpoint of reflection" on the I's "*essence*" and the realistic maxim as assuming the "*absolutely given fact*" of the I's "*existence*." Since each maxim "one-sidedly" regards itself as absolutely valid, each "annul[s] the other" while offering only an arbitrary starting point. This yields a "disjunction" between "two terms absolutely demanding unification."[81] Without unifying the idealist and realist aspects of our cognition of the I, there is no genuine, unified insight into the I's oneness and therefore no principle to ground philosophy.

Cognizing the I's oneness requires removing the "conflict of maxims" that arises between thinking the I from the standpoint of reflection and intuiting the I as an absolutely given fact. Fichte says that this conflict is "alleviated only by setting out a law of maxims."[82] In the Second Lecture, he states that "[t]he *Wissenschaftslehre*'s own maxim is to admit absolutely nothing inconceivable."[83] We can see how this statement prescribes a "law" that can resolve the conflict between the idealistic and realistic maxims once we see that neither maxim can conceive of what it posits. On the one hand, one cannot conceive of the I as cognized simply by thinking its idea, since any such act of thought assumes the I's actuality as its ground. On the other hand, one cannot conceive the I as cognized simply by intuiting its actuality, since an intuition of the I as the I must be an act of apperception, that is, of self-conscious thought. Hence, neither maxim posits something conceivable and so neither is as yet admissible into philosophy.

Since we must cognize the I's oneness in order to ground philosophy, we must render jointly conceivable that which the idealistic and realistic maxims posit, namely, the I's idea and actuality, or its concept and light, or its essence and

[79] Fichte GWL | SW I: 91.

[80] Fichte WL04 | GA II/8: 234–5. Cf. Fichte: "Do not think of 'idealism' and 'realism' here as artificial philosophical systems which the *Wissenschaftslehre* wants to oppose: having arrived in the circle of science, we have nothing more to do with the criticism of systems . . . [They] arise only in philosophy and especially in the *Wissenschaftslehre*" (Fichte GA II/8: 178–9). On the dialectical opposition between idealism and realism in the Twelfth, Thirteenth, and Fourteenth Lectures, see Schüz 2022: 317–33.

[81] Fichte WL04 | GA II/8: 178–81; cf. 170–3.

[82] Fichte WL04 | GA II/8: 172–3.

[83] Fichte WL04 | GA II/8: 32–3.

existence. Fichte does precisely this in the Eighteenth Lecture by relinquishing the one-sidedness of that which each maxim posits and reconceiving them as "*grounded*" in the I's own "*nature*."[84] The I's own nature alone can explain the unity of the thought of its essence and the intuition of its existence. This is because the I alone makes possible this thought and this intuition. In other words, the I alone explains how it is possible to cognize its actuality because it is presupposed by all cognition as unconditionally actual. If we distinguish between thinking and intuiting the I, we only divide that which must originally be a unity.[85] Hence, whereas neither of the factical terms that yield a disjunction in the cognition of the I posit anything conceivable in isolation, we can reconceive these as genetic terms, that is, as jointly expressive of the I's own "*self-genesis*."[86]

In keeping with the Jena period's view that the I as first principle is not merely a fact, but also an act, that is, not merely a truth to be grasped, but also a commitment to be performed, Fichte concludes in the Twenty-First Lecture that the "principle of absolute idealism" must be "presupposed . . . as something to be enacted and by no means as something to be understood."[87] To cognize the I's oneness is actively to exhibit the actuality of the principle on which all cognition rests, a presupposition that, unlike the factical terms of the idealist and realist maxims, cannot be derived from anything more basic. This explains Fichte's otherwise puzzling attribution of "absolute facticity" and "*primordial facticity*" to the I.[88] Hence he declares in the following lecture: "our task has been completed in its highest principle."[89] We can see that this conclusion is the result of Fichte taking a self-critical stance toward his Jena doctrine of intellectual intuition, whose factical terms are now genetically mastered.[90]

Cognizing the I's oneness demonstrates the practical standpoint from which, on pain of nihilism, we cannot be driven. But it also enables us to overcome facticity

[84] Fichte WL04 | GA II/8: 280–1.

[85] See Fichte's 1800 review of Christoph Gottfried Bardili's 1800 *Outline of the First Logic Purified of the Errors of Previous Logic in General and of the Kantian in Particular; Not a Criticism, But a* Medicina Mentis *Mainly Useful for Germany's Critical Philosophy*: "pure thinking does not at all stand above the I . . . [for] the latter signifies—to express myself this way—the *intelligizing* κατ' ἐξοχήν [*par excellence*], of which *thinking, intuiting, willing*, etc., are only subspecies, which are not posited absolutely, but must be derived from the former" (Fichte RG | GA I/6: 447, translated by Zöller 2000: 70).

[86] Fichte WL04 | GA II/8: 322–3. Cf. Fichte: "I have touched here on the very important distinction between a merely *factical regarding*, like our thinking of the in-itself, and *genetic insight*, like that into the in-itself's self-construction" (Fichte GA II/8: 196–7).

[87] Fichte WL04 | GA II/8: 322–3. Cf. Fichte's letter to Reinhold, July 2, 1795: "What I am trying to communicate is something which can be neither *said* nor *grasped conceptually*; it can only be *intuited*. My words are only supposed to guide the reader in such a way that the desired intuition is formed within him" (Fichte B | 1988: 398). Cf. also his letter to Reinhold, March 21, 1797: "My philosophy should be expounded in an infinite number of different ways. Everyone will have a different way of thinking it—and each person must think of it in a different way, in order to think it at all" (Fichte B | 1988: 417).

[88] Fichte WL04 | GA II/8: 46–7, 298–9; cf. 358–9.

[89] Fichte WL04 | GA II/8: 298–9.

[90] Cf. Talbot's examination of the 1804 Berlin lectures in her 1898 doctoral thesis, published as 1906's *The Fundamental Principle of Fichte's Philosophy* (Talbot 1906: 89–90).

within even the highest philosophical distinction, namely, between the thinkable essence and the intuitable existence of the I. By raising this distinction from the factical terms of one-sided maxims that attempt to posit the inconceivable to expressions that are derivative of the I's own nature, we can deduce the oneness of the I and thereby achieve genetic insight into philosophy's first principle. In this, we overcome the perhaps surprising new challenge that motivates the methodological clarification in the Berlin *Wissenschaftslehre*.

2.6 Toward a Hermeneutics of Facticity

We have seen in Part I that Fichte's philosophy sets the terms of the post-Kantian question of whether a science of intelligibility can tolerate brute facts by bearing the twin birth of coining 'facticity', so as to name the alleged problem of groundless or radically contingent conditions of intelligibility, and inventing dialectical logic, so as to derive such conditions from the contradictions of reason. Although it is usually associated with Heidegger's phenomenological conception of the necessary yet undeducibly groundless conditions of our existing in an intelligible world, Fichte coins 'facticity' over a century earlier in order to name the architectonically problematic contingency of putatively brute conditions of intelligibility. The term signals the methodological continuity of Fichte's Jena and Berlin periods insofar as it names the problem of the rhapsodic determination of the categories, even as what answers to this term comes to include the one-sidedly construed intellectual and intuitional aspects of the cognition of the first principle from which the categories are to be derived. Tracing the origin of the concept of facticity consequently serves to clarify the unity of Fichte's overall method throughout his career.

Tracing the origin of 'facticity' also promises to reveal an issue of shared concern for German idealism and phenomenology, since, after Fichte, it soon becomes an open question whether this term in fact names a real problem. This is to say that it soon becomes an open question for post-Kantian philosophers whether facticity requires positing a first principle for its elimination or instead characterizes the thrownness of finitude that is presupposed by positing as such and, accordingly, whether philosophy should ultimately satisfy architectonic or existentialist interests. As we will see in Parts II and III, respectively, this question shapes both Schelling's internal critique of the German idealist project of pursuing an absolute, that is, presuppositionless, science of intelligibility and Heidegger's phenomenological rejection of this same project.

I will conclude this chapter by observing that Heidegger shares the anti-nihilistic spirit of Fichte's idealism despite endorsing a diametrically opposed conception of facticity. This will set the stage for my analysis, in Part III, of Heidegger's hermeneutics of facticity and his related critique of Fichte's intolerance for facticity.

In order to show that Fichte and Heidegger exhibit a common anti-nihilistic spirit, it is necessary to trace the development of this spirit back to Jacobi's coining of 'nihilism.'

As we saw in the Introduction, Jacobi coins 'nihilism' to name the consequence of Spinoza's systematic commitment to the principle of sufficient reason, namely, the thoroughgoing determination of finite beings by external conditions, from which follows the denial of intrinsic capacities and properties, for example, freedom and purposiveness, and thus the annihilation of true individuals.[91] If nature ventriloquizes our belief and action, then we are merely the passage of fungible moments and empty of purpose, that is, we "accompan[y] the mechanism of efficient causes" with no "final" causes for our thinking, acting, and feeling. Before coining 'nihilism,' Jacobi ignites the Spinozism dispute when, in the *Doctrine of Spinoza*, he reports Gotthold Ephraim Lessing's 1780 private declaration to him that "[t]here is no other philosophy than the philosophy of Spinoza," to which he immediately yet pregnantly replies that "[t]hat might be true."[92] For Jacobi, there is indeed "no other philosophy" if philosophers are committed to "the proposition: 'Everything conditional must have a condition,'" that is, to the principle of sufficient reason, since the consequence of systematic commitment to this principle is precisely the nihilistic consequence of Spinozism.[93]

Jacobi's reply to Lessing indicts what I will call the 'philosopher's imperative,' which is to subordinate reason's perceptual faith in the immediacy of individuals with intrinsic capacities and properties to the understanding's inferential certainty in the system of the external conditions that mediate our access to existence. As he says in the Preface to the 1815 second edition of *David Hume on Faith, or Idealism and Realism: A Dialogue*, the intended introduction to his collected works, "since Aristotle, the growing tendency among the schools has always been to subordinate

[91] Jacobi claims that while every being is "connected with an infinite multitude of other singular beings," "[a]ll truly actual things are *individuals* or singular things, and, as such, they are living beings (*principia perceptiva et activa*) that are external to one another" (Jacobi DH 173–4 | 1994: 317–8). Individuals are not ultimately conditioned by external conditions, for they are principles that explain their perceptions and actions and are, in this sense, "living" powers. Earlier Jacobi describes the pre-philosophical conception of "a living, self-manifesting, freely acting, personal power" and says that "without the living experience of such a power in us . . . we should not have the slightest idea of cause and effect" (Jacobi DH 103–4 | 1994: 291). Not only, then, do we experience "actual things" as individuals and thus as living powers, but we also do so because we initially experience ourselves as living powers. As Jacobi says, we are not "beings who were *only capable of intuition and judgment*," for "we can *also act*!" (Jacobi DH 102 | 1994: 290). Cf. his letter to Johann Paul Friedrich Richter, a.k.a. Jean Paul, May 11, 1817: "freedom [is the] fundamental article of my teachings" (Jacobi B | 1827: 463, translated by Sandkaulen 2023: 3).

[92] Jacobi LS 13–4 | 1994: 187. See Kant's letter to Herz, April 7, 1786: "The Jacobi controversy is nothing serious; it is only an affection of *inspired enthusiasm* trying to make a name for itself and is hardly worthy of a serious refutation. It is possible that I shall publish something in the *Berlin Monthly* to expose this humbug" (Kant B | AA 10: 442). Kant's published response is 1786's "What Does It Mean to Orient Oneself in Thinking?". On the Spinozism dispute, see Beiser 2002, Franks 2005, Sandkaulen 2023, and Snow 1987.

[93] Jacobi LS 416 | 1994: 372.

immediate cognition to mediated cognition," that is, to subordinate the "*faculty of perception*," namely, "reason," to the "*faculty of reflection*," namely, the "understanding." According to Jacobi, reason is "the faculty of presupposing the true, the good, and the beautiful" as nature immediately reveals these to us. This is the faculty that the 1787 first edition of *David Hume* calls a "power of faith." By contrast, the understanding counts as true only that which is "demonstrable" on the basis of "*proofs*," that is, on the basis of inferences to external conditions, from which proofs it follows that finite beings with intrinsic capacities and properties, for example, freedom and purposiveness, are impossible.[94] By numbing reason's perceptual faith with the understanding's inferential certainty, philosophy annihilates true individuality.

Moreover, according to Jacobi, annihilation results regardless of whether philosophy invests certainty in the series of causally necessitated modes of nature, as in Spinozism, or invests it in the series of rationally necessitated acts of the I, as in idealism.[95] For both philosophical sciences, we grasp a thing not immediately, that is, as an individual that brutely manifests intrinsic capacities and properties, but rather mediately, that is, in terms of its external conditions, be they causal or rational. The philosopher's imperative is therefore demanding and disastrous irrespective

[94] Jacobi DH 4, 10–1 | 1994: 538, 541. Both editions of *David Hume* bear an epigraph that quotes from Blaise Pascal's posthumous 1670 *Thoughts* and is also cited in the *Doctrine of Spinoza*: "Nature confounds the Pyrrhonists, and reason the dogmatists.—We have an incapacity of proof that no dogmatism can overcome. We have an idea of truth that no Pyrrhonism can overcome" (Jacobi DH ii, 1 | 1994: 254, 537; Jacobi LS 180 | 1994: 237). On the one hand, insofar as nature reveals final causes to us, it cannot be doubted by skepticism. On the other hand, insofar as reason must presuppose this revelation, it cannot be proven by dogmatism. As Jacobi says, "[e]xplanation" is "a proximate—never a final—goal" for the scientist, whose "final goal" is "what cannot be explained: the unanalyzable, the immediate, the simple," and whose "greatest service" is ultimately "to unveil *existence*" (Jacobi LS 31–2 | 1994: 194). And as he tells Moses Mendelssohn in a letter, April 26, 1785, "immediate certainty . . . not only needs no proof, but excludes all proofs absolutely, and *is* simply and solely *the representation itself agreeing with the thing being represented.* Conviction by proofs is certainty at second hand . . . But if every *assent to truth* not derived from rational grounds is faith, then conviction based on rational grounds must itself derive from faith, and must receive its force from faith alone" (Jacobi LS 162–3 | 1994: 230).

[95] In his 1811 *Of Divine Things and their Revelation*, Jacobi claims that "Kantian criticism, rigorously carried through to its consequences, had to have the ***Wissenschaftslehre*** for result, and this science, in turn rigorously carried through, had to result in the doctrine of the **unitotality**, an inverted or transfigured Spinozism, an **ideal-materialism**" (Jacobi GD | forthcoming: 80). The second edition of *David Hume* describes the first edition as charging that Kant's first *Critique* "leads to nihilism" (Jacobi DH 19 | 1994: 544). In "On Transcendental Idealism," a supplement to the first edition, Jacobi cites passages in which Kant claims that space and time are forms of sensibility that are "in us," any appearance "separated" from which being "nothing" (Kant KrV A370–3), and infers that this reduces "actual objects" to "*internal beings*" that are "*merely subjective determinations of the mind*" (Jacobi DH 217 | 1994: 334). However, this inference neglects Kant's distinction, which Jacobi even cites, between things as "empirically external," i.e., "encountered in space," and as "'external' in the transcendental sense," i.e., "distinct from us," which is to say, from any possible experience (Kant KrV A373, cited by Jacobi DH 214 | 1994: 333). On Jacobi's neglect of this distinction, see Bruno 2020c and Franks 2005: 49–51. Cf. Jacobi's implicit comparison of Spinozistic nature and the Kantian I when, during an exposition of Spinoza's monism, he cites Kant's claim that "no cognitions can occur in us . . . without the unity of consciousness," i.e., "**transcendental apperception**" (Kant KrV A107, corrected citation from Jacobi LS 140n43 | 1994: 223).

of one's chosen philosophy.[96] As Jacobi says, "once one has fallen in love with certain explanations, one accepts blindly every consequence that can be drawn from an inference that one cannot invalidate—even if one must walk on one's head." Having committed to the principle of sufficient reason and "accept[ed] blindly" the consequences of the inferences that are made in its name, a philosopher forsakes their perceptual faith in the immediacy of "the true, the good, and the beautiful," substituting "explanations" for those presuppositions which ordinarily keep them grounded, as if to "walk on [their] head." Although presuppositions might seem absurd to philosophy insofar as they are inexplicable, for Jacobi it is only when one "wants to explain all things absolutely" that one "must run into absurdities," namely, the absurdity of denying those "conviction[s]" which are most "vital," for example, the conviction in one's freedom.[97] In order to avoid philosophy's groundless inversion, he "extricate[s] [himself] from the problem through a *salto mortale*," which is not an irrational leap of faith, but is rather a humane reversal of this inversion and a return of one's feet to solid ground.[98] Such a return requires what Jacobi calls a " 'non-philosophy', which has its essence in 'non-knowledge'."[99] Here non-knowledge consists not in ignorance, but rather in the absence of inferential certainty and the acceptance of "vital" presuppositions. In other words, it consists in perceptual faith in the existence of that which we cannot explain without explaining it away.[100] As Jacobi says: "I love Spinoza because he, more than any other philosopher, has led me to the perfect conviction that certain things admit of no explication: one must therefore not keep one's eyes shut to them, but must take them as one finds them."[101]

As we saw in Section 2.3, it is Fichte who leads the German idealist campaign, not only against facticity, but also against nihilism. It is also Fichte with whom Jacobi first explicitly charges nihilism, coining the term in his open letter in order to depict the *Wissenschaftslehre* as an "*inverted* Spinozism" that reduces objects not to causally necessitated modes of nature, but rather to rationally necessitated acts of the I, that is, of "pure and empty consciousness."[102] However, Fichte clearly aims

[96] For a reconstruction of Jacobi's master argument that philosophy entails nihilism, see Bruno (manuscript).

[97] Jacobi LS 29–30 | 1994: 193–4. Cf. Jacobi: "I can doubt [my freedom] just as much as I can doubt that I perceive *anything* outside me. If it is in you to be disturbed by such doubts, then there is nothing I can say to you. But I think that your *faith* triumphs over them just as easily as mine" (Jacobi DH 108 | 1994: 292).

[98] Jacobi LS 17 | 1994: 189. See Crowe 2009.

[99] Jacobi BF 1 | 1994: 501.

[100] Cf. Jacobi's view that inferential certainty presupposes perceptual faith with Thomas Nagel's view that "[w]hat sustains us, in belief as in action, is not reason or justification, but something more basic than these," a view that Nagel traces to Hume, after whom Jacobi names one of his main texts. Nagel articulates the nihilistic world-loss that Jacobi attributes to understanding when he says that "[i]f we tried to rely entirely on reason, and pressed it hard, our lives and beliefs would collapse—a form of madness that may actually occur if the inertial force of taking the world and life for granted is somehow lost. If we lose our grip on that, reason will not give it back to us" (Nagel 1971: 724).

[101] Jacobi LS 29 | 1994: 193.

[102] Jacobi BF 4 | 1994: 502.

to refute Spinozism's nihilistic consequence. He expresses solidarity on this matter in a letter to Jacobi, April 26, 1796:

> we are in complete agreement, and this agreement with you proves to me more than anything else that I am on the right track. You too seek all truth where I seek it: in the innermost sanctuary of our own being. But whereas you promote the revelation of the spirit *as spirit*, insofar as human speech allows, my task is to construe this spirit in the form of a system, so that it may be introduced into the schools in place of pseudo-wisdom . . . For you have shown in dealing with Spinoza that you are able to divest a system of its artificial trappings in order to present its spirit in its purity and are able to extrapolate from the parts to the whole to which they belong.[103]

Like Jacobi, Fichte regards the "sanctuary of our own being," namely, our capacity for freedom and hence for moral responsibility, as an irreducible "truth" insofar as he posits it as the first principle of experience. Since Fichte posits freedom as a first principle, it is not only exempt from the philosopher's imperative of explaining objects according to the principle of sufficient reason, but it also conditions the very intelligibility of this imperative, since without the absolute freedom of reason or the I, there is no apperceptive unity for the experience of explicable objects. Nevertheless, for Fichte, it is necessary for philosophy to "construe" the truth of freedom "in the form of a system," namely, idealism, given the nihilistic threat that Spinoza's opposing system poses to that truth. Moreover, Fichte takes himself to follow Jacobi in this respect, for it is the latter who shows him that, in order to "dea[l] with Spinoza," one must divest philosophical systems of "artificial trappings." This is to say, as we saw in Section 1.6, that one must show that a system is not merely "artificial[ly]" or theoretically consistent, which both idealism and dogmatism boast yet which leaves them in a stalemate, but rather is also practically livable, which, according to Fichte, is exclusively the virtue of idealism.[104]

It is therefore crushing to be publicly accused of nihilism in Jacobi's open letter, as Fichte tells Reinhold in a letter, April 22, 1799:

> I am disgusted with everything that pertains to this conflict, and I feel absolutely powerless. In view of this, perhaps the clearest way for me to explain my position to you is to say that I subscribe completely to all of Jacobi's statements. For a long

[103] Fichte B | 1988: 413. Cf. Fichte's first letter to Jacobi, September 29, 1794, which accompanies a copy of the first two Parts of the *Foundations*: "If there is any thinker in Germany with whom I wish and hope to be in agreement concerning my personal convictions, it is you" (Fichte B | 1998: 412n).

[104] See Fichte: "something stable, at rest, and dead can by no means enter the domain of what *I* call philosophy, within which all is act, movement, and life . . . [O]ne of the distinctive features of my philosophy is the fact that it deals only with what is living and by no means with what is dead" (Fichte AP | SW V: 381–2). Cf. Fichte GWL | SW I: 274.

> time I have known and clearly realized everything that he says in his letter. As pleased as I am that he wrote this excellent piece *for* me, at the same time I find it incomprehensible how he could have believed that it was directed *against* me.[105]

Admittedly, Fichte does not in fact subscribe to "all of Jacobi's statements," since, rather than endorse a "non-philosophy," he expresses the "spirit" of freedom in the "form" of a philosophical system.[106] However, he is compelled to adopt this form precisely because nihilism is the consequence of that system which purports to offer a rigorous, that is, facticity-free, account of the conditions of intelligibility, namely, Spinozism. Notwithstanding the *Wissenschaftslehre*'s systematic form, then, Fichte can plausibly profess the same love for Spinoza that Jacobi professes, for he can agree that the truth of freedom is absolute and so, in this respect, "admit[s] of no explication."

We find that Fichte's anti-nihilistic spirit is apparent in the work of a phenomenologist who has a major impact on Heidegger, namely, Edmund Husserl. In a letter to Heinrich Rickert, December 20, 1915, Husserl implies that he finds in Fichte and the other German idealists a kindred and, as we will see, anti-nihilistic spirit:

> It was only from the moment when, climbing up the paths that were for me very daunting, I found myself, without realizing it, in the realm of idealism, that I was able to . . . grasp what is great and eternally important in German idealism. (It is Fichte who, logically, attracts me more and more.) Thus, for the last decade, I feel tightly bound to the main figures of the German idealist schools: we are allies in the battle against the naturalism of our era, our common adversary. We serve, each of us in his own way, the same gods, and since this is something serious and holy to us, something to which we committed our entire life, each of these ways harbours in itself its own necessities and is bound to be indispensable for the advancement of philosophy.[107]

It is not surprising that Husserl should be "attract[ed]" to Fichte's philosophy, since he lectures on various aspects of the *Wissenschaftslehre* in Göttingen during the 1900s and 1910s. In 1917–18's winter lectures in Freiburg, "Fichte's Ideal of Humanity," he includes Fichte with Plato as "one of the great diviners" who "does not merely satisfy theoretical curiosity," but rather "transform[s] and elevate[s]"

[105] Fichte B | 1988: 429.
[106] As Fichte tells Reinhold in the same letter: "[Jacobi] rightly refuses to tolerate *logical enthusiasm*, and so do I. But he appears at the same time to harbour an opposite sort of enthusiasm, which I may term the enthusiasm of *real life*. It is this enthusiasm which forbids him to abstract dispassionately and impartially from real life, even for the sake of experiment . . . I consider such apathy to be absolutely necessary if one is to understand transcendental philosophy completely, without being either angered by it or lured by it into despair" (Fichte B | 1988: 429).
[107] Husserl B | 1994: 178, translated by Schnell 2018: 68–9. On late Husserl's proximity to German idealism, see Tolley 2017.

the reader to "a higher spiritual dignity and power."[108] However, it is to the constellation of German idealism's "main figures" that Husserl reports "feel[ing] tightly bound."[109] What he regards as "great and eternally important" in the German idealist system is that it shares with his own phenomenological system both a "common adversary," namely, "naturalism," and a common advantage, namely, the "same gods" that each system "serve[s]" in its "own way."[110] But what is the naturalism of the "era" that includes German idealism and phenomenology? And in their "battle" against this foe, which gods do they jointly serve?

We can answer these questions by consulting Husserl's 1910 "Philosophy as Rigorous Science" and his 1935 winter lectures in Prague, "Philosophy in the Crisis of European Humanity," whose 1936 publication is the basis for his posthumous 1954 *The Crisis of European Sciences and Transcendental Phenomenology*.

The arguments in "Rigorous Science" are "based on the conviction that the highest interests of human culture demand the development of a rigorously scientific philosophy." While this demand might seem too abstract for the "interests of human culture," Husserl claims that naturalism "dominates" the "present age" precisely because it purports to satisfy this demand by providing an entire worldview. According to naturalism's worldview, there is "only nature, and primarily physical nature," on which psychical phenomena are "dependent" and "at best a secondary 'parallel accompaniment.'" Moreover, physical and psychical phenomena are "subject to the exact laws of nature," which govern efficient causation and exclude final causes. The cultural promise of naturalism, then, is that it is a causally closed and therefore "rigorou[s] scien[ce]." However, the threat is that naturalism satisfies the cultural demand with a nihilistic picture of nature as a purposeless substance, that is, as a machine to which, echoing Jacobi, Husserl says we are a merely passive "accompaniment." Hence Husserl says that naturalism poses, "from a practical point of view," a "growing danger for our culture."[111]

[108] Husserl FM | 1995: 114. See Husserl's letter to Roman Ingarden, December 13, 1933: "Fichte was right: one can do other things because of secondary or egotistical motives; the philosopher is only as an ethical personality or he is nothing" (Husserl B | 1994: 294). On Husserl's lectures on Fichte, see Hart 1995.

[109] Husserl says relatively little about Hegel and Schelling. In the Introduction to his 1898–99 "Epistemology and the Main Points of Metaphysics," he argues that "natural scientists cannot escape" the "great need" for metaphysics, since "[a]s soon as they begin to reflect on the principles of their science, they also get into metaphysics, only they do not want to call the child by the frowned upon name." It is in this context that he claims that, despite the fact that metaphysics "is not at all adequately represented by a Hegel or Schelling," natural scientists fail to distinguish the "good and significant aspects" of metaphysics from the "wrong" aspects and thereby overlook the "proud series of metaphysical systems from Plato and Aristotle to Hegel" (Husserl EHM | 2001: 230, 232–3).

[110] Although, in his 1887–88 "Historical Overview of the Philosophy of Mathematics," Husserl refers to the "murky haze of the idealistic or, better, mystical after-philosophy" that follows Kant (Husserl GU | 1983: 220), he names no idealist and, moreover, makes his remark in Halle, prior to his Göttingen lectures on Fichte.

[111] Husserl P | 1965: 78–9.

However, Husserl argues that by "naturalizing" not only the "data of consciousness," but also the "absolute ideals and norms" for whose sake we consciously think, act, and feel, namely, the "tru[e]," the "good," and the "beautiful," the naturalist rules out the very point of thinking, acting, and feeling, including the point of their own naturalistic argument. Despite the naturalist's "purpose," which is to "make scientifically known" our epistemic, ethical, and aesthetics ends, their argument rules out purposes as such and consequently "refutes itself."[112] Evoking Fichte's argument in Section 1.6 that dogmatism is self-refuting, Husserl puts the point by saying that the naturalist "teaches, preaches, moralizes, reforms," yet "denies what every sermon, every demand, if it is to have a meaning, presupposes," namely, final causes.[113] Naturalism's folly, then, is that by posing the practical "danger" of undermining human culture's "highest" interest, namely, a rigorous science that enshrines rather than eliminates the freedom and purposiveness of consciousness, it refutes itself in a performative contradiction. According to Husserl, phenomenology is the only science that, by accounting for the way in which consciousness is "teleologically ordered,"[114] is rigorous in the required sense.

"Rigorous Science" prefigures *Crisis* in several respects. In §2 of *Crisis*, Husserl announces a "*crisis*" whereby the "*positivistic reduction of the idea of science to mere factual science*" results in "*the loss of [science's] meaning for life.*" He clarifies the crisis by explaining that factual science is a "science of bodies" that is "exclusively" concerned with "what the world . . . is in fact," namely, an aggregate of entities that, physical and psychical alike, "form and dissolve themselves like fleeting waves." On this view of the world, nothing abides insofar as everything is ceaselessly replaced by something else. It follows that there is nothing abidingly intrinsic in the world. In particular, it follows that knowledge follows no intrinsic norm, action emulates no intrinsic ideal, and history exhibits no intrinsic progress. As Husserl puts it, according to factual science, the "norms" and "ideals" on which we "rel[y]" for knowledge and action "must turn into nonsense" and "historical occurrence is nothing but an unending concatenation of illusory progress and bitter disappointment." Consequently, factual science "excludes in principle the questions" that we find "most burning: questions of the meaning or meaninglessness of the whole of this human existence." These questions concern the intrinsic conditions of knowledge, action, and history, that is, their purposes or final causes, namely

[112] Husserl P | 1965: 79–80. Husserl argues that if "physical natural science" cannot "serve as a foundation for philosophy," then neither can "psychology," for the latter ascribes to psychical phenomena "a never-failing physical connotation" (Husserl P | 1965: 86–7). In other words, if naturalism is self-refuting, then so is psychologism. For Husserl's refutation of psychologism, see his 1900–01 *Logical Investigations, Volume 1* (Husserl LU1 | 2001: Chapter One, §§17–51).

[113] Husserl P | 1965: 81. Thus, naturalism banishes questions about how experience can be objective and, indeed, how natural science itself can be "comprehensible" to mere "riddles" that are "inherent in principle" in naturalism and whose solution therefore "in principle transcends" naturalism (Husserl P | 1965: 87–8).

[114] Husserl P | 1965: 90.

and respectively, truth, virtue, and progress. Moreover, our "most burning" questions are those which, "[i]n the final analysis," concern ourselves as "free," namely, free in our "rationally shaping" the knowable world, free in our "behavior" toward other moral agents, and free in our advance "within the horizon of [our] historicity." Accordingly, factual science must exclude the intrinsic conditions by which subjects freely pursue truth, virtue, and progress. By "abstract[ing] from everything subjective" in this manner, factual science "has nothing to say" about the "meaning" of subjectivity and thereby loses its meaning for us.[115] The crisis of the "*positivistic reduction of the idea of science*" consists, then, in the mutual estrangement of science and subjectivity.

Husserl's clarification of the crisis enables us to answer the two questions that arise from his letter to Rickert.

Regarding the first question, although Husserl does not use the term, the naturalistic adversary that faces German idealism and phenomenology is a guise of nihilism. We can see why this is so when we consider that factual science poses a naturalistic threat insofar as it identifies explicable reality with the natural world to the exclusion of subjectivity. Such a world is exclusively composed of physical and psychical entities that rise and fall like "waves." Insofar as subjectivity finds meaning in questions that concern the intrinsic conditions of knowledge, action, and history, that is, their final causes, it falls outside nature and is therefore inexplicable according to factual science, leaving us with what Husserl calls the "*enigma of subjectivity*."[116] This naturalistic threat is a guise of nihilism, for it renders subjectivity enigmatic precisely by treating the world as an aggregate of entities that are subject to external conditions yet with no intrinsic conditions. To borrow Jacobi's phrase, the naturalistic threat that is posed by factual science is nihilistic because this science reduces truth, virtue, and progress to non-entities, annihilating these final causes and, with them, the freedom by which we think, act, and persevere for their sake.[117]

[115] Husserl K | 1970a: 5–7. Cf. Husserl's claim that the "positivistic concept of science" has "excluded questions" whose "inseparable unity" consists in the fact that "they contain . . . the *problems of reason*," which concern "knowledge," "valuation," and "action" and so bear on questions concerning "history," "God," "immortality," and "freedom" (Husserl K | 1970a: 9).

[116] Husserl K | 1970a: 5.

[117] Cf. Gurwitsch: "nihilism is not a consequence of naturalism, but, on the contrary, the very basis thereof. To look upon man as a purely vital being means, as we have seen, the abandonment of the classical conception according to which man is an *animal rationale* . . . For the truth is that man does not correspond to the picture that nihilism presents of him. Man is not an impotent being driven by blind impulses, abandoned to the play of mechanical forces, subjected, with no means of defense, to conjunctions of historical forces, social forces, etc. On the contrary, man has the possibility of knowledge; he can put a distance between himself and the given historical situation; he can analyze the latter and is able to understand the functioning of the various mechanisms at work in the situation. In short, he can consider this situation in the light of a system of reason and rationality. It is untrue that man can do nothing but undergo the situation in which he is involved; on the contrary, he is capable of making it the object of knowledge: it is in this possibility of knowledge that man's liberty resides" (Gurwitsch 1945: 176, 194). For a comparison of Husserl and Gurwitsch, see Kassab 1990.

Crucially, a momentous cultural shift separates the relevant guises of nihilism. As Husserl indicates, “in the second half of the nineteenth century” the initially academic encounter with nihilism expands into a “total worldview of modern man” that “let[s] itself be determined by the positive sciences and be blinded by the ‘prosperity’ they produced.” No longer confined to the participants in the Spinozism dispute of the late eighteenth century, by the beginning of the twentieth century nihilism afflicts an entire culture that, dazzled by the technological advances that factual science affords, unwittingly acquiesces in “an indifferent turning-away from the questions which are decisive for a genuine humanity,” which include questions about the epistemic, ethical, and historical value of technology. Forgetting questions of value in this manner leaves in its wake a culture that is saddled with unquestioned facts, which is to say, a culture that is informed without being enlightened. As Husserl puts the point, “[m]erely fact-minded sciences make merely fact-minded people.”[118]

Moreover, whereas Jacobi regards nihilism as the result of indulging the philosopher’s imperative, Husserl’s concern about nihilistically restricting our worldview to “the universe of mere facts” is that it “decapitates philosophy,”[119] where philosophy is not restricted to determining the external conditions of things, that is, their efficient causes, since it also and primarily determines their intrinsic conditions, that is, their final causes. *Pace* Jacobi, it is for philosophy to ask what orientation in scientific thinking is, namely, in light of our “burning” questions about truth, virtue, and progress. It is philosophical reason, not Jacobian faith, that keeps these questions alive. As Husserl says in 1935’s “Philosophy and the Crisis of European Humanity,” a lecture given to the Vienna Cultural Society:

> The reason for the failure of a rational culture, however, as we said, lies not in the essence of rationalism itself but solely in its being rendered superficial, in its entanglement in ‘naturalism’ and ‘objectivism.’ There are only two escapes from the crisis of European existence: the downfall of Europe in its estrangement from its own rational sense of life, its fall into hostility toward the spirit and into barbarity; or the rebirth of Europe from the spirit of philosophy through a heroism of reason that overcomes naturalism once and for all.[120]

[118] Husserl K | 1970a: 5–6.

[119] Husserl K | 1970a: 9.

[120] Husserl PK | 1970b: 299. In 1966’s *Negative Dialectics*, Theodor Adorno observes that, by the twentieth century, the choice between enlightenment and barbarism is a false dichotomy: “That [culture’s failure] could happen in the midst of the traditions of philosophy, of art, and of the enlightening sciences says more than that these traditions and their spirit lacked the power to take hold of men and work a change in them. There is untruth in those fields themselves, in the autarky that is emphatically claimed for them . . . Whoever pleads for the maintenance of this radically culpable and shabby culture becomes its accomplice, while the man who says no to culture is directly furthering the barbarism which our culture showed itself to be” (Adorno 1973: 366–7). In light of Adorno’s observation, see Husserl’s ascription of philosophy to “spiritual Europe,” to the exclusion of India, China, Babylonia, and indigenous peoples (Husserl PK | 1970b: 155–71).

Following Fichte, Husserl attributes the nihilistic "failure" of modern culture not to reason as such, but rather to reason's "entanglement" with "naturalism," that is, its susceptibility to the naturalistic threat that is posed by unchecked factual science. Moreover, reason provides the only "escap[e]" from a crisis that otherwise entails culture's "downfall" into a "barbarity" in which our burning questions are totally extinguished, since only a "heroism of reason" can remind us of these questions and thereby correct our "estrangement" from ourselves. Notwithstanding Jacobi's appeal to non-philosophy, it is precisely because the "spirit of philosophy" is equipped with the concepts of freedom and purposiveness that it is capable of correcting the naturalistic guise of nihilism. Indeed, Husserl says, philosophy can only realize itself by realizing "a genuine humanity."[121]

Regarding the second question, the gods that German idealism and phenomenology serve in their battle against nihilism are freedom and purposiveness, that is, the very things that are threatened with annihilation. Our burning questions concern the point of knowledge, action, and history and so concern their final causes, namely, truth, virtue, and progress. Moreover, such questions concern, in the "final analysis," our freedom to know, act, and exist for the sake of these causes. To serve such gods requires demonstrating their irreducibility, that is, their primacy.

We saw that, for Fichte, freedom and purposiveness are primary insofar as the absolute freedom of reason or the I is the first principle of experience. For Husserl, freedom and purposiveness are primary insofar as they are essential features of what he calls the "life-world," which the title of §9h of *Crisis* declares is the presupposed yet "forgotten meaning-fundament of natural science." He argues that the "natural scientist" can "put all [their] practical and theoretical questions only to . . . the pre-given world" of "pre-scientific life," since it is only for this life that questions about knowledge, action, and history, which include the questions of natural science, have any value in the first place.[122] Throughout scientific research, the life-world "remains unchanged as what it is, in its own essential structure," which essential structure, as we have seen, is intrinsically conditioned by the final causes of knowledge, action, and history and, ultimately, by the freedom by which we know, act, and exist for their sake. Natural science must accordingly "grow out of" and "serve" the life-world as its own condition of intelligibility, which is to say that it must presuppose the life-world.[123] It would therefore be nihilistic and, as we have

[121] Husserl PK | 1970b: 291.

[122] Husserl K | 1970a: 48, 50. Cf. Husserl K | 1970a: 56. Cf. Husserl's claim that only by being "rooted" in the life-world does "objective science" have "a constant reference of meaning to the world," including "the total community of scientists." In this respect, "objective science itself belongs to the life-world," whose "concreteness" accordingly includes not just "things" such as "stones, houses, or trees," but also "theories" and "logical constructs" (Husserl K | 1970a: 130).

[123] Husserl K | 1970a: 51. Cf. Husserl's claim that the life-world "constantly functions as subsoil" such that "its manifold pre-logical validities," namely, truth, virtue, and progress, "act as grounds for the logical ones, for theoretical truths" (Husserl K | 1970a: 124). On Husserl's concept of the life-world, see Staiti 2014: 222–63.

seen, a performative contradiction to employ natural science to causally reduce the life-world, whose essential features include the freedom and purposiveness in virtue of which natural science has its value.

Crucially, Husserl argues in §34a that the science of the life-world, namely, phenomenology, is "a peculiar one, one which is precisely not objective and logical, but which, as the ultimately grounding one, is not inferior but superior in value." The science in question is neither objective nor logical because it concerns the life-world, that is, the world insofar as it is lived by subjects. It is only in virtue of such a world that questions about objective and logical knowledge have value.[124] Hence Husserl says that the science of the life-world is "subjective-relative." This "grounding" science concerns a "realm" that the natural scientist cannot "disdain," but rather "must be satisfied with . . . whenever he has recourse, as he unavoidably must have recourse, to it."[125] No knowledge, not even natural-scientific knowledge, floats free of the questions that drive subjects to strive to achieve it. This is just to say that no knowledge is absolute, that is, without relation, but rather is always and specifically relative to subjectivity. The life-world is the world insofar as it is lived by subjects, whose consciousness is intrinsically conditioned by final causes and the freedom to pursue them. Phenomenology is a "peculiar" science, then, because its topic is. In what we might call a 'philosophical *salto mortale*,' phenomenologically grasping the foundational role that the life-world plays affords a humane reversal of naturalism's nihilistic inversion that returns natural science to solid ground and thereby remedies the mutual estrangement of science and subjectivity.

While Husserl finds in German idealism a kindred anti-nihilistic spirit, he does not regard it as an adequate science of the life-world. In "Rigorous Science," he says:

> However much Hegel insists on the absolute validity of his method and his doctrine, still his system lacks a critique of reason, which is the foremost prerequisite for being scientific in philosophy. In this connection it is clear that this philosophy, like romantic philosophy in general, acted in the years that followed either to weaken or to adulterate the impulse toward the constitution of rigorous philosophical science.[126]

Although he does not clarify the charge that Hegel's system "lacks a critique of reason," he seems to imply that this purportedly presuppositionless system fails to recognize its presupposition of the life-world and so, not unlike natural science, forgets its own "meaning-fundament." Husserl is somewhat clearer on this point in "Crisis of European Humanity" when he says:

[124] Husserl K | 1970a: 124. This argument applies to objective knowledge of the brain, on which, see Zahavi 2018.
[125] Husserl K | 1970a: 125.
[126] Husserl P | 1965: 76–7.

> the way of philosophy passes through naiveté . . . [T]he most general title for this naiveté is *objectivism*, taking the form of the various types of naturalism, of the naturalization of the spirit. Old and new philosophers were and remain naively objectivist. In fairness we must add, though, that the German idealism proceeding from Kant was passionately concerned with overcoming this naiveté, which had already become very troublesome, though it was unable to attain the higher stage of reflexivity which is decisive for the new form of philosophy and of European humanity.[127]

As we saw, phenomenology battles alongside German idealism against a common adversary, namely, nihilism. In its various guises, this foe "naively" reduces to a mere entity that which is free and purposive, namely, subjectivity, thereby "naturaliz[ing]" the latter, which is to say, annihilating it. In this battle, however, German idealism falls short of a "higher stage of reflexivity," one that is "decisive" for "humanity." Recall that the crisis that Husserl signals consists in the mutual estrangement of science and subjectivity such that, on the one hand, science cannot say anything about subjectivity's burning questions and, on the other hand, subjectivity cannot be anything but enigmatic to science. This is not an academic problem, but is rather a crisis for humanity's capacity for meaning, a crisis whose solution requires an adequate recognition of the ground that is presupposed by objective and logical sciences alike, namely, the life-world.[128] It is this solution that Husserl seems to imply is lacking in German idealism, presumably insofar as the latter, ultimately through Hegel's efforts, pursues a presuppositionless science of intelligibility.

Like Husserl, Heidegger finds himself bound to the main figures of German idealism. Heidegger's 1915 "*Curriculum Vitae*" reports that studying the work of Fichte, Hegel, Rickert, and Dilthey reveals to him that philosophy must be "oriented" by the "history of spirit."[129] According to 1927's "Heidegger, Martin," a lexicon article in *Religion in History and the Present: Concise Dictionary of Theology and Religious Studies* that is attributed to Rudolph Bultmann yet is written by Heidegger at the former's request, Heidegger develops the "fundament" of "universal ontology" from "the 'subject' properly understood as 'human Dasein'" so that "the true motives of German idealism come into their own."[130]

[127] Husserl PK | 1970b: 292.

[128] See Husserl: "The life-world is the world that is constantly pregiven, valid constantly and in advance as existing, but not valid because of some purpose of investigation, according to some universal end. Every end presupposes it; even the universal end of knowing it in scientific truth presupposes it, and in advance; and in the course of [scientific] work it presupposes it ever anew, as a world existing, in its own way [to be sure], but existing nevertheless. The scientific world (nature in the sense of natural science, world in the sense of philosophy as universal positive science) is a purposeful structure extending to infinity—a structure [made by] men who are presupposed, for the presupposed life-world" (Husserl K | 1970a: 382).

[129] Heidegger CV | 2009: 9.

[130] Heidegger HM | 2009: 335.

And in a letter to Karl Jaspers, June 25, 1929, Heidegger says: "I am lecturing for the first time on Fichte, Hegel, Schelling—and a world is dawning for me again."[131] Indeed, Heidegger lectures extensively on the German idealists during the 1920s, 1930s, 1940s, and 1950s.

We can see that Heidegger shares the anti-nihilistic spirit of Fichte's idealism in particular when we consult the opening of Division One of *Being and Time*. In §9, Heidegger announces that the text is "task[ed]" with analyzing the being that is "always we ourselves," which he calls "Dasein." He explains that the characteristics of Dasein are not the "'attributes' of an objectively present being," which, for such a being, are simply "a matter of 'indifference,'" but rather are the "possible ways for [Dasein] to be," about which it is always "concerned."[132] As Dasein, my being is not insignificant to me, but rather is "always *mine*" in that it has been "always already decided" by me to exist "in this or that way."[133] In other words, my being is something that I do. This is why Heidegger says that Dasein "does not 'have'" its possibility in the passive manner of an object, but rather "*is* always its possibility" in the active manner of a subject who "*can* 'choose' itself in its being." This is also why "*authenticity* and *inauthenticity*" are appropriate terms for describing how Dasein chooses and avoids choosing how it exists.[134]

Although it does not rely on Fichte's dual method of intellectual intuition and genetic deduction, the analytic task of *Being and Time* shares the anti-nihilistic spirit of his idealism. This is because grasping this task requires refusing to construe the being that is "we ourselves" as merely one object among many, externally conditioned *ad infinitum*. Such a construal would be a guise of nihilism. Dasein is neither what Jacobi would call a "witness" that idly adorns a purposeless machine nor what Husserl would call a "wave" that passes in an aimless sea. Instead, Dasein exhibits two irreducible features of subjectivity, namely, freedom and purposiveness, since it strives for possible ways of being and does so for the sake of the being that it chooses to be.[135] As Heidegger explains, the being that Dasein chooses to be is its primary final cause or "*what-for*." On the one hand, a secondary what-for is a "work to be produced," since producing a work, for example, a text, is an episodic project that occasionally concerns Dasein. On the other hand, the "primary 'what-for' is a for-the-sake-of-which," namely, the being that Dasein chooses to be, since choosing oneself is an existential project that "always concerns" Dasein.[136]

[131] Heidegger BJ | 2003: 119.

[132] Heidegger SZ | GA 2: 41–2.

[133] Heidegger SZ | GA 2: 42. Cf. Heidegger: "when we speak of Dasein, we must always use the *personal* pronoun along with whatever we say: 'I am', 'You are'" (Heidegger SZ | GA 2: 42).

[134] Heidegger SZ | GA 2: 42–3.

[135] See Heidegger: "a for-the-sake-of-which, a purposiveness, is only possible where there is a willing. Now insofar as transcendence, being-in-the-world, constitutes the basic structure of Dasein, being-in-the-world must also be primordially bound up with or derived from the basic feature of Dasein's existence, namely, *freedom*. Only where there is freedom is there a purposive for-the-sake-of, and only here is there world. To put it briefly, Dasein's transcendence and freedom are identical!" (Heidegger MA | GA 26: 237).

[136] Heidegger SZ | GA 2: 70, 84.

Thus, by maintaining the irreducibility of Dasein's freedom and purposiveness, Heidegger serves, in his "own way," the same gods that Fichte and the German idealists serve in their battle against nihilism.

Moreover, Fichte and Heidegger's shared anti-nihilistic spirit has a common ontological consequence. In the *New Presentation*, Fichte claims that "the only type of being with which we can be concerned is a *being for us*."[137] For an idealist, being is meaningful only if it is structured by conditions of intelligibility, which conditions are necessary only if they are deduced from the I. The ontological consequence is that an understanding of being depends on an understanding of our being.[138] Similarly, Heidegger claims that "*fundamental ontology* . . . must be sought in the *existential analysis of Dasein*."[139] He supports this claim by observing that an inquiry into being unavoidably implicates the "constitutive attitudes" of the inquirer, for example, "understanding and grasping." These attitudes are "modes of being of a particular being, of *the* being we inquirers ourselves in each case are. Thus to work out the question of being means to make a being—he who questions—transparent in its being."[140] No account of being can deny, ignore, or suspend the being of we who account. It follows that an analytic of Dasein is "a task whose urgency is hardly less than that of the question of being itself."[141] Interest in the meaning of being essentially involves attitudes that are characteristic of our inquisitive sort of being. Crucially, such attitudes include not only understanding and grasping, but also purposive striving, which Heidegger follows Fichte in defending against guises of nihilism.

However, while Heidegger shares Fichte's anti-nihilistic spirit, he crucially does not share the latter's anti-factical spirit. The post-Kantian question of whether a science of intelligibility can tolerate brute facts receives starkly opposed answers from German idealists and phenomenologists. For Fichte, facticity presents intolerable contingency that must be eliminated through a deduction of the conditions of intelligibility from reason or the I. For Heidegger, by contrast, facticity is "*characteristic of the being of Dasein taken on in existence*," any attempt to eliminate which, for example, via deduction, is an evasion of what it is to be Dasein, that is, to be thrown brutely into the standpoint of finitude. Such an evasion is not

[137] Fichte VND | SW I: 500. Cf. Fichte's claim in *System of Ethics* that freedom is "the sole true being and the ground of all other being," a truth "according to which all other truth must be directed and judged" (Fichte SS | SW IV: 26, 53).

[138] See Gardner 2007.

[139] Heidegger SZ | GA 2: 13. Just as, for Heidegger, ontology is only fundamental when we pursue an existential analytic of Dasein, so too, for Kant, ontology is only critical when we pursue a transcendental analytic of the understanding. On the latter, see de Boer 2011.

[140] Heidegger SZ | GA 2: 7.

[141] Heidegger SZ | GA 2: 45. Cf. Heidegger's letter to Karl Löwith, August 20, 1927: "I am also convinced that ontology can only be grounded ontically, and believe that no one before me has grasped or articulated this. But ontic founding does not mean arbitrarily pointing to an ontic thing and then moving backward—rather, the ground for ontology can only be located when one knows what ontology is and then allows it, as ontology, to efface itself" (Heidegger BL | 2021: 121).

unique to philosophers, for, he says, facticity is "*initially thrust aside*" by Dasein as such.[142] If this is true, then, as I will explore in detail in Chapter 6, German idealism's apparent victory over facticity expresses a more general tendency to escape or cover over what we are, that is, to prefer a slumber of sorts. Thus, whereas Fichte is as convinced as ever in 1800's *Vocation of Man* that we always "remain" in the "hand" of reason,[143] Heidegger will insist that Dasein "never gets back behind its thrownness."[144]

As I suggested in the Introduction, while the concepts of reason, freedom, nihilism, and systematicity are essential for understanding the trajectory of post-Kantian philosophy, these concepts are maximally organized by the concept of facticity. We can see that this suggestion is borne out by Fichte and Heidegger's opposition regarding facticity, which coordinates their otherwise shared anti-nihilistic commitment to the irreducibility of freedom and purposiveness. Whereas Fichte takes this irreducibility to entail the primacy of the practical, as we saw in Section 1.1, Heidegger reframes this irreducibility within the factical situation in which Dasein always already finds itself. This difference exhibits the post-Kantian transition from the primacy of the practical to the primacy of the factical. We will see, in Part II, that this transition commences with Schelling's critique of Hegel's logic and, in Part III, that it culminates with Heidegger's critique of the German idealist project as a whole.

Before turning to Part II, it is worth registering Husserl's rejection of the foundational role that facticity plays in Heidegger's phenomenology. We will see that Husserl's disappointment both with German idealism and with Heideggerian phenomenology places him at a midway point in the transition from the primacy of the practical to the primacy of the factical.

The initial bond and gradual break between Husserl and Heidegger are professional, philosophical, and personal in nature.[145] As a theology student at the University of Freiburg in 1909, Heidegger begins to study Husserl's work, continuing this study under Rickert. After serving in the First World War, Heidegger succeeds Edith Stein as Husserl's assistant in 1919. In the Foreword to his 1923 summer lectures in Freiburg, *Ontology: The Hermeneutics of Facticity*, he claims that Husserl "opened [his] eyes."[146] With Husserl's support, Heidegger is appointed

[142] Heidegger SZ | GA 2: 135.

[143] Fichte BM | SW II: 302.

[144] Heidegger SZ | GA 2: 284. In 1929's "On the Essence of Ground," Heidegger claims that "the Dasein in human beings" "occurs" in freedom, which consists not "negative[ly]" in "a kind of causality" for which "there is no determinative cause lying further back," but rather "more originar[ily]" in "transcendence," which "is not only a unique 'kind' of ground, but the *origin of ground in general. Freedom is freedom for ground.*" Later, he repeats this definition of 'freedom' and says that "freedom is the *abyss of ground*" in that it "places Dasein, as potentiality for being, in possibilities that gape open before its finite choice." Finally, Heidegger claims that Dasein "is, *as free* potentiality of being, *thrown* among beings," where this "thrownness" is what "determines Dasein's being as such." The free "projection of world is therefore *thrown*," owing to "the *essence of finitude* in Dasein" (Heidegger WG | W: 59–60, 69–70).

[145] See Sheehan 1997.

[146] Heidegger OHF | GA 63: 4.

as professor at the University of Marburg in 1923. However, in a letter to Karl Löwith, February 20, 1923, Heidegger claims to have "publicly burned and destroyed [Husserl's] *Ideas*" and concludes that "never in his life, not even for a second, was Husserl a philosopher."[147] Heidegger dedicates *Being and Time* to Husserl, who edits the *Yearbook for Philosophy and Phenomenological Research* in which the text's first edition also appears, although the dedication is removed by the 1941 fifth edition. In 1928, Heidegger takes up the chair at the University of Freiburg that Husserl vacates upon retiring. In a letter to Ludwig Landgrebe, May 28, 1932, Husserl observes that "Heidegger has gone over to national socialism and to crude anti-Semitism."[148] In 1933, Heidegger joins the Nazi Party, whose legislation denies any public platform to Husserl, who is born into a Jewish family. In 1938, Heidegger declines to attend Husserl's funeral.

When *Being and Time* appears, Husserl begins to have serious misgivings about Heidegger's combination of phenomenology and facticity. In a letter to Alexander Pfänder, January 6, 1931, Husserl describes Heidegger as an "extraordinary talent" in whom he initially places "the great, uplifting hope" of no less than "the future of phenomenological philosophy." However, reading Heidegger's text brings him to the "distressing conclusion" that his "one true student" and sole apparent "successor" is a "brilliant unscientific genius" who "may be involved in the formation of a philosophical system" that he considers it his "life's work to make forever impossible."[149] Similarly, in a letter to Dietrich Mahnke, January 8, 1931, Husserl states: "by a close and repeated study of *Being and Time* I came to the conclusion that [Heidegger's] 'phenomenology' has not the least thing to do with my own, and I view its pseudo-scientific character as an obstacle to the development of philosophy . . . I separate my phenomenology entirely from Heidegger's so-called phenomenology."[150] Already in a letter to Georg Misch, August 3, 1929, Husserl claims that Heidegger's text "abandons" phenomenology as a "radical and universal 'human science'" for mere "anthropology."[151] Husserl's charge of philosophical pseudo-science against Heidegger is thus specifically a charge of anthropologism.

Without naming Heidegger, Husserl elaborates his charge of anthropologism in 1931's "Phenomenology and Anthropology," a lecture given to the Kant Society in Frankfurt and Halle. There Husserl observes that phenomenology is "caught" in a "trend" among "German philosophers," namely, "philosophical anthropology," which he defines as the view that the "foundation of philosophy lies in human being alone, and more specifically in a doctrine of the essence of human

[147] Heidegger BL | 2021: 63. In another letter to Löwith, May 8, 1923, Heidegger speaks of Husserl while envisioning a future publication: "the old man will then truly see that I am wringing his neck—and then any possibility of succession is over" (Heidegger BL | 2021: 68).

[148] Husserl BL | 1997: 408.

[149] Husserl BP | 1997: 480–2.

[150] Husserl BM | 2009: 404.

[151] Husserl BMi | 2009: 397.

being's concrete worldly Dasein." This trend threatens a "complete reversal" of phenomenology's standpoint because it confuses *a priori* conditions with what they condition, which latter includes the merely human. Phenomenology seeks "apodictic insight" into "the pure *a priori*," that is, the "intrinsically true qualities" in any possible experience, irrespective of factically human peculiarities. "Prior to knowledge of the factical world" is knowledge of these qualities, that is, the *a priori* conditions "without which no world whatever, and this includes the factical world as well, can be thought of as existing."[152] Heidegger's combination of phenomenology and facticity is apparently pseudo-scientific, then, because it satisfies itself with knowledge of the "factical world," that is, with human peculiarities, falling short of knowledge of this world's *a priori* conditions. By confusing conditioned and condition in this way, he anthropologizes phenomenology.[153]

Husserl rightly suspects that Heidegger intends *Being and Time* to surpass his phenomenology. As Heidegger tells Jaspers in a letter, December 26, 1926: "If the treatise is written against anyone, it is against Husserl, who saw this immediately but stayed positive from the very beginning."[154] However, the text explicitly serves "a task whose urgency is hardly less than that of the question of being itself: the exposition of *the a priori* which must be visible if the question 'What is human being?' is to be discussed philosophically. The existential analytic of Dasein is *prior* to any psychology, anthropology, and especially biology."[155] By Heidegger's lights, "*the a priori*" that Husserl seeks is to be found precisely in the factical conditions of intelligibility that make possible Dasein's openness to objects, including the objects of anthropological inquiry. Despite Husserl's charge of anthropologism, it seems that Heidegger's appeal to facticity respects the distinction between conditioned and condition and thereby avoids anthropologizing phenomenology.

Husserl's charge of anthropologism becomes sharper if we consider two 1908 manuscripts that previously extend this charge to Kant. In "On the Confrontation of My Transcendental Phenomenology with Kant's Transcendental Philosophy," he says that "Kant does not know the phenomenological *a priori*" because "in his transcendental considerations the factical and the *a priori* are mixed up."[156] In "Against Kant's Anthropological Theory," he says that Kant "confounds" the "necessity" of "the human specificity" with that of "evidence" that "cannot be otherwise."[157] Kant

[152] Husserl PA | 1997: 485–7.

[153] Cf. Husserl's 1900–01 *Logical Investigations, Volume 2*: "Here we must rather stress that the so-to-say facticity of a fact belongs to sensibility, and that to call in sensibility to help provide a basis for purely categorial laws—laws whose very meaning excludes all sensibility and facticity, which make pure assertions of essence about categorial *forms*, as forms of possible correctness and truth as such—represents a most obvious μετάβασις εἰς ἄλλο γένος [category mistake]" (Husserl LU2 | 2001: 316). Insofar as Husserl holds that categorial laws "exclud[e] all . . . facticity" yet are immediately given to categorial intuition, he seems to occupy an ambiguous position between regarding bruteness as impermissible and as unavoidable, i.e., between *Ich bin* and *Es gibt.*

[154] Heidegger BJ | 2003: 73.

[155] Heidegger SZ | GA 2: 45. Cf. Heidegger BH | 1997: 138.

[156] Husserl A | 1956: 390, translated by Serban 2021: 55, translation modified.

[157] Husserl GK | 1956: 358–9, translated by Serban 2021: 55, translation modified.

apparently "mix[es] up" apriority and facticity due a confusion about necessity. For Husserl, *a priori* conditions of intelligibility are absolutely necessary, for they have no thinkable contrary and so "cannot be otherwise" in thought.[158] By contrast, factical conditions of intelligibility are relatively necessary, for, being radically contingent or brute features of "human specificity," they have thinkable contraries and so can be otherwise in thought.[159] Kant's anthropologistic error thus consists in masquerading an interest in facticity as an insight into apriority.

Husserl's charge of anthropologism against Kant helps to sharpen his subsequent extension of the charge to Heidegger. While Heidegger does not straightforwardly confuse conditioned and condition, as we will see in Chapter 6, he does follow Kant in regarding an interest in facticity as the only means to an insight into apriority. However, whether facticity is philosophically problematic is precisely the post-Kantian question about whether a science of intelligibility can tolerate brute facts. And Husserl would beg this question by simply dismissing Heidegger's affirmative answer as "unscientific."

The rupture between Husserl and Heidegger is complete by the time of their failed collaboration on "Phenomenology," Husserl's 1927 article for the *Encyclopedia Britannica*. In a letter to Husserl, October 22, 1927, concerning Draft B of the article, Heidegger underscores their disagreement over facticity's role in phenomenology. He concurs that "entities . . . cannot be explained in their transcendental constitution by returning to an entity of the same mode of being." This is to say that seeking the conditions of the intelligibility of entities in entities yields a regress, indeed, a regress that Husserl will liken to "fleeting waves" in *Crisis*. But Heidegger notes that this "does not mean what makes up the place of the transcendental is not an entity at all," for there is an entity whose "mode of being" is such that some of its features are not explicable by other entities. This, of course, is Dasein, whose freedom and purposiveness are irreducible features of subjectivity. Moreover, Heidegger says, "the mode of being of human Dasein is totally different from that of all other entities" because it "harbors right within itself the possibility of transcendental constitution." In other words, Dasein harbors the possibility of intelligibility, that is, of rendering entities intelligible. But then the possibility of intelligibility would belong not to a mere entity, which is indifferently "present-at-hand," but rather to the "factical self, the concrete human being," which "eksists," that is, which stands out among entities as the sole kind of entity for whom intelligibility matters.[160] As Heidegger says in *Being and Time*,

[158] The thinkable denial of conditions of intelligibility assumes a low bar for thinkability, namely, general logic. A higher bar would be categorial intuition, the method by which Husserl grasps conditions of intelligibility. For an account of why, for Husserl, the denial of these conditions is unthinkable in this more demanding sense, see Dika 2020. On Husserl's method of categorial intuition, see Heidegger's 1925 summer lectures in Marburg, *Prolegomena to the History of the Concept of Time* (Heidegger PGZ | GA 20: 64–99), Berghofer 2018, Cobb-Stevens 1990, Dahlstrom 2001: 74–8, and Sokolowski 1981.

[159] Cf. Husserl's 1925 summer lectures *Phenomenological Psychology*, in which he implies that "facticities" are "empirical contingencies of human act-living" (Husserl PP | 1977: 27).

[160] Heidegger BH | 1997: 138.

> Dasein is a being that does not simply occur among other beings. Rather it is ontically distinguished by the fact that in its being this being is concerned *about* its very being. Thus it is constitutive of the being of Dasein to have, in its very being, a relation of being to this being. And this in turn means that Dasein understands itself in its being in some way and with some explicitness. It is proper to this being that it be disclosed to itself with and through its being. *Understanding of being is itself a determination of being of Dasein.* The ontic distinction of Dasein lies in the fact that it *is* ontological.[161]

It is a false dichotomy to suppose that phenomenology must choose between an anti-factical insight into conditions of intelligibility and an anthropological observation of mere entities. This is because the "factical self" of Dasein is "ontically distinguished" among all entities by the fact that it alone raises the question of the conditions of intelligibility, that is, by "the fact that it *is* ontological."

Like Husserl, Heidegger shares Fichte's anti-nihilistic spirit. However, unlike both Fichte and Husserl, Heidegger, in pursuing fundamental ontology via an existential analytic of Dasein, regards the latter's conditions of intelligibility as radically contingent, brute, and groundless, that is, as factical. As we will see in Chapter 6, the life-world that constitutes Dasein as a meaning-fundament is not a stone foundation, but rather is soil that is meant to be turned, hermeneutically revealing ever-determinate conditions of intelligibility whose necessity is not logical, but whose contingency is not empirical.

Fichte's argument for the self-refutation of dogmatism and hence for the incoherence of its nihilistic consequence prefigures phenomenological approaches to the science of intelligibility. However, he predicates the possibility of such a science on the elimination of facticity, which phenomenologists will reject, at least after Husserl. As we will see in Part II, as early as 1801, it becomes a central question among Fichte's German idealist successors precisely how, but also whether, philosophy should follow his attempt to eliminate facticity.

[161] Heidegger SZ | GA 2: 12.

PART II
A CRISIS OF METHOD
Dialectical Logic

3

Nullifying Oppositions

Hegel's Radicalization of Fichte's Deductive Method

3.1 Introduction

As we saw in Part I, Fichte's genetic deduction of the conditions of intelligibility sets the agenda for post-Kantians who seek to remove rhapsody from the science of intelligibility and thereby eliminate the apparent facticity of such conditions.

First, by deriving the forms of the faculties of sensibility, understanding, and reason from the I as first principle, Fichte transforms the very idea of a science of intelligibility, overcoming its Kantian division into logical and aesthetic sciences. For Kant, the "matter" of an appearance is given *a posteriori*, while its "form" lies in the mind *a priori*. The science of the *a priori* forms of sensibility is transcendental aesthetic and the science of the *a priori* forms of the understanding is transcendental logic.[1] Since, according to Kant, the faculties of sensibility and understanding "cannot exchange their functions," that is, since, as a brute fact, the understanding cannot intuit and the senses cannot think, transcendental aesthetic and transcendental logic are irreducible sciences.[2] However, we can eliminate the facticity of this two-stem view of the faculties and of their respective sciences, as well as the facticity of the respective forms of these faculties, if we can vindicate the *Wissenschaftslehre* as the singular science of intelligibility.

Second and more specifically, by deriving the forms of the faculties through a dialectical movement of thought, Fichte advances logic beyond its Kantian division into general and transcendental varieties. For Kant, general logic is the science of the form of "the relation of cognitions to one another," which determines "the form of thinking in general," whereas transcendental logic is the science of the form of the relation of cognition "to objects *a priori*," which determines "the form of a possible experience."[3] As we saw in Section 1.2, according to Kant, there is no further ground, that is, no cognizably ultimate ground or first principle, for deriving either the forms of judgment that structure our thinking as such or the categories that structure our thinking about objects of possible experience, just as there is no such ground for deriving the forms of sensibility that structure our intuition of objects of possible experience. Consequently, general-logical and

[1] Kant KrV A20/B34.
[2] Kant KrV A51–2/B75–6; cf. B146–7.
[3] Kant KrV A52–7/B76–82.

Facticity and the Fate of Reason After Kant. G. Anthony Bruno, Oxford University Press.
 DOI: 10.1093/9780191987533.003.0004

transcendental-logical science, no less than aesthetic science, contain brutely presupposed forms, that is, formal facticity. However, we can purge science of formal facticity if we follow the *Wissenschaftslehre*'s logical turn toward dialectical logic as the method of a self-grounding and thus absolute science of intelligibility.

In Section 1.6, we saw that Hegel lauds Fichte in the *Encyclopedia* for "the profound and enduring merit" of advancing critical philosophy toward a presuppositionless logic and thereby toward a systematically satisfying response to the question *quid facti* concerning the origin of our possession of the categories. Such a response would proceed by "*deduc[ing]*" the categories not from a radically contingent origin that is "apprehended only empirically" or, as Fichte says, is observed inductively, namely, "traditional logic," but rather from an absolutely necessary origin, namely, what Hegel calls "thinking itself."[4] A deduction that proceeds in this manner is a method that belongs to a truly absolute science of intelligibility, that is, a logic whose formal content arises *sui generis* and so neither is factically received nor has any factical remainder. This logic alone can lay claim to "total *presuppositionlessness*."[5]

Hegel expresses his admiration for Fichte's logical turn during the former's Heidelberg period. However, it is during his earlier Jena period, particularly in 1801's *The Difference Between Fichte's and Schelling's System of Philosophy in Connection with the First Fascicle of Reinhold's Contributions to a More Convenient Survey of the State of Philosophy at the Beginning of the Nineteenth Century* and in 1802's "Faith and Knowledge, or the Reflective Philosophy of Subjectivity in the Complete Range of its Forms as Kantian, Jacobian, and Fichtean Philosophy," that he launches an intense criticism of Fichte's system as an expression and, indeed, the pinnacle of subjectivism. In what does Hegel's early charge of subjectivism consist? How can we reconcile his early charge against Fichte with his late praise of Fichte?

I will argue that Hegel's early charge of subjectivism against Fichte amounts to a charge of vestigial facticity, that is, of residual bruteness in a system that ostensibly pledges itself to the elimination of bruteness from philosophy.[6] As we saw in Section 2.3, according to Fichte the "overall gist" of the *Wissenschaftslehre* is the absolute freedom of reason, that is, the I is absolutely self-determining insofar as no brute fact is imposed on it. The logical turn that this gist demands inspires Hegel's pursuit

[4] Hegel EL | GW 20: §42 Remark. Cf. Hegel: "Concern with such pure determinations does, to be sure, presuppose a superior level of education. Studying them in and for themselves signifies further that we deduce them from thinking itself, and see from their own [development] whether they are *genuine*. We do not take them up in an external way, and then define them or exhibit their value and validity by comparing them with how they actually occur in consciousness. If we did that we would be starting from observation and experience" (Hegel EL | GW 20: §24 Addition 2).

[5] Hegel EL | GW 20: §78 Remark.

[6] Hegel's subjectivism charge is distinct from his charge of subjective idealism against Kant and Fichte in the *Encyclopedia*, according to which consciousness is restricted to mere appearances (Hegel EL | GW 20: §131 Addition).

of a true science of the conditions of intelligibility, which is presuppositionless in that such conditions are not received from any radically contingent source, but rather are necessary determinations of this science alone, which science is accordingly without contrary and therefore absolute. However, Hegel criticizes Fichte for tolerating the radical contingency not of the conditions of intelligibility, but rather of their derivational source in the I, which the *Wissenschaftslehre* openly presupposes. Moreover, he criticizes Fichte for the equally basic or equiprimordial presupposition of the not-I and, consequently, for presupposing the absolute opposition between the I and the not-I. The radical contingency or facticity of the absolute opposition with which Fichte's system begins ultimately undermines the necessity of its subsequent deduction of the conditions of intelligibility, for, insofar as this opposition is groundless, it renders the ensuing deduction rhapsodic and thus unscientific, thereby repeating the very error that he attributes to Kant and that Kant attributes to Aristotle. Fichte consequently falls short of an absolute science, betraying the gist, which is to say the spirit, of the *Wissenschaftslehre*. As I will show, Hegel charges Fichte's system with subjectivism, not because it fails somehow to be objective, but rather because it fails by its own lights to be scientific. It is the final vestige of facticity in the *Wissenschaftslehre* that compels Hegel to radicalize Fichte's deductive method by adopting a dialectical movement of thinking that presupposes neither the forms of any faculty nor any first principle nor, indeed, any opposition whatsoever.[7] In this way, Hegel aims to redeem the spirit of the *Wissenschaftslehre* and bring the post-Kantian response to the question *quid facti* to a philosophically defensible close.

In this chapter, I will articulate Kant's enlightenment ideal of rational cognition, according to which reason is the sole source of the form of cognition, and I will demonstrate Fichte's radicalization of this ideal (Section 3.2). I will then analyze Hegel's charge of subjectivism as the claim that Fichte abandons the enlightenment ideal by restricting his system to the standpoint of the understanding, which posits absolute oppositions, principally, the brute dichotomy between the I and the not-I. According to Hegel, philosophy demands the standpoint of reason to nullify all allegedly absolute oppositions of the understanding and thus to satisfy what he calls the 'principle of speculation,' namely, the identity of subject and object. I will apply this analysis to the *Difference* essay (Section 3.3) and to "Faith and Knowledge" (Section 3.4) in turn. Next, I will show that what Hegel calls 'bad infinity,' whereby Fichte's system endlessly strives to transcend the opposition between the I and the not-I, is a logical consequence of the vestigial facticity with which that system begins (Section 3.5). I will conclude by situating Hegel's early critique of subjectivism within the context of his burgeoning dialectical method, according to which the understanding's refusal to nullify opposition signals philosophy's failure to

[7] Cf. Hegel's claim that it is the "essence of dogmatism" to posit as "absolute" something that is merely relative, namely, "something finite, something burdened with an opposition" (Hegel VSP | 2000: 335).

embrace the necessity of contradiction, that is, to embrace the simultaneous truth of the contradictory terms in an absolute opposition, and thus its failure to advance to the speculative standpoint of reason, for which necessary contradictions dialectically yield their own resolution. We will see that philosophy's failure in this regard, and Fichte's failure in particular, consist in stalling at the first of what Hegel designates in the *Encyclopedia* as the three moments of logic (Section 3.6).

3.2 The Enlightenment Ideal of Rational Cognition

Fichte identifies the gist of the *Wissenschaftslehre* with the spirit of transcendental idealism, according to which reason is absolutely free. As we saw in Section 2.3, he rests his identity claim on an interpretation of §§16–7 of Kant's transcendental deduction, according to which the apperceptive I grounds "a systematic derivation of all consciousness or, what comes to the same, a system of philosophy."[8] Given that, as Fichte acknowledges,[9] Kant provides no such derivation, we should wonder where the alleged spirit and actual letter of transcendental idealism might more closely align.

As I hinted in Section 1.6, Fichte's conception of the absolute freedom of reason can be seen as radicalizing Kant's theory of enlightenment.[10] We will now see that while, for Kant, advancing the project of enlightenment depends on the resolve to use the understanding without external direction, for Fichte, grasping the truth of transcendental idealism depends on the resolve to exhibit the activity of reason without external determination. Whereas Kant's enlightenment dictum is "*Sapere aude!*,"[11] that is, dare to be wise, what I will call Fichte's enlightenment dictum is '*Agere aude!*,' that is, dare to act. As we will see, the Kantian and Fichtean dares similarly exhort us to be free.

Kant preliminarily answers the titular question of 1784's "An Answer to the Question: What is Enlightenment?" in the first sentence, stating that enlightenment consists in one's "*emergence*" from "*self-incurred minority.*" Minority is an "inability to make use of one's own understanding without direction from another" and is self-incurred in that it results from a "lack of resolution and courage."[12]

[8] Fichte VND | SW I: 477.

[9] Fichte VND | SW I: 479n.

[10] While scholars often read Fichte in light of Kant's practical texts, particularly the *Groundwork* and the second *Critique*, the importance of the "Enlightenment" essay is typically overlooked. For a recent exception, see Ware 2020: 150–1.

[11] Kant A | AA 8: 35.

[12] Kant A | AA 8: 35. Cf. Kant: "To think for oneself . . . is the first maxim of the **unprejudiced** way of thinking . . . [i.e.,] the maxim of a reason that is never **passive**. The tendency toward the latter, hence toward heteronomy of reason, is called **prejudice**; and the greatest prejudice of all is that of representing reason as if it were not subject to the rules of nature on which the understanding grounds it by means of its own essential law: i.e., **superstition**. Liberation from superstition is called **enlightenment**" (Kant KU | AA 5:294).

Freedom is a condition of the possibility of both minority and the maturity that characterizes enlightenment, for one must be free in order both to fail and to resolve to use one's understanding under one's own direction. On the one hand, minority is not causally necessitated, since only free individuals can incur it, namely, through reticence or cowardice. Hence, Kant says that our minority can, at most, become "almost nature" to us, but never actual nature, since we are always already capable of freely emerging from it. On the other hand, Kant claims that an enlightened public is "almost inevitable," so long as "it is left its freedom."[13] Maturity is not actually inevitable, however, since it is not causally necessitated. Nevertheless, a public that is ripe for maturity has "its freedom" as a condition of the possibility of maturation.

It is crucial to distinguish between the mere capacity for freedom that conditions the possibility of maturation and the actual exercise of this capacity toward the actualization of maturity. Kant describes the exercise of freedom as the "public use of one's reason in all matters," whether theoretical or practical. He clarifies that one makes public use of reason "*as a scholar* before the entire public of the *world of readers*."[14] This clarification assumes two things. First, reason's public use is subject to norms of communication, that is, maturity is an intersubjective end insofar as what I say and do must be comprehensible to my audience.[15] Second, reason's public use is subject to norms of validity, that is, maturity is a justificatory end insofar as what I say and do must be able to survive the critical scrutiny of my audience. So long as the public use of reason does not fully satisfy the norms of communication and validity, one cannot be said to live in "an *enlightened* age," but at most lives in "an *age of enlightenment*."[16]

In the first *Critique*, in Chapter III of the Transcendental Doctrine of Method, "The Architectonic of Pure Reason," Kant makes a related and, as we will see, momentous distinction between "rational cognition," that is, "*cognitio ex principiis* [cognition from principles]," and "historical cognition," that is, "*cognitio ex datis* [cognition from data or from what is given]." When we consider the form of cognition, we can ask whether this form "arise[s] from reason" or is "given . . . from elsewhere." In the first case, we cognize the form of cognition rationally, "draw[ing]" this form "out of the universal sources of reason" and thereby exhibiting an exercise of our "faculty" of "generation." In the second case, we cognize the form of

[13] Kant A | AA 8: 36.

[14] Kant A | AA 8: 36–7.

[15] Cf. Kant: "it is said that the freedom to *speak* or to *write* could be taken from us by a superior power, but the freedom to *think* cannot be. Yet how much and how correctly would we *think* if we did not think as it were in community with others to whom we *communicate* our thoughts, and who communicate theirs with us! Thus one can very well say that this external power which wrenches away people's freedom publicly to *communicate* their thoughts also takes from them the freedom to *think*—that single gem remaining to us in the midst of all the burdens of civil life, through which alone we can devise means of overcoming all the evils of our condition" (Kant O | AA 8: 144).

[16] Kant A | AA 8: 40.

cognition historically, drawing this form from immediate experience or external instruction and thereby exhibiting an exercise of our "faculty of imitation."[17] An example of rational cognition from the first *Critique* would be cognizing the principle of causality, which rests on the category of causality that originates in the understanding.[18] An example of historical cognition that Kant provides is learning a system of philosophy, for example, the Wolffian system. Although one may have "grasped and preserved well" the Wolffian system, since it is acquired, one is not its source, but rather its mouthpiece or instrument. It is in this sense that, as Kant says, one who cognizes historically is "a plaster cast of a living human being." Historical cognition consequently belongs to one who has "formed [oneself] according to an alien reason." Thus, historical cognition belongs to one who defers to the claims of others. By contrast, rational cognition belongs to one for whom "critique, indeed even the rejection of what has been learned, can also arise."[19] Thus, rational cognition belongs to one who scrutinizes the capacity of reason in oneself and can thereby secure reason's "rightful claims while dismissing all its groundless pretensions," which, Kant says, is precisely the task of "the critique of pure reason."[20]

By Kant's lights, rational cognition for us is not absolute. As we saw in Section 1.2, in the second *Critique*, he identifies a cognitive limit to "all human insight" into the conditions of possible experience such that, as he says in the first *Critique*, these conditions have no "further ground" in a cognizably ultimate ground from which they can be derived. We can see that this cognitive limit applies to rational cognition by briefly considering Kant's discussion of the conditions of possible experience in his lectures on logic.

In the 1800 *Jäsche Logic*, a manual that Gottlob Benjamin Jäsche edits at his request, Kant says that concepts "are either *given* (*conceptus dati*) or *made* (*conceptus factitii*)" and distinguishes between concepts that are given *a priori*, that is, "*notions*," and concepts that are given *a posteriori*, that is, "*concepts of experience*." He implies that the categories qualify as notions when he says that the "*pure concepts of the understanding* (*conceptus puri*) . . . arise merely from the understanding," since he thereby implies that the categories are, like all notions, given *a priori*.[21]

[17] Kant KrV A835–6/B863–4. Cf. Kant: "freedom in thinking signifies the subjection of reason to no laws except *those which it gives itself*... The natural consequence is that if reason will not subject itself to the laws it gives itself, it has to bow under the yoke of laws given by another; for without any law, nothing—not even nonsense—can play its game for long" (Kant O | AA 8: 145).

[18] See Kant KrV A188/B232–A211/B256.

[19] Kant KrV A836–7/B864–5. Cf. Kant: "Reason must regard itself as the author of its principles independently of alien influences" (Kant GMM | AA 4: 448).

[20] Kant KrV Axi–i.

[21] Kant JL | AA 9: 92–3. Cf. Kant's 1790's "On a Discovery Whereby Any New Critique of Pure Reason is to be Made Superfluous by an Older One," a response to Johann Augustus Eberhard's longstanding attack on the first *Critique*, in which he distinguishes an "originally acquired representation" or "*acquisitio* ... *originaria*," namely, space, time, and the categories, from a derivative acquisition or "*acquisitio derivativa*," namely, "the determinate *concep[t]*" of an object (Kant E | AA 8: 222–3). On this distinction, see Bruno 2018a.

Kant confirms this implication in the circa-1800 *Vienna Logic*, which is composed by a group of his lecture auditors, when he says that a concept that is given *a priori* is so given "merely in the understanding" and when, as an example of such a concept, he gives "the concept of cause."[22] He furthermore implies that the forms of sensibility are comparable to notions when, as another example of a concept that is given *a priori*, he gives the concept of "time."[23] Kant confirms this further implication in the early-1790s *Dohna-Wundlacken Logic*, a lecture transcript whose author is uncertain, when, as examples of concepts that are given *a priori*, that is, given "*rationati*," he gives the concepts of "cause, quantity, substance, action, time, and space," which latter he says we "cannot observe."[24] Like notions, then, the forms of sensibility are given *a priori*. This, of course, is no surprise, since space, time, and the categories are all given *a priori* as conditions of possible experience.

Clearly, we do not cognize conditions of possible experience historically, for they are not given *a posteriori*, that is, they are not "observe[d]." We must therefore cognize such conditions rationally. However, our rational cognition of them is not absolute. While we rationally cognize, for example, the principle of causality from a deeper principle or ground, namely, the category of causality, we do not cognize this category from any deeper ground than the categorical form of judgment, whose ultimate ground, like that of the forms of sensibility, exceeds the cognitive limit that applies to all insight of which we are capable, including the insight that is afforded by our rational cognition. Conditions of possible experience are accordingly factical insofar as their givenness is not just *a priori*, but also ultimately groundless or brute.

Crucially, we can find Kant's distinction from "The Architectonic of Pure Reason" between rational cognition and historical cognition at work in the "Enlightenment" essay. Minority essentially involves historical cognition, since it takes direction given from elsewhere regarding theoretical and practical matters. It is on the basis of another's instruction that the minor takes it as given that they must believe and act in certain ways. They do as they are expected. Moreover, insofar as the minor resembles a "*machine*" through their "mechanical" perpetuation of inherited precepts and formulas,[25] they instantiate the simulation or "plaster cast" of human living that characterizes historical cognition.[26] By contrast, maturation

[22] Kant WL | AA 24: 914. Cf. Kant: "the pure concept, insofar as it has its origin solely in the understanding (not in a pure image of sensibility), is called *notio*" (Kant KrV A320/B377).

[23] Kant WL | AA 24: 914.

[24] Kant DWL | AA 24: 756.

[25] Kant A | AA 8: 36, 42.

[26] Some cognition is properly historical, depending on the use of reason. Although "the *public* use of one's reason must always be free" to submit any claim to critique and thereby "bring about enlightenment among human beings," Kant acknowledges that the "*private use* of one's reason" is "that which one may make of it in a certain *civil* post or office to which [one] is entrusted." Cognition is properly historical insofar as one occupies one's post, since, for the sake of "the interest of a commonwealth" and of "public ends," whether, e.g., military, legal, or religious, one must "behave merely passively" and "obey." However, although "a certain mechanism is necessary" for the private use of reason, one must regard oneself not merely as a "part of the machine," but always also as a member of "the society of citizens of

requires the rational cognition that is achieved through the resolve to understand without another's direction. It is on the basis of principles that originate in their own reason that the mature believe and act in certain ways. They do as they must. Furthermore, the mature satisfy norms of communication and validity by cognizing the form of cognition in terms of principles to which, through the process of critique, they have a claim that is both comprehensible and justifiable.[27]

We will now see that Fichte champions the enlightenment spirit of transcendental idealism with a pioneering development of the connection between Kant's conceptions of maturity and rational cognition. Fichte's development not only comes to define the German idealist tradition, but also returns to haunt him in the form of Hegel's charge of subjectivism.

As we saw in Section 2.3, Fichte's interpretation of the transcendental deduction implies two criteria for systematic philosophy. The anti-nihilism criterion states that the I is absolutely self-determining, while the anti-rhapsody or scientific criterion states that the I is determinable by nothing radically contingent within consciousness. We also saw that Fichte articulates the anti-nihilism criterion in terms of two jointly necessary requirements. We can now see that these requirements are in fact identical.

This first articulated requirement is philosophy's first "task" of finding the "explanatory ground" or first principle of experience, while the second articulated requirement is philosophy's "first demand" of turning away from objects and "look[ing] within [one]self."[28] Philosophy's first task is *prima facie* in the service of rational cognition insofar as it requires a principle, rather than an external fact, by which to cognize the unity of experience. On its own, however, such a task leaves open the Spinozistic possibility that this principle is nature, that is, an ultimate cause of which experience, including reason itself, is an infinitely determined effect. Consequently, philosophy's first task is only in the service of rational cognition if, *contra* Spinozism, reason is the self-determining source of the first principle of experience, that is, only if, to borrow Kant's phrase, reason is a faculty of generation. However, I can only grasp reason as self-determining or generative by exhibiting its free activity myself, namely, through my rational autonomy, lest I be the infinitely determined effect of something merely called 'reason.' It follows that

the world" who, in one's capacity as a scholar addressing the public, "cannot fairly be prevented" from expressing one's thoughts on the "inappropriateness or even injustice" of the norms that are assigned to one's post (Kant A | AA 8: 37). The public use of reason is accordingly capable of qualifying or even overturning the historical cognition that is normally acquired through the private use of reason. Cf. Kant's distinction between public and private uses of reason with the distinction between what Richard Rorty calls a "private sense of mission" and "public rhetoric" (Rorty 1999: 128), respectively.

[27] Foucault complicates the relation between maturity and rational cognition by interpreting Kant's "Enlightenment" essay as asking who we are not as "unhistorical" subjects, but rather always in "this precise moment in which we are living" and so "in a very precise moment of history" (Foucault 1982: 785).

[28] Fichte VND | SW I: 422–3.

satisfying philosophy's first requirement of finding the first principle of experience is nothing other than satisfying its second requirement of looking within myself, for I can grasp this principle only insofar as I look within myself and posit myself as instantiating the freedom of reason, that is, insofar as I posit myself as self-positing. Thus, the anti-nihilism criterion of systematic philosophy expresses a singular requirement. Systematic philosophy singularly requires not just a first principle, but a first principle of freedom.

Freedom is not only required for systematic philosophy. It is also unavoidable. As we saw in Section 1.6, positing a principle in response to philosophy's first task, which we now see is simultaneously its first demand, is a normative and therefore "free act of thinking."[29] This is why a Spinozist's denial of freedom is a performative contradiction. While I can abstract from the content of experience in order to posit its first principle, I "freely determine myself" in positing either reason or nature as this principle. But then if I posit nature, the putative consequence of which is to rule out human freedom as illusory, "it is only because I have determined myself" to do so,[30] in which case I refute myself through a performative contradiction. Hence, just as I can "think that there are no objects" yet "can never represent that there is no space," as Kant argues in the transcendental aesthetic,[31] so too I can abstract from the content of experience yet can never abstract from my free standpoint on experience. My rational autonomy is inescapable. As Fichte puts the point: "I am only active. I cannot be driven from this position."[32]

We find that, insofar as philosophy's first task and first demand compose a singular requirement, this requirement exemplifies rational cognition. In order for philosophy to be systematic, I abstract from the content of cognition, that is, the content of experience, and posit cognition's ultimate form, that is, its first principle. Moreover, I freely posit this principle, given freedom's unavoidability in this matter. Drawing this principle from my rational autonomy is an exercise of a faculty of generation, not a faculty of imitation. As Fichte says in the *Nova Methodo*: "*Wissenschaftslehre* and philosophy are one and the same . . . Philosophy is not a collection of propositions that can be studied and memorized as such; instead, it is a certain way of looking at things, {a way of viewing things in accordance with certain principles,} a particular way of thinking, which one must generate

[29] Fichte VND | SW I: 425.
[30] Fichte VND | SW I: 427.
[31] Kant KrV A24/B38. Cf. Kant on time at Kant KrV A31/B46.
[32] Fichte VND | SW I: 467. Cf. Fichte: "It is contradictory to ask about a reality that supposedly remains after one has abstracted from all reason; for the questioner himself (we may presume) has reason, is driven by reason to question, and wants a rational answer; he, therefore, has not abstracted from reason. We cannot go outside the sphere of our reason; the case against the thing in itself has already been made, and philosophy aims only to inform us of it and keep us from believing that we have gone beyond the sphere of our reason, when in fact we are obviously still caught within it" (Fichte GN | SW III: 40).

within oneself."[33] I can attain historical cognition of, for example, Wolffian philosophy through "stud[y] and memor[ization]," which is to say that I can attain cognition from what is given.[34] However, this differs from the rational cognition that is specifically proper to systematic philosophy, namely, the rational cognition from those principles that I "generate within [my]self." Moreover, if philosophy and the *Wissenschaftslehre* are "one and the same," then the rational cognition that is proper to philosophy is cognition from a first principle that I generate, which, as we saw, is a first principle of freedom.[35] Hence, shortly after, Fichte says that "one will encounter absolutely nothing at all within philosophy unless one produces from within oneself everything about which one reasons. Philosophical ideas cannot be given to anyone; they have to be generated within one's own mind."[36] It is insufficient if one generates only part of what one reasons about in philosophy, for example, specific conditions of experience such as the categories, if this excludes the ultimate form or first principle of experience, about which, as we saw, it is philosophy's first requirement to reason.[37]

Fichte does not mention Kant's theory of enlightenment.[38] However, we can see how he develops the connection between maturity and rational cognition by considering what it means to adopt the standpoint of the *Wissenschaftslehre*.

On the one hand, I must deny, on pain of Spinozism, that my beliefs and actions are infinitely determined by external causes and hence that theoretical and practical cognition depend entirely on what is given. In Kantian terms, I must deny that

[33] Fichte NM | GA IV/2: 11. Cf. Fichte: "[The *Wissenschaftslehre*] is a system for persons who are able to think for themselves. {One of the features of [the *Wissenschaftslehre*] is that it cannot be learned in a historical manner.} It cannot be grasped merely by reading and study. Every person must produce it within himself, particularly since no fixed terminology will be introduced" (Fichte NM | GA IV/2: 21).

[34] See Fichte: "It is possible to know much, to study much, to read much, to hear much, and still to be no more than a machine. One can let authors or orators go to work upon one, while one remains in a state of comfortable repose, observing the way one representation succeeds another" (Fichte BE | SW VIII: 346).

[35] This is to be distinguished from what, in the "Announcement," Fichte calls "rational cognition based on concepts," which is merely analytic and to which he says philosophy cannot be confined (Fichte A | GA I/7: 156).

[36] Fichte NM | GA IV/2: 14.

[37] Compare Fichte's distinction between ideas that are "given," i.e., historically cognized, and ideas that are "generated," i.e., rationally cognized, with what Franks explains is the Kabbalistic distinction between *mesorah*, i.e., a "transmitted tradition" that anyone can inherit, and *kabbalah*, i.e., a "received tradition" that "must be received from someone who addresses it *to you*, in a manner designed to provoke your spontaneity, so that you are the one who 'understands spontaneously'" (Franks 2020: 11).

[38] Fichte seemingly evokes Kant's theory of enlightenment in Lecture II of *The Present Age*, which describes the "principle" of his epoch as the "*liberation from the compulsion of blind authority exercised by reason as instinct*" and states that the "fundamental maxim" of those who "stand at the head" of his epoch is "*to accept nothing as really existing or obligatory but that which one can understand and clearly comprehend*." However, he calls his epoch "the age of empty freedom" because, in applying its principle, it defers to "a certain fixed standard," namely, "an established *common sense of humankind*," and thus neglects that one must "learn *how to know*." Fichte infers that the "true character" of his epoch is "admirably expressed in a single phrase—would-be enlightenment" (Fichte GGZ | SW VII: 19–21, 39). Cf. Fichte ASL | SW V: 423–4. Cf. also Husserl PK | 1970b: 290.

cognition is exclusively historical.[39] On the other hand, I must affirm, given the singular requirement that is expressed by the anti-nihilism criterion of systematic philosophy, that my rational agency is the source of the first principle of experience and hence that I generate the cognition that is proper to philosophy. In Kantian terms, I must affirm that cognition is ultimately, if not exclusively, rational. Thus, adopting the standpoint of the *Wissenschaftslehre* demands the resolve to reject the minority that is characteristic of Spinozism and to use reason without direction from nature. In other words, for Fichte, the maturity of enlightenment consists in exhibiting the activity of reason without external determination, an activity that I exhibit by positing myself as self-positing. Like Kant, he regards maturity as conditioned by the capacity of freedom: "we cannot force anyone to accept [the *Wissenschaftslehre*], since the acceptance of this system is something that depends on freedom."[40]

Moreover, in 1794's *Some Lectures Concerning the Scholar's Vocation*, Fichte evokes norms that closely resemble the norms that Kant assumes in his theory of enlightenment. Recall that, for Kant, I exercise my capacity for freedom toward the actualization of maturity by making public use of reason as a scholar before a world of readers and that I do so in accordance with norms of communication and validity in order to ensure that what I say and do is comprehensible and justifiable, respectively. After arguing in the Second Lecture that the vocation of society is the "communal perfection" that characterizes the free interaction of individuals, Fichte claims that the "drive to interact with other free, rational beings" includes two sub-drives, namely, "*the drive to communicate*, that is, the drive to cultivate in other persons that aspect of personality in which *we* ourselves are especially strong" and "*the drive to receive*, that is, the drive to allow others to cultivate in us that aspect in which they are especially strong and we are especially weak."[41] We can hear in this claim Kant's idea that maturity is both an intersubjective and a justificatory end. On the one hand, in my "*drive to communicate*" with others, I aim to cultivate in them the comprehension of the reasons that I have for what I say and do, reasons my own grasp of which is or at least ought to be strong. On the other hand, in my "*drive to receive*" the critical scrutiny of others, I aim for them to

[39] See Fichte: "Philosophy cannot be established by attending to what is simply 'given'" (Fichte GA IV/2: 28).

[40] Fichte VND | SW I: 499. Cf. Fichte's claim that "one becomes an idealist only by passing through a disposition toward dogmatism [i.e., Spinozism]—if not by passing through dogmatism itself" (Fichte VND | SW I: 434) with Kant's account of our progression "in matters of pure reason" from the "childhood" of dogmatism, through the adolescence of skepticism, toward "the mature and adult power of judgment, which has at its basis firm maxims of proven universality" (Kant KrV A761/B789). On Kant's account, see Bruno 2018a.

[41] Fichte VBG | SW VI: 315. Cf. Fichte: "In order to fulfill this vocation [of society] and to do so ever more adequately, we require a skill that is acquired and increased only through culture. This skill has two aspects: the skill of *giving*, or affecting others as free beings, and the capacity for *receiving*, or for making the most of the effect which others have upon us" (Fichte SW VI: 310–1).

cultivate in me the awareness of the true extent of the validity of what I say and do, my awareness of which may be lacking or at least weak.[42]

The connection that Fichte develops between maturity and rational cognition positions us now to understand his identification of the *Wissenschaftslehre* not only with philosophy in general, but also with the spirit of transcendental idealism in particular.

The cognition that is proper to philosophy is cognition from a first principle, namely, the absolute freedom of reason or the I. For Fichte, this cognition expresses the spirit of transcendental idealism insofar as it grounds a system of philosophy. Although Kant constructs no such system, his theory of enlightenment exhorts the freedom that alone makes its construction possible, namely, the freedom of rational cognition. Fichte radicalizes Kant's theory of enlightenment by exhorting us to be free in such a way as to satisfy the anti-nihilism and anti-rhapsody criteria. We do so by affirming that the I is absolutely self-determining and determinable by nothing contingent within consciousness, respectively. But this is just to reject facticity, for it is to affirm that neither what the I is nor what it contains can be given to it. In other words, no historical cognition can limit the I, since to grasp the I, namely, by positing myself as self-positing, is to attain the rational cognition of a first principle that I generate. Kant's theory of enlightenment thus helps to clarify the spirit of transcendental idealism with which Fichte identifies the *Wissenschaftslehre*.[43]

Of course, concerns will remain about the alleged spirit of transcendental idealism, given, for example, the unavoidable transcendental illusion that Kant ascribes to human reason.[44] Nevertheless, Kant's enlightenment ideal of rational

[42] Fichte claims that Jean-Jacques Rousseau contradicts himself by imputing "human corruption" to "cultural advancement" and predicating human "salvation" on a return to the state of nature on the grounds that since his own theory of salvation relies on intellectual capacities that are "provided by his excellent education" and whose use aims to rationally "persuade" a community of scholars, it perpetuates "exactly what he so bitterly criticized . . . Thus, without realizing it, he transplanted himself and society as a whole into the state of nature *along with all of that cultivation which could not have been obtained except by emerging from the natural state*" (Fichte VBG | SW VI: 336, 342). Any return to nature can therefore only take a cultivated human form. Fichte also criticizes Rousseau's depiction of the pupil as "develop[ing] all by himself" at the mercy of "benevolent nature," for such a pupil requires a "teacher" who "furnishe[s] him with the enterprise, fire, and firm resolve to fight against and to subjugate nature" (Fichte SW VI: 345). On Fichte's critique of Rousseau, see Clarke 2013.

[43] Cf. Fichte: "Once, around the hour of midnight, a wondrous shape seemed to pass before me and speak to me: 'Poor mortal,' I heard it say, 'you heap mistakes upon mistakes in your reasoning and think yourself wise. You tremble before specters that you yourself have worked hard to create. Have the courage to become truly wise['] . . . I took courage. This voice appeals to my own understanding. I will take a chance on it. It cannot think anything into me; what I am to think, I myself have to think; a conviction that I am to come to hold, I myself have to produce within me" (Fichte BM | SW II: 199).

[44] See Fichte: "[Kant] refers in [the first *Critique*] *to a deception that continually recurs, despite the fact that one knows that it is a deception.* How can Kant know that this deception will always recur, particularly since he himself was the first person to bring this alleged deception to light? . . . To know that one is deceived and yet to remain deceived: this is not a state of conviction and harmony with oneself; instead, it is a state of serious inner conflict. In my experience, no deception recurs; for no deception whatsoever is present within reason. What then is the deception that is supposed to recur? Is it not this: that things in themselves exist outside of and independently of us? But who makes this assertion? . . . It is a false philosophy that attributes to ordinary consciousness this concept [of a thing in itself] it has

cognition provides a philosophical model that Fichte radicalizes for the purpose of systematizing transcendental idealism. We will now see why Hegel thinks that Fichte's radicalization of this ideal is not radical enough and how this shortcoming betrays the spirit of the *Wissenschaftslehre*.

3.3 Hegel's Critique of the Facticity of Absolute Opposition

A decade after sharing a room with Johann Christian Friedrich Hölderlin at the Evangelical-Lutheran seminary in Tübingen, Schelling and Hegel become the senior and junior editors, respectively, of the short-lived *Critical Journal of Philosophy*, which runs from 1802 to 1803. Hegel is the main author of its 1802 Introduction, "On the Essence of Philosophical Critique Generally and its Relationship to the Present State of Philosophy in Particular."[45] There Hegel claims that "critique transposes itself to a subjective situation" if it casts "the absolute (whether as God or in some other aspect as nature) as fixed in immovable and absolute opposition" to philosophical cognition, for, in that case, "essentially distinct" philosophies have "equal right to maintain [themselves] against the others," since, by virtue of their shared opposition to the absolute, they are equally "finite" or "one-sided," each depending on an "arbitrary starting point." In order for its "verdict" to instead be "objective," critique must adopt "a standard which is just as independent of the person who makes the judgment as it is of the thing that is judged," namely, "the idea of philosophy itself" according to which "reason is but one" such that "a wall cannot be set up between reason and its self-cognition."[46] In other words, the true standard of critique is that reason is the identity of subject and object. Ignoring this philosophical standard produces the "unphilosophy and unscientificity" that, according to Hegel, "the enlightenment already expresses" through "the vulgarity of the understanding and the vanity of its exaltation above reason."[47]

In what precisely do subjectivity and objectivity consist? What qualifies as a philosophical standard of critique that is independent of both "person[s]" and "thing[s]"? And what exactly is the difference between reason and the understanding such that the former's "self-cognition" can overcome the latter's "vulgarity"? Answers to these three questions emerge when we consult Hegel's

invented within its own philosophical domain. The deception in question here, which is quite avoidable and which can be completely extirpated by true philosophy, is, therefore, one you have created all by yourself; and as soon as you obtain a clear understanding of your philosophy, this delusion will fall away like scales from your eyes never to recur again" (Fichte VND | SW I: 512–4). Cf. Fichte UGB | 1988: 206.

[45] See di Giovanni and Harris 2000: 273–4.
[46] Hegel WPK | 2000: 275–6.
[47] Hegel WPK | 2000: 283.

contemporaneous charge of subjectivism against Fichte and recognize that subjectivism thwarts the enlightenment ideal of rational cognition specifically through its presupposition of an absolute opposition between the I and the not-I.

In order to answer the above three questions, I will analyze Hegel's subjectivism charge against Fichte in three steps. First, I will clarify the problem that 'subjectivism' names, namely, facticity in the form of an absolute opposition between two terms in a presupposed dichotomy. Second, I will articulate the philosophical goal whose attainment Hegel thinks this problem prevents, namely, the absolute identity of subject and object, that is, of thought and being. Third, I will explain Hegel's own solution to this problem, namely, reason's nullification of the oppositions that are posited by the understanding as absolute. I will trace these steps through each of the two early Jena texts in which the subjectivism charge principally occurs, focusing on the *Difference* essay in this section and on "Faith and Knowledge" in Section 3.4.

Before proceeding, it is worth noting that, although Hegel's charge of subjectivism does not use the term 'facticity,' we will see that it uses very closely related terms in order to signify putative conditions of intelligibility that are brutely 'external,' 'other,' or 'alien' to reason and, in this respect, are 'incomprehensible.'

In the Preface to the *Difference* essay, Hegel acknowledges that Fichte has "made an epoch" in philosophy with his distinction between the "letter" and the "spirit" of transcendental idealism. Hegel construes this as a distinction between the "reflection" of the understanding, which opposes the subject to the object, and the "speculation" of reason, which identifies the subject with the object. On the one hand, reflective opposition via the understanding characterizes Kant's transcendental deduction, which not only renders the categories "static" insofar as the table of their kind and number is fixed in accordance with an underived table of the forms of judgment, but also renders them "dead" insofar as their subjective use forms no living unity, that is, no identity, with the "absolute objectivity" of things in themselves, which consequently "destroy[s] the language that expresses the absolute itself." On the other hand, speculative identification via reason characterizes Fichte's logical turn, which renders transcendental idealism "purer, stricter," and "authentic" by positing the I both as the "purely speculative principle" of the transcendental deduction,[48] which generates the categories *sui generis*, and as the "self-reverting activity or subject-objectivity" that is limited by no thing in itself, whose concept Fichte regards as "utterly unreasonable."[49] Nevertheless, Hegel claims

[48] Hegel D | GW 4: 5–7.

[49] Fichte VND | SW I: 472, 502. Cf. Fichte VND | SW I: 529. Fichte takes seriously Jacobi's sarcastic dare in "On Transcendental Idealism," according to which, in order to avoid the alleged inconsistency of positing the existence of a thing in itself that we cannot cognize, the "transcendental idealist" must deny that there are "things present outside us in a transcendental sense," that is, that there are things in themselves, and "must have the courage, therefore, to assert the strongest idealism that was ever professed, and not be afraid of the objection of speculative egoism" (Jacobi DH 228–9 | 1994: 338; cf. Jacobi DH 37-8 | 1994: 553). On Jacobi's dare, see Bruno 2020c. On the structural analogy between Kant's concept of the thing in itself and Heidegger's concept of death, see Bruno 2014b.

that fortune has not "smiled on" Fichte's logical turn because, no less than Kant's Copernican turn, it fails to set reason "in harmony with nature," a failure that is the result of "presupposition, principles, and such like forms" that "still adorn the entrance to philosophy with their cobwebs" and whose removal is specifically what "occasion[s]" Hegel's essay.[50]

The Fichtean presupposition that sets reason and nature at odds and at whose removal the *Difference* essay aims is the opposition between the I and the not-I. In Chapter 2, "Exposition of Fichte's System," Hegel calls the "foundation" of Fichte's system "intellectual intuition, pure thinking of itself, pure self-consciousness, I = I, I am." He claims that this "pure consciousness" stands in the "highest opposition" to "empirical consciousness" insofar as the latter is "not determined" by the former and is therefore equally fundamental or "unconditioned."[51] This is because whereas pure consciousness apprehends "the I as infinite positing," empirical consciousness apprehends "an infinite not-I," that is, "an infinite objective world" as opposed to a finite spatio-temporal object, which has "the negative character of being something other, i.e., something opposite in general," to the I.[52] Thus, Hegel concludes that Fichte's system presupposes an "absolute opposition" between the I and the not-I.[53]

Hegel's conclusion accurately captures Fichte's view in the *Foundations*.[54] In §1, Fichte argues that the I is the ultimate ground of positing, that is, the necessary connection between subject and predicate in the identity proposition "A = A," for it is in virtue of the I's identity that subject and predicate constitute a valid unity.[55] In §2, he argues that the I is "the same connection" between subject and predicate in the opposition proposition "~A is not = A," for, again, it is in virtue of its identity that subject and predicate constitute a valid unity. Indeed, he says, the form of any proposition whatsoever stands "under the highest form, that of *formability as such*—the form of the unity of consciousness," that is, the identity of the I.[56] Fichte

[50] Hegel D | GW 4: 6–9. Cf. Hegel: "All . . . presuppositions or assumptions must equally be given up when we enter into the science, whether they are taken from representation or from thinking; for it is this science, in which all determinations of this sort must first be investigated, and in which their meaning and validity like that of their antitheses must be [re]cognized . . . Science should be preceded by *universal doubt*, i.e., by total *presuppositionlessness*" (Hegel EL | GW 20: §78 and Remark). Ng argues that Hegel's critique of Fichte in the *Difference* essay concerns the objective purposiveness that nature lacks in virtue of its disharmony with reason (Ng 2020: 88). We will see that the root cause of this disharmony is in fact the presupposition that Hegel says "occasion[s]" his essay, namely, the factical dichotomy between the I and the not-I.

[51] Hegel D | GW 4: 34.

[52] Hegel D | GW 4: 36–7, 42.

[53] Hegel D | GW 4: 34. Cf. Hegel: "in Fichte the pure unity of the I with itself presents itself immediately and from the very outset, as does the equally abstract thing-in-itself, the not-I, in its opposition to the I" (Hegel JW | GW 15: 18). Cf. also Schulze's anonymous 1803 "Aphorisms on the Absolute" (Schulze 2020: 19).

[54] A version of this discussion appears in Bruno 2021d.

[55] Fichte GWL | SW I: 95.

[56] Fichte GWL | SW I: 102. Not only would the terms in a proposition not form a unity without the I's identity, but also if the I that posits an identity proposition and an opposition proposition were not an identity, then positing the latter proposition "would not be an act of positing *in opposition*, but would

then observes that while "the *form* of ~A is determined purely and simply" by the I *qua* condition of "*formability as such*," ~A's "*matter*" is "determined by A," for it "is not what A is, and its entire essence consists in this: that it is not what A is." What ~A is can be known "only if I am acquainted with A." It follows that the I provides the form of what is posited, but not the matter. Such matter brutely opposes the I and, Fichte says, "that which is posited in opposition to the I = *not-I*."[57] Indeed, he later claims that the not-I's opposition to the I is a "postulated *factum*," that is, a brute fact that "underlies and grounds all derivation and grounding," for which "[n]o higher ground can be adduced from which one might derive" it.[58] As Fichte says in a letter to Reinhold, July 2, 1795:

> absolutely all operations of the mind presuppose that there is an I as well as something opposed to it, that is, a not-I. Only through the I and the not-I are any mental operations possible. There is no reason why the I is I and the thing is not-I; this opposition occurs absolutely . . . [T]he distinction is absolute, and only in consequence of this distinction are all *a priori* first principles and all experience possible."[59]

Hence we can say that acquaintance presupposes the matter of what I know, namely, the not-I, which matter irreducibly differs from and thus absolutely opposes the form by which I know, namely, the I. The not-I's opposition to the I is accordingly a fundamental presupposition of Fichte's system, an "absolute" opposition for which there is "no reason" and thus no "derivation."

Moreover, even acknowledging that Fichte publishes the *Foundations* strictly as "a manuscript for the use of [his] students"[60] and that he regards this text as an "extremely imperfect and defective" presentation of his system,[61] contemporaneous texts show that he regards as a fundamental presupposition not only the I's opposition to the not-I, but also the I itself. As we saw in Section 2.2, Fichte tells Reinhold in 1794 that he "cannot accept" the categories' deduction from "presuppose[d]" forms of judgment, since they must be deduced from the I on pain

be purely and simply an act of positing. Only in relation to an act of positing does it become an act of positing in opposition," namely, within the identity of the I (Fichte SW I: 103). Cf. Bernard Williams' argument that the "thought-event[s]" that compose a logical inference presuppose "the same thought-world" (Williams 2005: 80–1).

[57] Fichte GWL | SW I: 104. Cf. Fichte: "the second foundational principle [regarding the not-I] . . . presuppose[s] a *factum*, which can by no means be demonstrated *a priori*, but only through each person's own experience" (Fichte SW I: 252).

[58] Fichte GWL | SW I: 253. Cf. Fichte's claim in the *Foundations* that "[f]or the same reason that the first foundational principle could be neither proven nor derived, neither can the second foundational principle" (Fichte GWL | SW I: 101).

[59] Fichte B | 1988: 398–9.

[60] See Breazeale 1994: xi.

[61] Fichte GWL | SW I: 87. Cf. Fichte's description of the *Foundations* in the "Announcement" as "a text that does not appear to be readily able to dispense with oral assistance" (Fichte A | GA I/7: 153).

of rhapsody.[62] Yet, as we saw in Section 1.6, he tells Reinhold in 1795 that one enters the *Wissenschaftslehre* "by means of what is absolutely incomprehensible."[63] Fichte has good reason to deny that positing the I can be made comprehensible by some further fact. As a first principle, it is an unconditioned condition. And as a principle of freedom, it has no external cause. But then positing the I is a fundamental presupposition of his system rather than a derivable condition of intelligibility, that is, a brute fact whose determination is rhapsodic. Arguably, however, the arbitrariness of positing the I is virtuous insofar as it avoids the nihilistic consequence and, indeed, the performative contradiction of positing the first principle of Spinozism. As Fichte says in the *Nova Methodo*:

> Every philosophy presupposes something, something that it does not demonstrate and on the basis of which it explains and demonstrates everything else. This is also true of idealism. Idealism presupposes the previously mentioned free activity as its first principle, on the basis of which it must then explain everything else; but this principle itself cannot be explained any further. {To be sure, each of these two systems [namely, Spinozism and idealism] postulates something. But the idealist does not presuppose anything outside of his own consciousness; he merely postulates that this free activity of his I is that principle that cannot be derived from anything else. The first, immediate principle with which he begins is his consciousness of freedom.}[64]

Although *qua* philosophy idealism rests on the indemonstrable, by Fichte's lights it has the advantage of being "transcendental" rather than "*transcendent*," that is, of "remain[ing] within consciousness" rather than "soar[ing] beyond" it.[65]

Since, according to Fichte, the not-I, like the I, is presupposed, Hegel is correct to characterize positing the not-I as "absolute" and the not-I itself as "a fact" or "impact" that confronts the I as "absolutely alien" and that therefore "cannot be derived from the I."[66] He is consequently correct to conclude that, for Fichte, the opposition between the I and the not-I is absolute. As we will see, it is on the basis of this conclusion that Hegel will mount his charge of subjectivism against Fichte.

In Chapter 1, "Various Forms Occurring in Contemporary Philosophy," Hegel claims that the Fichtean I is "a *subjective* identity of subject and object."[67] We might take this to mean that the Fichtean I lacks something objective, namely, something beyond "intellectual intuition, pure thinking of itself, pure self-consciousness, I = I, I am." However, this would be mistaken, for there can be nothing beyond

[62] Fichte B | 1988: 376.
[63] Fichte B | 1988: 399.
[64] Fichte NM | GA IV/2: 17.
[65] Fichte NM | GA IV/2: 17.
[66] Hegel D | GW 4: 45–6.
[67] Hegel D | GW 4: 33.

reason or the I if we are to adopt the philosophical "standard" of critique, according to which, as we saw in the Introduction to the *Critical Journal*, "reason is but one" and not one among two.[68] Hegel's claim is rather that Fichte's system is unscientific insofar as it fails to rule out something that is "absolutely alien" to reason, that is, something that would render reason one among two. We can see why this is so if we consider Hegel's distinction between "dogmatic idealism," which "posits the subjective as the real ground of the objective," and "dogmatic realism," which "posits the objective as the real ground of the subjective." Hegel says that although Fichte's presentation of the *Wissenschaftslehre* might "mislead" us into classifying him as a dogmatic idealist, he in fact "does not deny the objective, but puts the subjective and the objective in the same rank of reality," namely, by positing the I and the not-I as equally "rank[ed]" or equiprimordial presuppositions. However, by positing the subjective and the objective "both at once but separately," that is, by fixing the I and the not-I as irreducible terms of an absolute opposition, Fichte fails to render them "equal," which Hegel says would require nullifying their opposition.[69] Instead, the I and the not-I lie at the ground of the *Wissenschaftslehre* as mutually external and mutually impenetrable brute facts, that is, they are factical. Insofar as they factically ground Fichte's system, it is "impossible to sublate their dichotomy."[70]

Hegel confirms that 'subjectivism' denotes not the absence of putative objectivity beyond the I, but rather the vestige of facticity when he says shortly before that philosophy is never "worse" than when it begins with "a definition, as Spinoza does." This is because presupposing definitions stands in "the starkest contrast" to providing a "deduction of the principles of knowledge," including definitions, from thinking itself. It is significant that Hegel attributes "Spinoza's artlessness" in this respect to "the subjectivity of reflection."[71] This implies that Fichte and Spinoza share a subjectivist error, namely, the error of presupposing undeduced principles that obstruct philosophy's entranceway like "cobwebs." However, if a transcendental idealist like Fichte, who begins from the I, and a transcendental realist like Spinoza, who begins from nature, are equally guilty of subjectivism, then subjectivism cannot consist in the absence or exclusion of putative objectivity beyond the I.

[68] Cf. Hegel: "Logic has nothing to do with a thought *about* something which stands outside by itself as the base of thought; nor does it have to do with forms meant to provide mere *markings* of the truth; rather, the necessary forms of thinking, and its specific determinations, are the content and the ultimate truth itself" (Hegel WL | GW 21: 34).

[69] Hegel D | GW 4: 41; cf. 45.

[70] Hegel D | GW 4: 34. In order to maintain terminological consistency between Hegel's early and late periods, I use 'sublate' to translate '*aufheben*,' diverging from Harris and di Giovanni's use of 'suspend' in both the *Difference* essay and "Faith and Knowledge."

[71] Hegel D | GW 4: 24. Cf. Hegel WL | GW 21: 33. Cf. also Hegel's Berlin lectures on the history of philosophy: "If the dogmatist has the right to presuppose an axiom as unproved, the sceptic has equally the right, or, if we choose to say so, equally no right, to presuppose the opposite as unproved. One is as good as the other. Thus all definitions are presuppositions. For instance, Spinoza presupposes definitions of the infinite, of substance, of attribute, etc.; and the rest follows consistently from them. Nowadays men prefer to give assurances and speak of facts of consciousness" (Hegel VGP2 | 1894: 359).

It must instead consist in the presence or inclusion of brute facts, whether these are definitions, as in Spinoza, or absolute oppositions, as in Fichte.[72] The scientific solution to this error is to eliminate facticity through a truly systematic deductive method that, according to Hegel, is lacking in the various presentations of the *Wissenschaftslehre*.

Hegel also clarifies a perhaps implied contrast to subjectivism by stating that the "objective totality" of knowledge that subjectivism fails to provide and that philosophy demands is "a system of science" that "finally frees itself from contingency." We can hear this as stating that the objectivity that subjectivism lacks is nothing, *per impossibile*, beyond the I or reason, but rather consists in reason's "free[ing]" or liberating itself from the imposition of radically contingent or brute facts, for example, the I's opposition to the not-I.[73] Hence Hegel describes the "construction" of a philosophical system as "reason's struggle for freedom."[74]

Our first step in analyzing Hegel's subjectivism charge against Fichte thus demonstrates that it targets the facticity of an absolute, that is, undeduced, opposition. Before taking our next step, however, it is important to observe that the subjectivism charge impugns Fichte's commitment to the enlightenment ideal of rational cognition and, consequently, his commitment to the stated gist of the *Wissenschaftslehre*.

Regarding the ideal of rational cognition, Hegel describes the "indifference" of an age whose "urge toward completeness of information" reduces spirit to a "curious collector" of "alien objects" and "contingent oddities." Cognition in such an information age is externally given or, in Kantian terms, historical, since it is received as the "lifeless product of alien ingenuity." By contrast, an age in which "reason comes to know itself and deals only with itself so that its whole work and activity are grounded on itself" alone "produces a true philosophy." Cognition in such an enlightened age is internally generated or, in Kantian terms, rational, since it is secured through reason's "putting its trust only in itself."[75] Fichte fails to fully

[72] See Hegel: "Spinoza further defines the attributes as *infinite*—infinite also in the sense of an *infinite multiplicity*. But only *two* are named in what follows, *thought and extension*, and no indication is given of how the infinite multiplicity necessarily reduces to opposition, specifically this opposition of thought and extension.—These two attributes are for this reason *empirically* assumed" (Hegel WL | GW 11: 377).

[73] See Hegel: "whim and contingency have their place only from subordinate standpoints and are banished from the concept of the science of the absolute. For whim is only the semblance of freedom; it is a freedom wholly abstracted from necessity or from freedom as a totality—and this abstraction can only take place where freedom is already posited within a single sphere—just as contingency, which is what corresponds to whim in the realm of necessity, is the positing of single parts as if they were for themselves, and did not exist solely in and through the objective totality" (Hegel D | GW 4: 72). Cf. Hegel EL | GW §14.

[74] Hegel D | GW 4: 30. Cf. Hegel: "the logical is to be sought in a system of thought-determinations in which the antithesis between subjective and objective (in its usual meaning) disappears. This meaning of thinking and of its determinations is more precisely expressed by the ancients when they say that *nous* governs the world, or by our own saying that there is reason in the world, by which we mean that reason is the soul of the world, inhabits it, and is immanent in it, as its own, innermost nature, its universal" (Hegel EL | GW 20: §24 Addition 1).

[75] Hegel D | GW 4: 9–11.

radicalize the enlightenment ideal of rational cognition, so as to transition from an information age to an enlightened age, because the opposition between the I and the not-I is received rather than generated, that is, a brute fact that, as he says, "underlies and grounds all derivation and grounding." Hegel evokes this failure when he says that "*the need of philosophy*" originates in response to "the unfree and given aspect" of thinking. This is the aspect of thinking that regards itself as constrained to presuppose an insuperable "dichotomy," a thinking that he attributes to the "understanding, as the capacity to set limits."[76] Insofar as Fichte's system begins with a factical dichotomy between the I and the not-I, one that explicitly restricts the scope of deduction, it rests on just such an "unfree and given aspect" of thinking. But then this system does not ultimately rest on the rational cognition that enlightenment idealizes and therefore does not begin with the cognition that is proper to philosophy.[77]

Regarding the gist of the *Wissenschaftslehre*, it is precisely by not radicalizing the enlightenment ideal that Fichte betrays the spirit of the *Wissenschaftslehre*, according to which reason is absolutely self-sufficient. By depending on the givenness of the presupposition of the opposition between the I and the not-I, Fichte's system adopts a "distorted perspective" in which reason is "not self-sufficient, but needy," and is, in this sense, not itself.[78] As we might put it, modifying a Jacobian criticism of Kant,[79] without the presupposition of this opposition, reason cannot enter Fichte's system, but with it, reason cannot remain. Hegel himself champions the spirit of the *Wissenschaftslehre*, according to which, "[w]ith the I's self-positing, everything is posited and outside of it is nothing."[80] However, he observes that, according to its letter, the *Wissenschaftslehre* is a "failure," given how freedom, which is the "characteristic mark of rationality," "appears" in its various presentations during Fichte's Jena period, namely, as "needy."[81] Rather than tolerate a brutely given and therefore "absolutely incomprehensible" opposition between the I and the not-I, philosophy's "sole concern" must be "to break out of this circle"

[76] Hegel D | GW 4: 12.

[77] On Hegel's commitment to intellectual freedom, see Bowman 2018. For an account of why Hegel's logic is not modeled on the theoretical cognition of what is given, see Werner 2020.

[78] Hegel D | GW 4: 29. Cf. Hegel: "this subject-object [i.e., the Fichtean I] is itself conditioned. Its standpoint is therefore not the highest. It is reason posited in a limited form" (Hegel D | GW 4: 64).

[79] See Jacobi: "*without* that presupposition [of the thing in itself] I could not enter into [Kant's] system, but *with* it I could not stay within it" (Jacobi DH 223 | 1994: 336).

[80] Hegel D | GW 4: 36. Contrast Jacobi's negative assessment of the *Wissenschaftslehre* as positing the I as "the all in all, outside of which there is *nothing*" (Jacobi BF 8 | 1994: 504).

[81] Hegel D | GW 4: 54. In the *Encyclopedia*, Hegel says that the Fichtean I "does not genuinely appear as free, spontaneous activity . . . having been aroused only by a check from outside" (Hegel EL | GW 20: §60 Addition 2). This refers to Fichte's claim in the *Foundations* that while the I determines its "*mode* and *manner*" of representing, "*that*" it represents "at all" is not determined by it, but rather "presuppos[es]" a "check or impetus" from "something or other external to it," namely, the "not-I," whose "reciprocal interaction" with the I is the "ultimate ground of all reality" (Fichte GWL | SW I: 248–9, 279).

of the "incomprehensible element."[82] This alone can vindicate the spirit of the *Wissenschaftslehre*.[83]

Moving to the second step of our analysis, we find that subjectivism prevents the attainment of what Hegel regards as the goal of philosophy, namely, the absolute identity of subject and object. This identity, he says, is the "principle of speculation."[84] We can hear this principle as expressing the standard of "objective" critique from the Introduction to the *Critical Journal*, according to which "reason is but one," not one in a pair, and therefore cognizes itself alone, for such cognition constitutes an identity of subject and object. We can accordingly hear the principle of speculation as expressing a truly radicalized ideal of enlightenment insofar as reason is not one among two and so cognizes nothing distinct and given, that is, nothing that it does not generate from itself. Hegel claims that the speculative identity of subject and object, that is, of "idea and being," is the point where "reflection," with its "style of thinking" in terms of brute or factical dichotomies, "ends" and where philosophy "begins."[85] If the "formal task of philosophy is the sublation of dichotomy," for example, of the allegedly absolute dichotomy between the I and the not-I, then subjectivism is an obstacle to the completion of this task. Indeed, Fichte's system cannot even hope to establish the absolute identity of subject and object, which is nothing other than reason's self-cognition, since, at its very foundation, this system enshrines "the different," namely, the pure consciousness of the I, on the one hand, and the empirical consciousness of the not-I, on the other hand.[86]

In the third step of our analysis, we find that reason nullifies the oppositions of the understanding by sublating their contradictory terms. Whereas the understanding's reflective "style" is to fix certain contradictory terms into rigid oppositions, reason's speculative urge is to sublate such terms, that is, to preserve them while causing their opposition to cease, thereby resolving their contradiction. We will see in Section 3.6 that, in his Nuremberg period, Hegel defines 'sublation' as an act of thinking that both preserves and causes to cease and that he places sublation at the heart of his dialectical method. For now, it is important to see that, according to Hegel in his Jena period, "relative identities" in which, for example, the I's identity depends on its opposition to "matter" and vice versa "can be nothing to philosophy" because they are mere "contingencies," that is, brute facts, which

[82] Hegel D | GW 4: 44.

[83] On the spirit of the *Wissenschaftslehre*, see Jacobi: "A *pure* philosophy, that is, a *thoroughly immanent* philosophy, a philosophy of *one piece*, a veritable *system* of reason, is only possible in the manner of Fichte. Obviously everything must be given in and through reason, in the I as I, in the *selfhood of the I* alone, and must be already contained in it, if pure reason is to be able to deduce everything alone, from itself alone" (Jacobi BF 14 | 1994: 507).

[84] Hegel D | GW 4: 6.

[85] Hegel D | GW 4: 29–30.

[86] Hegel D | GW 4: 62–3.

therefore have no place within cognition construed as an "absolute totality."[87] This is why reason must reject "the absolute fixity that the understanding gives to the dichotomy," for the terms in a dichotomy are limited or "finite" insofar as they are mutually external and mutually impenetrable. Such equally limited terms cannot "embrace totality," but at best constitute a mere aggregate.[88] Reason is the "highest law" of the "totality" or "system" of knowledge because, unlike the understanding, it alone "sublates" the "contradictories" within putatively absolute oppositions.[89]

Insofar as reason's "sole interest" is to "sublate such rigid antitheses" as the understanding posits,[90] it must somehow overcome the understanding. According to Hegel, reason's "secret efficacy" is to make the understanding "boundless" in its pursuit of "thoroughgoing determination." In this pursuit, the understanding "stubbornly" allows opposites to "subsist side by side in their opposition," each determining and thus limiting the other. However, "to posit the one is to cancel the other," for example, the I is only insofar as the not-I is not, and vice versa. Such opposites precisely cannot "subsist" as two in a pair, for each rules out the other. By "fix[ing] these opposites," then, the understanding undermines the stability of their opposition at every turn. The understanding thereby destroys its own absolute oppositions and so "destroys itself." But it is by observing this activity that reason "seduces the understanding into producing an objective totality," that is, a "totality of necessity" in which all allegedly factical oppositions have shown themselves to be unstable and, ultimately, to be self-nullifying.[91]

We can now answer the three questions that arise from the Introduction to the *Critical Journal*. First, subjectivity is the character of the factically dichotomous thinking that excludes an objective totality of necessity, that is, a "system of science" that is free from factical dichotomies.[92] Second, the standard of critique that

[87] Hegel D | GW 4: 21–2. Hegel distinguishes between "absolute identity," i.e., "the identity of subject and object," and "*pure* identity, i.e., an identity originating through abstraction and conditioned by opposition, the abstract intellectual concept of unity, one of a pair of fixed opposites" (Hegel D | GW 4: 18–9).

[88] Hegel D | GW 4: 14, 22.

[89] Hegel D | GW 4: 23. As Hegel puts the point, whereas a "transcendent" identity is one in which "the absolute contradiction of the opposites would be meant to subsist," leaving these opposites accidentally united, a "transcendental" identity is one in which this contradiction is "sublated" and a "true synthesis" is constructed from its component terms (Hegel D | GW 4: 38).

[90] Hegel D | GW 4: 13.

[91] Hegel D | GW 4: 17–8. Cf. Hegel's claim in the *Phenomenology* that "knowing" is the "cunning that, while seeming to abstain from activity, looks on and watches how determinateness, with its concrete life, just where it fancies it is pursuing its own self-preservation and particular interest, is in fact doing the very opposite, is an activity that results in its own dissolution, and makes itself a moment of the whole" (Hegel PG | W 3: 53–4). Cf. also Hegel's 1830–31 Berlin lectures on the philosophy of world history: "Particular interests contend with one another, and some are destroyed in the process. But it is from this very conflict and destruction of particular things that the universal emerges, and it remains unscathed itself. For it is not the universal idea which enters into opposition, conflict, and danger; it keeps itself in the background, untouched and unharmed, and sends forth the particular interests of passion to fight and wear themselves out in its stead. It is what we may call the cunning of reason that it sets the passions to work in its service, so that the agents by which it gives itself existence must pay the penalty and suffer the loss" (Hegel VPW2 | 1975: 89).

[92] See Hegel: "philosophy's task [consists in] sublating the dichotomy" (Hegel D | GW 4: 64).

transcends persons and things is the speculative principle of the identity of subject and object that is expressed by reason's self-cognition, which cognition is exclusively rational as opposed to historical and which alone comprehends the objective totality that characterizes science. Third, reason's self-cognition emerges from the understanding's unwitting destruction of its own fixed dichotomies and, indeed, of itself.

Having answered these questions by providing a three-step analysis of Hegel's subjectivism charge against Fichte in the *Difference* essay, I will now provide the same analysis for "Faith and Knowledge."

3.4 Facticity and the Philosophy of Subjectivity

As before, our three-step analysis will show that 'subjectivism' names the problem of factical opposition, which is a problem that prevents the attainment of the absolute identity of subject and object and whose solution is the nullification of all opposition. Moreover, we will see that, in "Faith and Knowledge," which appears in the *Critical Journal*, Hegel locates Fichte's subjectivist error at the pinnacle of what the text's subtitle announces is the "Complete Range" of the "Forms" of the "Philosophy of Subjectivity," preceded only by Kant and Jacobi.

In the Introduction, Hegel observes that, following "earlier times" during which philosophy is the "handmaid" of religion, "[e]nlightened reason" secures victory over religious faith. However, after this victory, reason's foe "is no longer religion" and, indeed, reason "is no longer reason." This is because reason has "become mere understanding," namely, by reviving, in reflective fashion, "the old distinction" between reason and an absolute that is "beyond" it and in which it can only have mere "*faith*." According to Hegel, it is "the *philosophies of Kant, Jacobi, and Fichte*," which he identifies with what "is now called German philosophy," that preside over reason's relegation to faithfully longing for an absolute that, as "a fixed realm of the incomprehensible," renders this faithful longing "non-rational."[93] The "fundamental principle common to the[se] philosophies" transforms the "old distinction" between reason and the absolute into an "absolute antithesis of finitude and infinity," namely, the finitude of a longing reason and the infinitude of an absolute beyond. However, Hegel observes that this "fundamental principle" itself conceals "the absoluteness of finitude," since "if infinity is thus set up against finitude, each is as finite as the other" insofar as each is limited by the other.[94] The philosophies of subjectivity absolutize the opposition between the finitude of reason and the infinitude of the absolute and hence absolutize their common limitedness and thus

[93] Hegel GuW | GW 4: 315–6, 320, 375. On the role of Hegel's distinction between the understanding and reason in his resolution of Kant's antinomies, see Kreines 2015 and Winegar 2016.

[94] Hegel GuW | GW 4: 321–2. Cf. Hegel GuW | GW 4: 383.

their common "finitude." These philosophies consequently fall short of the "idea," according to which finitude itself "vanish[es]," namely, when, ultimately, "finite and infinite are one."[95] Before turning to the third of these philosophies, namely, Fichte's philosophy, it is instructive to review the first two.

In Chapter 1, "Kantian Philosophy," Hegel describes Kant's subjectivism as an "antithesis" between "the I" and "the thing in itself," which are "completely heterogeneous" and "exist each for itself." This brute opposition abandons the "absolute identity" of subject and object by rendering them "only formally" identical in accordance with the unity of the apperceptive I, which, via the forms of the faculties of cognition, combines representations to which sensible matter must be given externally to the I, namely, by the thing in itself. Hence Hegel says that "transcendental idealism" thereby "passe[s]" into "formal or, more properly, psychological idealism," that is, an idealism that presupposes a "dualism" of form and matter, where matter's givenness is "incomprehensible," that is, "a *plus*," "something empirical," and "something alien."[96] Such a dualism expresses the factically dichotomous thinking of the understanding that, as we saw, is the root cause of subjectivism. Hegel clarifies that the "double meaning" of Kantian subjectivism includes the "quite correct meaning" that the understanding posits the "abstraction of finitude," whereby opposites are fixed in relations of mutual limitation, but "also the other meaning," namely, that finitude is specifically "absolute in humans."[97] This clarification draws the factical dichotomy of form and matter into a wider context of various presupposed Kantian dichotomies that includes the distinction between human or discursive understanding and divine or intuitive understanding, but also related distinctions between possibility and actuality, concept and intuition, and sensible intuition and intellectual intuition.[98] Thus, whereas Fichte launches

[95] Hegel GuW | GW 4: 324.

[96] Hegel GuW | GW 4: 331, 333, 343. Cf. Hegel: "Inwardly, then, the understanding is, and should be, a speculative idea, inasmuch as universal and particular are one in it. For the positing of the opposites in the judgment should be *a priori*, i.e., necessary and universal, which is to say that the opposites should be absolutely identical. But the matter comes to rest with the 'should.' For as opposed to empirical sensibility, this thinking [as conceived by Kant] is once more [only] an [activity of] understanding. The entire deduction is [merely] an analysis of experience and it posits an absolute antithesis and a dualism" (Hegel GuW | GW 4: 334).

[97] Hegel GuW | GW 4: 334. On Hegel's subjectivism charge against Kant in "Faith and Knowledge," see Longuenesse 2007: 165–217 and Sedgwick 2012. Cf. de Boer 2011 on Hegel's subjectivism charge against Kant in the *Science of Logic*.

[98] See Kant KU | AA 5: 401–8. In 1802's "On Criticism's Endeavour to Reduce Reason to the Understanding and Give Philosophy in General a New Purpose," Jacobi detects factical elements in Kant's philosophy while repeating his accusation of nihilism: "Kantian philosophy is the ideal of empiricism. The two chemical binding agents, form and substance, are factically given, factically taken, and factically processed in the melting pot. Sensibility arrives at its pure forms as some men arrive at their official dress, without knowing how, and in its good-naturedness is continually teased and ridiculed by the treacherous things in themselves. The things in themselves are real humorists, they get away from under our hands, and we respectable school systematists constantly claim that they are still there because they could not have gotten away, for where would they have gone? The understanding presents us with its document of investiture in the table of categories, but when we question it about the peculiarity of the same and about the way in which it lends the unity of its apperception of sensibility precisely through this number of theses, it is unable to explain its own privilege. We must therefore

a revolutionary campaign against facticity within the ranks of the forms of the faculties of cognition, namely, sensibility, understanding, and reason, Hegel envisions an unwavering extension of this campaign to the most basic oppositions that define transcendental idealism, prefiguring his assertion in the *Encyclopedia* that "[a]ll . . . presuppositions or assumptions must equally be given up when we enter into the science."[99]

In Chapter 2, "Jacobian Philosophy," Hegel describes Jacobi's subjectivism as "presuppos[ing] straight off, in the spirit of the most vulgar empiricism," a "community" between "a thing that senses," namely, consciousness, and "a thing that is sensed," namely, the object, the "unanalyzed and absolute assumption" of which community is a brute fact from which "all speculation must recoil." By regarding sensing consciousness and sensed object as absolutely opposed and thus equally finite things, Jacobi indulges the "absolute dogmatism" of "the elevation of the finite to an in-itself." Indeed, whereas Kant has the "immortal merit" of recognizing that appearances, whose representations the apperceptive I combines, are "nothing at all *in themselves*," Jacobi succumbs to dogmatic slumber by positing consciousness and object as mutually external and mutually impenetrable things in themselves, each with irreducibly intrinsic properties. Hegel remarks that "[w]ith this dream as his weapon, [Jacobi] fights Spinoza wide awake," evoking Jacobi's defense of the intrinsic properties of conscious subjects and of objects against the nihilistic consequence of their Spinozistic reduction to modes of nature that are infinitely determined by external conditions.[100] While Jacobi finds it "horrifying" that Spinozism "negate[s]" the "absoluteness" of consciousness and objects by reducing them to "nothing in themselves," that is, to "appearances and ghosts," Hegel claims that his "abhorrence" is as "fixed," that is, as brute or groundless, as his "absolute certainty of the finite."[101] Moreover, to Jacobi's argument that, because an object is "not

recognize sensibility in its pure dignity of form, things in themselves in their hybrid nature between ghost and body, and the understanding with its occupancy right, for they do indeed appear before our eyes in this way. But how on earth, without the gift of divination, could we have suspected this strange society in advance, only in a dream? Their empirical appearance can certainly please us, but it is not necessary to demand that we find the only instructive thing in them, for otherwise there may be many an absent form-bearer, witty mind, and feudal lord whose association and dealings give us as much to think about and of which we had just as little idea *a priori*. If a philosophy is empiricism in its foundations, then at the same time all *a priori* halo is nihilism, and the act of canonization will only be valid in a country where, according to the report of the printed works published there, one believes in a chosen, visible governor of the invisible philosophical church" (Jacobi UK | 2004: 319–20, my translation).

[99] Hegel EL | GW 20: §78.

[100] Hegel GuW | GW 4: 350, 352. See Jacobi LS 14 | 1994: 187, Jacobi DH 173–4 | 1994: 317–8, and Jacobi BF 3–5 | 1994: 502–3.

[101] Hegel GuW | GW 4: 351, 374. Jacobi's certainty extends to what Hegel calls the "eternal verities" about one's body and one's consciousness of others (Hegel GuW | GW 4: 377). See Jacobi: "Through faith we know that we have a body, and that there are other bodies and other thinking beings outside us. A veritable and wondrous revelation! For in fact we only sense our body, as constituted in this way or that; but in thus feeling it, we become aware not only of its alterations, but of something else as well, totally different from it, which is neither mere sensation nor thought; we become aware of *other actual*

allowed to lose the character of a datum, of being immovably opposite to the subject that thinks it," consciousness can only receive it via "supernatural revelation," Hegel objects, in an acknowledgment of Kant's "immortal merit," that an object is "*always already synthesized*" by consciousness in accordance with the "universal validity that belongs to scientific knowledge."[102] Left to his absolute opposition, however, Jacobi, not unlike Kant, reduces reason to faith in the absoluteness of things.[103]

Turning to Hegel's subjectivism charge against Fichte in "Faith and Knowledge," we find that it has the same form that it does in the *Difference* essay. In Chapter 3, "Fichtean Philosophy," Hegel describes Fichte's subjectivism as "beginning with the antithesis [of positing and oppositing]," that is, with the absolute opposition between the I and the not-I. Referring to the *Foundations*, he describes the I as "contain[ing] nothing but formal identity" and as "confronted" by the limitation or "finitude" of its opposition to a not-I that is "alien," "external and posterior" to it and whose reality it accordingly leaves "unexplained."[104] Hegel once again rightly surmises that, in this text, the not-I *qua* matter brutely opposes the I *qua* "highest form" when he claims that the I "does not alter the common and incomprehensible necessity of empirical existence in the slightest," but rather "supervenes incomprehensibly" on "something alien" that "does not originate" in it. Moreover, he rightly evokes from the *Foundations* the equiprimordiality of the I and the not-I when he claims that the "manifoldness of reality appears as an incomprehensible primitive fact, an empirical necessity,"[105] where, as we saw in Section 1.6, "empirical" for Hegel denotes the character of radically contingent or brute givenness in the way that 'inductive' does for Fichte.

Hegel not only captures the absolute opposition at the heart of the *Foundations*, but he also grasps the same in the *New Presentation*. In the First Introduction to that text, as we saw in Section 1.6, Fichte claims that one abstracts from experience in order to posit its first principle or explanatory ground, where an idealist posits the I and a dogmatist posits the not-I. Hegel observes that the idealist presupposes

things, and of that with the very same certainty with which we become aware of ourselves, for without the *thou*, the *I* is impossible" (Jacobi LS 163 | 1994: 231). Cf. Jacobi DH 31n9, 65 | 1994: 267n9, 277.

[102] Hegel GuW | GW 4: 371, 375.

[103] See Jacobi LS 162–3 | 1994: 230 and Jacobi DH v–vi | 1994: 256. Cf. Hegel: "It is hardly deniable that Jacobi's and Kant's common achievement was to have put an end to the metaphysics of the older school and thus to have established the necessity of a complete revision of logic. Jacobi thus initiated a new era in German philosophy and (since outside of Germany philosophy has degenerated to the point of extinction) in the history of philosophy as a whole. However, his contribution to knowledge goes no further than that, for whereas Kant cemented his *negative* result in opposition to the finite forms of knowledge, Jacobi cemented it against *knowledge in and for itself*. He abstained from taking the further step of replacing the understanding by reason and *spirit* as the *soul of cognition*, and having cognition born again in reason and spirit and baptized in the spirit after having before been baptized in the water of the understanding" (Hegel JW | GW 15: 25).

[104] Hegel GuW | GW 4: 388, 390, 396–7.

[105] Hegel GuW | GW 4: 389.

the "alien other," namely, the experiential world, from which they must abstract for the sake of positing the "pure knowing" of the I as this other's explanatory ground.[106] But then the act of abstraction permanently opposes the I to a world of experience from which it is abstracted and with which it strives for a reflectively unattainable point of identity that would "complet[e]" it. As Hegel says, beginning, as Fichte does, with the mutual limitation or "finitude" of the I and the world of experience "makes it impossible for the birth of cognition to be [the construction of] a genuine whole, for a genuine whole is only possible where no part exists in itself."[107] Moreover, as we also saw in Section 1.6, Fichte regards one's "decision" to abstract either the I or nature as first principle as "determined by *inclination* and *interest*." This decision is radically contingent on one's character. Hence Hegel observes not only that "intellectual intuition" of the I as first principle "[a]bstract[s] from everything alien in consciousness," but also that this act of abstraction is a brute "contingency" of character, one that Fichte renders "methodical," namely, by making it the way in which one satisfies philosophy's anti-nihilism criterion, but "without diminishing its contingency... in the least."[108]

In "Faith and Knowledge," just as in the *Difference* essay, Hegel's subjectivism charge against Fichte contrasts subjectivism with a certain kind of objectivity whose absence from the *Wissenschaftslehre* shows that the letter of this system fails the enlightenment ideal and hence fails itself. I will consider these points in turn.

Regarding objectivity, Hegel says of the factical opposition that defines subjectivism that "it does not matter" whether we regard the experiential world from which we abstract when positing a first principle "as ideal or as real."[109] The objectivity that subjectivism lacks accordingly does not concern the alleged reality of one term within a factical dichotomy, but rather is one that expunges factical dichotomy as such from the totality or system of science. As Hegel says in the Conclusion, what he now calls the "metaphysics of subjectivity" in the philosophies of Kant, Jacobi, and Fichte exhibits "the dogmatism of thinking" whereby, within a dichotomy, mutually limiting "finitudes" oppose each other in their "absoluteness," whereas it is the task of "true philosophy" to "nullify" any such presupposed absoluteness.[110]

[106] Hegel GuW | GW 4: 392.
[107] Hegel GuW | GW 4: 393.
[108] Hegel GuW | GW 4: 390–1.
[109] Hegel GuW | GW 4: 394. Cf. Hegel: "A defect of Schelling's philosophy is that the point of indifference of the subjective and the objective is presupposed, not proved. This proof could only be carried out by investigating the subjective and the objective each on its own account in its logical determinations, namely, in its essential determinations. From this investigation it then must follow that the subjective is self-transforming, that it does not remain subjective but makes itself objective, and that the objective is what does not remain objective but makes itself subjective. The result would thus be that each makes itself into its opposite, and only the identity of the two is the truth ... There must therefore be two fundamental sciences: the embodiment of everything objective is called nature, and that of everything subjective is the I, or intelligence. Either the one or the other can be made the starting point, and this must happen to each [in turn]—the I must be made the first principle, and nature as well" (Hegel VGP3 | V 9: 182–3).
[110] Hegel GuW | GW 4: 413.

Regarding the enlightenment ideal, Hegel says that the age of enlightenment restricts "positive knowledge" to "the finite and empirical" and thus restricts it to "the subjectivity of longing" for a factically opposed absolute in a "realm beyond" such knowledge. He observes that this restriction, since it reduces reason to dichotomously "renounc[ing]" and "excluding" the absolute, signals "the death of philosophy" and yet perversely has become "the zenith of philosophy."[111] On the one hand, philosophy's "zenith" is taken to consist in inheriting unquestioned oppositions, for example, between reason and the absolute. On the other hand, clinging to inherited oppositions is philosophy's "death" insofar as it "exalt[s]" the understanding over reason. Thus, the subjectivism that is "now called German philosophy" completes what, in the Introduction to the *Critical Journal*, he calls the "unphilosophy and unscientificity" whereby an information age clings to the inheritance of fixed distinctions. As the pinnacle of the philosophy of subjectivity, it is Fichte who oversees this completion. But the subordination of reason to the understanding, which Fichte exhibits by absolutely opposing the I to the not-I, demonstrates the failure of realizing the ideal of enlightenment, according to which reason's cognition is rational, not historical, that is, generated from itself, not dependent on brutely given facts.[112]

Regarding the gist of the *Wissenschaftslehre*, although Fichte regards reason or the I as absolutely self-sufficient, Hegel claims that it is "conditioned by something else," namely, the not-I that opposes it. The I's "absolute deficiency" here consists in its being "nothing but a part" of a brute composition of opposites. Although Fichte construes the I's "infinite possibility of wealth" as its being the deductive source of *a priori* forms, this ignores what Hegel calls the I's "infinite poverty," namely, the "acknowledged incompleteness" of its being one in a pair. Worse yet, the I can never produce a complete or unconditioned deduction, that is, a set of absolutely necessary categories, since the I's deduction rests on its own incompleteness and conditionality relative to the opposing not-I, a reflective and therefore "problematic style of philosophizing" that "simply does not resolve into a genuine identity."[113] "But

[111] Hegel GuW | GW 4: 316.

[112] See Hegel: "This reason which first recognizes itself in the object finds expression in the empty idealism which grasps reason only as it first comes on the scene; and fancies that by pointing out this pure 'mine' of consciousness in all being, and by declaring all things to be sensations or ideas, it has demonstrated this 'mine' of consciousness to be complete reality . . . This idealism therefore becomes the same kind of self-contradictory ambiguity as skepticism, except that, while this expresses itself negatively, the former does so positively; but it fails equally with skepticism to bring together its contradictory thoughts of pure consciousness being all reality, while the extraneous impulse or sensations and ideas are equally reality. Instead of bringing them together, it shifts from one to the other, and is caught up in the spurious, i.e., the sensuous, infinite . . . It is involved in a direct contradiction; it asserts essence to be a duality of opposed factors, the *unity of apperception* and equally a *thing*; whether the thing is called an extraneous impulse, or an empirical or sensuous entity, or the thing-in-itself, it still remains in principle the same, i.e., extraneous to that unity" (Hegel PG | W 3: 184–5).

[113] Hegel GuW | GW 4: 390–1, 397. Cf. Hegel: "Fichte's formal cognition . . . does not begin with the whole, but proceeds from the parts to other parts; so it cannot transcend its partiality . . . The task of constructing identity and integration simply cannot be performed" (Hegel GuW | GW 4: 393, 402).

then," Hegel says, since the I "shows itself immediately to be the principle of deduction only because it is strictly incomplete and finite, its truth and certainty are of a kind that is rejected by philosophy. For philosophy can only find truth and certainty in what is not incomplete, not an abstraction, not conditioned."[114] Crucially, Hegel does not illegitimately impose the desiderata of completeness, concreteness, and unconditionality on the *Wissenschaftslehre*, for they constitute its spirit, which Fichte betrays by articulating its letter on the basis of a factical opposition.

Once again, our first step in analyzing Hegel's subjectivism charge against Fichte shows that it targets facticity. Indeed, when Hegel says that philosophy is "denuded of all reason" if its "principle" is the "absolute non-identity" of subject and object,[115] we can hear "non-identity" as denoting the terms of any factical opposition whose presupposition deprives philosophy of the self-cognition that belongs to reason. Fichte's system is the culmination of the philosophy of subjectivity precisely because it begins by presupposing the non-identity of the I and the not-I, that is, by enshrining "the different" at its very ground.[116]

In the second step of our analysis, we find again that what subjectivism undermines is the speculative identity of subject and object. Hegel infers from the "incomprehensible primitive fact" of the not-I and from the I's inability to "alter" the "incomprehensible necessity" of the not-I "in the slightest" that Fichte's system cannot secure "a genuine ideality of actuality." Since the not-I's matter is brutely given to the I's form, the I is not absolutely spontaneous in cognizing actuality. But then it cannot render actuality fully ideal, that is, fully intelligible in terms of the I's own activity. Crucially, Hegel describes Fichte's "formalism" as providing "so-called idealistic knowledge," implying that it fails to provide genuinely idealistic knowledge.[117] Genuine idealism would be such that reason or the I is not given any matter whatsoever, but rather generates matter from its own form. Genuine idealism would accordingly provide cognition of a speculative identity of subject and object. Moreover, and just as crucially, Hegel describes Fichte's "abstract[ion]" of the I from an "alien other" as an act of "so-called intellectual intuition," registering the "deficiency" of positing the I as "just one part" in an absolute opposition. By contrast, "genuine intellectual intuition" would be cognition that begins with the I as an "absolute [that] is neither a part nor incomplete," that is, as a form that wholly generates its own matter.[118] Genuine intellectual intuition would accordingly cognize a speculative identity of subject and object.

[114] Hegel GuW | GW 4: 390–1.
[115] Hegel GuW | GW 4: 404.
[116] See Gardner 2013: 124.
[117] Hegel GuW | GW 4: 389.
[118] Hegel GuW | GW 4: 391–2. Cf. Hegel: "Now since Jacobi dismisses the *mediation* inherent in cognition and fails to see how it restitutes itself as the essential moment *within* the nature of spirit itself, his *consciousness of absolute spirit* remains fixated in the form of *immediate*, merely *substantial knowledge*. The sole content of Spinoza's simple, fundamental intuition is substantiality. Now if the intuition of the absolute knows itself to be intellectual, i.e., cognitive intuition, and if furthermore its object is no longer

Finally, in the third step of our analysis, we find again that reason nullifies the absolute oppositions of the understanding. The philosophy of subjectivity fails to be genuinely idealistic because it presupposes a factical dichotomy, the consequence of which is that the I cannot be absolute and, hence, that actuality cannot be ideality. According to Hegel, "[p]hilosophy is idealism" only when it "does not acknowledge either of the opposites," namely, the I and the not-I, "as existing for itself in its abstraction from the other," but instead considers each to be "nothing" on its own.[119] By nullifying the contradictory terms of an absolute opposition, genuine idealism is able to grasp their identity in a higher unity. Hegel will eventually conceive of nullification in terms of the sublation of contradiction. However, he concludes "Faith and Knowledge" by describing nullification as the process of sinking "finitude," to which the contradictory terms of an absolute opposition are restricted in virtue of their mutual limitation, into the "abyss of nothingness." It is through the "harsh consciousness of loss" that "encompass[es] everything" that is finite that the "highest totality," namely, a system of science that is free from factical dichotomy, can emerge in "the most serene freedom of its shape."[120]

To conclude our analysis of the subjectivism charge, it is worth noting that Hegel connects the nullification of finitude with nihilism in a way that underscores the gap between the letter and the spirit of the *Wissenschaftslehre*.

In Chapter 1, Hegel acknowledges that the idea that, in philosophy, finitude is "consume[d] and consummate[d]" and the "actual and temporal as such disappear" is "called cruel dissection destructive of the wholeness of humanity," "violent abstraction that has no truth, and particularly no practical truth," and "the painful cutting off of an essential part from the completeness of the whole."[121] Here Hegel implicitly evokes Jacobi's indictment of the philosopher's imperative, which is to annihilate finitude by subordinating reason's perceptual faith in the immediacy of finite beings to the understanding's inferential certainty in the infinite conditions that mediate our access to such beings. As we saw in Section 2.6, the

substance in its motionless rigidity, but spirit, then it would also be necessary that knowledge dispense with the leftover form of substantiality, namely, the form of immediacy" (Hegel JW | GW 15: 13).

[119] Hegel GuW | GW 4: 325.

[120] Hegel GuW | GW 4: 413–4. Cf. Hegel: "In true faith [however], the whole sphere of finitude, of being something-on-[one's]-own-account, the sphere of sensibility sinks into nothing before the thinking and intuiting of the eternal. The thinking here becomes one with the intuiting, and all the midges of subjectivity are burned to death in this consuming fire, and *the very consciousness* of this surrender and nullification is nullified" (Hegel GuW | GW 4: 379). Cf. also Hegel: "The idealism of philosophy consists in nothing else than in the recognition that the finite is not truly an existent. Every philosophy is essentially idealism or at least has idealism for its principle, and the question then is only how far this principle is carried out" (Hegel WL | GW 21: 142). And cf. Hegel's claim that although the "great merit" of Spinozistic thinking is "the foundation of every authentic view," namely, the "renunciation of everything determinate and particular, and its orientation solely to the One," on the one hand, it leaves the One "fixed and immobile" and, on the other hand, it represents the particular "without being justified," that is, without "deduc[ing] or deriv[ing]" it from the One (Hegel VGP3 | V 9: 105).

[121] Hegel GuW | GW 4: 324.

annihilation of finitude is the nihilistic consequence of any philosophy, whether it takes the form of Spinozism, which reduces objects to causally necessitated modes of nature and thus to what, in the *Doctrine of Spinoza*, Jacobi calls "*non-entia*," or the form of idealism, which reduces objects to rationally necessitated acts of the I and thus is systematically represented by what, in the open letter, he calls Fichte's "*inverted* Spinozism."[122] Spinozism and its Fichtean inversion share the nihilistic consequence that finite things, in virtue of their systematic explicability by infinite external conditions, whether these are modes of nature or modes of consciousness, lack intrinsic capacities and properties, for example, freedom and purposiveness. In other words, finite things are determinable strictly as negations of the infinite, whether the infinite is nature or consciousness, on which they are ultimately conditioned.[123] After implicitly evoking Jacobi in Chapter 1, Hegel explicitly evokes him in Chapter 2 when he says that Jacobi "screams blue murder" about any philosophy, whether Spinoza's or Fichte's, that must bring finitude "to nothing."[124]

However, in Chapter 3, Hegel argues that Jacobi's nihilism charge against Fichte is ironically misguided. Jacobi defends the intrinsic properties of finite things by locating "*the true*" of finitude "*prior to* and *outside of*" the systems of conditions that compose philosophical "*truth*." It is on the basis of his distinction between the true and truth that he asserts that Fichte "sins against" the "majesty" of the true by grounding the intelligibility of things on the I such that "[n]othing must remain" in things "which is not our activity" of philosophically constructing the truth.[125] Hegel objects that although Jacobi "violently abhors the nihilism he finds in Fichte's philosophy," Fichte is "very far from sinning" against the true and, "on this point," is even "in full agreement" with Jacobi. This is because the I is a brute fact along with the not-I, that is, a "*correlatum*" within an opposition that "cannot be absolutely nullified." In other words, the I is a "*relatum*" in an "antithesis" with the not-I insofar as "fate has forged the pair of them together" into a factical dichotomy. But if neither the I nor the not-I is explanatorily reducible, then each exhibits the irreducible finitude of mutually limiting brute facts. It follows from this that Fichte is "as little able to transcend dualism as Jacobi could possibly want," which is to say that he is unable to consistently endorse a monism that is grounded on the I.[126] Hence Hegel says that "[n]othing could be plainer than the fact that Jacobi has misunderstood [the *Wissenschaftslehre*] when he says in his 'Letter to

[122] Jacobi BF 4 | 1994: 502.

[123] On Spinoza's phrase "*determinatio negatio est* [determination is negation]" in his letter to Jarig Jelles, June 2, 1674 (Spinoza 2002: 892), and its appropriation by post-Kantians including Hegel, who reformulates the phrase as "*omnis determinatio est negatio* [every determination is negation]" in his review of Jacobi's *Works* (Hegel JW | GW 15: 10), see Melamed 2012 and Stern 2016.

[124] Hegel GuW | GW 4: 377.

[125] Jacobi BF viii, 16 | 1994: 499, 508.

[126] Hegel GuW | GW 4: 397–9. See Jacobi: "the two main avenues, materialism and idealism, or the attempt to explain everything from a self-determining matter alone or from a self-determining intelligence, have the same aim . . . [A]part from dualism there is only egoism" (Jacobi BF 3 | 1994: 502). Cf. Jacobi LS 185 | 1994: 239.

Fichte' that he believes that the Fichtean way produced 'a philosophy of *one piece*, a veritable *system* of reason, [which] is only possible in the manner of Fichte.'"[127]

Thus, although Hegel ironically agrees with Jacobi that "nihilism is certainly implicit in pure thought as a task" insofar as Hegel himself affirms that the "first step in philosophy is to recognize the absolute nothing" in finitude, he rightly observes that "Fichte's philosophy does not achieve this, however much Jacobi may despise it," because, as philosophers of subjectivity, "both of [Fichte and Jacobi] dwell in the nothing that is the opposite of philosophy," namely, the nothing of the brutely true.[128] Fichte therefore fails to embrace the nihilism that, according to Hegel, philosophy sets as a "task" in response to the bruteness of finitude, that is, to the facticity of absolutely opposed and thus mutually limiting brute facts. However, whereas, with its vestigial facticity, the letter of the *Wissenschaftslehre* demonstrates the irony of Jacobi's nihilism charge, its spirit, as we have seen, demands reason's absolute freedom, that is, reason's unlimited power to eliminate facticity in all of its guises, whether as a form of a faculty of cognition such as space and time, a first principle that is contingent on inclination and interest, or an absolute opposition between the I and the not-I.

In a letter to Jens Baggessen, April/May 1795, Fichte declares:

> Mine is the first system of freedom. Just as France has freed man from external shackles, so my system frees him from the fetters of things in themselves, which is to say, from those external influences with which all previous systems—including the Kantian—have more or less fettered man. Indeed, the first principle of my system presents man as an independent being.[129]

This declaration expresses the gist of the *Wissenschaftslehre*. However, Fichte leaves reason or the I unfree concerning its opposition to the not-I, which it cannot derive, but which it presupposes as a brute fact, thereby restricting rational cognition, that is, the cognition that is proper to philosophy. Indeed, as we saw in Section 2.5, Fichte explicitly affirms the "absolute" or "*primordial facticity*" of the I in the 1804 Berlin lectures after genetically deducing the I's essence and existence from the I itself, which latter, in line with the *Foundations* and the *New Presentation*, he regards as a strict limitation on deduction. Hegel's subjectivism charge thus rightly attacks Fichte for not radicalizing his own deductive method, which alone would vindicate a "system of freedom."

In his 1825–26 Berlin lectures on the history of philosophy, Hegel offers a summary of Fichte's contribution to modern philosophy, a summary that combines the

[127] Hegel GuW | GW 4: 397, corrected citation from Jacobi BF 14 | 1994: 507.

[128] Hegel GuW | GW 4: 398. Cf. Hegel's critique of Jacobi's doctrine of immediate knowledge in the *Encyclopedia*'s "Preliminary Conception," on which see Westphal 1989.

[129] Breazeale 1994: vii–n1.

early charge of subjectivism from the *Difference* essay and "Faith and Knowledge" with the late praise of a logical turn from the *Encyclopedia*. In Section D, "Recent Philosophy: Kant, Fichte, Jacobi, Schelling," he says:

> Kant adopted the thought-determinations, the categories, empirically, just as they have been worked out in [traditional] logic, that is, just as the universal forms are found in the [table of] judgments. This procedure is empirical and philosophically unjustified. Fichte went beyond this, and that is his great merit. He called for, and sought to complete, the derivation or construction of the categories of thought from the I, and he did in part carry out this project . . . Fichte also posited philosophical consciousness or the aim of philosophy as the knowing of knowing. For that reason he called his philosophy the *Wissenschaftslehre* or the knowing of our knowing. And here 'knowing' means our activity or our knowing within the categories. Fichte *constructed* the categories as follows. The I is what is first . . . The second thesis is that I posit a not-I, an object, in opposition to myself . . . Fichte says this second thesis is just as absolute as the first . . . Fichte now seeks more precisely to derive from [the I] the particular categories in their necessity. That is what is important in Fichte's philosophy. No one else since Aristotle has thought about how to exhibit the determinations of thinking in their necessity . . . We can see, however, that his presentation is from the outset burdened with an antithesis—in Kant it was the I and the representation, and then the thing-in-itself; in Fichte it is the I and the not-I . . . [A]part from thinking, human beings are also dependent and finite, but we must not seek to carry this dependence over into reason, into thinking. [If we do,] then infinitude too can be very abstract, and in this way it too is finite in its turn . . . For Fichte the I is infinite, it is thinking. But this I finds that it is together with a not-I. It is an absolute contradiction that the I, which is supposed to be utterly alone with itself—this I that is defined as being utterly free—is now said to be together with another. In Fichte's thought the resolution of the contradiction is a resolution only called for [and not one achieved]. It remains a kind of resolution in which the I can constantly sublate the boundary but in which there always remains a limit, beyond which it can go forth once more, and so on *ad infinitum*, namely, into the bad infinite.[130]

Just as Kant charges Aristotle with rhapsodically deriving the categories only to have Fichte return the charge to him, so Hegel returns the charge to Fichte.[131]

[130] Hegel VGP3 | V 9: 157–62.

[131] Cf. Hegel: "since Aristotle, [logic] has taken no backward step, but also none forward, the latter because to all appearances it seems to be finished and complete. If logic has not undergone change since Aristotle . . . then surely the conclusion to be drawn is that it is all the more in need of a total reworking" (Hegel WL | GW 21: 25). Cf. also Hegel: "Just as the Kantian philosophy did not consider the categories in and for themselves, but declared them to be finite determinations unfit to hold the truth, on the only inappropriate ground that they are subjective forms of self-consciousness, still less did it subject to criticism the forms of the concepts that make up the content of ordinary logic. What it did, rather, is to pick a portion of them, namely, the functions of judgments, for the determination of categories, and simply

Fichte's "great merit" is recognizing that the "philosophically unjustified" appeal to "empirically" observed "[traditional] logic" undermines Kant's answer to the question *quid facti* and calls for a renewed metaphysical deduction. The cognition of how we know from "within the categories" must be an active and generative "knowing," not a passive and imitative observing, which is to say that this cognition must be rational, not historical. This requires that we "carry" no "dependence" or "finit[ude]" over "into reason," for rational cognition requires that reason is not "together with another," that is, not saddled with a brute datum, but rather is "utterly alone" and thus "utterly free," that is, lacking any external imposition. As the Introduction to the *Critical Journal* states, reason is but one, not one in a pair. But since the *Wissenschaftslehre* begins with a second principle that is "just as absolute as the first," namely, the not-I, it is "burdened with an antithesis," that is, with a factical dichotomy. Fichte's method of resolving what he explicitly acknowledges is the contradiction between the I and the not-I is the endless pursuit of what Hegel calls "the bad infinite." We will now see why bad infinity is a logical consequence of the commitment to facticity that defines subjectivism.

3.5 Bad Infinity

Hegel first uses the term 'bad infinity' in The Doctrine of Being in the *Science of Logic*. In Section I, Chapter 2, "Existence," he claims that it is "essential to distinguish the true concept of infinity from bad infinity, the infinite of reason from the infinite of the understanding," because the latter "is in fact a *finitized* infinite." Hegel evokes the early Jena texts by aligning true infinity with reason and bad infinity with the understanding. Whereas speculative identification characterizes reason's activity, reflective opposition characterizes the understanding's activity. We have seen that the contradictory terms in an absolute opposition of the understanding, by virtue of limiting each other, are equally finite. Infinity is "bad," then, if it is brutely opposed to and so mutually limited by something, for it is in this sense "*finitized*." Moreover, insofar as something finite, namely, reason, might transcend itself in order to attain something infinite, namely, the absolute, their shared finitude, which is the result of being "mere *others* to each other," renders this attainment impossible. This is because "the finite constantly resurfaces" at any stage of progress toward the infinite if the latter is finitized by virtue of its existing relatively

accepted them as valid presuppositions. Even if there were nothing more to the forms of logic than these formal functions of judgment, for that reason alone they would already be worth investigating to see how far, by themselves, they correspond to the *truth*. A logic that does not perform this task can at most claim the value of a natural description of the phenomena of thought as they simply occur. It is an infinite merit of Aristotle, one that must fill us with the highest admiration for the power of his genius, that he was the first to undertake this description. But it is necessary to go further and determine both the systematic connection of these forms and their value" (Hegel WL | GW 12: 28).

or "*with reference* to the finite" that strives for it. As Hegel puts the point, "*the transcending itself*" is never "*transcended*." Consequently, the "true" infinite never exists, but only ever "*ought to be*," which is to say that the "bad infinite is in itself the same as the perpetual *ought*." Hence Hegel claims that "the infinite of the understanding," since it is merely one of "*two* determinacies," is "*itself finite infinite*" and therefore "the *bad infinite*."[132]

Hegel clarifies his claim by distinguishing between the "bad infinite," which "lowers itself" to a determination "over against the finite" whereby the finite and the infinite are "*jointly the finite*," and the "*true infinite*," which "elevates" the distinction between the finite and the infinite to a "self-affirmation" whereby they are "only moments" of the true infinite. The proper image for the bad infinite is "the straight *line*" because, by maintaining a finitizing boundary between mutually limiting terms, it guarantees that the finite's "progression" toward the infinite is an endless repetition of mutual limitation and that its goal is accordingly "unattainable." By contrast, the proper image for the true infinite is "the *circle*" because, by rendering the finite and the infinite "moments" of itself, it excludes mutual limitation between these terms and is accordingly "without *beginning* and *end*." The "*unfulfilled reflections*" of the understanding mire themselves in the linear repetition of the "*contradiction*" between the finite and the infinite because they fail to simultaneously grasp "both" determinations of the true infinite, namely, the "*opposition*" and the "*unity*" of the finite and the infinite. Rather than posit these two determinations as genuinely "*together*," the understanding "lets them only *alternate*," namely, by positing, in one moment, the finite as a cause that draws the infinite into actuality and by positing, in a subsequent moment, the infinite as a cause that draws the finite into action, and so on *ad infinitum*.[133] Holding fast to opposition in this way, the understanding can think only of an antinomy, never of its resolution.

As Wayne Martin shows, although 'bad infinity' does not appear in the *Difference* essay, its concept is at work there, namely, in Hegel's charge that Fichte abandons the principle of speculation, that is, the absolute identity of subject and object. Martin's case rests on three passages from that text.[134] First, Hegel claims that Fichte demands that the I, that is, "reason or the subject = object," exercise "absolute causality" on the not-I, for only this can realize the principle of speculation, yet holds that the I cannot do so, for this would "imply sublating the not-I" to which the I remains primordially opposed. This means that the I's exercise of absolute causality is obligatory yet contradictory. Second, Hegel claims that Fichte's demand is "self-destructive," for it "postulates a union which still must not happen."

[132] Hegel WL | GW 21: 124–7, 129. Cf. Hegel: "the bad infinite . . . finds its restriction in its opposite, in the finitude of each side" (Hegel WL | GW 21: 316).

[133] Hegel WL | GW 21: 135–8. Cf. Hegel: "the truly infinite quantum . . . determines itself as infinite *within*; it is such because, as demonstrated, the finite quantum or the quantum as such and its beyond, the bad infinite, are *equally* sublated" (Hegel WL | GW 21: 241).

[134] Martin 2007: 174–6.

This means that the I's striving is unavoidable yet incompletable. Third, Hegel claims that by opposing the I and the not-I and thereby "surrender[ing] reason to the understanding," Fichte transforms the speculative identity "I = I," which alone exhibits "true infinity," into the reflective identity "I *ought* to be equal to I." This means that the *Wissenschaftslehre* acknowledges yet betrays the principle of speculation.[135] Martin rightly observes that the early term "true infinity" is an indirect correlate of the later term 'bad infinity.'[136] However, this leaves us with two interpretive tasks.

The first task is textual. There are, in fact, direct correlates of 'bad infinity' both in the *Difference* essay and in "Faith and Knowledge." I will draw these correlates from the early Jena texts in order to establish a clearer continuity between them and the *Science of Logic*. The second task is philosophical. Hegel's charge that Fichte abandons the principle of speculation, in which Martin rightly sees the concept of bad infinity at work, is none other than the charge of subjectivism, which Martin explicitly sidesteps.[137] This raises a question of how to understand the connection between subjectivism and bad infinity. I will argue that bad infinity is a logical consequence of subjectivism. Before completing these tasks, however, I will explicate Fichte's theory of the I's striving for absolute identity, which theory provokes Hegel's early charge of the abandonment of speculation.

As we saw in Part I, Fichte consistently adopts a methodological division between intellectually intuiting the I as first principle and genetically deducing the categories from this principle.[138] We can regard intellectual intuition as disclosing the essence of our existence as free and rational, but as not yet disclosing the purpose of our existence, that is, as specifying the formal cause of human experience, but as not yet specifying its final cause. Fichte evokes this causal distinction in the *New Presentation* by drawing a distinction between "the I as an intellectual intuition, with which the *Wissenschaftslehre* commences, and the I as an idea, with which it concludes." As intuition, the I "contains nothing but the form of I-hood," namely, self-activity. As idea, the I represents the ideal of the "completely cultivated" human being, namely, one who "has completely succeeded in exhibiting universal reason" by transcending "the limitations of sensibility." In other words, as intuition, the I is our formal cause, whereas, as idea, it represents our final cause. Fichte clarifies that in neither of these senses is the I considered as "an individual." As intuition, the I "has not yet been determined as individuality," for, *qua* first principle, it is absolutely self-active and not, like an individual person, relatively self-active.[139] As idea, the I represents that which "has vanished as a result of a

[135] Hegel D | GW 4: 6–7, 45–6.
[136] Martin 2007: 176.
[137] Martin 2007: 168.
[138] A version of this discussion appears in Bruno 2023d.
[139] Fichte VND | SW I: 515–6. Cf. Fichte's letter to Jacobi, August 30, 1795: "My *absolute I* is obviously not the individual, though this is how offended courtiers and irate philosophers have interpreted me, in order that they may falsely attribute to me the disgraceful theory of practical egoism. Instead, *the*

process of cultivation," for, *qua* practical ideal, it is a goal for which, *per impossibile*, an individual person no longer must strive.[140] Both non-individual senses of the I thus serve as poles between which our lived individuality is strung. Nevertheless, whereas the I as intuition is the constitutive ground of experience, the I as idea is the regulative goal of experience.

Crucially, Fichte states that since the I as intuition "contains nothing but the form of the I," its categorial "content . . . becomes thinkable only when the I thinks of a world," one whose moral perfection via human cultivation is a practical ideal. This ideal is accordingly "exhibited only within the practical portion of philosophy, where it is shown to be the ultimate aim of reason's striving," but an aim that is "only something to which we ought to draw infinitely nearer" and so "will never become anything real."[141] Fichte's earliest deduction of the necessity of this moral aim appears in the *Foundations*, that is, the text that elicits both Hegel's charge of subjectivism and, as we will see, his use of two direct correlates of 'bad infinity.'

In Part I of the *Foundations*, Fichte discovers that positing the I yields an originary contradiction whose solution is to be achieved not through the deduction of theoretical categories that he attempts in Part II, but ultimately through the deduction of practical categories that he provides in Part III.[142] Both stages of Fichte's deduction make productive use of this originary contradiction and thus proceed according to a pioneering dialectical logic that he develops throughout the Jena period and that, as we saw in Section 1.5, is governed by the principle of determinability.

As we saw in Section 3.3, in Part I of the *Foundations*, §§1–2, Fichte argues that while the I *qua* unity of consciousness provides the form of what is posited, it does not provide the matter, which he instead ascribes to the undeducible not-I. In §3, he says that this analysis yields "two conclusions stand[ing] in opposition to each other." On the one hand, "insofar as the not-I is supposed to be posited, the I must also be posited within [this same] identical consciousness." This is because "all positing . . . presupposes the identity of the I." On the other hand, "[i]nsofar as the

individual must be deduced from the absolute I, and the *Wissenschaftslehre* will immediately proceed to such a deduction in conjunction with its treatment of natural rights" (Fichte B | 1988: 411). Cf. also Fichte: "The word 'self' has frequently been employed of late to designate this same concept ['I']. If my derivation is correct, all the words in the family to which the word 'self' belongs (e.g., 'self-same,' 'the same,' etc.) signify a relationship to something that has already been posited, though insofar as it has been posited *through its mere concept*. If what has been posited is I, then the word 'self' is formed. Hence the word 'self' presupposes the concept of the I, and everything that is thought to be absolute within the former is borrowed from the concept of the latter" (Fichte SW I: 530n). Shortly before, Fichte claims that we can "abstract" from "ourselves," as viewed from "the standpoint of ordinary consciousness," but not from "the I," as viewed from "the philosopher's standpoint" (Fichte SW I: 501–2). On the similarity between Fichte's distinction between ordinary and philosophical abstraction and Kant's distinction between empirical and transcendental externality, see Franks 2016a.

140 Fichte VND | SW I: 516.
141 Fichte VND | SW I: 516.
142 On Fichte's deductions in the *Foundations*, see Förster 2012: 179–229.

not-I is posited, the I is not posited." This is because the not-I materially determines the I and, in this sense, "annul[s]" the I. Thus, insofar as the not-I is posited, the I both is and is not posited. The opposition between these conclusions reveals an originary contradiction and hence a disunity within consciousness, such that the I both is and is not an identity or, as Fichte puts it, both "I = I" and "I is not = I."[143]

The threat is that "the identity of consciousness, which is the sole, absolute foundation of our knowledge, is nullified" by the conclusions that compose the originary contradiction. This threat imposes a "task," namely, to "discover some X" through which both of these conclusions can be "correct without nullifying the identity of consciousness." Since the task is to preserve the unity of consciousness and thus the identity of the I, this X must be a "product" of the I.[144] Indeed, Fichte says, "*critical* philosophy" only "becomes *Wissenschaftslehre*" if it derives from the "absolute I" alone a system of categories in which the opposing "features" of the I and the not-I are united and that therefore includes X.[145] However, the statement in Part I of the task of discovering X "by no means determines *how*" the two opposed conclusions, namely, that the I is and is not posited insofar as the not-I is posited, are to be "thought together in a manner that does not annihilate and annul them."[146] It accordingly falls, in Parts II and III, to the second part of the *Wissenschaftslehre*, that is, to genetic deduction, to derive the categories, which, as Fichte says in the *Nova Methodo*, are the conditions that "make it possible for the I to posit itself and to oppose a not-I to itself." This deduction will culminate in an X that reconciles the contradictory conclusions and thereby preserves the unity of consciousness.

In Part II, a deduction of theoretical categories proves inadequate to the task of discovering X and resolving the contradiction within consciousness. After analyzing the co-determination of the I and the not-I in terms of the categories of limitation, division, and negation, Fichte observes that "the contradiction will not be completely resolved in this way, but only displaced and posited anew." This is because, with each deduced category,

> [o]ne inserts between [the I and the not-I] some X, upon which both have an effect and by means of which each therefore has a mediated or indirect effect upon the other. Nevertheless, one quickly discovers that this X must, in turn, also contain some point at which I and not-I come into immediate contact [and thus contradict each other]. In order to prevent this, one avoids this sharp boundary by inserting a new intermediate component = Y. But it soon becomes evident that, just as in the case of X, Y also must contain some point in which the two

[143] Fichte GWL | SW I: 106–7.
[144] Fichte GWL | SW I: 107.
[145] Fichte GWL | SW I: 115, 119.
[146] Fichte GWL | SW I: 108.

> components posited in opposition to each other come into immediate contact. And things would continue in this manner forever were the knot not loosened but severed by means of an absolute decree of reason, not a decree pronounced by the philosopher himself, but one to which he merely calls attention, namely, that since there is no way in which the not-I can be united with the I, *there ought to be* no not-I at all.[147]

Each theoretical category fails to condition the possibility of the I's positing of the not-I because it only reformulates their co-determination, namely, as co-limiting, co-dividing, and co-negating. Each category thereby echoes the terms of the originary contradiction, only to call for yet another category. We can escape this regress only by deducing the "absolute decree of reason," namely, that there ought to be "no not-I" determining the I "at all." Since this deduction cannot be theoretical, Fichte says, we must pursue the "infinity of the I" in the "practical part of our science."[148]

In Part III, §5, Fichte argues that since, for the sake of the unity of consciousness, the I must be posited "purely and simply by the I itself," the "contradiction" of a not-I that imposes a "check" on the I's activity "must be eliminated," namely, by conceiving of the I as the "*cause* of the not-I."[149] However, this causality cannot annul the not-I's primordial opposition to the I, for then the not-I would "cease to be not-I" and, indeed, would "itself become I." Rather, this causality must consist in the not-I's "conformity" to the I. Fichte understands conformity in the spirit of "Kant's categorical imperative," according to which everything "*ought* to be posited" through the "absolute being of the I."[150] The not-I conforms, in this sense, to the I's demand for "a world as it would be were all reality to be posited purely and simply through the I," that is, "an ideal world."[151] The causality whereby the not-I conforms to the I is therefore final, for it harnesses the not-I toward the realization of an end, namely, nature's moral perfection.[152]

However, since the not-I appears to us most directly in the guise of our natural inclinations, the I is the final cause of the not-I within us and is therefore the final

[147] Fichte GWL | SW I: 143–4.

[148] Fichte GWL | SW I: 217–8. On the *Vocation*'s account of the limits of theoretical reason, see Crowe 2013: 38–44.

[149] Fichte GWL | SW I: 248–50; cf. 210–2.

[150] Fichte GWL | SW I: 254, 260–60n.

[151] Fichte GWL | SW I: 269.

[152] The deductions in the *Foundations* do not exhaust Fichte's characterization of the contradictory relation between the I and the not-I. As we saw in Section 1.5, in *Natural Right*, he extends his dialectical reflection on this relation, arguing that the mutual limitation of the I and the not-I is grounded on the mutual recognition of self and other, thereby recasting the sensible world as always also social. Cf. Fichte: "The investigations that make up the *Wissenschaftslehre* will here be conducted in a new manner, just as if they had never been conducted before. This revised version will profit from the fact that, since the time of the original version [namely, the *Foundations*], the first principles have been further developed and extended, and this facilitates a clearer understanding of those principles themselves" (Fichte NM | GA IV/2: 10).

cause of human experience.[153] We must morally perfect nature because it is our own actions, swayed as they are by inclination, that must conform to the I, that is, that "*ought* to be posited" through the I. Hence Fichte says that "that everything be in harmony with the I" is a "demand" specifically of our "practical reason."[154] Moreover, since we are never rid of our inclinations, fully conforming to the I is impossible. This is why, in §§6–7, Fichte says that "striving" for nature's moral perfection merely aspires or "aims to exercise causality" on the not-I. Were we actually and fully to "exercise causality" on the not-I, we would "completely annihilate" it and so would cease to strive, that is, we would, *per impossibile*, achieve moral perfection.[155] As the final cause of our experience, then, the I represents an ideal our striving for which always presupposes the not-I and so is endless. As Fichte puts it, while the I "strives to fill infinity," this "cannot be posited unless an opposed striving of the not-I is [also] posited."[156] In the terms of the *New Presentation*, we can say that although conformity to the practical ideal of nature's moral perfection is "something to which we ought to draw infinitely nearer," this ideal "will never become anything real" and thus is regulative.[157]

After deducing the necessity of striving endlessly to satisfy the I's demand for nature's moral perfection, Fichte announces in §8 that "the most complete system in the entire human being" is derived from "the subordination" of "all *theoretical* laws" to "*practical laws*" or, "since there is indeed but one practical law," to "the same practical law,"[158] namely, the moral law. This law is the X that ultimately, albeit regulatively, resolves the originary contradiction between the I and the not-I and preserves the unity of consciousness.[159] On the one hand, the I determines

[153] See Fichte's 1795 "On the Linguistic Capacity and the Origin of Language": "Man proceeds to modify the raw or bestial nature according to his own purposes. This must be subordinated to the highest principle in man, which is: be always at one with yourself . . . Man thus seeks . . . to subjugate irrational nature so that everything will harmonize with his reason, since only under this condition can he come into harmony with himself" (Fichte SUS | GA I/3: 102).

[154] Fichte GWL | SW I: 263–4.

[155] Fichte GWL | SW I: 287; cf. 254.

[156] Fichte GWL | SW I: 288; cf. 270.

[157] See Fichte: "The universe no longer seems to me that circle returning to itself, that endlessly repeating game, that monster which devours itself so as to give birth to itself as it already was. For my eyes it has become spiritualized and bears the mark proper to spirit: constant progress to greater perfection in a straight line which goes on to infinity" (Fichte BM | SW II: 316).

[158] Fichte GWL | SW I: 294–5.

[159] Positing the I, the not-I, and the resolution of their contradiction is a dialectical method that Fichte describes as "*thetic*, *antithetic*, and *synthetic*" (Fichte GWL | SW I: 337). Cf. Georg Philipp Friedrich Freiherr von Hardenberg's, a.k.a. Novalis', 1795–96 *Fichte Studies*: "There has to be a not-I in order that I can posit the I as I. Thesis, antithesis, synthesis" (Novalis 2003: 7). As we saw in Section 1.6, Hegel demands that thought discover, not impose, this three-stage method: "*triplicity* must not be regarded as scientific when it is reduced to a lifeless schema, a mere shadow, and when scientific organization is degraded into a table of terms" (Hegel PG | W 3: 48). Cf. Hegel: "Formalism, it is true, has also seized hold of triplicity, attending to its empty *schema*; the shallow nonsense and the barrenness of the so-called *construction* of modern philosophy, that consists in nothing but fastening that formal schema everywhere for the sake of external order, with no concept or immanent determination, has rendered that form tedious and has given it a bad name. Yet the insipidity of this use cannot rob it of its inner worth, and the fact that the shape of reason was discovered, albeit without conceptual comprehension at first, is always to be highly valued" (Hegel WL | GW 12: 247–8). Cf. also Schulze 2020: 23.

the not-I by demanding that they "*ought* to be purely and simply the same."[160] On the other hand, the not-I determines the I by always subsisting alongside its aspiring cause. Both conclusions can now be granted as "correct," for, insofar as we strive for nature's moral perfection, the I both is and is not posited. It is posited *qua* final cause of human experience and is not posited *qua* complete actualization of this cause.

We can see that Fichte's deduction of the necessity of the demand that "*there ought to be* no not-I at all" exhibits the three features that Hegel identifies above, namely, that the I's exercise of absolute causality on the not-I is contradictory, incompletable, and a betrayal of the principle of speculation. We can also see that the Fichtean demand excludes true infinity, for, by positing a not-I that always opposes and so never conforms to the I, it guarantees that the I is always burdened by something alien. In other words, by stating that the not-I ought not to be unequal to the I, the demand effectively states that there ought only to be the I's equality with itself, which is just to express the reflective identity "I *ought* to be equal to I," as opposed to the speculative identity "I = I."[161]

While 'true infinity' is an indirect correlate of 'bad infinity,' we find two direct correlates in Hegel's early Jena texts.

First, in the *Difference* essay, Hegel remarks that when Fichte "steps outside" of the intellectual intuition of the I and "evolves" it into "a system" of categories that he "deduce[s]" from the I, that is, when he moves from the first part of the *Wissenschaftslehre* to the second part, the "finitude and opposition" of two contradictory terms, namely, the I and the not-I, is "not removed." Fichte's deduction yields the practical demand that the not-I not be unequal to the I, that is, that there should only be the I's equality with itself. Since this practical demand cannot be fulfilled, that is, since the practical ideal of the moral perfection of nature is regulative, the I must progress endlessly toward its self-equality. This means that the I is permanently "conditioned" by what Hegel calls "an objective infinity, namely, the temporal progression *ad infinitum*"[162] whereby the I aspires to exert absolute causality on the not-I without ever actually doing so. But then "objective infinity" is none other than bad infinity, for it exhibits both a fixed opposition between two terms and the perpetual progress by which one of these terms endlessly strives to transcend this opposition.

[160] Fichte GWL | SW I: 260.

[161] See Hegel on Fichte's dialectical logic: "As is well known, Fichte's system raised Kant's to a higher level of abstraction and developed it with greater logical consistency . . . [I]n Fichte the pure unity of the I with itself presents itself immediately and from the very outset, as does the equally abstract thing-in-itself, the not-I, in its opposition to the I. The further development of the forms taken on by the determination of the one by the other is consistently carried out on the basis of their opposition, such that every new form presents a richer synthesis of the opposition but nevertheless fails to overcome it. The resulting resolutions thus continue in their status as *relations* and *finite forms*, whose ultimate resolution is deferred to the practical realm—where, however, it also fails to be achieved, ending in a one-sided 'ought' and a striving that remains vitiated by a beyond" (Hegel JW | GW 15: 18).

[162] Hegel D | GW 4: 6–7.

Second, in "Faith and Knowledge" Hegel contrasts the "infinity of substance," from which "the particular and finite are not excluded . . . as opposites" and the cognition of which is "intellectual intuition," with the "infinite of imagination," which is reflectively opposed to and "brought into antithesis with" the finite. Hegel associates the infinity of substance with Spinoza and the infinite of imagination with Kant,[163] although he must also associate the latter with Fichte, who he regards as the culmination of the philosophy of subjectivity that Kant inaugurates.[164] It is because neither the infinite of imagination nor the finite is what it is without the other that "each is posited and not posited." Hegel argues that "[a]nything posited in this fashion runs to empirical infinity," since positing one term in this opposition presupposes its limitation by the other term and vice versa, and so on *ad infinitum*, which leaves intact an "absolute, unresolved contradiction."[165] But then "empirical infinity" too is none other than bad infinity, since, like objective infinity, it exhibits fixed opposition and perpetual progress.

As direct correlates of bad infinity, objective infinity and empirical infinity equally contrast with true infinity.[166] Their proper image is the line, not the circle. Moreover, Hegel's use of 'objective infinity' and 'empirical infinity' in the early Jena texts indicates a continuity with his use of 'bad infinity' in the *Science of Logic*. However, if the concept of bad infinity and its direct correlate terms are at work in Hegel's charge that Fichte betrays the principle of speculation, then, since this charge just is the charge of subjectivism, we must understand the connection between bad infinity and subjectivism. We will now see that the former is the logical consequence of the latter.

In the *Difference* essay, when remarking on the transition between the two parts of the *Wissenschaftslehre*, Hegel says that it "surrenders reason to the understanding and passes over into the chain of finite [acts and objects] of consciousness from which it never reconstructs itself again as identity and true infinity."[167] We saw that the surrender in question is the abandonment of speculation for reflection that Fichte displays by positing the absolute opposition between the I and the not-I. Crucially, Hegel claims that positing this opposition entails the inability to construct "true infinity." In other words, it is Fichte's presupposition of the factical dichotomy between the I and the not-I that condemns his philosophy to untrue, that is, bad, infinity. We should expect that, insofar as the I and the not-I finitize

[163] Hegel GuW | GW 4: 354–5.

[164] See Hegel EL | GW 20: §94 Addition and Hegel WL | GW 21: 123, 150, 227.

[165] Hegel GuW | GW 4: 355. Cf. Hegel: "The ideal is to be integrated through the real . . . The all-controlling basic principle of this integration consists in this: the one side is absolutely not what the other is, and no genuine identity emerges from any linkage between them" (Hegel GuW | GW 4: 401).

[166] Cf. objective and empirical infinity with what Hegel calls "sensuous" infinity (Hegel PG | W 3: 184).

[167] Hegel D | GW 4: 6. Cf. Hegel: "In [Fichte's] system, freedom does not succeed in producing itself; the product does not correspond to the producing. The system, which starts out from self-positing, leads intelligence to its conditioned condition in an endless sequence of finitudes, without re-establishing it [as self-positing] in and through them" (Hegel D | GW 4: 44).

each other by virtue of their absolute opposition, the I can never overcome this mutual finitization, but rather can only reproduce it through its endless pursuit of the I as idea. As we saw, the I as idea represents the practical ideal of nature's moral perfection, an ideal in which the I exercises absolute causality on the not-I. Moreover, the I as idea is infinite insofar as it cannot be considered as "an individual." But since our practical pursuit of this infinite I is originally marked by its opposition to and thus its limitation by the not-I, this infinite I is a finite infinite. The bad infinity that defines the progress of practical reason is therefore a logical consequence of the facticity with which Fichte's system begins. Hence Hegel asks: "What union is possible, though, once absolute opposites are presupposed? Strictly speaking none at all, obviously."[168] There is an "antithesis" between the I and the not-I at the ground of Fichte's system and, following "obviously" as a consequence from this, they "still contradict each other" at the zenith of his system.[169]

In "Faith and Knowledge," Hegel describes the philosophy of subjectivity as being "immovably impaled on the stake of the absolute antithesis" between reason and the absolute for which it yearns,[170] implying that this philosophy never overcomes the contradictory terms of the absolute opposition with which it brutely begins. Turning later on to the philosophy of subjectivity's highest expression in the *Wissenschaftslehre*, he claims that "yearning is itself turned into the infinite" because "no point of indifference can be recognized in it."[171] In other words, it is because this philosophy begins not with "indifference," but rather with "the different," namely, the factical dichotomy between the finitude of reason and the infinitude of the absolute, that reason's yearning for the absolute inexorably must be badly infinite, namely, by perpetually reproducing a fixed opposition and perpetually progressing toward its removal.

The letter of the *Wissenschaftslehre* takes the absolute opposition between the I and the not-I as factically given. By failing thereby to realize the enlightenment ideal of rational cognition, it betrays the spirit of the *Wissenschaftslehre*. It is consequently condemned to reproduce absolute opposition in the form of the mutually finitizing relation between reason and the absolute, that is, condemned to bad infinity. In other words, the vestigial facticity on which Fichte's system rests inevitably marks the goal for which it strives. To conclude this chapter, I will now situate Hegel's early critique of Fichte's subjectivism within the context of his burgeoning dialectical method, which radicalizes Fichte's deductive method by nullifying facticity, not only in the guise of the forms of the faculties of cognition and of the first principle of philosophy, but also in the guise of absolute opposition.

[168] Hegel D | GW 4: 40. Cf. Hegel: "From the standpoint of the dichotomy, the absolute synthesis is a beyond" (Hegel D | GW 4: 15).
[169] Hegel D | GW 4: 33. Cf. Hegel's analysis of the self-contradiction of the moral worldview in the *Phenomenology* (Hegel PG | W 3: 442–64).
[170] Hegel GuW | GW 4: 323.
[171] Hegel GuW | GW 4: 387.

3.6 Ancient Skepticism and the Three Moments of Logic

In the *Difference* essay, Hegel states that philosophy only "becomes a system, that is, an organic whole of concepts," when its "highest law is not the understanding, but reason." Whereas the understanding merely "exhibit[s]" the contradictions that are produced by radically contingent or brute "oppositions," reason "unites these contradictories, posits both together, and sublates them." In this, reason "purifie[s] itself of the subjectivity of reflection" that presupposes the fixed opposition of the contradictory terms of factical dichotomies, for example, the I and the not-I. By "separat[ing] what is one in the absolute identity" of subject and object, impure reflection "cannot express the absolute synthesis" of propositions that the understanding regards as opposing yet equally "valid," for example, 'if the not-I is posited, then the I is posited' and 'if the not-I is posited, then the I is not posited.' However, whereas, despite its yearning for the "absolute identity" of, for example, the I with itself, the reflective style of the understanding holds opposing propositions apart and inevitably reproduces their contradiction, the speculative style of reason expresses the "absolute synthesis" of opposing propositions by affirming and sublating their contradiction. Thus, instead of perpetually striving to transcend the antinomy that equally valid opposing propositions produce, reason brings "the formal essence of reflection under its control" precisely by acknowledging "antinomy" as "the explicit formula of truth." In other words, reason grasps that "antinomy, that is, the contradiction that cancels itself, is the highest formal expression of knowledge and truth."[172]

What exactly is the "contradiction that cancels itself"? And how could such a contradiction serve as both the "formula" and the "expression" of truth?

I will show that Hegel's early view of truth makes productive use of contradiction by adapting a form of ancient skepticism and that this enables him to radicalize Fichte's deductive method of deriving the conditions of intelligibility. I will then show that Hegel's adaptation of ancient skepticism informs the development of his dialectical method and, in particular, his conception of the three moments of logic. It will emerge that the vestigial facticity of absolute opposition strands Fichte's system at the first moment of logic, namely, prior to the affirmation and sublation of necessary contradictions that emerge in the science of intelligibility.

Hegel articulates the essential role of contradiction in formulating and expressing philosophical truth in 1802's "On the Relationship of Skepticism to Philosophy: Exposition of its Different Modifications and Comparison of the Latest Form with the Ancient One," his review of Schulze's 1801 *Critique of Theoretical Philosophy*.[173] There he claims that Schulze "is only acquainted with skeptical and dogmatic philosophizing" because he fails to recognize that, "apart

[172] Hegel D | GW 4: 23–4, 26.
[173] A version of this discussion appears in Bruno 2023c.

from skepticism and dogmatism," there is "a third possibility, to wit, a philosophy."[174] Schulze assumes that "what is given within the compass of our consciousness has *undeniable certainty*" and that theoretical philosophy is the science of the "*unconditioned cause of all conditioned things*," which cause he locates "outside and above our consciousness." This assumption makes it both necessary and impossible that "*existence*" is "*discoverable*" by means of "*concepts*," for theoretical philosophy seeks the non-conceptual existence of an unconditioned cause yet can find "*certainty*" only "within the compass of our consciousness," that is, within concepts. Since no inferential "bridge" can be built from concepts to existence, Schulze skeptically resigns himself to "a *philosophy which does not go beyond consciousness*."[175] However, his skeptical conclusion is guaranteed by the dogmatic assumption on which it rests, namely, the absolute opposition between consciousness and existence, that is, between concepts and causes. Hence Hegel says that "Schulzian skepticism integrates the crudest dogmatism into itself."[176] Schulze combines skeptical resignation and dogmatic assurance as if there were not another possibility, "to wit, a philosophy."

Hegel begins to introduce the possibility of philosophy by distinguishing between the "Latest" and "Ancient" forms of skepticism whose "Comparison" the "Skepticism" essay's subtitle advertises:

> modern skepticism lacks the noblest side of skepticism, its orientation against the dogmatism of ordinary consciousness . . . For the most recent skepticism . . . the ordinary consciousness with its whole infinite range of facts has an indubitable certainty . . . Furthermore, according to this latest skepticism, our physics and astronomy, and analytical thought, bid defiance to all rational doubtfulness; and thus it lacks also the noblest side of the later ancient skepticism, i.e., its orientation against limited cognition, against finite knowledge.[177]

Schulze exemplifies modern skepticism by attributing "indubitable certainty" not just to the contents of consciousness, namely, concepts, but also to their absolute opposition to the existence of an unconditioned cause. This is because, despite denying, for example, that existence is inferable from concepts, modern skeptics like Schulze defy "all rational doubtfulness" concerning the "infinite range of facts" to which ordinary consciousness gives credence. In other words, however doubtful of certain facts, modern skepticism dogmatically holds certain other facts

[174] Hegel VSP | 2000: 316, 325. Cf. Hegel's Berlin lectures, in which he charges Schulze with the error of "recogniz[ing] nothing but dogmatism and skepticism, and not the third philosophy" (Hegel VGP2 | 1894: 331).
[175] Hegel VSP | 2000: 317–8.
[176] Hegel VSP | 2000: 330.
[177] Hegel VSP | 2000: 339.

to be beyond question on the authority of ordinary consciousness.[178] It therefore lacks what Hegel regards as the "noblest side of skepticism," namely, an ancient skeptical "orientation against the dogmatism of ordinary consciousness," which he specifies is an "orientation against . . . finite knowledge."[179] But what is dogmatic about ordinary consciousness' claim to finite knowledge?

According to Hegel, it is the "essence of dogmatism" to posit as "absolute" something that is merely relative, namely, "something finite, something burdened with an opposition."[180] To be "burdened with an opposition" is, as we saw, to be finitized, that is, to exist merely in relation to something else that opposes and thus finitizes. For example, the absolute toward which, according to the philosophy of subjectivity, reason strives is in fact not absolute, but rather, by virtue of their mutually limiting opposition, is just as finite as reason. Now, Hegel says that ordinary consciousness asserts its "finite knowledge" of truth within the "phenomenal world," namely, the truth of "the given, the fact, the finite (whether this finite is called 'appearance' or 'concept')."[181] However, ordinary consciousness regards finite knowledge as absolute insofar as it regards this knowledge as beyond "all rational doubtfulness." It thereby exhibits dogmatism, since finite knowledge is not absolute, but rather relative. This is because finite knowledge is "burdened with an opposition," namely, an opposition to contrary finite knowledge, that is, to contrary assurances about truth within the phenomenal world. Moreover, ordinary consciousness cannot resolve the opposition between its finite knowledge and contrary finite knowledge by appealing to still more finite knowledge on pain of regress, for such an appeal would inevitably reproduce finitizing oppositions. Resolving the opposition that is internal to finite knowledge instead requires

[178] See Hegel: "*Hume's* skepticism . . . should be very carefully distinguished from *Greek skepticism.* In Humean skepticism, the *truth* of the empirical, the truth of feeling and intuition is taken as basic; and, on that basis, he attacks all universal determinations and laws, precisely because they have no justification by way of sense-perception. The old skepticism was so far removed from making feeling, or intuition, into the principle of truth that it turned itself against the sensible in the very first place instead" (Hegel EL | GW 20: §39 Remark). Contrast Schulze's suggestion in his *Critique* that the "genuine character of skeptical philosophy that once bloomed in Greece" finds "in modern times . . . an astute defender in David Hume" (Schulze 1911: 19).

[179] In the Preface to the *Phenomenology*, Hegel says that philosophy's attainment of scientific form is "the prize at the end of a complicated, tortuous path." In the Introduction, he describes this path as a "pathway of *doubt*," one that involves not the irresolute skepticism of "shillyshallying about this or that presumed truth, followed by a return to that truth again, after the doubt has been appropriately dispelled," but rather the "thoroughgoing skepticism" that is "directed against the whole range of phenomenal consciousness," specifically, consciousness' "so-called natural ideas" about truth. Irresolute skepticism risks only a temporary suspension of its commitment to its "natural" idea of truth in order to secure foundational certainty for that idea by means of a suitable meditation. By contrast, thoroughgoing skepticism "brings about a state of despair" in consciousness' ideas of truth by discovering contradictions within them and "bring[ing] to pass the *completion* of the series" of their resolutions (Hegel PG | W 3: 19, 72–3). We can therefore see that the distinction between irresolute and thoroughgoing skepticism aligns with Hegel's earlier distinction between modern and ancient skepticism.

[180] Hegel VSP | 2000: 335.

[181] Hegel VSP | 2000: 331–2. Cf. Hegel WL | GW 21: 29–30.

adapting an ancient skeptical orientation "against finite knowledge" as such. But how does ancient skepticism thereby offer a way toward philosophy?

Modern skepticism casts a dogmatic shadow by presupposing the absolute opposition between consciousness and existence.[182] Evoking the distinction between the reflective opposition of the understanding and the speculative identification of reason, Hegel states that the "sundering of the rational, in which thinking and being are one, and the absolute insistence on this opposition, in other words, the understanding made absolute, constitutes the endlessly repeated and universally applied ground of this dogmatic skepticism."[183] Modern skepticism is dogmatic insofar as it "absolut[izes]" the standpoint of the understanding, namely, by positing factical dichotomies. By contrast, ancient skepticism offers a way beyond dogmatic skepticism and toward philosophy insofar as it prepares for the standpoint of reason, namely, by nullifying factical dichotomies.[184] Indeed, Hegel claims that ancient skepticism is "in its inmost heart at one with every true philosophy" because it alone teaches us how "philosophy may possibly be something other than the dogmatism" with which modern skepticism is exclusively acquainted.[185] But in what way does ancient skepticism lie at the "heart" of "every true philosophy"?

Hegel invokes a principle that he says is "*explicit*" in Plato's *Parmenides* yet "*implicit* in every genuine philosophical system," namely, "the principle of skepticism," which states that "*panti logōi logos isos antikeitai* [against every argument there is an equal one on the other side]." Although applying the principle of skepticism yields contradictions, Hegel denies that such contradictions are unacceptable violations of the "principle of [non-]contradiction" on the grounds that "every proposition of reason must, in respect of concepts, contain a violation" of that principle. On the one hand, a proposition of the understanding posits the contradictory terms of a factical dichotomy, from which contradiction the understanding flees. A proposition of the understanding is thus defined by its fidelity to the principle of non-contradiction. On the other hand, a proposition of reason is one whose component "concepts," "assertions," or claims "contradict themselves," which

[182] See Hegel: "The turning of skepticism against philosophy, as soon as philosophy became dogmatism, illustrates how it has kept in step with the communal degeneration of philosophy and of the world in general, until finally in these most recent times it has sunk so far in company with dogmatism that for both of them nowadays the facts of consciousness have an indubitable certainty, and for both of them the truth resides in temporality; so that, since the extremes now touch, the great goal is attained once more on their side in these happy times, that dogmatism and skepticism coincide with one another *on the underside*, and offer each other the hand of perfect friendship and fraternity" (Hegel VSP | 2000: 300).

[183] Hegel VSP | 2000: 339.

[184] Cf. Schelling: "True skepticism is entirely directed against reflection's mode of cognizing, and it is so directed by the principle of true speculation—except that it cannot express this position categorically, since it would then cease to be skepticism" (Schelling FD | SW I/4: 365–6).

[185] Hegel VSP | 2000: 322–3. Cf. Hegel: "*Ancient* skepticism must be differentiated from the *modern* form; we are only dealing with the former, for it alone is of a true, profound nature" (Hegel PG | W 19: 360). On the role of Agrippan, Pyrrhonian, and Platonic skepticism in Hegel's early Jena period, as well as the connection between Agrippan skepticism and nihilism, see Franks 2008.

contradiction reason affirms. A proposition of reason is thus defined by its violation of the principle of non-contradiction and its fidelity to the principle of skepticism. But then whereas the philosophy of subjectivity includes only propositions of the understanding insofar as it surrenders reason to the understanding by positing factical dichotomies, "true philosophy" includes only propositions of reason insofar as it harnesses reason's "secret efficacy" of "seduc[ing] the understanding into producing an objective totality," that is, a system of science that is free from factical dichotomy. We see, then, how ancient skepticism lies at the "heart" of true philosophy. It eliminates factical dichotomies in accordance with the principle of skepticism, namely, by affirming the contradictory terms in these dichotomies as "equal" instead of fleeing from them. This is why Hegel says that "every genuine philosophy" has as its "negative side" that it "sublates" the principle of non-contradiction.[186] Indeed, as he states in the first of twelve theses that are published along with "Philosophical Dissertation on the Orbits of the Planets," his 1801 habilitation thesis: "*contradictio est regula veri, non contradictio falsi* [contradiction is the rule of truth, non-contradiction that of falsity]."[187] But what is the method by which ancient skepticism affirms the contradictory terms of factical dichotomies?

As Michael Forster shows,[188] the "Skepticism" essay adapts an ancient skeptical method of setting opposing arguments of equal force against each other in order to produce equipollence, suspend judgment, and achieve tranquility.[189] On Hegel's adaptation of this method, we discover opposing claims of equal validity within individual categories or thought-determinations, fall into the despair of being forced to affirm the contradiction that is produced by these opposing claims, resolve this contradiction by sublating these opposing claims, and ultimately attain a kind of repose by dialectically exhausting the totality of such contradictions and arriving at a stable set, that is, a system, of categories. Crucially, unlike modern skepticism, this adapted ancient skeptical method presupposes the indubitable certainty of no facts whatsoever.

We find this adapted ancient skeptical method at work in the *Phenomenology*. There Hegel observes that the "path" toward the scientific "goal" of achieving "insight into what knowing is" is a "complicated, tortuous," "despair[ing]" one in which natural consciousness suffers "the loss of its own self" by contradicting its own criterion of knowing, for example, when it takes knowing to consist in the immediate sensation of particulars, only to show that it unavoidably mediates sensation via universals.[190] Since natural consciousness "suffers" the "violence" of

[186] Hegel VSP | 2000: 324–5. For a Hegelian critique of the presupposition of the principle of non-contradiction by Aristotle, Sextus Empiricus, and Kant, and how this presupposition does not secure, but rather impedes, the determinacy of being and meaning, see Winfield 2018.

[187] Hegel OP | W 2: 533.

[188] Forster 1989: 10–2.

[189] See Book 1, Chapter 4, of Sextus Empiricus' *Outlines of Skepticism* (Annas and Barnes (ed.) 2000: 4–5).

[190] Hegel PG | W 3: 19, 33, 72.

this contradiction "at its own hands," it can only "strive to hold on to what it is in danger of losing," namely, by "entrench[ing] itself in sentimentality" for its current criterion, for so long. In spite of itself, a successor criterion of knowing "*issues from*" natural consciousness that "*dialectical[ly]*" resolves its self-contradiction, for example, when it discovers that knowing consists in the perception of things as bearing properties that are universal, that is, common to a plurality of things.[191] However, natural consciousness "can find no peace" until it "finds itself," namely, when it generates a contradiction-free criterion of knowing, which affords the repose of a self-consistent insight into what knowing is, which insight is absolute knowledge. This achievement marks the "*completion* of the series" of the self-contradictions of natural consciousness, which series composes the "history of the *education* of consciousness itself to the standpoint of science."[192]

We can now see why contradiction serves as the "formula" and "expression" of truth. Hegel's adapted ancient method yields the science of the categories, that is, the science of the conditions of intelligibility, which is to say, the science of truth. But since this method makes productive use of contradiction, contradiction is essential to truth's philosophical formulation and expression.

This does not yet explain why contradiction "cancels itself" in the deductive process. I will explain this by showing how Hegel's early adaptation of ancient skepticism informs the later development of both his dialectical method and his conception of logic, drawing special attention to logic's three moments and identifying Fichte's place among them.

Hegel concludes the "Preliminary Conception" in the *Encyclopedia* with "descriptive anticipations" of the text's main structure according to which "the *logical* has three sides: (α) *the side of abstraction* or *of the understanding*, (β) *the dialectical* or *negatively rational side*, [and] (γ) *the speculative* or *positively rational* one." In other words, logic has three moments, which are the "*moments of everything logically real*; i.e., of every concept or of everything true in general." First, the abstractive moment of the understanding "stops short" at fixed categories. Second, the negative moment of dialectic then discovers the "genuine nature" of the categories, namely, that each "passes over, of itself, into its opposite." Third, the positive moment of speculation finally grasps the "unity" of categories through the "dissolution" of their inner opposition. Crucially, Hegel warns that if these moments are "kept separate from each other . . . then they are not considered in their truth."[193] In order to see how contradiction functions and ultimately cancels itself in these moments, it is worth elaborating on them in turn.

[191] Hegel PG | W 3: 78.
[192] Hegel PG | W 3: 74–5.
[193] Hegel EL | GW 20: §§79–82. In the *Science of Logic*, Hegel says that the *Phenomenology* presents consciousness as "an example" of the "simple rhythm" of the "self-movement" of logic through its moments (Hegel WL | GW 21: 37–8).

In the first moment of logic, the understanding posits the categories as abstract concepts, that is, as universals that are "held onto in firm opposition" to particulars. Furthermore, it judges according to the "principle of identity," applying the categories such that a thing may be "grasped in its full precision" in contrast to other things and, hence, so that "nothing should remain vague and indeterminate" in the "domains either of theory or of practice."[194] Bringing an object or an action under a category in a judgment preserves the identity and thus the determinacy of that object or action, to the exclusion of other objects or actions.

In the second moment of logic, dialectic discovers that the categories do not in fact preserve the identity of what is judged because a category's own "nature" is dialectical in that it "passes over, of itself, into its opposite." Dialectic discovers the "*immanent* transcending" whereby a category "displays itself as what it is," namely, its own "negation." For example, being negates itself because it lacks inner differentiation and outer difference and thereby is indistinguishable from and collapses into nothing and vice versa. This produces the contradiction that being both is and is not nothing.[195] Evoking his adaptation of ancient skeptical method, Hegel asserts that dialectic is "high ancient skepticism" because it consists in "complete despair about everything that the understanding holds to be firm" concerning the categories and therefore "must not be confused" with "modern skepticism." By exposing the process whereby a category "*immanent[ly]* transcend[s]" itself for its own opposite, dialectic thus reveals itself to be "[s]kepticism proper."[196]

Hegel clarifies that dialectic is not merely negative, but also positive, for while it is the "genuine nature" of a category, like a proposition of reason, to contain contradictory claims, the "dissolution" of these claims and their "transition" toward "unity" in a successor category equally belong to its nature. Hence he calls dialectic "the principle through which alone *immanent coherence and necessity* enter into the content of science."[197] First, the development of the science of truth falters if a category negates itself into claims that remain in contradiction, for such claims lack "*coherence*." Second, Hegel says shortly after that "*necessity*" consists in thinking's "*drive* to find" a "stable meaning" for the opposing claims within a category.[198] A category's opposing claims accordingly lack necessity unless their contradiction is resolved by the stability of a successor category. As Hegel says at the end of his description of the second moment, while "philosophy . . . contains the skeptical as a moment within itself—specifically as the dialectical moment," it

[194] Hegel EL | GW 20: §80 Addition.
[195] See Hegel WL | GW 21: 69.
[196] Hegel EL | GW 20: §81 Addition 2. Crucially, whereas the opposing arguments that concern antiquity are related externally, Hegel's adapted ancient skeptical method concerns the opposing claims that are contained internally within a proposition of reason or a category. This signals a shift of logical focus from mere contradiction to self-contradiction. On the difference between the classical principle of non-contradiction and the speculative principle of self-contradiction, see de Boer 2010.
[197] Hegel EL | GW 20: §81 Remark.
[198] Hegel EL | GW 20: §87 Remark.

"does not stop at the merely negative result of the dialectic," namely, at contradiction. This is because dialectic "mistakes its result" if it "holds fast" to contradiction, which thwarts the scientific goals of "*coherence and necessity*." Instead, the negative result of dialectic must be "sublated" into a "positive" result, which occurs in the third moment of logic.[199]

"Sublation," Hegel says, is "one of the most important concepts in philosophy," for it has the "speculative meaning" that it signifies both "to 'preserve'" and "to cause to cease." This co-signification is exhibited, for example, by becoming, in which being and nothing both are preserved as "*moments*" of becoming and cease to be insofar as they thereby each come to "possess a different determination," namely, as "coming-to-be and ceasing-to-be," respectively.[200] Being and nothing are sublated into becoming like nourishment is incorporated into a body, their presently contradictory forms dissolving while being absorbed into a higher form. As Hegel says, "it is contradiction that moves the world, and it is ridiculous to say that contradiction cannot be thought. What is correct in this assertion is just that contradiction is not all there is to it, and that contradiction sublates itself by its own doing."[201] Thus, whereas, from the first moment of logic, dialectic derives a contradictory unity of opposing claims, from the second moment of logic, speculation derives a sublated unity of opposing claims. This, however, is not to say that logic simply rids itself of contradiction. Just as the plant no more rids itself of the bud when flowering than it rids itself of the flower when fruiting, these being "reciprocally necessary moments" of the plant's growth,[202] so too logic no more rids itself of the fixed claims of abstraction that dialectic unifies into contradiction than it rids itself of the contradictory claims of dialectic that speculation unifies into successor categories and, ultimately, into the absolute idea, these being reciprocally necessary moments of logic's growth.

[199] Hegel EL | GW 20: §81 Addition 2. Cf. Hegel: "The *second* negative at which we have arrived, the negative of the negative, is this sublating of contradiction" (Hegel WL | GW 12: 246). For an account of contradiction in the Doctrine of Essence in the *Science of Logic*, see de Boer 2010 and Pippin 1996.

[200] See Hegel WL | GW 21: 94–5. Cf. Hegel: "Becoming entails that nothing not remain nothing, but that it pass over into its other, being . . . The proposition, *nothing comes from nothing, nothing is just nothing*, owes its particular importance to its opposition to *becoming* in general and hence also to the creation of the world out of nothing . . . The philosophical view that accepts as principle that being is only being, nothing only nothing, deserves the name of 'system of identity'; this abstract identity is the essence of pantheism . . . For from now on this unity of being and nothing will stand once and for all as foundation, as first truth, and will thus constitute the element of all that follows. All further logical determinations besides *becoming* itself (existence, quality, and in general all the concepts of philosophy) are therefore examples of this unity" (Hegel WL | GW 21: 71–2).

[201] Hegel EL | GW 20: §119 Addition 2. Cf. Hegel: "*Speculative thought* consists only in this, in holding firm to contradiction and to itself in the contradiction, but not in the sense that, as it happens in ordinary thought, it would let itself be ruled by it and allow it to dissolve its determinations into just other determinations or into nothing" (Hegel WL | GW 11: 287–8). Cf. Hegel's 1820s lectures on aesthetics: "the power of life, and still more the might of the spirit, consists precisely in positing contradiction in itself, enduring it, and overcoming it. This positing and resolving of the contradiction between the ideal unity and the real separatedness of the members constitutes the constant process of life, and life *is* only by being a *process*" (Hegel A | 1975: 120).

[202] See Hegel PG | W 3: 12.

In the third moment of logic, then, the "*positive* result" of dialectic is the speculative unity of the opposing claims within a category. This, Hegel says, is "not *simple, formal* unity, but a *unity of distinct determinations*,"[203] for it contains not just the sameness, but also the distinctness of these claims. In other words, a speculative unity contains the identity and difference of a category's opposing claims. Were this unity strictly an identity of opposing claims, it would merely repeat the contradiction with which dialectic negatively results, as if contradiction were "all there is." Thus, for example, being and nothing are moments of becoming because, in becoming, they are both "*the same*," since each has "passed over into" the other, and "*not the same*," since each is distinguished by its "distinct" mode of vanishing into the other.[204]

According to Hegel, logical thinking "gets entangled in contradictions" in a "conscious loss of its being at home with itself" when it posits categories that contain contradictory claims. However, he insists that "thinking will not give up, but remains faithful to itself," namely, through "the resolution of its own contradictions." If thinking "despairs of being able to bring about, *from its own resources*, the resolution of the contradiction in which it has put itself, then it returns to the solutions and appeasements in which the spirit has participated in its other modes and forms." But this despair lies on a path that leads toward the repose that, according to Hegel's adapted ancient skeptical method, is achieved by exhausting the totality of categorial contradictions and deriving a coherent and necessary set, that is, a system, of categories. This is why thinking's despair does not "degenerate into *misology*."[205] As Hegel says, "spirit is the one which is strong enough that it can endure contradiction" and "knows how to resolve it."[206] It is in this sense, then, that contradiction "cancels itself" in the deductive process.

As we saw, the three moments of logic can only be "considered in their truth" if they are "kept separate from each other." There are three ways of artificially separating these moments and thereby reducing logic to unscientificity.

First, one can leap to the third, positive moment of speculation, in which the science of intelligibility is simply asserted to be immediately crystal clear.[207] However, this is for thinking to exhibit what in the Preface to the *Phenomenology* Hegel calls "the rapturous enthusiasm which, like a shot from a pistol, begins straight away with absolute knowledge, and makes short work of other standpoints by declaring that it takes no notice of them."[208] Such a "royal road to science," he says, finds "no

[203] Hegel EL | GW 20: §82 Remark.

[204] See Hegel WL | GW 21: 69–70. Cf. Rödl 2019.

[205] Hegel EL | GW 20: §11 Remark. Cf. Kant on skeptical despair and misology, on which see Callanan 2019.

[206] Hegel WL | GW 21: 232. Cf. Hegel: "the life of spirit is not the life that shrinks from death and keeps itself untouched by devastation, but rather the life that endures it and maintains itself in it. It wins its truth only when, in utter dismemberment, it finds itself" (Hegel PG | W 3: 36).

[207] For an account of why John McDowell's quietist appropriation of Hegel makes this error and thus fails to consider the three moments of logic in their truth, see Bruno 2023c.

[208] Hegel PG | W 3: 31.

more easy-going way than to rely on sound common sense." Given the inherent dogmatism of common sense, that is, of ordinary consciousness, Hegel infers that the "scientific insight" of philosophy is "only to be won through the labour of the concept."[209]

Second, one can rest at the second, negative moment of dialectic, in which the contradictoriness of the opposing claims within a category is alleged to be unresolved.[210] However, this is for thinking to despair "of being able to bring about, *from its own resources*, the resolution of the contradiction in which it has put itself." Given that such despair threatens to "degenerate into *misology*," it must be endured for the sake of the coherence and necessity that the science of intelligibility requires.

Third, one can stall at the first, abstractive moment of the understanding, in which the opposing terms of an absolute opposition produce a contradiction from which thinking endlessly flees. However, this is to embody the philosophy of subjectivity, which, as we have seen, culminates in the vestigial facticity of the letter of the *Wissenschaftslehre*. Thus, despite launching the post-Kantian logical turn toward dialectical logic, Fichte undermines logic's scientific character, since he fails to consider the three moments of logic in their truth by stalling at its first moment.

Like Kant's deduction of the categories, Hegel's deduction generalizes a variety of skepticism. However, whereas Kant generalizes Humean skepticism in order to deduce our right to the categories in the service of a logic of truth,[211] Hegel generalizes a form of ancient skepticism in order to deduce our right to the system of the categories in the service of a science of truth. Moreover, like Fichte's deduction of the categories, Hegel's deduction makes productive use of contradiction. However, whereas Fichte derives the categories in a minimally empirical or inductive manner, namely, by presupposing a factical dichotomy between the I and the not-I, Hegel radicalizes Fichte's deductive method by deriving the categories in a presuppositionless manner.[212] As we saw in Section 1.6, a presupposition is

[209] Hegel PG | W 3: 65. Cf. Hegel: "Common sense cannot understand speculation; and what is more, it must come to hate speculation when it has experience of it" (Hegel D | GW 4: 21). Cf. also Hegel: "With science and common sense working hand in hand to cause the downfall of metaphysics, the singular spectacle came into view of *a cultivated people without metaphysics*—like a temple richly ornamented in other respects but without a holy of holies" (Hegel WL | GW 21: 6). And cf. Hegel: "[philosophy] only is philosophy in virtue of being directly opposed to the understanding and hence even more opposed to healthy common sense, under which label we understand the limitedness in space and time of a race of men; in its relationship to common sense the world of philosophy is in and for itself an inverted world" (Hegel VSP | 2000: 283).

[210] For an account of why Graham Priest's dialetheist appropriation of Hegel makes this error and thus fails to consider the three moments of logic in their truth, see Bruno 2023c.

[211] See Kant P | AA 4: 258–61, 310. On Kant's generalization of Humean skepticism, see de Boer 2019. On Kant's recognition of the Pyrrhonian element of Hume's skepticism, see Stern 2006.

[212] Houlgate interprets Hegel's commitment to presuppositionlessness as "the Cartesian conviction that all assumed certainties must be suspended before we may begin philosophy" (Houlgate 2006: 401) and as "exemplifying a Cartesian willingness to suspend his cherished beliefs and habits of thought, and to accept as true only what reason itself determines to be true" (Houlgate 2005: 39). This interpretation draws Stern's objection that Hegel rejects the skeptical impetus of Cartesian philosophy (Stern 2009: 218–25), which impetus, as we saw, is problematic insofar as it is modern as opposed to ancient.

"an arbitrary *assurance*,"[213] since it lacks a further ground, and thus "takes its *start* from the *contingent*."[214] Rather than derive the categories from an "arbitrary" or "*contingent*" origin, that is, rather than appeal to a brute fact, Hegel derives them from thinking itself, that is, he appeals to thinking alone. He thereby completes the German idealist response to the question *quid facti*.

To conclude this last section, it is crucial to notice that, insofar as Fichte fails to secure an absolute science of intelligibility, he fails to fully advance logic beyond its Kantian division into general and transcendental varieties. By contrast, Hegel transcends the Kantian division by embracing the nullification of finitude and hence of any finitizing opposition. In particular, he nullifies the opposition that the Kantian division within logic presupposes, namely, between the form and the content of cognition. For Kant, general logic abstracts from the content of cognition in order to determine the laws of what is thinkable, whereas transcendental logic abstracts from the content of cognition in order to determine the laws, that is, the categories, of what is experienceable. In the Preface to the second edition of the *Science of Logic*, Hegel rejects the view that, in logic, the categories are "*forms*" that attach to "*content*." Since the "*nature*" or "*essence*" of a thing just is its "*concept*," "there is no saying" what a thing is without its concept. Hence, the concept "cannot be regarded as *just* an indifferent form that attaches *to* a content," for it is rather "the innermost moment" of things, that is, "their simple life pulse."[215] If concepts are not merely the form, but rather the very essence of things, then a "science of logic" must investigate this essence. Although concepts "instinctively and unconsciously pervade our spirit everywhere," the "task" of logic is the "reconstruction" of the "multitude" of concepts whereby "*a* concept" is shown to be a "form determination" or "moment" of "*the concept itself*." This reconstruction produces "*the concept*" as a totality of concepts, namely, the categories, that constitute "the truth of what we call things."[216] Hence Hegel says in the *Encyclopedia* that logic is "capable of proving its very own peculiar content, and able to gain insight into the necessity of this content."[217] Moreover, since logic treats the categories as the essential content of things, it need not abstract from content in the manner of either general logic or transcendental logic. As Hegel says, abstraction is "the confusion in which

Stern instead interprets Hegel as driven to avoid presuppositions because they threaten to impose an external, unfathomable authority on thinking (Stern 2009: 229), a drive that, as we have seen, is originally Fichtean.

[213] Hegel EL | GW 20: §78.

[214] Hegel WL | GW 11: 388.

[215] Hegel WL | GW 21: 15. Cf. Hegel WL | GW 21: 29. See Heidegger's 1927 summer lectures in Marburg, *The Basic Problems of Phenomenology*: "When Hegel treats the concept in his *Logic* he takes the term 'Begriff,' 'concept,' contrary to the customary usage of his time, in the scholastic sense as *conceptus formalis*. In Hegel, concept means the conceiving and the conceived in one, because for him thinking and being are identical, that is to say, belong together" (Heidegger GP | GA 24: 117).

[216] Hegel WL | GW 21: 17–8.

[217] Hegel EL | GW 20: §42 Remark.

formalism invariably falls." Logic instead considers "the categories *in and for themselves*" through "a speculative form of philosophizing."[218]

Hegel succeeds Fichte at the University of Berlin in 1818 following the latter's death, becoming the new voice of the science of intelligibility and the champion of a truly absolute science. The exclusive role that dialectical logic plays in this science is meant to overcome the letter of the *Wissenschaftslehre* by vindicating its spirit, that is, by demonstrating thought's independence from presuppositions at all costs. However, as Schelling will soon argue, the hidden cost of pursuing a presuppositionless science of intelligibility is the presupposition that anything at all exists whose intelligibility might be an issue and, moreover, that this issue matters enough for us to endorse and develop this science. We will see in Chapter 4 that whereas Hegel provides the most thoroughgoing campaign against facticity among the German idealists, Schelling offers the most impactful defense of facticity for post-Kantian philosophy.

[218] Hegel WL | GW 12: 27.

4

Negative Philosophy

Schelling on Hegel's Factical Presuppositions

4.1 Introduction

In 1841, Schelling takes up the chair that is previously held by Fichte and Hegel at the University of Berlin, accepting an offer from King Wilhelm IV whose ambassador, Christian Karl Josias von Bunsen, intends the new chair to silence the "facile omniscience" of the still dominant Hegelian philosophy.[1] Schelling's inaugural lectures, whose attendees include Mikhail Bakunin, Carl Jacob Christoph Burckhardt, Friedrich Engels,[2] Alexander von Humboldt, Kierkegaard,[3] Leopold

[1] Schelling BV-A | 1977: 486. See Ralph Waldo Emerson's July 1842 and January 1843 journal entries for the New England Transcendentalist journal *The Dial*: "From Berlin, 'The City of Criticism', we learned in the past months that the king of Prussia was gathering around him a constellation of men of science. . .The king is discontented with the Hegel influence, which has predominated in Berlin, and, we regret to say, set himself to suppress the 'Hallische Jahrbucher', which, though published at Halle, depended for its support mainly on Berlin. With this view, also, he summons the great Schelling, now nearly seventy years old, to lecture on the Philosophy of Revelation. We have private accounts of these lectures, which began in the last November. The lecture room was crowded to suffocation, the pale professor, whose face resembles that of Socrates, was greeted with thunders of acclamation, but he remained pale and unmoved as if in his own study, and apparently quite unconscious that he was making a new epoch in German history. . .There are three questions on which Germany seems to be alive. 1st, The question between Catholicism and Protestantism. . .2nd, The question between Schelling and Hegel. . .3rd, The liberty of teaching" (Emerson, Fuller, and Ripley (ed.) 1842–43: 136, 396).

[2] Toward the start of the lectures, Friedrich Engels publishes a bitter response in December 1841 in the *Telegraph for Germany*: "Schelling as Hegel's successor can only lay claim to a certain piety and will demand calm and coolness least of all from me, for I am standing up for a dead man, and it is fit for a fighter to have a certain amount of passion: he who draws the sword in cold blood rarely has much enthusiasm for the cause for which he is fighting. . .[I]t is a little too much when Schelling asks the century to take back forty years of effort and work, forty years of thinking, of sacrifice of the dearest interests and the most sacred traditions, as a waste of time, an erroneous trend, only so that he shall not have lived these forty years too long. . .This is not the place to prove against him that existence belongs indeed to thought, that being is immanent in the mind, and that the foundation of all modern philosophy, the *cogito, ergo sum*, cannot thus be stormed and overrun; but I may be permitted to ask whether a power which itself has no being can produce a being" (Engels 2010: 185–7). For Engels' critique of Schelling's concept of positive philosophy, see his anonymous 1842 "Schelling and Revelation: Critique of the Latest Attempt of Reaction Against the Free Philosophy" (Engels 2010: 189–240).

[3] As his letters indicate, Kierkegaard's enthusiasm for the lectures diminishes markedly: "I am so happy to have heard Schelling's second lecture—indescribably. . .I remember almost every word he said after that. Here, perhaps, clarity can be achieved. . .I have put my trust in Schelling and at the risk of my life I have the courage to hear him once more. . .Schelling talks the most insufferable nonsense. . .I am too old to attend lectures, just as Schelling is too old to give them. His whole doctrine of potencies betrays the highest degree of impotence. . .I have never in my life felt like traveling as much as I do now. I owe that to Schelling. Had Schelling not lectured in Berlin, I would not have gone, and had Schelling not been so nonsensical, I would probably never have traveled again" (Kierkegaard 1989: xxi–xxiii). Despite the tone of the letters, Kosch argues that Schelling's

Facticity and the Fate of Reason After Kant. G. Anthony Bruno, Oxford University Press.
 DOI: 10.1093/9780191987533.003.0005

von Ranke, Friedrich Carl von Savigny, and Friedrich Adolph Trendelenburg, provide a momentous assessment of the first fifty years of the German idealist pursuit of the system of intelligibility.[4]

Schelling mounts an internal critique of German idealism, one that is sympathetic to the systematic aims of the philosophical movement that he helps to initiate, but which corrects the confinement of those aims to the method of what he calls 'negative philosophy.' Negative philosophy is a science of the conditions and, ultimately, the unconditioned condition or absolute first principle of the intelligibility of existence. Such a principle can be grasped as philosophy's starting point, as we saw in Chapters 1 and 2 regarding Fichte's doctrine of intellectual intuition, or as its end point, as we saw in Chapter 3 regarding Hegel's method of dialectical logic.[5] In either case, a first principle is intended to render existence systematically intelligible, that is, rational without remainder. But Schelling observes that existence itself constitutes this principle's remainder. Since "there could very well be nothing,"[6] it cannot be in virtue of a principle alone that there is any existence to render intelligible, that is, that there is any actuality to be rational. In the absence of existence, a principle would be an empty form, lacking reality. As Schelling puts it in the final lecture, negative philosophy holds that the actuality that realizes a first principle "necessarily exists," not unlike God, but only on the assumption that it exists, that is, only "*if it exists*."[7] In other words, negative philosophy can no more affirm the antecedent in its claim that if anything exists, then it exists according to its essence, that is, its principle, than pre-Kantian rationalism can affirm the antecedent in its claim that if God exists, then it exists according to its essence,

lectures have an evident impact on Kierkegaard's 1844 publications, namely, *The Concept of Anxiety* and *Philosophical Fragments* (Kosch 2006: 122–38).

[4] On Schelling's late philosophy, see Beach 1990, Bracken 1977, Bowie 1993, Dews 2022, Fackenheim 1954, Fackenheim 1996, Frank 1989, Gabriel 2009, Gardner 2020, McGrath 2016a, and Tritten 2012.

[5] According to Franks, Fichtean intuition and Hegelian dialectic are "competing interpretations of the same underlying methodological idea: the idea of a metaphysical deduction that begins with the *ens realissimum* and proceeds to trace the necessary delimitations or determinate negations of the 'space' of all possible transcendental realities. . .Whereas [Hegel] and Schelling had previously insisted that the system must begin with the absolute—by which they meant the idea of the *ens realissimum* from which the totality of the real is to be derived—Hegel now says [in the *Phenomenology*] that the absolute 'is essentially a *result*, that only in the *end* is it what it truly is' [Hegel PG | W 3: 24]. This might mislead one into thinking that Hegel has given up the project of a progressive derivation from the idea of the *ens realissimum*. But this would be incorrect. What he means is that the first principle disclosed through the *Factum* of 'thoroughgoing skepticism' [Hegel PG | W: 72] is an initial and still inadequate expression of the first principle, which achieves adequate expression only through its dialectical articulation in the system. Hegel's system is still progressive and, moreover, still progresses from the idea of God, although this idea is at first expressed in its most impoverished form, as mere 'being.' For 'being' and all the other determinations of Hegelian logic are 'the *metaphysical definitions of God*' [Hegel EL | GW 20: §85]" (Franks 2005: 373, 377). See Hegel: "There is a period in the formation of an epoch in which, just as in the formation of the individual, the foremost concern is the acquisition and reinforcement of the principle in its undeveloped intensity. But the higher demand is that such a principle should be made into science" (Hegel WL | GW 21: 7).

[6] Schelling BV-B | SW II/3: 59.

[7] Schelling BV-B | SW II/3: 168.

that is, its concept. It is an assumption that there is anything rather than nothing and, hence, that there is anything for negative philosophy to render intelligible. Negative philosophy cannot independently justify this assumption.

In order to resolve this issue, Schelling enlists what he calls 'positive philosophy.' Positive philosophy is a science that begins from the fact of existence and progresses toward the proof of the application, that is, of the reality, of its first principle.[8] However, Schelling recognizes that such a proof is faced with the "extra-logical nature" or bruteness of existence,[9] that is, the radical contingency that there is "anything at all."[10] In the absence of a principle, existence would be absurd, that is, nothing for reason. The final two lectures put this point in strikingly Fichtean terms. While positive philosophy must prove that the first principle or "*prius*" exists absolutely, namely, like "God," this must be proved not "*a priori*," but rather "*a posteriori*," that is, "*factically* [*faktisch*]."[11] In other words, the *prius* has absolute existence, "not necessarily, but *factically* [*faktisch*]," that is, without any ground.[12] Schelling will accordingly conclude that negative and positive philosophy are reciprocally dependent sciences, that is, that rendering existence rational and proving a first principle's reality are individually necessary and jointly sufficient elements of systematic cognition.[13] As I will put the point, repurposing a Kantian slogan,[14] 'a first principle without existence is empty and existence without a first

[8] McGrath argues that nature philosophy is not positive philosophy, since it concerns "an ideal, not an existing, nature" (McGrath 2016b: 123). Contrast Grant 2014.

[9] Schelling BV-B | SW II/3: 95.

[10] Schelling BV-B | SW II/3: 7. Cf. Ludwig Wittgenstein's 1921 *Tractatus Logico-Philosophicus*: "It is not how things are in the world that is mystical, but that it exists" (Wittgenstein 1994: 6.44). Cf. also Wittgenstein's Cambridge lecture on ethics, November 17, 1929: "it is nonsense to say that I wonder at the existence of the world, because I cannot imagine it not existing. I could, of course, wonder at the world around me being as it is. If for instance I had this experience while looking into the blue sky, I could wonder at the sky being blue as opposed to the case when it is clouded. But that is not what I mean. I am wondering at the sky being, *whatever it is*. One might be tempted to say that what I am wondering at is a tautology, namely, at the sky being blue or not blue. But then it is just nonsense to say that one is wondering at a tautology" (Wittgenstein 2014: 48). And cf. Wittgenstein's remark to Friedrich Waismann and Moritz Schlick, December 30, 1929: "Man feels the urge to run up against the limits of language. Think for example of the astonishment that anything at all exists. This astonishment cannot be expressed in the form of a question, and there is also no answer whatsoever. Anything we might say is *a priori* bound to be mere nonsense. Nevertheless we do run up against the limits of language" (Wittgenstein 1979: 68).

[11] Schelling BV-B | SW II/3: 128. Cf. Schelling: "what the consequences are that follow from [the absolute *prius*], these must be *factically* proved, and only thereby do we prove the divinity of that *prius*—that it is God, and that *God* therefore exists" (Schelling BV-B | SW II/3: 129).

[12] Schelling BV-B | SW II/3: 169. See Holz 1970: 49–51, 351, 365.

[13] See Schelling: "both philosophies are demanded—a science that grasps the essence of things and the content of all being and a science that explains the actual existence of things. Once this antithesis is present, one cannot get around it by somehow suppressing one of the two demands any more than by mixing both demands, whereby only more contradictions and confusion will arise. There remains, therefore, nothing else to do than to assume that each of these demands must be put forth and considered in its own right, that is, in a particular science. This of course does not prevent one from maintaining the association and perhaps even the unity of the two" (Schelling BV-B | SW II/3: 95).

[14] See Kant: "Without sensibility no object would be given to us, and without understanding none would be thought. Thoughts without content are empty, intuitions without concepts are blind" (Kant KrV A51/B75).

principle is blind.' We will see that whereas Kant's slogan expresses the concept of empirical cognition, which is a success term for a task that can in fact be satisfied by particular experiential episodes, its Schellingian repurposing expresses the concept of systematic cognition, which is a regulative ideal that guides experience as a whole, but can never be realized.

Schelling anticipates his core distinction between negative philosophy and positive philosophy in 1804's *Philosophy and Religion*,[15] which is a response to Adam Karl August von Eschenmayer's 1803 *Philosophy in its Transition to Non-Philosophy*.[16] There Schelling distinguishes between the "absolute" and the "actual world," that is, the "infinite" ground of objectivity and the "sensate universe" of finite objects, and argues that the world emerges not through a "continuous transition from the absolute," but rather through a "complete falling-away from absoluteness" that cannot be "*explained*." The world's emergence is inexplicable because "*pure absoluteness, without any further determination*," contains no differentiation and thus no "positive cause" for the emergence of anything at all. Schelling infers that the absolute and the world are equally "eternal (outside of time)," that is, equiprimordial. In other words, he infers that the opposition of the absolute and the world is a brute fact, thereby effectively positing an analogue of Fichte's underived opposition between the I and the not-I. Schelling then claims that the principle of the fallen world of objects "can only result in a negative philosophy" and that, since negative philosophy is "the realm of nothingness," it is "separated from the positive realm of reality by an incisive boundary."[17] We can clarify this obscure claim by drawing on the core distinction from the 1841–42 Berlin lectures. Insofar as negative philosophy proceeds from the unconditioned condition of the intelligibility of existence, it concerns not entities, but rather their first principle, which on pain of regress is not an entity, that is, is no genuine thing.[18] It is in this sense that the principle of the sensate universe of entities consists in "nothingness." This principle consequently lacks reality, which instead belongs to a "positive

[15] But cf. Schelling: "Some have wanted to explain my proposition of a positive philosophy as a change of mind. But since my studies of the Kantian philosophy, it has been clear to me that the latter could not be the whole of philosophy. I wrote in my *Letters on Dogmatism and Criticism* that a mightier, more majestic dogmatism would rise up against Kant's criticism, and this was the positive philosophy. Thus, *the notion of a positive philosophy* has been inscribed in me for a long time" (Schelling BV-C | 2020: 88). Cf. also Schelling: "I maintained already in 1795, in the *Letters on Dogmatism and Criticism*, that—not without turning to Fichte's momentary and obvious contradiction—in opposition to this criticism (and thus was the critical philosophy labeled as a system), there will someday appear an entirely different, far more adroit dogmatism than that of the mistaken and half-hearted former metaphysics" (Schelling BV-B | SW II/3: 82).

[16] On Schelling's response to Eschenmayer, see Bruno 2023a: 8–9. On Schelling's early correspondence with Eschenmayer, see Berger and Whistler 2020.

[17] Schelling PR | SW I/6: 29–43.

[18] Cf. Schelling: "an unconditioned thing [*unbedingtes Ding*] is a contradiction in terms. Unconditioned is what has not been turned into a thing, and what cannot at all become a thing. . .The principle of dogmatism contradicts itself because it presupposes an unconditional thing, that is, a thing that is not a thing" (Schelling IPP | SW I/1: 166, 170–1).

realm," namely, the factical existence whose science Schelling will call 'positive philosophy.'[19]

The reciprocal dependence of negative and positive philosophy gradually emerges in the course of Schelling's response to the "question of the meaning of philosophy itself." Early on in the Berlin lectures, he claims that, in order to answer this question, "one must once again return to Kant."[20] How are we to understand this claim? What insight does Kant offer into the limitations of negative philosophy and how does he point toward the need for its cooperation with positive philosophy? Moreover, what Kantian precedent is there for positive philosophy, which is a particularly unexpected science given that its topic, namely, facticity, by definition transcends scientific lawfulness?

I will argue that Schelling's alignment of negative and positive philosophy adapts a reciprocal relation that Kant expounds in the first *Critique*. For Schelling, a first principle depends for its reality on there being existence that requires intelligibility, while the fact of existence requires a first principle to demonstrate its rationality. I will call this Schelling's 'doctrine of infinite reciprocity.' A precedent for this doctrine is Kant's doctrine of epistemic reciprocity, according to which the categories depend for their cognitive significance on a given sensory manifold and, in turn, a sensory manifold requires the categories to determine its unity for consciousness. Furthermore, I will argue that Schelling's proof of the reality of a first principle adheres to Kant's threefold criterion for the proof of the principles that rest on the categories, that is, "those synthetic judgments that flow *a priori* from

[19] Contrast Schelling during his identity philosophy in 1801's *Presentation of My System of Philosophy*, which appears in the *Journal for Speculative Physics* that he founds in 1800: "*Absolute identity is absolute totality*...It might still be asked here what [an] individual is in relation to absolute totality. *In this relation, however, it simply does* **not** *subsist as individual*, since viewed from the standpoint of absolute totality only totality itself *is* and outside it is ***nothing***" (Schelling D | SW I/4: 125, 133). Frank shows that Schelling subsequently draws on Gottfried Wilhelm Leibniz, Christian Wolff, and Gottfried Ploucquet in order to develop the idea of absolute identity into a theory of predication in which an identity statement is the reduplication of the identity that the subject term and predicate term each bear to an underlying ground (Frank 2014). See the 1815 draft of Schelling's *Ages*: "The true meaning of every judgment, for instance, A is B, can only be this: *that which* is A is *that which* is B, or *that which* is A and *that which* is B is one and the same. Therefore, a doubling already lies at the bottom of the simple concept: A in this judgment is not A, but 'something = x, that A is.' Likewise, B is not B, but 'something = x, that B is', and not this (not A and B for themselves) but the 'x that is A' and 'the x that is B' is one and the same, that is, the same x. There are actually three propositions contained in the above-cited proposition. The first, 'A = x', the second, 'B = x', and, following first from this, the third, 'A and B are one and the same', that is, 'both are x'" (Schelling WA15 | SW I/8: 213–4). Cf. Schelling's 1809 *Philosophical Investigations into the Essence of Human Freedom and Matters Connected Therewith*: "'This body is blue' does not have the meaning that the body is, in and through that in and through which it is a body, also blue, but rather only the meaning that the same thing which is this body is also blue, although not in the same respect" (Schelling PU | SW I/7: 341). Cf. also Schelling's 1810 *Stuttgart Private Lectures* (Schelling SP | SW I/7: 422). On Schelling's theory of predication, see Gabriel 2014, Hogrebe 2024, and Thomas 2014.

[20] Schelling BV-B | SW II/3: 32. Schelling continues: "I most definitely have to dispute the opinion that any position can be advanced that is completely removed from a connection to Kant. . .Whoever wishes to make philosophy their major field of study must always begin with Kant" (Schelling SW II/3: 32–3; cf. 44–5).

pure concepts of the understanding," for example, the principle that everything that happens follows from something in accordance with a rule, which "flow[s]" from the category of causality.[21] Tracing this precedent will reveal the Kantian character of Schelling's internal critique of German idealism and thereby clarify his "return to Kant." This explanation, however, is not complete without articulating the skeptical challenge that prefigures Schelling's intervention with negative philosophy, a challenge that originates with Maimon.

After reviewing a manuscript that is sent to him by Herz and that becomes Maimon's 1790 *Essay on Transcendental Philosophy*, Kant tells Herz in a letter, May 26, 1789: "not only had none of my critics understood me and the main questions as well as Mr. Maimon does, but also very few men possess so much acumen for such deep investigations as he." This praise comes in spite of Maimon's criticism of Kant's division of cognition into two sources, namely, understanding and sensibility, for which reason Kant declines to recommend the manuscript's publication.[22] Kant dismisses the criticism in the letter by claiming that, whereas Maimon assumes that we must regard the understanding as a faculty that both thinks and intuits if we are to avoid the apparent problem of explaining the "agreement" of "such heterogeneous manners of representation" as concepts and intuitions, the cooperation of the distinct faculties of understanding and sensibility is the necessary condition of "experiential knowledge," without which objects of experience "would be nothing for us."[23]

Yet it is precisely the cooperation of understanding and sensibility as distinct faculties that Maimon denies. In the *Essay* and in other texts from the early 1790s, he argues that it is dubious whether we actually apply the categories to sensible intuitions and hence whether the categories are not merely empty forms, a doubt that he will extend to German idealism's first principle.[24] The challenge of empty formalism leads Maimon to reject the very idea of applying concepts to representations that belong to a brutely opposed faculty of sensibility,[25] a move that will encourage Fichte's deductive campaign against facticity.[26]

21 Kant KrV A136/B175.

22 Kant B | AA 11: 49, 54. See Maimon's letter to Kant, April 7, 1789: "I was lucky enough to see your immortal book, to study it, and to reconstruct the whole of my thinking in order to come into accord with it. . .These comments summarize the content of the manuscript that I venture to submit to you. My good friends have urged me for a long time to publish this book, but I did not want to comply without having subjected it to your priceless judgment" (Kant B | AA 11: 16–7).

23 Kant B | AA 11: 50–1.

24 On Maimon's empty formalism challenge, see Franks 2005.

25 While Maimon skeptically denies that we apply concepts to intuitions, he dogmatically asserts that sensibility is merely a confused use of the understanding. In the *Essay*, he describes sensibility as rule-conforming rather than rule-comprehending and says that it has the same cognitive source as the understanding, differing from the latter only in degree of cognitive completeness (Maimon VT | 2010: 23, 38, 98). In 1791's *The Hill of the Guide*, Maimon denies that sensibility and understanding are really distinct faculties (Maimon GH | 1965: 107, translated by Franks 2003: 206). On Maimon's self-description as an empirical skeptic and a rational dogmatist, see Franks 2003 and Thielke 2008.

26 The first sentence of the *Concept of the Wissenschaftslehre* credits Schulze and Maimon with convincing Fichte that, "despite the recent efforts of the most perspicacious men, philosophy has not yet

Schelling draws a restricted lesson from the Maimonian challenge. Empty formalism is a genuine threat to negative philosophy, which cannot justify its presupposition of the existence that would enmatter its first principle. For Schelling, however, negative philosophy's vulnerability to emptiness should inspire critical hope, not skeptical despair, in the possibility of realizing its first principle. The challenge that is posed by empty formalism does not force us to collapse the science of intelligibility into negative philosophy, but rather invites us to discover the sciences that properly compose the systematic cognition of the intelligibility of existence.[27] Such an undertaking requires pursuing a positive science whose topic can support the presupposition of existence, even as that science depends on an opposing negative science that can render existence rational. As we will see, Schelling employs Maimonian skepticism in a mood of hope in order to correct the one-sidedly negative character of the prevailing absolute science of intelligibility, namely, Hegel's logic, and thereby to save the German idealist project from the pitfalls of "dogmatizing rationalism."[28]

Of course, we saw in Section 3.6 that, for Hegel, categories are not forms that stand "indifferent[ly]" to content such that their "attach[ment]" to content can be dogmatically asserted as much as skeptically denied, but rather are the "life pulse" of all things. As he says in the *Phenomenology*, the existence of things "is directly a logical existence" in that, by making their content ever determinate and thus ever intelligible, things exhibit a "self-moving concrete shape" in such a way that their existence "raises itself to logical form." For this reason, he concludes, it is "unnecessary to clothe the content in an external [logical] formalism; the content is in its very nature the transition into such formalism, but a formalism that ceases to be external, since the form is the innate development of the concrete content itself."[29] Nevertheless, the empty formalism challenge arises with Schelling's Maimonian observation that the system of categories itself, that is, the science of intelligibility, presupposes the very existence whose intelligibility such conditions are meant to provide and that, without this presupposition, they would lack actuality. In other words, these conditions and this existence are equally essential components of

been raised to the level of a clearly evident science" (Fichte BWL | SW I: 29). In a fragment of a letter to Reinhold, March/April 1795, Fichte says: "My respect for Maimon's talent knows no bounds. I firmly believe that he has completely overturned the entire Kantian philosophy as it has been understood by everyone until now, including you, *and I am prepared to prove it*" (Fichte B | 1988: 383–4). Nevertheless, against Maimon, Fichte defends our right to use the categories by claiming in the *Foundations* that we derive them from "the I, as absolute subject" (Fichte GWL | SW I: 99). This is also to claim that we derive our right to use the categories, given Fichte's simultaneously genealogical and jurisprudential conception of deduction. Cf. Fichte's rebuttal of Maimon's skepticism in 1795's *Outline of the Distinctive Character of the Wissenschaftslehre with Respect to the Theoretical Faculty* (Fichte GE | SW I: 387–9) and 1797's *Lectures on Logic and Metaphysics* (Fichte GA IV/1: 212). Cf. also Fichte GWL | SW I: 227, although here Maimon is unnamed.

[27] On Kant's hopeful transmutation of Hume's skeptical despair, see Franks 2005: 148–52.
[28] Schelling BV-B | SW II/3: 119; cf. 82–3, 170.
[29] Hegel PG | W 3: 55.

intelligibility in that they jointly contribute to intelligibility. Since, for Hegel, philosophy can presuppose nothing that contributes to intelligibility, then, by his own lights, he cannot presuppose existence. And yet, as we will see in Section 4.6, he cannot but presuppose it and so cannot lay claim to total presuppositionlessness. Schelling's response will be to argue that the conditions of intelligible existence and existence itself are reciprocally dependent, which necessitates a conception of systematic philosophy as composed of corresponding, reciprocally dependent sciences, namely, negative and positive philosophy.

In this chapter, I will explain the doctrine of epistemic reciprocity that Kant develops in the first *Critique* (Section 4.2) and show how it is meant to answer the question of the objective reality of the categories, namely, the question *quid indicii* (Section 4.3). I will then articulate Maimon's skeptical argument for the empty formalism of both the categories and the first principle of German idealism (Section 4.4). Next, I will turn to Schelling's critique of negative philosophy and explain the twofold pressure that it exerts on Hegel's claim to an absolute, that is, presuppositionless, science of intelligibility. First, I will reconstruct the argument in the 1813 and 1815 drafts of Schelling's *Ages of the World* that any science of intelligibility, including Hegel's negative science, presupposes the facticity of time (Section 4.5). Second, I will reconstruct Schelling's argument in the Berlin lectures that, on pain of empty formalism, Hegel's negative science mutually depends on a science of our experiential openness to factical existence, namely, positive philosophy (Section 4.6).

4.2 Epistemic Reciprocity

Schelling's internal critique of German idealism adapts a reciprocal relation that Kant establishes in the first *Critique* between the categories and sense experience, a relation that he will extend to the first principle of a negative science that Kant does not indulge. The opening of the B-edition Introduction states:

> There is no doubt whatever that all our cognition begins with experience. . .But although all our cognition commences **with** experience, yet it does not on that account all arise **from** experience. For it could well be that even our experiential cognition is a composite of that which we receive through impressions and that which our own cognitive faculty (merely prompted by sensible impressions) provides out of itself.[30]

[30] Kant KrV B1–2.

This passage draws a crucial distinction from an analysis of the assumption that cognition begins with experience. On Kant's analysis, the sense of "begins with" is ambiguous between commencing and arising. In the sense of commencing, experience is the domain or context in which our body of cognitions develops insofar as it is necessary for that body's formation and perfection.[31] Cognition thus commences with experience just as cognition of German idealism commences with undertaking an academic degree, during which it can develop through careful study and become perfected through reading, writing, and discussion. In the sense of arising, experience is an origin or source of cognition insofar as we must be given a sensory manifold in order to cognize objects. Cognition thus arises from experience just as a passage arises from a philosophical text, which serves as the origin of definitions, premises, and references. For Kant, then, experience plays two roles in the beginning of cognition, namely, as cognition's formative context and as its sensory source.[32]

How are experience's roles as formative context and sensory source to be related? Whatever their relation, it must be both clearly defined and sufficiently motivated. I will argue that the relation between experience's two roles is defined by Kant's doctrine of epistemic reciprocity and that this relation is motivated by Kant's responses to two varieties of skepticism.

As Graciela de Pierris shows, there is a reciprocal relation in the first *Critique* between the *a priori* forms of cognition, of which I will focus on the categories, and sense experience. On the one hand, experience is "essentially dependent" on the categories because the latter make possible or "*constitut[e]*" the former. On the other hand, "the sensory ingredient of experience in turn gives meaning to and legitimizes" the categories, since, without the former, the latter "would not amount

[31] See Engstrom: "cognition does not simply abide within itself, like always-already-complete intellectual intuition, staying indoors, as it were. It must rather, without abandoning its concept, depart from it and 'run about' outside it to secure a further concept that is not already actually thought in the original yet suited to it, a concept it then combines with the original in the act of synthetic judgment. Because it involves this running about, it merits the appellation 'discursive'. Thus the expressions 'discursive cognition' and 'cognition from concepts' are but two ways of capturing the distinctive feature that belongs to this type of cognition and distinguishes it from the infinite cognition of an intuiting intellect—namely, its character as *learning*, or as cognition that comes to be and grows" (Engstrom 2006: 12–3). Cf. Stang's account of Kant's distinction between perceptual and universal experience (Stang 2015).

[32] The opening of the A-edition Introduction is less clear about these roles: "Experience is without a doubt the first product that our understanding brings forth as it works on the raw material of sensible sensations. It is for this very reason the first teaching, and in its progress it is so inexhaustible in new instruction that the chain of life in all future generations will never have any lack of new information that can be gathered on this terrain. Nevertheless it is far from the only field to which our understanding can be restricted. It tells us, to be sure, what is, but never that it must necessarily be thus and not otherwise" (Kant KrV A1). Despite the claim that the understanding produces experience by bringing sensations under concepts, the role of experience as the formative context of cognition is expressed by its identification with a "terrain" that affords "inexhaustible" instruction. And despite the claim that experience is not the only "field" in which the understanding functions, the role of experience as a sensory source of cognition is expressed by the implication that it discloses "what is," that is, what exists.

to knowledge" and "would even be devoid of meaning."[33] In §23 of the Analytic, Kant says that the

> extension of concepts beyond **our** sensible intuition does not get us anywhere. For they are then merely empty concepts of objects, through which we cannot even judge whether the latter are possible or not—mere forms of thought without objective reality—since we have available no intuition to which the synthetic unity of apperception, which they alone contain, could be applied, and that could thus determine an object. **Our** sensible and empirical intuition alone can provide them with sense and significance.[34]

Like the wind rustling a field of wheat, the categories shape the movement of experience. And like wheat displaying the wind's force, experience exhibits the ordering structure of the categories. The articulation of this reciprocal relation is Kant's doctrine of epistemic reciprocity. The doctrine helps to clarify the roles that experience plays with respect to cognition. While experience must play its role as sensory source in order to show that the categories apply to something, that is, that they have "sense and significance" and are not "mere forms of thought without objective reality," it must also subordinate its role in this regard to the understanding, which is a source of cognition in its own right insofar as it is the faculty that supplies the categories on which experience depends for its possibility. Thus, with Kant's doctrine of epistemic reciprocity, a deeper relation emerges than the one that is announced at the opening of the B-edition Introduction, namely, a relation between experience as the formative context and sensory source of cognition, on the one hand, and the categories as the non-sensory sources of cognition, on the other hand.

The key passage in which Kant discusses epistemic reciprocity arises in Chapter I of the Transcendental Doctrine of Method, "The Discipline of Pure Reason," where he says that, "through concepts of the understanding," speculative reason

> erects secure principles, but not directly from concepts, but rather always only indirectly through the relation of these concepts to something entirely contingent, namely **possible experience**; since if this (something as object of possible experience) is presupposed, then they are of course apodictically certain, but in themselves they cannot even be cognized *a priori* (directly) at all. Thus no one can have fundamental insight into the proposition 'Everything that happens has its cause' from these given concepts alone. Hence it is not a dogma, although from another point of view, namely, that of the sole field of its possible use, i.e., experience, it

[33] De Pierris 1992: 180.

[34] Kant KrV B148–9; cf. A19b/B33b, A84c/B116c, A139/B178, A145–7/B185–7, A155–6/B194–5, A219/B266–7, A239–42/B299–300, B305–8, A348–9, B431, A609/B637, A635/B663, A677/B705.

> can very well be proved apodictically. But although it must be proved, it is also called a **principle** and not a **theorem** because it has the special property that it first makes possible its ground of proof, namely, experience, and must always be presupposed in this.[35]

This passage articulates a relation in which experience proves the significance and objective reality of the principles that are grounded on the categories, while these principles make experience, and hence their own experiential proof, possible. According to this relation, principles cannot secure their own significance and objective reality without experience, just as experience cannot constitute itself without these principles. This passage also provides a threefold criterion for the proof of a principle and the category on which it is grounded. As we will see, such a proof must be indirect, incomplete, and reciprocal.

First, a proof must relate a principle to experience because we can have no direct "insight" into the significance of a synthetic principle like 'all events are caused,' namely, on the basis of "concepts alone." Sense experience is required. As Kant says in the A-edition Chapter III of the Analytic of Principles, "On the Ground of the Distinction of All Objects in General into *Phenomena* and *Noumena*," regarding the category of causality and its related principle, "if I leave out the time in which something follows something else in accordance with a rule," there is "nothing through which cause and effect could be distinguished" and so the category and its related principle must lack "any determination through which to apply to any object." Categories and the principles that are grounded on them "contain nothing but the logical function for bringing the manifold under a concept" precisely because they can have "determinate significance and relation to any object only by means of the general **sensible condition**."[36] A principle's proof therefore must be indirect because it must be mediated by sense experience.

Second, since the proof of a principle has a sensible condition, it relies on "something entirely contingent, namely, **possible experience**." Proving a principle, that is, proving that it has real application and hence significance, depends on what we happen to be given in a sensory manifold. Moreover, such a proof depends on something whose contingency can never definitively express the significance of a principle, since no amount of sense experience can non-arbitrarily be regarded as sufficient for this proof. A proof therefore must be incomplete because it must be mediated by endless experience.

Third, since a principle conditions the possibility of the very experience that mediates its proof, the relation between a principle and experience within a proof is one of reciprocal dependence. A series of causal conjunctions contributes to the proof of the significance of the causal principle yet it is only on the presupposition

[35] Kant KrV A736–7/B764–5.

[36] Kant KrV A243–5/B301–2. Cf. Kant NF | AA 18: 111 (R5184).

of that principle that this series is intelligibly of causal conjunctions. A principle's proof therefore must consist of a reciprocal relation between that principle and experience.[37]

We can now fully define the deeper relation between experience as the formative context and sensory source of cognition and the categories as the non-sensory sources of cognition. It is a relation that serves both to constitute sense experience with synthetic *a priori* judgments, for example, the causal principle, and the pure concepts on which they rest, for example, the category of causality, and to prove the significance and objective reality of these principles and concepts through sense experience. And it is a relation whose proof is marked by indirectness, incompleteness, and reciprocity. But what motivates Kant to cast experience within this relation? To answer this, we must clarify two skeptical problematics to which he responds in the first *Critique.*

4.3 The Question *Quid Indicii*

As James Conant shows, skepticism is not a position, but is rather a "*dialectical space*" or "*problematic*" in which one can adopt a range of opposing positions on a central question.[38] One finds that Kant participates in two skeptical problematics that address what I will call 'inverse questions.' I will abstract these two problematics from Conant's formulation of them in order to explain Maimonian skepticism and its employment by Schelling in the remaining sections of this chapter.

Conant identifies two varieties of skepticism that he calls "Kantian" and "Cartesian." He clarifies that one participates in these skeptical problematics by engaging with its central question, but need not thereby espouse any skeptical viewpoint.[39] The Kantian problematic addresses the question of the conditions of a purported cognition, that is, it asks how an actual cognition is possible. The Cartesian problematic addresses the question of whether a purported cognition is borne out by existence, that is, it asks whether a possible cognition is actual. The

[37] In "The Architectonic of Pure Reason," Kant divides metaphysics, according to the "**speculative**" and "**practical**" uses of pure reason, into the "**metaphysics of nature**" and the "**metaphysics of morals,**" respectively. He divides the metaphysics of nature into "**transcendental philosophy**" and "the **physiology** of pure reason." While transcendental philosophy "considers only the **understanding** and reason itself in a system of all concepts and principles that are related to objects in general, without assuming objects that **would be given,**" the physiology of pure reason "considers **nature**, i.e., the sum total of **given** objects (whether they are given by the senses or, if one will, by another kind of intuition)" (Kant KrV A841/B869, A845/B874). Insofar as a physiology concerns reason in regard to objects that are given to sensible intuition, it concerns the formation of cognition through the categories' application in experience.

[38] Conant 2004: 101. Cf. Cavell 1999: 46.

[39] Thus, Kant critiques dogmatic metaphysics, but only in order to set metaphysics on the path to a science, and Descartes doubts his cognitive faculties, but only in order to secure them through divine intervention.

inverse questions that these problematics address apply to various contexts of empirical cognition.[40] I will examine these questions within the context of the two skeptical problematics that motivate Kant's doctrine of epistemic reciprocity. To this end, I must first introduce Kant's distinction between logical possibility and real possibility.

In a footnote[41] to Book II, Chapter III of the Transcendental Dialectic, "The Ideal of Pure Reason," Kant issues "a warning not to infer immediately from the possibility of the concept (logical possibility) to the possibility of the thing (real possibility)." Logical possibility is the mark of a non-contradictory concept. Such a concept is "empty" if it lacks the "objective reality" of its synthesis with an intuition. Real possibility, by contrast, is the mark of a non-contradictory concept that can be synthesized with the intuition of an object of possible experience and can thereby attain objective reality.[42] Now, the "principles of analysis," primary among which is the principle of non-contradiction, govern logical possibility because they govern the form of thinking in general, which abstracts from the content of thinking and hence is indifferent to that content so long as that thinking is non-contradictory. Such principles are accordingly too weak to govern real possibility, which requires thinking whose content is not merely non-contradictory, but also potentially objectively real. As I noted in Section 0.1, general logic is the science of the rules of thinking in general or, to use the language of Kant's warning, the science of the principles of analysis. General logic is ontologically over-permissive insofar as it tolerates any non-contradictory metaphysical doctrine, which is why it is powerless to resolve the controversies of metaphysics. By contrast, the "principles of possible experience," which are composed of the *a priori* forms of cognition that include the categories, govern real possibility because they govern the form of a possible experience, within which the content of thinking can grasp objective reality. Thought grasps objective reality, then, by synthesizing concepts with intuitions in empirical cognition.

Following Kant's terminology, we find that thought grasps objective reality just if it cognizes the actuality of that which is really as opposed to logically possible. As he says in a footnote to Chapter II of the Analytic of Principles, "System of All Principles of Pure Understanding," "while [real] possibility was merely a positing of a thing in relation to the understanding (to its empirical use), actuality is at the same time its connection with perception."[43] As I noted in Section 0.1,

[40] Conant considers the contexts of perception, other minds, and meaning. In the Cartesian problematic, I may misperceive an object, falsely take you to be a subject, or mistakenly interpret a text's meaning. In the Kantian problematic, I may boggle over how I can perceive objects, how you can appear to me as a subject, or how a text can have interpretable meaning (Conant 2004).

[41] See Kant KrV A596n/B624n.

[42] Cf. Kant: "the possibility of a thing can never be proved merely through the non-contradictoriness of a concept of it, but only by vouching for it with an intuition corresponding to this concept" (Kant KrV A252/B308).

[43] Kant KrV A235n/B287n.

transcendental logic is the science of the rules of thinking of objects of experience or, to use the language of Kant's warning, the science of the principles of possible experience.[44] Unlike the principles of general logic, the principles of transcendental logic are strong enough to govern real possibility, within which actuality can be cognized, namely, in experience. Kant's logical turn in the first *Critique* can thus be viewed as raising the standard for possibility in metaphysics from non-contradictoriness to object-relatedness such that possibility signifies not merely the system of conceivability, whose members are mostly not cognizably actual insofar as they include objects that transcend possible experience, but rather the system of objectivity, whose members are cognizably actual insofar as they are objects of possible experience.

Now, Kant can ask, within the dialectical space of the Kantian problematic, how an actual cognition is possible. This is to ask which system of objectivity must be presupposed by a purported member of that system, that is, how that which is actual is really possible. But Kant can also ask, within the dialectical space of the Cartesian problematic, whether a possible cognition is actual. This is to ask whether a system of objectivity in fact has any members, that is, whether that which is really possible is actual. We find that Kant addresses guises of these inverse questions about possibility and actuality in, respectively, the question *quid juris* and the question *quid indicii*.

It is in the Kantian problematic that Kant asks the question *quid juris* regarding our right to use the categories. Hume's 1748 *An Enquiry Concerning Human Understanding* teaches Kant the importance of this question by assuming our actual practices of causal inference and asking what justifies their possibility.[45] Hume concludes that nothing justifies this on the empiricist assumption that our two allegedly exhaustive modes of cognition are "demonstrative" and "moral," that is, the assumption that our cognition is either analytic *a priori* or synthetic *a posteriori*.[46] Kant generalizes Hume's justificatory question from the category of causality to all categories in order to eliminate dogmatism in metaphysics. However, he avoids Hume's skeptical answer by rejecting its empiricist assumption, namely, by substituting Hume's cognitive fork with a cognitive trident so as to pursue an account of the possibility of the synthetic *a priori* cognition that is expressed by our use of the categories and the principles that rest on them.[47] As we saw in Section 1.2, Kant

[44] Cf. Kant's distinction between the principles of analysis and the principles of experience with his distinctions, in reflections from the 1770s and 1780s, between the analytic and synthetic criteria of possibility, analytic and synthetic possibility, and the possibility of things and the possibility of the existence of things (Kant NF | AA 18: 111–12 (R5184), 232 (R5556), 349-50 (R5772)).

[45] On Kant's endorsement of Hume's critique of special metaphysics, see de Boer 2019. On Hume's role in Kant's formulation of the question *quid juris*, see Bruno 2018a. On Hume and Kant's recognition of reason's natural illusion, see Thielke 2003.

[46] Hume 2007: 25–6, 32.

[47] See Hume: "In vain do you pretend to have learned the nature of bodies from your past experience. Their secret nature, and consequently, all their effects and influence, may change, without any change in their sensible qualities. This happens sometimes, and with regard to some objects: Why may it not happen always, and with regard to all objects? What logic, what process of argument secures you

transcendentally deduces our right to use categories like 'causality' by showing that they are necessary for the possibility of experience. Thus, insofar as it contributes to the determination of the principles of possible experience, a transcendental deduction serves to delimit real possibility, that is, to demarcate the system of objectivity in which actuality is cognizable.

I suggest that it is in the Cartesian problematic that Kant answers the question *quid indicii*, from the Latin '*indicium*,' which means 'evidence' or 'proof.'[48] Whereas the question *quid facti* demands the origin of our possession of a category and the question *quid juris* demands our right to use a category, the question *quid indicii* demands the proof of the objective reality, that is, the non-emptiness and hence the sense and significance, of a category and its related principle, namely, through its application to a sensory manifold. This question arises in the Cartesian problematic because it concerns whether the system of objectivity, that is, real possibility as governed by the categories, has actual members. Hence, the question *quid indicii* addresses the problem of whether the objective reality of a category is proven by its synthesis with an intuition and the related problem of whether a practice that presupposes that category actually cognizes anything with it. Although Kant does not mention this question, he is well aware of its importance given his doctrine of epistemic reciprocity, which predicates the significance of a category and its related principle on a synthesis with intuition.

In the face of the question *quid indicii*, Kant is confident that the categories apply to intuition and thus that real possibility is actual. In the B-edition Introduction, he says that pure mathematics and pure natural science are "actually given" as "sciences," that is, that they have "actuality" as sciences.[49] Earlier he says:

> it is easy to show that in human cognition there actually are such necessary and in the strictest sense universal, thus pure *a priori* judgments. If one wants an example from the sciences, one need only look at all the propositions of mathematics; if one would have one from the commonest use of the understanding, the proposition that every alteration must have a cause will do...[H]ere we can content ourselves with having displayed the pure use of our cognitive faculty as a fact.[50]

against this supposition?" (Hume 2007: 27–8). Kant invents transcendental logic and transcendental argument precisely in order to secure our right to use the category of causality and thereby to cognize nature's causal regularity.

[48] This expression extends the juridical terminology of the questions *quid juris* and *quid facti*, on which see Henrich 1989.

[49] Kant KrV B20. In contrast to mathematics and natural science, metaphysics, Kant says, is "actual, if not as a science yet as natural predisposition (*metaphysica naturalis*)" (Kant KrV B21).

[50] Kant KrV B5.

For Kant, we can "content ourselves" with the "fact" that our "use" of synthetic *a priori* judgments and thus of the categories is "displayed" in cognitions from both "the sciences" and the "commonest" experience. In §14 of the Analytic, he says that those who, like John Locke and Hume, derive the categories empirically and so fail to see that they originate in the understanding and apply to intuitions are "refuted by the fact," namely, "the actuality of the scientific cognition *a priori* that we possess, that, namely, of **pure mathematics** and **general natural science.**"[51] And in the *Prolegomena*, Kant says:

> we can confidently say that some pure synthetic cognition *a priori* is actual and given, namely, *pure mathematics* and *pure natural science*; for both contain propositions that are fully acknowledged, some as apodictically certain through bare reason, some from universal agreement with experience (though these are still recognized as independent of experience). We have therefore some at least *uncontested* synthetic cognition *a priori*, and we do not need to ask whether it is possible (for it is actual), but only: *how it is possible*, in order to be able to derive, from the principle of the possibility of the given cognition, the possibility of all other synthetic cognition *a priori*.[52]

According to Kant, we can answer the question *quid indicii* regarding whether the categories have objective reality or actuality in the affirmative, for the proof of their application lies in "the fact" that, in mathematics and natural science, synthetic *a priori* cognition, that is, the synthesis of categories and intuition, is "actual and given," "fully acknowledged," and "*uncontested*." But exactly what sort of fact is this?

The fact of the actuality of synthetic *a priori* cognition, that is, of the objective reality of the categories, if indeed it is a fact, is neither general-logically necessary nor empirically contingent. On the one hand, it is no violation of the principle of non-contradiction to deny this fact, since otherwise Hume's skepticism about synthetic *a priori* cognition would be not merely misguided, but rather unintelligible. And yet his skepticism must be intelligible for Kant to generalize it for the sake of eliminating dogmatism. On the other hand, an empirically contingent fact is cognizable only in virtue of the application and hence the objective reality of the categories, which is the very fact in question. The fact of the actuality of synthetic *a priori* cognition is accordingly a fact whose necessity is not logical yet whose contingency is not empirical, which is to say that it occupies precisely the modal space of brute facts. Kant's answer to the question *quid indicii* is accordingly an appeal to an example of facticity, that is, to something that cannot be proven and is simply

[51] Kant KrV A95/B128.
[52] Kant P | AA 4: 275.

"*uncontested*." As we saw in Part I, this does not constitute Kant's first or only such appeal.[53]

This will not satisfy Maimon, who will accuse Kant of begging the question *quid indicii* on the grounds that it is doubtful whether we in fact apply the categories to a sensory manifold. For Maimon, we cannot simply assume that real possibility, construed as a system of objectivity, has any actuality. As we will see, he extends his skeptical doubt to whether the system of objectivity that is grounded on the first principle of German idealism has any actuality. This will be Schelling's clue that existence must be presupposed alongside this principle, however factically.

4.4 Maimonian Skepticism

Kant's transcendental deduction is apparently a successful *reductio ad absurdum* of Hume's skeptical answer to the question *quid juris*, that is, of his despair about reason's capacity to justify its metaphysical claims. By generalizing Hume's pursuit of justifying our use of the category of causality to all categories and showing that this conceptual repertoire makes our standpoint on experience possible, Kant exposes the self-refuting character of Hume's skeptical answer insofar as the latter undermines its own experiential standpoint. As Kant says in the *Prolegomena*, such doubt is "a mode of thinking in which reason moves against itself with such violence that it never could have arisen except in complete despair as regards satisfaction of reason's most important aims" and thus, as a mode of thinking, "promises us absolutely nothing at all, not even the tranquility of a permitted ignorance."[54]

For Maimon, however, Kant's is a limited victory because it answers one question while begging another. On Maimon's interpretation, in the Kantian problematic, Kant indeed demonstrates what would make actual experience possible, namely, by showing that the categories are necessary conditions of experience. However, in the Cartesian problematic, Kant does not demonstrate that possible experience is actual, for he assumes that we actually apply the categories to a sensory manifold, taking this to be a brute fact that is acknowledged by all. In other words, Maimon holds that the success of Kant's answer to the question *quid juris* coincides with his begging the question *quid indicii*. In 1794's *Attempt at a New Logic, or Theory of Thinking with Appended Letters of Philalethes to Aenesidemus*, Maimon puts this point by saying that Kant answers the question *quid juris* by showing that we have the "right" to use the categories because they condition the possibility of experience, but that there remains what Maimon misleadingly calls the "question *quid facti*," which is in fact the question *quid indicii*, namely, "whether

[53] On the Kantian idea of a fact that cannot be proven, but rather is only illustrated through an experiment, see Ware 2014.
[54] Kant P | AA 4: 271, 274.

in fact we do use them with respect to empirical objects. Their employment cannot be taken as an undoubted fact of consciousness, for this consciousness might rest on an illusion to be explained on psychological grounds."[55] Kant's apparently limited victory against Hume consists in the fact that while he justifies our possible and even subjective use of the categories, he does not prove their actual and genuinely objective use. This, according to Maimon, leaves us in the Humean predicament that we simply believe, but cannot know, that the categories have "*objective reality*."[56] As we saw in Section 4.3, "*objective reality*" is Kant's term for a concept that is not merely logically possible, that is, not empty, but rather is synthesized with the intuition of an object. This indicates that Maimon confronts Kant with an empty formalism challenge. I turn now to consider Maimon's challenge in more detail in order to see how it both threatens Kant's doctrine of epistemic reciprocity and provokes Schelling's successor doctrine of infinite reciprocity.

As Paul Franks shows,[57] Maimon's empty formalism challenge exploits a distinction that Kant draws in the *Prolegomena* between judgments of experience and judgments of perception. A judgment is experiential and thus "*objectively valid*" if it applies a category of the understanding, for example, when I judge that the sun warms the stone, but perceptual and thus "*subjectively valid*" if it involves no categories, but rather only the logical connection among one's perceptions, for example, when I judge that the sun shines on the stone and that the stone becomes warm.[58] In other words, a judgment of experience proves that real possibility is actual, that is, that the system of objectivity has actual members, whereas a judgment of perception leaves this question open.[59] But then the question of whether a judgment is experiential rather than perceptual just is the question *quid indicii*, a point that Maimon registers in the *Essay*.

[55] Maimon VNL | 2000: 191. I use 'the question *quid indicii*' for what Maimon calls 'the question *quid facti*' (see also Maimon VT 70, 129 | 2010: 42, 72) in order to distinguish the latter from Kant's usage of it, which concerns the fact not of a concept's objective reality, but rather of its original acquisition (see Kant KrV A84–5/B116–17 and Kant NF | AA 18: 267 (R5636)).

[56] Maimon GW 7: 58, translated by Franks 2005: 183n83. Cf. Maimon's 1791 *Philosophical Dictionary, or Illumination of the Most Important Objects of Philosophy in Alphabetical Order*: "[whereas Kant] holds that the categories are transcendental concepts of the understanding, I. . .hold them to be transcendental fictions of the imagination" (Maimon PW | GW III: 20, translated by Thielke 2001: 114). Cf. Jacobi's criticism of Kant: "Our universal representations, concepts, and principles express only the essential form to which every particular representation and every particular judgment must conform because of the constitution of our nature. . .Neither the principle of sufficient reason, nor even the proposition that nothing can come from nothing, apply to things in themselves. In brief, our entire cognition contains nothing, nothing whatsoever, that could have any *truly* objective meaning at all" (Jacobi DH 225-6 | 1994: 337).

[57] See Franks 2005: 176–89.

[58] Kant P | AA 4: 298, 301n.

[59] For Kant, judgments of perception do not even purport to successfully apply categories to objects, for they "refer merely to feeling—which everyone acknowledges to be merely subjective and which must therefore never be attributed to objects." Judgments of perception "hold only for us, i.e., for our subject, and only afterward do we give them a new relation, namely, to an object, and intend that the judgment should also be valid at all times for us and for everyone else." They are accordingly "completely different" from judgments of experience (Kant P | AA 4: 298–9, 299–n).

In Chapter 2, Maimon says:

> we have presumably abstracted [a category] from its use with real objects, and transferred it into logic; as a result we must put the reality of its use beyond doubt before ascribing reality to it as a form of thought in logic; but the question is not whether we can use it legitimately, which is the question: *quid juris?*, but whether the fact is true, namely, that we do use it with actual objects. Yes, it will be said, the fact is indubitable. We say, for example: the fire warms (makes warm) the stone and this signifies not merely perception of the succession of the two appearances in time, but the necessity of this succession. But to this **David Hume** would reply: it is not true in this case that I perceive a necessary succession; I certainly use the same expression that others use on this occasion, but I understand by it only the often perceived succession of the warming of the stone upon the presence of the fire and not the necessity of this succession. It is merely an association of perceptions, not a judgment of the understanding. It is just what in animals we call the expectation of similar cases; and even if **Kant** has proved that we cannot have abstracted these forms from experience because experience only becomes possible in the first place by means of them, **David Hume** (or his representative) can gladly admit this. . .From this we see that logic is unable to yield a trustworthy distinguishing mark of the reality of these forms (insofar as the fact, or the use of its forms, is itself doubtful); and that concepts like these that determine particular objects must be completely excluded from logic, which abstracts from all matter.[60]

Drawing on Kant's example in the *Prolegomena*, Maimon argues that it cannot be assumed to be "indubitable" that my judgments are experiential simply because I use "the same expression that others use" when judging that the sun warms the stone, for that an expression is shared does not guarantee that it is not empty, that is, that its use is not merely subjectively valid. If my judgment does not apply the category of causality to a sensory manifold, but rather expresses "merely an association of perceptions," then it is dogmatic to "put the reality of its use beyond doubt." Maimon's move here is from the question of the rightful use of the categories to the question of their actual use. Even if Kant can answer the former in the affirmative, proving that we "legitimately" use the categories is distinct from proving that we "do" use them, which is just to say that answering the question *quid juris* is distinct from answering the question *quid indicii*.[61] As Maimon puts the point, a category's

[60] Maimon VT 72–4 | 2010: 42-3. Cf. van Cleve 1999: 89.

[61] In this connection, another misleading use of a Kantian phrase occurs when Maimon says that the question *quid juris* is "one and the same as the important question that has occupied all previous philosophy, namely, the explanation of the community between soul and body, or again, as the explanation of the world's arising (with respect to its matter) from an intelligence" (Maimon VT | 2010: 37). This "important question" concerns whether the use of a category, namely, 'causality,' is actual, not whether its use is legitimate, that is, it is in fact the question *quid indicii*. Thus, when Maimon then argues that

application to intuition cannot be "assumed *materialiter*," even if, for the sake of the possibility of experience, it must be "assumed *formaliter*."[62] In general, we can remove doubt regarding our capacity to use a concept yet remain in doubt regarding whether this capacity is ever actualized. This is why Maimon says that Hume can "gladly admit" the conclusion of Kant's transcendental deduction and still doubt whether our judgments are experiential as opposed to perceptual.[63]

That the question *quid indicii* arises in the Cartesian problematic is clear from Maimon's claim that transcendental logic offers no "distinguishing mark" of the reality of the forms of the understanding. This claim is analogous to the claim that is under consideration in Meditation One of René Descartes' 1641 *Meditations on First Philosophy*, namely, that perception offers no "sure signs" of the reality of the world.[64] Both claims respond in the negative to the question of the actuality of a kind of possibility, namely, real possibility and waking life, respectively.

Maimon's empty formalism challenge signifies a crossroads for post-Kantian participants in the Cartesian problematic who recognize the limits of logic as a science of intelligibility, for it is possible to draw two opposing inferences from the observation that logic, insofar as it is a formal abstraction "from all matter," cannot provide a distinguishing mark or sure sign of actuality beyond possibility.

On the one hand, Maimon's own inference is to seek the elimination of any limits on transcendental logic that appear to be posed by the science of any faculty that is allegedly distinct from the understanding, for example, transcendental aesthetic *qua* science of the rules of sensibility. As Frederick Beiser shows, this inference leads Maimon to regard sensibility as a confused expression of the understanding, not a distinct faculty, and to correct this confusion by thinking of empirical cognition under the regulative idea of an infinite understanding that, rather than sensibly receiving its objects, creates them merely by thinking of them.[65] Hence he argues in the *New Logic* and in 1794's *Aristotle's Categories* that the rules of sensibility, namely, space and time, are in fact forms of the understanding. Maimon's refusal to consign any forms of cognition to any faculty that is apparently brutely

since "[i]n the Kantian system, namely, where sensibility and understanding are two totally different sources of our cognition, this question [*quid juris*] is insoluble," whereas it is "easily resolved" by the "Leibnizian-Wolffian system," in which these faculties "flow from one and the same cognitive source" and differ "only in the degree of completeness of this cognition" (Maimon VT | 2010: 38), he in fact refers to the question *quid indicii*. Kant tells Herz in a letter, May 26, 1789, that Maimon's conception of the difference between sensibility and understanding as one of degree rather than of kind is not Leibnizian-Wolffian, but is rather "Spinozis[tic]" (Kant B | AA 11: 50).

62 Maimon VT 41–2 | 2010: 27. Hence, unlike Schulze's skeptical challenge to Kant in *Aenesidemus*, Maimon's challenge is internal to critical philosophy. On this, see Beiser 2003: 238–9 and Thielke 2001: 106, 113.

63 Cf. Maimon's letter to Kant, April 7, 1789: "The question, *Quid facti?* You seem to have touched on this, but it is, I think, important to answer it fully, on account of the Humean skepticism" (Kant B | AA 11: 17). On the Humean background of Maimon's skepticism, see Thielke 2008.

64 Descartes 1996: 13.

65 Beiser 1987: 291–5. On the Leibnizian background of Maimon's idea, see Fincham 2015.

opposed to the understanding, in combination with his explicit subordination of the allegedly complete science of general logic, with its inherited and groundless forms of judgment, to a new and genuinely critical logic,[66] crucially prefigure the German idealist campaign against facticity.

On the other hand, as we will see in Section 4.6, in the Munich and Berlin lectures, Schelling makes the Maimonian observation of the limits of logic as a science of the conditions of intelligible existence. However, rather than collapse this science into a negative philosophy that is guided by the idea of an infinite understanding, he infers that this science, for the sake of its sense and significance, mutually presupposes a positive science of factical existence.

It is worth noting that Maimon explicitly formulates Kant's doctrine of epistemic reciprocity yet rejects Kant's threefold criterion of the proof of the reality of a category and its related principle. In Chapter 2, Maimon says:

> experiences and these concepts (cause and effect) are in a reciprocal relation that is asymmetrical: on the one hand, experience does not first make these concepts possible, but only shows that they are in themselves possible; on the other hand, these concepts not only show that experience in itself is possible, but they make it possible.[67]

Maimon's formulation of Kant's doctrine states that while pure concepts like 'causality' make experience possible, sense experience "shows" that such concepts are "in themselves possible," namely, as actually applying to objects. Their relation is "asymmetrical" insofar as the categories constitute experience, whereas experience can only exhibit their constituting function. Nevertheless, it is a "reciprocal" relation insofar as the categories cannot exhibit themselves, just as experience cannot constitute itself. The relation's reciprocal feature might suggest that Maimon, like Kant, espouses the threefold criterion according to which an exhibition or proof is indirect, incomplete, and reciprocal. Maimon dispels this appearance by arguing that the categories cannot be shown to apply to intuitions at all, and hence cannot be shown to apply either indirectly or incompletely, given their heterogeneity as *a priori* and *a posteriori* representations, respectively. If an intuition is empirical and I attempt to give its matter categorial form and thereby "make it into an object," then my procedure is "manifestly illegitimate because the intuition has arisen *a posteriori* from something outside me, not *a priori* from myself, and so I can no longer prescribe a rule for it to arise."[68] If heterogeneous representations generally

[66] See Maimon VNL | 2000: 191. Cf. Beiser 1987: 300, 309–10.
[67] Maimon VT 42 | 2010: 27.
[68] Maimon VT 49 | 2010: 31.

cannot follow the same rules, then the categories in particular cannot apply to intuitions and consequently no judgments can be experiential.[69]

We could only avoid this conclusion, Maimon says,

> if our understanding could produce objects out of itself according to its self-prescribed rules or conditions without needing to be given something from elsewhere. But this is not the case. . .We assume an infinite understanding (at least as idea), for which the [*a priori*] forms are at the same time objects of thought, or that produces out of itself all possible kinds of connections and relations of things (the ideas). Our understanding is just the same, only in a limited way.[70]

Maimon denies that proof of the objective reality of a category and its related principle is possible for our finite understanding, for which, unlike an infinite understanding, the form and matter of cognition are not homogeneous. Nevertheless, he holds that our understanding resembles an infinite understanding in one special case, namely, mathematics. Mathematical concepts are uniquely capable of being constructed wholly *a priori* insofar as an *a priori* intuition, for example, the intuition of space, can "arise in conformity" with an *a priori* rule, for example, the concept of a circle.[71] This is why Maimon says in 1793's *On the Progress of Philosophy* that

> [God] does not think as we do, that is, discursively; rather his thoughts are at one and the same time presentations [of their objects]. If someone objects that we have no conception of such a style of thinking, my answer is: We do in fact have a concept of it, since we partly have this style in our possession. All mathematical

[69] In §21 of the Analytic, i.e., the Remark that signals the move from the first step or "beginning" to the second step or "sequel" of the B-edition transcendental deduction, Kant announces that "it will be shown from the way in which the empirical intuition is given in sensibility that its unity can be none other than the one the category prescribes to the manifold of a given intuition in general" (Kant KrV B144–5). He conceives of a transcendental deduction as ruling out the heterogeneity of the unity of an intuition and the unity of a category on the grounds that these unities are identical in their use, namely, when an intuition is "given" and a category is "prescribe[d]" to what is given, and so are at most rationally distinct. Maimon's empty formalism challenge against Kant thus seems to ignore the one unity at which the deduction aims. For a Kantian rebuttal of Maimon that distinguishes between distinct faculties and distinct exercises of faculties, see Franks 2005: 51–61. For the view that intuition presents an object to thought only if it bears categorial unity, see McDowell 2009. For the argument that rational perception must be explained not additively by combining our rational power with a perceptual system that we allegedly share with non-rational animals, but rather transformatively by distinguishing our rationally informed species of animal powers from non-rationally informed species of animal powers, see Boyle 2016. For a critique of the assumption that, for Kant, the difference between sensible and discursive representations entails that sensibility and understanding, like layers of a cake, compose a *compositum* of self-standingly intelligible capacities as opposed to the *totem* of a unified capacity for cognition, see Conant 2016. Cf. Schafer 2021.

[70] Maimon VT 63–5 | 2010: 37–8.

[71] Maimon VT 50 | 2010: 31.

> objects are at the same time thought by us and exhibited as real objects through *a priori* construction. Thus we are in this respect *similar to God*.[72]

Unless a concept can "be made intuitive and thereby obtain objective reality," as it does for a finite understanding in mathematics and for an infinite understanding in general, it is "merely symbolic" and its objective reality is accordingly "merely problematic."[73] Hence, far from being answered by the fact of successful, if endless, epistemic reciprocity in non-mathematical cognition, it seems that the question *quid indicii* is unanswered by Kant, if not begged. Without a non-question-begging answer to the question *quid indicii*, Kant's answer to the question *quid juris* thus appears at best to secure the mere subjective indispensability of the categories.[74]

The possibility that our judgments are merely perceptual indicates the existential weight of Maimon's empty formalism challenge, for the potential unreality of the categories confronts us with the loss of a cognitively significant world. This is especially clear when we register the threat that the challenge poses to the German idealist thought of a first principle.

The first principle of the system of intelligibility would appear to be ideally positioned to meet the empty formalism challenge because it serves as the unconditioned condition of intelligibility and, in particular, the derivational source of the faculties of cognition, understanding and sensibility included. Moreover, a first principle would seem to justify our judgments of experience precisely insofar as it functions for the German idealists as a kind of infinite understanding for which the form and matter of cognition are ultimately homogeneous. No serious skeptic, it seems, could doubt the proof of such a principle. As Fichte says in the *Foundations*, skepticism

> would not be a system at all, since it denies the very possibility of any system whatsoever. But it can deny this only systematically; hence it contradicts itself and is quite irrational. The nature of the human mind has seen to it in advance that skepticism is also impossible. No one has yet been such a skeptic in earnest. The critical skepticism of Hume, Aenesidemus [i.e., Schulze], and Maimon, which exposes the inadequacy of the grounds that have been offered heretofore and, in doing so, indicates where more tenable ones may be discovered, is something else. Science profits from such critical skepticism, if not always with respect to its content, then certainly with respect to its form; and anyone who denies the

[72] Maimon SGP | GW 4: 20, translated by Socher 2006: 91. Cf. Giambattista Vico's 1709 *On the Study Methods of Our Time*: "We are able to demonstrate geometrical propositions because we create them; were it possible for us to supply demonstrations of propositions of physics, we would be capable of creating them *ex nihilo* as well" (Vico 1990: 23).

[73] Maimon VT 48 | 2010: 30.

[74] On the connection of this problem to post-Fregean philosophy, see Franks 2007.

perspicacious skeptic his due respect exhibits a poor understanding of what is to the advantage of science.[75]

By Fichte's lights, Maimonian skepticism, while self-contradictory as a system, is instructive because it draws our attention to the proper grounds of cognition, for example, Maimon's idea of an infinite understanding or Fichte's own idea of the I as "absolute," "*infinite* and *unlimited*."[76] By exposing Kant's failure to answer the question *quid indicii*, this skepticism helpfully points us toward philosophy's redemption in a first principle.

However, Maimon is just as skeptical about the reality of a first principle, telling Reinhold in 1793's *Philosophical Correspondence*, which he publishes without Reinhold's permission, that such a first principle faces the same empty formalism challenge as do the categories. Reinhold posits the principle of consciousness in order to ground the system of intelligibility and asserts that this principle describes a "fact." For Maimon, this leaves open two questions, namely, how we know that it describes a fact and how we know that it describes "a primary and immediate fact rather than a derived and mediate one."[77] Without a satisfactory answer to the first question, a first principle is "a castle in the air,"[78] that is, an empty form whose logical possibility lacks objective reality. But even assuming a satisfactory answer to the first question, without a satisfactory answer to the second question, the fact that is described by a first principle could be explained on psychological grounds as an illusion, our belief in which is at best subjectively valid. This, for Maimon, shows that a first principle is no less vulnerable than the categories to the question *quid indicii*, without an answer to which that principle is an empty form whose objective reality cannot simply be posited as a brute fact.

The crisis of Maimonian skepticism now reaches its height. The objective reality of the first principle of the system of intelligibility, which is sought by German idealism in order to provide the missing premise for Kant's conclusions and to save human freedom and purposiveness from the nihilistic consequence of Spinozism, is no more capable of proof than the categories. This jeopardizes the idea that reality is rational at all, let alone rational without remainder. The threat that is posed by the empty formalism challenge will consequently lead Schelling to establish a new reciprocity between a first principle and the fact of existence.

[75] Fichte GWL | SW I: 121n5. Cf. Fichte's fragment from April 1795: "Anyone who has not yet understood Hume, Aenesidemus (where he is right), and Maimon and has failed to come to terms with the issues they pose is by no means ready for the *Wissenschaftslehre*; *it answers questions he has not yet raised and bandages him where he has suffered no injury*" (Fichte GA II/3: 389, translated by Breazeale 2013: 41).

[76] Fichte GWL | SW I: 255. On the connection between Maimon's and Fichte's ideas, see Beiser 2003: 243–7 and Thielke 2001. On Fichte's engagement with skepticism, see Breazeale 1991 and Horstmann 2015. For Fichte's distinction between critical skepticism, mere skepticism, and dogmatism, see Bruno 2021e.

[77] Maimon SGP | GW 4: 213–4, 263, translated by Beiser 1987: 318.

[78] Maimon SGP | 1793: 208n.

4.5 Schelling on Negative Philosophy

Schelling assigns to positive philosophy the topic about which negative philosophy can make only an unjustified presupposition, namely, existence as such. The topic of negative philosophy, namely, the necessary conditions of the intelligibility of existence, exhibits a necessity that is not general-logical insofar as it demarcates a system of objectivity as opposed to a mere system of conceivability. By contrast, the topic of positive philosophy exhibits a contingency that is not empirical, since empirical reality obeys the necessary conditions of intelligibility, but rather is radical, insofar as existence as such is given groundlessly, brutely, or factically. This might suggest that facticity is a feature that is exclusive to the topic of positive philosophy. However, we will see in this section that it is also a feature of the topic of negative philosophy, after which, in Section 4.6, I will turn to facticity in positive philosophy.

Schelling's Maimonian challenge to Hegel in Munich in the 1830s and in Berlin in the 1840s is that he leaves the science of intelligibility open to the threat of empty formalism by developing a negative philosophy that, while it dialectically articulates the conditions of intelligible existence, presupposes the existence that it is meant to render intelligible, taking for granted an existence that could well not be.[79] Having radicalized Fichte's method of eliminating radical contingency from the science of intelligibility and thereby securing absolute premises for Kant's conclusions, Hegel presupposes the reality that dialectical logic is meant to rationalize, that is, the existence that contributes to intelligibility and that therefore, by his own lights, cannot be presupposed. Hegel is consequently led to mistake the conditions of intelligible existence for existence itself, that is, to confuse their necessity with their reality. This is why Schelling argues in the Berlin lectures that Hegel's negative science requires a mutually complementary positive science, whose proper topic is our experiential openness to the brute givenness of existence.[80] However, there is textual support in drafts of the *Ages*, which are composed three decades before these lectures, to show that Schelling argues that negative philosophy also bears the mark of facticity, namely, in its own basic conditions. I will reconstruct this argument in order to portray Schelling as a pivotal figure in the history of the concept of facticity, one who inaugurates a post-Kantian shift from architectonic to existentialist interests. By turning away from Fichte and Hegel's German idealist project of employing the absolute freedom of reason in order to eliminate radical

[79] Cf. James' 1882 "On Some Hegelisms": "if the [common] man ask how self-contradiction *can* do all this, and how its dynamism may be seen to work, Hegel can only reply by showing him the space itself and saying: 'Lo, *thus*.' In other words, instead of the principle of explanation being more intelligible than the thing to be explained, it is absolutely unintelligible if taken by itself; and must appeal to its pretended product to prove its existence" (James 1882a: 194–5).

[80] On Schelling's Hegel-critique, see Bowie 1993: 127–77, Bowie 2014, Dews 2022, Matthews 2007: 57–60, and Rush 2014.

contingency, Schelling marks the beginning of the transition from the primacy of the practical to the primacy of the factical. In this respect, Schelling prefigures facticity's embrace and analysis by Heidegger, which will be my focus in Part III.[81]

For Schelling, pursuing a science of intelligibility is essential to philosophy.[82] However, he holds that pursuing this science with the pretense to total justification, that is, to total presuppositionlessness, inevitably confronts the question of why there is such a science in the first place. Indeed, it raises a permutation of the question, to which Schelling returns throughout his life, of why there is something rather than nothing, namely, why there is systematic intelligibility at all. Scholars recognize that this question motivates Schelling's claim against Hegel that reason is not self-justifying, but rather is bounded by something other than itself.[83] But what kind of claim is this? Assuming that it is not a bare assurance, for what sort of argument could it be the conclusion? I propose that Schelling's claim is the conclusion to a transcendental argument that is discernible in the *Ages*, according to which the past and the future are brute facts that condition the possibility of a science of intelligibility. As I reconstruct it, this argument represents the past as the free decision to derive a science of intelligibility and the future as the completeness that guides this derivation. In their role as brutely underivable conditions of possibility, the past and the future undermine any science's claim to presuppositionless.

Before turning to Schelling's argument, four points are worth noting.

First, Schelling's why-question and Kant's how-question, namely, how experience is possible, both arise within the dialectical space of the Kantian problematic, for they both assume something actual, namely and respectively, that there is systematic intelligibility and that there is experience, and ask after its possibility. They therefore contrast with whether-questions that arise within the dialectical space of the Cartesian problematic, for example, whether there is an external world or other minds, which assume a possibility and ask after its actuality.

Second, Schelling's answer to his why-question, by adducing brute facts about we who pursue science, qualifies as a long argument to idealism. As Karl Ameriks shows,[84] Reinhold pioneers a short argument to idealism that begins from the concept of "representation in general," from which it trivially follows that the thing in itself, which he defines as unrepresentable, is unknowable. Reinhold thereby

[81] See Heidegger's 1968 seminar in Le Thor: "Philosophy, as a totality of knowledge produced by reflection, becomes a system, that is, an organic whole of concepts, whose highest law is not the understanding, but reason. . .In thinking this notion of system, we are able to measure the distance that separates Hegel from Kant. Kant speaks of system in the 'Doctrine of Method'; nevertheless, a system is only possible after Fichte. This possibility is brought to its highest degree of completion by Hegel himself, since, at the end of his life, Schelling again fell outside the system. Thus in philosophy there is no system in the strict sense other than that of these two thinkers [namely, Fichte and Hegel]" (Heidegger VS | GA 15: 35–6).

[82] A version of this discussion appears in Bruno 2020a.

[83] See Franks 2005: 380–3, Kosch 2006: 107–8, Matthews 2007: 67, Snow 1996: 6, Stern 2009: 311–2, Stern 2007: 13–4, and Tritten 2012: 26.

[84] Ameriks 2000: 125–35.

offers "a shorter route" to Kant's conclusion against transcendental realism,[85] one that bypasses Kant's premise in the Transcendental Aesthetic that space and time are brute facts of our peculiar kind of sensibility to which appearances must conform.[86] The short argument to idealism prefigures Fichte and Hegel's project of eliminating presuppositions about peculiar features of our sensibility by deriving such features from a dialectical movement of thought.[87] After the period of his identity philosophy, Schelling takes a longer path to idealism, one that begins with a transcendental argument for the facticity of time, that is, for the past and the future as conditions of the science of intelligibility whose necessity is not logical and whose contingency is not empirical.

Third, we must distinguish intra-logical presuppositions, which are derivable moments within a science of intelligibility, from extra-logical presuppositions, which are radically contingent or brute facts that outstrip the dialectical method of scientific derivation. Although, in the *Science of Logic*, Hegel says of the beginning of logic that "there is *nothing* that it may *presuppose*,"[88] there is a sense in which earlier stages within logic are discovered to presuppose later stages. At the start of the logic, for example, the concept of "*pure being*—without further determination" is shown to contain no determinable content, lest it "fail to hold fast to its purity," and thus to contain "[j]ust as little" as the concept of "*pure nothingness*." The truth that it turns out is presupposed by these two now indistinguishable and unstable concepts is the "*movement* of the immediate vanishing of the one into the other: *becoming*."[89] For Hegel, such intra-logical presuppositions are not radically contingent, that is, unscientific, for they are entailed by contradictions that emerge from the dialectically unfolding structure of thinking itself.[90] Intra-logicality also characterizes the presuppositions that natural consciousness betrays in the *Phenomenology*,[91] as well as the natural and historical presuppositions that emerge in the philosophy of nature and philosophy of spirit, respectively. As Hegel argues in his 1822–23 Berlin lectures, intra-logicality constitutes "history as the development of spirit," in which "the ladder of stages that spirit climbs" proceeds "through the sublation and reworking of the previous, lower stage, which,

[85] Reinhold VNT 244, 254–5 | 2011: 114, 119.

[86] See Kant KrV A42/B59.

[87] See Fichte VND | SW I: 487–9 and Hegel PG | W 3: 82–92.

[88] Hegel WL | GW 21: 57.

[89] Hegel WL | GW 21: 68–70. On the consistency between logic's beginning with being and its being presuppositionless, see Hentrup 2019.

[90] On why, for Hegel, contingency is the necessity that is generated by the self-negation of possibility, see Houlgate 1995. Cf. Burbidge 1980 and Henrich 1958.

[91] That the *Phenomenology* begins with the apparently factical givenness of particulars to sense-certainty is not evidence of an extra-logical presupposition, for sense-certainty's criterion of knowing reveals itself intra-logically to presuppose that knowing consists in mediating particulars via universals. The opening of the text instead shows that Hegel begins with the elimination of merely apparent facticity and that, in this respect, he follows the spirit of Fichte's idealism, whereas Schelling will argue that such elimination is illusory.

once transformed by time, falls into the past."[92] Intra-logicality even characterizes the relation between the *Science of Logic* and the *Phenomenology*, which latter Hegel says "traverses all the forms of the *relation of consciousness to the object*" and thereby supplies "nothing other than" the "deduction," that is, the "justification," of "the *concept of science*" that the *Science of Logic* subsequently articulates.[93] The *Phenomenology* "has the *concept* of science. . .for its result," since, as we saw in Section 3.6, it details the "history of the *education* of consciousness itself to the standpoint of science" at which consciousness realizes that the subject and object of knowing are not distinct, a "liberation from the opposition of consciousness" that yields "[p]ure science," which Hegel says "contains *thought insofar as thought is equally the fact as it is in itself*; or the *fact in itself* insofar as this *is equally pure thought*." "To this extent," he concludes, logic has the *Phenomenology* "for its presupposition." However, he immediately clarifies this claim by saying that a "beginning is *logical*" if it is made "*in pure knowledge*," that is, in "a free, self-contained thought" that presupposes no externally imposed fact. He then says that logic is "pure knowledge in the full compass of its development." It follows from this that, "in the full compass of its development" and hence in its beginning in particular, logic is "free, self-contained thought," presupposing nothing extra-logical. This is why Hegel then says that the *Phenomenology* is, for logic, a presupposition that "has proved itself to be the result" of pure knowledge.[94] In other words, the deduction of the concept of science in the *Phenomenology* is not an extra-logical presupposition of the thinking that composes the *Science of Logic*, but rather is an earlier moment in the overall science of intelligibility of which the *Science of Logic* is a later moment.[95] As we will see in this section, Schelling will argue that the past and the future are extra-logical presuppositions, for they underivably condition the possibility that a science of intelligibility could be so much as freely valued and purposefully pursued, respectively.

Fourth, it is crucial that Schelling's why-question ultimately concerns the conditions of the possibility of a science of intelligibility. Espousing the facticity of time is his response to the question of why there is something rather than nothing, a question to which he continually returns in various connected permutations.[96]

[92] Hegel VPW1 | GW 18: 39.

[93] Hegel WL | GW 21: 32–3. On the relation between the *Phenomenology* and the *Science of Logic*, see the Introduction to Heidegger's 1930–31 Freiburg lectures, *Hegel's Phenomenology of Spirit* (Heidegger HPG | GA 32: 1–47). For the argument that the *Phenomenology* facilitates the presuppositionlessness of the *Science*, see Maker 1994: 78, 93, but contrast Dunphy 2020.

[94] Hegel WL | GW 21: 33, 54–5.

[95] See Houlgate 2003: 380.

[96] See Schelling PB | SW I/1: 310, 313–4, Schelling S | SW I/6: 38, Schelling WA15 | SW I/8: 255–6, Schelling MV33 | SW I/10: 143, and Schelling BV-B | SW II/3: 7–8. Schelling twice dismisses the why-question, namely, in 1804's *System of Philosophy in General and of the Philosophy of Nature in Particular* (Schelling S | SW I/6: 155) and 1805's *Aphorisms as an Introduction to Philosophy of Nature* (Schelling A | SW I/7: 174). However, these dismissals occur during his identity philosophy at the height of his confidence in our ability to cognize the absolute, whose necessary existence allegedly renders nothingness inconceivable.

The question does not ask why certain finite things exist, but rather why there is finite existence as such. However, since, for post-Kantian idealism in general, finite existence is nothing apart from its meaningfulness for the standpoint of experience, it has the more determinate form of the question of why there is meaningful experience. Moreover, since, for German idealism in particular, meaningful experience is nothing apart from the thought-determinations that compose an absolute science of intelligibility, it has the even more determinate form of the question of why there is systematic intelligibility. Since the permutations of Schelling's why-question take on these increasingly determinate forms, his transcendental argument will ultimately concern the factical conditions of the science of intelligibility.

Schelling expresses the meaning and science permutations of the why-question in his 1832–33 Munich lectures during a criticism of Hegel:

> What [Hegel's] argument concerns. . .is that everything is in the logical idea and therefore the meaningless can exist nowhere. But. . .[w]hy is there meaning at all, why is there not meaninglessness instead of meaning?. . .The logical represents itself as the negative, as that without which nothing could exist. . .The entire world, so to speak, lies caught in the nets of the understanding or reason, but the question is: How did it come into these nets?[97]

As we saw in Chapter 3, for Hegel the conditions of the meaning or intelligibility of existence are determined by logic, a science whose lack of a contrary and hence absoluteness rules out the very idea of meaninglessness, that is, the very idea of a standpoint from which meaning could be put into question.[98] If, as he says in the *Encyclopedia*, "*logic* coincides with *metaphysics*"[99] and, as he says in *Philosophy of Nature*, Part II of *Encyclopedia of the Philosophical Sciences*, "metaphysics is nothing else but the entire range of the universal determinations of thought, as it were, the diamond net into which everything is brought and thereby first made intelligible,"[100] then it seems that we cannot so much as pose the permutations of

[97] Schelling MV32 | 1972: 222.

[98] See Longuenesse on Hegel's system: "reflection is the process by which thought as a 'function of unity'. . .brings to unity the multiple determinations it finds within itself, only to go beyond the unity thus found towards more determinations to be unified anew, and so on *ad indefinitum*. . .[A]lterity is no longer the alterity of a given with respect to another given, but the alterity of thought with regard to itself" (Longuenesse 2007: 51–2).

[99] Hegel EL | GW 20: §24.

[100] Hegel EPN | 2004: 11. Cf. Hegel's 1820 introduction to his Berlin lectures: "everyone possesses and uses the wholly abstract category of *being*. The sun *is* in the sky; the grapes *are* ripe, and so on *ad infinitum*. Or, in a higher sphere of education, we proceed to the relation of cause and effect, force and its manifestation, etc. All our knowledge and ideas are entwined with metaphysics like this and governed by it; it is the net which holds together all the concrete material which occupies us in our action and endeavour. But this net and its knots are sunk in our ordinary consciousness beneath numerous layers of stuff. This stuff comprises our known interests and the objects that are before our minds, while the universal threads of the net remain out of sight and are not explicitly made the subject of our reflection" (Hegel VGP1 | 1985: 27–8).

Schelling's why-question. Not surprisingly, Hegel implicitly dismisses the why-question in the *Science of Logic*: "It is customary to oppose *nothing* to *something*. Something is however already a determinate existent that distinguishes itself from another something; consequently, the nothing which is being opposed to something is also the nothing of a certain something, a determinate nothing."[101] However, we can see that Hegel disregards the senses of 'nothing' and 'something' that are relevant to the why-question. He construes their senses in terms that are internal to and hence already incipiently justified by his science. Yet the why-question is raised by that very science. Assuming that we find experience to be meaningful in accordance with the thought-determinations of an absolute science, that we do so, that is, that there is "not meaninglessness," is, for that science, a brute fact. Hegel's allegedly presuppositionless account of meaningfulness cannot explain why, but rather can only presuppose that, this account is itself meaningful, which is to say, it can only presuppose that this account matters or has value. But this is just to say that the commitment to presuppositionlessness presupposes something, namely, the value of presuppositionlessness itself.[102]

Negative philosophy, that is, the absolute science of intelligibility, discloses a world that lies caught in reason, which raises the question of why it lies so caught. This forces us to face the bounds of reason, that is, to confront the thought that, as Schelling says, "there is obviously something other and something *more* than mere reason in the world."[103] In the *Ages*, he conceives of reason's other in temporal terms as the past and the future that condition the possibility of a science of intelligibility. Grasping the concept of reason's other requires that we adopt a critical standpoint on the very idea of scientific intelligibility, that is, the very idea of a "diamond net" whose luminosity is meant to render existence rational without remainder. Schelling will put this point in his 1833–34 Munich lectures by saying that "Hegel threw himself into the methodological discussion in such a way

[101] Hegel WL | GW 21: 70. Hegel also interprets the why-question in the form 'how does something finite emerge from something infinite?,' on which see Hegel WL | GW 21: 139 and Hegel PG | W 3: 132.

[102] Cf. Bowie: "forms of sense-making. . .cannot be reduced to a nomological account of sense-making, as such an account itself depends on a certain prior direction of sense-making that cannot be grounded in its own terms without the sense dissolving" (Bowie 2014: 187). Cf. Sheehan: "For [Heidegger], every human act is an act of making sense. But the most he can say about such pan-hermeneutics is that the phenomenological correlation of man and meaning, which is its basis, is an irreducible given. To ask for the cause of sense-making is itself a sense-making act; and therefore the question about why there is meaning-at-all gets caught up in circular reasoning and cannot be answered. Whether practically or theoretically, we can in principle make sense of everything—except why we can make sense of anything" (Sheehan 2013: 392). Some argue that Hegel at most presupposes enabling conditions, e.g., language, which his science subsequently justifies (see Houlgate 2006: 78–9 and Winfield 1989: 63, 87–8). However, this does not show that science incorporates a justification of its own value, which value would be presupposed by that very justification.

[103] Schelling MV33 | SW I/10: 143–4. Cf. Schelling's 1832–33 Munich lectures: "what we call the world, which is so *completely contingent* both as a whole and in its parts, cannot possibly be the impression of something which has arisen by the *necessity of reason*. . .[I]t contains a *preponderant* mass of *unreason*" (Schelling FS | 1972: 99, translated by Bowie 1993: 148–9). Contrast Fichte: "the only thing that exists in itself is reason" (Fichte VND | SW I: 505).

that he thereby completely forgot the questions which lay outside it."[104] One such question, to which I now turn, arises within the dialectical space of the Kantian problematic insofar as it asks after a specific possibility, namely, why there is philosophical science at all.

We can divide the transcendental conditions that Kant identifies in the first *Critique* into two kinds. The first includes the grounds that give experience its structure, namely, space, time, and the categories. The second includes the ends that give experience its purpose, namely, the systematic ideals that are represented by the ideas of reason. I will call these kinds of conditions 'grounding' and 'teleological,' respectively. We can see that they are individually necessary, but only jointly sufficient, for what they condition. On the one hand, experience cannot rest on the forms of sensibility and the categories without also satisfying reason's desire for ideals that lie beyond appearances.[105] On the other hand, experience cannot pursue these ideals without aesthetic and logical structure. We can also see that each kind of transcendental condition bears a unique temporality. Grounding conditions signify an immemorial past for experience insofar as the latter is essentially belated with respect to them. There can be no empirical derivation of space, time, or the categories because experience cannot but have exhibited their structure, that is, they have always already made possible any experience that we might have.[106] By contrast, teleological conditions signify an unrealizable future for experience insofar as the latter will never reach a point where the cognition that it affords is adequate with respect to them. There can be no empirical actualization of the ideas of reason because experience cannot but fall short of intuiting their content, that is, they are the receding horizon of any experience that we might have.[107]

The past and the future that are signified by grounding and teleological conditions, respectively, are not empirical, for this is a past that could never have been present and a future that could never come. They are rather transcendental. Grasping the unique temporality of transcendental conditions enables us to grasp what I will call Schelling's 'idealism of ages,' that is, his doctrine of the factical times that condition the possibility of a science of intelligibility. I will now reconstruct from drafts of the *Ages* his three-step argument that a free decision to derive a science signifies the past that grounds this derivation, turning thereafter to his

[104] Schelling MV33 | SW I/1: 143.

[105] See Kant: "our power of cognition feels a far higher need than that of merely spelling out appearances according to a synthetic unity in order to be able to read them as experience, and. . .our reason naturally exalts itself to cognitions that go much too far for any object that experience can give ever to be congruent" (Kant KrV A314/B370–1).

[106] For Kant, the categories are "ancestral concepts" (Kant KrV A13/B27, A81/B107), which must be deduced transcendentally and which, moreover, make possible the "ancestry from experiences" (Kant KrV A86/B119) to which an empirical deduction is restricted.

[107] For a practical interpretation of the regulative principles that rest on the ideas of reason, see Mudd 2013.

three-step argument that the complete derivation of a science signifies the future that guides this derivation.

First, Schelling says that if the past is exclusively thought of as a phase in "a chain of causes and effects," then the world is a "mechanistic system."[108] This is the thought of empirical time, that is, the thought of an efficient-causal series of moments in which the past is qualitatively identical to the present, preceding the latter within a uniform succession. Such a thought rules out the possibility of a science of intelligibility insofar as it entails that that science is the product of a causal mechanism rather than an expression of the autonomy of reason. In order to avoid this mechanistic scenario, Schelling invites us to "rise above" the succession of "time-parts flowing continuously into each other" and to conceive of an "authentic past," one that makes science possible.[109] Insofar as this is a past that lies outside of empirical time, we require the concept of a non-empirical past.

Second, Schelling describes the concept of a non-empirical past as follows: "different times (a concept that, like many others, has gotten lost in modern philosophy) can certainly be, as different, at the same time, nay, to speak more accurately, they are necessarily at the same time. . .The past certainly cannot be as the present, but it must be, as the past, at the same time with the present."[110] Schelling conceives of a past that is not present yet is simultaneous with the present. This is precisely the unique temporality of a grounding transcendental condition. Construed in this transcendental register, the past precedes science by grounding its possibility yet cannot fail to coincide with science, since otherwise the latter would lack its structure. Thus, we can say that science is never without its transcendental past.

Third, Schelling casts freedom in the role of the transcendental past. He describes "freedom" as the "life of obsession and craving" and posits it as "a past that did not first become past, but which was the past from the primordial beginning and since all eternity."[111] This past is qualitatively distinct from the present, for it was never present, but rather has been from "eternity." However, if this past is eternal, then it cannot but be simultaneous with the present. Again, we find the temporality of a grounding condition. But in what sense does freedom *qua* craving function as such a condition? An answer lies in Hegel's own description of the beginning of logic in Book One of the *Science of Logic*, The Doctrine of Being. He says that in order to ensure that the beginning of logic will "remain immanent" to it, we must first consider "*what is there before us*" in its "*simple immediacy*," namely, "*pure being*."[112] He then adds that "if no presupposition is to be made, if the beginning is itself to be taken *immediately*, then the only determination of this beginning is

[108] Schelling WA13 | 1997: 110.
[109] Schelling WA13 | 1997: 120–1.
[110] Schelling WA15 | SW I/8: 302.
[111] Schelling WA15 | SW I/8: 254.
[112] Hegel WL | GW 21: 55.

that it is to be the beginning of logic, of thought as such. There is only present the resolve, which can also be viewed as arbitrary, of considering *thinking as such*."[113] To "resolve" to think of intelligibility systematically, that is, with "no presupposition," is to decide to pursue a science without contrary. This decision is "arbitrary" insofar as it is voluntary. More importantly, its arbitrariness expresses a craving for systematicity, that is, a desire to "conside[r] *thinking as such*" and thereby to eliminate radical contingency from the science of intelligibility, without which desire such a science would have no value. I express this desire by removing an opposition within myself between permitting and refusing presuppositions in science. Schelling describes the experience of this opposition as involving a "doubling of ourselves. . .in which there are two beings, a questioning being and an answering being."[114] In order to pursue absolute science, I must put myself into question regarding what I value. However I answer confronts me with my freedom, that is, with what I value enough to resolve, arbitrarily and with desire, to pursue.[115] As Schelling puts the point in his 1820–21 Erlangen lectures:

> Here nothing more can be explained by necessity; rather, the transition into being is a free deed. Here all deduction ceases, to the extent to which it is a deduction of something absolutely given from premises that have been determined in advance. Here we separate ourselves from the concept of the dialectician. Here is the point where not the concept but only the deed is decisive.[116]

Science depends for its value on the "decisive" freedom to pursue its derivation. By signifying the free decision to derive an absolute science, the transcendental past thus serves as science's grounding condition, that is, one of its underivable presuppositions or brute facts.[117]

I will now reconstruct Schelling's three-step argument that the complete derivation of a science of intelligibility serves as that science's teleological condition.

First, Schelling says that

[113] Hegel WL | GW 21: 56.

[114] Schelling WA15 | SW I/8: 201.

[115] See Schelling: "the concept for its own part would lie completely immobile if it were not the concept of a thinking subject, i.e., if it were not thought" (Schelling MV33 | SW I/10: 132). Pippin rejects Schelling's critique of Hegel in this regard by claiming that "[t]he topic of pure thinking, the logic of thinking, has nothing to do with, in no way rests on some view about, the thinker, the subject, consciousness, the mind" (Pippin 2022: 314). We will see that Schelling's Hegel critique is more complex than this suggests.

[116] Schelling EV | 1969: 116, translated by Bowie 1993: 139. On Schelling's Erlangen lectures, see Moss 2018.

[117] The philosophical significance of decision begins for Schelling as early as the "Philosophical Letters," in which he solves the antinomy between Fichtean criticism and Spinozistic dogmatism: "If we want to establish a system and, therefore, principles, we cannot do it except by an anticipation of the practical decision. We should not establish those principles unless our freedom had already decided about them" (Schelling PB | SW I/1: 312–3). On Schelling's solution, see Bruno 2014a and Bruno 2020d.

> it is no less the case with true science than it is with history that there are no. . .assertions that would have a value or an unlimited and universal validity in and for themselves or apart from the movement through which they are produced. Movement is what is essential to knowledge. When this element of life is withdrawn, propositions die like fruit removed from the tree of life. Absolute propositions, that is, those that are once and for all valid, conflict with the nature of true knowledge, which involves progression.[118]

In the previous argument, we saw that science depends for its value on freedom. The present argument begins with an inference from this dependence, namely, that the assertions of science have no value "in and for themselves or apart from the movement through which they are produced." The movement of freedom not only initiates the pursuit of science, but also sustains the results of science, which otherwise would "die like fruit removed from the tree of life." It is not obvious how this supports a criticism of Hegel, whose Preface to the *Phenomenology* somewhat ironically denies that a philosophical work can contain a preface that announces bare results on the grounds that

> the real issue is not exhausted by stating [philosophical cognition of the truth] as an *aim*, but by *carrying it out*, nor is the *result* the *actual* whole, but rather the result together with the process through which it came about. The aim by itself is a lifeless universal, just as the guiding tendency is a mere drive that as yet lacks an actual existence; and the bare result is the corpse which has left the guiding tendency behind it.[119]

Bare results cannot be announced in a preface because they are empty without "the guiding tendency" that produces them, that is, they are the fruit that cannot sustain themselves in isolation, but rather relate to the flower and the bud as "reciprocally necessary moments".[120] Nevertheless, Hegel regards final results as achievable in philosophy, whose "goal" as science is to "lay aside the title '*love* of *knowing*' and be *actual knowing*." He characterizes this goal as absolute knowledge, which is the contradiction-free insight into what knowing is that, he holds, is "capable of being the property of all self-conscious reason."[121] Schelling rejects this view, for his claim is not simply that freedom is the initiating and sustaining "element of life" for science, but also that this element precludes the very idea of "[a]bsolute propositions," that is, propositions whose validity no longer depends on the activity

[118] Schelling WA15 | SW I/8: 208.
[119] Hegel PG | W 3: 13.
[120] Hegel PG | W 3: 12.
[121] Hegel PG | W 3: 14, 65. For dialetheist interpretations that deny that Hegel's science is ever free of contradiction, see Moss 2020, Priest 1989, and Priest 2019. For critiques of Priest's interpretation, see Bordignon 2019, Bruno 2023c, Schick 2020, and Stang (manuscript).

in which we consider and potentially reject candidate conditions of intelligibility. In other words, it is precisely because freedom grounds the derivation of science that derivation is interminable. The content of science is at no point "once and for all valid," then, because the "nature of true knowledge" consists in "progression." As Schelling puts the point in the Fifth Letter of the 1795–96 "Philosophical Letters on Dogmatism and Criticism," were I to bring my science's derivation to a close, it "would become an object of *knowledge*, and therewith it would cease to be an object of *freedom*," which would belie its own grounding condition. Of the "genuine philosopher," he adds: "The whole sublimity of his science has consisted in just this, that it would never be complete. He would become unbearable to himself the moment he came to believe that he had completed his system. That very moment he would cease to be *creator* and would be degraded to an instrument of his own creature."[122] Given the nature not only of knowledge, but also of freedom, I must strive endlessly to derive the conditions that compose science.[123] In this, I am led by the regulative idea of a future that, paralleling the previous three-step argument about an "authentic past," Schelling calls an "authentic future."[124] This is a future in which the derivation of science would be complete, a completeness that, given the nature of knowledge and freedom, is unattainable. Such a pursuit accordingly demands the concept of a non-empirical future.

Second, Schelling describes the concept of a non-empirical future as follows: "What is future is certainly not something that has being now, but it is a future. . .at the same time with the present."[125] Schelling conceives of a future that is not present yet is simultaneous with the present. This is precisely the unique temporality of a teleological transcendental condition. Construed in this transcendental register, the future in which science's derivation would be complete is an unrealizable ideal lying beyond the present yet is "at the same time" as the present, since otherwise science's derivation would lack a guiding purpose. Thus, we can say that science is never without its transcendental future.

Third, Schelling casts the actualization of character in the role of the transcendental future. He says that "the person who doubts whether they should be utterly

[122] Schelling PB | SW I/1: 306–6n. Cf. Schelling: "*Philosophy*, an admirable word! If this author has a vote, he casts it for the retention of this old word. For, as far as he sees, our whole knowledge will always remain *philosophy*, i.e., always merely progressing knowledge, whose higher or lower degrees we owe only to our *love* for wisdom, i.e., to our freedom" (Schelling PB | SW I/1: 307n). Cf. also Schelling BV-B | SW II/3: 131. See Ivan Sergeevich Turgenev's letter to Leo Tolstoy, January 3, 1857: "The only people who treasure systems are those whom the whole truth evades, who want to catch it by the tail. A system is just like truth's tail, but the truth is like a lizard. It will leave the tail in your hand and escape; it knows it will soon grow another tail" (Turgenev 1958: 304).

[123] In the "Philosophical Letters," Schelling claims that the "merit" of the skeptic consists in their insight into the essential incompleteness of a science of intelligibility (Schelling PB | SW I/1: 307). On how Schelling's claim prefigures Cavell's view of the "truth" of skepticism (Cavell 1999: 7, 241), see Bruno 2021f.

[124] Schelling WA13 | 1997: 121.

[125] Schelling WA15 | SW I/8: 302.

one thing or the other is without character," whereas "a decisive person, in whom something definitely expressive of the entire being is revealed, has character."[126] Recall that I must value an absolute science of intelligibility enough to resolve to take up its pursuit. By pursuing it, I exhibit what I value. This can be seen as the exhibition of a certain philosophical character, for example, I can express a systematic philosophical character by valuing the elimination of extra-logical presuppositions. However, I cannot actualize my character once and for all, since I can always waver. As Schelling says, we assess character "as a work of freedom, as, so to speak, an eternal (incessant, constant) deed."[127] In striving to actualize my character, I pursue an ideal self, for example, one who would completely satisfy the value of deriving an absolute science of intelligibility yet who will never come to be insofar as one can never claim authentically to have fully actualized one's character. The future in which I would fully actualize my character is thus qualitatively distinct from the present, for it does not lie with the present along an efficient-causal series, simply arriving later. This is why Schelling says that we strive toward this future in an "inexorable progression" toward an "eternal end." To achieve it would be, *per impossibile*, to achieve a will that is "free of all desire," one that is fully satisfied and so "does not will."[128] Thus, by signifying the ideal of the complete derivation of science, the transcendental future serves as the teleological condition of the latter, that is, another of science's underivable presuppositions or brute facts.

Schelling's transcendental argument for the facticity of time reveals a limit to Hegel's commitment to the enlightenment ideal of rational cognition. According to this argument, any science of intelligibility presupposes the transcendental past and the transcendental future, that is, it presupposes the freedom to value the pursuit of that science and the character that would completely satisfy the value that this pursuit exhibits. Insofar as Hegel resolves to pursue a presuppositionless science, he presupposes the value of that pursuit, that is, he presupposes the value of presuppositionlessness. As Schelling says in the 1833–34 Munich lectures, "Hegel. . .pretend[s] that [dialectical] thought is driven forward only by a necessity which lies in itself, although it obviously has a goal that it is striving towards."[129] While

[126] Schelling WA15 | SW I/8: 304. Indicating the groundlessness by which one decides one's character, Schelling adds: "most people are frightened precisely by this abyssal freedom in the same way that they are frightened by the necessity to be utterly one thing or another. And where they see a flash of freedom, they turn away from it as if from an utterly injurious flash of lightning and they feel prostrated by freedom as an appearance that comes from the ineffable, from eternal freedom, from where there is no ground whatsoever" (Schelling WA15 | SW I/8: 304). On the groundlessness of freedom in Schelling's *Philosophical Investigations*, see Bruno 2017a, Bruno 2021b, Dews 2017, Gardner 2017, and Welchman 2013.

[127] Schelling WA15 | SW I/8: 304.

[128] Schelling WA15 | SW I/8: 234, 237. Cf. Schelling: "every man in particular strives, in truth, only to return to the condition of non-willing; not only he who strips himself away from all desirable things, but—though unknowingly—also he who abandons himself to all desires. For this man, too, desires only the state in which he has nothing more to wish for, nothing more to want, even if that state retreats immediately from him; and the more zealously he pursues, the further away it is" (Schelling WA13 | 1997: 134).

[129] Schelling MV33 | SW I/10: 132.

valuing a science of intelligibility neither undermines the coherence[130] nor determines the content[131] of this "goal," it makes scientific determinacy and coherence so much as possible to matter. For this reason, value does not arise from pure thinking, but rather is extra-logically presupposed by it.[132] As we will see in more detail in Part III, the enlightenment ideal must face up to this facticity.[133]

I will conclude this section by considering two objections to Schelling's transcendental argument.

First, one might object that, by entertaining the why-question, particularly its science permutation, Schelling indulges a question that cannot be answered and is therefore distracted by a pseudo-question. The objection is that simply posing the why-question guarantees that it cannot be answered, since any meaningful or scientific answer will raise the question anew. This, one might argue, dooms philosophy to chasing a receding horizon, that is, to a limitation that bars it from attaining systematic form. However, this objection begs the question against Schelling, for it appeals to systematicity in order to dismiss the why-question, which is to insist on precisely what is in question. Schelling asks why there is a truly absolute, that is, systematic, science of intelligibility. Appealing to systematicity in order to dissolve his question shows not that it is a pseudo-question, but rather that one does not find that question pressing. At best, such an appeal leaves matters in a stalemate. At worst, it betrays a prejudice.

[130] Rush says that Schelling fails to prove that Hegel's science is "internally incoherent" (Rush 2014: 225). However, Schelling's point is that the question of why there is an internally coherent science at all points to the free act that conditions its possibility.

[131] Houlgate rebuts Kierkegaard's Schellingian critique of Hegel by saying "the particular resolve or decision presupposed by the *Logic* is a free act *of* thought, not an act that interrupts thought from a position 'outside' thought" so as to determine its content (Houlgate 2006: 90). However, Schelling's point is that the question of why there is science points to the free act that conditions its possibility, which, as such a condition, is in no meaningful sense "outside" of thought determining its content.

[132] See Kierkegaard: "If I really have a conviction. . .then to me my conviction is higher than reasons; it is actually the conviction which sustains the reasons, not the reasons which sustain the conviction. . .'Reasons' can lay an egg no more than a rooster can. . .and no matter how much intercourse they have with each other they never beget or bear a conviction. A conviction arises elsewhere. This is what I. . .have meant with the problem: 'on the distinction between a pathos-filled and a dialectical transition'" (Kierkegaard JP III: 3608).

[133] Schelling's legacy on this matter is discernible in Nietzsche's unmasking of presuppositions. In 1882's *The Gay Science*, Nietzsche says that "in order that this cultivation [of the scientific spirit] begin, must there not be some prior conviction—and indeed one so authoritative and unconditional that it sacrifices all other convictions to itself? We see that science, too, rests on a faith; there is simply no 'presuppositionless' science" (Nietzsche 2001: 200). In 1886's *Beyond Good and Evil*, he says that philosophers "act as if they had discovered and arrived at their genuine convictions through the self-development of a cold, pure, divinely insouciant dialectic. . .while what essentially happens is that they take a conjecture, a whim, an 'inspiration' or, more typically, they take some fervent wish that they have sifted through and made properly abstract—and they defend it with rationalizations after the fact. They are all advocates who do not want to be seen as such; for the most part, in fact, they are sly spokesmen for prejudices that they christen as 'truths'" (Nietzsche 1989: 8). And in 1887's *On the Genealogy of Morality*, he states: "Strictly speaking, there is no 'presuppositionless' science—the very idea is unthinkable, paralogical: a philosophy, a 'faith' must always be there first, so that from it science can acquire a direction, a sense, a limit, a method, a right to exist" (Nietzsche 2006: 112).

Second, one might object that asking the why-question is useless because no meaningful answer to it can be definitive. Since any meaningful answer, including Schelling's own transcendental argument, will raise the question anew, asking it is an endless process and therefore useless. This objection accurately captures the endlessness of asking the why-question. However, it is misguided to infer that such endlessness is useless, for this neglects what is ultimately at stake in the asking, namely, making sense of ourselves. As we see in its intensifying permutations, Schelling's why-question is not merely theoretical, but rather bears on who we are. This explains the human permutation of the question that he raises early on in the Berlin lectures:

> far from man and his endeavours making the world comprehensible, it is man himself that is the most incomprehensible and who inexorably drives me to the belief in the wretchedness of all being, a belief that makes itself known in so many bitter pronouncements from both ancient and recent times. It is precisely man that drives me to the final desperate question: Why is there anything at all? Why is there not nothing? That there should be a science that responds to these questions, which would snatch us from this despair, is unquestionably a compelling, indeed a necessary, longing—a longing not of this or that individual person but of human nature itself. What other science should it be that is capable of this if not philosophy? For all other sciences known by man—invented or developed by him—each has its specific task and none responds to this final and most universal question. So there will be no doubt about this: philosophy is in itself and at all times the most longed for of sciences, since through it all other knowledge receives both its first highest reference and its final support. If I cannot answer this final question, then for me everything else sinks into the abyss of a bottomless void.[134]

The "wretchedness of all being" consists in the fact that, whereas we can use "other sciences" than philosophy to make "comprehensible" the "world" insofar as it is composed of classes of beings, that there is being "at all" and "not nothing" is incomprehensible. The grounds that these sciences discover for beings end in the "abyss of a bottomless void" because being as such exists groundlessly, that is, as a brute fact. The "despair" that this bruteness causes is uniquely human, for it afflicts only us. We are the sole beings for whom the groundlessness of being is an issue. This is why Schelling says that we are the "most incomprehensible," for we alone give voice to such a disturbing fact. It is exclusively "human nature" to make "bitter pronouncements" about being's wretchedness, that is, to ask the various permutations of the "final desperate question," namely, the why-question. It is accordingly

[134] Schelling BV-B | SW II/3: 7–8.

our peculiar fate to "lon[g]" for a science of being, that is, for philosophy.[135] To be sure, this science can only defer a definitive answer to the why-question, since its answers will unavoidably exhibit the meaning, the systematicity, and, indeed, the humanity that provoke that question in the first place. However, this deferral shows that asking the question is not useless, but rather is deeply, if frustratingly, human. In that case, the proper image for our confrontation with the why-question is not the circle, but rather the line, which is to say that the endlessness of our asking it is badly infinite. This may well be the only infinitude that is appropriate to human reason.[136]

What, then, should we make of Schelling's transcendental argument as an answer to the why-question? Indeed, what is an answer that unavoidably raises the very question to which it is a response? I suggest that such an answer is comparable to what, in the third *Critique*, Kant calls a "**reflecting** judgment," for it is an incompletable attempt to shed light on a topic, namely, being, and is, in this sense, a judgment about a particular whose universal "is to be found" yet never definitely arrives.[137] Like a reflecting judgment that searches endlessly for a universal with which to determine the meaning of a particular, Schelling makes repeated attempts to make sense of being. His attempts draw not only on the concepts of the past and the future in the *Ages*, but also on the concept of value in the "Philosophical Letters" and the concept of the will in 1809's *Philosophical Investigations into the Essence of Human Freedom and Matters Connected Therewith*. Moreover, Schelling's attempts take on the shifting form of treatises, letters, dialogues, and myths. As his answer to the why-question develops, it exhibits the meaning, systematicity, and humanity that raise the question anew, embodying the very particular for which he continuously searches for the definitive yet elusive universal.[138] Schelling's endless engagement with the why-question can accordingly be seen as an intentional exposure to the ceaseless challenge that is posed by the topic of an unparalleled reflective judgment, an exposure in which, as the changing shape of his corpus suggests, his transcendental argument is a wittingly provisional answer.

[135] Cf. Schopenhauer's 1844 *The World as Will and Representation, Volume 2*: "even the most perfect philosophy will always contain an unexplained element, like an insoluble precipitate or the remainder that is always left behind by the irrational proportion of two quantities. Therefore, if anyone ventures to raise the question why there is not nothing at all rather than this world, then the world cannot be justified from itself; no ground, no final cause of its existence can be found in itself; it cannot be demonstrated that it exists for its own sake, in other words, for its own advantage" (Schopenhauer 1969: 579).

[136] See Martin 2007: 180–2.

[137] Kant KU | AA 5: 179.

[138] For an account of Schelling's various responses to the why-question, see Bruno 2020a: 187–91.

4.6 Schelling on Positive Philosophy

We have seen that facticity is a feature of the topic of negative philosophy insofar as a science of intelligibility presupposes the past and the future as radically contingent or brute facts. This partly clarifies Schelling's claim that an answer to the question of the meaning of philosophy demands a return to Kant, who, as we saw in Part I, is a philosopher of facticity *avant la lettre*, given his commitment to radically contingent conditions of intelligibility, for example, the forms of sensibility and the forms of judgment. But, as we will now see, facticity is also a feature of the topic of positive philosophy insofar as that topic, namely, existence itself, is a brute fact. This will further clarify Schelling's demand for a return to Kant and further position Schelling as a philosopher of facticity in his own right.

As we saw in Sections 4.2 and 4.3, Kant's doctrine of epistemic reciprocity identifies a relation of mutual dependence, in accordance with a threefold criterion of proof, between the categories as the necessary conditions of intelligibility and sense experience as the contingent source of the categories' objective reality. In light of Maimon's empty formalism challenge, Schelling will adapt this relation and its threefold criterion to a mutual dependence between the unconditioned condition of intelligibility, that is, the first principle that is negative philosophy's topic, and this condition's reality, that is, the existence that is positive philosophy's topic. As mentioned in Section 4.1, Schelling's successor doctrine of infinite reciprocity will suggest the repurposed Kantian slogan that a first principle without existence is empty and existence without a first principle is blind.

Before turning to Schelling's adaptation of epistemic reciprocity, it is important to explain his pivotal role in the history of the concept of facticity. Schelling follows Jacobi in charging Kant with the apparent inconsistency of denying our cognition of things in themselves and affirming our knowledge of their existence.[139] Although he will ultimately transpose the concept of uncognizable existence from the context of transcendental idealism to that of German idealism, Schelling observes that this concept precipitates a crisis for Kant, namely, that despite "maintain[ing] that there is an *a priori* knowledge of things," Kant "remove[s] from this *a priori* knowledge that which is precisely the most important thing, namely, that which exists," which leaves him with "no answer" to the question of what remains in existence that is "independent of the determinations of our faculty of knowledge."[140]

[139] See Jacobi DH 209–30 | 1994: 331–8. For responses to Jacobi's charge, see Bruno 2020c, Franks 2005: 154–74, and Stang 2015. On Kant's distinction between cognition and knowledge, see Willaschek and Watkins 2020.

[140] Schelling BV-B | II/3: 49–50. Cf. Schelling: "Here it would first be asked: how *this* supersensuous [namely, the thing in itself] relates to the supersensuous of the other kind which Kant always presents at least as the object of the *endeavour* of our cognition, although he denies that it can *really* be known, how it relates to that supersensuous which Kant recognizes in God, in the human soul, in the freedom of the will, etc. Nothing is more noticeable than the fact that in the famous critical procedure Kant never came across this obvious and pressing question: how the one extra-sensuous or the merely intelligible relates to the other, the really supersensuous; nothing is more noticeable than that he calmly leaves these two

Schelling registers the philosophical significance of the Kantian crisis for the first generation of post-Kantians, which, of course, includes himself, in a passage that immediately follows:

> The unavoidable next step was therefore the insight that if there is a knowledge at all of things *a priori*, and even if that *which exists itself* can be known *a priori*, then the matter and form of things must be derived together and from the same source. This thought came to fruition in the work of Fichte, whose greatest, most unforgettable service will always remain to have first grasped within his spirit the idea of a *completely a priori* science. Even though he did not carry out this idea in reality, he nonetheless bequeathed a great legacy for philosophy, namely, the concept of an absolute philosophy that presupposes nothing, in which nothing is assumed from *any other source* as a *given*, but rather everything is to be derived, in intelligible succession, from one general *prius*, from that which alone is to be immediately posited.[141]

The Kantian crisis consists in the fact that Kant posits an existence that, by transcending "*a priori* knowledge," imposes itself on reason as a brute fact, not unlike the forms of sensibility and the forms of judgment. Fichte's "insight" is that "the matter and form of things must be derived together and from the same source," namely, the absolute freedom of reason or "the '*I am*.'"[142] Schelling identifies Fichte's "great legacy" with the pursuit of a "completely *a priori* science" whose formal and material constituents are not "assumed from *any other source* as a *given*," but rather are derived from reason alone. This is why he calls the Fichtean goal a "*science of reason*."[143] In this regard, Schelling echoes Hegel, who, as we saw in Section 1.6, identifies Fichte's "profound and enduring merit" with deducing the categories independently of observed logical tradition and hence with opening a path toward a true, that is, presuppositionless, science or what Schelling here calls "an absolute philosophy that presupposes nothing."

standing side by side, without in some way either distinguishing them or connecting them" (Schelling MV33 | SW I/10: 83–4).

[141] Schelling BV-B | II/3: 50–1.

[142] See Fichte: "The not-I is thus nothing other than another way of looking at the I" (Fichte NM | GA IV/2:42). Cf. Fichte GWL | SW I: 482–3, 488, 499.

[143] Schelling BV-B | SW II/3: 57. See Wilfrid Sellars' undated manuscript on Schelling's philosophy: "The Kantian philosophy. . .involved a dualism of form and matter in its analysis of the nature and origin of experience. Clearly a theory which avoided this duality, which denied that sensation was the result of the modifications of the faculty of sense by things in themselves, and yet held to the same general doctrines, would be an advance upon that of Kant. Schelling attempts to form exactly such a theory. He feels that Kant did not do enough justice to this universal noumenal self, and believes that with it he can account for both the matter and the form of human experience in a coherent and logical manner" (Sellars 2017: 209–10).

Crucially, Schelling indicates that Fichte's "unavoidable next step" after the Kantian crisis generates a new, post-Kantian crisis. He observes that Fichte derives the conditions of intelligibility from the I yet leaves the I "immediately posited," namely, as an underived presupposition, which we saw in Section 2.5 is why Fichte reserves the term 'facticity' exclusively for his first principle.[144] As we saw in Chapter 3, Hegel complains that this vestigial facticity vitiates the *Wissenschaftslehre*'s scientific promise. We might hear Schelling as echoing Hegel's complaint when he asserts that Fichte "did not carry out" the idea of a presuppositionless science "in reality," for we might hear this as asserting that Fichte fails to satisfy the scientific criterion of removing radical contingency from the conditions of intelligibility and achieving a philosophy that "presupposes nothing." However, this would be mistaken, for Schelling regards this criterion as misguided. Shortly after describing Fichte's "unforgettable service" to philosophy, he says:

> it is two entirely different things to know what a being is, *quid sit*, and that it is, *quod sit*. The former—the answer to the question *what* it is—accords me insight into the *essence* of the thing, or it provides that I understand the thing, that I have an understanding or a concept of it, or have it *itself* within the concept. The other insight, however, *that* it is, does not accord me just the concept, but rather something that goes beyond just the concept, which is existence.[145]

Evoking Thomas Aquinas' distinction between a thing's essence and its being,[146] Schelling distinguishes between "*what*" a thing is and "*that*" it is, that is, between its "*essence*" and its "existence." This is a distinction in kind, for whereas a thing's "*whatness*" is a "question" that "directs itself to *reason*," "*that* [a thing] exists—can

[144] See Schopenhauer's implicit detection of the I's facticity in his 1813 doctoral thesis *On the Fourfold Root of the Principle of Sufficient Reason*: "the identity of the subject of willing with the cognizing subject, by means of which (and, indeed, necessarily), the word 'I' includes and indicates both, is the knot of the world and therefore inexplicable. For to us, only relations among objects are conceivable; among these, however, two can be one only insofar as they are part of a whole. In contrast, here, when speaking of the subject, the rules for cognition of objects no longer apply, and an actual identity of the cognizer with that which is cognized as willing, thus of the subject with the object, is *immediately given*. But whoever truly realizes the inexplicability of this identity will with me call it the miracle *par excellence*" (Schopenhauer 2012: 136). Cf. his 1819 *The World as Will and Representation, Volume 1*: "object and subject precede all knowledge, and hence even the principle of sufficient reason in general, as the first condition. For this principle is only the form of every object, the whole nature and manner of its appearance; but the object always presupposes the subject, and hence between the two there can be no relation of reason and consequent. My essay 'On the Principle of Sufficient Reason' purports to achieve just this: it explains the content of that principle as the essential form of every object, in other words, as the universal mode and manner of all objective existence, as something which pertains to the object as such. But the object as such everywhere presupposes the subject as its necessary correlative, and hence the subject always remains outside the province of the validity of the principle of sufficient reason" (Schopenhauer 1969: 14).

[145] Schelling BV-B | SW II/3: 57–8.

[146] See Aquinas 1968: 55.

only be taught by experience."[147] In other words, no conceptual analysis of whatness can prove the actuality of thatness. It follows from this that while the science of reason must logically determine the whatness of things, it must also presuppose the thatness of things as a brute fact. Such a science fails to "carry out" the criterion of presuppositionlessness, then, not because it suffers from vestigial facticity, but rather because this criterion is misguided insofar as facticity is ineradicable.

For Schelling, then, the post-Kantian crisis consists in the fact that, despite its campaign against facticity, the science of reason unavoidably presupposes existence as a brute fact the experience of which is required to realize the conditions of intelligibility. The terms of this crisis are, of course, Maimonian, since they describe the threat that the conditions that compose absolute philosophy are empty forms without the presupposition of brutely given existence. However, as mentioned in Section 4.4 and as we will see in this section, whereas Maimon collapses the science of reason into a negative philosophy that pursues the ideal of an infinite understanding, Schelling infers that this science, for its sense and significance, must mutually presuppose a positive science of experience.

Moreover, the post-Kantian crisis threatens not just Fichte, but also Hegel. As mentioned in Section 4.1, the conditions of intelligibility and the existence that realizes them jointly contribute to intelligibility. As we have seen, this is so on pain of empty formalism. In order to be presuppositionless, Hegel's philosophy can presuppose nothing that contributes to intelligibility, since this would be to admit that reason is saddled with a brute fact and thus is one in a pair, which, as we saw in Section 3.3, he explicitly rejects. According to Schelling, however, Hegel presupposes precisely that there is existence. Referring to the "first pages" of Hegel's *Encyclopedia*, Schelling interprets the "dictum that reason concerns itself with the 'in itself' of things" as claiming that reason concerns the "essence," as opposed to the "being," of things, since, for example, the essence of the human "remains the same even if there were no people at all on the earth."[148] The claim is that whereas the essence or whatness of things is a condition whose necessity is such that it "remains the same," the being or thatness of things is an existence whose contingency is such that it need not "remai[n]" insofar as there need not be anything. Thus, it is precisely in deducing what things are in themselves that absolute philosophy, that is, the science of reason, presupposes that there is something rather than nothing.

[147] Schelling BV-B | SW II/3: 58.

[148] Schelling BV-B | SW II/3: 59. See Hegel: "We said earlier that it has been man's ancient faith that it is the vocation of the spirit to know the truth. This has the further implication that the objects, both the outer and the inner nature, the object in general, is in-itself just as it is in thought, and that thinking is therefore the truth of what is objective. The business of philosophy consists only in bringing into consciousness explicitly what people have held to be valid about thought from time immemorial" (Hegel EL | GW 20: §22 Addition). Cf. Hegel: "when we speak of *things*, we call their *nature* or *essence* their *concept*...[T]hat which is truly *permanent* and *substantial* in the manifold and accidentality of appearance and fleeting externalization, is the *concept* of the thing" (WL | GW 21: 14–5).

But this is to presuppose the existence that contributes to intelligibility and thereby to admit that reason is saddled with a brute fact and is therefore not "but one."[149]

To be clear, Schelling's extension of the post-Kantian crisis to Hegel does not illegitimately demand that the science of reason provide a deduction of existence. That error belongs to Wilhelm Traugott Krug's 1801 "Outline of a New Organon of Philosophy, or Essay on the Principles of Philosophical Cognition," which Hegel reviews in 1802's "How the Ordinary Human Understanding Takes Philosophy (as Displayed in the Works of Mr. Krug)." Krug both figuratively and literally asks for the moon by charging that German idealism breaks its "promise" to deduce "the whole system of our presentations," including "definite presentation[s], e.g., of the moon with all its characteristics or of a rose, a horse, a dog, or of wood, iron, clay, an oak tree, or even just of his pen." The charge is that the science of reason fails to deduce not only the conditions of intelligibility, but also the existence of individuals. Hegel rebuts the charge by arguing that it is "most vulgar" to demand the deduction of individuals because, since "it is philosophy we are talking about here," individuals simply cannot be "comprehended" independently of the "philosophical construction" of the system of the conditions of their intelligibility. In other words, there is nothing for philosophy to deduce beyond such a system. The "most sublime task of reason" consists strictly in cognizing the practical system in which Krug's pen finds its intelligibility, the historical system in which "a Cyrus, a Moses, an Alexander, or a Jesus" finds their intelligibility, the "solar system" in which the moon finds its intelligibility, and, ultimately, the logical system in which everything finds its intelligibility.[150] Hegel's rebuttal anticipates his view in the *Science of Logic*, which we saw in Section 3.6, that the concept is not "an indifferent form that attaches" to an individual, but rather is the latter's "life pulse."[151] If philosophy has no requirement to deduce existence, then it cannot be charged with failing to provide such a deduction.

Nevertheless, by Hegel's own lights, philosophy may not presuppose anything that contributes to intelligibility. However, this includes both the deducible conditions of intelligibility and the existence that they render intelligible. Since the latter

[149] Schelling's charge that Hegel presupposes the actuality that realizes the conditions of intelligibility differs from his charge that Hegel "*must* come to actuality" via the "transition" from logic to nature that the *Encyclopedia* announces, whereby the absolute idea is said to "*release*" nature "*out of itself*" (Schelling MV33 | SW I/10: 153, 159, cited from Hegel EL | GW 20: §244). Cf. this second charge with "On the Source of the Eternal Truths," Schelling's lecture at the Berlin Academy of Sciences, January 17, 1850 (Schelling QW | SW II/1: 584). On the second charge, see Bowie 1993: 175–7, Horstmann 1986, and Rush 2014: 225.

[150] Hegel GM | 2000: 298–9. Cf. Hegel's claim that Krug is "quite naive" to "challeng[e] the philosophy of nature to perform the feat of deducing *only* his pen" (Hegel EPN | 2004: 23n).

[151] Cf. Hegel: "what in ordinary reflection is, as content, at first separated from the form cannot in fact be in itself formless, devoid of determination (in that case it would be a vacuity, the abstraction of the thing-in-itself)" (Hegel WL | GW 21: 17). Cf. also Hegel: "The concept of logic has hitherto rested on a separation, presupposed once and for all in ordinary consciousness, of the *content* of knowledge and its *form*, or of *truth* and *certainty*. . .[T]he subject matter remains a thing in itself, utterly a 'beyond' of thought" (Hegel WL | GW 21: 28–9).

cannot but be presupposed, philosophy cannot be presuppositionless. Indeed, Hegel takes for granted that there are writing implements, human beings, celestial bodies, and existence as such, without which the conditions of their intelligibility would be empty forms. This faces not the spurious Krugian challenge of providing a deduction of existence, but rather the genuine Maimonian challenge of tracing the boundary of deduction. For Schelling, this boundary consists in reason's factical limitation by experience, by which alone we are "taught" that, not what, things are. This is why he says, as we saw in Section 4.5, that there is "something *more* than mere reason." Intelligibility demands not just the deduction of the whatness of things, but also the presupposition of the thatness of things.[152]

We see, then, that whereas Fichte critiques Kant for failing to live up to what he regards as the spirit of transcendental idealism, according to which reason is absolutely free, and Hegel critiques Fichte for failing to live up to the spirit of the *Wissenschaftslehre*, according to which reason's absolute freedom demands philosophy's presuppositionlessness, Schelling critiques Fichte and especially Hegel for indulging a misguided demand that ignores the unavoidable presupposition of factical existence. For Schelling, this presupposition is not a threat to philosophy, but rather represents philosophy's sensitivity to the question of why there is something rather than nothing.[153]

Hegel's claim to presuppositionlessness leads him to confuse negative philosophy's discursive determinations of the conditions of intelligibility with positive philosophy's non-discursive openness to the givenness of existence. As Schelling says, Hegel's philosophy "is the negative driven beyond its limits: it does not exclude the positive, but thinks it has subdued it within itself."[154] We overstep

[152] Houlgate claims that Schelling and Ludwig Feuerbach establish an "orthodox" interpretation of Hegel that is "hugely influential on later readers," according to which the *Logic* presupposes concrete truth as its goal. He objects that they fail either to "tak[e] seriously" Hegel's demand of presuppositionlessness or to "accep[t] that Hegel lives up to his own deman[d]" (Houlgate 2006: 54, 56–7). However, this is unlikely. On the one hand, Schelling takes seriously Hegel's demand for presuppositionlessness, since he interprets Hegel as championing Fichte's pursuit of an "absolute philosophy that presupposes nothing." On the other hand, Schelling denies that Hegel satisfies this demand, since he argues that Hegel presupposes not only truth as the transcendental future of philosophy, but also existence as a necessary though insufficient contribution to intelligibility. Crucially, Schelling's denial abides by what Houlgate describes as Hegel's "prohibition on external criticism," that is, on imposing onto philosophy a "prior *assumption*" about what is "ontologically, epistemologically, or politically fundamental" (Houlgate 2006: 62). First, Schelling argues rather than assumes that the transcendental future is a brute fact. Second, he argues rather than assumes that what contributes to intelligibility must include existence.

[153] Hegel and Schelling might seem to beg the question against each other in that the former denies while the latter affirms that existence transcends conceptual determination. Pippin claims that Schelling begs the question, since, insofar as his invocation of brute existence is "a thinking, a judging, and a claim to know," it is "always already a manifestation of a dependence on pure thinking and its conditions" (Pippin 2022: 314). Schelling can break the apparent impasse if he can show that we have a non-discursive, non-spontaneous openness to being, namely, what he calls 'sensibility.' We will see in Chapter 6 that Heidegger appeals to mood as a primary instance of such openness. For the argument that Spinoza and Kant face a similar impasse regarding whether existence transcends predication, see Boehm 2014.

[154] Schelling BV-B | II/3: 80.

the bounds of negative philosophy if we mistake thought's ability to derive conditions of intelligibility for an ability to justify its assumption of the existence that would give these conditions reality and significance. As "a science that is in a crisis," negative philosophy cannot advance through a "hasty" conflation of conditions with their reality, which is the characteristic flaw of "*pure* rationalism." This is why Schelling will conclude that, in order to resolve the crisis of negative philosophy, which is to say, the post-Kantian crisis, a philosophy that begins from existence, namely, positive philosophy, must become "its own science."[155]

En route to resolving the post-Kantian crisis, Schelling turns to "The Ideal of Pure Reason" in the first *Critique*. There Kant argues that being is "the true abyss" for human reason because, as "the ultimate sustainer of all things," it is unconditioned, that is, without a ground, and could therefore only rhetorically ask itself "**but whence** am I?" There can be no answer. In imagining this self-interrogation, Kant concludes, "everything gives way beneath us."[156] As Schelling interprets this argument, being is "groundless."[157] In other words, it is "[t]hat which just exists," which is to say, that which exists factically. He calls the idea of being "the inverted idea, the idea in which reason is set *outside* itself, absolutely ecstatic."[158] We can make sense of this claim by observing that, insofar as being is groundless or radically contingent and reason consists in the self-derivation of absolutely necessary conditions of intelligibility, being is precisely reason's inversion. Schelling also describes being as "*unprethinkable*," for, although it is thinkable, it is thinkable precisely as that which "*precedes all activity of thought*" insofar as it is always already given to thought, which therefore cannot ground it.[159] Being accordingly cannot be derived "in mere thought," a rationalist error that Schelling attributes to "Fichtean idealism," but rather is that from which "we *must* proceed" as a presupposition, a starting point of which he says "Hegelian philosophy knows nothing."[160] Again, we see that the post-Kantian crisis consists not in the failure to achieve presuppositionlessness, but rather in the very pursuit of presuppositionlessness.

[155] Schelling BV-B | SW II/3: 83–4; cf. 71, 79, 94–5, 120, 125–6, 128, 130–1, 146, 150–3, 159.

[156] Kant KrV A613/B641, cited by Schelling BV-B | II/3: 163. Cf. Kant: "Perhaps nothing more sublime has ever been said, or any thought more sublimely expressed, than in the inscription over the temple of Isis (Mother Nature): 'I am all that is, that was, and that will be, and my veil no mortal has removed'" (Kant KU | AA 5: 316).

[157] Schelling BV-B | SW II/3: 164.

[158] Schelling BV-B | SW II/3: 162.

[159] Schelling BV-C | 2020: 124–5. See Tritten 2012: 66.

[160] Schelling BV-B | SW II/3: 164. Houlgate argues that Schelling's critique of Hegel begs the question of whether being exceeds thought, that is, whether actuality surpasses the concept. For Hegel, being does not exceed thought because thinking "is the awareness that there is and must be existence as such" (Houlgate 1999: 117). However, part of Schelling's critique is that thought can without contradiction think the non-necessity of being, from which it follows that the fact that there is anything cannot be in virtue of thinking. As he says in the Berlin lectures, "*that which has being* is completely indifferent to accepting or not accepting being; it is the being that is prior to all concept and all potence. It is indifferent to adopting or not adopting being. . .It is found in that **blind** *being*. . .which has *necessity by accident*. . .[I]t exists only *actu, i.e., only blindly, which accidentally has existence*" (Schelling BV-C | 2020: 128, 132–3).

This pursuit displays negative philosophy "driven beyond its limits," within which it determines the conditions or thought-determinations that compose the system of objectivity, and into the bounds of positive philosophy, which begins from our openness and continued commitment to the actuality of that system. As Schelling says toward the end of the Berlin lectures: "What has once begun in thought can only continue in thought and can never advance any further than to the *idea*. What shall reach reality must then also proceed directly from reality and, indeed, from *pure* actuality, thus, from the actuality that precedes all possibility."[161] We can now begin to see precisely how Schelling's solution to the post-Kantian crisis relies on a return to Kant.

In Section 4.2, we saw that Kant analyzes the roles that experience plays in cognition, namely, its formative context and its sensory source, and reciprocally relates these roles to the categories as non-sensory sources of cognition. In Section 4.3, we saw that while Kant establishes this epistemic reciprocity in response to the question *quid indicii* in order to prove the application and hence the significance or non-emptiness of the categories and their related principles, he takes this reciprocity to be a brute fact. And in Section 4.4, we saw that Maimon denies that this fact objectively obtains with respect to not only the categories, but also the first principle of Reinhold's elementary philosophy, which threatens to reduce the latter to an empty form. Schelling is sensitive to Maimon's empty formalism challenge as early as 1795's "Of the I as Principle of Philosophy, or On the Unconditioned in Human Knowledge." After noting that "the I in the logical sense has no significance except inasmuch as it is the principle of the unity of thinking, and thus it disappears with thinking itself and has no other than thinkable reality," he remarks in a footnote:

> [Reinhold's] principle of consciousness automatically vanishes as a principle of philosophy. For it is clear that through it neither subject nor object is determined except *logically*, so that the principle has no real significance, at least as long as it is supposed to be the *highest* principle. No philosopher has pointed out more emphatically this lack of reality in the principle of consciousness than Salomon Maimon.[162]

This remark occurs during a discussion in which Schelling makes it clear that his first principle safely avoids the threat of empty formalism:

> the absolute I is neither a merely formal principle, nor an idea, nor an object, but pure I determined in intellectual intuition as absolute reality. He who demands

[161] Schelling BV-B | SW II/3: 162.

[162] Schelling IPP | SW I/1: 208–8n, translation modified. In response to Johann Benjamin Erhard's 1796 review of "Of the I" in the *General Literary Journal*, Schelling writes "Anti-Critique" that same year.

> proof 'that something else besides our idea should match it' does not know what he is demanding, because (1) it is not given by any idea, (2) it realizes itself, it creates itself, and therefore does not need to be realized beforehand. Even if it were realizable in advance, the very action by which it became realizable would already presuppose it. In other words, to make it real as something posited outside of itself would mean to annul it. It is either nothing, or else realized through itself and in itself not as an object but *as I*.[163]

Crucially, Schelling's confidence in avoiding empty formalism depends on his endorsement of intellectual intuition.[164] This is a doctrine that he critiques continually and as early as the "Philosophical Letters."[165] By critiquing this doctrine, he

[163] Schelling IPP | SW I/1: 208. Schelling begins "Of the I" by arguing that unless knowledge rests on "an ultimate point of reality," its conditions are circular, arbitrary, or regressive, i.e., they fall into "an eternal cycle," rest on an arbitrary condition that "dissolv[es] in its opposite," or compose a regress in which no condition "crystallize[s]" (Schelling IPP | SW I: 162). This evokes both Aristotle's discussion in *Posterior Analytics* of the threat that understanding rests on demonstrations that "proceed in a circle or reciprocally," "come to a stop" with what is "unknowable," or "le[a]d back *ad infinitum*" (Aristotle 2002: 4–5) and three of Agrippa's five modes of suspending judgment (see Book 1, Chapter 15 of Sextus Empiricus' *Outlines of Skepticism* in Annas and Barnes (ed.) 2000: 40–1). On the role of Agrippan skepticism in the development of German idealism, see Franks 2005.

[164] In 1865's *Kant and the Epigones*, Otto Liebmann quips that "'intellectual intuition' was not first discovered by [Schelling], but was picked out of Kant's dirty laundry" (Liebmann 1912: 93).

[165] In the Preface to the *Phenomenology*, Hegel appears to attack Schelling implicitly for espousing intellectual intuition in the identity philosophy when he says that the "coming-to-be of *science as such*" will "least of all. . .be like the rapturous enthusiasm that, like a shot from a pistol, begins straight away with absolute knowledge, and makes short work of other standpoints by declaring that it takes no notice of them" (Hegel PG | W 3: 31). In a letter to Schelling, May 1, 1807, he implies that his attack targets Schelling's acolytes: "In the Preface you will not find that I have been too hard on the shallowness that makes so much mischief with your forms in particular and degrades your science into a bare formalism." Schelling acknowledges this implication in his final letter to Hegel, November 2, 1807: "Insofar as you yourself mention the polemical part of the Preface, given my own justly measured opinion of myself I would have to think too little of myself to apply this polemic to my own person. It must therefore, as you have expressed in your letter, apply only to further bad use of my ideas and to those who parrot them without understanding, although in this writing itself the distinction is not made" (Hegel B | 1984: 80). Drawing on the Preface and Hegel's 1803 fragmentary manuscript, in which he says "I know well enough that *Schelling's ideas* must be very clearly distinguished from the use *that his school makes of them*, and I honor *Schelling's* genuine service to philosophy just as much as I despise this formalism" (Hegel F | 1979: 259, cited from Rosenkranz 1963: 185), Harris offers a "loose interpretation" of "Schelling's school" as including Bardili, Johann Joseph Görres, Reinhold, and Johann Jakob Wagner (Harris 1997: 51). Schelling in fact anticipates Hegel's attack on "enthusiasm" in 1802's *Further Presentations from the System of Philosophy*: "most people see in the essence of the absolute nothing but empty night and can discern nothing in it. It disappears for them into the mere negation of difference and is for itself entirely a privative entity; therefore they prudently make it the end of their philosophy. . .I wish to show here in a more detailed way how for cognition the night of the absolute is changed into day" (Schelling FD | SW I/4: 404). Cf. the *Stuttgart Private Lectures*: "all of philosophy is properly speaking the progressive demonstration of the absolute, which therefore cannot be demanded from the outset of philosophy" (Schelling SP | SW I/7: 424). Despite the assurance of their last correspondence, Hegel reiterates his attack on enthusiasm in his Berlin lectures and explicitly directs it at Schelling: "Schelling's philosophy makes its beginning from immediate knowing, from intellectual intuition. . .Since the presupposition of [his] philosophy is that the subject has an immediate intuition of this identity of the subjective and the objective, philosophy thus appears as an artistic talent or genius in individuals that comes only to 'Sunday's children' [namely, to the favored few]. By its very nature, however, philosophy can become universal, for its soil is thinking, the universal, and that is the very thing that makes us all human. The principle therefore is one that is utterly universal; but if a

gradually realizes that one can indeed think the mere "idea" of the I as first principle and that one therefore "know[s]" precisely what one "demands" if one demands a "proof" of this idea, whether the latter is construed, with Fichte, as the beginning or, with Hegel, as the end of the science of intelligibility. Hence Schelling announces in the Berlin lectures that philosophy's "astonishing challenge" is to prove that the "ultimate principle of the negative science. . .is not merely the highest idea, but is that which *actually exists*."[166] Moreover, he faces Maimon's empty formalism challenge not only as a live threat, but also as a lived threat, for he grasps its existential as opposed to merely speculative character, which we saw consists in the loss of a cognitively significant world. As Schelling says shortly after his announcement, "negative philosophy will predominately remain the philosophy of the *academy*, whereas the positive will be the philosophy for *life*. The complete dedication that one demands from philosophy will only be provided through the two in combination."[167] In order to see how combining negative and positive philosophy avoids the lived threat of empty formalism, we must analyze these components in light of Kant's doctrine of epistemic reciprocity.[168]

Schelling states that the "*true* thought of a philosopher," that is, the thought that expresses her deepest explanatory "intentions," is the "fundamental thought" from which she proceeds. Two such thoughts are "*whatness*," which refers to the essence or concept of a thing, that is, "what something is," and "*thatness*," which refers to the existence or actuality of a thing, that is, "that it exists."[169] I will consider these two thoughts in turn.

Whatness is a negative philosopher's fundamental thought insofar as her science "removes and eliminates the mere contingencies" from its content, leaving the concept of that which is "absolutely certain and unchanging."[170] Although Schelling claims that negative philosophy is "completely synonymous" with "rationalism,"[171] we can see that the latter is a genus of which one species is German idealism's elimination of radical contingency from the science of intelligibility, as exemplified by Fichte's deductive method and its radicalization by Hegel. Indeed, Schelling calls the negative philosophy of his day "the consequence of the standpoint philosophy

determinate intuition or consciousness is required such as consciousness or intuition of the identity of subject and object, then what is being required is a determinate or particular thinking" (Hegel VGP3 | V 9: 180–1). Schelling's 1833–34 Munich lectures provide a rebuttal shortly after Hegel's death (Schelling MV33 | SW I/10: 148–50). For an account of Schelling's rebuttal and the development of his doctrine of intellectual intuition, see Bruno 2023a. On Schelling's espousal of intellectual intuition and the identity philosophy, see Beiser 2002: 582–4, Bruno 2013, Forster 2014, Melamed 2020, Ostaric 2020, Vater 2012, Watkins 2014, and Whistler 2013: 132–5.

166 Schelling BV-B | SW II/3: 150.
167 Schelling BV-B | SW II/3: 155.
168 Versions of this discussion appear in Bruno 2015b and Bruno 2016.
169 Schelling BV-B | SW II/3: 60, 83, 100.
170 Schelling BV-B | SW II/3: 67–8.
171 Schelling BV-B | SW II/3: 83.

obtains through Kant's critique of reason."[172] As we have seen, the "consequence" of Kant's philosophical "standpoint" is the German idealist campaign against facticity. Hence Schelling observes that Fichte is "determinative for all subsequent schools of philosophy" after Kant for whom the "unavoidable demand" is a principle from which to derive the forms of cognition, that is, a "common *prius* of sensibility, of the understanding, and of reason."[173] Fichte's deductive method generates "the concept of an unconditioned *science of reason*," that is, a science in which reason is the sole source of the conditions of intelligibility. However, with this science, one can ask only "what will exist, if anything at all exists," for it strictly speaking provides only a systematic account of the whatness of existence, whereas "*that* [anything] exists does not follow from this [science], for there could very well be nothing at all that exists." As we saw, the apotheosis of negative philosophy's restriction to whatness is Hegel, whose *Encyclopedia* concerns not "the fact" that things exist, but rather their "essence" or "concept," which "remains the same" even if there were nothing.[174]

Negative philosophy's fundamental thought becomes its highest achievement through the systematic articulation of the thought-determinations that compose the whatness or "*concept* of being itself." Schelling's Maimonian challenge is to the significance of this systematically articulated concept, for reason is "pathetic" if it has "nothing to do with being, thus only concerning itself with a chimera."[175] Despite our deducible right to the thought-determinations by which existence is intelligible, they are potentially empty. Avoiding this threat requires a capacity other than reason, one that can correct the "wrongful and improper expressions of a *self-movement* of the idea" of such thought-determinations.[176] A capacity other

[172] Schelling BV-B | SW II/3: 68–9.

[173] Schelling BV-B | SW II/3: 55.

[174] See Schelling: "the circumstance of whether [something] exists or not does not change my concept of [its] content in the least. . .Rational philosophy has its truth in the immanent necessity of its progress; as we said earlier, it is so independent of existence that it would be true even if nothing existed" (Schelling BV-B | SW II/3: 60, 128). In a symposium on Bowie 1993, White argues that Schelling cannot prove, *contra* Hegel, that being exceeds thinking merely by observing that there could be nothing, since Hegel assumes that there is actually something and provides a transcendental argument for its conditions of possibility (White 1994: 17–8). However, there is good reason to deny that Hegel provides a transcendental argument, on which see Houlgate 2015. Moreover, the assumption of actuality is precisely what fuels Schelling's critique of negative philosophy, on which see Bowie 1994: 27. Beiser accuses Bowie of indulging the false dichotomy that we must read Schelling "selectively in light of contemporary concerns," on the one hand, in order not to historically "pigeonhole him as a mere predecessor of Hegel," on the other hand, as there remains the third "hermeneutical" option of reconstructing Schelling's arguments in their historical context and evaluating them according to their own standards, which would reveal, *contra* Bowie, that they do not signal the "end of metaphysics," assuming that that were even possible (Beiser 1994: 2–4).

[175] Schelling BV-B | SW II/3: 60, 71. Cf. Schelling's 1796–97 *Treatises on the Explication of the Idealism of the Wissenschaftslehre*: "He who does not feel and recognize around himself anything real, who is merely feeding on or juggling with concepts, whose faculty of intuition has long since been deadened by memorization, dead speculation, or social degeneracy, and whose existence remains but a *dim thought*: how can he ever speak of reality (e.g., any more than the blind man about colours)?" (Schelling AE | SW I/1: 353).

[176] Schelling BV-B | SW II/3: 60, 73.

than reason is necessary in order to move this idea toward actuality. That capacity is experience. As Schelling says: "experience, through which we know what really exists, is a source of knowing independent of reason and, thus, travels right alongside it." Moreover, despite the necessity of the thought-determinations by which existence is intelligible, "*that*" there is existence "is something purely contingent."[177] If the science of reason provides the "[conceptual] *content* of what exists. . .but not, therefore, *actuality*,"[178] then a science distinct from the science of reason is needed, namely, one that can supplement knowledge of necessary whatness with knowledge of contingent thatness. A science distinct from the science of reason must grasp the actuality of the latter's conceptual content, namely, a science of experience. This science is positive philosophy. Accordingly, the thought of the experience of actuality, that is, the thought of our non-discursive openness to the thatness of existence, constitutes the positive philosopher's "fundamental thought."[179]

Schelling returns to "The Ideal of Pure Reason" in order to demarcate the method of positive philosophy. In that chapter, he says, Kant finds the idea of "groundless being" necessary for thinking the ground of finite existence yet incomprehensible because no experience is adequate to cognizing its reality.[180] Such an idea is what, earlier in the first *Critique*, Kant calls a "problematic" concept and a "concept of reason," whose content is non-contradictory yet whose reality is non-cognizable. Such an idea, moreover, is a "boundary concept" that serves to restrict the understanding's assertoric use to sensible intuition on pain of the dogmatism of "making thoughts into things and hypostatizing them."[181] Schelling extends Kant's critique of dogmatism to a criticism of Hegel's negative philosophy, which, by "hypostatiz[ing] the concept," fails to locate "what is positive *outside* itself."[182] And yet Schelling claims that positive philosophy aims to "transform" incomprehensible being into that which is "*a posteriori* comprehensible."[183] This claim seems to contradict Kant's commitment to the inadequacy of experience for cognizing that which is represented by the ideas, which, as the highest species on what he calls the "stepladder" of representations, represent that which exceeds possible experience.[184] How can the abyss of reason be made comprehensible? In what sense can reason reach "that being which overpowers" and "paralyze[s]" it and "which it cannot find in the phenomenal world as something actually known"?[185] Indeed, what is the experience by which positive philosophy can access the actuality of

[177] Schelling BV-B | SW II/3: 60.
[178] Schelling BV-B | SW II/3: 61.
[179] See Fackenheim: "the first principle of the positive philosophy cannot be an absolute Idea, but only an absolute Fact" (Fackenheim 1954: 571).
[180] Schelling BV-B | SW II/3: 165.
[181] Kant KrV A254–5/B310–1, A310–1/B367, A395.
[182] Schelling BV-B | SW II/3: 89. Cf. Schelling: "the nothing is the final result of [Hegel's] philosophy and therefore has done nothing" (Schelling MV32 | 1972: 236, my translation).
[183] Schelling BV-B | SW II/3: 165.
[184] Kant KrV A320/B376–7.
[185] Schelling BV-B | SW II/3: 165.

being, that is, the thatness of existence? What is the experience of which positive philosophy could be the science?

Answers to these questions emerge from a process of elimination. First, Schelling distinguishes positive philosophy from "philosophical empiricism," which denies that being, as opposed to beings, either is knowable or exists. Second, he distinguishes it from "*mystical empiricism*," which affirms being's existence through either the "certain[ty]" of "divine revelation," conceived as "an *external* datum," or "the inner fact of an irresistible *feeling*," an example of which he says is Jacobi's early conception of faith.[186] Third, he distinguishes it from "speculative or theoretical mysticism," which he associates with theosophy and which professes an "infallible vision" into the "essence of creation," that is, an "immediate intuition" that "renounces science."[187] These distinctions create a contrast space in which we can conceive of an experience that, first, grasps being as opposed to beings and, second, whose grasp of being is scientific as opposed to mystical. I will consider the two features of this experience in turn.

Regarding the first feature, the experience in question concerns not a being, whether an "*external* datum" or an "inner fact," but rather being as such. Schelling describes the science of this experience as follows:

> positive philosophy starts out just as little from something that occurs merely in thought (for then it would fall back into the negative philosophy) as it starts out from some being that is present in *experience*. If it does not start out from something that occurs in thought, and, thus, in no way from pure thought, then it will start out from that which is before and external to all thought, consequently from being, but not from an empirical being. For we have already excluded this, in that empirical being is external to thought only in the very relative sense, to the extent that every being that occurs in experience inherently carries with it the logical determinations of the understanding, without which it could never even be represented. If positive philosophy starts out from that which is external to all thought, it cannot begin with a being that is external to thought in a merely relative sense, but only with a being that is *absolutely* external to thought. The being that is external to all thought, however, is just as much beyond all experience as it is before all thought: positive philosophy begins with the *completely transcendent being*.[188]

[186] Jacobi's conception of faith in the first edition of *David Hume* provokes Kant in the "Orientation" essay to assert that his belief in God expresses a need of reason rather than of inclination, which leads Jacobi in the 1815 second edition to approve reason's priority over understanding in Kant's practical philosophy. On why Jacobi's belief in God expresses a need of inclination rather than of reason, see Bruno 2021e.

[187] Schelling BV-B | SW II/3: 115–9, 126. Contrast Schelling's assessment of the early Jacobi (Schelling MV33 | SW I/10: 169).

[188] Schelling BV-B | SW II/3: 126–7.

Being, insofar as it is "*completely transcendent*," is "*absolutely* external" both to "pure thought" and to "empirical being." On the one hand, being is external to pure thought insofar as the latter presupposes the former on pain of the threat that its categories lack being and thus are empty. On the other hand, being is external to empirical being insofar as the latter "could never even be represented" without "logical determinations of the understanding," that is, without the always potentially empty categories of pure thought. Thus, the experience in question concerns not beings, which have necessary categorial form as determined by negative philosophy, but rather being, that is, the very givenness of beings, which is radically contingent. In the 1832–33 Munich lectures, Schelling describes this givenness as "the experiential," which is "not just any individual being," but rather is being as such. The experiential is therefore the "starting point" of positive philosophy, which, unlike philosophical empiricism, does not deny the knowability or existence of being and, unlike mystical empiricism, does not concern a being.[189]

Regarding the second feature, if there is indeed a science of experience, then it would seem that it must specify certain laws. But this cannot be, since the topic of positive philosophy, namely, facticity, transcends lawfulness. How, then, are we to understand positive philosophy as a science? Schelling says that positive philosophy begins with a desire for the actuality of the idea of being. He then explains:

> Since it begins with a wanting, it is already justified as philosophy, that is, as a science that itself freely determines its object, a philosophy that in itself, and even according to its name, is a wanting. It can therefore also receive this demand *solely* from itself, and, likewise, it can provide itself with its own actual beginning. For this beginning is of the type that requires no foundation: it is that which through itself is the certain and absolute beginning.[190]

As we saw, a philosopher's fundamental thought expresses their deepest explanatory intention. Schelling describes the positive philosopher's explanatory intention here as a "wanting." Moreover, he regards the expression of this intention as sufficient to "justif[y]" the positive philosopher's inquiry as "a science," that is, as an inquiry that "determines its object." Insofar as this determination does not involve the specification of *a priori* laws, Schelling must conceive of science more broadly than Kant, who identifies both transcendental aesthetic and transcendental logic as sciences on the basis of their specification of *a priori* laws for sensing and thinking of objects, respectively. Indeed, Schelling is compelled to conceive of science more broadly in order for positive philosophy to count as a science because the specification of laws is the mark of negative philosophy in particular. We can see that his broader conception of science captures both negative philosophy

[189] Schelling MV32 | 1972: 239–40, 246, my translation.
[190] Schelling BV-B | SW II/3: 93.

and positive philosophy if we consider their distinguishing explanatory intentions, that is, the "object" that each "want[s]" to "determin[e]." In order to determine the whatness of being, negative philosophy specifies the laws that are necessary for thinking of being, namely, the categories or thought-determinations in virtue of which the intelligibility of existence is possible. In order to determine the thatness of being, positive philosophy specifies not laws, but rather a receptive capacity that is necessary for experiencing being, namely, the capacity of sensibility in virtue of which the experience of existence is possible. This is an unexpected science insofar as its topic is factical existence, which transcends lawfulness. Rather than being lawful, the sensibility that makes the experience of existence possible is characterized by our passivity or non-discursive openness toward thatness. As Schelling says: "If reason wants a real being, if it wants as something real any type of object discovered within itself in a concept. . .then it must submit to the authority of the senses. For the testimony of the senses is nothing other than an authority, since through it we know the present existence."[191] The "testimony" of the senses is an "authority" insofar as it bears witness to existence, that is, to the brute givenness of the actuality of that which would otherwise be merely formally or merely negatively intelligible. This authority thereby determines the object of positive science, which satisfies the "wanting" that distinguishes the positive philosopher's explanatory intention.[192] In this way, positive philosophy qualifies as a science, unlike theoretical mysticism.

We saw that the Berlin lectures take on the "astonishing" Maimonian challenge of proving the actuality of the first principle of negative philosophy, that is, the actuality of the articulated concept or whatness of being, and that this requires the combination of negative philosophy with positive philosophy, that is, with the science of the experience of the existence or thatness of being. Only such a combination can prove the reality of this principle. We will now see that, following Kant, Schelling's proof establishes a relation between a first principle and experience in accordance with the threefold criterion that such a proof is indirect, incomplete, and reciprocal.

[191] Schelling BV-B | SW II/3: 171. Cf. Schelling: "*Initium philosophiae est admiration* [the beginning of philosophy is wonder], or even more precisely after Plato: τὸ πάθος τοῦ φιλοσοφοῦ ἐστι τὸ θαυμάζειν [the affect of the philosopher is wonder]. This affect of the philosopher now has a place in positive philosophy" (Schelling BV-C | 2020: 125). For the argument that Schelling is a mystical Platonist from 1792 to 1802, see Fisher 2024.

[192] See James: "By what insatiate conceit and lust of intellectual despotism do I arrogate the right to know [the secrets of the nethermost bounds of the universe], and from my philosophic throne to play the only airs they shall march to, as if I were the Lord's anointed? Is not my knowing them at all a gift and not a right? And shall it be given before they are given? *Data! Gifts!* Something to be thankful for! It is a gift that we can approach things at all, and by means of the time and space of which our minds and they partake, alter our actions so as to meet them. . .Now to a mind like Hegel's such pusillanimous twaddle sounds simply loathsome. Bounds that we can't overpass! Data! Facts that say 'Hands off, till we are given'! Possibilities we can't control! A banquet of which we merely share! Heavens, this is intolerable; such a world is no world for a philosopher to have to do with. He must have all or nothing" (James 1882a: 191–2).

First, proving the reality of the *prius*, that is, of the fully articulated unconditioned condition or first principle of intelligibility, cannot be directly conceptual on pain of a tautology that Kant exposes in pre-critical rationalism,[193] but to which Schelling thinks German idealism's negative method is prone. Negative philosophy cannot infer existence as such from the concept as such, that is, thatness from whatness, any more than the ontological argument can infer God's existence from its concept. The conclusion to that argument, Schelling says, is simply that "God exists in a necessary manner, that is, *if* he exists, which then still leaves undecided whether he does or does not exist." In other words, the conclusion states what God must be like if God exists, which leaves open whether God in fact exists. Likewise, if one assumes that the *prius* is a fully articulated concept that contains its own existence, then to conclude with "the proposition *that it exists* is certainly nothing other than tautological."[194] The conclusion leaves open whether the *prius* in fact exists. Thus, negative philosophy exhibits the "dogmatizing" tendency of "reason to attempt through inferences to reach beyond itself to existence," a tendency that Schelling traces to "the old metaphysics" and whose futility he credits Kant with exposing.[195] It shows only how the *prius* would exist, given its whatness. The thatness of the *prius* must be sought not through illicit rational inference, but rather in "*transcendent being*,"[196] that is, in the experience of the existence on which the *prius* of negative philosophy depends if it is to render anything intelligible.[197] This is to say that a proof of the *prius*' reality cannot be directly conceptual, but rather must be indirect, that is, mediated by the experience of an opposing, "non-conceptual *prius*."[198] Otherwise, the proof invites the empty formalism challenge. As Schelling says: "the science of reason, contrary to excluding experience, requires it. . .[I]t is vital for [reason] to have a control through which

[193] See Kant KrV A592–602/B620–30.

[194] Schelling BV-B | SW II/3: 157–8. Cf. Schelling BV-B | SW II/3: 167. Hegel describes the transition from concept to objectivity in the *Science of Logic* as "essentially the same as the *proof* from the *concept*, that is to say, from the *concept of God* to his existence, that was formerly found in *metaphysics*, or the so-called *ontological proof*" (Hegel WL | GW 12: 127). The ontological argument's success depends on one's method of deriving contents from concepts, e.g., the early modern method of conceptual analysis and the German idealist method of dialectical analysis. Kant targets the early modern method, whereas Schelling targets the German idealist method.

[195] Schelling BV-B | SW II/3: 82–3. Cf. Schelling: "That everything in the world is determined through pure thinking is the position of rationalism" (Schelling MV32 | 1972: 243, my translation). Cf. Schelling's use of 'dogmatizing' with his use of his neologism 'dogmaticism' in the "Philosophical Letters." On the latter use, see Bruno 2020d. On Schelling's neologism, see Nieke 1972: 278–9.

[196] See Schelling: "Kant forbade metaphysics transcendence, but he forbade it only for dogmatizing reason, that is, for reason that of itself seeks, by means of inferences, to reach existence; he did not forbid reason to proceed conversely from that which *simply* and, thus, infinitely *exists* to the concept of the most supreme *being* as *posterius* (he had not thought of it, for this possibility had not even presented itself to him)" (Schelling BV-B | SW II/3: 170).

[197] Evoking Kant's conception of experience's role as the formative context of cognition, Schelling says that experience, while not the "*source*" of the science of reason, is its "escort" (Schelling BV-B | SW II/3: 63).

[198] Schelling BV-B | SW II/3: 167. Cf. Schelling: "it is no contradiction to subject what is first in thinking to what is first in being" (Schelling MV32 | 1972: 245, my translation).

it can demonstrate that what it has found *a priori* is *not* a chimera. This control is experience. For only experience, and not reason, can say that *that* which has been construed really exists."[199] Experience provides reason with an openness or receptivity to being, that is, to "actuality" as opposed to "potency," where actuality is what is "most worthy of knowing."[200] A positive science is accordingly required, one that proceeds from the experience of "that which just exists",[201] that is, from what Schelling says exists "*factically*," toward a proof of the applicability, and hence the reality and significance, of the first principle of negative science.

Second, proving a first principle's reality cannot be complete, for the existence on which it depends is factical. As we saw, that being exists is "purely contingent," since "there could very well be nothing." Thus, no proof that relies on the experience of being can ever be conclusive.[202] Moreover, since the principle at issue defines the intelligibility of being as such rather than that of a being, that is, the whatness of thatness as a whole, a conclusive proof would require an experience of unrestricted being, which no possible experience can furnish. As Schelling argues:

> The experience towards which positive philosophy proceeds is not just of a *particular kind*, but is the entirety of all experience from beginning to end. What contributes to the proof is not a part of experience, but all of experience. . .Because the realm of reality in which this proof moves is not finished and complete. . .but is a realm perpetually nearing its consummation, the proof is therefore also *never* finished, and for this very reason this science is only a *philo-sophie*.[203]

Positive philosophy facilitates a proof of the reality of the first principle of negative philosophy by beginning from the experience of "that which just exists," that is, being. But since being exceeds possible experience, comprehending this principle's reality is a regulative ideal, which, it turns out, adheres to Kant's denial, noted above, that experience is adequate for cognizing being. This is why Schelling says that positive philosophy never escapes the status of a love of wisdom, that is, of "a *philo-sophie*," which contradicts Hegel's advertised fulfillment of this love in the Preface to the *Phenomenology*. The proof at issue is therefore never complete, but rather is coextensive with the whole of history.[204]

199 Schelling BV-B | SW II/3: 63.
200 Schelling BV-B | SW II/3: 149.
201 Schelling BV-B | SW II/3: 158.
202 We might wonder how the experience of existence could fail to realize the first principle of its intelligibility. However, even if experience must realize this principle, it cannot do so conclusively, since the matter of its proof is contingent and unrestricted.
203 Schelling BV-B | SW II/3: 130–1.
204 Schelling describes positive philosophy as facilitating the revelation of God, whose existence negative philosophy by itself can prove only tautologically. He clarifies that revelation is not positive philosophy's "point of departure, as it is in the so-called Christian philosophy from which it is in this respect *toto coele* different," and is present in positive philosophy "in no other sense than nature or the entire history of the human race is also present within it; revelation will exert on it no different authority than what every other object exerts on the science that deals with it." He infers from this that

Third, the relation between a first principle and experience in a proof is one of reciprocal dependence. The proof aims to show both that rationality is real and that reality is rational, that is, both that intelligibility exists and that existence is intelligible. But just as a principle depends for its reality on the experience of existence, since there could "well be nothing," so too the experience of existence depends on a principle for its rationality, since it is only brutely the case that there is "anything at all." As we have seen, a first principle without existence is empty and existence without a first principle is blind. It is as one-sided to assume that existence is essentially rational as it is to assume that the *prius* is essentially real. We avoid one-sidedness by recognizing, negatively, that the experience of existence cannot prove the reality of the *prius* without presupposing the latter as the unconditioned condition of the intelligibility of existence and, positively, that the *prius* cannot function as this condition without the continuous and, as we have seen, endless experience of its reality and thus of its significance. As Schelling says: "Only the correctly understood negative philosophy leads to the positive philosophy; conversely, the positive philosophy is first possible only in contrast to the correctly understood negative."[205] A first principle's proof therefore consists in a reciprocal relation between it and the whole of experience.

In satisfying the Kantian threefold criterion of proof of the reality of a principle and its related category, we find an answer to Schelling's question about the meaning of philosophy, the union of whose "negative and positive facets" he says finally gives philosophy its "complete and altogether satisfying conclusion."[206] We find, in other words, that despite the fact that the "entire history of philosophy. . .presents a struggle between the negative and positive philosophies," "philosophy cannot help but be both negative and positive."[207] Schelling puts the point clearly toward the end of the Berlin lectures:

> although we realize in an indubitable manner that philosophy only completes itself in two sciences, the semblance, nonetheless, of two different philosophies existing side by side, which certainly would have to be called a scandal of philosophy, now disappears through this last exposition. For it has become apparent that the negative philosophy must posit the positive, but *by* positing this it only

while positive philosophy contains the "content of religion," it cannot be called "a *religious* philosophy" (Schelling BV-B | SW II/3: 133–4). Cf. Schelling: "For me it is not a matter of agreeing with any one church doctrine. I have no interest in being orthodox, as it is called, just as I would have no difficulty in being the opposite. For me, Christianity is merely a phenomenon that I seek to *explain*" (Schelling SW XIV: 201, translated by Snow 1996: 182).

205 Schelling BV-B | SW II/3: 80. Cf. Schelling: "The concept of the absolute *prius* and the concept of the experiential are by no means mutually exclusive concepts. The same thing can be recognized *a priori* and *a posteriori* from different standpoints" (Schelling MV32 | 1972: 241, my translation).

206 Schelling BV-B | SW II/3: 17.

207 Schelling BV-B | SW II/3: 145.

> makes itself into the consciousness of the positive, and is *to this extent* no longer *outside the positive*, but rather belongs to it itself, so that there is in fact but one philosophy.[208]

In philosophy, we may find ourselves motivated by one of two opposing "fundamental thought[s]," driven by one of two apparently irreconcilable explanatory intentions, and wanting scientifically to determine one of two seemingly incompatible objects, namely, whatness or thatness. However, we find that these thoughts are incomplete without each other, that these drives cannot satisfy themselves in isolation, and that these objects are unilaterally indeterminable.[209] It is only when we simultaneously cultivate our negative desire for speculation and our positive desire for actuality that we attain a stable philosophical position.

Schelling's announced "return to Kant" in the Berlin lectures is accordingly evident in at least four respects.

First, Schelling distinguishes between two irreducible faculties, that is, two "source[s] of knowing" that are "independent" of each other, namely, reason, which articulates the system of the categories, that is, the system of the whatness of being, and experience, which is sensibly receptive to the givenness of existence, that is, the givenness of the thatness of being. He thereby adapts Kant's two-stem faculty view, according to which the understanding and sensibility are "two stems of human cognition" whose respective cognitions differ not in "distinctness and indistinctness," that is, in degree, as the Leibnizian-Wolffian philosophy claims, but rather in "origin and content," that is, in kind, owing to their being two irreducible factors of "our subjective constitution."[210] Moreover, Schelling assigns two intra-philosophical sciences to each faculty, namely, the science of reason, that is, negative philosophy, and the science of experience, that is, positive philosophy. He thereby adapts Kant's intra-philosophical two-science view, according to which transcendental logic is the science that determines the rules by which the understanding thinks of objects, namely, the categories, and transcendental aesthetic is the science that determines the rules by which sensibility intuits objects, namely, space and time.[211]

Second, Schelling argues that negative philosophy must acknowledge what, for us, are underivable presuppositions, namely, the past *qua* free decision and the future *qua* complete derivation and actualized character, adapting Kant's argument that his "special science," namely, critique, must acknowledge what, for

[208] Schelling BV-B | SW II/3: 152.

[209] See Schelling: "should it really surprise us if such a double-sided nature of philosophy presents itself, since. . .it can be shown that both directions have been present in philosophy—the one right alongside the other—since time immemorial, and that when they have come into conflict, the one has nonetheless always held its own against the other[?]" (Schelling BV-B | SW II/3: 95).

[210] Kant KrV A43–4/B60–2; cf. A51/B75.

[211] On Schelling's repurposing of Kant's two-stem faculty view, see Bruno 2023a.

us, are underivable presuppositions, namely, the forms of sensibility, the forms of judgment, the categories of the understanding, and the ideas of reason. Returning to Kant in this second respect enables him to avoid the Hegelian fantasy, whose "concept" is "bequeathed" by Fichte, of "an absolute philosophy that presupposes nothing."

Third, Schelling argues that positive philosophy registers the non-conceptual givenness of existence, which alone can prove the actuality of the categories of negative philosophy, adapting Kant's argument that the threefold criterion of proof registers the non-conceptual givenness of objects of possible experience, which alone can prove the actuality of a principle and its related category. Returning to Kant in this third respect enables him to avoid the Hegelian error of "hypostatiz[ing] the concept."

Fourth, as we have seen, the Schellingian slogan is that, for the sake of systematic cognition, a first principle without existence is empty and existence without a first principle is blind, which repurposes the Kantian slogan that, for the sake of empirical cognition, concepts without intuitions are empty and intuitions without concepts are blind. However, whereas the Kantian slogan signifies a realizable achievement that constitutes individual episodes of experience, the Schellingian slogan signifies an unrealizable ideal that regulatively guides the whole of experience.

The four respects in which Schelling's return to Kant is evident yield the components of a five-step argument. First, philosophy is composed of two irreducible sciences, namely, negative and positive philosophy. Second, for the sake of systematic cognition, these intra-philosophical sciences are mutually dependent. Third, any attempt either to reduce one of these sciences to the other or to deny their mutual dependence undermines a "complete and altogether satisfying" science of intelligibility. Fourth, insofar as Hegel's logic rejects the brute givenness of existence, it must deny the irreducibility of positive philosophy and so must deny the latter's mutual dependence on negative philosophy. Fifth, therefore, as a science of intelligibility, Hegel's logic is neither complete nor satisfying.

Schelling expresses this five-step argument as follows:

> When through my public lectures something of the positive philosophy was first disclosed there were many who believed they must take up the negative against me, believing that I thought the negative should be entirely abolished, since I had certainly spoken of the Hegelian philosophy in such a way. This occurred, however, not because I considered the Hegelian philosophy to be the negative. I am not able to inflict this honour upon it, nor can I even concede that it is the negative, since, on the contrary, its fundamental error consists precisely in that it wants to be positive. The difference between Hegel and myself is no smaller in regards to the negative than to the positive philosophy. . .[T]he negative science, taken in isolation or in its own right, is not capable of making a claim to the name

> 'philosophy': it only becomes worthy of this name in its final moment, through its relationship to the positive science. This is a very important point that finally leads us to completely sublate this duality within philosophy. For the negative philosophy is, in its own right, not yet philosophy, but rather only in its relation to the positive.[212]

Schelling evokes the argument's first premise when he denies that his introduction of positive science is meant to "abolis[h]" negative science, since philosophy is composed of both a negative and a positive science. He evokes the second premise when he says that negative science is "worthy" of "the name 'philosophy'" only "through its relationship" to positive science and vice versa, since these sciences are mutually dependent. He evokes the third premise when he says that philosophy must "sublate" the "duality" of negative and positive science, since neither science is reducible or independent for a complete and satisfying philosophy. He evokes the fourth premise when he says that he and Hegel "diffe[r]" regarding not only the positive science that he introduces, but also the negative science that he places in mutual dependence with it, since Hegel ultimately denies their mutual dependence. And he evokes the conclusion when he says that Hegel's logic does not deserve the "honor" of being even a merely negative science, since Hegel denies the irreducibility and mutual dependence of negative and positive sciences that are jointly necessary for a complete and satisfying philosophy. Thus, according to Schelling, it is not only that Hegel locates his philosophical standpoint in a negative science that excludes a genuinely positive science and is consequently as one-sided as thinkers like Jacobi, who, by grounding their convictions "in a blind feeling, in faith, or even in revelation," locate "their standpoint *only* in the positive." Even worse, by being one-sided, Hegel, like Jacobi, renounces "all scientific philosophy."[213]

With the *Ages*, the Munich lectures, and the Berlin lectures in view, we can see that Schelling's full critique of Hegel is that he neglects facticity both insofar as it conditions negative philosophy in the form of the past *qua* free decision and the future *qua* complete derivation and actualized character and insofar as it orients negative philosophy toward the experience of existence as such. In both respects, Schelling raises the concept of facticity to an existential register such that it signifies the radically contingent freedom and character of one who pursues a science of intelligibility, on the one hand, and signifies one's openness to the bruteness of

[212] Schelling BV-B | SW II/3: 80, 151. Cf. Kierkegaard's notes on Schelling's Nineteenth Lecture in Berlin: "*for itself negative philosophy cannot be called philosophy; it becomes philosophy only in connection with positive philosophy*" (Kierkegaard 1989: 365).

[213] Schelling SW BV-B | II/3: 85. This is the latest in a series of criticisms between Schelling and Jacobi. Schelling's 1807 "On the Relation of the Fine Arts to Nature," a gala lecture at the Munich Academy of the Sciences, aggravates Jacobi, the Academy's president, for its implicit pantheism, which, without naming its author, Jacobi attacks in *Divine Things*, provoking Schelling's counterattack in 1812's "Monument to Mr. Friedrich Heinrich Jacobi's Writing 'Of Divine Things, Etc.'" On the pantheism dispute, see Ford 1965, Hammacher 1994, Jacobi 1994: 630n27, and McGrath 2023.

existence, on the other hand. He thereby provides a post-Hegelian revival and repurposing of the three factical elements of Fichte's philosophy, namely and as we saw in Sections 1.6 and 3.3, freedom as the ground for which "no reason can be given," the dependence of one's chosen philosophy on one's character or "the kind of person one is," and the not-I's opposition to the I as a "postulated *factum*" that is derivable from "[n]o higher ground." Crucially, Schelling revives and repurposes these factical elements without thereby raising the two threats that, as we saw in the Introduction, motivate the German idealist project, namely, facticity construed as marking the impossibility of a science of intelligibility and nihilism construed as marking the impossibility of human freedom and purposiveness.

As we will see in Part III, the existential register to which Schelling raises the concept of facticity is precisely the register at which classical phenomenology, particularly in the work of Heidegger, will engage in a deeper, tradition-defining analysis of the many facets of our factical life.

PART III
A CRISIS OF METHOD
Hermeneutics

5
Hiatus Irrationalis
Lask's Fateful Misreading of Fichte

5.1 Introduction

In the two decades after Schelling's death in 1854, neo-Kantianism begins to form as a philosophical movement whose major schools coalesce toward the end of the nineteenth century around Hermann Cohen, Paul Natorp, and Ernst Cassirer in Marburg, Wilhelm Windelband, Rickert, and Lask in Heidelberg, Leonard Nelson in Göttingen, and Friedrich Paulsen, Alois Riehl, and Benno Erdmann in Berlin. The neo-Kantians call for a return to Kant in response to the German idealist project of systematically deducing the conditions of intelligibility from reason alone and amid psychologism's emerging challenge to philosophy's authority regarding the normative character of intelligibility.[1]

Fichte occupies a complicated position in the neo-Kantian conception of the history of post-Kantian philosophy.[2] Despite his role in defining German idealism's systematic ambitions, Fichte allegedly comes to restrict these ambitions by discovering the insuperable bounds of reason, as Lask argues in his 1902 doctoral thesis *Fichte's Idealism and History*. According to Lask, as early as 1797–98, Fichte recognizes what he calls a '*hiatus irrationalis*' or irrational gap between the necessary conditions of intelligibility and the contingent existence of individuals, a gap whose removal presents an endless task. Notwithstanding Fichte's initial commitment to what Lask calls 'rationalism,' that is, to the deduction of the conditions of intelligibility from reason and to the explanatory priority of the logical generality of such conditions over the material particularity of actual individuals, Fichte's recognition of the irrational gap signals his turn toward what Lask calls 'critical anti-rationalism.' Crucially, Lask's reading of Fichte relies on a problematic interpretation of the meaning of Fichte's neologism 'facticity,' which, as we will see, directly figures in the term's transmission to the phenomenological tradition that succeeds neo-Kantianism.

As we saw in Section 2.2, Fichte coins 'facticity' on the eve of his Berlin period. The neologism names an architectonically unacceptable contingency, namely, the

[1] On the origins of neo-Kantianism, see Beiser 2014. On the neo-Kantian reception of Fichte, see Beiser 2018. On neo-Kantianism's anti-psychologism, see Anderson 2005. On the relation between neo-Kantianism and phenomenology, see Luft 2018.
[2] A version of this discussion appears in Bruno 2021d.

Facticity and the Fate of Reason After Kant. G. Anthony Bruno, Oxford University Press.
 DOI: 10.1093/9780191987533.003.0006

allegedly brute conditions of intelligibility, whose bruteness would undermine the necessity that is required for a true science of intelligibility. Such conditions would be externally imposed on reason or the I, thereby eliminating the latter's role as the first principle of idealism and leaving open its complete determination by nature, that is, leaving open the nihilistic consequence of Spinozism. The prehistory of 'facticity' in the *Wissenschaftslehre* lies in Fichte's rejection, throughout his Jena period, of any deduction of conditions that rests on radically contingent grounds, that is, any deduction that is rhapsodic and consequently an impediment to true science. 'Facticity' accordingly denotes false conditions of intelligibility whose determination is rhapsodic, whether perceptually, causally, historically, or merely intuitively so. In general, factical and thus false conditions of intelligibility lack the necessity of being either genetically deduced from a first principle or intellectually intuited as such a principle. Such radical contingency differs from the empirical contingency of facts, which could be otherwise yet must always conform to their rationally deducible and thus true conditions of intelligibility. Fichte diagnoses facticity in *Recollections*, the *Presentation*, the *Blessed Life*, the *Principles*, the Erlangen lectures, and especially the Berlin lectures, which latter are the textual focus of Lask's doctoral thesis and hence of my discussion below. As Fichte says in these lectures, facticity must be "master[ed]" and "expunge[d]" by showing that allegedly brute conditions of intelligibility are in fact deducible from the absolute freedom of reason or the I.

As a philosophical term, 'facticity' is familiar to most scholars, not via Fichte, but rather via the major figures of classical phenomenology, namely, Heidegger, Sartre,[3] de Beauvoir,[4] and Merleau-

[3] In *Being and Nothingness*, Sartre distinguishes between "being in-itself" and "being for-itself." Whereas being in-itself "can neither be derived from the possible nor reduced to the necessary," since it "is isolated in its being by its total positivity," "[t]he possible is a structure of" being for-itself, which is "the being which determines itself to exist inasmuch as it can not coincide with itself" and "perpetually effects in itself a break in being." Their relation is such that the for-itself is "sustained" by "the perpetually evanescent contingency of the in-itself," which contingency is thus "the facticity of the for-itself," which the latter must strive to transcend (Sartre 1956: lxv–vi, 78–9, 82–3). He provides an illustration of facticity when he says that "death . . . is a *contingent fact* which as such on principle escapes me and originally belongs to my facticity. I can neither discover my death nor wait for it nor adopt an attitude toward it, for it is that which is revealed as undiscoverable, that which disarms all waiting, that which slips into all attitudes (and particularly into those which are assumed with respect to death) so as to transform them into externalized and fixed conducts whose meaning is forever entrusted to others and not to ourselves. Death is a pure fact as is birth; it comes to us from outside and it transforms us into the outside. At bottom it is in no way distinguished from birth, and it is the identity of birth and death that we call facticity" (Sartre 1956: 545). Cf. Sartre on the "contingent necessity" of "the other's existence" (Sartre 1956: 250).

[4] See de Beauvoir's 1947 *The Ethics of Ambiguity*: "The goal toward which I surpass myself must appear to me as a point of departure toward a new act of surpassing. Thus, a creative freedom develops happily without ever congealing into unjustified facticity . . . However, man does not create the world. He succeeds in disclosing it only through the resistance which the world opposes to him. The will is defined only by raising obstacles, and by the contingency of facticity certain obstacles let themselves be conquered, and others do not . . . Life imprisonment is the most horrible of punishments because it preserves existence in its pure facticity but forbids it all legitimation" (de Beauvoir 1972: 27–8, 33).

Ponty,[5] if not via later thinkers.[6] Heidegger uses the term in *Being and Time* to denote the hermeneutically interpretable yet undeducibly brute conditions of Dasein's intelligible being in the world. Such conditions are neither logically necessary, since their denial is thinkable, nor empirically contingent, since they characterize Dasein's very being, a kind of existence to which Dasein is simply given. As he says in §29, "[Dasein] is thrown in such a way that it is the 'there' as being-in-the-world. The expression 'thrownness' is meant to suggest the *facticity of its being delivered over*."[7] In that same section, Heidegger distinguishes between two modes of disclosing Dasein's existence, namely, mood and knowledge.

On the one hand, "a fundamental existential mode of being" of Dasein is attunement, since, in it, "Dasein is always already brought before itself." Attunement's "most familiar" form is "mood," which "*always already disclose[s]*" Dasein and "*first makes possible directing oneself toward something*." One always finds oneself in some mood, which "makes manifest 'how one is and is coming along.'" Mood is thus the "primordial disclosure" of one's being in a particular situation in which "*directing oneself toward something*" that one understands as, for example, urgent or exciting is "*possible*." As we will see in Chapter 6, anxiety is unique among moods by "*disclos[ing] Dasein in its thrownness*," that is, by attuning Dasein to its "burdensome character," namely, that, in general, it is factically being-in-the-world, being-with-others, being-ahead-of-itself, being-toward-death, and being-time.[8] Thus, mood discloses Dasein as a being who not only finds itself in a particular situation that makes self-direction possible, but also finds itself in a general situation whose conditions of intelligibility are factical.[9]

[5] In *Phenomenology of Perception*, Merleau-Ponty declares "I can never fully justify the permanent thesis of my life that 'there is a world' or, rather, 'there is the world,'" since this thesis expresses "the facticity of the world." Hence he says that "the contingency of the world" is not "a problem to be resolved as soon as possible through the discovery of some deeper necessity" (Merleau-Ponty 2012: lxxxi, 419). Cf. Merleau-Ponty's posthumous 1964 *The Visible and the Invisible*: "the enigma of the brute world is finally left intact by science and by reflection" (Merleau-Ponty 1968: 156).

[6] By defining 'facticity' as "the property whereby everything and every world *is* without reason, and is thereby *capable of actually becoming otherwise without reason*" (Meillassoux 2008: 53), Quentin Meillassoux deprives it of the relative necessity that classical phenomenology accords to it. He does attribute a more classical definition of 'facticity' to Kant, although this attribution is incomplete, for he includes space and time yet does not specify why they are factical, includes the categories yet incorrectly denies that Kant regards them as deducible, and omits the ideas of reason (Meillassoux 2008: 38). On this, see Bruno 2017b.

[7] Heidegger SZ | GA 2: 135. Heidegger uses the term as early as notes for his undelivered 1918–19 Freiburg lectures, *The Philosophical Foundations of Medieval Mysticism* (Heidegger PGM | GA 60 3).

[8] Heidegger SZ | GA 2: 134–7.

[9] Since, in attunement, we find ourselves as being-there, we find more than merely a "psychical condition." In other words, since mood "*has always already disclosed*" our "*being-in-the-world*," it "comes neither from 'without' nor from 'within.'" As Heidegger says, mood attunes Dasein not only to its thrownness and to its being-there, but also "in such a way that what it encounters in the world can *matter*" under some "psychical condition" or other. Hence he lauds the second book of Aristotle's *Rhetoric* for interpreting πάθη not "in the scope of 'psychology,'" in which "[t]hey sink to the level of accompanying phenomena," but rather within "the first systematic hermeneutic of the everydayness of being-with-one-another" (Heidegger SZ | GA 2: 136–9). Cf. Heidegger's 1924 summer Marburg lectures, *Basic Concepts of Aristotelian Philosophy*: "πάθη, 'affects,' are not states pertaining to ensouled things, but are concerned with a *disposition of living things in their world*, in the mode of being

On the other hand, knowledge seeks the "why" for what mood "makes manifest," namely, Dasein's finding itself as situated. As Heidegger puts it, knowledge seeks the "whence and whither" for the "pure 'that it is'" of Dasein's being. Insofar as knowledge aims to provide reasons for why Dasein finds itself as it does, it aims at "minimizing the 'evidence' of attunement by measuring it against the apodictic certainty of the theoretical cognition of something merely objectively present." This is to say that knowledge aims at reducing what mood discloses to the terms of "objective presen[ce]," that is, to the features of that which, by being merely occurrent or extant as an object and thus not even available or useful as a tool, much less self-understanding or self-directing as a Dasein, lacks the capacity to find itself at all. Moreover, by "measuring" this situation "against" a "certainty" that is "apodictic," that is, a certainty that is logically demonstrable, knowledge rejects the very idea of the factical and therefore logically indemonstrable conditions of the intelligibility of the situation that mood purports to disclose. The idea that Dasein is constituted by factical conditions "stares at it with the inexorability of an enigma" whose elucidation through deduction knowledge demands under the banner of what Heidegger calls "rationalism."[10] In this way, knowledge discloses Dasein as a being whose conditions of intelligibility are, like those of any object, logically demonstrable and thus amenable to deductive elucidation.

Like Lask, Heidegger understands rationalism as affirming the explanatory priority of deducible conditions of intelligibility over existence, in this case, Dasein's existence. However, he argues that "rational enlightenment" is an evasion of facticity precisely when it asserts that it "knows" the "whence" of Dasein's being. Such an assertion assumes that "knowledge" has explanatory "priority" over and thus can "master" mood in its attempt to demonstrate that the kind of existence that mood discloses is an instance of rationally perspicuous objective presence. But this assumption is false because mood attunes Dasein to the worldly, social, concernful, mortal, and temporal existence on which the very possibility of theoretical and practical knowledge depends. As Heidegger says, mood is "a primordial kind of being of Dasein in which it is disclosed to itself *before* all cognition and willing." Although mood and knowledge are both ways of disclosing Dasein's existence, the latter depends on and is therefore limited by the former. This is why Heidegger

positioned toward something, allowing a matter to matter to it. The affects play a fundamental role in the determination of being-in-the-world, of being-with-and-toward-others . . . [T]he traditional conception of the affects . . . partitioned the phenomenon into bodily states and states of the soul—states that stand in some connection. On the other hand, it must be noted that Aristotle, in accordance with his orientation of treating the ensouled as the mode of being of living things, emphasizes that the πάθη express the *being of human beings*" (Heidegger GAP | GA 18: 122, 177).

[10] Heidegger SZ | GA 2: 134, 136. Heidegger observes that "[i]rrationalism," which "banishes" Dasein's factical mode of existence "to the sanctuary of the irrational," is "no better" than rationalism, for it "talks about the things to which rationalism is blind, but only with a squint" (Heidegger SZ | GA 2: 136).

says that while we might rationalistically aim to "master" mood "with knowledge," in fact "we never master a mood by being free of a mood, but always through a counter mood . . . Mood assails." If knowledge always presupposes being in some mood, then what knowledge discloses presupposes what mood discloses, namely, the possibilities of self-direction of Dasein's situation in particular and the factical conditions of Dasein's situation in general. Under the banner of rationalism, knowledge might aim to elucidate the apparent enigma of these conditions through deduction and thereby attain the "why" of what mood discloses. Nevertheless, "Dasein cannot know [this] why because the possibilities of disclosure belonging to cognition fall far short of the primordial disclosure of moods in which Dasein is brought before its being as the there."[11] As disclosive modes of being, then, mood limits knowledge.

Heidegger's distinction between mood and knowledge serves to contextualize his disagreement with Fichte, to whom he explicitly opposes himself concerning the nature of facticity in his 1941 summer lectures in Freiburg, *The Metaphysics of German Idealism*: "According to Fichte, it is the I that throws the world. But according to *Being and Time*, the I does not first throw the world; it is rather Dasein, essentially presencing before all humanity, that is thrown."[12] Fichte's systematic ambition is to demonstrate that apparently factical conditions of intelligibility, that is, conditions into which we are allegedly thrown, reveal themselves to be absolutely necessary conditions once they are deduced from reason or the I.[13] This ambition contradicts Heidegger's hermeneutics of facticity, according to which, as we saw in Section 2.6, Dasein "never gets back behind its thrownness." It is with a rationalist recoil from facticity that Fichte declares in the *Vocation*: "Only reason is . . . All our life is its life. We are in its hand and remain there, and no one can tear us out of it. We are eternal because it is."[14] Whereas Heidegger regards Dasein as thrown into existence, Fichte regards us as held by reason, whose reach no brute fact escapes. Fichte's deductive mastery of facticity is driven by revulsion at the idea of bruteness within the conditions of intelligibility. Heidegger's

[11] Heidegger SZ | GA 2: 134, 136. On Heidegger's conception of mood, see Elpidorou and Freeman 2015, Golob 2017, and Ratcliffe 2013.

[12] Heidegger MDI | GA 49: 161. Cf. Heidegger's 1929–30 winter lectures in Freiburg, *The Fundamental Concepts of Metaphysics: World, Finitude, Solitude*: "The fundamental concepts of metaphysics . . . are anchored in our being gripped, in which we do not represent before us that which we conceptually comprehend, but maintain ourselves in a quite different comportment, one which is originarily and fundamentally different from any scientific kind" (Heidegger GM | GA 29/30: 12–3).

[13] See Fichte: "[the I] is the circle within which every finite understanding, that is, every understanding that we can conceive, is necessarily confined. Anyone who wants to escape from this circle does not understand himself and does not know what he wants . . . [Critical] philosophy points out to us that circle from which we cannot escape. Within this circle, on the other hand, it furnishes us with the greatest coherence in all of our knowledge" (Fichte RA | SW I: 11, 15).

[14] Fichte BM | SW II: 302. Cf. Fichte: "in the *Wissenschaftslehre* . . . the only thing that exists in itself is reason, and individuality is something merely accidental. Reason is the end and personality is the means . . . [R]eason alone is eternal, whereas individuality must ceaselessly die off" (Fichte VND | SW I: 505). Cf. Jacobi: "Pure reason is a taking hold that *only* takes hold of itself" (Jacobi BF 14 | 1994: 507).

opposition to Fichte's rationalist recoil from facticity echoes Friedrich Schiller's letter to Johann Wolfgang von Goethe, October 26, 1794, which Heidegger quotes in *Metaphysics of German Idealism*: "To [Fichte], the world is only a ball which the I has thrown forth, and which it again catches in the act of reflexion!"[15] Thus, the emerging post-Kantian dispute regarding the nature of facticity centers on the question of whether reason's explanatory power is absolute or relative, that is, infinite or finite.[16]

In the development of post-Kantian philosophy from German idealism to phenomenology, the meaning of 'facticity' transforms from denoting intolerably contingent conditions that reason must annihilate to denoting radically contingent conditions that reason must presuppose. For Heidegger, facticity is a topic for hermeneutical interpretation and not, as for Fichte, something to be rationally expunged as far as possible. If, as Heidegger holds, 'facticity' signifies the arational conditions of Dasein's thrownness, then it is a delusion to pursue the rational derivation of factical conditions of intelligibility, which would be to transcend the explanatory limits of reason. This accordingly calls for philosophy's transition from an architectonic interest in logical systematicity to an existentialist interest in radical contingency. How, then, does Heidegger inherit and diametrically repurpose Fichte's neologism? Whence the reversed meaning of 'facticity' in post-Kantian thought?

The reversal of the term's meaning is the result of Heidegger reading Lask's doctoral thesis, whose impact on Heidegger's 1915 habilitation thesis *The Theory of Categories and Meaning in Duns Scotus* is noted in the thesis report that is filed by their shared supervisor, Rickert.[17] As we will see, Lask interprets 'facticity' as Fichte's term for what Lask calls the 'individuality problem,' that is, the resistance of the material particularity of individuals to explanation by the categories that

[15] Schiller and Goethe 1994: 19, cited by Heidegger MDI | GA 49: 161.

[16] See Heidegger's 1929 *Kant and the Problem of Metaphysics*: "[the first *Critique*] rattles the mastery of reason and the understanding . . . What does the struggle against the 'thing in itself,' which started with German idealism, mean, other than the growing forgetting of what Kant struggled for: that the inner possibility and necessity of metaphysics, i.e., its essence, are at bottom brought forth and preserved through the more original working-out and increased preservation of the problem of finitude?" (Heidegger KPM | GA 3: 243–4).

[17] See Kisiel 1995 and Sheehan 1998. On Heidegger's habilitation thesis, see Caputo 1974. In the Foreword to the 1972 first edition of his *Early Writings*, Heidegger quotes his 1957 lecture at the Heidelberg Academy of Sciences, which "discusses some features of the intellectual world that implicitly shaped [his] early efforts," including his introduction to Lask's work by Rickert in 1909 (Heidegger DS | GA 1: 55). In *Duns Scotus*, Heidegger describes Lask's 1911 *The Logic of Philosophy and the Doctrine of Categories* as "rich in problems," claiming that "it is Lask who first decisively" defines, demarcates, and determines the validity of reflexive and constitutive categories and that Lask's theory of judgment is similar to yet "far more comprehensive" than Scotus', although he sees in Lask's theory a "lack of intellectual freedom vis-à-vis the fetters of tradition" (Heidegger DS | GA 1: 205, 335–6, 383–4).

are genetically deduced from the absolute freedom of reason or the I. According to this interpretation, the neologism denotes radical contingency in the guise of haecceity, that is, the brute uniqueness of individuals, whose material particularity cannot be rendered fully intelligible by any category. For Lask, it is to Fichte's credit that he registers the problem of individuality, for he is deemed thereby to draw our attention to the world's irreducibly pre-categorial character.

This raises an important interpretive question. How is 'facticity' transmitted from Lask to Heidegger given their opposing interpretations of how Fichte understands his neologism's meaning? According to Lask, Fichte rightly understands 'facticity' to signify the undeducible bruteness of individuals' existence, whereas, according to Heidegger, Fichte wrongly understands it to signify conditions of Dasein's existence that can and must be rationally deduced. How can we make sense of this crucial Fichtean juncture between neo-Kantianism and phenomenology?

I will argue that the neologism's transmission is the result of a fateful misreading. Lask misreads Fichte as a proponent of facticity, that is, as a philosopher whose alleged accommodation of radical contingency dramatically deflates the deductive ambitions of the *Wissenschaftslehre*. Nevertheless, I will show that Lask's is a productive misreading, for, without deceiving Heidegger regarding the sincerity of Fichte's deductive ambitions, it prefigures Heidegger's distinctive non-rationalist conception of facticity.

In this chapter, I will first sketch Lask's claim that Fichte curtails his method of genetic deduction in 1797–98 after detecting the individuality problem, which allegedly prompts Fichte to coin 'facticity' in Berlin as the name for the underivable material particularity of individuals (Section 5.2). I will then show that Lask mistakes the task that Fichte sets for his deduction of the categories and thereby mistakes the specific problem that his neologism names (Section 5.3). In coining this term, Fichte is responsive not to the problem of deducing the material particularity of individuals, that is, the problem of haecceity, but rather to the problem of deducing the formal generality of the conditions of intelligibility, that is, the problem of rhapsody. As I will put the point, Fichte aims to avoid formal facticity, not material facticity, for it is the former alone that threatens philosophical systematicity as he conceives it. Indeed, the distinction between formal and material facticity is indispensable for understanding his express and sustained confidence that reason can annihilate facticity, at least beyond the presupposition of the I. I will then show that, despite this interpretive error, Lask's conception of the facticity of individuals prefigures Heidegger's conception of the facticity of Dasein (Section 5.4). I will conclude with the prehistory of Heidegger's hermeneutical method of analyzing the facticity of Dasein by introducing Dilthey's conception of hermeneutics in its relation to the human sciences (Section 5.5) and explaining why, for Heidegger, this concept demands a turn toward a hermeneutics of facticity (Section 5.6).

5.2 Lask on the Individuality Problem

Lask's doctoral thesis is divided into three parts, which successively concern Fichte's relation to Kant and Hegel, Fichte's critique of rationalism, and Fichte's philosophy of history. I will focus mainly on the first two parts.

By "rationalism," Lask means the view that "individual facts" must be subsumed under a "general concept," that is, the view that the logical generality of categories has explanatory priority over the material particularity of individuals.[18] A rationalist can demonstrate this priority by deducing the categories as necessary conditions for the cognition of individuals. This deduction takes one of two forms.

On the one hand, a rationalist can conduct a "rhapsodic" deduction of the categories by positing them as radically contingent or "hypothetical" elements of cognition, that is, as brute or "finished facts" about how we cognize individuals. According to this deduction, our use of the categories is unavoidable yet lacks absolute necessity insofar as they are not derived from "a highest principle."[19] Such a deduction exemplifies what I will call 'rhapsodic rationalism.' Lask follows Maimon and Fichte in ascribing rhapsodic rationalism to Kant's metaphysical deduction of the categories in particular and to his account of the forms of cognition in general.[20] This suggests that rhapsodic rationalism employs transcendental logic.

On the other hand, a rationalist can conduct a "systematic" deduction of the categories from a highest principle, in pursuit of the "system of reason" with which the German idealists aim to "progress beyond Kant."[21] According to Lask, a systematic deduction employs one of two logics.

Analytic logic allows a rationalist to avoid a rhapsodic determination of the categories because it governs the articulation of the "dialectical connection" that binds an absolutely necessary succession of categories.[22] A deduction that accords with analytic logic exemplifies what I will call 'analytic rationalism.' While analytic rationalism avoids rhapsody, it shares with rhapsodic rationalism the presupposition of the "non-actuality of the concept," that is, the presupposition of the categories' lack of "empirical" or "perceptual material."[23] By abstracting from "the region of the merely empirical" toward a "sphere of pure concepts," analytic rationalism entails "the content-poverty of the concept."[24] This, Lask says, makes it "incomprehensible" how we could ever transition from the "logical sphere" of

[18] Lask FIG | 1923 I: 11. Unless otherwise noted, translations of this text are my own.
[19] Lask FIG | 1923 I: 77, 83, 85.
[20] Lask FIG | 1923 I: 82. In a footnote, Lask cites Fichte's letter to Reinhold, July 2, 1795, which charges that Kant "does not answer even this subordinate question [of how to combine objects in a unity of consciousness] on the basis of a single principle; he picks up the forms of thought in a heuristic way, [and] only *guesses at* the forms of intuition, and conducts his proof inductively" (Lask FIG | 1923 I: 82n3, cited from Fichte B | 1988: 399).
[21] Lask FIG | 1923 I: 84, 86.
[22] Lask FIG | 1923 I: 81, 85.
[23] Lask FIG | 1923 I: 32.
[24] Lask FIG | 1923 I: 62, 84.

categorial generality to the "specific content" of individual particularity, that is, from apriority to aposteriority.[25] Closing the categories off from individuals in this way commits analytic rationalism to a "logical atomism" according to which categories and individuals are mutually external and mutually impenetrable, raising the threat of an irrational gap between them. Hegel's polemic against this threat, Lask says, is directed against Fichte.[26]

By contrast, emanationist logic allows a rationalist to avoid both rhapsodic determination and an irrational gap because it governs the articulation of the necessary internal structure of the "dialectical organism of total actuality," that is, of being as a dialectically self-developing whole.[27] A deduction that accords with emanationist logic exemplifies what I will call 'emanationist rationalism.' Rather than presuppose a brute origin of the categories, as rhapsodic rationalism does, and rather than presuppose the non-actuality of the categories and hence their externality to and impenetrability by individuals, as analytic rationalism does, emanationist rationalism treats categories and individuals as jointly forming an "indiscriminate dialectical mass," that is, a totality to which a dogmatically presupposed "dualism of concept and empirical actuality" does not antecedently apply. Deducing categories in accord with emanationist logic is thus a "dialectical self-movement" of thinking that is "capable of drawing even the individual and smallest" into the results of deduction and that is therefore free of even their presupposition.[28] Lask ascribes emanationist rationalism to Hegel.[29]

To summarize Lask's philosophical taxonomy, then, rhapsodic rationalism deduces the categories from a radically contingent origin, analytic rationalism avoids rhapsody by deducing the categories dialectically yet leaves an irrational gap between their content-poverty and the actuality of the material individuals, and emanationist rationalism avoids both rhapsody and irrationality by deducing categories and individuals alike from a single dialectical mass.

For our purposes, Lask's major claim is that Fichte initially espouses emanationist rationalism in the *Foundations*, but then shifts to analytic rationalism in the *New Presentation* after discovering the individuality problem, that is, the resistance of individuals to total explanation via the genetic deduction of the categories. Emanationist rationalism conceives of individuals not as "isolated, self-contained entit[ies]," but rather as "limitations" of a "transindividual whole." Such a whole does not succeed its parts as a "*compositum*" or "product," but rather precedes them as a "*totum*" or "ultimate ground."[30] Individuals are furthermore

[25] Lask FIG | 1923 I: 40.
[26] Lask FIG | 1923 I: 85, 85n1.
[27] Lask FIG | 1923 I: 85.
[28] Lask FIG | 1923 I: 84. On the connection between mathematical construction and emanationist logic, see Redaelli 2016: 53.
[29] Lask FIG | 1923 I: 84–5. Cf. Siep 1991.
[30] Lask FIG | 1923 I: 92.

neither external to nor impermeable by the categorial structure of this whole. According to Lask, although in Fichte's early work we find "the first traces of Hegel's approach" to emanationist rationalism,[31] Fichte subsequently rejects the latter for analytic rationalism when he recognizes that the "empirical" world is "separated" from the categories by a "gap of irrationality," that is, that, "despite all deduction," the uniqueness and richness of empirical individuals transcends the categories as "an undeducible remainder."[32] *Contra* emanationist rationalism, for analytic rationalism there can be no "equalization of concept and empirical actuality"[33] because the latter is "undeducible" from "the exhaustively deduced and comprehended forms of the I" and is consequently an "irrational remainder." Fichte thus allegedly comes to regard the material particularity of individuals as "a limit that is insurmountable for any transcendental explanation."[34]

For Lask, Fichte's rejection of emanationist rationalism amounts to a turn away from "absolute rationalism," but not thereby a turn toward "absolute irrationalism." It instead qualifies as a "critical anti-rationalism,"[35] for, rather than deny the deducibility of any necessary conditions of intelligibility from reason whatsoever, Fichte tempers his deductive ambition by acknowledging individuality as its strict limit. Categories are indeed deducible, but the individuality problem nevertheless admits of "no satisfactory or even rational result" because the material particularity of individuals cannot be deduced from "the 'sphere' of the general," that is, from "merely conceptual content."[36] Hence, rationalism "must be led back to critical modesty" in the face of the "inevitability" of the contingent existence of individuals, the concept of whose "perfect rationality" is at best "only an idea," that is, the concept of a "limit" whose overcoming by deduction "lies in infinity."[37] Lask identifies this limit-concept with the I as a regulative "idea,"[38] evoking Fichte's distinction, which we saw in Section 3.5, between "the I as an intellectual intuition, with which the *Wissenschaftslehre* commences, and the I as an idea, with which it concludes," where the former strictly apprehends the reality of the freedom of the I as first principle and the latter represents the total intelligibility of actuality as a whole, an idea that "will never become anything real" and is "something to which we ought to draw infinitely nearer."[39]

Before I address Fichte's alleged discovery of the individuality problem in Section 5.3, I will first assess Lask's claim that this discovery interrupts Fichte's prior commitment to emanationist rationalism.

[31] Lask FIG | 1923 I: 94.
[32] Lask FIG | 1923 I: 84.
[33] Lask FIG | 1923 I: 84.
[34] Lask FIG | 1923 I: 117.
[35] Lask FIG | 1923 I: 103.
[36] Lask FIG | 1923 I: 93–4.
[37] Lask FIG | 1923 I: 103.
[38] Lask FIG | 1923 I: 101.
[39] Fichte VND | SW I: 515–6.

Recall that, since emanationist rationalism presupposes neither a brute origin of the categories nor the non-actuality of the categories, it is incompatible with both rhapsodic rationalism and analytic rationalism. On the one hand, rhapsodic rationalism presupposes a factical source for the categories, for example, the forms of judgment. Like Hegel, Lask identifies Fichte's "merit" with treating "forms of cognition" like the categories not as an "aggregate" to be "read from" such "empirical" matters as observed canons of judgment, but rather as "an 'organism' structured through the purposes of reason."[40] Rather than presuppose an external source of the categories, an emanationist rationalist consults reason alone, whose "purposes" include the articulation of those conditions that are necessary for its realization in experience. In this way, such a rationalist deduces the categories without presupposing their source, unlike their rhapsodic counterpart. On the other hand, analytic rationalism deduces the categories through a dialectical movement of thought that presupposes no external authority regarding their precise kind and number. However, it does presuppose their non-actuality and hence their mutual externality to and impenetrability by actual individuals. An analytic rationalist is thereby able to deduce no more than the formal generality of the categories, whereas an emanationist rationalist aims to show that the material particularity, that is, the haecceity, of individuals is not a factical imposition on dialectical thinking about the categories, but rather emerges from the latter. We see, then, that emanationist rationalism rejects not only rhapsodic rationalism's presupposition of the categories' origin, but also analytic rationalism's presupposition of the particularity of individuals. In other words, emanationist rationalism is opposed to both rhapsodic presuppositions and haecceitic presuppositions.

Contrary to Lask's interpretation, it is clear that Fichte is not an emanationist rationalist in 1794–95.[41] As we saw in Section 3.3, Fichte's view in the *Foundations* is that the not-I is a fundamental presupposition insofar as it constitutes the matter with which we are acquainted in knowing, while the I serves as the form of the possibility of knowing. This is why he says that "[n]o higher ground can be adduced from which one might derive" the not-I's opposition to the I and hence why this opposition "grounds all derivation" as a brute fact. As we also saw, Fichte regards the I itself as a fundamental presupposition. As a first principle and, specifically, as a principle of freedom, it is an unconditioned condition. Positing the I is yet another brute fact, whose determination is thus rhapsodic. Fichte's position in 1794–95 therefore lacks an emanationist rationalist's opposition to rhapsodic presuppositions.

This does not completely undermine Lask's reading. Despite never espousing emanationist rationalism, it is possible that Fichte instead espouses critical

40 Lask FIG | 1923 I: 105.

41 This is also contrary to Bertrand Russell's assertion that, for Fichte, "everything is only an emanation of the ego" (Russell 2004: 8).

anti-rationalism as early as 1797–98, when he allegedly discovers the problem of individuality. In other words, it may be that Fichte always espouses analytic rationalism and simply curbs its deductive ambition when he finally reckons with haecceity in the *New Presentation.* I will now argue that Lask is wrong to detect such a reckoning in that text.

5.3 Haecceity or Rhapsody?

According to Lask, Fichte's *Foundations* are "exemplary" for "Hegel's dialectic of transferring the logic of the intuitive understanding," which is the understanding that cognizes actual individuals merely by thinking of them, from the "unattainable distance" of a merely regulative ideal "into scientific actuality."[42] The text is exemplary in this regard because it proves, first, that "nothing escapes the fate of being the content of consciousness," second, that "what is, is for the I," and, third, that "everything is I-like," that is, completely rational and hence non-factical.[43] We saw, however, that, for Fichte, such a proof is strictly formal. Whereas the I is the absolute form of positing, it presupposes the matter of what is posited. Thus, while Lask is technically not wrong to read the *Foundations* as arguing that "empirical actuality" is formally "contained" in the I,[44] the logic that supports this argument cannot be emanationist. Still, perhaps Lask is right to detect in the *New Presentation*, two years later, the insight that logic is unable to account for the material particularity of individuals, that is, the insight into the individuality problem. This, I will argue, is to misread that presentation of the *Wissenschaftslehre.*

The *New Presentation* consists only of a preface, two introductions, and one chapter. Its composition is interrupted by the atheism dispute that is begun by the 1798 publication of controversial essays on religion by Fichte and his colleague Friedrich Karl Forberg in *Philosophical Journal of a Society of German Scholars*, which Fichte co-edits with Friedrich Philipp Immanuel Niethammer. The ensuing dispute prompts both Jacobi's open letter publicly denouncing the *Wissenschaftslehre* as 'nihilism,' a term that he coins for that purpose, and Fichte's flight that year from the University of Jena to Berlin.

As we saw, Lask attributes to Fichte in the *New Presentation* the critical anti-rationalist discovery that the "insurmountable" limit of deduction is the material particularity of individuals, that is, material facticity. Lask cites the following passage from §6 of the Second Introduction as evidence of Fichte's case for the "mystery of empirical actuality": "the necessity of *some limitation of the I* has been

[42] Lask FIG | 1923 I: 90. On Hegel's early conception of imagination as the original unity of subject and object that mimics an intuitive understanding, see Wretzel 2018.
[43] Lask FIG | 1923 I: 89.
[44] Lask FIG | 1923 I: 95.

derived from the very possibility of the I. The *specific determinacy* of this limitation is, however, not something that can be derived in this way . . . Consequently, we have arrived at the point at which all deduction comes to an end."[45] In this passage, Fichte claims that the form of the I's limitation is deducible, whereas the matter of its limitation is not. That the I is formally limited, that is, that in general it must be limited in "*some*" way, is deducible from its own nature as a necessary condition of its realization in experience. By contrast, how the I is materially limited, that is, how in some particular instance it happens to be limited in some "*specific*" way, cannot be deduced from its nature, but rather is contingent on experience. As Fichte says at the end of the passage that Lask cites, it "appears" that the "determinacy" that "I am, of all possible rational beings, a *human being*, and that, of all human beings, I am this *specific* person" is a "*merely empirical* element" of cognition and thus "something absolutely contingent."[46] If Fichte recognizes that he cannot deduce the material particularity of how the I is specifically limited, that is, of how, in his own person, the I is empirically determined, then, Lask infers, 1797–98 must mark a "turning point" in his thinking toward a "pronounced empiricism."[47] In other words, in the *New Presentation*, Fichte must make the critically anti-rationalist discovery of the individuality problem, namely, that empirical actuality is "an unsystematizable immediacy" or brute fact.[48] This would amount to an acceptance of material facticity. Crucially, as we will see, Lask will claim that this alleged discovery heralds Fichte's coining of 'facticity,' which, on Lask's interpretation, denotes precisely the "brutality of actuality," whose "unpredictability" creates an epistemic gap that "no reflection can fill in," namely, the "lawlessness of the particular" that "we cannot deduce in its uniqueness."[49]

How does Fichte arrive at the conclusion that the "*specific determinacy*" of the limitation of the I is undeducible? Is the "end" of "all deduction" really marked by the "irrational remainder" of material facticity, as Lask suggests?

As we saw in Section 1.1, in §7 of the First Introduction, Fichte explains that a deduction

> *shows that what is postulated as the first principle and immediately established in consciousness is not possible unless something else occurs as well, and that this second thing is not possible apart from the occurrence of some third thing. It continues in this manner until all of the conditions of the first principle have been completely exhausted and its possibility has become completely comprehensible.*[50]

[45] Lask FIG | 1923 I: 117, cited from Fichte VND | SW I: 489.
[46] Lask FIG | 1923 I: 117–8, cited from Fichte VND | SW I: 489.
[47] Lask FIG | 1923 I: 140.
[48] Lask FIG | 1923 I: 158.
[49] Lask FIG | 1923 I: 172–3. Contrast Lask's reading of Fichte on this point with Talbot 1907: 494–5.
[50] Fichte VND | SW I: 446.

The dual method of Fichte's system is to intellectually intuit the I as a first principle and to genetically deduce from it the conditions of its intelligibility, which deduction must be "*completely exhausted*" if the I is to be "*completely comprehensible*." As we saw in Section 1.2, genetic deduction provides a simultaneous answer to the questions *quid facti* and *quid juris*, for it proves our right to conditions of intelligibility just if it derives them from the I's primary and irreducible freedom. Fichte's strategy is meant to rule out formal facticity, that is, the threat that the formal generality of the conditions of intelligibility is radically contingent insofar as their deduction lacks an absolute ground and is therefore haphazard or rhapsodic, a threat to which he thinks Kant, no less than Aristotle, is vulnerable. Hence he asks the Kantian: "how did you become aware that the laws of the intellect are precisely these laws of substantiality and causality?"[51] Moreover, in the same section from which Lask cites, Fichte says that the first *Critique* "by no means lacks a foundation. Such a foundation is very plainly present; but nothing has been constructed upon it, and the construction materials—though already well prepared—are jumbled together in a most haphazard manner."[52] We will see that the very passage that Lask cites as evidence that Fichte discovers and accepts material facticity as unavoidable is in fact the culmination of a discussion about how to avoid formal facticity.

The discussion begins in the Second Introduction with Fichte's claim that "the overall gist" of his system is that reason or the I is "absolutely self-sufficient," that is, "explicable solely on the basis of . . . itself," a claim that he summarizes by stating that "the *Wissenschaftslehre* is transcendental idealism."[53] With this statement, he purports to agree with Kant's argument in the transcendental deduction that the unity of apperception is the "supreme principle of the possibility of all intuition in relation to the understanding," which he interprets as the argument that thinking, intuiting, "and hence *all consciousness*" are subject to the condition of apperception.[54] As we saw in Section 2.3, Fichte regards the spirit of transcendental idealism as consisting in the demonstration that the apperceptive I is the derivational source of not only the categories, but also the forms of sensibility. This differs from its letter, which derives the categories from no higher than the forms of judgment and which does not derive the forms of sensibility at all. Fichte expresses this difference shortly after by introducing a distinction between consciousness as "conditioned" by the apperceptive I and consciousness as "determined" by the apperceptive I. If consciousness is merely conditioned by the I, as it is according to the letter of transcendental idealism, then its contents "have their foundation" outside of the I, which contents therefore limit, even if they do not "*contradict*," the I. By contrast,

[51] Fichte VND | SW I: 442.
[52] Fichte VND | SW I: 479n.
[53] Fichte VND | SW I: 474.
[54] Fichte VND | SW I: 475, cited from Kant KrV B136.

if consciousness is determined by the I, as it is according to the spirit of transcendental idealism, then its contents must be "*generated*" and so derivable from the I.[55] These contents include the forms of sensibility, of which Fichte says Kant provides no "derivation whatsoever" and at most entertains the mere "*thought*" of the system in which their derivation would figure.[56]

A deduction of space, time, the forms of judgment, and the categories from the I would solve the rhapsody problem insofar as the I is an absolutely necessary ground. In other words, it would remove the threat of formal facticity. However, such a deduction would not thereby solve the individuality problem, for it is precisely the formal generality of the conditions of intelligibility that abstracts from the material particularity, that is, the haecceity, of individuals. In other words, such a deduction would leave the threat of material facticity unaddressed. Even assuming that Fichte ought to take this threat seriously, he makes it clear that he does not when he gives a five-step argument for the deduction of the forms of intuition in §6 of the Second Introduction, which I will now reconstruct.

First, Fichte says that the understanding "*adds* the object in appearance" by synthesizing the manifold of intuition "*within a single consciousness*," that is, in apperception.[57] Second, if the object is a contribution of the understanding, then it is, in this regard, "*a mere thought*." Third, if the object is a mere thought, then insofar as the object exercises an effect on us, "*it is only thought of as exercising an effect*" on us. Fourth, if "affection itself is only something we think of, then everything associated with this affection [including, therefore, our own ability to be affected] is, undoubtedly, also something that is only thought of." Fifth, therefore, to think of objects in general as affecting us is nothing other than to think of ourselves "as *generally affectable*. In other words, it is *by means of this act of your own thinking* that you ascribe receptivity or sensibility to yourself."[58] Like "*all consciousness*," then, sensibility is subject to the condition of apperception, which is to say that it is determined by or derived from the I.[59] Rather than a brute fact imposed on

[55] Fichte VND | SW I: 477.

[56] Fichte VND | SW I: 478.

[57] Fichte VND | SW I: 487. Fichte's argument relies on citations of the first *Critique* from Jacobi DH 218–21 | 1994: 335–6.

[58] Fichte VND | SW I: 488.

[59] Fichte's argument here does not follow the dialectical movement of thought that, as we saw in Section 1.5, normally guides his genetic deductions, which determine a condition of intelligibility through the inner opposition of a prior condition. As we find in the deductions that are provided in the *Foundations*, the *Nova Methodo*, and *Natural Right*, this movement is guided by the principle of determinability. In 1810's *The Wissenschaftslehre in its General Outline*, Fichte claims that the *Wissenschaftslehre* must recognize itself as the "image or schema" of the "manifestation" of the "one" that "is absolutely through itself" by attaining "consciousness of that which is contained in the schema," namely, intuition, space, time, causality, matter, thought, individuality, mutual recognition, and a moral imperative (Fichte AU | SW II: 695, 698). In the *Blessed Life*, he claims that the "general properties and attributes" of the "special forms" with which consciousness "separat[es]" the "one reality . . . may be discovered by *a priori* investigation of the different laws of reflection, as we have already set forth its one fundamental law—and a systematic philosophy ought to do this, and must do it, in a complete and exhaustive manner." However, he clarifies that this presentation of the *Wissenschaftslehre* will not "critically deduce" these forms, but rather will "historically set forth and describe" them, namely, as

the I, sensibility is a condition by which the I renders intelligible its own actualization in experience. A corollary of this argument is that insofar as sensibility for us has a spatio-temporal form, space and time as forms of sensibility are themselves also deducible from the I. As Fichte notes in the next section of the Second Introduction, this corollary will be demonstrated in a subsequent "series of deductions," according to which:

> [o]n the one hand, spatial extension and subsistence will be ascribed to [the I], and in this respect it becomes a determinate body; on the other hand, temporal identity and duration will be ascribed to it, and in this respect it becomes a soul. It is, however, the task of philosophy to demonstrate this and to provide a genetic account of how the I comes to think of itself in these ways. Accordingly, this is not something philosophy has to presuppose, but rather is part of what has to be derived.[60]

Although the deduction of space and time is not provided in the truncated publication of the *New Presentation*, Fichte makes it clear in the text that the spirit of transcendental idealism cannot tolerate any rhapsodic determination of the conditions of intelligibility, including the forms of sensibility and the sensible faculty to which they belong, for they must be "derived," not "presuppose[d]." It is in order to satisfy the scientific criterion that a science of intelligibility must eliminate any apparent formal facticity.

The conclusion to the present argument is that the faculty of sensibility, that is, our "ability to be affected," is derivable from the I. We can see that Fichte expresses this conclusion when he says one page later, within the passage that Lask cites, that we can deduce only the "*limitation of the I*" and not the "*specific determinacy* of this limitation." The I's deducible limitation is, according to the present argument, its spatio-temporal form, as distinguished from that form's sensory matter. In what sense, then, does the derivation of this formal limitation of the I bring deduction to an end? Does this involve the admission, as Lask suggests, of an irrational remainder at the level of matter?

In §6, Fichte grants that one indeed might posit the existence of bare matter, that is, matter that is absolutely independent of spatio-temporal form, in order to provide an "explanation" of sensibility, that is, in order to explain the source of my "*feeling*" of the "determinate character of my limitation." But he argues that this is no more than to posit "the wretched 'thing in itself.'" Such an explanation,

standpoints on the world according to sensibility, lawful order, morality, religion, and science, which latter "thoroughly comprehends" these previous standpoints in their "transition," "order," and "relations" (Fichte ASL | SW V: 458–9, 462, 471),

[60] Fichte VND | SW I: 495.

he says, exhibits the "dogmatism" of "the Kantians" who restrict transcendental idealism to its letter, with its inclusion of the concept of a thing in itself.[61] But this concept is "a complete perversion of reason" and "utterly unreasonable,"[62] since it precludes reason's absolute self-sufficiency and thereby undermines the spirit of transcendental idealism, which is to say that it undermines the "overall gist" of the *Wissenschaftslehre*. Consequently, Fichte must derive the concept of the thing in itself, which he also calls the "concept of being," from "the form of sensibility," from which derivation it will follow that "all being is necessarily *sensible* being."[63] It will furthermore follow from this derivation that all being is necessarily sensible being for the apperceptive I, from which, as we saw, the form of sensibility is itself derivable. Fichte's derivation is as follows:

> It is undoubtedly an immediate fact of consciousness that I feel *myself* to be determined in a particular way. If certain widely celebrated philosophers now wish to *explain* this feeling, then how can they fail to see that they thereby wish to ascribe to feeling something not immediately included within the fact in question? And how can they do this except by means of thinking, and indeed, by thinking in accordance with a category, which, in the case we are considering, is the principle of a 'real ground'? Assuming they do not possess, as it were, an immediate intuition of the thing in itself and its relationships, then what more do they know about this principle than this: that *they* are required to think in accordance with it? It follows that they are asserting no more than this: that they are required to supply the thought of a thing as a ground or foundation [of the immediately felt determinations of their consciousness]. We are quite prepared to concede this claim and even to join them in affirming it, insofar as it pertains to the standpoint they occupy. Their thing is a product of their own thinking.[64]

Insofar as positing the thing in itself is a "means of thinking" of my feeling of being sensibly affected, it is nothing other than a categorial "principle" that is "required" in order to explain my capacity for sensible affection. But then, no less than the object whose effect on me is contributed by my understanding and no less than the form of sensibility that I ascribe to myself by means of my thinking of it, the thing in itself is solely "a product of [my] own thinking." This is the sole ground on which Fichte concedes the invocation of the thing in itself by "certain widely celebrated philosophers," including and in particular those who endorse transcendental

[61] Fichte VND | SW I: 489–90. Cf. Fichte's letter to Jacobi, August 30, 1795: "Kant clings to the view that the manifold of experience is something given—God knows how and why. But I straightforwardly maintain that even this manifold is produced by us through our creative faculty" (Fichte B | 1988: 411).

[62] Fichte VND | SW I: 472. Cf. Fichte's description of this concept in his *Aenesidemus* review as "a piece of whimsy, a pipe dream, a non-thought" (Fichte RA | SW I: 17).

[63] Fichte VND | SW I: 472.

[64] Fichte VND | SW I: 491.

idealism strictly according to its letter. Positing the thing itself strictly on these grounds remains faithful to the spirit of transcendental idealism insofar as it is committed to an explanation of all consciousness, including sensibility, on the basis of the I alone.

Fichte's anti-dogmatic strategy allows us to see in what sense deduction comes to an end regarding sensibility. According to this strategy, there can be no deeper explanation of sensibility than its deduction from the I as the latter's own formal limitation. As he says: "Since this limitation of mine conditions my positing of myself, it constitutes an original limitation."[65] Insofar as sensibility is a formal limitation that is genetically deducible from the I, it is a condition of intelligibility that is "original" to, rather than imposed on, the I. It therefore cannot originate in anything external to the I, on pain of a dogmatism that explains sensibility by positing the matter of a thing in itself that brutely limits the absolute freedom of reason and whose concept is, in this sense, a "perversion of reason."[66] In other words, sensibility *qua* formal limitation of the I is not factical because its determination is genetic as opposed to rhapsodic. But then Fichte's claim about the end of deduction concerns rhapsody, not haecceity. In that case, the proper context for understanding this claim is not, *contra* Lask, the individuality problem of the undeducibility of the material particularity of individuals, but is rather the question of whether transcendental idealism assigns any condition of intelligibility to "*something distinct from the I*," namely, to "*a thing in itself*."[67]

Admittedly, Fichte cites Jacobi's "On Transcendental Idealism," a supplement to the first edition of *David Hume*, as "the most thorough and complete proof" that, since transcendental idealism proscribes the categories' use beyond appearances, it must rule out the existence of a thing in itself.[68] Nevertheless, Fichte's primary

[65] Fichte VND | SW I: 489.

[66] While, for Fichte, no thing in itself explains the form of the I's limitation, further determinations of this form are still to be deduced, as his dialectical reflections show. In *Natural Right*, he argues that if the I is to be capable of self-determination, then the form of its limitation must be social rather than merely sensible, which is to say that the causality of this limitation must be final rather than merely efficient (Fichte GN | SW III: 33-6). Cf. Fichte VND | SW I: 476).

[67] Fichte VND | SW I: 480–1. Cf. Cohen's 1902 *Logic of Pure Cognition*: "Kant insists on distinguishing pure intuition from pure thinking. Not that they should remain separate, but rather that they should connect and become suitable for connection. By this plan of his methodical terminology, however, apart from intuition, an inner damage has been done to thinking. Thus, thinking was preceded by an intuition. This is also pure, therefore it is related to thinking. But thinking has its beginning in something outside of itself. Here lies the weakness of Kant's foundation. Here lies the reason for the apostasy which immediately broke into his school. By placing ourselves again on the historical ground of critique, we refuse to let logic be preceded by a doctrine of sensibility. We begin with thinking. Thought must have no origin outside itself, if its purity must be unrestricted and unclouded. Pure thinking in itself and exclusively must bring pure cognitions to generation. Consequently, the doctrine of thinking must become the doctrine of cognition. We seek here to construct logic as such a doctrine of thinking, which in itself is the doctrine of cognition" (Cohen 1914: 12, my translation).

[68] Fichte VND | SW I: 481–2, citing Jacobi DH 209–30 | 1994: 331–8. Cf. Fichte's letter to Reinhold, July 4, 1797: "Jacobi, to whom I refer in my essay [namely, the Second Introduction to the *New Presentation*], misunderstood one aspect of Kant's writings, although he understood another aspect of them very well; i.e., he misunderstood the empirical realism, although he correctly grasped the transcendental idealism" (Fichte B | 1988: 420).

reason for denying that idealism admits of factical conditions of intelligibility, such as a thing in itself, is that conditions of the intelligibility of experience are "laws of thinking" and so must be "*produced only by our own thinking*," that is, "by an act of thinking that is *necessary*," from which it follows that a thing in itself "exists only *for our thinking*."[69] Indeed, he acknowledges no problematic haecceity whatsoever when he later adds that what "constitutes" the system of transcendental idealism is specifically its investigation of "the laws in accordance with which [the] process of [empirical] explanation proceeds."[70]

Still, even if Fichte disregards haecceity in Jena, perhaps he finally confronts it when he coins 'facticity' in Berlin. According to Lask, Fichte's neologism denotes the "lawlessness" and "bruteness of the actual," that is, a "uniqueness and singularity" that cannot be "derived," but rather "can only be awaited and accepted" and "must always be 'new' and surprising."[71] In other words, on this interpretation of the neologism, facticity is material, not formal, and so pertains to haecceitic, not rhapsodic, presuppositions. In order to support his interpretation, Lask cites a passage from the Fifteenth Lecture of the 1804 Berlin lectures that announces an "irrational gap" between "an object whose origin is inexplicable" and our "projection" of that object.[72] This passage might be taken to suggest Fichte's acknowledgment of an inescapable haecceitic presupposition, that is, of an individual whose unique and singular actuality is undeducibly brute.

However, Fichte is clear in the Sixteenth Lecture not only that the irrational gap "is in essence nothing at all,"[73] but also that the gap, despite being "so far . . . presented only factically," must be removed by a "genetic principle."[74] Such a gap is no problem that cannot be solved by the deductive capacity of reason. Moreover, the context of the announcement of the irrational gap is Fichte's description, in the Fifteenth Lecture, of a realistic maxim and an idealistic maxim that "are at bottom *factical*,"[75] maxims whose factical terms, as we saw in Section 2.5, must be made "genetic."[76] But then the irrational gap between an inexplicable object and its projection is none other than the disjunction between the realistic maxim of an object that is absolutely given in intuition, namely, the I's existence, and the idealistic maxim of that object's projection in thought, namely, the I's essence. And the removal of this gap is none other than the genetic insight into the unification of these maxims, that is, an insight into the oneness of the I's existence and its essence. We saw that Fichte expunges this deeper facticity from the *Wissenschaftslehre* as a response to the threat of formal facticity, for the I's existence and essence cannot be

69 Fichte VND | SW I: 482–3.
70 Fichte VND | SW I: 490.
71 Lask FIG | 1923 I: 173.
72 Lask FIG | 1923 I: 173, cited from Fichte WL04 | GA II/8: 236–7.
73 Fichte WL04 | GA II/8: 246–7.
74 Fichte WL04 | GA II/8: 248–9.
75 Fichte WL04 | GA II/8: 234–5.
76 Fichte WL04 | GA II/8: 76–7.

rhapsodic presuppositions, but must rather be shown to be absolutely necessary, namely, on the basis of the I's own self-genesis.

Contrary to Lask's interpretation, Fichte's Berlin lectures do not discover a haecceitic presupposition that "can only be awaited and accepted," but rather reveal an insight into the I's oneness that removes the merely apparent irrational gap between its existence and essence. Indeed, on the very page from which Lask quotes the above passage, Fichte describes the "immediate consciousness" whose "effect" is an irrational gap and states that the "higher maxim" is that this consciousness must be "discarded" and "always removed from the truth." Moreover, underscoring the continuity of the anti-rhapsodic methods of his Jena and Berlin periods, he adds on the following page that this maxim "has ruled in every possible presentation of the *Wissenschaftslehre* from the very first hint which I gave in a 'Review of *Aenesidemus*' in the *General Literary Newspaper* [in 1794] because this maxim is identical with the principle of absolute genesis."[77] Genesis is absolute precisely insofar as facticity is annihilated, and the principle of genesis can lie nowhere but in the I's own nature, which is responsible for eliminating facticity from the conditions of its intelligibility. Although, as we saw in Section 2.5, Fichte affirms the "*primordial facticity*" of the I as a fundamental presupposition of the *Wissenschaftslehre*, Lask's reading of Fichte is mistaken in locating facticity in individuals.

Fichte's aim in 1804, as in 1797–98, is to expunge rhapsody, not haecceity, from the science of intelligibility, that is, to overcome formal facticity, not material facticity. This aim is guided by the essence of the *Wissenschaftslehre*, namely, that reason is absolutely free in deducing the conditions of its intelligibility. In a letter to Reinhold, January 8, 1800, written between his alleged discovery of the individuality problem and his coining of 'facticity,' Fichte writes: "My system is from beginning to end nothing but an analysis of the concept of freedom, and freedom cannot be contradicted within this system, since no other ingredient is added."[78] That same year, in "From a Private Letter," he declares: "the essence of *my* philosophy, and in my view of *all* genuine philosophy, consists exclusively in deducing!"[79] Deduction is the means by which reason makes its conditions of intelligibility explicit to itself, free from either purportedly factical sources of or purported authorities on such conditions. Lask misreads the role of deduction in this system by misconstruing the problem that 'facticity' names and thereby misconstruing Fichte's "exclusively" deductive solution to that problem. Nevertheless, this misreading is historically fortuitous, for, by thematizing material facticity, Lask prefigures Heidegger's own conception of facticity, which he will deploy against Fichte's rationalist ambition of getting behind our thrownness.

[77] Fichte WL04 | GA II/8: 238–9.
[78] Breazeale 1994: vii–n1.
[79] Fichte AP | SW V: 395.

5.4 Alogical Matter

Lask's two major works following his doctoral thesis are 1911's *The Logic of Philosophy and the Doctrine of Categories* and 1912's *The Doctrine of Judgment*, whose debt to Husserl he acknowledges in their correspondence.[80] A study of these texts reveals the development of an original account of material facticity, one that anticipates aspects of Heidegger's own conception of facticity even as its ultimate conclusion transgresses what he will regard as the critical bounds of a hermeneutics of facticity. We will first see, in the *Logic*, that Lask's conception of alogical matter inherits the role of facticity, that is, the role of the undeducible, irrational remainder that he assigns to individuality in his doctoral thesis.[81] We will then see, in the *Doctrine*, that he attributes to alogical matter a categorial structure that is absolutely independent of the subject's act of judging. I will argue that this independence raises a doubt, in the dialectical space of the Cartesian problematic, about how subjects could ever affirm such a structure. Denying the absolute independence of categorial structure will be Heidegger's way, in the dialectical space of the Kantian problematic, of retaining a philosophical role for facticity within strictly critical bounds.

In Section 2 of the Introduction to the *Logic*, Lask says that Hermann Lotze's "liberating and clarifying achievement" consists, first, in rejecting the "two-world theory" according to which everything thinkable is either a sensible being or a non-sensible being, and, second, in conceiving "the totality of what is at all thinkable in terms of an ultimate duality; in terms, namely, of a gulf between that which is and that which holds, the realm of beings and the realm of validities," that is, "that which is and occurs and that which is valid without having to be."[82] In Book III of 1874's *System of Philosophy, First Part: Logic*, Lotze draws a crucial distinction between the "being" of things that occur and the "validity" of true assertions, a distinction whose components are "ultimate and underivable" because, on the one hand, no modification of beings can generate the validity of a true assertion and, on the other hand, the validity of a true assertion cannot generate the existence of any being, whether sensible or non-sensible.[83] In the First Part of the *Logic*, "The Logic of the Categories of Being," Lask argues that since a two-world theory is exclusively concerned with something that is, namely, being, whether sensible or non-sensible, it necessarily excludes logic as the "science of validity," which is "concerned with something that is not" insofar as validity is properly construed as holding of that which is. This is devastating for a two-world theory because the "guiding concepts" of validity include no less than "the concepts of meaning, of

[80] See Schuhmann and Smith 1993. On the limits of Lask's debt to Husserl, see Crowell 2001.
[81] On the continuity of Lask's early and late work, see Redaelli 2016: 69–70.
[82] Lask LPK | 1923 II: 6, translated by Crowell 1996: 73.
[83] Lotze 1884: 440.

sense, and above all of value." If logic is the "home" of such concepts, then we must "wrench logic out of its isolation," namely, by rejecting the two-world theory and widening our philosophical view to include the non-being of validity.[84]

Lask describes Kant's Copernican turn as the discovery that validity is the "very essence of being," that is, that objectivity is only ever "disclosed" to us "with a corresponding claim to validity" in accordance with the laws of transcendental logic, namely, the categories. The "Copernican achievement" is the proof that logic neither mirrors nor shadows nor harmonizes with nor corresponds to objectivity, but rather constitutes or "coincide[s]" with objectivity as the necessary condition of its possibility and, hence, is the proof that "every duality of objectivity and logical validity is destroyed."[85] However, Lask charges Kant with failing to locate logical validity in a "third realm" in which it rightly has neither sensible nor non-sensible being, thereby leaving the science of validity "homeless" within "his two-world metaphysics" of phenomena and noumena.[86] The task for neo-Kantians, then, is that the "two-world theory is to be reformed into a two-element theory" in which being, which exists, and validity, which holds of that which exists, are the basic elements composing a "single 'realm.'"[87]

Lask conceives of these elements in hylomorphic terms, such that validity consists of the "logical form" that is supplied by the categories and being consists of the "alogical matter" that is supplied by sensibility, and he conceives of the "single" realm that they compose, that is, "the homogeneous type of structure that is constituted of form and matter," as the realm of "*sense*."[88] He also gives hylomorphic expression to Lotze's conception of the "absolute opposition"[89] between validity and being by arguing for the ultimacy or irreducibility of the distinction between form and matter. First, Lask evokes Maimon's empty formalism challenge by arguing that validity is always "validity *with regard to*" and is, in this regard, always dependent on "something foreign," since validity cannot "constitute a 'world' for itself" and is thus "a mere empty form awaiting fulfilment from 'matter.'"[90] In other words, while form can become enmattered, it cannot enmatter itself. Second, he argues that matter "is able to indeed stand in the logical, but without thereby transforming into something logical," since matter by itself "can neither be valid nor 'mean' anything."[91] In other words, while matter can become formed, it cannot become formal. Hence, alogical matter's distinctness from logical form is irreducible. Moreover, alogical matter is factically given to logical form, not unlike, as we saw in Lask's doctoral thesis, the material particularity of individuals is factically given

[84] Lask LOC | 2015: 401.
[85] Lask LOC | 2015: 403–4, 410.
[86] Lask LPK | 1923 II: 260. Cf. Lask BT | 2015: 425.
[87] Lask LOC | 2015: 410–1.
[88] Lask LOC | 2015: 405, 409–10.
[89] Lask LOC | 2015: 413.
[90] Lask LOC | 2015: 404–5.
[91] Lask LOC | 2015: 406.

to the categories. This explains why he now says that, although it contributes to the world of sense, matter as such is defined by its "non-rationalizability."[92]

We can see that the critical anti-rationalism that Lask attributes to Fichte, albeit in the course of a misreading of the latter, characterizes to a certain extent his own defense of material facticity. In arguing that logical form depends on alogical matter on pain of emptiness, he rejects the "*panlogism*" of pre-Kantian "rationalism."[93] However, his anti-rationalism is critical, for he affirms the "Copernican thesis" that the proper object of philosophical cognition is "*categorial form*," which *a priori* governs and so cannot be "reduced" to "intuitive material," and he thereby affirms the "*panarchy of the logos*" for the world of sense.[94] And yet, as we saw in Section 5.3, Lask's critical anti-rationalism cannot be Fichtean, given his case for material facticity.

Lask expands his case for material facticity by imposing a brute limit on the deductive capacity of transcendental logic, the science that is responsible for determining the categories. In Section 4 of the First Part, he claims that the categories are "not thoroughly logical" in that "they do not derive from the logical, but from the alogical material," by which he means that the "principle of differentiation" whereby we determine the categories is "a purely 'empirical' one" because their functional role as logical forms is discernible only by abstracting from the alogical matter that they inform. If the categories are "determined by the material that is foreign to *logos*, and their place can only be determined by taking a detour across this material,"[95] then they cannot be said to derive solely from the I, in which case matter constitutes a brute limit on logic's capacity to deduce the categories. Lask rightly observes that this claim is "irreconcilable with the Hegelian dialectical principle," for, according to this claim, the categories "do not point dialectically to each other," but rather "point to the material . . . even if the dialectical philosopher thinks he can spin speculative connecting threads around them retrospectively."[96]

[92] Lask LPK | 1923 II: 65. It is important to situate Lask's conception of the non-rationalizability of matter, i.e., the facticity of individuals, in the southwestern neo-Kantian context. In 1870's *Doctrines of Chance*, Windelband describes facticity's relation to necessity and the factical limits of science (Windelband 1870: 4, 26–9) and, in 1894's "Rectorial Address," he asserts that "in all the data of historical and individual experience a residuum of incomprehensible, brute fact remains, an inexpressible and indefinable phenomenon" (Windelband 1980: 184). In 1902's *The Boundaries of Natural-Scientific Concept Formation*, Rickert affirms the fundamental irrationality of empirical reality (Rickert 1913: 36) and explains how the facticity of individuals limits the ability of natural science to form concepts, make predictions, and render reality comprehensible (Rickert 1913: 186, 194–200, 207, 209, 257, 352, 363, 377).

[93] Lask A | 2015: 399, Lask LOC | 2015: 406.

[94] Lask A | 2015: 399. Cf. Lask: "When it has been asserted that an entity is impervious to being affected by the categories, such an entity already stands in the grip of categories as soon as one reflects upon it, even in those reflections that deny this to be the case . . . *Not panlogicism but rather the panarchy of the logos must be restored to its glory*" (Lask BT | 2015: 424, 426).

[95] Lask LPK | 1923 II: 62–3.

[96] Lask LPK | 1923 II: 63.

Lask's expanded case for material facticity naturally rules out Hegel's emanationist rationalism, given the latter's intolerance for haecceitic presuppositions, including that of alogical material. But it also rules out Fichte's analytic rationalism, given the latter's intolerance for rhapsodic presuppositions. This is because the expanded case appeals not only to the haecceity of alogical material, but also to the rhapsodic determination of logical form on the basis of that material. Indeed, Lask's demand for a factical "detour" would provoke a version of Fichte's complaint in the *New Presentation* that Kant's metaphysical deduction makes a "detour" through factical forms of judgment,[97] just as Lask's commitment to an "empirical" principle for determining the categories would provoke a version of Hegel's explicitly Fichtean complaint in the *Encyclopedia* that Kant's metaphysical deduction proceeds "empirically."[98] But what exactly does it mean for matter to restrict the deductive capacity of transcendental logic? In what does matter's brute limit on deduction consist?

As Steven Crowell shows, for Lask, logical form does not relate to alogical matter externally, as if they were distinct beings, which the two-world theory assumes at its peril. Instead, form relates to matter within the hylomorphic unity in which they play their functional roles, as stipulated by the two-element theory. Just as we might say that the soul is nothing but the way in which the body composes a system of abilities for performing vital functions, so too, in its functional role as logical form, a category is "*nothing but* a way the material is in itself deployed or involved," that is, nothing but the exhibition of matter's "structures and relations."[99] As Lask puts the point in Section 4, to know "the logical at its source" is to grasp it "in its original application" and thus to "immerse" oneself in the "sensible material" in which alone logical form can play its part.[100] He articulates this thought in the Second Part of the *Logic*, "The Logic of the Philosophical Categories," Chapter 3, by saying that the "strangeness between life and speculation" consists in the fact that, on the one hand, "the non-sensible," that is, the category, finds its "first and original" home in life while, on the other hand, speculation raises us out of our "ethical, aesthetic, and religious" immersion in life by "elevating" us "into consciousness" of the non-sensible itself. In other words, whereas we have "immediate experience" of the categories in their concrete, everyday application, it is only in "reflection" that we consider them in abstraction from that application.[101] Thus, as Lask explains in Chapter 1, we are pre-reflectively directed toward "categorially engaged material" such that the "validity character" of a category "remains unrecognized."[102] This is because, when we are absorbed in life, sensible matter is simply

[97] Fichte VND | SW I: 422–3.
[98] Hegel EL | GW 20: §42.
[99] Crowell 1992: 228.
[100] Lask LPK | 1923 II: 69.
[101] Lask LPK | 1923 II: 190–1.
[102] Lask LPK | 1923 II: 122.

transparent to us, that is, "logically naked."[103] It is only when matter's transparency is disturbed through reflection that we thematize the category that renders it intelligible, thereby logically clothing it.[104]

This, then, is why the categories are "not thoroughly logical" and "derive" from "alogical material," and, consequently, why they cannot be deduced from the I. The matter in whose experience we are normally immersed and on which the categories depend for their functional roles restricts the content of a deduction. Moreover, since this matter is factical or non-rationalizable, it cannot itself be deduced. For Lask, a deduction of the categories simply amounts to a reflection on the categories' functional role, that is, to a higher iteration of the hylomorphic unity of form and matter at which the categories that ordinarily inform sensible matter themselves become the material for deductive reflection.[105]

Early Heidegger finds in Lask a kindred spirit who is attuned to our factical situation and to the limits of deduction. However, in the Introduction to the *Doctrine*, Lask subordinates subjectivity in a way that, as we will see, transgresses the critical bounds within which Heidegger will develop his mature philosophical view.

Lask posits a "hierarchy" according to which what is "original" and "primary" is the categorial form of an object's factical matter insofar as it is "completely untouched by subjectivity," whereas what is "artificial" and thus "secondary and supplementary" is the subject's judgment of categorial form.[106] In Chapter 3, "Subjectivity as the Ground of the Emergence of Opposition," Lask explains that this hierarchy involves a "peculiar intertwining" of "aletheiology" and "gnoseology" in that it concerns, respectively, what objects are in truth and how subjects cognize objects, but crucially prioritizes the former concern over the latter concern.[107] The prioritization of objective truth over subjective cognition is meant to capture the sense in which subjectivity submits the ontologically prior or "transcendent" structure of objects to "atomization," that is, to "fragmentation" into the hylomorphic elements of logical form and alogical matter.[108] The object's

[103] Lask LPK | 1923 II: 74. Hence Lask says just prior: "The analogy of Kant's saying would therefore be: form without content is empty, content without form is naked" (Lask LPK | 1923 II: 74).

[104] See Crowell 1992: 229.

[105] Emundts 2008 argues that Lask's position in the *Doctrine* radically reconceives the priority of transcendental logic over general logic. Ainbinder 2015 argues that Lask's conception of reflection circumvents the questions *quid facti* and *quid juris* and thereby any need for Kant's metaphysical and transcendental deductions.

[106] Lask LU | 1923 II: 287–8, 291. In 1908's "Is There A 'Primacy of Practical Reason' in Logic?," Lask's address to the Third International Congress for Philosophy in Heidelberg, he answers his address' titular question in the negative by distinguishing between objective validity, which provides a "transsubjective" criterion of truth that enables us to distinguish successful theoretical "cognition" from mere "artistic looking," and subjective value, which is represented by a "valuable action" whose practical worth depends on "the personal sphere" and is therefore "never objectively valid." Confusing objective validity with subjective value, he says, only yields a "disturbing ethicizing" of truth (Lask G | 1923 I: 349–56).

[107] Lask LU | 1923 II: 424.

[108] Lask LU | 1923 II: 417–8. Crowell 2009 argues that Lask's subordination of gnoseology to aletheiology distinguishes his image of the "limitlessness of truth" (Lask FIG | 1923 I: 125, 128–9, 153, 223) from German idealism's image of the boundlessness of the concept (see Fichte GN | SW III: 40,

transcendent structure is "archetypal" and, insofar as it precedes "all contact with subjectivity," is the "highest goal of recognition." But this structure can only be a "lost paradise" due to subjectivity's role as "disintegrator," which Lask calls the "original sin of cognition."[109]

Lask's prioritization of objective truth over subjective cognition, that is, of alethiology over gnoseology, is dogmatic insofar as it sacrifices the critical purpose of a Copernican turn, which is to mark the transformation of objectivity that occurs through our reorientation from objects toward our subjective constitution.[110] As Kant says in the B-edition Preface to the first *Critique*, just as Copernicus' success in astronomy requires registering a shift in the motion of celestial bodies given our revolving position, so too our success in metaphysics requires registering a shift in the character of empirical objects given "the constitution of our faculty of intuition" and its *a priori* forms, namely, space and time.[111] Subjectivity's contribution of form to objectivity is primary rather than secondary precisely because it is essential to objectivity. Evading or even subordinating a critical investigation of this form only leaves us mired in whichever dogmatic "prejudice" regarding objectivity happens to prevail.[112] Already in his habilitation thesis, Heidegger recognizes that the subject is essential to any view about objectivity: "consciousness may be oriented toward 'truth,' but only through the judgment does it become aware of it as true, valid meaning . . . [O]bjecthood has meaning only for a judging subject, a subject without consideration of which it will never be possible to elucidate that which one designates as 'validity.'"[113] Heidegger's refusal to adopt Lask's hierarchy will be driven by a commitment to conducting philosophical investigation within

Hegel EL | GW 20: §45, and McDowell 1996: 13, 34). Crowell views the latter image in light of Kant's claim that there is "no other use of . . . concepts than that of judging by means of them" (Kant KrV A68/B93). If the concept is boundless, but presupposes the act of judging in pursuit of cognition, then the German idealist image is gnoseological. By contrast, Lask aletheiologically construes the categories not merely as concepts that are deployable by the judging subject, but rather ultimately as the form of objects insofar as they are in themselves "truths" (Lask FIG | 1923 I: 41).

[109] Lask LU | 1923 II: 424–6. Cf. Lask: "The scope of the categorical form investigated by logic extends as far as legitimate cognition. But this proposition cannot be reversed: cognition need not extend as far as the categorical form itself. Behind this requirement of logical research to secure in its complete breadth and comprehensiveness the categorical form that extends into the whole of cognition, lies the axiom of the universal dominion of the logical. This axiom is to be distinguished from, and is independent of, the question of the capacity of the logical to be actually encountered in cognition. The dominion of the logical in itself is boundless, although the domain of the logical that is accessible to cognition is perhaps bounded" (Lask BT | 2015: 424).

[110] See Beiser 2008.

[111] Kant KrV Bxvi–i.

[112] Kant KrV Bxxx.

[113] Heidegger FS | 1972: 227, 347, translated by Crowell 1992: 230. Cf. Heidegger: "If finitude is placed at the point of departure for transcendence as clearly as it is by Kant, then it is not necessary, in order to escape an alleged 'subjective idealism,' to invoke a 'turn to the object'—a turn which is praised again today all too noisily and with all too little understanding of the problem" (Heidegger KPM | GA 3: 73).

critical bounds, a commitment that, as we will see, is informed by Dilthey's concept of hermeneutics.

To clarify Heidegger's divergence from Lask, consider the different skeptical problematics in which they figure on the issue of subjectivity. For Lask, the categorial structure of objects transcends subjectivity, which "atomiz[es]," "fragment[s]," or disintegrates that structure into the formal components of judgment. This leaves us with the question, arising in the Cartesian problematic, of whether our possible grasp of transcendent categorial structure is ever actual. Even worse, it leaves us with the further question of how we could ever non-dogmatically affirm the transcendent categorial structure of factical matter from our allegedly distorting standpoint as judging subjects, that is, how we could ever affirm the existence of such a permanently lost paradise.[114] Worse still, objectivity's absolute transcendence of subjectivity makes it difficult to see how Lask avoids resurrecting the two-world theory that he initially aims to reject.

By contrast, Heidegger's approach to facticity denies such transcendence from the outset. As he argues in *Hermeneutics of Facticity*:

> The relationship here between hermeneutics and facticity is not a relationship between the grasping of an object and the object grasped, in relation to which the former would simply have to measure itself. Rather, interpreting is itself a possible and distinctive how of the character of being of facticity. Interpreting is a being that belongs to the being of factical life itself. If one were to describe facticity—improperly—as the 'object' of hermeneutics (as plants are described as the objects of botany), then one would find this (hermeneutics) in its own object itself (as if analogously plants, what and how they are, came along with botany and from it). This relationship with its 'object' which, as we have just indicated, hermeneutics enjoys on the level of being makes the inception, execution, and appropriation of hermeneutics prior ontologically and factico-temporally to all accomplishments in the sciences . . . The theme of this hermeneutical investigation is the Dasein which is in each case our own and indeed as hermeneutically interrogated with respect to and on the basis of the character of its being and with a view to developing in it a radical wakefulness for itself.[115]

Our interpretation of the factical being of Dasein cannot but exhibit that very being, since we ourselves are Dasein. In this sense, our interpretation "belongs to the being" of that which we interpret. Unlike empirical science, which presupposes the difference between its inquiry and "the object grasped," a hermeneutics

[114] See Beiser 2011: 462–7 and Crowell 2001. Cf. the problem of Dennett's view of consciousness as a "user-illusion" (Dennett 2017: 3b–4b), on which, see Bruno 2021c.

[115] Heidegger OHF | GA 63: 15.

of facticity is a first-personal inquiry, one that "interrogate[s]" itself.[116] Moreover, such an inquiry is "prior" to empirical science insofar as it supplies an answer to a question that arises in the Kantian problematic, namely, how empirical science is possible. The hermeneutical answer involves an inquiry into our factical being, for example, our being-in-the-world, being-with-others, being-ahead-of-ourselves, being-toward-death, and being-time, without which no meaningful world could be open to us, *a fortiori* open to our scientific investigations.[117] Indeed, reflecting the Kantian character of the problematic in which he figures, Heidegger ascribes "radical wakefulness" to hermeneutics, implying the latter's interruption of a dogmatic slumber of sorts. Moreover, a hermeneutics of facticity shares with a critique of reason the crucial feature of a genitive that is simultaneously subjective and objective. Unlike a tribunal of experience, in which interrogator and interrogated differ and for which the genitive is therefore objective and at best only accidentally subjective, a critique of reason is, as Kant says in the A-edition Preface, "a court of justice" in which reason occupies both the bench and the stand, interrogating itself for its right to its own claims.[118] Just as a critique of reason both thematizes and belongs to reason, so too a hermeneutics of facticity both thematizes and belongs to facticity.

Thus, while Lask's impact on Heidegger is acknowledged by Heidegger himself and documented by Rickert, it is also fairly circumscribed. First, Lask's misreading of the *Wissenschaftslehre* does not impede Heidegger's awareness of Fichte's rationalist recoil from facticity. Heidegger is thereby able to assign new, anti-Fichtean meaning to 'facticity' in his analysis of Dasein. Second, Lask's subordination of subjectivity and prioritization of aletheiology over gnoseology does not encourage Heidegger to indulge the dogmatic idea of a transcendent categorial structure of factical matter.[119] Heidegger is thereby able to analyze the facticity of Dasein

[116] We might worry that Lask and Heidegger both face a problem of correspondence. While Lask sacrifices objectivity by regarding our subjectivity as essentially distorting, Heidegger might also sacrifice objectivity by regarding our subjectivity as potentially distorting insofar as we are prone to the inauthenticity of reifying and thus de-vivifying lived experience. However, we can overcome the threat of inauthenticity, if provisionally, precisely through the self-understanding that hermeneutic interpretation affords.

[117] Cf. Husserl: "natural science (like all science generally) is a title for spiritual accomplishments, namely, those of the natural scientists working together; as such, they belong, after all, like all spiritual occurrences, to the region of what is to be explained by humanistic disciplines. Now is it not absurd and circular to want to explain the historical event 'natural science' in a natural-scientific way, to explain it by bringing in natural science and its natural laws, which, as spiritual accomplishment, themselves belong to the problem? . . . For true nature in the sense of natural science is a product of the spirit that investigates nature and thus presupposes the science of the spirit" (Husserl PK | 1970b: 272–1, 297).

[118] Kant KrV Axi–xii. Cf. Kant: "pure reason . . . represents the supreme court of justice for all disputes" (Kant KrV A740/B768).

[119] In his 1919 summer lectures in Freiburg, *Phenomenology and Transcendental Philosophy of Value*, Heidegger claims that although, in "value," Lask discovers "*the* world" as "something non-material" yet "also not unmaterial," that is, as something "factual," he goes "further than Rickert, without, however, taking the step into phenomenology" (Heidegger PTW | GA 56/57 2: 122, 177). He nevertheless asserts: "Emil Lask, to whose investigations I personally owe very much . . . was one of the strongest philosophical personalities of our time, a serious man who in my view was on the way to phenomenology" (Heidegger PTW | GA 56/57 2: 180). Cf. Heidegger IP | GA 56/57 1: 88 and Heidegger DS | GA 1: 192.

within the critical bounds of hermeneutics. However, this leaves us with the question of how Heidegger comes to adopt a hermeneutical method of analyzing the facticity of Dasein. We will now see that while he inherits the concept of facticity from Lask, he inherits the hermeneutical method from Dilthey. Just as Heidegger repurposes that concept, so too he repurposes that method.

5.5 Dilthey and the Hermeneutic Tradition

After studying with Kuno Fischer at the University of Heidelberg, Dilthey transfers to the University of Berlin where he studies with Trendelenburg and August Böckh, both students of Friedrich Daniel Ernst Schleiermacher, and eventually takes up the chair that is previously held by Fichte, Hegel, and Schelling. Dilthey's students include Leo Baeck, Martin Buber, and William Edward Burghardt Du Bois. His engagement with the history of hermeneutics begins with his 1860 Schleiermacher Society prize essay "Schleiermacher's Hermeneutical System in Relation to Earlier Protestant Hermeneutics" and includes the 1870 first volume of an unfinished intellectual biography of Schleiermacher.

In the posthumous 1838 *Hermeneutics and Criticism*, Schleiermacher seeks to transform hermeneutics from its traditional role as the philological discipline of interpreting canonical texts into "the art of understanding," which establishes rules for the validity of any form of interpretation.[120] The principal rule, without which he says interpretation cannot secure "scientific" and therefore "[c]omplete knowledge," is the hermeneutic circle, that is, the "apparent circle" in which "each particular can only be understood via the general, of which it is a part, and vice versa." The hermeneutic circle is "apparent" in that it appears vicious, but is in fact virtuous. Whereas a vicious circle is closed, restricting our understanding by turning from a phenomenon toward a condition of intelligibility that never arrives, a virtuous circle opens, expanding our understanding by cycling between a phenomenon and a condition of intelligibility that reciprocally intensify each other's clarificatory power. The circle that delimits valid interpretation accordingly does not merely defer our understanding by passing between particular and general as mutually indifferent terms. Instead, it extends our understanding by showing how particular and general are mutually illuminating terms. Hence Schleiermacher says that nothing we interpret "can be understood all at once," since, according to its principal rule, interpretation moves between part and whole such that the knowledge that is secured through "each reading" of the one in terms of the other "makes us capable of better understanding by enriching that previous knowledge." The example that he gives is the mutually illuminating relation between a part,

[120] Schleiermacher 1998: 5. On the modern history of hermeneutics, see Grondin 2005.

namely, an author's "*writings*," and a whole, namely, their "*vocabulary*" and "*era*," where the part "*must be understood as the part*" of the whole, such as when we interpret a text within a linguistic or historical context, and "*the whole must, in turn, be understood from the part*," such as when we interpret that text's transformative impact on that context.[121]

For Dilthey, Schleiermacher's transformation of hermeneutics affords an insight into the method that distinguishes the human sciences from the natural sciences. On the one hand, natural sciences, for example, physics, chemistry, and biology, aim to explain worldly events third-personally by reducing them to their external causes. On the other hand, human sciences, for example, history, political theory, and jurisprudence, aim to understand human life first-personally by interpreting it from the standpoint of lived experience.[122] As Dilthey says in Book Six, Section Three of a draft of the 1880–90 *Introduction to the Human Sciences, Volume 2*, whereas "explanation" denotes the natural sciences' "reduction" of "human affairs" to "exactly definable (and preferably quantitatively determinable) external facts," "understanding" denotes the human sciences' "interpretation" of such affairs within "the context of the whole of psychic life and conditioned by its milieu."[123] Natural science explains the affairs of human life as mere events whose intelligibility directs scientific thinking outward toward a series of further "facts." By contrast, human science interprets these affairs as lived experiences whose intelligibility directs scientific thinking inward toward the "context" of lived experience. Crucially, natural-scientific explanation does not content itself with any particular fact, but rather, not unlike the vicious circle although not circularly, pursues a reductive conclusion that never arrives. Just as crucially, human-scientific understanding does not restrict itself to the "psychic life" of an individual, but rather, like the virtuous and specifically hermeneutic circle, pursues an interpretive unity in which that life is reciprocally clarified by "its milieu," namely, human life as a "whole."[124] Even more crucially, since the human sciences are themselves part of this whole, their interpretations of life provide an understanding that both accords with and exhibits the hermeneutic circle.

The interpretive method that distinguishes human science is hermeneutic, then, because what it aims to understand, namely, human life, is not really distinct from it. As Dilthey puts it, "understanding is the domain of all who are actively involved

[121] Schleiermacher 1998: 24. On the hermeneutic circle, see Grondin 2016 and Mensch 2018.

[122] On Johann Gustav Droysen's role in developing the distinction between explanation and understanding, see Beiser 2011: 289–321. On the contrast between Dilthey's conception of the human sciences and the neo-Kantians' conception of the cultural sciences, see Makkreel 1969.

[123] Dilthey EG | 1989: 439. On Dilthey's divergence from Schleiermacher concerning the role of interpretation in natural science, see Forster 2019.

[124] Cf. Dilthey's "On Understanding and Hermeneutics," which is based on transcripts of his 1867–68 lecture *Logic and the System of Philosophical Sciences*: "A whole should be understood on the basis of the particular and the particular on the basis of the whole. This contradiction generates the procedure of the hermeneut. He operates with hypotheses. When we apply this to a work, it becomes obvious that we never understand a work on a first reading" (Dilthey VH | 1996: 231).

in human affairs, and differs from explanation by participating in life, which is possible only on the basis of life. Life is the great object as well as the organon of those who are concerned with human affairs."[125] Insofar as we are scientifically "concerned with human affairs," we seek understanding rather than explanation, since, unlike those physical, chemical, and biological events that we passively accompany and endure, we are "actively involved in" and "participat[e] in" those historical, political, and jurisprudential affairs that elicit our scientific interest. Human life is thus both the "organon" and the "great object" of the human sciences. In other words, the sciences of human life exhibit a genitive that is both subjective and objective. Insofar as there is no real distinction between the subject and object of the human sciences, their interpretations follow a hermeneutical method. Hence Dilthey says in the Appendix to 1910's *The Formation of the Historical World in the Human Sciences* that the "human scientist . . . develops the technique of hermeneutics and its scientific discipline, thereby making understanding rule-guided."[126]

In 1900's "The Rise of Hermeneutics," Dilthey reiterates the claim that interpretation is governed by the hermeneutic circle, according to which "[t]he whole of a work is to be understood from the individual words," whose "comprehension . . . presupposes comprehension of the whole." He observes that this "circle" of comprehension "is then reduplicated in the relationship between the individual work itself and the spiritual tendencies of its creator" and "returns again in the relationship between the work and its literary genre." As we saw, the circle is reduplicated yet again to include the hermeneut's own interpretation of a work, which interpretation is itself part of human life as a whole. Recognizing this endless exhibition of the hermeneutic circle, Dilthey says that "all understanding remains partial and can never be terminated." However, he infers from the interminability of understanding that "*[i]ndividuum est ineffabile* [the individual is ineffable]."[127] The inference is that since interpretation never transcends the mutual illumination of part and whole, it is closed within a circle that, while virtuous insofar as it genuinely expands our understanding, never incorporates the "individual," which exceeds interpretive intelligibility and is, in this sense, "ineffable." The individual that outstrips interpretation is accordingly a scientifically underivable or brute fact, that is, it is factical. But what precisely is this factical individual?

The individual in question might seem comparable to the alogical matter that Lask regards as factically given to logical form. However, we find that Diltheyan individuality is unlike Laskian individuality in that the latter is haecceitic and multitudinous, whereas the former is horizonal and singular. As we saw in Section 5.4, Lask construes facticity as the undeducible particularity or haecceity of objects. By

[125] Dilthey EG | 1989: 439.
[126] Dilthey A | 2002: 335.
[127] Dilthey EH | 1972: 243. See Goethe's 1780 letter to Johann Kaspar Lavater: "Have I written to you already the phrase '*Individuum est ineffabile*'? I derive a whole world from it" (Goethe 1957: 121).

contrast, Dilthey construes facticity as the undeducible background or horizon of life. In *Human Sciences, Volume 2*, he ascribes "facticity" to "life" or "*lived experience*," which serves as the insuperable boundary within which part and whole, for example, "self-consciousness" and "world," can be mutually illuminating.[128] Life is a factical individual because it is the presupposed space without which there can be no understanding of parts and wholes. As Dilthey puts it, the "orientation" of "cognition" within "life" is a "facticity" from which "[w]e cannot abstract."[129] While understanding expresses the "vitality" of human science, this vitality itself "is bound by facticity," namely, the brute givenness of life.[130]

In opposition to the German idealist campaign of eliminating facticity, Dilthey expresses the undeducible facticity of life in *Formation of the Historical World* as follows:

> Life . . . is what is given in lived experience and understanding. In this sense, life thus extends over the whole range of objective spirit insofar as it is accessible through lived experience. Life is the basic fact that must form the starting point of philosophy. Life is that with which we are acquainted from within and behind which we cannot go. We cannot bring life before the tribunal of reason.[131]

Like any human science, philosophy offers interpretations of human life, but only by "starting" from life as a "basic fact." Philosophy cannot abstract from life so as to deduce its conditions of intelligibility, for there is no "range of objective spirit" that does not fall within and so is not always already "acquainted" with the space of lived experience. Insofar as reason cannot get "behind" life, it cannot stand above it as a "tribunal." Thus, whereas, for Lask, we cannot deduce the givenness of objects, for Dilthey we cannot deduce the givenness of life. But if interpretation grounds out in the facticity of life, which discipline is responsible for pointing to this ground?

In a draft of a letter to Richard Schöne, mid-1882, Dilthey says:

> The quarrel between idealism and realism can be resolved by psychological analysis, which can demonstrate that the real world given in experience is not a phenomenon in my representation; it is rather given to me as something distinct from myself, because I am a being that does not merely represent, but also wills and feels. The real world is what the will possesses in reflexive awareness when it meets resistance or when the hand feels pressure. This reflexive awareness of the

[128] Dilthey EG | 1989: 330.
[129] Dilthey EG | 1989: 355.
[130] Dilthey EG | 1989: 454–5. Cf. 1883's *Introduction to the Human Sciences, Volume 1*, where Dilthey claims that the "facticity" of "our experience" is "unfathomable" (Dilthey EG | 1989: 62).
[131] Dilthey A | 2002: 280. Cf. Dilthey: "understanding does not disclose how the logical content that has been thought is related to the dark background and fullness of psychic life" (Dilthey A | 2002: 227).

> will is as much of this real world as of itself. Both self and the real world are therefore given in the totality of psychic life.[132]

If philosophy cannot abstract from the fact of lived experience, then it cannot vindicate an "idealis[t]" or "realis[t]" account of the priority of, respectively, the "self" or the "real world," for we only encounter these as "given" jointly within the factical "totality of psychic life." Dilthey claims that it falls to "psychological analysis" to "demonstrate" this joint givenness and thereby to "resolv[e]" the old philosophical "quarrel." He clarifies this claim in 1883's *Introduction to the Human Sciences, Volume 1* by classifying psychology as an "analytic science" that understands "the individual as a component of society." Psychology does not begin with the "fiction" of an individual that is "immersed in [themselves]" and that must somehow be shown to relate to the world, which would only perpetuate the old quarrel. Instead, psychology secures "analytic knowledge of the universal characteristics" of life construed as the experiential totality within which individuals are intelligible in the first place. By analyzing the characteristics that, as social "component[s]," all individuals must exhibit, psychology "provides the basis of all knowledge of historical life" and so qualifies as "the first and most fundamental of the particular human sciences." Thus, for Dilthey, psychology is the discipline that points to life as the factical ground of the interpretations that the human sciences offer in accordance with their principal rule of interpretation, namely, the hermeneutic circle.

5.6 First-Personal Hermeneutics

As we saw in Section 5.4, Heidegger seeks a method of interpreting facticity that avoids Lask's problematic appeal to archetypal, that is, transcendent, categorial structures. We will now see that Heidegger finds the basic elements of this method in Dilthey's hermeneutics, which invites the idea that an interpretation of facticity is itself always already situated, that is, immanent, in factical life. We will also see that just as Heidegger redirects Lask's concept of facticity from the existence of individuals to the existence of Dasein, so too he redirects Dilthey's method of hermeneutics from psychological analysis to phenomenological analysis. Together, these modifications enable a hermeneutics of facticity that remains within critical bounds, *contra* Lask, and is properly philosophical, *contra* Dilthey.

In 1953–54's "A Dialogue on Language," Heidegger's reconstruction of his conversation with Tezuka Tomio, he tells his interlocutor that he is introduced to hermeneutics during his early theological studies, when he is "agitated over the question of the relation between the word of holy scripture and

[132] Dilthey EG | 1989: 493–4. Although the letter is often regarded as being addressed to Friedrich Althoff, see Dilthey EG | 1989: 493n1 concerning its likely addressee.

theological-speculative thinking," which he says is "the same" as the relation between "language and being." He returns to hermeneutics when he studies Dilthey's "theory of the history of ideas."[133] These studies yield a critical engagement with Dilthey that covers the decade leading up to the publication of *Being and Time*, in which Heidegger will announce in §7 that "phenomenology," that is, "the science of the being of beings—ontology," is "*hermeneutics* in the original sense of that word, which designates the work of interpretation," and whose "*logos*" accordingly "has the character of *hermēneuein*."[134]

Heidegger begins to engage with Dilthey in his 1919 summer lectures in Freiburg, *Phenomenology and Transcendental Philosophy of Value*. In Part One, Chapter Two, "Windelband's Grounding of Modern Transcendental Philosophy of Value," Heidegger says that "we are indebted" to Dilthey for defending the human sciences' "autonom[y]" from the natural sciences, but objects that his "valuable intuitions . . . do not reach down to ultimate and primordial principles and to radical purity and novelty of method. Phenomenology, whose basic founding he of course did not live through, but the far-reaching meaning of whose first breakthroughs and researches he was one of the first to recognize, is now beginning to fulfil the secret longing of his life."[135] Although this objection is somewhat implicit, recall that, for Dilthey, psychology points to the facticity of lived experience as the horizon within which individuals and society stand in relations of mutual illumination. We can see that this position restricts itself to an ontic inquiry into a class of beings, namely, social beings. But such an inquiry is one whose principles are derivative relative to the "primordial principles" of an ontological inquiry into being as such. Thus, Dilthey's turn to psychology leaves us without an inquiry that can provide an interpretation of being, which, for Heidegger, is the task of "[p]henomenology."

Heidegger develops his objection in 1920's summer lectures in Freiburg, *Phenomenology of Intuition and Expression*, which displays extensive familiarity with Dilthey's work.[136] In Part Two, Section Two, "The Destructing Consideration of the Diltheyian Position," Heidegger claims that Dilthey is not "a proper philosopher" because he does not "determine the concept of philosophy from out of its proper motive," which is "to interpret life from out of itself."[137] We saw in Section 5.5 that Dilthey regards human life as not really distinct from the human sciences, whose interpretations of life would exhibit a subjective and objective genitive and would in this respect be first-personal. Such interpretations would accordingly express philosophy's "proper motive" of interpreting life "from out of itself." However,

[133] Heidegger GS | 1971: 9–10.
[134] Heidegger SZ | GA 2: 37. On Heidegger's early turn to hermeneutics, see Arrien 2018. On Heidegger's critical engagement with Dilthey, see Bambach 2019, Grondin 2019, Nelson 2013, and Scharff 2013. On the connection between Heidegger's conceptions of phenomenology and hermeneutics, see Claudio and Djian 2018 and Crowe 2019.
[135] Heidegger PTW | GA 56/57 2: 164–5.
[136] See Heidegger PA | 2010: 119–20.
[137] Heidegger PA | 2010: 118–9.

while Dilthey recognizes this motive, his psychological analysis of the "structural complexes" of life does not proceed from it. This is because he interprets life as composed of a "bundle of drives," for example, the drive to resist external forces. But this is to treat life not only as an ontic class of beings, but also third-personally as an object that is distinct from the interpreting subject, who is no mere bundle. Dilthey thus fails to interpret life first-personally.[138] Nevertheless, Heidegger sees in him "an instruction that is not yet exhausted,"[139] namely, to pursue a genuinely first-personal hermeneutics in which the interpretation of life exhibits a genitive that is truly subjective and objective.

Moreover, Heidegger implies that Dasein, that is, our being-there, is the proper topic of first-personal hermeneutics when he complains that, on Dilthey's view, "[a]ctual Dasein does not come to its primordial due."[140] Dasein is not given "primordial due" if it is confined to a class of beings, for example, social components or psychological drives, since an understanding of this or any such class is derivative relative to a primordial understanding of being as such, which Dasein alone provides. Accordingly, Dasein must be interpreted not merely ontically as a class of beings, but rather ontologically as uniquely disclosive of being. Hence, anticipating his analysis of Dasein in *Being and Time* as constituted *inter alia* by being-in-the-world, being-with-others, and being-ahead-of-itself, Heidegger says that "[e]nvironing world, with-world, and self-world are no areas of being, not determined in something. All reality receives its primordial sense through the worry of the self."[141] The "self" here is Dasein's worldly, social, and concernful existence, which does not occupy one of many ontic "areas of being" that are "determined" in relation to other such areas, but rather gives the "reality" of any area its "primordial sense," namely, by disclosing that area's ground in an understanding of being. In this brief characterization of Dasein, then, we see a glimpse of the primordiality that Heidegger entrusts to phenomenology and charges Dilthey with failing to fathom.

Finally, Heidegger indicates a crucial disagreement with Dilthey when he says that "[p]hilosophy has the task of preserving the facticity of life and strengthening the facticity of Dasein."[142] On the one hand, philosophy must "preserv[e] the facticity" of life against its third-personal misconstrual, for example, its natural-scientific reduction to external causes, by pursuing a first-personal interpretation of life "from out of" itself. This expresses the hermeneutical spirit, although not the psychological letter, of Dilthey's work. On the other hand, philosophy must "strengthe[n]" the facticity of life by recognizing that facticity essentially belongs to "Dasein." But philosophy does not strengthen facticity by consigning it to

[138] Heidegger PA | 2010: 121, 128–9.
[139] Heidegger PA | 2010: 124.
[140] Heidegger PA | 2010: 130.
[141] Heidegger PA | 2010: 132–3.
[142] Heidegger PA | 2010: 133.

unspeakable ineffability, as Dilthey does, for this is in fact to weaken facticity by abandoning it to a questionable and, indeed, dogmatic silence. Instead, philosophy strengthens facticity through an enriching and transformative interpretation of its structural components, that is, through a hermeneutical account of the worldly, social, concernful, mortal, and temporal conditions of Dasein's existence. Crucially, since philosophy is itself situated in and therefore exhibits the conditions of factical life, its interpretation of the latter is necessarily first-personal.

Dilthey and Heidegger agree that lived experience is undeducibly brute or factical. However, whereas Dilthey regards the facticity of life as the ineffable limit of hermeneutics, Heidegger regards it as the interpretable topic of hermeneutics. In 1922's introduction to a planned book on Aristotle, "Phenomenological Interpretations in Connection with Aristotle: An Indication of the Hermeneutical Situation," also known as the Natorp Report, Heidegger describes the hermeneutical method as it applies to facticity:

> The basic problem of philosophy concerns the *being* of factical life. In this respect, philosophy is a *fundamental ontology that deals with principles*, so that this ontology of facticity provides the particular specialized regional ontologies of the world with a foundation for their problems and a clarification of the sense of these problems . . . Due to its tendency toward falling, factical life lives for the most part in what is inauthentic, in what has been handed down to it, in what has been transmitted and reported to it from the past, in what it has appropriated and learned in an average way . . . In the ways it formulates questions and finds answers to them, philosophy too is situated in this movement of facticity, since it is only the explicit interpretation of factical life. Accordingly, it is necessary for the philosophical hermeneutics of facticity to begin within its factical situation by inserting itself into the particular state of the having-been-interpreted of factical life given in advance for hermeneutics. This having-been-interpreted initially supports hermeneutics and can never be completely eradicated.[143]

Two points are salient in this passage. First, Heidegger makes explicit his implicit claim in *Philosophy of Value* that philosophy's "basic problem" concerns not beings, but rather "*being*," and so is not a "regional ontolog[y]," but rather is "a *fundamental ontology*." Accordingly, whereas Dilthey's psychological analysis applies to a region of beings, a properly philosophical analysis applies to being, that is, "the *being* of factical life," within which beings are encountered.

Second, Heidegger says that factical life is constituted by the "state" of "having-been-interpreted" by methods that are "handed down" and "appropriated" in uncritically "average" and thus "inauthentic" ways, methods that include

[143] Heidegger PIAA | 2002: 121–3.

natural-scientific explanation and, as we will see in Chapter 6, dialectical logic. Philosophy's "questions" and "answers" are vulnerable to this averageness insofar as they always already find themselves in the ongoing history of typically inauthentic interpretations of factical life. A philosophical interpretation of facticity must accordingly be an articulation of its own historicity.[144] Crucially, this opens a hermeneutic circle in which part and whole potentially stand in a relation of mutual illumination. On the one hand, a particular philosophical interpretation of facticity can only be understood as "begin[ning]" from the "factical situation" of the general historicity of interpretation. On the other hand, the historicity of interpretation can only be understood as typically average and inauthentic in light of a particular philosophical interpretation that explicitly thematizes averageness and inauthenticity. Thus, while a "philosophical hermeneutics of facticity" can never "completely eradicat[e]" the historicity of interpretation, which "support[s]" the former "in advance," it nevertheless can reveal a path toward interpretive authenticity.[145]

By the time of 1925's spring lectures in Kassel, "Wilhelm Dilthey's Research and the Contemporary Struggle for a Historical Worldview," Heidegger's objection to Dilthey is fully developed in a way that combines the above points into the claim that a hermeneutical interpretation of facticity must be ontological, first-personal, and articulate. While Dilthey's "critique of metaphysics" relies on "French positivism," he rejects the latter's conception of the mind as "a product of nature" in order to grasp the mind as capable of the self-determination whereby it "investigates itself in its history" and so attains "a distinct form of self-knowledge."[146] Nevertheless, he construes the mind ontically and third-personally "under the traditional heading of psychology" as "a spiritual being" and so, despite avoiding a positivistic denial of the mind as "living, free, and historical," he fails to "pose the question ... concerning the being of beings," which is precisely the question of "the being of our own Dasein".[147] It therefore falls to "*phenomenology*" to "advanc[e]

[144] See Heidegger: "What is required of philosophical research is that it be a critique of the present. In disclosing the past in a primordial manner, the past is no longer seen to be merely a present that preceded our own present. Rather, it is possible to emancipate the past so that we can find in it the authentic roots of our existence and bring it into our own present as a vital force. Historical consciousness liberates the past for the future, and it is then that the past gains force and becomes productive" (Heidegger WD | 2002: 174–5).

[145] See Gadamer's 1960 *Truth and Method*: "Heidegger describes the [hermeneutic] circle in such a way that the understanding of the text remains permanently determined by the anticipatory movement of fore-understanding. The circle of whole and part is not dissolved in perfect understanding but, on the contrary, is most fully realized. The circle, then, is not formal in nature. It is neither subjective nor objective, but describes understanding as the interplay of the movement of tradition and the movement of the interpreter. The anticipation of meaning that governs our understanding of a text is not an act of subjectivity, but proceeds from the commonality that binds us to the tradition. But this commonality is constantly being formed in our relation to tradition. Tradition is not simply a permanent precondition; rather, we produce it ourselves inasmuch as we understand, participate in the evolution of tradition, and hence further determine it ourselves. Thus the circle of understanding is not a 'methodological' circle, but describes an element of the ontological structure of understanding" (Gadamer 2006: 293–4).

[146] Heidegger WD | 2002: 152, 155.

[147] Heidegger WD | 2002: 155–6.

further than Dilthey's own position" and to provide a hermeneutical interpretation of the facticity of Dasein that articulates the conditions by which we exist not simply as spiritual beings, but rather as the disclosure of being.[148] Heidegger then rehearses the articulation of Dasein's being-in-the-world, being-with-others, being-ahead-of-itself, being-toward-death, and being-time on which he will expand in *Being and Time* two years later.[149]

The culmination of Heidegger's critical engagement with Dilthey in *Being and Time* begins with a restatement of the "limits" of his "humanistic psychology," namely, that it "does not reach the dimension of the question of being in Dasein."[150] While a "descriptive and analytic psychology" can elaborate the phenomenon of the will's resistance to reality, its "foundation" is left "ontological[ly] indefinit[e]" by its failure to ask "[w]hat kind of being belongs" to this phenomenon. As Heidegger says, in willing anything, "something must already have been disclosed, something which drive and will are *out to get*," which "is itself already *together with* a totality of relevance" that in turn presupposes "*the disclosedness of world* . . . The 'against' and the 'counter to' are supported in their ontological possibility by disclosed being-in-the-world."[151] A hermeneutical interpretation of facticity that is genuinely ontological, first-personal, and articulate consists of a philosophical analysis of the factical conditions of Dasein, on the basis of which alone spiritual beings such as "drive and will" can be psychologically analyzed. As Heidegger says, the "*primary* meaning" of hermeneutics is as an "interpretation of the being of Dasein," whose "ontological priority over all other beings" is such that hermeneutics "contains the roots of what can be called 'hermeneutics' in a derivative sense: the methodology of the historical humanistic disciplines," including psychology.[152]

We have seen that the hermeneutical method "reduplicate[s]" the hermeneutic circle and that this occurs in philosophy's interpretation of factical life, which, being situated in life, unavoidably exhibits its own factical conditions. In §63 of *Being and Time*, Heidegger addresses the circularity of the "hermeneutical situation" of "fundamental ontology," in which "the ontologically clarified idea of being" depends on an understanding of the being of Dasein, which in turn must be "guided by the idea of existence." This invites the charge that ontology "is moving in a 'circle,'" that is, that it is viciously circular. I will conclude this chapter by

[148] Heidegger WD | 2002: 159, 162.
[149] Heidegger WD | 2002: 163–74.
[150] Heidegger SZ | GA 2: 46–7. As we saw, historicity factically conditions the being of Dasein. While Heidegger regards an interpretation of historicity as Dilthey's "constant goal," he claims that it is "illuminated more penetratingly" by Dilthey's friend, Count Hans Ludwig Paul Yorck von Wartenburg (Heidegger SZ | GA 2: 397).
[151] Heidegger SZ | GA 2: 209–11. Cf. Heidegger: "The authentic correlation of world and Dasein (if we can speak here of correlation at all, which is not my opinion) is not that of impulse and resistance or, as in [Max] Scheler, will and resistance, but rather *care and meaningfulness*. This correlation is the basic structure of life, a structure which I also call *facticity*" (Heidegger PGZ | GA 20: 304).
[152] Heidegger SZ | GA 2: 37–8.

explaining Heidegger's aim of "clarif[ying]" ontology's hermeneutical situation in light of the charge of vicious circularity.[153]

As we saw in Section 2.6, fundamental ontology depends on an existential analysis of Dasein in that no inquiry into being can bracket the being of we who inquire. Already in §2, Heidegger considers the charge that the "enterprise" of ontology "fall[s] into an obvious circle" if an answer to the question of the meaning of being depends on an "explication of a being (Dasein) with regard to its being," since this would seem to "presuppose something that only the answer can provide," namely, an understanding of being. His reply is that "there is no circle at all" because an analysis of Dasein "grows out of the average understanding of being in which we are always already involved *and which ultimately belongs to the essential constitution of Dasein itself*." This reply reiterates the claim in "Phenomenological Interpretations in Connection with Aristotle" that the being of factical life is constituted by its having-been-interpreted in average, that is, inauthentic, ways and that philosophy, while vulnerable to averageness given its situation in life, is no less capable of thematizing averageness so as to enable an authentic interpretation of being. As Heidegger now puts it, the analysis of Dasein "grows out of the average understanding of being," which is to say that it expands an understanding that is initially restricted to what has been handed down. He indicates that this expansion is hermeneutical when he distinguishes between "circular reasoning," in which one "posit[s] a principle from which a series of propositions is deduced" that invalidly includes that principle, and a "'relatedness backward or forward' of what is asked about (being) to asking as a mode of being of a being," in which "being" and Dasein's "mode of being" stand in a relation of mutual illumination.[154] Fundamental ontology's method is hermeneutical rather than "deduc[tive]" because it moves "forward" from an average understanding of being to the factical conditions of Dasein's existence, whose analysis cycles "backward" to a correction of that understanding. But then the idea of being with which this analysis begins differs from the idea that it yields and so does not presuppose "the answer" that it "provide[s]" to the question of the meaning of being. Thus, when Heidegger says that "there is no circle" in ontology, it is rather like Schleiermacher's claim that hermeneutics is only "apparently" circular, that is, only apparently vicious in its circularity, since ontology's hermeneutical method instead enables the virtuously circular, that is, cyclical, expansion of our understanding of being.[155] The proper image for ontology is accordingly neither the line nor the circle, recalling the figures in Hegel's *Science of Logic*, but is rather the spiral.

[153] Heidegger SZ | GA 2: 314.
[154] Heidegger SZ | GA 2: 7–8.
[155] See Heidegger: "our attempt must aim at leaping into this 'circle' primordially and completely, so that even at the beginning of our analysis of Dasein we make sure that we have a complete view of the circular being of Dasein" (Heidegger SZ | GA 2: 315). Cf. Heidegger SZ | GA 2: 152–3.

When Heidegger later returns to the charge that fundamental ontology is viciously circular if the idea of "being in general" is "presupposed" by the "existential interpretation" of Dasein that is meant to clarify that idea, he distinguishes between two meanings of 'presuppose.' The first meaning denotes a relation between propositions such that, "according to the formal rules of consistency," one proposition can be "deduce[d]" from another. This is a logical relation that prevents a proposition from grounding a deduction of that proposition, on pain of vicious circularity. The second meaning denotes a relation between Dasein and its projection of itself onto "possibilities of its existence," which expresses its "*disclosive*" being and, Heidegger adds, is exhibited in "*all research*," including ontological research into the meaning of being. This is a hermeneutical relation between Dasein and being that expands our presupposed and initially average understanding of being in a mode of virtuous circularity. Such a relation "is *not* proving anything according to the rules of the 'logic of consistency' *at all*,"[156] but rather is disclosing the meaning of being according to the principal rule of hermeneutics, which, in light of his critique of Dilthey, Heidegger puts to ontological, first-personal, and articulate use.

We might demand that an answer to the question of the meaning of being contains nothing from its starting point, that is, nothing about being. Thus, we might "'star[t] out with' a worldless I in order then to provide that I with an object." However, according to Heidegger, this would be to presuppose "[n]ot too much, but *too little*," since it would ignore ontology's historicity, that is, its inheritance of inauthentic interpretations of being. Indeed, as his quotation marks indicate, it would be, *per impossibile*, for philosophy to "star[t] out" from nowhere. Avoiding this error and the charge of vicious circularity that it invites requires that we grasp not the logical meaning of 'presupposition,' which serves the "formal" ideal of "consistency" in thinking about beings, but rather the hermeneutical meaning of 'presupposition,' which serves the "existential" ideal of "authenticity" in an understanding of being.[157]

When Dilthey argues that philosophy cannot get back behind lived experience, he prefigures Heidegger's claim that Dasein cannot get back behind its own thrownness. Unlike Dilthey, Heidegger seeks a method of articulating the structural components of factical life, that is, the factical conditions of the intelligibility of Dasein's existence. He finds it in the hermeneutical method that Dilthey develops, but he puts it to philosophical rather than psychological use, namely, by investigating being rather than beings. Insofar as a hermeneutics of facticity is a philosophical interpretation that exhibits its own factical conditions, it is not really distinct from what it interprets and so is first-personal. Moreover, such a

[156] Heidegger SZ | GA 2: 314–5, translation modified.
[157] Heidegger SZ | GA 2: 315–6.

hermeneutics makes no problematic reference to Laskian transcendence and so remains within critical bounds. As we will now see, this positions Heidegger methodologically to critique the German idealist project of deductively eliminating facticity from the science of intelligibility and thereby to complete the transition from the primacy of the practical to the primacy of the factical.

6
The Nothing
Heidegger on Being Attuned to Facticity

6.1 Introduction

Kant invents transcendental logic as the science of the rules for thinking about objects of experience, a logic that is responsible for deducing the categories as universal and necessary conditions of intelligibility. The rhapsody problem, which he regards as inherited unsolved from Aristotle, is that the kind and number of the categories is equivalently brute, groundless, radically contingent, or, as it comes to be known, factical. This motivates Kant to provide, in addition to a transcendental deduction of our right to use the categories, a metaphysical deduction of the origin of our possession of the categories from the forms of judgment. Crucially, he thinks it is neither possible nor necessary to provide a metaphysical deduction of either the forms of judgment or the forms of sensibility insofar as they appear to be factical conditions of intelligibility. As we saw in Parts I and II, Fichte and Hegel subsequently regard the rhapsody problem as inherited unsolved from Kant, for they predicate the possibility of philosophy as a science on the elimination of facticity from all conditions of intelligibility. In order to realize this possibility, Fichte invents, and Hegel thereafter develops, dialectical logic as the method of the absolute science of intelligibility, which deduces the conditions of intelligibility from contradictions that reason, that is, thinking, discovers in itself.

In this final chapter, I will show that Heidegger dissolves rather than solves the rhapsody problem, namely, by pursuing an account of the conditions of intelligibility that is hermeneutical as opposed to deductive.[1] Moreover, I will also show that, in the process of substituting hermeneutical interpretation for dialectical logic, Heidegger makes significant philosophical improvements on various aspects of Schelling's, Lask's, and Dilthey's own critical responses to the German idealist confidence in reason. In particular, I will provide support for three important observations, which I will anticipate for now.

First, recall that Schelling, Lask, and Dilthey affirm the facticity of existence. Schelling holds that reason presupposes the existence of being for the sake of the

[1] Heidegger's account of the conditions of intelligibility arguably substitutes the juridical approach of Kant's transcendental deduction of the categories with the phenomenological approach of his metaphysical exposition of space and time, on which latter, see Carson 1997 and Parsons 1992. This has the effect of foreclosing not only the Cartesian demand for a proof of the world's reality (see Heidegger SZ | GA 2: 205, 211), but also the Humean demand for a justification of our use of the categories.

Facticity and the Fate of Reason After Kant. G. Anthony Bruno, Oxford University Press.
 DOI: 10.1093/9780191987533.003.0007

actuality, that is, the non-emptiness, of dialectically derived categories. Lask holds that reason presupposes the existence of individuals for the sake of the content, that is, the matter, of rationally deduced categories. And Dilthey holds that reason presupposes the existence of life for the sake of our understanding, that is, our interpretation, of human affairs. The first important observation will be that while Heidegger follows Schelling, Lask, and Dilthey by affirming the facticity of our existence as worldly, social, concernful, mortal, and temporal, his philosophical improvement in doing so is to assign the interpretation of facticity to hermeneutics. We saw in Chapter 5 that the hermeneutical method allows Heidegger to avoid the dogmatism of both Lask's appeal to alethiology and Dilthey's appeal to ineffability. But it also allows him to avoid the dualism of Schelling's appeal to the distinction between negative and positive philosophy. As we saw in Chapter 4, Schelling concedes that the conditions of intelligibility are dialectically derivable, even if existence is not. By contrast, Heidegger will deny that these conditions are so derivable insofar as dialectic presupposes and so reproduces its own factical conditions. As he says, "[w]hen today the attempt is made to connect the authentic fundamental tendency of phenomenology with dialectic, this is as if one wanted to mix fire and water."[2] Thus, whereas Schelling dualistically posits an irreducible difference between negative philosophy's derivation of conditions of intelligibility and positive philosophy's experiential openness to existence, Heidegger espouses no such two-stem science of intelligibility, but rather espouses a singular science, namely, phenomenology, whose hermeneutical method posits the irreducible identity of conditions of intelligibility and existence.

Second, recall that Schelling and Lask affirm our non-rational capacity for openness to the facticity of existence, which they identify as sensibility and life, respectively. The second important observation will be that while Heidegger follows Schelling and Lask by identifying mood and, in particular, anxiety as our non-rational capacity for openness to the facticity of existence, his philosophical improvement in doing so is to identify a capacity that is transformative rather than merely passive. Just as, for Schelling, sensibility is our passive receptivity to the givenness of being, so too, for Lask, life is our passive absorption in the givenness of individuals. By contrast, Heidegger will claim that anxiety does not simply open us to the givenness of being, but rather transforms us by moving us to ask why there is not nothing.

Third, recall that Schelling's critique of Hegel and, indeed, his entire philosophy are oriented primarily by the question of why there is something rather than nothing. The third important observation will be that while Heidegger follows Schelling in according orientational primacy to the why-question, his philosophical improvement in doing so is to construe this question as asking not simply

[2] Heidegger OHF | GA 63: 42.

why there is being, but rather why there is being-there, that is, why there is Dasein, and thus as demanding a hermeneutical interpretation of the facticity of Dasein. Such an interpretation concerns not just factical matters that Schelling does indeed register, namely, temporality and existence, but also, and more comprehensively, sociality, care, and mortality. Moreover, such an interpretation articulates an unspoken truth in '*nihil ulterius*' or 'nothing further,' which we saw in Section 1.2 is Kant's phrase for the ultimate groundlessness of intelligibility. In "What Is Metaphysics?," Heidegger says that "[t]he nothing itself nothings," a strange phrase that he immediately reformulates as the claim that the nothing "manifests. . .beings in their full but heretofore concealed strangeness," namely, "that they are beings—and not nothing." In other words, the nothing nothings insofar as it "unveils" the fact that the rationality or intelligibility of beings as a whole is radically contingent or factical in that they could well not be.[3] As Heidegger says in his 1935 summer lectures in Freiburg, *Introduction to Metaphysics*, beings are not "unquestionably given" and, in this respect, are groundless.[4] It is by moving us to ask the why-question and thereby grasp the groundlessness of being that anxiety facilitates a more comprehensive hermeneutical interpretation of the facticity of Dasein.

Before proceeding, it is worth recalling from Section 2.1 three aspects of Heidegger's conception of facticity in *Being and Time*.[5]

First, the facticity of Dasein's existence is "*not the factuality*" of "*something objectively present*," for it is "never to be found by looking." In other words, facticity is not an empirically contingent feature of Dasein, that is, something that is accidentally lived, for example, being in Freiburg. It is rather "*a characteristic of the being of Dasein taken on in existence*," for it is that to which Dasein is "*delivered over*" or "thrown."[6] In other words, facticity is an existentially necessary feature of Dasein, that is, something that is unavoidably lived, for example, being-in-the-world,

[3] Heidegger WM | W: 8, 11, translation modified. In 1931's "The Elimination of Metaphysics Through the Logical Analysis of Language," Rudolph Carnap charges that Heidegger's phrase 'the nothing' is meaningless or, at best, the expression of an unskilled artist (Carnap 1959: 69, 80). Contrast Wittgenstein: "To be sure, I can imagine what Heidegger means by being and anxiety. Man feels the urge to run up against the limits of language. Think for example of the astonishment that anything at all exists" (Wittgenstein 1979: 68). For an account of the seriousness of Carnap's charge, see Stone 2006. For a defense of Heidegger against the charge, see Inwood 1999, Käufer 2001, and Suarez 2023. See Käufer 2001 for an account of the neo-Kantian context of Heidegger's appeal to the nothing and his critique of logic.

[4] Heidegger EM | GA 40: 21.

[5] See Heidegger's letter to Löwith, August 20, 1927: "The problems of facticity exist for me just as they did in the beginning in Freiburg, only much more radically and now seen from the perspectives that were also guiding me there" (Heidegger C | 2021: 121).

[6] Heidegger SZ | GA 2: 135. Cf. Heidegger's 1925–26 winter lectures in Marburg, *Logic: The Question of Truth*: "By 'facticity' we understand a specific determination of the being of existence. The term does not have an indifferent meaning that would be the same as the factuality of something merely there. Nonetheless, it is, in a specific sense, a *factum* and we designate this specificity as facticity and will determine it more precisely later" (Heidegger L | GA 21: 233).

being-with-others, being-ahead-of-itself, being-toward-death, and being-time.[7] However, as we have seen, while the contingency of this feature is not empirical, its necessity is not logical, for it derives from no rational principle.[8]

Second, the "factuality" of a "stone" is "ontologically totally different" from the "*facticity*" of Dasein, since a stone is a "*what*" whose features are "of no importance to its existence" and which "comes into being and passes away 'with time,'" whereas Dasein is a "*who*" who "can understand itself as bound up in its 'destiny'" as "a being that has to be as it is and can be" and who "constantly *is* as having been."[9] In other words, Dasein differs in kind from an object that is indifferent toward its being because it has ineluctable concern for the being into which it is thrown, for its possibilities of being, and for the temporal horizon of these possibilities.[10] As Heidegger says, although Dasein is "never more than it is factically," it is "constantly 'more'" than "something objectively present."[11]

Third, Dasein's facticity is manifested, that is, "seen phenomenally," in the constitutive ways in which it is thrown, namely, as a being that is "always already thrown *into a world*" and is "sucked into the eddy" of the "inauthenticity" of others and so "*essentially falls prey to the world*."[12] In other words, Dasein is factically constituted by an average and uncritical understanding of itself in which what is "ontically nearest and familiar" is "ontologically the farthest, unrecognized, and constantly overlooked."[13]

I propose to situate Heidegger's conception of facticity in *Being and Time* at the midpoint of a two-stage development. In the first stage, during the eight years preceding *Being and Time*,[14] Heidegger argues that an interpretation of Dasein's

[7] See Heidegger's claim that the "constitutive characteristics of facticity" include "caring, the tendency toward falling, and the how of having death imminently before one" (Heidegger PIAA | 2002: 119).

[8] Cf. Merleau-Ponty's formulation of facticity's modal character: "there is no unconditioned possession in human existence, and yet neither is there any fortuitous attribute" (Merleau-Ponty 2012: 174).

[9] Heidegger SZ | GA 2: 45, 56, 276, 328. Contrast Spinoza's letter to Georg Hermann Schuller, October 1674: "A stone receives from the impulsion of an external cause a fixed quantity of motion whereby it will necessarily continue to move when the impulsion of the external cause has ceased. . .[C]onceive, if you please, that while continuing in motion the stone thinks, and knows that it is endeavouring, as far as in it lies, to continue in motion. Now this stone, since it is conscious only of its endeavour and is not at all indifferent, will surely think it is completely free, and that it continues in motion for no other reason than that it so wishes. This, then, is that human freedom which all men boast of possessing, and which consists solely in this, that men are conscious of their desire and unaware of the causes by which they are determined" (Spinoza 2002: 909).

[10] See Heidegger: "Existentials and categories are the two fundamental possibilities of the characteristics of being. The being which corresponds to them requires different ways of primary interrogation. Beings are a *who* (existence) or else a *what* (objective presence in the broadest sense)" (Heidegger SZ | GA 2: 45).

[11] Heidegger SZ | GA 2: 145.

[12] Heidegger SZ | GA 2: 179, 192, 222.

[13] Heidegger SZ | GA 2: 43.

[14] Kisiel divides the writing of *Being and Time* into the "hermeneutic" or "Dilthey" draft, i.e., the 1924 Marburg Theologians' Society public address "The Concept of Time," the "phenomenological-ontological" or "Husserl" draft, i.e., *History of the Concept of Time*, and the "existentialist" or "Kantian" draft, i.e., the final draft of *Being and Time* itself (Kisiel 1993: 9, 313).

factical life, since it presupposes that life for its very possibility, must be hermeneutical. Reconstructing this argument will not only further clarify Heidegger's phenomenological redirection of Dilthey's method of hermeneutics, which we saw in Section 5.6, but it will also bear out the first important observation that Heidegger improves on Schelling's, Lask's, and Dilthey's positions regarding the undeducibility of facticity. In the second stage, during the eight years following *Being and Time*,[15] Heidegger argues that mood attunes us to facticity, specifically, our anxiety before the nothing. Reconstructing this argument will bear out the second and third important observations that Heidegger improves on Schelling's and Lask's positions regarding our non-rational openness to facticity and on Schelling's position on the why-question. We will see that the two-stage development of Heidegger's conception of facticity yields a powerful objection to German idealism's anti-factical response to the question *quid facti*, namely, that the pursuit of a rationally cognized and exhaustively articulated origin for the conditions of intelligibility must be critiqued rather than indulged.

In this chapter, I will first reconstruct Heidegger's argument in his 1919 war emergency summer lectures in Freiburg, *The Idea of Philosophy and the Problem of Worldview*, that Hegelian dialectic is not presuppositionless because it presupposes the brute fact of lived experience (Section 6.2). I will then show that *Hermeneutics of Facticity* supplants the enlightenment ideal of rational cognition with the existential ideal of authenticity by showing how factical life expresses itself in modes of self-interpretation, including Hegelian philosophy, whose "inauthenticity" requires "*historical critique*" (Section 6.3).[16] Having thereby established the first stage of the development of Heidegger's conception of facticity, I will then begin to establish the second stage by examining his claim in 1929's *Kant and the Problem of Metaphysics* that we are "seized with vertigo when we try to determine [being]"

[15] Heidegger's 1930 "On the Essence of Truth" ends with a Note that reports that "[e]very kind of anthropology and all subjectivity of the human being as subject is not merely left behind—as it was already in *Being and Time*—and the truth of being sought as the ground of a transformed historical position; rather, the movement of the lecture is such that it sets out to think from this other ground (Dasein)" (Heidegger WW | W: 97). According to 1946's "Letter on 'Humanism,'" this Note "provides a certain insight into the thinking of the turning from 'Being and Time' to 'Time and Being'. This turning is not a change of standpoint from *Being and Time*, but in it the thinking that was sought first arrives at the locality of that dimension out of which *Being and Time* is experienced, that is to say, experienced in the fundamental experience of the oblivion of being" (Heidegger BüH | W: 159). Cf. Heidegger's 1969 seminar in Le Thor: "[b]y ek-sisting, Dasein includes *meaning*. The thinking that proceeds from *Being and Time*, in that it gives up the word 'meaning of being' in favour of 'truth of being', henceforth emphasizes the openness of being itself, rather than the openness of Dasein in regard to this openness of being" (Heidegger VS | GA 15: 83). Sheehan argues that "Heidegger's basic and abiding question is this: What makes intelligibility-at-all—*Sein*, which is always the *Sein* of things—necessary and possible? The early Heidegger's response was: our *a priori* thrown-openness as the clearing, and the later Heidegger's answer was the same: our structural appropriation to being the open space for discursive intelligibility. Thrownness and appropriation are identical, simply earlier and later names for the same existential structure." He infers that the turn is "only another name for Heidegger's abiding topic," about which his "thinking. . .underwent a change from a transcendental to a *seinsgeschichtlich* model in the 1930s" (Sheehan 2015: 236, 239).

[16] Heidegger OHF | GA 63: 74–6.

because it strikes us as "something like the nothing" (Section 6.4).[17] Next, I will articulate Heidegger's ironically anti-Hegelian claim in "What Is Metaphysics?" that asking about the nothing is only misguided if we are "misled" by the understanding's intolerance for contradiction (Section 6.5).[18] I will conclude by explicating Heidegger's claim in *Introduction to Metaphysics* that one "must necessarily become unscientific" in order to speak "truly" of the nothing, from which he infers that "scientific thinking" is "derivative" of "philosophical thinking," that is, derivative of "authentic, rigorous thinking" (Section 6.6).[19]

6.2 The Idea of a Presupposition

In *The Idea of Philosophy*, Heidegger pursues a "critical, scientific conception" of philosophy as "primordial science."[20] In Part One, Chapter One, "The Search for a Methodological Way," he says that primordial science investigates not "separate object-domains," but rather "what is common to them all," namely, "universal being." By contrast, a non-primordial or "particular" science investigates a definite "field of objects." Since no non-primordial science "encompasses all fields" of objects, it follows that primordial science is not derivable from any non-primordial science.[21] It follows, furthermore, that grasping the concept of a primordial science requires that one "deliver oneself over to the circle which lies within" this concept. This is to say that one must embrace the "circularity" of grasping the concept of primordial science from the standpoint of that science alone, a circularity that is "necessary" rather than "artificial" given the unavailability of any alternative, that is, any non-primordially scientific, access to this concept.[22]

In Chapter Two, "Critique of Teleological-Critical Method," Heidegger observes that, for the sake of its "unitary sense *as* knowledge," the "diversity and specificity" of the knowledge that the particular sciences afford us presuppose "*first* (fundamental) principles" that, since they "ground all proof," are "themselves unprovable" by these sciences. It is philosophy as primordial science that is tasked with demonstrating the validity of such principles. However, this raises the question of which "method" is appropriate for this task.[23] Heidegger claims that "philosophy begins" only with "the *teleological* method or, as it is otherwise called, the *critical method*," since, unlike the "genetic method (of psychology)," which investigates the "natural laws" that govern "how we in fact" think, the teleological-critical method

[17] Heidegger KPM | GA 3: 225–9.
[18] Heidegger WM | W: 6.
[19] Heidegger EM | GA 40: 19–20.
[20] Heidegger IP | GA 56/57 1: 9, 12. See Kisiel 1986.
[21] Heidegger IP | GA 56/57 1: 26.
[22] Heidegger IP | GA 56/57 1: 16.
[23] Heidegger IP | GA 56/57 1: 31–3.

investigates the principles or "norms" that govern "how we *ought to* think," where thinking has "the *telos* of *truth*."[24] In other words, demonstrating the validity of the principles of knowledge requires a method that grasps the normative role that these principles play for knowledge.

Heidegger credits Fichte with being "the first to recognize teleology as the method of the *Wissenschaftslehre*, i.e., as the method of philosophy." This is because,

> [f]or the first time, Fichte sought to derive systematically the forms of intuition and thought, the axioms and fundamental principles of the understanding, and the ideas of reason (all of which Kant, in the metaphysical and transcendental deduction, attempted to establish as the conditions of the possibility of the knowing consciousness) from a unitary principle and according to rigorous method, as the system of necessary actions of reason demanded by the very goal of reason. Reason can and must be understood only from itself; its laws and norms cannot be derived from a context external to it. The ego is egological fact-act [*Tathandlung*], it has to be active, its goal is the ought. In acting it sets itself a limit, but only in order to be able to sublate it again. The ought is the ground of being. Fichte did indeed work out the teleological idea in a radical manner, seeking the goal of reason in itself, as it gives itself in absolute self-knowing and self-insight. But he was also convinced that from this simple primordial act of the ego the multiplicity and diversity of qualitatively different functions of reason could be derived through pure deduction, i.e., through a constant and repeated overcoming of the posited limit. His teleological method was transformed into a constructive dialectic.[25]

This is an apt description of the *Wissenschaftslehre*. As we saw in Section 2.3, the gist of Fichte's system is that reason is absolutely free. As Heidegger puts it, Fichtean reason is "understood only from itself" such that the principles, that is, the "laws and norms," of knowledge "cannot be derived from a context external" to reason, but rather must be derived "systematically" from a "unitary principle" of reason "according to a rigorous method," namely, a "constructive dialectic." Although such a derivation is merely "attempted" by Kant in the "metaphysical and transcendental deduction[s]", Fichte's derivation serves the "goal of reason," which, as we saw in Section 3.5, is the regulative ideal of resolving the originary contradiction between the I and the not-I.

However, Heidegger charges that Fichte "overlook[s]" the fact that in order to demonstrate the validity of the principles of knowledge and their normative bearing on true thinking, the teleological-critical method

[24] Heidegger IP | GA 56/57 1: 35–6. Cf. Husserl LU1 | 2001: Chapter One, §§19, 22.
[25] Heidegger IP | GA 56/57 1: 37.

> requires a substantive material guideline in which the goal of reason might realize itself, and in which the actions of reason are themselves to be discovered in their universal character. This material, the empirical psychic context, does provide the determinations of content for thought-forms and norms, but it does not *ground* their validity. It is, so to speak, only an occasion and impetus for finding them—they are *grounded* in a teleological manner.[26]

Fichte neglects the fact that reason's pursuit of its regulative "goal" depends on "a substantive material guideline," namely, the "psychic context" that, although it does not "*ground*" the "validity" of the principles of knowledge, "occasion[s]" the "determination" of their "content." What precisely is this context?

We can begin to answer this question by observing that Heidegger specifies his charge against Fichte in a way that implies its extension to Hegel. Heidegger claims that "the inner impossibility of a *dialectical*-teleological deduction of the system of necessary actions and necessary forms of reason" results from the fact that

> [d]ialectic in the sense of resolving ever newly posited contradictions is *substantively uncreative*; moreover, the positing of contradictions is itself possible only through a hidden non-dialectical principle which on account of its own hiddenness and unclarity is not in a position to ground the character and validation of the deduced forms and norms as genuine ones. The dialectic of antithesis and synthesis cannot be activated by itself: it remains condemned to an unproductive standstill, or else it unfolds itself on the implicit and methodologically arbitrary basis of something substantively given, or at least presupposed.[27]

Like Fichte, Hegel provides a dialectical deduction of the conditions of intelligibility that makes productive use of "contradictions" in order to "validat[e]" these conditions. Heidegger's charge is that dialectic is "*substantively uncreative*" because contradictions neither emerge from nor are resolved by reason alone. Rather, their "unfold[ing]" is "activated" by and thus "presuppose[s]" a "hidden non-dialectical principle," namely, "something substantively given." Shortly after, Heidegger claims that it is the "*methodological function*" of psychology to provide this "something," that is, this "*already given material*." Acknowledging that a psychological determination of the content or material of dialectical deduction suggests the invocation of a non-primordial science, he immediately asks: "does this not involve a fundamental *deformation of method* from the very beginning?" Indeed, we might worry that a psychological approach would repeat the ontic error with which he charges Dilthey. Heidegger aims to remove this worry by claiming that once

[26] Heidegger IP | GA 56/57 1: 37.
[27] Heidegger IP | GA 56/57 1: 40.

psychology provides the matter of deduction, it "has nothing more to do" and, "as it were, withdraws."[28] How can we make sense of this claim?

We can see that psychology's "withdraw[al]" reflects Heidegger's earlier claim that it merely occasions the determination of the content, but does not ground the validity, of the principles of knowledge, since grounding validity is the task of philosophy. Hence he says that psychology cannot fulfill "the complete characterization of material giving," which completeness demands both determining the content and grounding the validity of principles.[29] However, it is not yet clear how precisely to characterize the matter that psychology's withdrawal leaves to deduction, where this matter is supposed to contain the non-dialectical principle that "activate[s]" and so is "given" to and "presupposed" by Fichte's and Hegel's dialectical deductions.

Heidegger characterizes the matter in question by raising a regress problem for description. Psychology describes psychic phenomena. But description "is surely a psychic phenomenon and thus itself belongs to the sphere of the material thing." This leads Heidegger to ask whether description is merely a phenomenon, that is, merely "one thing" among many, a question that he answers rhetorically: "Is there even a single thing when there are only things? Then there would be no thing at all; not even *nothing*, because with the sole supremacy of the sphere of things there is not even the 'there is.'"[30] If psychological descriptions are strictly psychical phenomena, then a regress threatens, since such phenomena will in turn require their own descriptions, and so on *ad infinitum*, in which case there can be no standing or abiding descriptive perspective on phenomena. Consequently, description cannot be one among many things. Heidegger's rhetorical expression of this response to the regress problem is to say that if "there are only things," then "there is not even a 'there is'" that could be intelligible to some descriptive perspective. But, in that case, there is not even intelligibly "a single thing." How should we understand this response?

We can compare Heidegger's response to the regress problem with Kant's argument in the A-edition transcendental deduction that if there are only "determinations of our state," which are "merely empirical, forever variable," then there is "no standing or abiding self," which is the apperceptive condition of the possibility of "empirical data," in which case there is not even empirical data.[31] As Kant reformulates this argument in the B-edition transcendental deduction, if there is only "empirical consciousness", then there is no apperceptive "**I think**" that is "**able** to accompany all my representations," in which case these representations are "nothing."[32] Heidegger's response to the regress problem for description and

[28] Heidegger IP | GA 56/57 1: 41–2.
[29] Heidegger IP | GA 56/57 1: 57–8.
[30] Heidegger IP | GA 56/57 1: 61–2.
[31] Kant A107.
[32] Kant B131–3.

the two formulations of Kant's argument in the deduction each express what I will call the 'transcendental idealist insight' that things alone cannot be intelligible because they afford no perspective on their intelligibility, whether descriptive or apperceptive.[33]

Now, Heidegger infers from the transcendental idealist insight that the matter that contains the non-dialectical principle that dialectical deduction presupposes cannot be grasped "empirical[ly]", that is, by a non-primordial science, as being composed solely of things. Rather, this matter must be grasped by "primordial science,"[34] which investigates universal being. This implies that the matter in question is not restricted to any particular domain of things, which avoids Dilthey's ontic error. But then such matter cannot be something of which we have theoretical knowledge, since theoretical knowledge consists in knowledge of things in particular domains. Hence, regarding this matter, Heidegger says that the "primacy of the theoretical" must be "broken" because it in fact "refers back to something pre-theoretical."[35] We can therefore finally say that the matter that dialectical deduction presupposes is accessible pre-theoretically, namely, as lived experience. Whereas a "psychic process in itself, isolated as a thing, explains nothing," since, as the transcendental idealist insight shows, mere things afford no perspective on their intelligibility, the matter in question is something that "lives."[36] It is pre-theoretical lived experience, then, that serves as the "material guideline" or "hidden" principle of Fichte's and Hegel's dialectical deductions.[37]

In Part Two, Chapter One, "Analysis of the Structure of Experience," Heidegger states that philosophy stands at a "methodological crossroad" between "nothingness, that is, absolute reification, pure thingness," and "the leap into the world as such."[38] In other words, philosophy must decide between, on the one hand, an empirical, that is, non-primordial, investigation of a particular object-domain that neglects the transcendental idealist insight that there cannot intelligibly be only things or "pure thingness" and, on the other hand, a "leap" that reaffirms the standpoint of our lived experience of the world. Heidegger invites us to "remain with the sense of the lived experience, keeping a firm hold on what it gives," which he

[33] Cf. Novalis: "I is basically nothing—Everything has to be given to it—But it is to it alone that something can be given and the given only becomes something via the I" (Novalis 1978: 185, translated by Bowie 2003: 22).
[34] Heidegger IP | GA 56/57 1: 60.
[35] Heidegger IP | GA 56/57 1: 59.
[36] Heidegger IP | GA 56/57 1: 64–6.
[37] Cf. Windelband's 1883 "Critical or Genetic Method?": "the deeper error of the *Wissenschaftslehre* consists in that it supposes itself able from the determination of the end alone. . .to *deduce* all the means to its realization. This is why, in order to teleologically construct the progress from one 'action of reason' to the other, it had to lay down contradictions from one step to the next, whose dissolution was supposed to propel it onward, and so the critical method became the *dialectical* method. But this can no more retrieve the manifold of the specific out of its principle than any other form of deduction" (Windelband 2015: 282).
[38] Heidegger IP | GA 56/57 1: 63.

reports is not something that "pass[es] in front of me like a thing" that is meaninglessly received, but rather is something that "I appropriate" as a meaningful situation.[39] Faced with a lectern, for example, I am not given things that I first perceive as adjacent brown surfaces, then conceive as a "box," and finally "label" with "lectern-hood." This, he says, is "simply bad and misguided interpretation, diversion from a pure seeing into the experience." Rather, I experience the lectern "in one fell swoop" from within an "environmental milieu" as having a "meaning" that is "primary and immediately given to me without any mental detours across thing-oriented apprehension" and as serving a vital function, namely, public speaking.[40] As Heidegger says in Chapter Two, "The Problem of Presuppositions," it is a "theoretical infringement" to regard "environmental experience" as "a mere thing" that is "*given*" to us initially as meaningless, for this is a "de-vivification" of our normally situated grasp of the meaning of things.[41]

In response to the "repeated objection" that lived experience "*presuppose[s]*" the "reality of the external world," Heidegger partially prefigures his distinction in *Being and Time* between the logical and hermeneutical meanings of 'presupposition,' which we saw in Section 5.6, by claiming that 'pre-' in 'presupposition' "refers to a relation of logical ordering" that holds between "theoretical propositions," a relation in which a proposition posits the validity of the proposition that "ground[s]" it. He infers from this that experience cannot presuppose reality because experience contains "*no theoretical positing* at all." The objection expresses "the point of view of epistemology," which conflates the experienced world, that is, the world in which Dasein is always already meaningfully absorbed, with the "theorized world," that is, the world that is composed of relations of propositions about

[39] Heidegger IP | GA 56/57 1: 67, 76.

[40] Heidegger IP | GA 56/57 1: 71–3. Cf. Heidegger: "What is there in *the* room there at home is *the* table (not 'a' table among many other tables in other rooms and houses) at which one sits *in order to* write, have a meal, sew, play. Everyone sees this right away, e.g., during a visit: it is a writing table, a dining table, a sewing table—such is the primary way in which it is being encountered in itself. This characteristic of 'in order to do something' is not merely imposed on the table by relating and assimilating it to something else which it is not" (Heidegger OHF | GA 63: 90). Cf. also Heidegger: "the ontological distinction between *res cogitans* and *res extensa*, between I and not-I, to speak formally, cannot in any way be conceived directly and simply, as for instance in the form that Fichte uses to initiate the problem when he says, 'Gentlemen, think the wall, and then think the one who thinks the wall.' There is already a constructive violation of the facts, an unphenomenological onset, in the request 'Think the wall.' For in our natural comportment toward things we never think a *single* thing, and whenever we seize upon it expressly for itself we are taking it *out* of a contexture to which it belongs in its real content: wall, room, surroundings. The request 'Think the wall,' understood as the beginning of a return to the one who is thinking the wall, as the beginning of the philosophical interpretation of the subject, is saying: 'Make yourselves blind to what is already given to you in the very first place and for all apprehending that is explicitly thinking.' But what is thus antecedently given? How do the beings with which we dwell show themselves to us primarily and for the most part? Sitting here in the auditorium, we do not in fact apprehend walls—not unless we are getting bored. Nevertheless, the walls are already present even before we think them as objects. Much else also gives itself to us before any determining of it by thought. Much else—but how? Not as a jumbled heap, but as an environs, a surroundings, which contains within itself a closed, intelligible contexture" (Heidegger GP | GA 24: 231–2).

[41] Heidegger IP | GA 56/57 1: 88, 90.

things.[42] But just as experience is not a thing that is meaninglessly received, but rather is a situation that is meaningfully appropriated, so too experience exceeds the logical order of propositions about things. Thus, by exceeding relations of logical ordering, lived experience escapes Hegel's project of presuppositionlessness insofar as this project employs dialectic in order to establish the immanence of intelligibility within logically ordered relations. Indeed, Heidegger implicitly relies on a version of the Schellingian distinction from Section 4.5 between intra-logical presuppositions, which are dialectically derivable moments of the science of intelligibility, and extra-logical presuppositions, which are radically contingent or brute facts that transcend that science by making it possible. This is because while lived experience is not composed of relations in which some propositions presuppose the validity of others, it is, as we saw, the "hidden non-dialectical principle" that is "presupposed" by dialectic as a brute fact.[43] Insofar as dialectic presupposes lived experience, then, the meaning of this presupposition is not logical, but rather, as we will see in more detail, hermeneutical.[44]

We saw that lived experience, that is, the matter that psychology provides to deduction and from which it withdraws, must be grasped by primordial science. We also saw that lived experience exceeds relations of logical ordering that hold between theoretical propositions as determined by dialectic. It follows that dialectic cannot be primordial science. Thus, in Chapter Three, "Primordial Science as Pre-Theoretical Science," Heidegger says that "the very idea of a *system* that would essentially absolutize the theoretical" is "illusory," from which he concludes that, "in one of the most difficult confrontations, we stand on the front against Hegel."[45] Whereas Hegel employs dialectic in order to establish a truly absolute,

[42] Heidegger IP | GA 56/57 1: 93. Cf. Heidegger: "Even if one wanted to fall back on the fact that the subject must presuppose, and indeed always already does unconsciously presuppose, the fact that the 'external world' is objectively present, one would still be starting with the construct of an isolated subject. The phenomenon of being-in-the-world would no more be met with than it would be by demonstrating that the physical and the psychical are objectively present together. With such presuppositions, Dasein always already comes 'too late', because, in that it carries out this presupposition as a being (and otherwise this would not be possible), *as a being*, it is always already in a world. 'Earlier' than any presupposition that Dasein makes, or any of its ways of behavior, there is the '*a priori*' of its constitution of being in the mode of being of care" (Heidegger SZ | GA 2: 205–6).

[43] See Heidegger's letter to Hannah Arendt, February 15, 1972: "You are right: Schelling is much more difficult than Hegel; he risks more and sometimes leaves dry land entirely behind. Hegel always stays safely on the rails of the dialectic" (Arendt and Heidegger 2004: 191).

[44] See Heidegger: "Ontology and logic need to be brought back to their original unity in the problem of facticity and understood as offshoots of fundamental research into principles that can be described as 'the *phenomenological hermeneutics* of facticity'" (Heidegger PIAA | 2002: 121).

[45] Heidegger IP | GA 56/57 1: 96. Cf. Heidegger's 1935–36 winter lectures in Freiburg, *The Question Concerning the Thing: On Kant's Doctrine of the Transcendental Principles*: "Hegel alone seemingly succeeded in leaping over this shadow—but only in such a way that he eliminated the shadow (i.e., the finitude of the human being) and leapt into the sun itself. Hegel leapt over the shadow, but he did not thereby surpass the shadow" (Heidegger FD | GA 41: 153). Cf. also Heidegger: "there exists. . .the legitimate demand to start anew, to understand the finiteness of the Hegelian system" (Heidegger GP | GA 24: 400). On the role of temporality in Heidegger's critique of Hegel, see de Boer 2000. For an analysis of Heidegger's still unpublished 1925 winter lectures on Hegel, see Gonzalez 2022.

that is, presuppositionless, science of intelligibility, Heidegger argues that dialectic presupposes lived experience as a brute fact, that is, as the pre-theoretical "origin" from which dialectical theorizing "spring[s]." Hence Heidegger says that the possibility of a primordial science, which he calls "a science of experiences," "cannot be decided by dialectical exercises."[46] Were we to construct the science of experience dialectically, experience would be "no longer lived, but looked at," that is, we would " 'still the stream' as Natorp says."[47] Conditions of intelligibility would be shown to be absolutely necessary, but only by evading the manifest facticity or thrownness of our lived experience. Just as we de-vivify our situated grasp of the meaning of things by reducing experience from an "environmental milieu" to an indifferent space, so too we de-vivify experience by reducing it from an environing situation in which we are immediately open to the meaning of, for example, a lectern, to a general type of interaction in which we represent objects as mediated by concepts, for example, 'brown' and 'box-shaped.' In this, we theorize about the pre-theoretical, freezing our normally absorbed dealings with equipment into logical relations among propositions about things. As we saw, this "mental detour" deadens our grasp of meanings that are "primary and immediately given" to us.

Heidegger concludes *The Idea of Philosophy* by announcing that the "scientific disclosure of the sphere of lived experience" is the "fundamental methodological problem of phenomenology." As we saw, the science of experience must be primordial. Heidegger claims that phenomenology qualifies as primordial science because it begins from what, in 1913's *Ideas Pertaining to a Pure Phenomenology and to a Phenomenological Philosophy, First Book: General Introduction to a Pure Phenomenology*, Husserl calls the "*principle of all principles: that everything originally* (so to speak, in its 'personal' actuality) *offered* to us *in 'intuition' is to be accepted simply as what it is presented as being*, but also *only within the limits in which it is presented there*."[48] According to Heidegger, "although Husserl does not

[46] Heidegger IP | GA 56/57 1: 97–8. Cf. Heidegger: "To be sharply separated therefore are: the pre-worldly something of life in itself, the formally objective arising from this (only from this?) as de-vivification, and the object-like theoretical. The first sphere, as that of life, is absolute, the two others are relative, conditioned" (Heidegger IP | GA 56/57 1: 116).

[47] Heidegger IP | GA 56/57 1: 100–1, cited from Natorp 1912: 190–1. Ironically, by predicating philosophy on the idea that all "particular directions of knowledge. . .must proceed as necessary emanations" from "the object-relation in general" (Natorp 1918: 432), Natorp, according to Heidegger, is guilty of "radically logiciz[ing] the sphere of experience" and hence of the "most radical absolutization of the theoretical and logical, an absolutization that has not been proclaimed since Hegel. (Unmistakable connections with Hegel: everything unmediated is mediated.)" (Heidegger IP | GA 56/57 1: 108). Nevertheless, see Natorp: "Hegel presumes to have brought the lawfulness of thinking to an absolute conclusion, which he invariably describes as circular and which is expected to produce the entire contents of thought. It is for this reason that his philosophy could adopt the outrageous pretense of itself being the conclusion of philosophy, in the form of absolute philosophy, which is at the same time absolute science. Transcendental idealism, as we view it, is legions away from such pretense; in an entirely non-Hegelian manner, it presents philosophy with the modest task of critique, or, positively applied, of method. This method is thought to be immanent to research and quite generally to cultural achievement, but also to be open to infinite further development" (Natorp 2015: 189).

[48] Heidegger IP | GA 56/57 1: 109, corrected citation from Husserl IRP1 | 1982: 44.

explicitly say so," this principle expresses "absolute *sympathy with life*" because it posits the "primordial bearing of life-experience," which is "not achieved by any constructed system of concepts," but rather is intuited. It is accordingly "separated by a chasm from every kind of *logicism*," including Hegelian dialectic. Heidegger immediately adds that the principle "has not the slightest connection with the *philosophy of feeling*," which, by isolating subjective states from objective scenarios, violates the principle's demand that we accept what is intuited "*within the limits in which it is presented*," namely, the environmental milieu that situates, for example, a lectern's meaning in relation to the vital function of public speaking.[49] Phenomenology is the science of experience, then, because it begins with neither "concepts" nor "*feeling*," but rather with intuition, which Heidegger clarifies is "the understanding intuition, the *hermeneutical intuition*, the originary phenomenological back-and-forth formation of the recepts and precepts from which all theoretical objectification, indeed every transcendent positing, falls out."[50] Faced with a lectern, I have an "understanding intuition" of it insofar as I am competent in using it for the various purposes of lecturing. My intuition is "*hermeneutical*," moreover, since I acquire this competence through a series of mutually illuminating encounters with the lecture notes, lecture hall, and audience with which the lectern is situated, that is, a "back-and-forth" flow in which a whole, namely, the activity of public speaking, sheds light on one of its parts, namely, the lectern, and vice versa. It is only by suspending this flow that I am able to offer a "theoretical objectification" of the lectern as parts that are arranged lectern-wise. Intuition is my access to an environmental milieu and, ultimately, a livable world, that is only derivatively conceivable in terms of domains of objects. Phenomenology is accordingly primordial science because, in the terms of Chapter 1, it investigates lived experience not as one among many "object-domains," but rather as "what is common to them all." It is through this science that, Heidegger says, "the puzzling presence of determination prior to all theoretical description is clarified."[51]

The final sentence of *The Idea of Philosophy* states that the "[p]roblem of material giving is not genuine, but only comes from theory."[52] We can see why this

[49] Heidegger IP | GA 56/57 1: 110.
[50] Heidegger IP | GA 56/57 1: 117. Cf. Husserl: "And above all—to dispose of an important point right away—one must not go straight back to the supposedly immediately given 'sense-data', as if *they* were immediately characteristic of the purely intuitive data of the life-world. What is actually first is the 'merely subjective-relative' intuition of pre-scientific world-life" (Husserl K | 1970a: 125). Cf. Husserl PK | 1970b: 295.
[51] Heidegger IP | GA 56/57 1: 117. Heidegger implies a criticism of Husserl's method of categorial intuition: "By showing how all sight is primarily based on understanding—the circumspection of taking care of things is understanding as *common sense*—we have taken away from pure intuition its priority which noetically corresponds to the traditional ontological priority of objective presence. 'Intuition' and 'thought' are both already remote derivatives of understanding. Even the phenomenological 'intuition of essences' is based on existential understanding" (Heidegger SZ | GA 2: 147). On Heidegger's criticism, see Carman 2007.
[52] Heidegger IP | GA 56/57 1: 117.

is so. We saw that psychology provides the matter that dialectical derivation presupposes as a brute fact, namely, lived experience. This might invite the charge that psychology's "material giving" is problematic insofar as this giving is brute or groundless. However, this charge is "not genuine," for it makes the unwarranted theoretical assumption that the meaning of the presupposition of lived experience is restricted to "relation[s] of logical ordering" among propositions, whereas, as we will soon see, its relevant meaning is hermeneutical insofar as lived experience is that which is originally, that is, pre-logically, interpretable. For Heidegger, psychology is only a partial contribution to a "complete characterization of material giving," which completeness requires not only determining the content, but also grounding the validity, of the principles of knowledge. This grounding is to be provided by the science of experience, namely, phenomenology, whose method of the analysis of principles consists in hermeneutical interpretation. Thus, by withdrawing from its provision of lived experience, psychology leaves a truly primordial science in its wake.[53]

By arguing that dialectical derivations presuppose lived experience as a brute fact whose structural analysis falls to hermeneutical method, *The Idea of Philosophy* opens the first stage of the development of Heidegger's conception of facticity. This bears out the first important observation, namely, that, by turning to the method of hermeneutics, Heidegger improves on Schelling's, Lask's, and Dilthey's positions regarding the undeducibility of facticity, which appeal, respectively, to dualism, alethiology, and ineffability.

6.3 Authenticity After Enlightenment

In the 1921–22 winter lectures in Freiburg, *Phenomenological Interpretations of Aristotle: Initiation into Phenomenological Research*, Heidegger provides an account of philosophy's flight from facticity. It is worth considering this account, for it prefigures his critique of inauthenticity in *Hermeneutics of Facticity* the following year.

In Part II, Chapter Two, "The Appropriation of the Situation in which Understanding is Rooted," Heidegger says:

> insofar as we understand that factical life is actually always in flight from matters of principle, then it is no wonder that the appropriating turn toward matters does not happen readily and without further ado. The frequent appearance of

[53] See Heidegger's 1919–21 "Comments on Karl Jasper's 'Psychology of Worldviews'": "the concrete self should be taken up into the starting point of our approach to philosophical problems, and brought to 'givenness' at the genuinely fundamental level of phenomenological interpretation, namely, that level of interpretation that is related to the factical experience of life as such" (Heidegger AKJ | 1998: 30)

> one who, it is claimed, 'champions principles' is not evidence against what we have just said, but rather supports it, insofar as such a person's loud invocation of principles on every occasion is actually a sure announcement of the flight in question.[54]

Factical life is the lived experience into which we are thrown. Heidegger claims that factical life is "always in flight from matters of principle." It is important that "the flight in question" is from "matters of principle," not from "principles" as such. As we saw, the matter of dialectical derivations of the principles of knowledge is a brute fact, namely, lived experience or what Heidegger here calls "factical life." Fichtean and Hegelian dialectic rationalistically recoils from this matter due to its radical contingency, "champion[ing]" principles, namely, intelligibility conditions of absolute necessity, in an "eviden[t]" flight from facticity. Thus, while it is not difficult to observe a flight from facticity in commonsensical, religious, and natural-scientific appeals to varieties of necessity,[55] it is just as easily observable in philosophy's "loud invocation of principles." As Kant says in the B-edition Introduction to the first *Critique*, "nothing is more natural" than that a critique of our capacity for *a priori* cognition "should long have been neglected" by philosophers and so is not "that which usually happens."[56] Similarly, Heidegger says that "it is no wonder" that "appropriating" the bruteness of lived experience "does not happen readily" for philosophers. Crucially, since philosophers are not really distinct from the factical life from which they flee, we can say that factical life flees from itself.

In Part III, Chapter One, "The Basic Categories of Life," Heidegger registers a constitutive relationship between life and world. When we "concretely" grasp the verb 'to live,' its "intransitive" sense gives way to the transitive sense of living in, out of, for, with, or against "something," which something "we call 'world.'" As a "phenomenological category," 'world' names "*what* is lived" in these ways. Indeed, Heidegger says, it is "the basic category of the content-sense in the phenomenon, life."[57] World thus indicates itself as categorially constituting life.[58]

Heidegger then notes that although a category is in general a "principle" that "brings the phenomenon to intelligibility," when that phenomenon is life, a category is understood "only insofar as factical life itself is compelled to interpretation," that is, only insofar as we are compelled to interpret life.[59] However, as we saw, we

[54] Heidegger PIA | GA 61: 71.
[55] See Heidegger: "Common sense has its own necessity; it asserts its rights with the weapon peculiarly suitable to it, namely, appeal to the 'obviousness' of its claims and considerations" (Heidegger WW | W: 74).
[56] Kant KrV A3–4/B7–8.
[57] Heidegger PIA | GA 61: 85–6.
[58] On the role of formal indication in Heidegger's interpretation of the categories, see Burch 2013, Dahlstrom 1994, Nir 2021, and Shockey 2010.
[59] Heidegger PIA | GA 61: 86.

are not "readily" so "compelled," given our natural flight from factical life. Thus, understanding a category of life, which is precisely the task of phenomenology as the science of lived experience, demands our resolve to interrupt our self-flight and turn toward ourselves.[60]

As we saw, resistance to taking this turn afflicts philosophy, namely, when it is concerned "primarily" with the "universal validity" of the categories. Heidegger claims that philosophy's concern with validity is driven by fear of the "danger" of "[s]kepticism," one guise of which is the doubt that motivates the rhapsody charge and its successor charge against facticity and that yearns for the dialectical deduction of absolutely necessary conditions of intelligibility. Philosophy thereby becomes "closed off" to facticity as "the basic sense of the being of life." However, if philosophy instead faces up to the facticity of its life, then it can recognize that the categories are "*alive in life itself*," that is, that their content and use presuppose factical life and so presuppose a radically contingent origin. Consequently, although a "progressive interpretation" of the categories serves to clarify life's initial "haziness," that is, the original unclarity about the conditions of its intelligibility, the categories always presuppose life such that this clarification is never independent of the phenomenon whose intelligibility they provide. The interpretation of the categories of life, which Heidegger will call the 'existentials' of Dasein, therefore "must essentially be *repeated*," namely, by increasingly intensifying the richness of the intelligibility that the category of the world initially brings to the phenomenon of life.[61] Hence, in Division One of *Being and Time*, Heidegger's phenomenological interpretation of the world in which Dasein exists reveals that it is a "*with-world*" that Dasein shares with others and, moreover, is "taken care of" through Dasein's concernfulness.[62] And in Division Two, insofar as Dasein is ceaselessly concerned for its "potentiality-of-being" and so is "constitut[ed]" by a "*constant unfinished quality*," which raises the question of what brings "Dasein as a whole into view," this interpretation reveals that the social and concerning world

[60] Cf. Kant: "the reader must be convinced of the unavoidable necessity of such a transcendental deduction [of the categories] before he has taken a single step in the field of pure reason; for he would otherwise proceed blindly, and after much wandering around would still have to return to the ignorance from which he had begun" (Kant KrV A88/B121).

[61] Heidegger PIA | GA 61: 88–9. In his 1921 summer lecture *Augustine and Neo-Platonism*, Heidegger says that "all explicates of sense" in factical life are "*existentiale*, that is, 'categories' formally viewed, and indeed *enactment-historically hermeneutic* categories" (Heidegger AN | GA 60 2: 232).

[62] Heidegger SZ | GA 2: 118, 184. Cf. Heidegger: "where something *strange* presses into the world closest to us and we happen across it. . .the question 'what is it?' explicates itself into a 'What is it for? What are we supposed to do with it? Who is it for? What is it supposed to be? Who made it?'. . .*Spatiality*, which is saturated in a factical manner with concern, has its distances—it is there as: too far, nearby, through this street, through the kitchen, a stone's throw, behind the cathedral, and the like" (Heidegger OHF | GA 63: 95, 101–2). Cf. also Heidegger's argument that, since 'being-ahead-of-itself' signifies neither "a worldless 'subject'" nor a subject not "entangled" in "publicness," being-in-the-world and being-with-others "are *also posited*" in being-ahead-of-itself (Heidegger SZ | GA 2: 192–3). And cf. Heidegger WD | 2002: 163.

comes to an "end" for Dasein, namely, in resolute anticipation of death.[63] Finally, insofar as Dasein's being-ahead-of-itself is "grounded in the future" and thereby "makes known" its "being *present*" and "having-been," this interpretation reveals that Dasein's social, concerning, and mortal world has the "*primordial unity*" of "*temporality*."[64] This is why Heidegger calls the existentials "pregnant structures."[65]

Finally, in Chapter Two, "Ruinance," Heidegger describes life's flight from itself in terms of "ruinance," which signifies life's movement "*against* itself" and is a correlate term for 'fallenness.'[66] He predicates a "counter-ruinant" movement on philosophy's openness to "questioning" rather than evading its factical life, that is, its openness to recognizing that facticity is "the main issue in philosophy."[67] Heidegger clarifies that philosophy's "*struggle*. . .*against its own factical ruinance*," that is, against its natural flight from itself, requires that it pursue a "genuine questioning" of facticity, namely, by not relying "mechanically" on "an empty maxim" of questioning "in any way whatsoever," but rather by relying on "motives" that "receive their direction from factical life."[68] We can hear in this clarification of philosophy's struggle against self-flight an implicit critique of the enlightenment ideal of rational cognition, one that Heidegger will develop in *Hermeneutics of Facticity*.

Recall that Kant contrasts enlightenment with minority, which is characterized by the mechanical perpetuation and thus tacit endorsement of the received wisdom of shared precepts and formulas, and that he identifies enlightenment with maturity, which is characterized by understanding without another's direction. There is, it turns out, a sense in which maturity itself can be pursued "mechanically," namely, according to the "empty maxim" of refusing to take direction "in any way whatsoever," that is, of refusing to take direction not only from others, but also "from factical life." As we saw in Chapter 3, Fichte and Hegel offer radicalized enlightenment ideals that are mechanical in precisely this sense. Consequently, they entrench life's ruinant evasion of itself. By contrast, the "genuine" questioning on which Heidegger rests counter-ruinance, even if it refuses to take direction from others, nevertheless "receive[s]" its direction from life in the form of an awareness that, since the categories presuppose the phenomenon of life as their radically contingent origin, their interpretation is never independent of this phenomenon and so must be "*repeated*" in a way that intensifies the intelligibility that they bring to

[63] Heidegger SZ | GA 2: 233–4, 236. Cf. Heidegger: "Death is not pieced on to Dasein as its 'end', but, as care, Dasein is the thrown (that is, null) ground of its death. . .Care contains death and guilt equiprimordially" (Heidegger SZ | GA 2: 306).

[64] Heidegger SZ | GA 2: 326–7.

[65] Heidegger SZ | GA 2: 44. We might wonder whether existentials are endlessly fertile and so might worry that phenomenology assists with the birth of implausibly many structures. A plausible guideline for intensifying the intelligibility that the category of the world brings to life is that it can only yield conditions of intelligibility without which our pre-reflective engagement with the world is unimaginable.

[66] See Campbell 2012.

[67] Heidegger PIA | GA 61: 99, 131.

[68] Heidegger PIA | GA 61: 152–4.

life. We will now see that, quickly following the *Phenomenological Interpretations of Aristotle*, Heidegger develops his implicit critique of enlightenment into a historical critique of inauthenticity.

Hermeneutics of Facticity begins by evoking the distinction between primordial and non-primordial science. In the Introduction, Heidegger describes a twofold "*inadequacy*" of traditional ontology. First, whereas traditional ontology takes as its theme "being-an-*object*," ontology is properly the "doctrine of being," whose "secure basis," he says, only phenomenology provides. Phenomenology is thus primordial science. Second, traditional ontology takes as its theme the object-domain of "particular," that is, non-primordial, "sciences of nature," which "blocks access to that being which is decisive within philosophical problems, namely, *Dasein*, from out of which and for the sake of which, philosophy 'is.'"[69] If, at its "methodological crossroad," philosophy makes a "leap into the world" as it is lived, then it begins phenomenologically from our experience of the world, that is, from our Dasein or being-there. By making this leap, phenomenology investigates pre-theoretical experience not as an object-domain about which to theorize, but rather as "what is common" to all such domains, that is, as the factical origin that they all presuppose. Phenomenology is therefore primordial science just insofar as it is the science of experience. It is to the interpretive method by which phenomenology investigates experience that I now turn.

Prefiguring his conception of facticity in *Being and Time* as the mark of a thrown existence for whose possibilities we have ineluctable concern within a temporal horizon, in Part One, "Paths of Interpreting the Being-There of Dasein in the Awhileness of Temporal Particularity," Heidegger says that 'facticity' designates "the character of the being of 'our' 'own' *Dasein*," which is "never" there "primarily as an *object*," but rather is "*there* for itself."[70] In Chapter One, "Hermeneutics," he assigns phenomenology's method of interpreting facticity to hermeneutics, which alone can interpret facticity in a "unified manner" because it explicates factical life "out of" and "on the basis of" that which is to be explicated. No less than dialectic, a hermeneutics of facticity presupposes lived experience. However, it does so wittingly, for it recognizes that its "conceptual explicata," namely, the "*existentials*" that constitute Dasein's possibility of being, are not really distinct from the matter that they explicate.[71] This is because hermeneutical interpretation, which is itself a meaningful pursuit of Dasein, manifests the very brute fact that it interprets. Hermeneutics thereby exhibits the "back-and-forth" character of providing mutually illuminating interpretations of that which makes its own interpretations

[69] Heidegger OHF | GA 63: 1–3.
[70] Heidegger OHF | GA 63: 5–6.
[71] Heidegger OHF | GA 63: 8, 6. Cf. Heidegger: "A '*concept*' is not a schema, but rather a possibility of being, of how matters look in the moment, i.e., is constitutive of the moment—a meaning drawn out of something. . .Fundamental concepts are not later additions to Dasein, but rather ex-press it in advance and propel it forward" (Heidegger OHF | GA 63: 16).

possible. We find ourselves thrown into lived experience, then, and it is only on the presupposition of this thrownness that we are ever able to interpret the existential structures of this experience. Hence, as we saw in Section 5.4, Heidegger says that a hermeneutics of facticity is not the grasping of a really distinct object, like botany is of plants, but rather is a "how of the character of being of facticity" and so "belongs to the being of factical life itself," just as a critique of reason, for Kant, belongs to reason. In other words, a hermeneutics of facticity, like a critique of reason, exhibits a genitive that is simultaneously subjective and objective.

Heidegger indicates that hermeneutics provides philosophy with the "counter-ruinant" movement that is necessary for correcting its natural flight from itself. The "task" of hermeneutics, he says, is to secure for Dasein "an *understanding* of itself," which understanding is "defined" as "the *wakefulness* of Dasein to itself." Dasein's flight from itself is a kind of slumber of which philosophy is one type, one token of which is dialectic. Hermeneutics is tasked with "hunting down" Dasein's "alienation from itself," that is, with exposing its evasion of its factical life.[72] In philosophy, this involves Dasein waking to itself by pursuing a genuine questioning whereby it turns toward its life in the recognition that "[p]hilosophy is a mode of knowing which is in factical life itself."[73] Thus, just as, for Kant, critique corrects reason's dogmatic and evil alienation from its experiential and moral laws by bringing it to theoretical and practical self-knowledge, respectively, so too, for Heidegger, hermeneutics corrects Dasein's ruinant alienation from its factical life by bringing it to self-understanding.[74]

Hermeneutics is accordingly "*the self-interpretation of facticity*,"[75] for it manifests the very fact that it interprets, namely, Dasein's factical life. But then interpretation in general manifests this fact. As Heidegger says, interpretation is Dasein's "primordial act" of making that which it understands "*explicitly* understood" and yet "is itself *part and parcel* of the 'being there' of Dasein."[76] In manifesting Dasein's factical life, however, interpretation can nevertheless come to obscure it.

In Chapter Two, "The Idea of Facticity and the Concept of 'Man,'" Heidegger says that an interpretation can become a ubiquitous kind of "*talk*," that is, a "mode

[72] Heidegger OHF | GA 63: 15.

[73] Heidegger OHF | GA 63: 17–8. Cf. Heidegger: "Factical life experience is very peculiar; in it, the path to philosophy is made possible and the turning around which leads to philosophy is enacted" (Heidegger EPR | G 60 1: 11). Cf. also Heidegger: "A philosophical reflection does not fall out of the sky, nor is it an arbitrarily concocted undertaking. Like all knowledge it grows out of our factical existence and its everydayness" (Heidegger L | GA 21: 248).

[74] We might compare ruinance, construed as our natural flight from factical life, with what Kant calls 'self-conceit,' construed as our natural flight from our experiential and moral laws. Moreover, we might compare hermeneutical counter-ruinance with Kant's definition of critique as the correction of self-conceit. On the theoretical and practical guises of self-conceit, namely, dogmatism and evil, and how, for Kant, they constitute our original fall in metaphysics and our original sin in ethics and thereby call for a critique of theoretical and practical reason, respectively, see Bruno 2023b.

[75] Heidegger OHF | GA 63: 14.

[76] Heidegger OHF | GA 63: 16, 149, 157.

of discourse" that provides "a definite comprehension which Dasein in advance has of itself," according to which Dasein is, for example, created, rational, or natural. Such talk is that "out of which [Dasein] lives," pervading Dasein's everyday speech about itself. When an interpretation rises to the "public and average manner" in which we all speak, it prescribes a certain description of our factical life, that is, a certain self-interpretation. It ventriloquizes our discourse about life by speaking for and through us. Since, by manifesting our factical life, this interpretation is "*part and parcel*" of our being-there, it is no mere story, but rather constitutes our "mode of being." Moreover, it is a mode of being in which "everyone" says, hears, thinks, expects, and favors the same things on the basis of talk whose proliferation "belongs to no one" and is no one's "responsibility." But since a "public and average" interpretation is one that we have "in advance" and one that constitutes our "mode of being," its authority is both anonymous and unquestioned. As Heidegger says, the author of this interpretation is "*the* 'no-one' which circulates in factical Dasein and haunts it like a specter," while the interpretation itself is a "hearsay" to which Dasein habitually "pays tribute." The dominion of such an interpretation stifles the genuine questioning of facticity on which counter-ruinance depends. It is therefore ruinant, for it inhibits our resolve to face our factical life. Hence Heidegger says that, in parroting how everyone talks, "Dasein speaks about itself and sees itself in such and such a manner, and yet this is only a *mask* which it holds up before itself in order not to be frightened by itself."[77] In manifesting Dasein's factical life, then, interpretation can obscure it by solidifying our natural self-alienation.

In §27 of *Being and Time*, Heidegger describes the "no-one" from *Hermeneutics of Facticity*, that is, the spectral public whose interpretation of life we unwittingly perpetuate, as "*the they*," which "*disburdens*" Dasein of genuine questioning by "suppl[ying] the answer to the *who* of everyday Dasein." Heidegger calls the "self of everyday Dasein" the "*they-self*," since it exists "in the manner of dependency and inauthenticity," and he calls the "self which has explicitly grasped itself" through liberation from the they the "*authentic self*."[78] Exposing ruinant self-interpretation so as to question facticity and thereby attain a wakeful "gras[p]" of oneself is accordingly a matter of overcoming inauthenticity. We will now see that *Hermeneutics of Facticity* provides a critique of the inauthenticity of philosophy, specifically, of dialectic.

In Chapter Three, "Being-Interpreted in Today's Today," Heidegger distinguishes between two modes of interpretation, namely, history, which classifies cultures across time, and philosophy, which classifies regions of being, and he cites

[77] Heidegger OHF | GA 63: 31–2. Cf. Kierkegaard's 1846 "The Present Age": "the basic tendency of our modern age has been toward leveling. . .For leveling really to take place, a phantom must first be raised, the spirit of leveling, a monstrous abstraction, an all-encompassing something that is nothing, a mirage—and this phantom is *the public*. . .[T]o adopt the same opinion as the public is a deceptive consolation, for the public exists only *in abstracto*" (Kierkegaard 2009: 90–2).

[78] Heidegger SZ | GA 2: 126–9.

"*dialectic*" as an instance of the latter mode. Turning to the dispute between dialectic and phenomenology, he then considers the view that dialectic is superior because, first, its cognition reaches beyond the "immediacy" of hermeneutic intuition to the "mediated immediacy" of conceptually sublated contradictions and, second, its cognition "penetrat[es] the irrational," that is, the radically contingent or brute fact that arguably "transcend[s]" conceptual sublation. Heidegger acknowledges that phenomenology places a "*limit*" on reason, namely, the lived experience whose primordial disclosure, as we saw in Section 5.1 and will see in more detail in Section 6.5, mood affords. However, he says that "the question is whether such a limit" is "a defect," which yields the deeper question of where the dialectical idea of unlimited rationality "come[s] from" in the first place.[79]

Heidegger's posing the deeper question about where the idea of unlimited rationality comes from might suggest that he will charge dialectic with rhapsody because it cognizes its idea historically, that is, via imitation, and so violates the enlightenment ideal of rational cognition. Indeed, he gives this impression when he says that dialectic "lives from the tables of others," the "shining example" of which is "Hegel's logic," which, as he quotes from the second edition Preface to the *Science of Logic*, holds that

> [t]o display the realm of thought philosophically, that is, in its own immanent activity. . .the received material, the known thought-forms, must be regarded as an extremely important fund, even a necessary condition, a presupposition to be gratefully acknowledged even though what it offers here and there is only a bare thread, the dead bones of a skeleton thrown together in a disorderly heap.[80]

That thought "receive[s]" categories or "thought-forms" from tradition, even if they are "dead bones" that the science of intelligibility must animate, might suggest that dialectic rests on historical cognition of the categories, violating its enlightenment ideal. However, this is neither what Hegel means in the Preface, as we saw in Chapter 3, nor, more importantly, why Heidegger concludes that dialectic "lacks radicality, i.e., is fundamentally unphilosophical." It is crucial that Heidegger reaches his conclusion on the basis of the claim that the "eloquence" of "Hegelese" relies on "readymade material,"[81] which claim we are well-positioned to grasp.

First, recall that philosophy's flight from factical life is a flight not from principles, but rather from "matters of principle," namely, the matters that compose the brute fact of lived experience. This fact is the "readymade material" on which Hegelese relies, that is, the table from which dialectic "lives." Lived experience, then, is where dialectic's idea of unlimited rationality comes from. Second, recall

[79] Heidegger OHF | GA 63: 42–5.
[80] Heidegger OHF | GA 63: 46, expanded citation from Hegel GW 21: 10.
[81] Heidegger OHF | GA 63: 46.

that ruinant interpretation obscures life by alienating us from it. Philosophy fosters ruinance by supplying an "eloquen[t]" interpretation that "circulates everywhere and about everything", which "*disburdens*" Dasein of questioning factical life. Dialectic in particular supplies a ruinant interpretation by "mechanically" refusing to take direction not only from others, but also from factical life and thus by neglecting the latter as its "hidden" principle. The first refusal successfully avoids rhapsody according to the enlightenment ideal of rational cognition. However, the second refusal evades facticity according to the very same ideal. It is therefore precisely by honoring, not violating, its enlightenment ideal that dialectic ignores the brute fact on which it rests and consequently "lacks radicality."

This reveals a crucial feature of Heidegger's critique of dialectic. We saw that facing up to factical life by questioning it is the mark of an "*authentic self*." We can accordingly say that, far from charging dialectic with failing to avoid rhapsody, Heidegger charges its successful avoidance of rhapsody with a ruinant flight from facticity and thus with inauthenticity. Moreover, instead of charging Hegel with leaving the rhapsody problem unsolved, as Hegel does to Fichte, Fichte does to Kant, and Kant does to Aristotle, Heidegger dissolves the rhapsody problem by replacing the enlightenment ideal of rational cognition, on which the rhapsody charge rests, with the existential ideal of authenticity. This is because Heidegger shows that it is a false dichotomy to regard the origin of the conditions of intelligibility as either external to reason and thus rhapsodically determined or internal to reason and thus absolutely necessary, for he argues that this origin, while not really distinct from the lived standpoint of the philosopher, is nevertheless radically contingent or factical.

Returning to the dispute between dialectic and phenomenology, Heidegger says that it "must be decided vis-à-vis the *object* of philosophy" and observes that dialectic "sets itself on the sideline regarding this task" by not "staying with the object and allowing it to prescribe the right mode of grasping it and the limits to this."[82] Philosophy is primordial science, whose "*object*" is lived experience and whose proper form is phenomenology. The latter demonstrates its superiority to dialectic by not fleeing the facticity of lived experience and instead receiving from lived experience the "right mode of grasping" the object of philosophy.

Heidegger's ruinance charge against dialectic contextualizes his claim that it is "[n]o accident that [Franz] Brentano, from whom came the first impulses for the development of phenomenology, sensed in German idealism the deepest ruin of philosophy."[83] As noted above, 'ruinance' is a precursor to 'fallenness.' I will

[82] Heidegger OHF | GA 63: 47.

[83] Heidegger OHF | GA 63: 46. Brentano's 1889 "On Schelling's Philosophy" describes Hegel's dialectical method as a "three-mirror kaleidoscope" and asserts that German idealism "lack[s] everything and every value from a scientific point of view" (Brentano 1968: 125). Cf. the Foreword to his 1894 lecture to the Literary Society in Vienna: "[i]t would be a fatal misunderstanding if anybody were to think that I deny the unusual talents of those epoch-making philosophers whom I cannot consider to have made real contributions to the advancement of philosophy. I agree with Schopenhauer in his judgment

conclude this section by considering how Heidegger's analysis of ruinance in *Hermeneutics of Facticity* prefigures his discussion of the three moments of fallenness in *Being and Time* and how, in doing so, it implicates German idealism.

In Division One, Chapter V of *Being and Time*, Heidegger says that Dasein has "always already fallen away from itself." He describes this as Dasein's having "fallen prey to the 'world,'" which "means being absorbed in the being-with-one-another as it is guided by idle talk, curiosity, and ambiguity."[84] First, idle talk is the discourse by which, through "*gossiping* and *passing the word along*," an interpretation "spreads in wider circles and takes on an authoritative character" that "divests us of the task of genuine understanding," which is to understand our Dasein, by encouraging and proliferating "average understanding."[85] Second, in the absence of any felt need for genuine understanding, curiosity fills this lack with the "restlessness and excitement" of "leap[ing]" among different topics, which is to say that it responds to the abandonment of understanding with the "constant possibility of *distraction*."[86] Third, ambiguity is the product of idle talk and curiosity insofar as idle talk, for which nothing is "not understood" in an average way, and curiosity, to whose superficial intrigue nothing is "closed off," yield the inability to "decide what is disclosed in genuine understanding and what is not."[87] Falling prey to the they through these moments, Dasein's "*entanglement*" tightens as it creates itself in the they's image by pursuing the "*tempting*" prospect of satisfying the they's ubiquitous and tacitly accepted expectations of a "full and genuine 'life.'" Although satisfying these expectations can produce success and thereby the "*tranquilizing*" feeling that "everything is in 'the best order,'" since it begins with an abandonment of self-understanding, it "*alienat[es]*" Dasein from "its authenticity."[88] It is because this process yields an I that does not own its existence that Heidegger says, in strikingly Fichtean terms, that "'not I' by no means signifies something like a being which is essentially lacking 'I-hood', but means a definite mode of being of the 'I' itself; for example, having lost itself."[89] We can now find the three moments of fallenness prefigured in *Hermeneutics of Facticity*.

as to the scientific value of the Hegelian system; I cannot, however, consent to his contempt for the intellectual capacity of the man" (Brentano 1998: 2).

[84] Heidegger SZ | GA 2: 175.
[85] Heidegger SZ | GA 2: 168–9.
[86] Heidegger SZ | GA 2: 172.
[87] Heidegger SZ | GA 2: 173.
[88] Heidegger SZ | GA 2: 175, 177–8.
[89] Heidegger SZ | GA 2: 116. Cf. Heidegger: "'Being like an I' belongs to each situation. With that it is not said that the 'like an I' of a situation is that which unifies the diversity. Nothing is expressed about the relation of the I and the not-I. One should not here read into this a subject-object relationship, nor claim in the wake of Fichte that 'The I posits the not-I.' About that, we express nothing. Apparently the Fichtean relation is entirely general, but it nevertheless prejudices already entirely particular connections; it says: 'The I posits the form of non-I-ness'—not the factical world is posited" (Heidegger EPR | GA 60 1: 91–2).

First, as we have seen, a public and average interpretation of life consists in "*talk*" that ventriloquized Dasein simply "*pass[es]. . .along*," thereby preserving the they's anonymous and unquestioned authority.

Second, in Chapter Four, "Analysis of Each Interpretation Regarding its Mode of Being-Related to its Object," Heidegger says that "*curiosity*" is "*at work*" both in historical interpretation, which is "*pulled along*" by "its object," namely, cultural forms, and in philosophical interpretation, which "*leads itself along*," namely, through categorial forms. Evoking Lask's distinction from Section 5.2 between rhapsodically and systematically deduced categories, Heidegger adds that it is "a difference of a secondary order" whether the categories compose a "finished and static system" or emerge from the "self-development" of "knowing."[90] We can see why this difference is "secondary," for both instances of philosophical interpretation share with historical interpretation the "restlessness and excitement" of classifying categorial and cultural forms, respectively. More importantly, recalling Kant's theory of enlightenment in Section 3.2, although both instances of philosophical interpretation, by "*lead[ing] itself along*," exhibit the maturity of rational cognition, which generates its object, whereas historical interpretation, by being "*pulled along*," exhibits the minority of historical cognition, which imitates its object, nevertheless philosophical and historical interpretation share the core feature of ruinance, namely, the flight from factical life. Thus, the presence of enlightenment in philosophical interpretation, no less than its absence in historical interpretation, is at least typically a case of inauthenticity. The relevant ideal for correcting enlightened and unenlightened ruinance alike, as we have seen, is authenticity.

Third, although Heidegger does not use the term 'ambiguity' in the text, in Part Two, Chapter One, "Preliminary Reflections: Phenomenon and Phenomenology," he describes a "discipline" whose object of study "becomes so restricted and fixed through *tradition* that this inauthenticity is no longer able to be recognized."[91] This implies a discipline, for example, dialectic, that, by idly passing along ubiquitous talk and curiously following speculative paths, suffers the ambiguity of being unable to determine whether such paths lead to "genuine understanding." Moreover, having established its interpretive credentials, dialectic can be seen as "offer[ing] to Dasein an objective refuge, the prospect of the tranquilizing certainty and security of agreement" with dialectic's scientific method and scientific community. Dasein, now entangled, abandons itself to what I will call 'the I that is they and the they that is I.'[92] Turning to Hegel and citing, once again, the second edition Preface to the

[90] Heidegger OHF | GA 63: 54–5, 61–4.

[91] Heidegger OHF | GA 63: 75.

[92] See Heidegger: "Initially and for the most part, we are not ourselves. We live in terms of what *everyone* says, what *everyone* judges to be the case, how *everyone* sees things, what *everyone* wants. It is this indeterminate 'everyone' that rules over Dasein. Initially and for the most part, this everyone enjoys a thorough dominance over Dasein. Even science lives in terms of it. In tradition, we are shown how *everyone* asks questions and how everyone takes up research. . .The more rote saying dominates,

Science of Logic, Heidegger describes this self-abandonment as a "freedom from need," which he sarcastically paraphrases as an "authentic freedom" from "feelings, goals, interests," that is, from the matter of lived experience.[93] Such hollow freedom is facilitated by the I that is they and the they that is I.

Heidegger concludes that inauthenticity in philosophy must be "critically dismantled" by a hermeneutics of facticity via what he calls "*historical critique*," which traces philosophy's "*falling away*" through the ages since antiquity. While historical critique might suggest an inquiry whose object is really distinct from it, Heidegger indicates that the opposite is the case when he says that "the mode of *covering-itself-up*" that marks historical cases of fallenness "constitutes the object of philosophy."[94] Since, as we have seen, philosophy's object is inseparable from lived experience, it cannot be really distinct from the standpoint of the historically critical philosopher. Historical critique is accordingly a legitimate interpretive tool of hermeneutics and therefore proper to phenomenology as primordial science, that is, as the science of experience.[95]

Having traced the development of Heidegger's conception of facticity prior to *Being and Time*, I will now establish the second stage of this development by explicating his increasing focus, following *Being and Time*, on anxiety and the nothing.

the more the world is covered over. It is in this way that Dasein has the tendency to cover over the world and, along with this, itself. This tendency to cover over is nothing other than Dasein's flight from itself into publicness, a flight that has important consequences for understanding the phenomenon of time" (Heidegger WD | 2002: 164–5). Contrast Hegel: "What still lies ahead for consciousness is the experience of what spirit is—this absolute substance which is the unity of the different independent self-consciousnesses which, in their opposition, enjoy perfect freedom and independence: 'I' that is 'We' and 'We' that is 'I'" (Hegel PG | W 3: 145).

[93] Heidegger OHF | GA 63: 63–4, corrected citation from Hegel WL | GW 21: 12. Contrast Hegel's claim in the *Encyclopedia* that "spirit is [in the Logic] purely at home with itself, and thereby free, for that is just what freedom is: being at home with oneself in one's other, depending upon oneself, and being one's own determinant" (Hegel EL | GW 20: §24 Addition 2; cf. Hegel WL | GW 21: 43) with Heidegger's claim that "[p]hilosophy is the opposite of all comfort and assurance. It is turbulence, the turbulence into which man is spun, so as in this way alone to comprehend Dasein without delusion" (Heidegger GM | GA 29/30: 28–9).

[94] Heidegger OHF | GA 63: 75–7.

[95] See Heidegger: "We have to look around in factical life experience in order to obtain a motive for its turning around. It is, to be sure, possible to find this motive, but it is very difficult. For this reason, we will choose a more convenient route, since we possess knowledge of past and contemporary philosophy. The factical existence of the history of philosophy is, in itself, certainly no motivation to philosophize. Nevertheless, as a cultural possession, one can take it as a starting point and, with its help, clarify for oneself motivations to philosophize" (Heidegger EPR | GA 60 1: 18). Cf. Heidegger's presentation "For Edmund Husserl on his Seventieth Birthday", April 8, 1929: "The decisive element of your work has not been this or that answer to this or that question, but instead this breakthrough into a new dimension of philosophizing. But this breakthrough is nothing less than the radicalizing [of how to do] philosophy, the bending of philosophy back onto the hidden path of its authentic historical happening as this announces itself in the inner communion of the great thinkers" (Heidegger EH | 1997: 476).

6.4 Heidegger on the Vertigo of Being-There

In the *Jäsche Logic*, Kant says that philosophy can be "brought down" to the questions "*What can I know?*," "*What ought I to do?*," "*What may I hope?*," and "*What is man?*," the answers to which he assigns to metaphysics, morality, religion, and anthropology, respectively. He adds that "we could reckon all of this as anthropology because the first three questions relate to the last one."[96] To ask about knowledge, action, and hope is, it seems, anthropological insofar as it must be done from and for the human standpoint.

In *Kant and the Problem of Metaphysics*, Part Four, "The Laying of the Ground for Metaphysics in a Retrieval," Heidegger raises a problem for Kant's organization of philosophy around these four basic questions. Granting that anthropology is methodologically philosophical insofar as it differentiates "the being called man" from the "remaining regions of beings," he claims that philosophical anthropology is nevertheless a "regional ontology" because it lies outside "the centre of philosophy."[97] In the terms of *The Idea of Philosophy*, philosophical anthropology investigates a region of beings, namely, "man," and thus is not yet primordial science, whereas philosophy "centr[ally]" investigates universal being and is therefore primordial science. This is why, instead of "searching for the answer" to Kant's fourth question, Heidegger says that we must ask how we can "have *asked about* man" in the first place, that is, on what "ground" we must stand in order to be able to pose the fourth or, indeed, any of Kant's philosophical questions. The ground of questioning, he claims, is one that Kant "himself unveiled" yet "falls back from," namely, finitude. Asking, for example, what I can know or what I ought to do "betrays thereby a finitude," for, unlike an "all-powerful entity," namely, a divine understanding or a holy will, I pose my question as a "creature" who is situated between "an ability," namely, knowledge or virtue, and "a disability," namely, ignorance or vice, respectively. Heidegger concludes that we ask Kant's philosophical questions only because we are finite, from which it follows that Kant's first three questions are in fact "no different from" his fourth question.[98]

There is, however, one question that is unlike Kant's questions, namely, the question of the meaning of being, for it alone has "an inner relation to finitude in human beings." This is because it is through our finitude that "there occurs an irruption into the totality of beings," that is, into being. We are finitely being-there, that is, Dasein, insofar as we exist in the midst of being.[99] As Heidegger says, evoking his concept of thrownness, our finitude consists not merely in existing

96 Kant JL | AA 9: 25. Cf. Kant's letter to Karl Friedrich Stäudlin, May 4, 1793 (Kant B | AA 11:429).
97 Heidegger KPM | GA 3: 211.
98 Heidegger KPM | GA 3: 213–8.
99 See Heidegger: "To characterize with a *single* term both the relation of being to the essence of man and the essential relation of man to the openness ('there') of being as such, the name of 'Dasein' was chosen for the essential realm in which man stands as man" (Heidegger WM | W: 202).

"among other beings," but rather in being "*surrendered to*" and "*delivered up*" to being.[100] Our finitude and being co-manifest, then, because our being-there essentially is what I will call our 'being-amid-being.'[101] Hence Heidegger says that we have a "pre-conceptual understanding of being," since, "[w]ith every mood wherein 'something is this way or that', our being-there becomes manifest to us."[102]

Heidegger infers from the fact that our understanding of being is "the innermost essence of finitude" that this understanding "make[s] possible the so-called 'creative' capacities of the finite human creature" as Kant conceives of them, namely, knowledge, action, and hope. Such capacities are themselves only expressions of and thus presuppose our finitude. Since these capacities concern Dasein *qua* human, the dependence of their possibility on the "essence of finitude," namely, our understanding of being, indicates that "*the finitude of the Dasein*" in us is "*[m]ore original*" than the humanity in us. But then "the question as to what is more original" than the humanity in us "cannot be anthropological," since philosophical anthropology "has already assumed" that Dasein is human. The question is rather metaphysical, which is why Heidegger pursues a "metaphysics of Dasein."[103]

[100] Heidegger KPM | GA 3: 226, 228. Cf. Heidegger: "Hegel's step from Kant to absolute idealism is the sole consequence of Western philosophy. It becomes *possible* and *necessary* through Kant because the problem of human Dasein, the problem of finitude, did not properly become a problem for Kant himself. That is to say, this did not become a central problem of philosophy because Kant himself, as the second edition of the *Critique of Pure Reason* reveals, helped to prepare the turn away from an uncomprehended finitude toward a comforting infinitude" (Heidegger GM | GA 29/30: 306).

[101] Cf. Heidegger: "This *schema* must be avoided: *What exists are subjects and objects*. . .The relation between subject and object needs to be explained and is a problem for epistemology. . .This problem. . .fundamentally and forever obstructs access to that which we have indicated with the term 'factical life' ('Dasein')" (Heidegger OHF | GA 63: 81). Cf. also Heidegger: "what is more obvious than the fact that a 'subject' is related to an 'object' and the other way around? This 'subject-object-relation' must be presupposed. But that is a presupposition which, although it is inviolate in its own facticity, is truly fatal, perhaps for that very reason, if its ontological necessity and especially its ontological meaning are left in obscurity. . .[S]ubject and object are not the same as Dasein and world" (Heidegger SZ | GA 2: 59–60). And cf. Heidegger's 1955 "On the Question of Being": "the subject-object relation. . .says that to every subject (human being) there belongs an object (being), and vice versa. Certainly; were it not for the fact that all of this—the relation, the subject, and the object—already resides within the essence of what we are representing. . .Subjectivity and objectivity are for their part already grounded in a peculiar manifestness of 'being' and of the 'human essence'" (Heidegger ZS | W: 236). On Meillassoux's misattribution of the epistemological schema to Heidegger, see Bruno 2018d.

[102] Heidegger KPM | GA 3: 227.

[103] Heidegger KPM | GA 3: 229; cf. Heidegger BüH | W: 172. Heidegger claims that Kant grasps the question of the ground of metaphysics "all too little," despite being more "awake" to it than anyone "before or after him," as evinced by his remark in a letter to Herz, May 11, 1781, that the first *Critique* "includes the *metaphysics of metaphysics*," which remark, Heidegger says, "puts to rest any attempt to search, even partially, for a 'theory of knowledge' in the *Critique of Pure Reason*" (Heidegger KPM | GA 3: 230, cited from Kant B | 10: 269). Cf. Kant KrV A850/B878. Cf. also Rickert: "the *Critique of Pure Reason*. . .should not be viewed as a *merely* epistemological work. It belongs to the worst mistakes of some (but not all) of the representatives of so-called 'neo-Kantianism' that they have allowed this view to arise, and have even strengthened it. The days in which a view like this is possible are, hopefully, forever a thing of the past. Even in his 'theoretical' philosophy in the *Critique of Pure Reason*, Kant treated philosophy not as a specialized discipline, but as a *science of the whole*. He tackled the old question of the being of the world with a new method, thereby practicing metaphysics or ontology *in his particular manner*. For him, epistemological investigations were never anything more than a *means* to gain an answer, in his unprecedented and utterly singular way, to the question of what the world as a whole is" (Rickert 2015: 384).

He notes that this phrase is "ambiguous in a positive sense." This is because metaphysics is not "'about' Dasein" like "zoology is about animals," that is, it is not a "fixed and ready-for-use organon" that is really distinct from and applicable to its object. Instead, metaphysics belongs to Dasein, namely, by presupposing and expressing the latter's finitude.[104] Since, as we saw, a hermeneutics of facticity belongs to facticity, we can say that a metaphysics of Dasein must be methodologically hermeneutical given its exhibition of a simultaneously subjective and objective genitive.

Heidegger's critical response to Kant's organization of philosophy contains a perhaps unexpected pair of questions: "are we not seized with vertigo when we [try to] determine [being], even if we should comprehend it properly? Is being then not something like the nothing?"[105] He immediately passes over these startling questions, returning to their topic only briefly in the antepenultimate section of *Kant and the Problem of Metaphysics* when he says that "[a]nxiety is the basic disposition which places us before the nothing" and that being is "only understandable" if Dasein "holds itself into the nothing."[106] What is anxiety? What is the nothing? What role does our anxiety before the nothing play in our understanding of being? And how does this bear on the facticity of our being-there, that is, of our being-amid-being?

Contemporaneous texts also posit a relation between anxiety and the nothing. However, they similarly shed little light on this relation's role in our understanding of being. In 1925's summer lectures in Marburg, *Prolegomena to the History of the Concept of Time*, Heidegger describes "anxiety" as a "being afraid" whose object or "of-which" is "indefinite." In anxiety, "one feels *uncanny*," that is, one "no longer feels at home" in one's "most familiar environment." Since what threatens in anxiety is "nothing definite and worldly," he calls it "*being-in-the-world as such*" yet also refers to it as "nothing."[107] Two years later in *Being and Time*, Heidegger says that since "*anxiety*" is about "*being-in-the-world as such*" rather than "an innerworldly being," it makes manifest "the nothing."[108] And in the 1929 winter lectures in Davos that he and Cassirer deliver as part of a disputation, Heidegger asserts that "[i]t is only possible for me to understand being if I understand the nothing or anxiety. Being is incomprehensible if the nothing is incomprehensible." He adds that this represents "the most elementary and the most concrete of problems" to which "the

[104] Heidegger KPM | GA 3: 230–1.
[105] Heidegger KPM | GA 3: 226.
[106] Heidegger KPM | GA 3: 238.
[107] Heidegger PGZ | GA 20: 399–402. On Heidegger's concept of uncanniness, see Withy 2015.
[108] Heidegger SZ | GA 2: 186–7. Cf. Heidegger's 1935–36 "The Origin of the Work of Art": "In the midst of beings as a whole an open place comes to presence. There is a clearing. Thought from out of beings, it is more in being than is the being. This open center is, therefore, not surrounded by beings. Rather, this illuminating center itself encircles all beings—like the nothing that we scarcely know" (Heidegger UK | 2002: 30).

whole analytic of Dasein has been oriented."[109] Apparently, there is nothing more "elementary" for primordial science, that is, for phenomenology, than the question of the meaning of being, where this is essentially the question of the meaning of the nothing and where this essentially involves the mood of anxiety. However, this raises the same questions with which *Kant and the Problem of Metaphysics* leaves us. It is not until later in 1929, in "What Is Metaphysics?," that we find the answers.

6.5 Anxiety and Apperception

"What Is Metaphysics?" has three parts. The first part, "The Unfolding of a Metaphysical Inquiry," begins by claiming that "science," by which Heidegger means non-primordial science, consists in a "submission to beings" insofar as it gives beings "the first and last word." In order not to misconstrue its proper domain, it is natural to say that science concerns "beings themselves—and beyond that, nothing." I will call this the 'natural saying'. Heidegger observes a Cartesian ambiguity in the natural saying. In one sense, science must reject the nothing, which is not a being, as "an outrage and a phantasm," for it is unspeakable on the assumption that the "first and last word" belongs to beings. That is, the natural saying strictly offers clarity in that it refers exclusively to that which is present to science, namely, beings. In another sense, however, science "speaks, whether explicitly or not, of something different" than beings and so "has recourse to what it rejects" with the word 'beings.' That is, the natural saying jointly offers clarity and distinctness in that it refers simultaneously to the beings that are present to science and to that which is separate or excluded from beings, namely, the nothing. But then if the natural saying speaks both of and "beyond" beings, then we must ask: "How is it with the nothing?"[110]

The second part, "The Elaboration of the Question," addresses the charge that asking about the nothing is misguided because, since it "deprives itself of a being" about which to ask, it is a contradictory question. The charge assumes that "understanding" is the "taskmaster" of thought, which latter cannot violate the understanding's logical principles, in particular, the principle of non-contradiction. Heidegger refutes the charge by claiming that asking about the nothing is only misguided if we are "misled" by the understanding's intolerance for contradiction.[111] This refutation is ironically anti-Hegelian, for while it may seem to echo Hegel's subordination of the understanding to reason, which, as we saw in Section 3.6, affirms contradiction within a dialectical movement of thought, it

[109] Heidegger KPM | GA 3: 284. On the Davos disputation, see Friedman 2000, Gordon 2010, and Truwant 2022.

[110] Heidegger WM | W: 3–4. On the difference between clarity and distinctness, see Descartes 1982: 20.

[111] Heidegger WM | W: 5–6.

in fact subordinates both the understanding and reason, as modes of knowledge, to mood.

As we saw in Section 5.1, Heidegger argues in *Being and Time* that mood's disclosure of our kind of existence makes possible knowledge's disclosure of the same. In Chapter V, he says that mood is the "primordial disclosure" of the being to which Dasein is "delivered over," that is, of the "*facticity*" of Dasein's "*thrownness*." Mood discloses Dasein in its "naked" or "pure 'that it is,'" whereas "know[ing]" offers a "why" in order to explain such an already given "that." This is not unlike how, for Schelling, negative philosophy provides the whatness to explain the already given thatness to which positive philosophy is open, as we saw in Section 4.6. Hence Heidegger says that "cognition fall[s] far short of the primordial disclosure of moods in which Dasein is brought before its being as the there."[112] In mood, Dasein finds itself as being-there and can thereby project itself toward possibilities of being. It is on this basis alone that "knowledge" or "cognition" is possible according to principles of either contradiction-intolerant understanding or contradiction-affirming reason. As Heidegger says, "the purest *theōria* does not abandon all moods."[113]

In "What Is Metaphysics?," Heidegger argues that we circumvent the understanding's intolerance for the contradiction of inquiring beyond beings when the appropriate mood attunes us to that which is not a being. On the one hand, it "does seem as though we cling to this or that particular being" and so "can never comprehend absolutely the whole of beings," which is not itself a being.[114] As Heidegger says in his 1962 winter lecture in Freiburg, "Time and Being", "[n]owhere among things do we find being."[115] On the other hand, we "do find ourselves stationed in the midst of beings" such that our "everyday existence. . .always deals with beings in a unity of the 'whole', if only in a shadowy way." Whereas we "comprehend" nothing beyond beings, we have a "shadowy" mode of access beyond them, namely, in an appropriate mood. Certain moods attune us beyond beings to "beings as a whole," for example, "boredom," which "removes" beings into "a remarkable indifference," and "joy," which delights in "the Dasein," as opposed to "the person," of the beloved. However, these moods "conceal from us the nothing we are seeking." According to Heidegger, anxiety alone is the "originary

[112] Heidegger SZ | GA 2: 134–5. Since Dasein is never mood-free, in attunement it "must always already have found itself." Heidegger notes that this finding "comes not from a direct seeking, but from a fleeing," since, "[f]or the most part, mood does not turn toward the burdensome character of Dasein." As we saw, we naturally flee from factical life. Hence he says that attunement discloses our thrownness "*in the mode of an evasive turning away*" (Heidegger SZ | GA 2: 135–6).

[113] Heidegger SZ | GA 2: 136, 138. Understanding according to logical principles must be distinguished from Heidegger's own conception of understanding, according to which, like attunement, understanding is an "existential structur[e]" that discloses the "significance" of the "potentiality of being" to which Dasein "projects" itself (Heidegger SZ | GA 2: 142–5). Cf. Heidegger SZ | GA 2: 336.

[114] Heidegger WM | W: 7.

[115] Heidegger ZuS | 1972: 3. Cf. Novalis: "We everywhere *seek* the unconditioned, and always only *find* things" (Novalis 1978: 226, translated by Bowie 2003: 94).

attunement" in which we are "brought before the nothing itself," that is, the sole attunement that "makes manifest the nothing."[116]

The nothing is "at first and for the most part distorted" because we "usually lose ourselves altogether among beings in a certain way." Anxiety is the "peculiar calm" of the "uncanny" feeling of "the slipping away of beings as a whole," which "makes manifest the nothing." In the third part, "The Response to the Question," Heidegger clarifies that this slipping away is not the "annihilation" that, by removing beings individually, "submit[s] to calculation." Rather, it is the "repelling gesture" whereby the nothing "nothings," that is, manifests the "full but heretofore concealed strangeness" that beings, however intelligibly existent, could well not be.[117] In other words, the nothing reveals that beings "are beings—and not nothing." Heidegger returns here to the Cartesian ambiguity of the natural saying in order to motivate its second sense. Science investigates beings by speaking, "explicitly or not," of the nothing that reveals their radical contingency or ultimate groundlessness, that is, their facticity. In this sense, the natural saying offers both clarity and distinctness by referring both to accessible beings and, even if implicitly, to that which marks these beings in their facticity. Hence Heidegger explains that "this 'and not nothing'. . .is not some kind of appended clarification. Rather, it makes possible in advance the manifestness of beings in general."[118] While we avoid error by clearly saying what is manifest to science, namely, beings, we grasp phenomenological truth by distinctly saying what "makes" this manifestness "possible," namely, the nothing. Saying the former requires the appropriate knowledge. Saying the latter requires the appropriate mood.

Anxiety attunes us to the nothing, which moves us to ask why there is something rather than nothing or, as Heidegger asks in *Introduction to Metaphysics*,

[116] Heidegger WM | W: 7–8.

[117] Heidegger WM | W: 9, 11–3. Cf. Heidegger: "Calculative thinking. . .is unable to foresee that everything calculable by calculation. . .is already a whole, a whole whose unity indeed belongs to the incalculable that withdraws itself and its uncanniness from the claws of calculation. Yet that which everywhere and always from the outset has closed itself off from the intent behind calculation and yet, in its enigmatic unfamiliarity, is at all times nearer to the human being than all those beings in which he establishes himself and his intentions can at times attune the essence of the human being to a thinking whose truth no 'logic' is capable of grasping" (Heidegger WM | W: 104–5). For an argument that Heidegger's discussion of anxiety in *Being and Time* is an implicit methodological use of breakdown experiences, see Ward 2021.

[118] Heidegger WM | W: 11–2. Heidegger describes the nothing that reveals the facticity of beings as a "clear night" (Heidegger WM | W: 11), evoking a vision of stars against a black sky. Contrast Fichte's positive description, in 1801's "A Crystal Clear Report to the General Public Concerning the Actual Essence of the Newest Philosophy: An Attempt to Force the Reader to Understand," of our intellectual intuition of the "unconditioned" in self-consciousness as "a fortunate flash of insight" that "makes itself immediately clear" (Fichte SB | 1987: 70) and Hegel's satirical description of intellectual intuition of the absolute as a "night in which, as the saying goes, all cows are black" (Hegel PG | W 3: 22). Cf. Hegel's description of Spinozistic substance as "the dark, shapeless abyss, so to speak, in which all determinate content is swallowed up as radically null and void" (Hegel EL | GW 20: §151 Addition). Harris observes earlier uses of the night metaphor by Friedrich Schlegel in the 1790s and Jean Paul in 1804 (Harris 1987: 628). Cf. the night metaphor with Meister Eckhart's metaphor of "the quiet desert, into which distinction never gazed," i.e., "where no one dwells" and there is "a simple silence" (Eckhart 1981: 198).

"Why are beings torn from the possibility of not-being? Why do they not fall back into it constantly with no further ado?"[119] In moving us to ask the why-question, anxiety dares us to remain in the lightness of the intelligibility of beings, that is, their groundless givenness, so as to resolve to attain an authentic awareness of that groundlessness. This is why Heidegger says that anxiety's "breath quivers. . .most assuredly in those who are basically daring."[120] We saw in Section 3.2 that Kant's and Fichte's respectively explicit and implicit enlightenment dicta, namely, '*Sapere aude!*' and '*Agere aude!*,' dare us to be wise and to act. By replacing the enlightenment ideal of rational cognition with the existential ideal of authenticity, Heidegger pivots to observe in anxiety a mood that, by disclosing the factical or groundless ground of the intelligibility of beings, dares us to stay in that mood long enough to ask the why-question and thereby resolve to authentically acknowledge that ground. In this respect, anxiety issues what I will call the authenticity dictum '*Sollicitari aude!*,' that is, dare to be anxious. Daring to be anxious consists in opening oneself to the transformational potential of being awoken from inauthentic commitment to interpretations that deny, whether commonsensically, religiously, natural-scientifically, or philosophically, the factical character of the conditions of intelligibility and of beings themselves.

When we register the power of anxiety to throw the facticity of beings into relief, we come to speak about the nothing. We thereby employ a mode of speech that is "deprive[d]" of a being. While this mode of speech circumvents the principle of non-contradiction, it does so without indulging German idealism's ruinant program of dialectically affirming contradictions for the purpose of eliminating facticity. As Heidegger says in "Time and Being":

> [p]hilosophy knows a way out of [contradictions]. One allows the contradictions to stand, even sharpens them and tries to bring together in comprehensive unity what contradicts itself and thus falls apart. This procedure is called dialectic. Supposing the contradictory statements about being and about time could be reconciled by an encompassing unity, this indeed would be a way out—it would be a way out which evades the matters and the issues in question; for it allows itself to become involved neither with being as such nor with time as such nor with the relation of the two.[121]

As we saw in Section 6.3, dialectic is "fundamentally unphilosophical," since, as Heidegger now says, it offers a "way out" that "evades" the "matters" at hand, namely, the facticity of life, which our anxiety before the nothing reveals to include the facticity of beings, that is, the "concealed strangeness" that they could well not

[119] Heidegger EM | GA 40: 21.
[120] Heidegger WM | W: 14.
[121] Heidegger ZuS | 1972: 4.

be. If we dare to face this strangeness, we can acknowledge the nothing from which dialectic flees. We can thereby ironically affirm and thus fundamentally transform the Hegelian claim that dialectic presupposes nothing.

Our mode of speaking about the nothing not only circumvents the principle of non-contradiction. It also inverts the principle of sufficient reason, whose negative formulation, that is, "*ex nihilo nihil fit* [from nothing, nothing comes to be]," Heidegger says is "found to contain another sense," namely, "*ex nihilo omne ens qua ens fit* [from the nothing all beings as beings come to be]."[122] Anxiety reveals to us that beings exist questionably, that is, by the grace of the nothing. Thus, while the principle of sufficient reason states that nothing comes from nothing, anxiety indicates that, in "another sense," it states that everything comes from nothing. In other words, while this principle contains the statement that there is nothing without reason, it is also "found to contain" the statement that there is no reason without the nothing. The "power of the understanding" and the "reign of 'logic'" are thereby "shattered,"[123] although, again, not in favor of dialectic, whose primary aim is to expunge facticity from the science of intelligibility. We saw that this science is neither primordial nor authentic insofar as it evades its factical ground. We also saw that this factical ground is the lived experience of our being-amid-being. We can now finally see that the strangeness of this factical ground is what is revealed to us in anxiety about the nothing.

"What Is Metaphysics?" thus answers the questions with which *Kant and the Problem of Metaphysics* leaves us. But it also shows why, in Davos, Heidegger asserts that being is only comprehensible if the nothing is. He argues that being and nothing "belong together" not because, as Hegel says in the *Science of Logic*, they "agree in their indeterminateness and immediacy," but rather because being "manifests itself only in the transcendence of a Dasein that is held out into the nothing." Boredom and love afford a partial comprehension of being, since it is only through anxiety about the nothing that "belongs" with being that the "total strangeness" of beings as such, namely, their facticity, can "overwhelm us" and "evoke wonder." Hence Heidegger says that the nothing "brings Dasein for the first time before beings as such."[124] Indeed, he goes so far as to identify being and nothing in the 1943 Postscript to "What Is Metaphysics?":

[122] Heidegger WM | W: 17. Cf. Heidegger's 1955–56 *The Principle of Reason*: "Being 'is' in essence: ground/reason. Therefore being can never first have a ground/reason which would supposedly ground it. Accordingly, ground/reason is missing from being. Ground/reason remains at a remove from being. Being 'is' the abyss in the sense of such a remaining-apart of reason from being. To the extent that being as such grounds, it remains groundless. 'Being' does not fall within the orbit of the principle of reason, rather only beings do" (Heidegger SG | GA 10: 92).

[123] Heidegger WM | W: 14. Casati 2022 argues that this entails that Heidegger endorses dialetheism; Witherspoon 2022 and Withy 2022 deny this entailment.

[124] Heidegger WM | W: 12, 17–8. Cf. Heidegger: "The nothing is not an empty nothingness that allows nothing to be present at hand, but is that power which constantly thrusts us back, which alone thrusts us into being and lets us assume power over our Dasein" (Heidegger GM | GA 29/30: 434).

> As that which is altogether other than all beings, being is that which is not. But this nothing essentially prevails as being. We too quickly abdicate thinking when, in a facile explanation, we pass off the nothing as a mere nullity and equate it with the unreal. Instead of giving way to the haste of such empty acumen and relinquishing the enigmatic ambiguities of the nothing, we must prepare ourselves solely in readiness to experience in the nothing the pervasive expanse of that which gives every being the warrant to be. That is being itself. Without being, whose abyssal but yet to be unfolded essence dispenses the nothing to us in essential anxiety, all beings would remain in an absence of being.[125]

Being is not simply not a being. It "itself" is "the nothing" that "prevails" as the "pervasive expanse" against which it is manifest that all beings could well not be and by whose grace "every being" has its peculiar and unsettling "warrant." This raises "enigmatic ambiguities" that include not only the grace of the nothing, but also how we can "prepare ourselves" to be attuned to it in "essential anxiety." Dialectic banishes such ambiguities from philosophy. But this exhibits the "empty acumen" of a reason that, while it overcomes the restricted logic of the understanding, evades both its being conditioned by mood and its presupposition of the brute fact to which mood attunes us.[126] Heidegger elaborates on this point in the 1949 Introduction to "What Is Metaphysics?" by claiming that "cognition" affords a "derivative form" of truth, whose "primordial" form depends on a non-cognitive thinking that, "instead of implementing a higher degree of exertion," for example, what Hegel calls "the labour of the concept," is rather "directed toward another provenance," namely, by being "in thrall to being," which is to say, to the nothing.[127] In anxiety, we are attuned to the nothing that "overwhelm[s]" our reason, which leads us to ask why there is being. This bears out the second important observation, namely, that, by drawing on the transformative mood of anxiety, Heidegger

[125] Heidegger WM | W: 101–2; cf. 211. Cf. Heidegger: "if we want to lay hold of being it is always as if we were reaching into a void. . .[B]eing remains undiscoverable, almost like nothing, or in the end *entirely* so" (Heidegger EM | GA 40: 27).

[126] The Postscript refutes three objections to "What Is Metaphysics?," namely, that it is nihilistic by focusing on the nothing, depressing by focusing on anxiety, and illogical by focusing on mood. Refuting the first objection, Heidegger says that we "abdicate thinking" by confusing the nothing with "unreal[ity]," for it is rather the factical ground of the reality of beings. Refuting the second objection, he says that although anxiety is "the silent voice that attunes us toward the horror of the abyss," readiness for anxiety is readiness for experiencing "the wonder of all wonders: *that* beings *are*. . .For close by essential anxiety. . .dwells awe," which "cherishes" that Dasein "endures," and which the lecture itself states "cannot be opposed to joy," for it "stands. . .in secret alliance with the cheerfulness and gentleness of creative longing." Refuting the third objection, he says that "'logic' is only *one* interpretation of the essence of thinking," whereas a phenomenological interpretation posits as essential that thinking whose thoughts "are in general determined by that which is other than beings" (Heidegger WM | W: 15, 101–5).

[127] Heidegger WM | W: 199, 201.

improves on Schelling's and Lask's positions on our non-rational openness to facticity, which appeal, respectively, to the passivity of sensibility and life.[128]

I will conclude this section by considering how Heidegger radicalizes Kant's humility regarding the science of intelligibility.

We saw in Section 2.3 that Kant defines 'apperception' as the spontaneous activity whereby the I synthesizes representations within a single consciousness, a synthesis that is original insofar as it is not a product of experience. In §17 of the Analytic, he states that the "first principle" of human understanding is that "all the manifold of intuition stand under conditions of the original synthetic unity of apperception." In §19, he adds that the "aim of the copula" in a judgment is to bring representations to the unity of apperception.[129]

Heidegger signals the bounds of apperception at three junctures in "What Is Metaphysics?" First, he says that, in anxiety, not only beings but also "we ourselves" slip away. It is not " 'you' or 'I' " who is left to feel uncanny, but rather "some 'one,' " for, in an "unsettling experience. . .where there is nothing to hold on to, pure Dasein is all that is still there." Anxiety is not synthesized by the I into a single consciousness, for it is the uncanny exposure of consciousness to the radical contingency of beings and, indeed, of being-there. Second, he says that anxiety "robs us of speech" such that "all utterance of the 'is' falls silent." Insofar as anxiety is an experience that deprives the aim of the copula, it severs all representations from the unity of apperception. Third, he says that "[w]ithout the original manifestness of the nothing," the anxious exposure to which puts Dasein "beyond beings as a whole," there is "no selfhood and no freedom."[130] Heidegger here claims that anxiety not only transcends apperception, but also makes the latter possible, for it makes possible the "freedom" of "selfhood," which primarily consists in spontaneously synthesizing representations within the single consciousness of the I. This echoes Heidegger's claim in the 1925–26 winter lectures in Marburg, *Logic: The Question of Truth*, that "[t]he 'I think'. . .is the autonomous but derivative mode of an original making-present on the part of factical existence itself."[131] The I's

[128] Houlgate notes that while Heidegger is known as a "philosopher of *Gelassenheit*, or letting-be. . .Hegel employs the word *lassen* frequently, especially when characterizing the basic attitude of mind required of the philosopher" (Houlgate 2006: 61), e.g., when Hegel says, in the *Phenomenology*, that "instead of being the arbitrarily moving principle of the content of [science]," the philosopher "sink[s] [their] freedom in [this] content" (Hegel PG | W 3: 56), in the *Encyclopedia*, that the philosopher "give[s] up" their "subjective particularity" and "let[s] thought follow its own course" (Hegel EL | GW 20: §24 Addition 2) and, in the *Logic*, that the philosopher allows "pure knowledge" to "step back from its content, allowing it free play. . .without determining it further" (Hegel SL | GW 21: 59). However, as we saw in Section 3.6, the result of Hegelian letting-be is spirit's being at home in the world, i.e., the total intelligibility of its world, which would make spirit immune to the anxiety that discloses Dasein's facticity and to which, for Heidegger, Dasein is permanently vulnerable. In other words, whereas dialectic begins by giving up control in thinking and ends with the absolute freedom of thinking, hermeneutics is a thinking that resolves to inescapably reproduce the factical situation into which it is uncannily thrown.

[129] Kant KrV B136, 139, 142.

[130] Heidegger WM | W: 9–10, 12.

[131] Heidegger L | GA 21: 407. Cf. Heidegger SZ | GA 2: 318–21.

"autonomous" mode of the "making-present" of a world is "derivative" because it depends on a deeper condition of intelligibility, namely, the "factical existence" on the basis of which we apperceptively synthesize our representations, but which we only authentically grasp in resolute responsiveness to our anxious attunement to the nothing.

Heidegger signals the bounds of apperception by positing the nothing as its condition of intelligibility. He thereby articulates an unspoken truth in '*nihil ulterius*,' Kant's phrase for the ultimate groundlessness of intelligibility. While the nothing conditions the making-present of a world of beings, it is itself radically contingent and thus groundless. It is the 'nothing further,' that is, the lack of a rational principle, on which rests not only the forms of judgment and the forms of sensibility, whose bruteness Kant acknowledges, but also, and more fundamentally, the bruteness of our apperceptively being-there. Heidegger therefore radicalizes Kant's humility regarding the science of intelligibility by showing that the nothing to which anxiety attunes us grounds apperception itself and hence the unity of our consciousness of the world. In other words, Heidegger surpasses Kant's tolerance for radical contingency by showing that not even the I can get back behind its thrownness as being-amid-being. This is not to deny that, as we saw in Part I, Kant is a philosopher of facticity *avant la lettre*, but is rather to suggest that Heidegger is the philosopher of facticity *par excellence*.[132]

By articulating an unspoken truth in Kant's factical phrase, Heidegger underscores his view that the German idealist campaign against facticity is a ruinant evasion of its alogical presupposition. Hence Heidegger says that science, if it truly "understands itself," cannot "surrender the nothing."[133] Self-understanding, as we saw in Section 6.3, is the "*wakefulness*" that we exhibit when we resolve to turn toward and interpret our factical life. Taking this turn in philosophy demands the "readiness to experience in the nothing the pervasive expanse of that which gives every being the warrant to be," that is, the readiness to be attuned in anxiety to the radical contingency of being-there.[134] Moreover, the hermeneutical interpretation of being-there in terms of the existentials that condition the intelligibility of being-there, if it is to methodologically serve phenomenology *qua* primordial science, must sustain our readiness for anxious attunement. It can do so only by refusing to "surrender the nothing" to the "empty acumen" of ruinant philosophy, that is, by refusing to surrender facticity to its supposed dialectical elimination.

The final sentence of "What Is Metaphysics?" concludes that "the nothing itself compels" the "fundamental question of metaphysics," namely: "why are there

[132] See Heidegger: "We can say that Fichte and Hegel are looking for a ground where for Kant there could only be an abyss" (Heidegger VS | GA 15: 38).

[133] Heidegger WM | W: 18.

[134] Shockey worries that Heideggerian anxiety offers an ontical disclosure of one's life, not an ontological disclosure of life itself (Shockey 2016: 13). However, this seems to be a false dichotomy, given that, for Heidegger, Dasein's "ontic distinction" is that it "*is* ontological."

beings at all and not rather nothing?"[135] In the last section of this chapter, I will show that Heidegger investigates this question six years later in the *Introduction to Metaphysics* as part of an argument for the claim that thinking philosophically about the nothing must be authentic and therefore, in some sense, unscientific.

6.6 Philosophy and Unscientificity

In *Introduction to Metaphysics*, Chapter One, "The Fundamental Question of Metaphysics," Heidegger gives three reasons for the claim that the question "[w]hy are there beings at all instead of nothing?" is the "first of all questions," not chronologically, but rather "in rank." First, it is "the broadest in scope," for, since it "comes to a halt at no being of any kind" and is "limited" only by the nothing, "we can never exceed it." Since the question concerns neither any particular being nor the sum of all beings, no other question can exceed its scope. Second, it is the "deepest," for it seeks not the "causes" of beings, but rather their "ground." The question concerns the ground on which it is so much as possible for beings to causally interact. Third, it is the "most originary," for it abstracts "from every particular, individual being" in order to disclose the "ground" through which "beings as a whole are first opened up *as such*." Since all beings could well not be, no being could be the origin of the nothing, which means that no question could be more originary.[136]

Heidegger observes three corollaries of this claim. First, "[p]hilosophizing means asking" the why-question.[137] Insofar as it inquires into that which is common to all object-domains, philosophy *qua* primordial science ultimately and unavoidably "means" inquiring into the nothing. Second, the why-question "recoils upon itself" so as to ask: "[w]hat is the ground of this why-question itself?"[138] In asking why there are beings, the question cannot exclude its own being, that is, why it is posed. Third, however "strange" philosophy's question seems to "everyday understanding," its real "achieve[ment]" consists in "burdening" Dasein with the "weight" of all beings.[139] Under the "reign of 'logic,'" everyday understanding, like non-primordial science, regards the question about the nothing as "outrage[ous]." But logic thereby serves the they's spectral capacity for "*disburden[ing]*" Dasein of genuine questioning. Philosophy's essential, burdensome question invites Dasein's "*authentic self*" to see that the "weight" of beings consists in their weightlessness,

[135] Heidegger WM | W: 19; cf. 210.
[136] Heidegger EM | GA 40: 1–3.
[137] Heidegger EM | GA 40: 6.
[138] Heidegger EM | GA 40: 4, 10. Cf. Heidegger: "thus not only what is asked about is extraordinary, but also the questioning itself" (Heidegger EM | GA 40: 10). This implies, as we saw in Section 4.5, that Schelling's answer to the why-question in his Berlin lectures cannot but invite its return, such that he must defer a definitive answer.
[139] Heidegger EM | GA 40: 9. Cf. Heidegger: "True talk of nothing always remains unfamiliar. It does not allow itself to be made common" (Heidegger EM | GA 40: 20).

that is, in their radically contingent or factical grounding in the nothing. Such a question ultimately confronts Dasein with its own facticity. This bears out the third important observation, namely, that, by construing the why-question as asking about being-there, Heidegger improves on Schelling's position on the why-question, which restricts itself to asking about being.

Shortly after, Heidegger elaborates on the third corollary of his claim in a way that not only underscores his radicalization of Kant's humility regarding the science of intelligibility, as we saw in Section 6.5, but also clarifies the scientific character of this science. I will analyze this elaboration in two parts.

In the first part of the elaboration, Heidegger says:

> it cannot be decided so readily whether logic and its fundamental rules can provide any measure for the question about beings as such. It could be the other way around, that the whole logic that we know and that we treat like a gift from heaven is grounded in a very definite answer to the question about beings, and that consequently any thinking that simply follows the laws of thought of established logic is intrinsically incapable of even beginning to understand the question about beings, much less of actually unfolding it and leading it toward an answer. In truth, it is only an illusion of rigor and scientificity when one appeals to the principle of contradiction, and to logic in general, in order to prove that all thinking and talk about nothing is contradictory and therefore senseless. 'Logic' is then taken as a tribunal, secure for all eternity, and it goes without saying that no rational human being will call into doubt its authority as the first and last court of appeal. Whoever speaks against logic is suspected, implicitly or explicitly, of arbitrariness. This mere suspicion already counts as an argument and an objection, and one takes oneself to be exempted from further, authentic reflection.[140]

A science that gives beings "the first and last word" must respect logic as "the first and last court of appeal" if it is to speak about its particular object-domain consistently, that is, without contradiction. It would seem, then, that the why-question, by "depriv[ing] itself" of an object-domain, is "contradictory and therefore senseless." In any case, a thinking that "simply follows" logical principles is "intrinsically incapable of even beginning to understand" such a question. Nevertheless, it is possible that logical consistency is not the appropriate "measure" for the why-question, particularly if logic is "treat[ed] like a gift from heaven" and "secure for all eternity." If logical principles were heaven-sent and eternally secured, then they would apparently be absolutely necessary. But then they would fail to contribute to Dasein's intelligibility, the conditions of which are precisely not absolutely necessary, but rather are radically contingent, including, as they do, the nothing. Asking about

[140] Heidegger EM | GA 40: 19.

the latter accordingly demands a non-logical measure, which we find in the mood of anxiety. Only phenomenology's "authentic reflection" on our being-there can indicate anxiety's capacity to attune us to the nothing as that which "overwhelm[s] us" and "evoke[s] wonder."[141] Absent such reflection, our fidelity to logic secures consistency yet "is only an illusion of rigor and scientificity." Heidegger puts this final point in strikingly Hegelian terms. As we saw in Section 3.3, Hegel attributes "unscientificity" to "the vulgarity of the understanding and the vanity of its exaltation above reason." Rather than follow Hegel by reserving scientificity for reason, however, Heidegger implicitly ascribes scientificity to the authentic reflection according to which mood conditions the possibility of knowledge in the guises of understanding and reason alike.

In the second part of the elaboration, which continues immediately after the first part, Heidegger says:

> One cannot, in fact, talk about and deal with the nothing as if it were a thing, such as the rain out there, or a mountain, or any object at all; the nothing remains in principle inaccessible to all science. Whoever truly wants to talk of the nothing must necessarily become unscientific. But this is a great misfortune only if one believes that scientific thinking alone is the authentic, rigorous thinking, that it alone can and must be made the measure even of philosophical thinking. But the reverse is the case. All scientific thinking is just a derivative and rigidified form of philosophical thinking. Philosophy never arises from or through science. Philosophy can never belong to the same order as the sciences. It belongs to a higher order, and not just 'logically', as it were, or in a table of the system of sciences. Philosophy stands in a completely different domain and rank of spiritual Dasein.[142]

Since the nothing is "in principle inaccessible" to any ontic science whose speech exclusively refers to "thing[s]" or "object[s]," that is, to beings, anyone who purports to speak about it "must necessarily become unscientific." But this assumes that such an ontic science is "authentic" and is therefore the "measure" of "philosophical thinking." We have seen that this science is not authentic, for, by referring to beings alone, it clarifies an object-domain at the expense of "remain[ing] with"

[141] See Heidegger's 1928–29 winter lectures in Freiburg, *Introduction to Philosophy*: "But one will say: why not leave metaphysics in the safe and definite guard of logic? Why then the struggle against rationalism, when it has given the history of metaphysics such great impetus? However, it is not about the fight against rationalism, nor about partisanship with irrationalism, but solely about enabling a more radical interpretation of transcendence, of the understanding of being, in view of the fact that the λόγος only has an interpretive and determining function, which does not mean that it has no role at all in the problem of being. It is important to see that the understanding of being lies above all logical statements and determinations and makes this possible in the first place" (Heidegger EP | GA 27: 320, partly translated by Käufer 2001: 470).

[142] Heidegger EM | GA 40: 19–20.

the lived standpoint on things and, by making logic the sole measure of thinking, it secures logically consistent thinking at the expense of attunement to the nothing that grounds the very possibility of logically consistent thinking about beings. A science that is restricted to beings and logic lacks authenticity and therefore cannot be the measure of philosophy.

It is in the light of this final point that we should understand Heidegger's claims that philosophy belongs to a different "order" than "the sciences" and that a philosophical investigation of the nothing must be "unscientific." Such claims might suggest that science and philosophy are mutually exclusive. However, we have seen that a science can be either non-primordial and thus non-philosophical, namely, when it concerns beings and takes logic as its sole measure, or primordial and thus philosophical, namely, when it concerns that which is beyond beings and takes logic as its subordinate measure. As the science of intelligibility, philosophy is unscientific strictly insofar as it is not non-primordial and so not beholden exclusively to logical consistency. It nevertheless exhibits scientificity, namely, in virtue of its authentic reflection on the facticity of our being-there. We can therefore say that the scientific character of philosophy *qua* science of intelligibility consists in its being authentic.[143]

We have seen that authenticity demands the resolve to turn toward our factical life and to hermeneutically interpret its conditions of intelligibility. Insofar as this turn requires interrupting our natural flight from life, it is not given, but is rather a task. Heidegger describes asking the fundamental question of metaphysics in these terms when he says that the why-question is "not given like shoes, clothes, or books," but rather "only" is as it is "actually asked," where asking it is "a *willing*-to-know" and thus requires a will that "*is* resolute."[144] I will conclude this chapter by considering a question about Heidegger's conception of the authentic turn.

In Division Two, Chapter II of *Being and Time*, Heidegger says that insofar as the they "disburden[s] Dasein of the explicit *choice*" of the "tasks, rules, standards," "urgency," and "scope" of its "possibilities-of-being," Dasein is "'lived' by the commonsense ambiguity of publicness" and thereby "lost" in "inauthenticity." In order to "*find* itself," Dasein must first be "summoned" by what he calls the "call of conscience." Conscience summons one "[t]o one's *own self*," that is, to one who is "awakened" to the fact that the correctness, significance, and extent of one's possibilities-of-being depend not on an anonymous public, but rather on one's own freedom, which itself depends on interpretable yet brute conditions of

[143] Heidegger indicates that the authenticity of philosophical science consists partly in its irreducibility to a fixed doctrine: "Because philosophy is the universal science, as opposed to the so-called individual sciences, it will give our studies the right breadth and round them off. . .Is there a falseness and a hidden despair somewhere in all this activity? What if it were a *prejudice* that metaphysics is a fixed and secure discipline, and an *illusion* that philosophy is a science that can be taught and learned?" (Heidegger GM | GA 29/30: 1–2).

[144] Heidegger EM | GA 40: 15–6.

intelligibility, that is, on a situation into which one is factically thrown. The call of conscience thus invites one to resolve to turn from one's "they-self" toward "*authentic* being-one's-self" and, in doing so, to grasp the existential structure of one's thrown being.[145]

Heidegger identifies three core features of the call of conscience. First, the call is not an "utterance," but rather "*speaks solely and constantly in the mode of silence*," which he clarifies is an "uncanny mode of silence." Since anxiety is associated with uncanniness, namely, the uncanny feeling of the "slipping away" of beings, we must hear the call in a mood of anxiety. Hence Heidegger says that conscience requires "a readiness for anxiety." Second, the call is "neither planned nor prepared for nor willfully brought about," but rather is made "against our expectations and even against our will." Since, as we saw in Section 5.1, mood is generally something that "assails" us, we must hear the call in the passivity of being struck by anxiety. Third, the call does not come from "someone else," but rather "comes *from* me, and yet *over* me." Since the call strikes us with anxiety yet not externally, we must hear it in being struck by our own standpoint, that is, by our own being-there. Hence Heidegger says that the "caller" is "the naked 'that'" of "Dasein."[146] Thus, it is in being internally struck by the call of conscience in a mood of anxiety that we can resolve not to return in flight to our "they-self" and instead to turn authentically toward our "*own self*."

Heidegger's conception of authenticity raises the question of what could justify my turn from they-self to own-self. One indeed finds justifications for analogous philosophical turns. For Kant, it is judgment's demand for self-knowledge that justifies the Copernican turn from dogmatism to criticism.[147] For Fichte, it is philosophy's demand for a first principle that justifies the idealist turn from objects to the freedom of reason.[148] For Hegel, it is consciousness' demand for science that justifies the dialectical turn from alienation to absolute knowledge.[149] By contrast, nothing justifies the turn from inauthenticity to authenticity, for nothing is authorized to demand it. In resolving to "*mak[e] up for not choosing*" who and

[145] Heidegger SZ | GA 2: 268, 273, 275, 299. Heidegger says that conscience is only possible given Dasein's "primordial being-guilty" for the fact that it "closes itself off from itself as thrown and fallen prey," i.e., from its "lostness in the they." To conscientiously acknowledge this guilt, i.e., to find oneself lost, is to make genuine moral propriety possible. Hence Heidegger says that "essential being guilty is, equiprimordially, the existential condition of the possibility of the 'morally' good and evil" and so "cannot be defined by morality because morality already presupposed it for itself" (Heidegger SZ | GA 2: 286–7). While the call of conscience resembles the call in Kant's enlightenment dictum to summon the "resolution and courage" that is necessary in order to be mature, a crucial difference, as we saw in Section 6.3, is that the latter call, when taken to its German idealist conclusion as a radicalized enlightenment ideal of rational cognition, becomes the "empty maxim" of taking direction from nothing, not even factical life.

[146] Heidegger SZ | GA 2: 273, 275, 277, 296. On Heidegger's conception of conscience, see Blattner 2015, Crowell 2013, Han-Pile 2013, and Kukla 2002.

[147] See Kant KrV Axi.

[148] See Fichte VND | SW I: 422–3.

[149] See Hegel PG | W 3: 20.

how to be, namely, by "choosing to make this choice,"[150] I heed a wordless, unbidden, and unpredictable call. There is no court to which my heeding can appeal, since recognizing the authority of any such court itself depends on my resolutely choosing to choose.[151] Heeding the call of conscience consists not in being responsible to a putatively authoritative norm, but rather in committing to be responsible for norms as such, that is, in "*wanting to have a conscience*."[152] The turn to authenticity is simply a matter of decision, that is, a matter of whether one commits to being a being whose fundamental question concerns the facticity of being, a question to whose topic we may be attuned by anxiety. Intensifying Fichte's dictum that "the kind of philosophy one chooses. . .depends upon the kind of person one is," Heidegger's conception of the authentic turn shows that the kind of person one is remains radically open.

As I have tried to show, the fate of reason after Kant is to transform from a pure activity that derives absolutely necessary conditions of intelligibility from its own contradictions into a lived activity whose conditions of intelligibility are interpretable yet ultimately brute, which is to say, groundless or radically contingent.[153] Philosophy can fruitfully interpret such conditions. However, it can never transcend them, since, by interpreting them, philosophy forever exhibits its own facticity.[154]

[150] Heidegger SZ | GA 2: 268.

[151] See Heidegger: "It would be a complete misunderstanding of the phenomenon of resoluteness if one were to believe that it is simply a matter of receptively taking up possibilities presented and suggested" (Heidegger SZ | GA 2: 298).

[152] Heidegger SZ | GA: 288.

[153] See Merleau-Ponty's 1950s lecture notes: "There are two directions in Kant. Within human contingency (*quid facti*) he discovers a positing power (*quid juris*). Human being is a facticity that gives itself validity *de jure*" (Merleau-Ponty 2003: 22).

[154] See Merleau-Ponty: "Human existence will lead us to revisit our usual notion of necessity and of contingency, because human existence is the change of contingency into necessity through the act of taking up. All that we are, we are on the basis of a factual situation that we make our own and that we ceaselessly transform through a sort of *escape* that is never an unconditioned freedom" (Merleau-Ponty 2012: 174).

Conclusion

The cover of this book features a reproduction of Hendrick Goltzius' 1588 drawing of his right hand. A printmaker, draftsman, and painter who came from a long line of artists, Goltzius was a leading engraver of the early Baroque period. The drawing portrays an adult hand that, when he was a child, was burned and fixed into the depicted position. Although the result of an injury, the position was suited to holding and guiding the burin that he used to produce the engravings for which he became well known.

The book's cover is a metaphor for the ambiguity of its epigraph. As we have seen, the parting of the ways after Kant centrally concerns the question of whether we remain in reason's hand, as Fichte holds, or are arationally thrown into existence, as Heidegger holds. Goltzius' half-closed hand symbolizes the openness of this question. As post-Kantians, we must ask whether we are held by reason or thrown into being, that is, whether we are supported by the all or by the nothing. *Ich bin* or *Es gibt*.

Fichte's *Wissenschaftslehre* is the main source of the post-Kantian parting of the ways. It bears the twin birth of the coining of 'facticity,' which signifies the alleged problem of the radical contingency of the conditions of intelligibility, and the invention of dialectical logic, which serves as the putatively absolute science of deriving such conditions from the contradictions of reason. Fichte's system points directly toward Hegel's presuppositionless logic, as we saw in Chapters 1 and 2, and indirectly, via Lask and Dilthey, toward Heidegger's hermeneutics of facticity, as we saw in Chapter 5. Fichte and Hegel radicalize Kant's theory of enlightenment by daring reason to take direction from itself alone, as we saw in Chapter 3, but provoke Heidegger's critique of inauthenticity by not daring to take direction from factical life, as we saw in Chapter 6. Finally, as we saw in Chapter 4, it is only with Schelling's defense of facticity that post-Kantian philosophy begins its transition from German idealism's architectonic interest in logical systematicity toward phenomenology's existentialist interest in radical contingency, that is, from the primacy of the practical to the primacy of the factical. Such a transition positions us today to use the concept of facticity in order to address persistent philosophical problems.

The hitherto untold history of the concept of facticity traces a line from Kant, through the rise and fall of German idealism and the emergence of neo-Kantianism, to the flourishing of phenomenology. Admittedly, this history is one chapter in philosophy's ancient and abiding confrontation with brute facts. However, in light

Facticity and the Fate of Reason After Kant. G. Anthony Bruno, Oxford University Press. © G. Anthony Bruno 2025. DOI: 10.1093/9780191987533.003.0008

of the Copernican turn that opens that chapter, philosophy's confrontation with bruteness takes the form of a quite specific question, namely, whether a genuine science of the conditions of intelligibility can tolerate extra-logical presuppositions, that is, whether critique is consistent with facticity. This question is decisive for the kind of philosophy that one chooses after Kant, for it concerns our resoluteness in the face of human finitude. The radical contingency, that is, the bruteness or groundlessness, of the conditions of intelligibility, of the freedom and character with which we might pursue a science of intelligibility, of intelligible existence itself, and of our thrownness into intelligible existence all refer to our inescapably finite standpoint on intelligibility. We ourselves are radical contingency incarnate. How we choose to answer the post-Kantian question therefore inevitably exhibits whether and to what extent we own up to our finitude.

Post-Kantian thinkers, including Schelling and Heidegger, who interpret rather than recoil from facticity, that is, who tarry with the groundless ground of intelligibility, are committed philosophers of finitude. The example that they set, however, is not only one of resoluteness. It is also one of humility, since any interpretation of our factical situation can only reproduce that very situation, thereby inviting further, hermeneutical interpretation. The precise character of critique's consistency with facticity is accordingly marked by a constitutive incompleteness of interpretation. We should find in this incompleteness an opening for our own contributions in thinking with and beyond the post-Kantian philosophers of finitude.

References

Main Primary Sources

Wilhelm Dilthey (1833–1911)

A (1910). *Der Aufbau der geschichtlichen Welt in den Geisteswissenschaften* (2002). *The Formation of the Historical World in the Human Sciences*, ed. Rudolph A. Makkreel and Frithjof Rodi. Princeton: Princeton University Press.

EG (1883). *Einleitung in die Geisteswissenschaften.* (1989). *Introduction to the Human Sciences*, ed. Rudolph A. Makkreel and Frithjof Rodi. Princeton: Princeton University Press.

EH (1900). "Die Entstehung der Hermeneutik." (1972). "The Rise of Hermeneutics" in *New Literary History* 3 (2).

VH (1867–68). "Über Verstehen und Hermeneutik" (1996). "On Understanding and Hermeneutics" in *Hermeneutics and the Study of History*, ed. Rudolph A. Makkreel and Frithjof Rodi. Princeton: Princeton University Press.

Johann Gottlieb Fichte (1762–1814)

Fichte, J. G. (1965). *Sämmtliche Werke* [SW], ed. I. H. Fichte. Berlin: de Gruyter.

Fichte, J. G. (1962–2012). *J. G. Fichte: Gesamtausgabe der Bayerischen Akademie der Wissenschaften* [GA], ed. Erich Fuchs, Hans Gliwitzky, Reinhard Lauth, and Peter K. Schneider. Stuttgart-Bad Canstatt: Frommann-holzboog.

A (1801). "Ankündigung." (1994). "Public Announcement of a New Presentation of the *Wissenschaftslehre*" [GA I/7] in *Introductions to the Wissenschaftslehre and Other Writings*, trs. Daniel Breazeale. Indianapolis: Hackett.

AP (1800). "Aus einem Privatschreiben." (1994). "From a Private Letter" [SW V] in *Introductions to the Wissenschaftslehre and Other Writings*, trs. Daniel Breazeale. Indianapolis: Hackett.

ASL (1806). *Die Anweisung zum seligen Leben oder auch die Religionslehre.* (1889). *The Way Towards the Blessed Life, or the Doctrine of Religion* [SW V] in *The Popular Works of Johann Gottlieb Fichte, Volume 2*, trs. William Smith. London: Trubner and Co.

AU (1810). *Die Wissenschaftslehre in ihrem allgemeinen Umrisse dargestellt.* (1889). *The Wissenschaftslehre in its General Outline* [SW II] in *The Popular Works of Johann Gottlieb Fichte, Volume 2*, trs. William Smith. London: Trubner and Co.

B (1790–99). "Briefwechsel." (1988). "Selected Correspondence, 1790–99" in *Early Philosophical Writings*, trs. Daniel Breazeale. Ithaca: Cornell University Press.

BE (1795). "Über Belebung und Erhöhung des reinen Interesse für Wahrheit." (1988). "On Stimulating and Increasing the Pure Interest in Truth" [SW VIII] in *Early Philosophical Writings*, trs. Daniel Breazeale. Ithaca: Cornell University Press.

BM (1800). *Die Bestimmung des Menschen.* (1931). *The Vocation of Man* [SW II], trs. William Smith. Chicago: Open Court.

BS (1800–02). "Briefweschsel." (2012). "Correspondence" in *The Philosophical Rupture Between Fichte and Schelling: Selected Texts and Correspondence (1800–02)*, trs. Michael Vater and David W. Wood. Albany: SUNY Press.

BWL (1794). "Über den Begriff der Wissenschaftslehre." (1988). "Concerning the Concept of the *Wissenschaftslehre*" [SW I] in *Early Philosophical Writings*, trs. Daniel Breazeale. Ithaca: Cornell University Press.

DWL (1801–02). *Darstellung der Wissenschaftslehre* [*Presentation of the Wissenschaftslehre*] [SW II].

EM (1793–94). "*Eigne Meditationen über ElementarPhilosophie*" ["Personal Meditations on Elementary Philosophy"] [GA II/3].

GE (1795). *Grundriss des Eigenthümlichen der Wissenschaftslehre in Rücksicht auf das theoretische Vermögen.* (1988). *Outline of the Distinctive Character of the Wissenschaftslehre with Respect to the Theoretical Faculty* in *Early Philosophical Writings* [SW I], trs. Daniel Breazeale. Ithaca: Cornell University Press.

GGW (1798). "Über den Grund unsers Glaubens an eine göttliche Weltregierung." (1994). "On the Basis of Our Belief in a Divine Governance of the World" [SW V] in *Introductions to the Wissenschaftslehre and Other Writings*, trs. Daniel Breazeale. Indianapolis: Hackett.

GGZ (1806). *Der Grundzüge des gegenwärtigen Zeitalters.* (1889). *The Characteristics of the Present Age* [SW VII] in *The Popular Works of Johann Gottlieb Fichte, Volume 2*, trs. William Smith. London: Trubner and Co.

GN (1796). *Grundlage des Naturrechts nach Principien der Wissenschaftslehre.* (2000). *Foundations of Natural Right* [SW III], trs. Michael Bauer. Cambridge: Cambridge University Press.

GWL (1794–95). *Grundlage der gesamten Wissenschaftslehre.* (2021). *Foundation of the Entire Wissenschaftslehre* [SW I] in *Foundation of the Entire Wissenschaftslehre and Related Writings (1794–95)*, trs. Daniel Breazeale. Oxford: Oxford University Press.

NB (1800). *Neue Bearbeitung der Wissenschaftslehre.* (2012). *New Version of the Wissenschaftslehre* in *The Philosophical Rupture Between Fichte and Schelling: Selected Texts and Correspondence (1800–02)*, trs. Michael Vater. Albany: SUNY Press.

NM (1796–99). *Wissenschaftslehre Nova Methodo.* (1992). *Foundations of Transcendental Philosophy (Wissenschaftslehre) Nova Methodo* [GA IV/2], trs. Daniel Breazeale. Ithaca: Cornell University Press.

PE (1805). *Propädeutik Erlangen* [*Erlangen Propaedeutics*] [GA II/9].

PGSR (1805). *Principien der Gottes-, Sitten- und Rechtslehre* [*Principles of the Doctrine of God, Ethics, and Jurisprudence*] [GA II/7].

RA (1794). "Rezension von Aenesidemus." (1988). "Review of *Aenesidemus*" [SW I] in *Early Philosophical Writings*, trs. Daniel Breazeale. Ithaca: Cornell University Press.

RAF (1799). *Rückerinnerungen, Antworten, Fragen* [*Recollections, Answers, Questions*] [SW V; GA II/5].

RG (1800). *Rezension: Grundriß der ersten Logik, gereiniget von den Irrthümern bisheriger Logiken überhaupt, der Kantischen insbesondre; keine Kritik, sondern eine Medicina mentis, brauchbar hauptsachlich für Teutschlands kritische Philosophie, von C. G. Bardili* [*Review: Outline of the First Logic Purified of the Errors of Previous Logic in General and of the Kantian in Particular; Not a Criticism, but a* Medicina Mentis *Mainly Useful for Germany's Critical Philosophy, by C. G. Bardili*] [GA I/6].

S (1800–01). "Bei der Lectüre von Schellings tr. Idealismus," "Vorarbeiten gegen Schelling," "Zur Darstellung von Schelling's Identitätssysteme." (2012). "Commentaries on Schelling's *Transcendental Idealism* and *Presentation of My System of Philosophy*" in *The Philosophical Rupture Between Fichte and Schelling: Selected Texts and Correspondence (1800–02)*, trs. Michael Vater. Albany: SUNY Press.

SB (1801). "Sonnenklarer Bericht an das größere Publikum über das eigentliche Wesen der neuesten Philosophie. Ein Versuch, die Leser zum Verstehen zu zwingen." (1987). "A Crystal Clear Report to the General Public Concerning the Actual Essence of the Newest Philosophy: An Attempt to Force the Reader to Understand" in *Philosophy of German Idealism*, ed. Ernst Behler. New York: Continuum.

SS (1798). *Das System der Sittenlehre nach den Principien der Wissenschaftslehre.* (2005). *The System of Ethics According to the Principles of the Wissenschaftslehre* [SW IV], trs. Daniel Breazeale and Günter Zöller. Cambridge: Cambridge University Press.

SUS (1795). "Von der Sprachfähigkeit und dem Ursprung der Sprache." (1996). "On the Linguistic Capacity and the Origin of Language" [GA I/3] in *Language and German Idealism: Fichte's Linguistic Philosophy*, trs. Jere Paul Surber. New Jersey: Humanities Press.

TB (1817). *Die Thatsachen des Bewusstseyns.* (2017). *Facts of Consciousness*, trs. Adolph Ernst Kroeger. UK: Anados.

UGB (1794). "Über den Unterschied des Geistes und des Buchstabens in der Philosophie." (1988). "Concerning the Difference Between the Spirit and the Letter within Philosophy" in *Early Philosophical Writings*, trs. Daniel Breazeale. Ithaca: Cornell University Press.

VBG (1794). "Einige Vorlesungen über die Bestimmung des Gelehrten." (1988). "Some Lectures Concerning the Scholar's Vocation" [SW VI] in *Early Philosophical Writings*, trs. Daniel Breazeale. Ithaca: Cornell University Press.

VND (1797–98). *Versuch einer neuen Darstellung der Wissenschaftslehre.* (1994). *Attempt at a New Presentation of the Wissenschaftslehre* [SW I] in *Introductions to the Wissenschaftslehre and Other Writings*, trs. Daniel Breazeale. Indianapolis: Hackett.

WL04 (1804). *Die Wissenschaftslehre: Zweiter Vortrag im Jahre 1804.* (2005). *The Science of Knowing* [GA II/8], trs. Walter E. Wright. Albany: SUNY Press.

ZFK (1798). "Zu 'Fichte und Kant, oder Versuch einer Ausgleichung der Fichteschen und Kantischen Philosophie.'" (1994). "Note to 'Fichte and Kant, or An Attempted Comparison between the Fichtean and the Kantian Philosophy'" [GA I/4] in *Introductions to the Wissenschaftslehre and Other Writings*, trs. Daniel Breazeale. Indianapolis: Hackett.

Georg Wilhelm Friedrich Hegel (1770–1831)

Hegel, G. W. F. (1986). *Vorlesungen: Ausgewählte Nachschriften und Manuskripte* [V], ed. Pierre Garniron and Walter Jaeschke. Hamburg: Meiner.

Hegel, G. W. F. (1970). *Werke in 20 Bänden* [W], ed. Eva Moldenhauer and Karl Markus Michel. Frankfurt: Suhrkamp.

Hegel, G. W. F. (1968). *Gesammelte Werke* [GW], Deutsche Forschungsgemeinschaft. Hamburg: Meiner.

A (1823, 1826, 1829–29). *Vorlesungen über die Ästhetik I.* (1975). *Aesthetics: Lectures on Fine Art, Volume 1*, trs. T. M. Knox. Oxford: Oxford University Press.

B (1793–1831). *Briefe.* (1984). *The Letters*, trs. Clark Butler and Christiane Seiler. Bloomington: Indiana University Press.

D (1801). *Differenz des fichte'schen und schelling'schen Systems der Philosophie.* (1977). *The Difference Between Fichte's and Schelling's System of Philosophy* [GW 4], trs. Walter Cerf and H. S. Harris. Albany: SUNY Press.

EL (1830). *Enzyklopädie der philosophischen Wissenschaften I: Der Logik mit Zusatze.* (1991). *The Encyclopedia Logic (with the Zusätze)* [GW 20], trs. T. F. Geraets, W. A. Suchting and H. S. Harris. Indianapolis: Hackett.

EPN (1830). *Enzyklopädie der philosophischen Wissenschaften II: Die Philosophie der Natur.* (2004). *Hegel's Philosophy of Nature*, trs. A. V. Miller. Oxford: Clarendon.

F (1803). *Fragment* in (1979) *System of Ethical Life (1802/03) and First Philosophy of Spirit (Part III of the System of Speculative Philosophy 1803/04)*, trs. H. S. Harris and T. M. Knox. Albany: SUNY Press.

GM (1802). "Wie der gemeine Menschenverstand die Philosophie nehme, dargestellt an den Werken des Herrn Krug." (2000). "How the Ordinary Human Understanding Takes Philosophy (as Displayed in the Works of Mr. Krug)" in *Between Kant and Hegel: Texts in the Development of Post-Kantian Idealism*, trs. George di Giovanni and H. S. Harris. Indianapolis: Hackett.

GuW (1802). "Glauben und Wissen." (1977). "Faith and Knowledge" [GW 4], trs. Walter Cerf and H. S. Harris. Albany: SUNY Press.

JW (1816). "Friedrich Heinrich Jacobis Werke, Dritter Band." (2009). "Review, *Friedrich Heinrich Jacobi's Works, Volume 3*" in *Heidelberg Writings*, trs. Brady Bowman and Allen Speight. Cambridge: Cambridge University Press.

OP (1801). "*De Orbitis Planetarum.*" (2002). "Philosophical Dissertation on the Orbits of the Planets and the Habilitation Theses" [W 2] in *Miscellaneous Writings of G. W. F. Hegel*, ed. Jon Stewart. Evanston: Northwestern University Press.

PG (1807). *Die Phänomenologie des Geistes.* (1977). *Phenomenology of Spirit* [W 3], trs. A. V. Miller. Oxford: Oxford University Press.

VGP1 (1823–24, 1825–26, 1827–28). *Vorlesungen über die Geschichte der Philosophie I.* (1985). *Introduction to the Lectures on the History of Philosophy*, trs. T. M. Knox and A. V. Miller, Oxford: Oxford University Press.

VGP2 (1894). *Lectures on the History of Philosophy, Volume 2*, trs. E. S. Haldane and Frances H. Simson. London: Kegan Paul, Trench, Trübner, and Co.

VGP3 (1825–26). *Vorlesungen über die Geschichte der Philosophie III.* (1990). *Lectures on the History of Philosophy 1825–26, Volume 3: Medieval and Modern Philosophy* [V 9], trs. R. F. Brown and J. M. Stewart. California: University of California Press.

VPW1 (1822–23). *Vorlesungen über die Philosophie der Weltgeschichte.* (2011). *Lectures on the Philosophy of World History, Volume 1* [GW 18], trs. Robert F. Brown and Peter C. Hodgson. Oxford: Clarendon.

VPW2 (1830–31). *Vorlesungen über die Philosophie der Weltgeschichte.* (1975). *Lectures on the Philosophy of World History. Introduction: Reason in History*, trs. H. B. Nisbet. Cambridge: Cambridge University Press.

VSP (1802). "Verhältnis des Skeptizismus zur Philosophie. Darstellung seiner verschiedenen Modifikationen und Vergleichung des neuesten mit dem alten." (2000). "On the Relationship of Skepticism to Philosophy, Exposition of its Different Modifications and Comparison of the Latest Form with the Ancient One" in *Between Kant and Hegel: Texts in the Development of Post-Kantian Idealism*, trs. George di Giovanni and H. S. Harris. Indianapolis: Hackett.

WL (1812–16). *Wissenschaft der Logik.* (2010). *Science of Logic* [GW 11, 12, 21], trs. George di Giovanni. Cambridge: Cambridge University Press.

WPK (1801). "Über das Wesen der philosophischen Kritik überhaupt und ihr Verhältnis zum gegenwärtigen Zustand der Philosophie insbesondere." (2000). "On the Essence of Philosophical Critique Generally and its Relationship to the Present State of Philosophy in Particular" in *Between Kant and Hegel: Texts in the Development of Post-Kantian Idealism*, trs. George di Giovanni and H. S. Harris. Indianapolis: Hackett.

Martin Heidegger (1889–1976)

Heidegger, Martin (1975–). *Gesamtausgabe* [GA]. Frankfurt am Main: Klostermann.

Heidegger, Martin (1967). *Wegmarken* [W]. Frankfurt am Main: Klostermann.

AKJ (1919–21). "Anmerkungen zu Karl Jaspers 'Psychologie der Weltanschauungen.'" (1998). "Comments on Karl Jasper's 'Psychology of Worldviews'" in *Pathmarks*, ed. William McNeill. Cambridge: Cambridge University Press.

AN (1921). *Augustinus und der Neuplatonismus.* (1995). *Augustine and Neo- Platonism* [GA 60 2] in *The Phenomenology of Religious Life*, trs. Matthias Fritsch and Jennifer Anna Gosetti-Ferencei. Bloomington: Indiana University Press.

BH (1927). "Brief an Husserl." (1997). "Letter to Husserl, October 22, 1927, with Appendices" in *Psychological and Transcendental Phenomenology and the Confrontation with Heidegger (1927–1931)*, trs. Thomas Sheehan and Richard E. Palmer. Dordrecht: Springer.

BJ (1926). *Martin Heidegger/Karl Jaspers: Briefwechsel 1920–1963.* (2003). *The Heidegger-Jaspers Correspondence (1920–1963)*, ed. Walter Biemel and Hans Saner. New York. Humanity Books.

BL (2015). *Martin Heidegger/Karl Löwith, Briefweschsel 1919–1973*, ed. Alfred Denker. Freiburg im Breisgau: Karl Alber. (2021). *Correspondence: 1919–1973*, trs. J. Goesser Assaiante and S. Montgomery Ewegen. New York. Rowman and Littlefield.

BüH (1946). "Brief über den Humanismus." (1998). "Letter on 'Humanism'" [W] in *Pathmarks*, ed. William McNeill. Cambridge: Cambridge University Press.

CV (1915). "*Curriculum Vitae.*" (2009). "*Curriculum Vitae*" in *Becoming Heidegger: On the Trail of his Early Occasional Writings, 1019–1927*, ed. Theodore Kisiel and Thomas Sheehan. London: Routledge.

DS (1915). *Die Kategorien- und Bedeutungslehre des Duns Scotus.* (2022). *Duns Scotus' Doctrine of Categories and Meaning* [GA 1], trs. Joydeep Bagchee and Jeffrey D. Gower. Bloomington: Indiana University Press.

EH (1929). "Edmund Husserl zum 70. Geburtstag." (1997). "For Edmund Husserl on his Seventieth Birthday" in *Psychological and Transcendental Phenomenology and the Confrontation with Heidegger (1927–1931)*, trs. Thomas Sheehan and Richard E. Palmer. Dordrecht: Springer.

EM (1935). *Einführung in die Metaphysik.* (2000). *Introduction to Metaphysics* [GA 40], trs. Gregory Fried and Richard Polt. New Haven: Yale University Press.

EP (1928–29). (1996). *Einleitung in die Philosophie* [*Introduction to Philosophy*] [GA 27], ed. Frankfurt am Main: Klostermann.

EPR (1920–21). *Einleitung in die Phänomenologie der Religion.* (1995). *Introduction to the Phenomenology of Religion* [GA 60 1] in *The Phenomenology of Religious Life*, trs. Matthias Fritsch and Jennifer Anna Gosetti-Ferencei. Bloomington: Indiana University Press.

EOW (2007). *Becoming Heidegger: On the Trail of His Early Occasional Writings, 1910–1927*, ed. Theodore Kisiel and Thomas Sheehan. Evanston: Northwestern University Press.

FD (1935–36). *Die Frage nach dem Ding. Zu Kants Lehre von den transzendentalen Grundsätzen.* (2018). *The Question Concerning the Thing: On Kant's Doctrine of the Transcendental Principles* [GA 41], trs. James D. Reid and Benjamin D. Crowe. London: Rowman & Littlefield.

FS (1972). *Frühe Schriften*, ed. Friedrich-Wilhelm. von Herrmann. Frankfurt am Main: Klostermann.

GAP (1924). *Grundbegriffe der aristotelischen Philosophie.* (2009). *Basic Concepts of Aristotelian Philosophy* [GA 18], trs. Robert D. Metcalf and Mark B. Tanzer. Bloomington: Indiana University Press.

GM (1929–30). *Die Grundbegriffe der Metaphysik. Welt—Endlichkeit—Einsamkeit* [GA 29/30]. (1995). *The Fundamental Concepts of Metaphysics: World, Finitude, Solitude*, trs. William McNeill and Nicholas Walker. Bloomington: Indiana University Press.

GP (1927). *Die Grundprobleme der Phänomenologie.* (1975). *The Basic Problems of Phenomenology* [GA 24], trs. Albert Hoftsadter. Bloomington: Indiana University Press.

GS (1953–54). "Aus einem Gespräch von der Sprache." (1971). "A Dialogue on Language" in *On the Way to Language*, trs. Peter D. Hertz. San Francisco: Harper & Row.

HM (1927). "Heidegger, Martin." (2009). "Heidegger, Martin" in *Becoming Heidegger: On the Trail of his Early Occasional Writings, 1019–1927*, ed. Theodore Kisiel and Thomas Sheehan. London: Routledge.

HPG (1930–31). *Hegels Phänomenologie des Geistes.* (1988). *Hegel's Phenomenology of Spirit* [GA 32], trs. Parvis Emad and Kenneth Maly. Indiana: Indiana University Press.

IP (1919). *Die Idee der Philosophie und das Weltanschauungsproblem.* (2008). *The Idea of Philosophy and the Problem of Worldview* [GA 56/57 1] in *Towards the Definition of Philosophy*, trs. Ted Sadler. London: Continuum.

KPM (1929). *Kant und das Problem der Metaphysik.* (1997). *Kant and the Problem of Metaphysics* [GA 3], trs. Richard Taft. Bloomington: Indiana University Press.

L (1925–26). *Logik. Die Frage nach der Wahrheit.* (2010). *Logic: The Question of Truth* [GA 21], trs. Thomas Sheehan. Bloomington: Indiana University Press.

MA (1928). *Metaphysische Anfangsgründe der Logik im Ausgang von Leibniz.* (1992). *The Metaphysical Foundations of Logic* [GA 26], trs. Michael Heim. Bloomington: Indiana University Press.

MDI (1941). *Die Metaphysik des deutschen Idealismus: Zur erneuten Auslegung von Schelling: Philosophische Untersuchungen über das Wesen der menschlichen Freiheit und die damit zusammenhängenden Gegenstände (1809).* (2021). *The Metaphysics of German Idealism* [GA 49], trs. Ian Alexander Moore and Rodrigo Therezo. UK: Polity.

OHF (1923). *Ontologie. Hermeneutik der Faktizität.* (1999). *Ontology: The Hermeneutics of Facticity* [GA 63], trs. John van Buren. Bloomington: Indiana University Press.

PA (1920). *Phänomenologie der Anschauung und des Ausdrucks. Theorie der philosophischen Begriffsbildung.* (2010). *Phenomenology of Intuition and Expression: Theory of Philosophical Concept Formation*, trs. Tracy Colony. New York: Continuum.

PGM (1918–19). *Die philosophischen Grundlagen der mittelalterlichen Mystik.* (1995). *The Philosophical Foundations of Medieval Mysticism* [GA 60 3] in *The Phenomenology of Religious Life*, trs. Matthias Fritsch and Jennifer Anna Gosetti-Ferencei. Bloomington: Indiana University Press.

PGZ (1925). *Prolegomena zur Geschichte des Zeitbegriffs.* (1985). *History of the Concept of Time* [GA 20], trs. Theodore Kisiel. Bloomington: Indiana University Press.

PIA (1921–22). *Phänomenologische Interpretationen zu Aristoteles. Einführung in die phänomenologische Forschung.* (2001). *Phenomenological Interpretations of Aristotle: Initiation into Phenomenological Research* [GA 61], trs. Richard Rojcewicz. Bloomington: Indiana University Press.

PIAA (1922). "Phänomenologische Interpretationen zu Aristoteles (Anzeige der hermeneutischen Situation)." (2002). "Phenomenological Interpretations in Connection with Aristotle: An Indication of the Hermeneutical Situation" in *Supplements: From the Earliest Essays to* Being and Time *and Beyond*, ed. John van Buren. Albany: SUNY Press.

PTW (1919). *Phänomenologie und transzendentale Wertphilosophie.* (2008). *Phenomenology and Transcendental Philosophy of Value* [GA 56/57 2] in *Towards the Definition of Philosophy*, trs. Ted Sadler. London: Continuum.

SG (1955–56). *Der Satz vom Grund.* (1991). *The Principle of Reason* [GA 10], trs. Reginald Lilly. Indianapolis: Indiana University Press.

SZ (1927). *Sein und Zeit.* (1996). *Being and Time* [GA 2], trs. Joan Stambaugh. Albany: SUNY Press.

UK (1935–36). "Der Ursprung des Kunstwerkes." (2002). "The Origin of the Work of Art" in *Off the Beaten Path*, ed. and trs. Julian Young and Kenneth Haynes. Cambridge: Cambridge University Press.

VS (1966, 1968, 1969). *Vier Seminare: Seminar in Le Thor.* (2003). *Four Seminars: Le Thor 1966, 1968, 1969, Zähringen 1973* [GA 15], trs. Andrew Mitchell and François Raffoul. Indianapolis: Indiana University Press.

WD (1925). "Wilhelm Diltheys Forschungsarbeit und der gegenwartige Kampf um eine historische Weltanschauung." (2002) "Wilhelm Dilthey's Research and the Contemporary Struggle for a Historical Worldview" in *Supplements: From the Earliest Essays to* Being and Time *and Beyond*, ed. John van Buren. Albany: SUNY Press.

WG (1929). "Vom Wesen des Grundes." (1998). "On the Essence of Ground" [W] in *Pathmarks*, ed. William McNeill. Cambridge: Cambridge University Press.

WM (1929, 1943, 1949). "Was ist Metaphysik?"; "Nachwort zu 'Was ist Metaphysik?'"; "Einleitung zu 'Was ist Metaphysik?'" (1998). "What Is Metaphysics?"; "Postscript to 'What Is Metaphysics?'"; "Introduction to 'What Is Metaphysics?'" [W] in *Pathmarks*, ed. William McNeill. Cambridge: Cambridge University Press.

WW (1930). "Vom Wesen der Wahrheit." (1998). "On the Essence of Truth" [W] in *Pathmarks*, ed. William McNeill. Cambridge: Cambridge University Press.

ZS (1955). "Zur Seinsfrage." (1998). "On the Question of Being" [W] in *Pathmarks*, ed. William McNeill. Cambridge: Cambridge University Press.

ZoS (1959–72). *Zollikoner Seminare.* (2001). *Zollikon Seminars: Protocols, Conversations, Letters* [GA 89], trs. Franz K. Mayr and Richard R. Askay. Evanston: Northwestern University Press.

ZuS (1962). "Zeit und Sein." (1972). "Time and Being" in *On Time and Being*, trs. Joan Stambaugh. New York: Harper.

Edmund Husserl (1859–1938)

A (1908). "Zur Auseinandersetzung meiner transzendentalen Phänomenologie mit Kants Transzendentalphilosophie" ["On the Confrontation of My Transcendental Phenomenology with Kant's Transcendental Philosophy"] in *Erste Philosophie (1923/24)*, ed. Rudolph Boehm. Haag: Nijhoff.

B (1994). *Briefwechsel* [*Correspondence*] in *Edmund Husserl Dokumente 3/5*, ed. Karl Schuhmann. Dordrecht: Kluwer.

BL (1932). "Brief an Ludwig Landgrebe." (1997). "Letter to Ludwig Landgrebe" in *Psychological and Transcendental Phenomenology and the Confrontation with Heidegger (1927–1931)*, trs. Thomas Sheehan and Richard E. Palmer. Dordrecht: Springer.

BM (1931). "Brief an Dietrich Mahnke." (2009). "Letter to Dietrich Mahnke" in *Becoming Heidegger: On the Trail of his Early Occasional Writings, 1019–1927*, ed. Theodore Kisiel and Thomas Sheehan. London: Routledge.

BMi (1929). "Brief an Georg Misch." (2009). "Letter to Georg Misch" in *Becoming Heidegger: On the Trail of his Early Occasional Writings, 1019–1927*, ed. Theodore Kisiel and Thomas Sheehan. London: Routledge.

BP (1931). "Brief an Alexander Pfänder." (1997). "Letter to Alexander Pfänder" in *Psychological and Transcendental Phenomenology and the Confrontation with Heidegger (1927–1931)*, trs. Thomas Sheehan and Richard E. Palmer. Dordrecht: Springer.

EHM (1898–99). "Aus der Einleitung der Vorlesung 'Erkenntnistheorie und Hauptpunkte der Metaphysik" [Introduction to "Epistemology and the Main Points of Metaphysics"] in (2011) *Allgemeine Erkenntnistheorie Vorlesung 1902/03*, ed. Elisabeth Schuhmann. Dordrecht: Springer.

FM (1917–18). "Fichtes Menschheitsideal." (1995). "Fichte's Ideal of Humanity," trs. James G. Hart, in *Husserl Studies* 12.

FT (1929). *Formale und Transzendentale Logik Versuch Einer Kritik der Logischen Vernunft.* (1969). *Formal and Transcendental Logic*, trs. Dorion Cairns. The Hague: Nijhoff.

GK (1908). "Gegen Kants anthropologische Theorie" ["Against Kant's Anthropological Theory"] in (1956) *Erste Philosophie (1923/24)*, ed. Rudolph Boehm. Haag: Nijhoff.

GU (1887–88). "Geschichtlicher Überblick über die Philosophie der Mathematik" ["Historical Overview of the Philosophy of Mathematics"] in (1983) *Studien zur Arithmetik und Geometrie: Texte aus dem Nachlass (1886–1901)*, ed. Ingeborg Strohmeyer. The Hague: Nijhoff.

IRP1 (1913). *Ideen zu einer Reinen Phänomenologie und Phänomenologischen Philosophie: Erstes Buch: Allgemeine Einführung in die Reine Phänomenologie* (1982). *Ideas Pertaining to a Pure Phenomenology and to a Phenomenological Philosophy, First Book: General Introduction to a Pure Phenomenology*, trs. F. Kersten. The Hague: Nijhoff.

IRP2 (1912) *Ideen zu einer Reinen Phänomenologie und Phänomenologischen Philosophie: Phänomenologische Untersuchungen zur Konstitution* (1989). *Ideas Pertaining to a Pure Phenomenology and to a Phenomenological Philosophy, Second Book: Studies in the Phenomenology of Constitution*, trs. Richard Rojcewicz and André Schuwer. The Hague: Nijhoff.

K (1954). *Die Krisis der europäischen Wissenschaften und die transzendentale Phänomenologie: Eine Einleitung in die phänomenologische Philosophie* (1970a). *The Crisis of European Sciences and Transcendental Philosophy*, trs. David Carr. Evanston: Northwestern University Press.

LU1 (1900–01). *Logische Untersuchungen. Erster Teil: Prolegomena zur reinen Logik.* (2001). *Logical Investigations, Volume 1*, trs. J. N. Findlay. London: Routledge.

LU2 (1900–01). *Logische Untersuchungen. Zweiter Teil: Untersuchungen zur Phänomenologie und Theorie der Erkenntnis.* (2001). *Logical Investigations, Volume 2,* trs. J. N. Findlay. London: Routledge.

P (1910). "Philosophie als strenge Wissenschaft." (1965) "Philosophy as Rigourous Science" in *Phenomenology and the Crisis of Philosophy,* trs. Quentin Lauer. New York: Harper.

PA (1931). "Phänomenologie und Anthropologie." (1997). "Phenomenology and Anthropology" in *Psychological and Transcendental Phenomenology and the Confrontation with Heidegger (1927–1931),* trs. Thomas Sheehan and Richard E. Palmer. Dordrecht: Springer.

PK (1935). "Philosophie und die Krisis des europäischen Menschentums" (1970b). "Philosophy and the Crisis of European Humanity" in *The Crisis of European Sciences and Transcendental Philosophy,* trs. David Carr. Evanston: Northwestern University Press.

PP (1925). *Phänomenologische Psychologie.* (1977). *Phenomenological Psychology,* trs. John Scanlon. The Hague: Nijhoff.

Friedrich Heinrich Jacobi (1743–1819)

B (1827). *Friedrich Heinrich Jacobis auserlesener Briefwechsel, Zweiter Band* [*Friedrich Heinrich Jacobi's Selected Correspondence, Volume 2*]. Leipzig: Gerhard Fleischer

BF (1799). "Brief an Fichte." (1994). "Jacobi to Fichte" in *The Main Philosophical Writings and the Novel* Allwill, trs. George di Giovanni. Montreal/Kingston: McGill-Queen's University Press.

DH (1787/1815). *David Hume über den Glauben oder Idealismus und Realismus.* (1994). *David Hume on Faith, or Idealism and Realism: A Dialogue* in *The Main Philosophical Writings and the Novel* Allwill, trs. George di Giovanni. Montreal/Kingston: McGill-Queen's University Press.

GD (1811). "Von Den Göttlichen Dingen und Ihrer Offenbarung." (2024). *Of Divine Things and their Revelation,* trs. Paolo Livieri. Montreal/Kingston: McGill-Queen's University Press.

LS (1785/1789). *Über die Lehre des Spinoza in Briefen an den Herrn Moses Mendelssohn.* (1994). *Concerning the Doctrine of Spinoza in Letters to Mr. Moses Mendelssohn* in *The Main Philosophical Writings and the Novel* Allwill, trs. George di Giovanni. Montreal/Kingston: McGill-Queen's University Press.

UK (1802). "Über das Unternehmen des Kriticismus, die Vernunft zu Verstande zu bringen, und der Philosophie überhaupt eine neue Absicht zu geben" ["On Criticism's Endeavour to Reduce Reason to the Understanding and Give Philosophy in General a New Purpose"] in (2004) *Schriften zum transzendentalen Idealismus,* ed. Walter Jaeschke and Irmgard Maria Piske. Hamburg: Meiner.

Immanuel Kant (1724–1804)

Kant, Immanuel (1900–). *Kants gesammelte Schriften* [AA, except for *Critique of Pure Reason,* cited in A/B pagination for 1781/1787 editions]. Berlin: de Gruyter.

A (1784). "Beantwortung der Frage: Was ist Aufklärung?" (1996). "An Answer to the Question: What is Enlightenment?" [AA 8] in *Practical Philosophy,* trs. and ed. Mary J. Gregor. Cambridge: Cambridge University Press.

B (1749–1800). *Briefe.* (1999). *Correspondence* [AA 10–13], trs. Arnulf Zweig. Cambridge: Cambridge University Press.

DWL (early 1790s). *Dohna-Wundlacken Logik.* (1992). *Dohna-Wundlacken Logic* [AA 24] in *Lectures on Logic,* ed. J. Michael Young. Cambridge: Cambridge University Press.

E (1790). "Über eine Entdeckung, nach der alle neue Kritik der reinen Vernunft durch eine ältere entbehrlich gemacht werden soll." (2002). "On a Discovery Whereby Any New Critique of Pure Reason is to be Made Superfluous by an Older One"

[AA 8] in *Theoretical Philosophy After 1781*, trs. Henry Allison. Cambridge: Cambridge University of Press.

GMM (1785). *Die Grundlegung der Metaphysik zur Moral.* (1996). *Groundwork of the Metaphysics of Morals* [AA 4] in *Practical Philosophy*, trs. and ed. Mary J. Gregor. Cambridge: Cambridge University Press.

IAG (1784). "Idee zu einer allgemeinen Geschichte in weltbürgerlicher Absicht." (2007). "Idea for a Universal History With a Cosmopolitan Aim" [AA 8] in *Anthropology, History, and Education*, ed. Günter Zöller and Robert B. Louden. Cambridge: Cambridge University Press.

JL (1800). *Jäsche Logik.* (1992). *Jäsche Logic* [AA 9] in *Lectures on Logic*, ed. J. Michael Young. Cambridge: Cambridge University Press.

KpV (1788). *Kritik der praktischen Vernunft.* (1996). *Critique of Practical Reason* in *Practical Philosophy* [AA 5], trs. and ed. Mary J. Gregor. Cambridge: Cambridge University Press.

KrV (1781/1787). *Kritik der reinen Vernunft.* (1998). *Critique of Pure Reason*, trs. Paul Guyer and Allen W. Wood. Cambridge: Cambridge University Press.

KU (1790). *Kritik der Urteilskraft.* (2000). *Critique of the Power of Judgment* [AA 5], trs. Paul Guyer and Eric Matthews. Cambridge: Cambridge University Press.

NF (2005). *Notes and Fragments*, trs. Curtis Bowman, Paul Guyer, and Frederick Rauscher. Cambridge: Cambridge University Press.

O (1786). "Was heißt: Sich im Denken orientiren?" (1996). "What Does It Mean to Orient Oneself in Thinking?" [AA 8] in *Religion and Rational Theology*, trs. and ed. Allen W. Wood and George di Giovanni. Cambridge: Cambridge University Press.

P (1783). *Prolegomena zu einer jeden kunftigen Metaphysik die als Wissenschaft wird auftreten können.* (2002). *Prolegomena to Any Future Metaphysics That Will Be Able to Come Forward as Science* [AA 4] in *Theoretical Philosophy After 1781*, trs. Gary Hatfield. Cambridge: Cambridge University Press.

RI (1785). "Rezension von 'Ideen für eine Philosophie der Geschichte der Menschheit.'" (2007) "Review of 'Ideas for the Philosophy of the History of Humanity'" [AA 8] in *Anthropology, History, and Education*, ed. Günter Zöller and Robert B. Louden. Cambridge: Cambridge University Press.

RS (1783). "Rezension von Schulz's 'Versuch einer Anleitung zur Sittenlehre für alle Menschen ohne Unterschied der Religion.'" (1999). "Review of 'Attempt at an Introduction to a Doctrine of Morals for All Human Beings Regardless of Different Religions'" [AA 8] in *Practical Philosophy*, trs. and ed. Mary J. Gregor. Cambridge: Cambridge University Press.

W (1804). "Welches sind die wirklichen Fortschritte, die die Metaphysik seit Leibnizens und Wolfs Zeiten in Deutschland gemacht hat?" (2002). "What Real Progress Has Metaphysics Made in Germany since the Time of Leibniz and Wolff?" [AA 20] in *Theoretical Philosophy After 1781*, trs. Gary Hatfield. Cambridge: Cambridge University Press.

WL (circa 1800). *Wiener Logik.* (1992). *Vienna Logic* [AA 24] in *Lectures on Logic*, ed. J. Michael Young. Cambridge: Cambridge University Press.

Emil Lask (1875–1915)

A (2015). "Announcement" in *The Neo-Kantian Reader*, ed. Sebastian Luft. London: Routledge.

BT (2015). "The Boundlessness of Truth" in *The Neo-Kantian Reader*, ed. Sebastian Luft. London: Routledge.

FIG (1902). *Fichtes Idealismus und die Geschichte* [*Fichte's Idealism and History*] in (1923) *Gesammelte Schriften Band I.* Tübingen: Mohr.

G (1908). "Gibt es einen 'Primat der praktischen Vernunft' in der Logik?" ["Is There A 'Primacy of Practical Reason' in Logic?"] in (1923) *Gesammelte Schriften Band I.* Tübingen: Mohr.

LOC (2015). "The Logic of the Ontological Categories" in *The Neo-Kantian Reader*, ed. Sebastian Luft. London: Routledge.

LPK (1911). *Die Logik der Philosophie und die Kategorienlehre* [*The Logic of Philosophy and the Doctrine of the Categories*] in (1923) *Gesammelte Schriften Band II* . Tübingen: Mohr.

LU (1912). *Die Lehre vom Urteil* [*The Doctrine of Judgment*] in (1923) *Gesammelte Schriften Band II* . Tübingen: Mohr.

Salomon Maimon (1753–1800)

GH (1791). *Giv'at Hammore* [*The Hill of the Guide*]. (1965). Jerusalem: Israel Academy of Sciences and Humanities.

PW (1791). *Philosophisches Worterbuch* [*Philosophical Dictionary, or Illumination of the Most Important Objects of Philosophy in Alphabetical Order*].

SGP (1793). *Streifereien im Gebiete der Philosophie. Erster Theil.* Berlin: Wilhelm Vieweg. *Wanderings in the Region of Philosophy.* Includes *Über die Progressen der Philosophie* [*On the Progress of Philosophy*] and *Philosophischer Briefwechsel* [*Philosophical Correspondence*].

VNL (1794). *Versuch einer neuen Logik, oder Theorie des Denkens. Nebst angehängten Briefen des Philalethes an Aenesidemus.* (2000). *Attempt at a New Logic, or Theory of Thinking with Appended Letters of Philalethes to Aenesidemus* in *Between Kant and Hegel: Texts in the Development of Post-Kantian Idealism*, trs. George di Giovanni and H. S. Harris. Indianapolis: Hackett.

VT (1790). *Versuch über die Transcendentalphilosophle.* (2010). *Essay on Transcendental Philosophy*, trs. Nick Midgley, Henry Somers-Hall, Alistair Welchman and Merten Reglitz. London: Continuum.

Karl Leonhard Reinhold (1757–1823)

BB (1790). *Beyträge zur Berichtigung bisheriger Missverständnisse der Philosophen, Band 1* [*Contributions to Correcting Previous Misunderstandings of the Philosophers*]. Jena: Mauke.

FPW (1791). *Über das Fundament des philosophischen Wissens.* (2000). *The Foundation of Philosophical Knowledge* in *Between Kant and Hegel: Texts in the Development of Post-Kantian Idealism*, ed. George di Giovanni and H. Harris. Indianapolis: Hackett.

VNT (1789/1795). *Versuch einer neuen Theorie des menschlichen Vorstellungsvermögens.* (2011). *Essay on a New Theory of the Human Capacity for Representation*, trs. Tim Mehigan and Barry Empson. Berlin: de Gruyter.

Friedrich Wilhelm Joseph von Schelling (1775–1854)

Schelling, F. W. J. (1856–61). *Friedrich Wilhelm Joseph Schellings Sämmtliche Werke* [SW], ed. K. F. A. Schelling. Cotta: Stuttgart.

A (1805). *Aphorismen zur Einleitung in die Naturphilosophie* [*Aphorisms as an Introduction to Philosophy of Nature*] [SW I/7]. (1968). Darmstadt: Wissenschaftliche Buchgesellschaft.

AE (1796–97). *Abhandlungen zur Erlauterung des Idealismus der Wissenschaftslehre.* (1994). *Treatises on the Explication of the Idealism of the Wissenschaftslehre* [SW I/1] in *Idealism and the Endgame of Theory: Three Essays by F. W. J. Schelling*, ed. Thomas Pfau. Albany: SUNY Press.

BS (1800–02). "Briefweschsel." (2012). "Correspondence" in *The Philosophical Rupture Between Fichte and Schelling: Selected Texts and Correspondence (1800–02)*, trs. Michael Vater. Albany: SUNY Press.

BV-A (1841–42). *Berliner Vorlesungen.* (1977). *Philosophie der Offenbarung 1841/42*, ed. Manfred Frank. Frankfurt am Main: Suhrkamp.

BV-B (1841–42). *Berliner Vorlesungen.* (2007). *The Grounding of Positive Philosophy* [SW II/3], trs. Bruce Matthews. Albany: SUNY Press.

BV-C (1841–42). *Berliner Vorlesungen.* (2020). *Philosophy of Revelation (1841–42) and Related Texts*, trs. Klaus Ottmann. Connecticut: Spring Publications.

D (1801). *Darstellung meines Systems der Philosophie.* (2001). *Presentation of My System of Philosophy* [SW I/4], trs. Michael Vater in *The Philosophical Forum* 32 (4).

EV (1820–21). *Erlanger Vorlesungen.* (1969). *Initia Philosophiae Universae.* Bonn: Bouvier.

FD (1802). *Fernere Darstellungen aus dem System der Philosophie.* (2001). *Further Presentations from the System of Philosophy* [SW I/4], trs. Michael Vater in *The Philosophical Forum* 32 (4).

IPN (1797). *Ideen zu einer Philosophie der Natur als Einleitung in das Studium dieser Wissenschaft.* (1988). *Ideas for a Philosophy of Nature as Introduction to the Study of this Science*, trs. Errol E. Harris and Peter Heath. Cambridge: Cambridge University Press.

IPP (1795). "Vom Ich als Prinzip der Philosophie, oder über das Unbedingte im menschlichen Wissen." (1980). "Of the I as Principle of Philosophy, or On the Unconditioned in Human Knowledge" [SW I/1] in *The Unconditioned in Human Knowledge: Four Early Essays 1794–1796*, trs. Fritz Marti. Lewisburg: Bucknell University Press.

MV32 (1832–33). *Münchener Vorlesungen: Grundlegung der positiven Philosophie* [*Munich Lectures: Grounding of Positive Philosophy*]. (1972). Turin: Bottega D'Erasmo.

MV33 (1833–34). *Münchener Vorlesungen.* (1994). *On the History of Modern Philosophy* [SW I/10], trs. Andrew Bowie. Cambridge: Cambridge University Press.

PB (1795–96). "Philosophische Briefe über Dogmatismus und Kriticismus." (1980). "Philosophical Letters on Dogmatism and Criticism" [SW I/1] in *The Unconditioned in Human Knowledge: Four Early Essays 1794–1796*, trs. Fritz Marti. Lewisburg: Bucknell University Press.

PR (1804). *Philosophie und Religion.* (2010). *Philosophy and Religion* [SW I/6], trs. Klaus Ottmann. Putnam, Conn.: Spring.

PU (1809). *Philosophische Untersuchungen über das Wesen der menschlichen Freiheit und die damit zusammenhängenden Gegenstände.* (2006). *Philosophical Investigations into the Essence of Human Freedom and Matters Connected Therewith* [SW I/7], trs. Jeff Love and Johannes Schmidt. Albany: SUNY Press.

QW (1850). "Abhandlung über die Quelle der ewigen Wahrheiten." (1990). "On the Source of Eternal Truths" [SW II/1], trs. Edward A. Beach in *The Owl of Minerva* 22 (1).

S (1804). *System der gesammten Philosophie und der Naturphilosophie insbesondere.* (1994). *System of Philosophy in General and of the Philosophy of Nature in Particular* [SW I/6] in *Idealism and the Endgame of Theory: Three Essays by F. W. J. Schelling*, ed. Thomas Pfau. Albany: SUNY Press.

SP (1810). *Stuttgarter Privatvorlesungen.* (1994). *Stuttgart Private Lectures* [SW I/7] in *Idealism and the Endgame of Theory: Three Essays by F. W. J. Schelling*, ed. Thomas Pfau. Albany: SUNY Press.

WA13 (1813). *Die Weltalter.* (1997). *Ages of the World (1813)/The Abyss of Freedom* (with Slavoj Žižek), trs. Judith Norman. Ann Arbor: University of Michigan Press.

WA15 (1815). *Die Weltalter.* (2000). *Ages of the World (1815)* [SW I/8], trs. Jason M. Wirth. Albany: SUNY Press.

Other Primary Sources

Adorno, Theodor W. (1973). *Negative Dialectics*, trs. E. B. Ashton. London: Routledge.

Annas, Julia and Jonathan Barnes (ed.) (2000). *Sextus Empiricus: Outlines of Scepticism.* Cambridge: Cambridge University Press.

Aquinas, Thomas (1968). *On Being and Essence*, trs. Armand Maurer. Toronto: Pontifical Institute of Medieval Studies.

Arendt, Hannah and Martin Heidegger (2004). *Letters 1925–1975*, ed. Ursula Ludz. USA: Harcourt.

Aristotle (2002). *Posterior Analytics*, trs. Jonathan Barnes. Oxford: Clarendon.

Bacon, Francis (1829). *The Works of Francis Bacon, Lord Chancellor of England, Volume 11*, ed. Basil Montagu. London: Pickering.

Beck, Jakob Sigismund. (2000). *The Only Possible Standpoint from which Critical Philosophy Must be Judged* in *Between Kant and Hegel: Texts in the Development of Post-Kantian Idealism*, ed. George di Giovanni and H. Harris. Indianapolis: Hackett.

Brentano, Franz (1998). *The Four Phases of Philosophy*, trs. Balász M. Mezei and Barry Smith. Amsterdam: Rodopi.

Brentano, Franz (1968). "Über Schellings Philosophie" in *Über die Zukunft der Philosophie*. Hamburg: Meiner, 101–32.

Carnap, Rudolf (1959). "The Elimination of Metaphysics Through Logical Analysis of Language" in *Logical Positivism*, ed. A. J. Ayer. New York: Macmillan, 60–81.

Cohen, Hermann (1914). *Logik der reinen Erkenntnis*. Berlin: Cassirer.

Colledge, Edmund and Bernard McGinn (ed.) (1981). *Meister Eckhart: The Essential Sermons, Commentaries, Treatises, and Defense*. New Jersey: Paulist Press.

De Beauvoir, Simone (1972). *The Ethics of Ambiguity*, trs. B. Frechtman. New Jersey: The Citadel Press.

Descartes, René (1996). *Meditations on First Philosophy with Selections from the Objections and Replies*, trs. John Cottingham. Cambridge: Cambridge University Press.

Descartes, René (1982). *Principles of Philosophy*, trs. Valentine Rodger Miller and Reese P. Miller. Dordrecht: Kluwer.

Emerson, Ralph Waldo, Margaret Fuller, and George Ripley (ed.) (1842–43). *The Dial: A Magazine for Literature, Philosophy, and Religion* 3 (1, 3), 132–6, 387–404.

Engels, Friedrich (2010). "Schelling on Hegel" in *Marx and Engels: Collected Works, Volume 2: Friedrich Engels 1838–42*. Lawrence and Wishart, 181–8.

Foucault, Michel (2001). *Fearless Speech*. Los Angeles: Semiotext(e).

Foucault, Michel (1982). "The Subject and Power" in *Critical Inquiry* 8 (4).

Gadamer, Hans-Georg (2006). *Truth and Method*, trs. Joel Weinsheimer and Donald G. Marshall. London: Continuum.

Goethe, Johann Wolfgang von (1957). *Letters from Goethe*. Edinburgh: Edinburgh University Press.

Gurwitsch, Aron (1945). "On Contemporary Nihilism" in *The Review of Politics* 7 (2), 170–98.

Hume, David (2007). *An Enquiry Concerning Human Understanding*. Oxford: Oxford University Press.

James, William (1884). "The Dilemma of Determinism" in *The Unitarian Review and Religious Magazine* 22, 193–224.

James, William (1882b). "Rationality, Activity, and Faith" in *The Princeton Review* 58, 58–86.

James, William (1882a). "On Some Hegelisms" in *Mind* 7 (26), 186–208.

Jonas, Hans (2001). *The Phenomenon of Life: Toward a Philosophical Biology*. Evanston: Northwestern University Press.

Kierkegaard, Søren (2009). *Two Ages: The Age of Revolution and the Present Age*, trs. Howard V. Hong and Edna H. Hong. Princeton: Princeton University Press.

Kierkegaard, Søren (1989). *The Concept of Irony, With Continual Reference to Socrates, Together With Notes of Schelling's Berlin Lectures*, trs. and ed. Howard V. Hong and Edna H. Hong. Princeton: Princeton University Press.

Kierkegaard, Søren (1967–78). *Søren Kierkegaard's Journals and Papers: Volumes 1–6* [JP]. Ed. and trs. Howard V. Hong and Edna A. Hong. Bloomington: Indiana University Press.

Liebmann, Otto (1912). *Kant und die Epigonen*. Berlin: Reuther & Reichard.

Lotze, Hermann (1884). *Logic in Three Books: Of Thought, Of Investigation, and Of Knowledge*, trs. R. L. Nettleship, F. H. Peters, F. C. Conybeare, R. G. Tatton, and B. Bosanquet. Oxford: Clarendon.

Merleau-Ponty, Maurice (2012). *Phenomenology of Perception*, trs. Donald A. Landes. London: Routledge.

Merleau-Ponty, Maurice (2003). *Nature: Course Notes from the Collège de France*, trs. Robert Vallier: Evanston: Northwestern University Press.

Merleau-Ponty, Maurice (1968). *The Visible and the Invisible*, trs. Alphonso Lingis. Evanston: Northwestern University Press.

Mill, John Stuart (2018). *Autobiography*. Oxford: Oxford University Press.

Natorp, Paul G. (2015). "Kant and the Marburg School" in *The Neo-Kantian Reader*, ed. Sebastian Luft. London: Routledge, 180–97.

Natorp, Paul G. (1918). "Bruno Bauchs 'Immanuel Kant' und die Fortbildung des Systems des kritischen Idealismus" in *Kant-Studien* 22, 426–59.

Natorp, Paul G. (1912). *Allgemeine Psychologie nach kritischer Methode, Band 1*. Tübingen: Mohr Siebeck.

Nietzsche, Friedrich (2006). *On the Genealogy of Morality*, trs. Carol Diethe. Cambridge: Cambridge University Press.

Nietzsche, Friedrich (2001). *The Gay Science*, trs. Josefine Nauckhoff. Cambridge: Cambridge University Press.

Nietzsche, Friedrich (1989). *Beyond Good and Evil*, trs. Walter Kaufmann. New York: Vintage.

Novalis (2003). *Fichte Studies*. ed. Jane Kneller. Cambridge: Cambridge University Press.

Novalis (1978). *Band 2: Das philosophisch-theoretische Werk*, ed. Hans-Joachim. Mähl. Munich: Hanser.

Rickert, Heinrich (2015). "Knowing and Cognizing: Critical Remarks on Theoretical Intuitionism" in *The Neo-Kantian Reader*, ed. Sebastian Luft. London: Routledge, 384–95.

Rickert, Heinrich (1913). *Die Grenzen der naturwissenschaftslichen Begriffsbildung*. Tübingen: Mohr Siebeck.

Rorty, Richard (1999). *Philosophy and Social Hope*. London: Penguin.

Russell, Bertrand (2004). *History of Western Philosophy*. London: Routledge.

Sartre, Jean-Paul (1956). *Being and Nothingness*, trs. Hazel E. Barnes. New York: Washington Square Press.

Schiller, Friedrich and Johann Wolfgang von Goethe (1994). *Correspondence Between Goethe and Schiller 1794–1805*, trs. Liselotte Dieckmann. Germany: Lang.

Schleiermacher, Friedrich (1998). *Hermeneutics and Criticism and Other Writings*, trs. Andrew Bowie. Cambridge: Cambridge University Press.

Schopenhauer, Arthur (2012). *On the Fourfold Root of the Principle of Sufficient Reason and Other Writings*, trs. and ed. David E. Cartwright, Edward E. Erdmann, and Christopher Janaway. Cambridge: Cambridge University Press.

Schopenhauer, Arthur (1969). *The World as Will and Representation, Volumes 1–2*, trs. E. F. J. Payne. New York: Dover.

Schulze, Gottlob Ernst (2020). "Aphorisms on the Absolute," trs. Caleb Faul, James Sares, and Kenneth R. Westphal, in *The Owl of Minerva* 51 (1–2), 13–34.

Schulze, Gottlob Ernst (1911). *Aenesidemus oder über die Fundamente der von dem Herrn Professor Reinhold in Jena gelieferten Elementar-Philosophie Nebst einer Verteidigung des Skeptizismus gegen die Anmaßungen der Vernunftkritik*. Berlin: Reuther and Reichard.

Sellars, Wilfrid (2017). "Introduction to the Philosophy of Schelling," trs. Jesper Lundsfryd Rasmussen, in *Schelling-Studien* 5, 197–215.

Spinoza, Baruch (2002). *Complete Works*, trs. Samuel Shirley. Indianapolis: Hackett.

Trendelenburg, Friedrich Adolf (1862). *Logische Untersuchungen*. Leipzig: Hirzel.

Turgenev, Ivan Sergeevich (1958). *The Essential Turgenev*, ed. Elizabeth C. Allen. Evanston: Northwestern University Press.

Vico, Giambattista (1990). *On the Study Methods of Our Time*, trs. Elio Gianturco and Donald Phillip Verene. Ithaca: Cornell University Press.

Williams, Bernard (2005). *Descartes: The Project of Pure Inquiry*. London: Routledge.

Windelband, Wilhelm (2015). "Critical or Genetic Method?" in *The Neo-Kantian Reader*, ed. Sebastian Luft. London: Routledge, 271–86.

Windelband, Wilhelm (1980). "Rectorial Address" in *History and Theory* 19 (2), 169–85.

Windelband, Wilhelm (1870). *Die Lehren vom Zufall*. Berlin: F. Henschel.

Wittgenstein, Ludwig (2014). *Lecture on Ethics*, ed. Edoardo Zamuner, Ermelina Valentina di Lascio, and D. K. Levy. UK: Wiley-Blackwell.

Wittgenstein, Ludwig (1994). *Tractatus Logico-Philosophicus*, trs. D. F. Pears and B. F. McGuinness. London: Routledge.
Wittgenstein, Ludwig (1979). *Wittgenstein and the Vienna Circle: Conversations Recorded by Friedrich Waismann*, trs. Brian McGuinness and Joachim Schulte. New York: Barnes and Noble.

Secondary Sources

Ainbinder, Bernardo (2015). "From Neo-Kantianism to Phenomenology: Emil Lask's Revision of Transcendental Philosophy" in *Studia Phaenomenologica* 15, 433–56.
Ameriks, Karl (2000). *Kant and the Fate of Autonomy*. Cambridge: Cambridge University Press.
Anderson, R. Lanier (2005). "Neo-Kantianism and the Roots of Anti-Psychologism" in *British Journal for the History of Philosophy* 13 (2), 287–323.
Arrien, Sophie-Jan (2018). "The Hermeneutical Turn of Phenomenology in the Young Heidegger's Thought" in *Hermeneutics and Phenomenology: Figures and Themes*, ed. Saulius Geniusas and Paul Fairfield. London: Bloomsbury, 138–48.
Balog, Katalin (2012). "In Defense of the Phenomenal Concept Strategy" in *Philosophy and Phenomenological Research* 84 (1), 1–23.
Bambach, Charles (2019). "Hermeneutics and Historicity: Dilthey's Critique of Historical Reason" in *Interpreting Dilthey: Critical Essays*, ed. Eric S. Nelson. Cambridge: Cambridge University Press, 82–102.
Beach, Edward A. (1990). "The Later Schelling's Conception of Dialectical Method in Contradistinction to Hegel's" in *The Owl of Minerva* 22 (1), 35–54.
Beiser, Frederick (2018). "Neo-Kantianism as Neo-Fichteanism" in *Fichte-Studien* 45, 309–37.
Beiser, Frederick (2014). *The Genesis of Neo-Kantianism, 1796–1880*. Oxford: Oxford University Press.
Beiser, Frederick (2013). *Late German Idealism: Trendelenburg and Lotze*. Oxford: Oxford University Press.
Beiser, Frederick (2011). *The German Historicist Tradition*. Oxford: Oxford University Press.
Beiser, Frederick (2008). "Emil Lask and Kantianism" in *The Philosophical Forum* 39 (2), 283–95.
Beiser, Frederick (2003). "Maimon and Fichte" in *Salomon Maimon: Rational Dogmatist, Empirical Skeptic*, ed. Gideon Freudenthal. Dordrecht: Kluwer, 233–48.
Beiser, Frederick (2002). *German Idealism: The Struggle Against Subjectivism, 1781–1801*. Cambridge, Mass.: Harvard University Press.
Beiser, Frederick (1994). "Bowie on Schelling" in *Hegel Bulletin* 15 (2), 1–5.
Beiser, Frederick (1987). *The Fate of Reason: German Philosophy from Kant to Fichte*. Cambridge, Mass.: Harvard University Press.
Berger, Benjamin and Daniel Whistler (2020). *The Schelling-Eschenmayer Controversy, 1801: Nature and Identity*. Edinburgh University Press.
Berghofer, Philipp (2018). "Why Husserl's Universal Empiricism is a Moderate Rationalism" in *Axiomathes* 28, 539–63.
Berry, Jessica N. (2022). "Sextan Skepticism and the Rise and Fall of German Idealism" in *Epistemology After Sextus Empiricus*, ed. Katja Maria Vogt and Justin Vlasits. Oxford: Oxford University Press, 154–72.
Blattner, William (2015). "Essential Guilt and Transcendental Conscience" in *Heidegger, Authenticity, and the Self*, ed. Denis McManus. London: Routledge, 116–34.
Boehm, Omri (2014). *Kant's Critique of Spinoza*. Oxford: Oxford University Press.
Bordignon, Michela (2019). "Hegel: A Dialetheist? Truth and Contradiction in Hegel's Logic" in *Hegel Bulletin* 40 (2), 1–17.
Bowie, Andrew (2014). "Nature and Freedom in Schelling and Adorno" in *Interpreting Schelling: Critical Essays*, ed. Lara Ostaric: Cambridge: Cambridge University Press, 180–99.
Bowie, Andrew (2003). *Aesthetics and Subjectivity: From Kant to Nietzsche*. Manchester: Manchester University Press.
Bowie, Andrew (1994). "Reply: The Schellingian Alternative" in *Hegel Bulletin* 15 (2), 23–42.

Bowie, Andrew (1993). *Schelling and Modern European Philosophy: An Introduction.* London: Routledge.
Bowman, Brady (2018). "Autonomy, Negativity, and the Challenge of Spinozism in Hegel's *Science of Logic*" in *Journal of the History of Philosophy* 56 (1), 101–26.
Boyle, Matthew (2016). "Additive Theories of Rationality: A Critique" in *European Journal of Philosophy* 24 (3), 257–55.
Bracken, Joseph A. (1977). "Schelling's Positive Philosophy" in *Journal of the History of Philosophy* 15 (3), 324–30.
Brandt, Reinhard (1995). *The Table of Judgments: Critique of Pure Reason A67–76; B92–101*, trs. Eric Watkins. Atascadero: Ridgeview Press.
Breazeale, Daniel (2018). "Fichte's Spinoza: 'Common Standpoint', 'Essential Opposition', and 'Hidden Treasure'" in *International Yearbook of German Idealism* 14, 103–38.
Breazeale, Daniel (2013). *Thinking Through the Wissenschaftslehre.* Oxford: Oxford University Press.
Breazeale, Daniel (1994). "Editor's Introduction" in *Introductions to the Wissenschaftslehre*, ed. Daniel Breazeale. Indianapolis: Hackett, vii–xxxii.
Breazeale, Daniel (1991). "Fichte on Skepticism" in *Journal of the History of Philosophy* 29 (3), 427–53.
Breazeale, Daniel (1982). "Between Kant and Fichte: Karl Leonhard Reinhold's 'Elementary Philosophy'" in *The Review of Metaphysics* 35 (4), 785–821.
Breazeale, Daniel (1981). "Fichte's 'Aenesidemus' Review and the Transformation of German Idealism" in *The Review of Metaphysics* 34 (3), 545–68.
Breazeale, Daniel and Tom Rockmore, ed. (2008). *After Jena: New Essays on Fichte's Later Philosophy.* Chicago: Northwestern University Press.
Bruno, G. Anthony (manuscript). "Jacobi's Master Argument: Nihilism, Individuals, and the Distinction between Reason and Understanding."
Bruno, G. Anthony (forthcoming). "Schelling and Early German Idealism" in *The Palgrave Schelling Handbook*, ed. Sean McGrath, Joseph Carew, and Kyla Bruff. London: Palgrave.
Bruno, G. Anthony (2024b). "Metametaphysical Monism, Dualism, Pluralism, and Holism in the German Idealist Tradition" in International Journal of Philosophical Studies.
Bruno, G. Anthony (2024a). "Post-Kantian Idealism and Self-Transformation" in *Transformation and the History of Philosophy*, ed. G. Anthony Bruno and Justin Vlasits. London: Routledge, 205–22.
Bruno, G. Anthony (2023d). "'All is Act, Movement, and Life': Fichte's Idealism as Immortalism" in *Life, Organisms, and Human Nature: New Perspectives on Classical German Philosophy*, ed. Luca Corti and Johannes-Georg Schülein. Berlin: Springer, 121–39.
Bruno, G. Anthony (2023c). "Quietism, Dialetheism, and the Three Moments of Hegel's Logic" in *Metaphysics as a Science in Classical German Philosophy*, ed. Robb Dunphy and Toby Lovat. London: Routledge, 315–38.
Bruno, G. Anthony (2023b). "Logical and Moral Aliens Within Us: Kant on Theoretical and Practical Self-Conceit" in *Limits of Intelligibility: Issues from Kant and Wittgenstein*, ed. Jens Pier. London: Routledge, 109–34.
Bruno, G. Anthony (2023a). "'From Time into Eternity': Schelling on Intellectual Intuition" in *Philosophy Compass* 18 (4), 1–15.
Bruno, G. Anthony (2022b). "From Being to Acting: Kant and Fichte on Intellectual Intuition" in *British Journal for the History of Philosophy* 31 (4), 762–83.
Bruno, G. Anthony (2022a). "Review of *Reason and Conversion in Kierkegaard and the German Idealists*, by Ryan S. Kemp and Christopher Iacovetti" in *Kantian Review* 27 (1), 169–73.
Bruno, G. Anthony (2021f). "Schelling, Cavell, and the Truth of Skepticism" in *Journal for the History of Analytical Philosophy* 9 (9), 22–41.
Bruno, G. Anthony (2021e). "Review of *For the Love of Metaphysics: Nihilism and the Conflict of Reason from Kant to Rosenzweig*, by Karin Nisenbaum" in *Mind* 131 (522), 733–42.
Bruno, G. Anthony (2021d). "*Hiatus Irrationalis*: Lask's Fateful Misreading of Fichte" in *European Journal of Philosophy* 30 (3), 977–95.

Bruno, G. Anthony (2021c). "The Parallactic Leap: Fichte, Apperception, and the Hard Problem of Consciousness" in *Parallax: The Dialectics of Mind and World*, ed. Dominik Finkelde, Christoph Menke, and Slavoj Žižek. London: Bloomsbury, 93–106.

Bruno, G. Anthony (2021b). "Schelling on the Unconditioned Condition of the World" in *Schellings Freiheitsschrift: Methode, System, Kritik*, ed. Thomas Buchheim, Thomas Frisch, and Nora C. Wachsmann. Tübingen: Mohr Siebeck, 17–33.

Bruno, G. Anthony (2021a). "Facticity and Genesis: Tracking Fichte's Method in the Berlin *Wissenschaftslehre*" in *Fichte-Studien* 49, 177–97.

Bruno, G. Anthony (2020d). "Schelling's Philosophical Letters on Doctrine and Critique" in *Critique in German Philosophy: From Kant to Critical Theory*, ed. María del Rosario Acosta López and J. Colin McQuillan. Albany: SUNY Press, 133–54.

Bruno, G. Anthony (2020c). "Jacobi's Dare: McDowell, Meillassoux, and Consistent Idealism" in *Idealism, Relativism and Realism: New Essays on Objectivity Beyond the Analytic-Continental Divide*, ed. Dominik Finkelde and Paul M. Livingstone. Berlin: de Gruyter, 35–55.

Bruno, G. Anthony (2020b). "The Thought of a Principle: Rödl's Fichteanism" in *The Bloomsbury Companion to Fichte*, ed. Maria Bykova. New York: Bloomsbury, 521–38.

Bruno, G. Anthony (2020a). "The Facticity of Time: Conceiving Schelling's Idealism of Ages" in *Schelling's Philosophy: Freedom, Nature, and Systematicity*, ed. G. Anthony Bruno. Oxford: Oxford University Press, 185–206.

Bruno, G. Anthony (2018d). "Meillassoux, Correlationism, and the Ontological Difference" in *PhaenEx: Journal of Existential and Phenomenological Theory and Culture* 12 (2), 1–12.

Bruno, G. Anthony (2018c). "Genealogy and Jurisprudence in Fichte's Genetic Deduction of the Categories" in *History of Philosophy Quarterly* 35 (1), 77–96.

Bruno, G. Anthony (2018b). "Determinacy, Indeterminacy, and Contingency in German Idealism" in *The Significance of Indeterminacy: Perspectives from Asian and Continental Philosophy*, ed. Gregory S. Moss and Robert H. Scott. London: Routledge, 67–83.

Bruno, G. Anthony (2018a). "Skepticism, Deduction, and Reason's Maturation" in *Skepticism: Historical and Contemporary Inquiries*, ed. G Anthony Bruno and A. C. Rutherford. London: Routledge, 203–20.

Bruno, G. Anthony (2017b). "Empirical Realism and the Great Outdoors: A Critique of Meillassoux" in *Continental Realism and its Discontents*, ed. Marie-Eve Morin. Edinburgh: Edinburgh University Press, 21–37.

Bruno, G. Anthony (2017a). "Schelling on the Possibility of Evil: Rendering Pantheism, Freedom and Time Consistent" in *Northern European Journal of Philosophy* 18 (1), 1–18.

Bruno, G. Anthony (2016). "'As From a State of Death': Schelling's Idealism as Mortalism" in *Comparative and Continental Philosophy* 8 (3), 1–14.

Bruno, G. Anthony (2015b). "Epistemic Reciprocity in Schelling's Late Return to Kant" in *Rethinking Kant, Volume 4*, ed. Oliver Thorndike. UK: Cambridge Scholars Publishing, 74–95.

Bruno, G. Anthony (2015a). "Varieties of Transcendental Idealism: Kant and Heidegger Thinking Beyond Life" in *Idealistic Studies* 45 (1), 81–102.

Bruno, G. Anthony (2014b). "A Peculiar Fate: The Unity of Human Life in Kant and Heidegger" in *Dialogue: Canadian Philosophical Review* 53 (4), 715–35.

Bruno, G. Anthony (2014a). "Freedom and Pluralism in Schelling's Critique of Fichte's Jena *Wissenschaftslehre*" in *Idealistic Studies* 43 (1/2), 71–86.

Bruno, G. Anthony (2013). "The Appearance and Disappearance of Intellectual Intuition in Schelling's Philosophy" in *Analecta Hermeneutica* 5, 1–14.

Burbidge, John (1980). "The Necessity of Contingency: An Analysis of Hegel's Chapter on 'Actuality' in the *Science of Logic*" in *Proceedings of the Hegel Society of America* 4, 201–17.

Burch, Matthew I. (2013). "The Existential Sources of Phenomenology: Heidegger on Formal Indication" in *European Journal of Philosophy* 21 (2), 1–21.

Callanan, John (2019). "Kant on Misology and the Natural Dialectic" in *Philosophers' Imprint* 19 (47), 1–22.

Campbell, Scott M. (2012). *The Early Heidegger's Philosophy of Life: Facticity, Being, and Language*. New York: Fordham University Press.

Caputo, John D. (1974). "Phenomenology, Mysticism and the '*Gramatica Speculativa*': A Study of Heidegger's '*Habilitationsschrift*'" in *Journal of the British Society for Phenomenology* 5 (2), 101–17.
Carman, Taylor (2007). "Phenomenology as Rigourous Science" in *The Oxford Handbook of Continental Philosophy*, ed. Michael Rosen and Brian Leiter. Oxford: Oxford University Press, 9–29.
Carson, Emily (1997). "Kant on Intuition in Geometry" in *Canadian Journal of Philosophy* 27 (4), 489–512.
Carvalho, M. Jorge de (2010). "Fichte, Heidegger, and the Concept of Facticity" in *Fichte and the Phenomenological Tradition*, ed. Violetta Waibel, Daniel Breazeale, and Tom Rockmore. Berlin: de Gruyter, 233–60.
Casati, Filippo (2022). *Heidegger and the Contradiction of Being: An Analytic Interpretation of the Late Heidegger*. London: Routledge.
Cavell, Stanley (1999). *The Claim of Reason: Wittgenstein, Skepticism, Morality and Tragedy*. Oxford: Oxford University Press.
Clarke, James A. (2013). "Fichte's Critique of Rousseau" in *The Review of Metaphysics* 66 (3), 495–517.
Cobb-Stevens, Richard (1990). "Being and Categorial Intuition" in *The Review of Metaphysics* 44 (1), 43–66.
Conant, James (2016). "Why Kant Is Not a Kantian" in *Philosophical Topics* 44 (1), 75–125.
Conant, James (2004). "Varieties of Skepticism" in *Wittgenstein and Skepticism*, ed. Denis McManus. London: Routledge, 97–136.
Cooper-Simpson, Charlie (2021). "Is There a Deduction in Hegel's *Science of Logic*?" in *Hegel Bulletin* 43 (1), 69–92.
Crowe, Benjamin (2019). "Hermeneutics and Phenomenology" in *The Cambridge Companion to Hermeneutics*, ed. Michael N. Forster and Kristin Gjesdal. Cambridge: Cambridge University Press, 211–36.
Crowe, Benjamin (2013). "Fichte's Philosophical *Bildungsroman*" in *Fichte's* Vocation of Man: *New Interpretive and Critical Essays*, ed. Daniel Breazeale and Tom Rockmore. Albany: SUNY Press, 33–44.
Crowe, Benjamin (2009). "F. H. Jacobi on Faith, or What It Takes to Be an Irrationalist" in *Religious Studies* 45 (3), 309–24.
Crowe, Benjamin and Gabriel Gottlieb, ed. (2024). *Fichte's 1804 Wissenschaftslehre Essays on the "Science of Knowing."* Albany: SUNY Press.
Crowell, Steven (2013). "Conscience and Reason" in *Normativity and Phenomenology in Husserl and Heidegger*. Cambridge: Cambridge University Press, 191–213.
Crowell, Steven (2009). "Transcendental Logic and Minimal Empiricism: Lask and McDowell on the Unboundedness of the Conceptual" in *Neo-Kantianism in Contemporary Philosophy*, ed. Rudolph A. Makkreel and Sebastian Luft. Bloomington: Indiana University Press, 150–76.
Crowell, Steven (2002). "Facticity and Transcendental Philosophy" in *From Kant to Davidson: Philosophy and the Idea of the Transcendental*, ed. Jeff Malpas. London: Routledge, 100–21.
Crowell, Steven (2001). *Husserl, Heidegger, and the Space of Meaning: Paths Toward Transcendental Phenomenology*. Evanston: Northwestern University Press.
Crowell, Steven (1996). "Emil Lask: Aletheiology as Ontology" in *Kant-Studien* 87 (1), 69–88.
Crowell, Steven (1992). "Lask, Heidegger, and the Homelessness of Logic" in *Journal of the British Society for Phenomenology* 23 (3), 222–39.
Dahlstrom, Daniel O. (2001). *Heidegger Concept of Truth*. Cambridge: Cambridge University Press.
Dahlstrom, Daniel O. (1994). "Heidegger's Method: Philosophical Concepts as Formal Indications" in *The Review of Metaphysics* 47 (4), 775–95.
De Boer, Karin (2019). "Kant's Response to Hume's Critique of Pure Reason" in *Archiv für Geschichte der Philosophie* 101 (3), 376–406.

De Boer, Karin (2011). "Transformations of Transcendental Philosophy: Wolff, Kant, and Hegel" in *Hegel Bulletin* 32 (1–2), 50–79.

De Boer, Karin (2010). "Hegel's Account of Contradiction in the *Science of Logic* Reconsidered" in *Journal of the History of Philosophy* 48 (3), 345–74.

De Boer, Karin (2000). *Thinking in the Light of Time: Heidegger's Encounter with Hegel.* Albany: SUNY Press.

Denker, Alfred (2000). "The Young Heidegger and Fichte" in *Heidegger, German Idealism, and Neo-Kantianism*, ed. Tom Rockmore. New York: Humanity, 103–22.

Dennett, Daniel (2017). "A History of Qualia" in *Topoi* 39 (1), 5–12.

De Pierris, Graciela (1992). "The Constitutive *A Priori*" in *Canadian Journal of Philosophy* 22 (supplement 1), 179–24.

Dews, Peter (2022). *Schelling's Late Philosophy in Confrontation with Hegel.* Oxford. Oxford University Press.

Dews, Peter (2017). "Theory Construction and Existential Description in Schelling's Treatise on Freedom" in *British Journal for the History of Philosophy* 25 (1), 157–78.

Di Giovanni, George and H. S. Harris (2000). "Editors' Notes" in *Between Kant and Hegel: Texts in the Development of Post-Kantian Idealism*, ed. George di Giovanni and H. Harris. Indianapolis: Hackett.

Dika, Tarek (2020). "*Auch für Gott*: Finitude, Phenomenology, and Anthropology" in *Phenomenology to the Letter: Husserl and Literature*, ed. Rochelle Tobias, Kristina Mendicino, and Philippe P. Haensler. Berlin: De Gruyter, 45–59.

Dunphy, Robb (2023). "Schulze's Scepticism and the Rise and Rise of German Idealism" in *Metaphysics as a Science in Classical German Philosophy*, ed. Robb Dunphy and Toby Lovat. London: Routledge, 226–50.

Dunphy, Robb (2020). "On the Incompatibility of Hegel's *Phenomenology* with the Beginning of his *Logic*" in *The Review of Metaphysics* 74 (1), 81–119.

Elpidorou, Andreas and Lauren Freeman (2015). "Affectivity in Heidegger I: Moods and Emotions in Being and Time" in *Philosophy Compass* 10 (10), 661–71.

Emundts, Dina (2008). "Emil Lask on Judgment and Truth" in *The Philosophical Forum* 39 (2), 263–81.

Engstrom, Stephen (2006). "Understanding and Sensibility" in *Inquiry* 49 (1), 2–25.

Fackenheim, Emil L. (1996). "Schelling's Philosophy of Religion" in *The God Within: Kant, Schelling, and Historicity*, ed. John Burbidge. Toronto: University of Toronto Press, 92–108.

Fackenheim, Emil L. (1954). "Schelling's Conception of Positive Philosophy" in *The Review of Metaphysics* 7 (4), 563–82.

Fahrenbach, Helmut (1972). "Faktizität" in *Historisches Wörterbuch der Philosophie, Band 2*, ed. Joachim Ritter, Karlfried Gründer, and Gottfried Gabriel. Basel/Stuttgart: Schwabe & Co.

Fincham, Richard Mark (2015). "Reconciling Leibnizian Monadology and Kantian Criticism" in *British Journal for the History of Philosophy* 23 (6), 1033–55.

Fisher, Naomi (2024). *Schelling's Mystical Platonism: 1792–1802.* Oxford: Oxford University Press.

Ford, Lewis S. (1965). "The Controversy Between Schelling and Jacobi" in *Journal of the History of Philosophy* 3 (1), 75–89.

Forster, Michael (2019). "Dilthey's Importance for Hermeneutics" in *Interpreting Dilthey: Critical Essays*, ed. Eric S. Nelson. Cambridge: Cambridge University Press, 61–81.

Forster, Michael (2014). "Schelling and Skepticism" in *Interpreting Schelling: Critical Essays*, ed. Lara Ostaric. Cambridge: Cambridge University Press, 32–47.

Forster, Michael (1989). *Hegel and Skepticism.* Cambridge, Mass.: Harvard University Press.

Förster, Eckart (2012). *The Twenty-Five Years of Philosophy: A Systematic Reconstruction*, trs. B. Bowman. Cambridge, Mass.: Harvard University Press.

Förster, Eckart (2005). "Fichte, Beck, and Schelling in Kant's *Opus Postumum*" in *Kant and His Influence*, ed. George MacDonald Ross and T. McWalter. London: Continuum, 146–69.

Frank, Manfred (2019). "From 'Fichte's Original Insight' to a Moderate Defense of Self-Representationalism" in *ProtoSociology* 36, 36–78.

Frank, Manfred (2014). "'Identity of Identity and Non-Identity': Schelling's Path to the 'Absolute System of Identity'" in *Interpreting Schelling: Critical Essays*, ed. Lara Ostaric. Cambridge: Cambridge University Press, 120–44.
Frank, Manfred (1989). "Schelling's Critique of Hegel and the Beginnings of Marxian Dialectics" in *Idealistic Studies* 19 (3), 251–68.
Franks, Paul (2020). "The Rationality of History and the History of Rationality: Menachem Fisch on the Analytic Idealist Predicament" in *Open Philosophy* 3, 1–17.
Franks, Paul (2016b). "Fichte's Kabbalistic Realism: Summons as ẓimẓum" in *Fichte's Foundations of Natural Right: A Critical Guide*, ed. Gabriel Gottlieb. Cambridge: Cambridge University Press, 92–116.
Franks, Paul (2016a). "Fichte's Position: Anti-Subjectivism, Self-Awareness, and Self-Location in the Space of Reasons" in *Cambridge Companion to Fichte*, ed. Günter Zöller. Cambridge: Cambridge University Press, 374–404.
Franks, Paul (2008). "Ancient Skepticism, Modern Naturalism, and Nihilism in Hegel's Early Jena Writings" in *Cambridge Companion to Hegel and Nineteenth-Century Philosophy*, ed. Frederick Beiser. Cambridge: Cambridge University Press, 52–73.
Franks, Paul (2007). "From Quine to Hegel: Naturalism, Anti-Realism, and Maimon's Question *Quid Facti*" in *German Idealism: Contemporary Perspectives*, ed. Espen Hammer. London: Routledge, 50–69.
Franks, Paul (2005). *All or Nothing: Systematicity, Transcendental Arguments, and Skepticism in German Idealism*. Cambridge, Mass.: Harvard University Press.
Franks, Paul (2003). "What Should Kantians Learn from Maimon's Skepticism?" in *Salomon Maimon: Rational Dogmatist, Empirical Skeptic*, ed. Gideon Freudenthal. Dordrecht: Kluwer, 200–32.
Friedman, Michael (2000). *A Parting of the Ways: Carnap, Cassirer, and Heidegger*. Chicago: Open Court.
Gabriel, Markus (2014). "Aarhus Lecture 2: Schelling's Ontology in the *Freedom Essay*" in *Northern European Journal of Philosophy* 15 (11), 75–98.
Gabriel, Markus (2009). "The Mythological Being of Reflection: An Essay on Hegel, Schelling and the Contingency of Necessity" in *Mythology, Madness, and Laughter*, M. Gabriel and S. Žižek. New York: Continuum, 15–94.
Gardner, Sebastian (2020). "Thought's Indebtedness to Being: From Kant's *Beweisgrund* to Schelling's *Quelle*" in *Schelling's Philosophy: Freedom, Nature, and Systematicity*, ed. G. Anthony Bruno. Oxford: Oxford University Press, 209–30.
Gardner, Sebastian (2017). "The Metaphysics of Human Freedom: From Kant's Transcendental Idealism to Schelling's *Freiheitsschrift*" in *British Journal for the History of Philosophy* 25 (1), 133–56.
Gardner, Sebastian (2013). "Transcendental Philosophy and the Possibility of the Given" in *Mind, Reason, and Being-in-the-World: The McDowell-Dreyfus Debate*, ed. Joseph Schear. London: Routledge, 110–42.
Gardner, Sebastian (2007). "The Status of the *Wissenschaftslehre*: Transcendental and Ontological Grounds in Fichte" in *International Yearbook of German Idealism: Metaphysics in German Idealism* 5, 90–125.
Genova, A. C. (1974). "Kant's Epigenesis of Pure Reason" in *Kant-Studien* 65 (3), 259–73.
Gentry, Gerad (2020). "Review of *Hegel's Concept of Life: Self-Consciousness, Freedom, Logic*, by Karen Ng" in *Notre Dame Philosophical Reviews*.
Golob, Sacha (2017). "Methodological Anxiety: Heidegger on Moods and Emotions" in *Thinking About the Emotions: A Philosophical History*, ed. Alix Cohen and Robert Stern. Oxford: Oxford University Press, 253–71.
Gomes, Anil, A. W. Moore, and Andrew Stephenson (2022). "On the Necessity of the Categories" in *Philosophical Review* 131 (2), 129–68.
Gonzalez, Francisco (2022). "Heidegger and Gadamer on Hegel's Greek Conception of Being and Time in an Unpublished 1925/26 Seminar" in *Archiv für Geschichte der Philosophie* 104 (4), 735–58.

Gordon, Peter E. (2010). *Continental Divide: Heidegger, Cassirer, Davos.* Cambridge, Mass.: Harvard University Press.
Gottlieb, Gabriel (2015). "Fichte's Deduction of the External World" in *International Philosophical Quarterly* 55 (2), 217–34.
Gram, Moltke (1981). "Intellectual Intuition: The Continuity Thesis" in *Journal of the History of Ideas* 42 (2), 287–304.
Grant, Iain Hamilton (2014). "The Hypothesis of Nature's Logic in Schelling's *Naturphilosophie*" in *The Palgrave Handbook of German Idealism*, ed. Matthew C. Altman. London: Palgrave Macmillan, 478–98.
Grondin, Jean (2019). "Dilthey's Hermeneutics and Philosophical Hermeneutics" in *Interpreting Dilthey: Critical Essays*, ed. Eric S. Nelson. Cambridge: Cambridge University Press, 252–65.
Grondin, Jean (2016). "What Is the Hermeneutic Circle?" in *The Blackwell Companion to Hermeneutics*, ed. Niall Keane and Chris Lawn. UK: John Wiley and Sons, 299–305.
Grondin, Jean (2005). "Hermeneutics" in *New Dictionary of the History of Ideas, Volume 3*, ed. Maryanne C. Horowitz. New York: Thomson Gale, 982–7.
Gueroult, Martial (1930). *L'Évolution et la Structure de la Doctrine de la Science chez Fichte.* Paris: Les Belles Lettres.
Gurofsky, Simon R. (2020). "On the Putative Possibility of Non-Spatio-Temporal Forms of Sensibility in Kant" in *European Journal of Philosophy* 28 (4), 841–56.
Hammacher, Klaus (1994). "Jacobis Schrift Von den göttlichen Dinge" in *Religionsphilosophie und spekulative Theologie. Der Streit um die göttlichen Dinge (1799–1812)*, ed. Walter Jaeschke. Hamburg: Meiner, 129–41.
Han-Pile, Béatrice (2013). "Freedom and the 'Choice to Choose Oneself' in Being and Time" in *Cambridge Companion to Heidegger's* Being and Time, ed. Mark A. Wrathall. Cambridge: Cambridge University Press, 291–319.
Harris, H. S. (1997). *Hegel's Ladder, Volume 1: The Pilgrimage of Reason.* Indianapolis: Hackett.
Harris, H. S. (1987). "The Cows in the Dark Night" in *Dialogue* 26, 627–44.
Hart, James G. (1995). "Husserl and Fichte: With Special Regard to Husserl's Lectures on 'Fichte's Ideal of Humanity'" in *Husserl Studies* 12, 135–63.
Helbig, Daniela and Dalia Nassar (2016). "The Metaphor of Epigenesis: Kant, Blumenbach, and Herder" in *Studies in History and Philosophy of Science* 58, 98–107.
Henrich, Dieter (2003). *Between Kant and Hegel: Lectures on German Idealism*, trs. D. S. Pacini. Cambridge, Mass.: Harvard University Press.
Henrich, Dieter (1989). "Kant's Notion of a Deduction and the Methodological Background of the First *Critique*" in *Kant's Transcendental Deductions: The Three "Critiques" and the "Opus Postumum,"* ed. Eckart Förster. Stanford: Stanford University Press, 29–46.
Henrich, Dieter (1982). "Fichte's Original Insight" in *Contemporary German Philosophy, Volume 1*, ed. Darrel E. Christensen, Manfred Riedel, Robert Spaemann, and Wolfgang Wieland. Pennsylvania: Pennsylvania State University Press, 15–53.
Henrich, Dieter (1958). "Hegels Theorie Über den Zufall" in *Kant-Studien* 50, 131–48.
Hentrup, Miles (2019). "Hegel's Logic as Presuppositionless Science" in *Idealistic Studies* 49 (2), 145–65.
Hoeppner, Till (2022). "Kant's Metaphysical and Transcendental Deductions of the Categories: Tasks, Steps, and Claims of Identity" in *Kant's Transcendental Deduction and the Theory of Apperception: New Interpretations*, ed. Giuseppe Motta, Dennis Schulting, and Udo Thiel. Berlin: de Gruyter, 461–92.
Hogrebe, Wolfram (2024). *Predication and Genesis: Metaphysics as Fundamental Heuristic After Schelling's* The Ages of the World, trs. Iain Hamilton Grant and Jason Wirth. Edinburgh: Edinburgh University Press.
Holz, Harald (1970). *Spekulation und Faktizität: Zum Freiheitsbegriff des mittleren und späten Schelling.* Bonn: Bouvier.
Horstmann, Rolf-Peter (2015). "Fichte's Anti-Skeptical Programme: On the Anti- Skeptical Strategies in Fichte's Presentations of the *Wissenschaftslehre* 1794 to 1801/2" in *The*

Transcendental Turn, ed. Sebastian Gardner and Matthew Grist. Oxford: Oxford University Press, 96–134.
Horstmann, Rolf-Peter (1986). "Logifizierte Natur oder naturalisierte Logik? Bemerkungen zu Schellings Hegel-Kritik" in *Hegels Philosophie der Natur*, ed. Rolf-Peter Horstmann and Michael John Petry. Stuttgart: Klett-Cotta, 190–207.
Houlgate, Stephen (2022). "Review of *Hegel's Concept of Life: Self-Consciousness, Freedom, Logic*, by Karen Ng" in *Philosophical Review* 131 (2), 226–30.
Houlgate, Stephen (2015). "Is Hegel's Phenomenology of Spirit an Essay in Transcendental Argument?" in *The Transcendental Turn*, ed. Sebastian Gardner and Matthew Grist. Oxford: Oxford University Press, 173–94.
Houlgate, Stephen (2006). *The Opening of Hegel's* Logic: *From Being to Infinity*. Indiana: Purdue University Press.
Houlgate, Stephen (2005). *An Introduction to Hegel: Freedom, Truth, and History*. UK: Blackwell.
Houlgate, Stephen (2003). "Thinking Philosophically Without Begging the Question" in *The Classics of Western Philosophy: A Reader's Guide*, ed. Jorge J. E. Garcia, Gregory M. Reichberg, and Bernard N. Schumacher. Oxford: Blackwell, 364–82.
Houlgate, Stephen (1999). "Schelling's Critique of Hegel's *Science of Logic*" in *The Review of Metaphysics* 53 (1), 99–128.
Houlgate, Stephen (1995). "Necessity and Contingency in Hegel's *Science of Logic*" in *The Owl of Minerva* 27 (1), 37–49.
Hyppolite, Jean (1971). *Figures de la pensée philosophique. Écrits de Jean Hyppolite (1931–1968)*, Tome I. Paris: Quadrige.
Inwood, Michael (1999). "Does the Nothing Noth?" in *Royal Institute of Philosophy Supplement* 44, 271–90.
Kassab, E. Suzanne (1990). "Husserl's Crisis and Gurwitsch's Nihilism: A Common Preoccupation—A Common Call" in *International Sociology* 5 (3), 267–77.
Käufer, Stephan (2001). "On Heidegger on Logic" in *Continental Philosophy Review* 34, 455–76.
Kemp, Ryan S. and Christopher Iacovetti (2020). *Reason and Conversion in Kierkegaard and the German Idealists*. New York: Routledge.
Kisiel, Theodore (2010). "Hermeneutics of Facticity" in *Martin Heidegger: Key Concepts*, ed. Bret W. Davis. UK: Acumen, 17–32.
Kisiel, Theodore (2008). "On the Genesis of Heidegger's Formally Indicative Hermeneutics of Facticity" in *Rethinking Facticity*, ed. François Raffoul and Eric S. Nelson. Albany: SUNY Press, 41–68.
Kisiel, Theodore (2000). "Heidegger—Lask—Fichte" in *Heidegger, German Idealism, and Neo-Kantianism*, ed. Tom Rockmore. New York: Humanity, 239–70.
Kisiel, Theodore (1995). "Why Students of Heidegger Will Have to Read Emil Lask" in *Man and World* 28, 197–240.
Kisiel, Theodore (1993). *The Genesis of Heidegger's Being and Time*. Berkeley: University of California Press.
Kisiel, Theodore (1986). "Das Entstehen des Begriffsfeldes 'Faktizität' im Frühwerk Heideggers" in *Dilthey-Jahrbuch für Philosophie und Geschichte der Geisteswissenschaften* 4, 91–120.
Kosch, Michelle (2006). *Freedom and Reason in Kant, Schelling and Kierkegaard*. Oxford: Oxford University Press.
Kreines, James (2015). *Reason in the World: Hegel's Metaphysics and its Philosophical Appeal*. Oxford: Oxford University Press.
Krüger, Lorenz (1968). "Wollte Kant die Vollständigkeit seiner Urteilstafel beweisen?" in *Kant Studien* 59, 333–56.
Kukla, Rebecca (2002). "The Ontology and Temporality of Conscience" in *Continental Philosophy Review* 35, 1–34.
Lafont, Cristina (2015). "Transcendental versus Hermeneutic Phenomenology in *Being and Time*" in *The Transcendental Turn*, ed. Sebastian Gardner and Matthew Grist. Oxford: Oxford University Press, 278–93.

Lauth, Reinhard (1998). "Eine Bezugnahme Fichtes auf Hegels 'Wissenschaft der Logik' im Sommer 1812" in *Kant-Studien* 89 (4), 45664.

Longuenesse, Béatrice (2007). *Hegel's Critique of Metaphysics*, trs. N. J. Simek. Cambridge: Cambridge University Press.

Longuenesse, Béatrice (2006). "Kant on *A Priori* Concepts: The Metaphysical Deduction of the Categories" in *Cambridge Companion to Kant and Modern Philosophy*, ed. Paul Guyer. Cambridge: Cambridge University Press, 129–68.

Longuenesse, Béatrice (1998). *Kant and the Capacity to Judge*, trs. Charles T. Wolfe. Princeton: Princeton University Press.

Lu-Adler, Huaping (2016). "Kant on Proving Aristotle's Logic as Complete" in *Kantian Review* 21 (1), 1–26.

Luft, Sebastian (2018). "Kant, Neo-Kantianism, and Phenomenology" in *The Oxford Handbook of the History of Phenomenology*, ed. Dan Zahavi. Oxford: Oxford University Press, 45–67.

Majolino, Claudio and Aurélien Djian (2018). "What 'Phenomenon' for Hermeneutics? Remarks on the Hermeneutical Vocation of Phenomenology" in *Hermeneutics and Phenomenology: Figures and Themes*, ed. Saulius Geniusas and Paul Fairfield. London: Bloomsbury, 48–64.

Maker, William (1994). *Philosophy Without Foundations: Rethinking Hegel.* Albany: SUNY Press.

Makkreel, Rudolph (1969). "Wilhelm Dilthey and the Neo-Kantians: The Distinction of the *Geisteswissenschaften* and the *Kulturwissenschaften*" in *Journal of the History of Philosophy* 7 (4), 423–40.

Martin, Wayne (2007). "In Defense of Bad Infinity: A Fichtean Response to Hegel's *Differenzschrift*" in *Bulletin of the Hegel Society of Great Britain* 28 (55), 168–87.

Martin, Wayne (2003). "Nothing More or Less than Logic: General Logic, Transcendental Philosophy, and Kant's Repudiation of Fichte's *Wissenschaftslehre*" in *Topoi* 22, 29–39.

Martin, Wayne (1997). *Idealism and Objectivity: Understanding Fichte's Jena Project.* Stanford: Stanford University Press.

Matthews, Bruce (2007). "Translator's Introduction" in *The Grounding of Positive Philosophy*, F. W. J. Schelling, trs. B. Matthews. Albany: SUNY Press, 1–84.

McDowell, John (2009). "Hegel's Idealism as Radicalization of Kant" in *Having the World in View: Essays on Kant, Hegel, and Sellars.* Cambridge, Mass.: Harvard University Press, 69–89.

McDowell, John (1996). *Mind and World.* Cambridge, Mass.: Harvard University Press.

McGrath, Sean J. (2023). "The Jacobi-Schelling Debate" in *Friedrich Heinrich Jacobi and the Ends of the Enlightenment: Religion, Philosophy, and Reason at the Crux of Modernity*, ed. Alexander J. N. Hampton. Cambridge: Cambridge University Press, 104–23.

McGrath, Sean J. (2016b). "Is the Late Schelling Still Doing Nature-Philosophy?" in *Angelaki* 21 (4), 121–41.

McGrath, Sean J. (2016a). "On the Difference Between Schelling and Hegel" in *Rethinking German Idealism*, ed. Sean J. McGrath and Joseph Carew. London: Palgrave Macmillan, 247–70.

McNulty, Jacob (2023). *Hegel's Logic and Metaphysics.* Cambridge: Cambridge University Press.

Meillassoux, Quentin (2008). *After Finitude: An Essay on the Necessity of Contingency*, trs. Ray Brassier. New York: Continuum.

Melamed, Yitzhak (2021). "Salomon Maimon's 'Principle of Determinability' and the Impossibility of Shared Predicates" in *Revue de Métaphysique et de Morale* 1, 49–62.

Melamed, Yitzhak (2020). "*Deus Sive Vernunft*: Schelling's Transformation of Spinoza's God" in *Schelling's Philosophy: Freedom, Nature, and Systematicity*, ed. G. Anthony Bruno. Oxford: Oxford University Press, 93–114.

Melamed, Yitzhak (2012). "*Omnis Determinatio est Negatio*" in *Spinoza and German Idealism*, ed. Eckart Förster and Yitzhak Melamed. Cambridge: Cambridge University Press, 175–96.

Melamed, Yitzhak (2004). "Salomon Maimon and the Rise of Spinozism in German Idealism" in *Journal of the History of Philosophy* 42 (1), 67–96.

Mensch, James (2018). "Phenomenology and the Givenness of the Hermeneutic Circle" in *Hermeneutics and Phenomenology: Figures and Themes*, ed. Saulius Geniusas and Paul Fairfield. London: Bloomsbury, 65–77.
Mensch, Jennifer (2013). *Kant's Organicism: Epigenesis and the Development of Critical Philosophy*. Chicago: University of Chicago Press.
Messina, James (2011). "Answering Aenesidemus: Schulze's Attack on Reinholdian Representationalism and Its Importance for Fichte" in *Journal of the History of Philosophy* 49 (3), 339–69.
Moss, Gregory S. (2020). *Hegel's Foundation-Free Metaphysics*. London: Routledge.
Moss, Gregory S. (2018). "Free Thinking in Schelling's Erlangen Lectures" in *The Significance of Indeterminacy: Perspectives from Asian and Continental Philosophy*, ed. G. S. Moss and R. H. Scott. London: Routledge, 84–103.
Mudd, Sasha (2013). "Rethinking the Priority of Practical Reason in Kant" in *European Journal of Philosophy* 24 (1), 78–102.
Nagel, Thomas (1971). "The Absurd" in *The Journal of Philosophy* 68 (20), 716–27.
Nelson, Eric S. (2013). "Heidegger and Dilthey: A Difference in Interpretation" in *The Bloomsbury Companion to Heidegger*, ed. Francois Raffoul and Eric S. Nelson. London: Bloomsbury, 129–34.
Neuhouser, Frederick (2014). "Fichte's Methodology in the *Wissenschaftslehre* (1794–95)" in *The Palgrave Handbook of German Idealism*, ed. Matthew C Altman. London: Palgrave Macmillan, 300–19.
Neuhouser, Frederick (1990). *Fichte's Theory of Subjectivity*. Cambridge: Cambridge University Press.
Ng, Karen (2020). *Hegel's Concept of Life: Self-Consciousness, Freedom, Logic*. Oxford: Oxford University Press.
Nieke, Wolfgang (1972). "Dogmatismus" in *Historisches Wörterbuch der Philosophie, Band 2*, ed. Joachim Ritter, Karlfried Gründer, and Gottfried Gabriel. Basel/Stuttgart: Schwabe & Co, 278–9.
Nir, Gilad (2021). "Toward a Resolute Reading of Being and Time: Heidegger, Wittgenstein, and the Dilemma between Inconsistency and Ineffability" in *The Southern Journal of Philosophy* 59 (4), 572–605.
Nisenbaum, Karin (2018). *For the Love of Metaphysics Nihilism and the Conflict of Reason from Kant to Rosenzweig*. Oxford: Oxford University Press.
Nuzzo, Angelica (2010). "Fichte's 1812 Transcendental Logic: Between Kant and Hegel" in *Fichte, German Idealism, and Early Romanticism*, ed. Daniel Breazeale and Tom Rockmore. Amsterdam: Rodopi, 189–206.
Ostaric, Lara (2020). "Nature as the World of Action, Not of Speculation: Schelling's Critique of Kant's Postulates in His *Philosophical Letters on Dogmatism and Criticism*" in *Schelling's Philosophy: Freedom, Nature, and Systematicity*, ed. G. Anthony Bruno. Oxford: Oxford University Press, 11–31.
Parsons, Charles (1992). "The Transcendental Aesthetic" in *Cambridge Companion to Kant*, ed. Paul Guyer. Cambridge: Cambridge University Press, 62–100.
Philonenko, Alexis (1966). *La liberté humaine dans la philosophie de Fichte*. Paris: Vrin.
Piché, Claude (2010). "The Concept of Phenomenology in Fichte's *Wissenschaftslehre* of 1804/II" in *Fichte and the Phenomenological Tradition*, ed. Violetta Waibel, Danial Breazeale and Tom Rockmore. Berlin: de Gruyter, 25–40.
Pier, Jens (forthcoming). "Approximating Essence: On Kant's Successive Definitional Methodology" in *Kant's Project of Enlightenment: Proceedings of the 14th International Kant Congress*, ed. Christoph Horn and Rainer Schäfer. Berlin: de Gruyter.
Pippin, Robert (2024). *The Culmination: Heidegger, German Idealism, and the Fate of Philosophy*. Chicago: University of Chicago Press.
Pippin, Robert (2022). "The Idealism in German Idealism" in *Reason in Nature: New Essays on Themes from John McDowell*, ed. Matthew Boyle and Evgenia Mylonaki, Cambridge, Mass.: Harvard University Press, 309–28.

Pippin, Robert (2019). *Hegel's Realm of Shadows: Logic as Metaphysics in* The Science of Logic. Chicago: University of Chicago Press.

Pippin, Robert (2000). "Fichte's Alleged Subjective, Psychological, One-Sided Idealism" in *The Reception of Kant's Critical Philosophy: Fichte, Schelling and Hegel*, ed. Sally Sedgwick. Cambridge: Cambridge University Press, 147–70.

Pippin, Robert (1996). "Hegel's Metaphysics and the Problem of Contradiction" in *The Hegel Myths and Legends*, ed. Jon Stewart. Evanston: Northwestern University Press, 239–52.

Priest, Graham (2019). "Kant's Excessive Tenderness for Things in the World and Hegel's Dialetheism" in *Logic from Kant to Russell: Laying the Foundations for Analytic Philosophy*, ed. Sandra Lapointe. London: Routledge, 56–72.

Priest, Graham (1989). "Dialectic and Dialetheic" in *Science and Society* 53 (4), 388–415.

Proops, Ian (forthcoming). "Kant on Enlightenment" in *Oxford Handbook of Kant*, ed. Anil Gomes and Andrew Stephenson. Oxford: Oxford University Press.

Proops, Ian (2003). "Kant's Legal Metaphor and the Nature of a Deduction" in *Journal of the History of Philosophy* 41 (2), 209–29.

Radrizzani, Ives (2016). "The *Wissenschaftslehre* and Historical Engagement" in *Cambridge Companion to Fichte*, ed. David James and Günter Zöller. Cambridge: Cambridge University Press, 222–47.

Ratcliffe, Matthew (2013). "Why Mood Matters" in *Cambridge Companion to Heidegger's* Being and Time, ed. Mark A. Wrathall. Cambridge: Cambridge University Press, 157–76.

Redaelli, Roberto (2016). *Emil Lask: Il soggetto e la forma*. Macerata: Quodlibet.

Reich, Klaus (1986). *The Completeness of Kant's Table of Judgment*, trs. J. Kneller and M. Losonsky. Stanford: Stanford University Press.

Rockmore, Tom (2001). "Fichte on Deduction in the Jena *Wissenschaftslehre*" in *New Essays in Fichte's Foundation of the Entire Doctrine of Scientific Knowledge*, ed. Daniel Breazeale and Tom Rockmore. New York: Prometheus, 60–80.

Rödl, Sebastian (2019). "Logic, Being, and Nothing" in *Hegel Bulletin* 40 (1), 92–120.

Rödl, Sebastian (2018). *Self-Consciousness and Objectivity: An Introduction to Absolute Idealism*. Cambridge, Mass.: Harvard University Press.

Rödl, Sebastian (2014). "Intentional Transaction" in *Philosophical Explorations* 17 (3), 304–16.

Rödl, Sebastian (2013). "The Single Act of Combining" in *Philosophy and Phenomenological Research* 87 (2), 213–20.

Rödl, Sebastian (2007). "Eliminating Externality" in *International Yearbook of German Idealism* 5. Berlin: de Gruyter, 176–88.

Rosenkranz, Karl (1963). *Georg Wilhelm Friedrich Hegels Leben*. Darmstadt: Wissenschaftsliche Buchgesellschaft.

Rosenthal, Earl (1971). "*Plus Ultra, Non Plus Ultra*, and the Columnar Device of Emperor Charles V" in *Journal of the Warburg and Courtauld Institutes* 34, 204–28.

Rush, Fred (2014). "Schelling's Critique of Hegel" in *Interpreting Schelling: Critical Essays*, ed. Lara Ostaric. Cambridge: Cambridge University Press, 216–37.

Sandkaulen, Birgit (2023). *The Philosophy of Friedrich Heinrich Jacobi: On the Contradiction Between System and Freedom*, trs. Matt Erlin. London: Bloomsbury.

Schafer, Karl (2021). "A System of Rational Faculties: Additive or Transformative?" in *European Journal of Philosophy* 29 (4), 918–36.

Scharff, Robert C. (2013). "Becoming a Philosopher: What Heidegger Learned From Dilthey, 1919–25" in *British Journal for the History of Philosophy* 21 (1), 122–42.

Schick, Stefan (2020). "Dialetheism as Romanticism and the Hegelian Critique of True Contradictions" in *Symphilosophie: International Journal of Philosophical Romanticism* 2: 273–95.

Schlösser, Ulrich (2010). "Presuppositions of Knowledge versus Immediate Certainty of Being: Fichte's 1804 *Wissenschaftslehre* as a Critique of Knowledge and a Program of Philosophical Foundation" in *Fichte, German Idealism, and Early Romanticism*, ed. Daniel Breazeale and Tom Rockmore. Amsterdam: Rodopi.

Schmidt, Andreas (2004). *Der Grund des Wissens. Fichtes Wissenschaftslehre in den Versionen von 1794/95, 1804/II und 1812.* Paderborn: Schöningh, 103–16.
Schnell, Alexander (2018). "Phenomenology and German Idealism" in *The Oxford Handbook of the History of Phenomenology*, ed. Dan Zahavi. Oxford: Oxford University Press, 68–87.
Schuhmann, Karl and Barry Smith (1993). "Two Idealisms: Lask and Husserl" in *Kant-Studien* 83, 448–66.
Schüz, Simon (2022). *Transzendentale Argumente bei Hegel und Fichte: Das Problem objektiver Geltung und seine Auflösung im nachkantischen Idealismus.* Berlin: De Gruyter.
Sedgwick, Sally (2012). *Hegel's Critique of Kant: From Dichotomy to Identity.* Oxford: Oxford University Press.
Serban, Claudia (2021). "Transcendental Philosophy, Psychology, and Anthropology: Kant and Husserl on the 'Inner Man' and the Human Being" in *The Palgrave Handbook of German Idealism and Phenomenology*, ed. Cynthia D. Coe. Switzerland: Palgrave Macmillan, 41–62.
Sheehan, Thomas (2015). *Making Sense of Heidegger: A Paradigm Shift.* London: Rowman & Littlefield.
Sheehan, Thomas (2013). "What If Heidegger Were a Phenomenologist?" in *Cambridge Companion to Heidegger's Being and Time*, ed. Mark A. Wrathall. Cambridge: Cambridge University Press, 381–402.
Sheehan, Thomas (1998). "Heidegger's *Lehrjahre*" in *The Collegium Phaenomenologicum: The First Ten Years*, ed. John C. Sallis, Giuseppina Moneta, and Jacques Taminiaux. Dordrecht: Springer, 77–137.
Sheehan, Thomas (1997). "Husserl and Heidegger: The Making and Unmaking of a Relationship" in *Psychological and Transcendental Phenomenology and the Confrontation with Heidegger (1927–1931)*, trs. Thomas Sheehan and Richard E. Palmer. Dordrecht: Springer, 1–34.
Shockey, R. Matthew (2016). "Heidegger's Anxiety: On the Role of Mood in Phenomenological Method" in *Bulletin d'analyse phénoménologique* 12 (1), 1–27.
Shockey, R. Matthew (2010). "What's Formal about Formal Indication? Heidegger's Method in *Sein und Zeit*" in *Inquiry* 53 (6), 525–39.
Shuster, Martin (2014). "Kant's *Opus Postumum* and McDowell's Critique of Kant" in *Southern Journal of Philosophy* 52 (4), 427–44.
Siep, Ludwig (1991). "Hegel's Idea of a Conceptual Scheme" in *Inquiry* 34 (1), 63–76.
Snow, Dale (1996). *Schelling and the End of Idealism.* Albany: SUNY Press.
Snow, Dale (1987). "F. H. Jacobi and the Development of German Idealism" in *Journal of the History of Philosophy* 25 (3), 397–415.
Socher, Abraham P. (2006). *The Radical Enlightenment of Solomon Maimon: Judaism, Heresy, and Philosophy.* Stanford: Stanford University Press.
Sokolowski, Robert (1981). "Husserl's Concept of Categorial Intuition" in *Philosophical Topics* 12, 125–45.
Staiti, Andrea (2014). *Husserl's Transcendental Phenomenology: Nature, Spirit, and Life.* Cambridge: Cambridge University Press.
Stang, Nicholas F. (manuscript). "Determinacy, Contradiction, Movement: Towards a Reading of Hegel's Logic."
Stang, Nicholas F. (forthcoming). "Kant's Metaphysical Deduction of the Categories: Towards a Systematic Reconstruction" in *Oxford Handbook of Kant*, ed. Anil Gomes and Andrew Stephenson. Oxford: Oxford University Press.
Stang, Nicholas F. (2015). "Who's Afraid of Double Affection" in *Philosophers' Imprint* 15 (18), 1–28.
Stern, Robert (2016). "'Determination is Negation': The Adventures of a Doctrine from Spinoza to Hegel to the British Idealists" in *Hegel Bulletin* 37, 29–52.
Stern, Robert (2009). *Hegelian Metaphysics.* Oxford: Oxford University Press.
Stern, Robert (2007). "Pierce, Hegel, and the Category of Firstness" in *International Yearbook on German Idealism* (5), 276–308.
Stern, Robert (2006). "Metaphysical Dogmatism, Humean Scepticism, Kantian Criticism" in *Kantian Review* 11 (1), 102–16.

Stone, Abraham (2006). "Heidegger and Carnap on the Overcoming of Metaphysics" in *Martin Heidegger*, ed. Stephen Mulhall. London: Routledge, 217–44.

Suarez, David (2023). "Art, Authenticity, and Understanding" in *Limits of Intelligibility: Issues from Kant and Wittgenstein*, ed. Jens Pier. London: Routledge, 238–61.

Talbot, Ellen Bliss (1907). "The Philosophy of Fichte and its Relation to Pragmatism" in *The Philosophical Review* 16 (5), 488–505.

Talbot, Ellen Bliss (1906). *The Fundamental Principle of Fichte's Philosophy*. London: Macmillan.

Talbot, Ellen Bliss (1901). "The Relation of the Two Periods of Fichte's Philosophy" in *Mind* 10 (39), 336–46.

Talbot, Ellen Bliss (1900). "The Relation Between Human Consciousness and its Ideal as Conceived by Kant and Fichte" in *Kant-Studien* 4 (1–3), 286–310.

Thielke, Peter (2008). "Apostate Rationalism and Maimon's Hume" in *Journal of the History of Philosophy* 46 (4), 591–618.

Thielke, Peter (2006). "Fate and the Fortune of the Categories: Kant on the Usurpation and Schematization of Concepts" in *Inquiry* 49 (5), 438–68.

Thielke, Peter (2003). "Hume, Kant, and the Sea of Illusion" in *Hume Studies* 29 (1), 63–88.

Thielke, Peter (2001). "Getting Maimon's Goad: Discursivity, Skepticism, and Fichte's Idealism" in *Journal of the History of Philosophy* 39 (1), 101–34.

Thöle, Bernhard (2001). "Michael Wolff und die Vollständigkeit der kantischen Urteilstafel" in *Kant und die Berliner Aufklärung: Akten des IX. Internationalen Kant-Kongresses, Band II*, ed. Volker Gerhardt. Berlin: de Gruyter, 477–88.

Thomas, Mark (2014). "The Mediation of the Copula as a Fundamental Structure in Schelling's Philosophy" in *Schelling-Studien* 2, 20–39.

Tilliette, Xavier (1967). "Études Fichtéennes" in *Archive de Philosophie* 30, 114–32.

Tolley, Clinton (2017). "Husserl's Philosophy of the Categories in his Development toward Absolute Idealism" in *Grazer Philosophische Studien* 94, 460–93.

Tritten, Tyler (2012). *Beyond Presence: The Late F. W. J. Schelling's Criticism of Metaphysics*. Berlin: De Gruyter.

Truwant, Simon (2022). *Cassirer and Heidegger in Davos: The Philosophical Arguments*. Cambridge: Cambridge University Press.

Van Cleve, James (1999). *Problems from Kant*. Oxford: Oxford University Press.

Vater, Michael (2012). "Schelling's Philosophy of Identity and Spinoza's *Ethica more geometrico*" in *Spinoza and German Idealism*, ed. Eckart Förster and Yitzhak Melamed. Cambridge: Cambridge University Press, 156–74.

Von Herrmann, Friedrich-Wilhelm (1972). "Nachwort des Herausgebers" in *Heidegger, Martin: Frühe Schriften*. Frankfurt: Klostermann, 437–40.

Ward, Katherine (2021). "Breaking Down Experience: Heidegger's Methodological Use of Breakdown in *Being and Time*" in *European Journal of Philosophy* 29 (4), 712–30.

Ware, Owen (2020). *Fichte's Moral Philosophy*. Oxford: Oxford University Press.

Ware, Owen (2014). "Rethinking Kant's Fact of Reason" in *Philosophers' Imprint* 14 (32), 712–30.

Watkins, Eric (2014). "The Early Schelling on the Unconditioned" in *Interpreting Schelling: Critical Essays*, ed. Lara Ostaric. Cambridge: Cambridge University Press, 10–31.

Welchman, Alistair (2013). "Schelling's Moral Argument for a Metaphysics of Contingency" in *Nature and Realism in Schelling's Philosophy*, ed., Emilio C. Corriero and Andrea Dezi. Turin: Accademia University Press, 27–54.

Werner, Andrew (2020). "Hegel's Dialectical Method: A Response to the Modification View" in *Canadian Journal of Philosophy* 50 (6), 767–84.

Westphal, Kenneth R. (1989). "Hegel's Attitude Toward Jacobi in the 'Third Attitude of Thought Toward Objectivity'" in *Southern Journal of Philosophy* 27 (1), 135–56.

Whistler, Daniel (2013). *Schelling's Theory of Symbolic Language*. Oxford: Oxford University Press.

White, Alan (1994). "Hegel or Schelling?" in *Hegel Bulletin* 15 (2), 14–22.

Willaschek, Marcus and Eric Watkins (2020). "Kant on Cognition and Knowledge" in *Synthese* 197 (8), 3195–213.

Winegar, Reed (2016). "To Suspend Finitude Itself: Hegel's Reaction to Kant's First Antinomy" in *Hegel Bulletin* 37 (1), 81–103.

Winfield, Richard Dien (2018). "On Contradiction: Hegel versus Aristotle, Sextus Empiricus, and Kant" in *Hegel and Ancient Philosophy: A Re-Examination*, ed. Glenn Magee. New York: Routledge, 147–60.

Witherspoon, Edward (2022). "Logic and Attunement: Reading Heidegger through Priest and Wittgenstein" in *Heidegger on Logic*, ed. Filippo Casati and Daniel O. Dahlstrom. Cambridge: Cambridge University Press, 159–81.

Withy, Katherine (2022). "Review of *Heidegger and the Contradiction of Being: An Analytic Interpretation of the Late Heidegger*, by Filippo Casati" in *Notre Dame Philosophical Reviews*.

Withy, Katherine (2015). *Heidegger on Being Uncanny*. Cambridge, Mass.: Harvard University Press.

Wolff, Michael (2017). "How Precise Is Kant's Table of Judgments?" in *Kant's Critique of Pure Reason: A Critical Guide*, ed. James R. O'Shea. Cambridge: Cambridge University Press, 83–105.

Wolff, Michael (1995). *Die Vollständigkeit der kantischen Urteilstafel*. Frankfurt: Klostermann.

Wood, Allen (2012). "Fichte on Freedom: The Spinozistic Background" in *Spinoza and German Idealism*, ed. Eckart Förster and Yitzhak Melamed. Cambridge: Cambridge University Press, 121–35.

Wretzel, Joshua (2018). "Organic Imagination as Intuitive Intellect: Self-Knowledge and Self-Constitution in Hegel's Early Critique of Kant" in *European Journal of Philosophy* 26 (3), 958–73.

Zahavi, Dan (2018). "Brain, Mind, World: Predictive Coding, Neo-Kantianism, and Transcendental Idealism" in *Husserl Studies* 34 (1), 47–61.

Zöller, Günter (2016b). "Fichte's Later Presentations of the *Wissenschaftslehre*" in *Cambridge Companion to Fichte*, ed. David James and Günter Zöller. Cambridge: Cambridge University Press, 139–67.

Zöller, Günter (2016a). "Fichte's Original Insight: Dieter Henrich's Pioneering Piece Half A Century Later" in *Debates in Nineteenth-Century European Philosophy: Essential Readings and Contemporary Responses*, ed. Kristin Gjesdal. London: Routledge, 45–56.

Zöller, Günter (2000). "The Unpopularity of Transcendental Philosophy: Fichte's Controversy with Reinhold (1799-1801)" in *Pli* 10, 50–76.

Zöller, Günter (1998). *Fichte's Transcendental Philosophy: The Original Duplicity of Intelligence and Will*. Cambridge: Cambridge University Press.

Index

For the benefit of digital users, indexed terms that span two pages (e.g., 52–53) may, on occasion, appear on only one of those pages.